Corporations Law

Text and Essential Cases

Corporations Law

Text and Essential Cases

Julie Cassidy
LLB (Hons) (Adel); PhD (Bond)
Barrister and Solicitor of the Supreme Court of Victoria
Barrister of the Supreme Court of Queensland
Barrister of the High Court of Australia
Associate Professor in Law, Deakin University

THE FEDERATION PRESS
2005

Published in Sydney by

The Federation Press
PO Box 45, Annandale, NSW, 2038.
71 John St, Leichhardt, NSW, 2040.
Ph (02) 9552 2200. Fax (02) 9552 1681.
E-mail: info@federationpress.com.au
Website: http://www.federationpress.com.au

National Library of Australia
Cataloguing-in-Publication entry

Cassidy, Julie.
Corporations Law: text and essential cases.

Includes index.
ISBN 1 86287 548 0.

1. Corporation law – Australia. I. Title.

346.94066

© The Federation Press

This publication is copyright. Other than for the purposes of and subject to the conditions prescribed under the Copyright Act, no part of it may in any form or by any means (electronic, mechanical, microcopying, photocopying, recording or otherwise) be reproduced, stored in a retrieval system or transmitted without prior written permission. Enquiries should be addressed to the publisher.

Typeset by The Federation Press, Leichhardt, NSW.
Printed by Ligare Pty Ltd, Riverwood, NSW.

Preface

This text is adapted from the publication *Concise Corporations Law* and is designed for teaching/learning within a semester (13 week) corporations law unit. This has influenced the extent of coverage of various topics, the selection of cases and presentation. To this end the detailed commentary in *Concise Corporations Law* has been decreased and instead the text includes fuller case extracts. Review Questions and Further Readings are detailed at the end of each chapter. While a Plain English style is still used in the text, these added features are designed to make the text an effective teaching tool. The fuller extracts also make the text suitable for legal practitioners who may use it when preparing written submissions and legal opinions.

While the text tries to maintain some evenness between topics to reflect the norm of a 13 week semester, some topics by their very nature, such a directors' duties, require greater attention. This, however, simply reflects the increased attention temporally that this topic would receive in the classroom.

The text is current to January 2005 and includes important changes, such as those effected by the *Corporate Law Economic Reform Program (Audit Reform and Corporate Disclosure) Act* 2004 (Cth).

Julie Cassidy
January 2005

List of Chapters

Chapter 1	Introduction to Corporations Law	1
Chapter 2	Choosing Between Business Organisations	17
Chapter 3	Corporate Personality	39
Chapter 4	Promoters and Pre-registration Contracts	61
Chapter 5	Registration of Corporations	79
Chapter 6	The Corporate Constitution	89
Chapter 7	Shares and Dividends	107
Chapter 8	Corporate Fundraising	146
Chapter 9	Appointment and Removal of Directors	169
Chapter 10	Directors' Duties	204
Chapter 11	Meetings	270
Chapter 12	Members' Remedies	293
Chapter 13	External Administration	331

For detailed Table of Contents *see over*

Contents

Preface	v
Table of Cases	xxi
Table of Statutes	xxxiii

Chapter 1 Introduction to Corporations Law — 1
Overview — 1
A Select History of Corporations Law — 1
    Historical development of the corporate entity — 1
    Joint stock companies — 2
    Development of corporations law in Britain — 3
    Development of corporations law in Australia — 4
        Companies Act 1981 — 4
        Corporations Act 1989 — 5
        Corporations Law — 5
        Corporations Act 2001 — 6
Commonwealth's Legislative Power to Enact a Federal
    Corporations Regime — 7
    Corporations Act 1989 — 7
    Corporations Law — 10
    Cross-vesting — 12
Current Jurisdictional and Administrative Arrangements — 14
    Review questions — 15
    Further reading — 16
    References Chapter 1 — 16

Chapter 2 Choosing between Business Organisations — 17
Overview — 17
Sole Proprietorship — 18
    Defining a sole proprietorship — 18
    Benefits and shortcomings of a sole proprietorship — 18
Trading Trust — 19
    Defining a trust — 19
    Benefits and shortcomings of a trust — 20
    Corporate trustee — 22
Partnership — 22
    Defining a partnership — 22
    Limited partnerships — 25
    Benefits and shortcomings of a partnership — 26
Joint Ventures — 27
    Defining a joint venture — 27
    Benefits and shortcomings of a joint venture — 29
Company — 29
    Defining a company — 29
    Liability of members — 30
    Company limited by shares — 30
    Company limited by guarantee — 30

Unlimited company	31
No-liability company	31
Public and proprietary companies	32
Public companies	32
Proprietary companies	32
Small and large proprietary companies	33
Benefits of registration	33
Separate legal identity	33
Limited liability	33
Perpetual succession	34
Flexibility	34
Finance	34
Shortcomings of registration	34
Formalities	34
Costs	35
Participation in management	35
Benefits of proprietary companies	35
Benefits of public companies	36
Review question	36
Further reading	38
References Chapter 2	38

Chapter 3 Corporate Personality   39

Overview	39
Corporate Personality	39
Defining corporate personality	39
Limited liability	40
Multiple capacities	42
Distinguishing company and shareholder property	43
Company Liability	44
Difficulties in determining corporate liability	44
Strict liability	44
Vicarious liability	44
Primary liability: The organic theory	45
Privilege against self-incrimination	48
Piercing the Corporate Veil	49
Piercing the corporate veil	49
Sham	49
Statutory directives to pierce the corporate veil	49
Insolvent trading	49
Debts incurred as trustee	51
Common law rules regarding piercing the corporate veil	51
Avoiding a legal obligation	52
Fraud	52
Agency	53
Corporate groups	56
Trusts	58
Public policy: The enemy	59
Review questions	59
Further reading	59

Chapter 4 Promoters and Pre-Registration Contracts — 61
Overview — 61
Promoters — 61
    Defining a promoter — 61
    Promoter's duties — 65
    Consequences of a breach of duty — 65
Pre-Registration Contracts — 66
    Pre-registration contracts at common law — 66
        Liability of the company — 66
        Liability of the promoter — 66
        Breach of warranty of authority — 67
    Reimbursement of promoter's costs — 68
    Pre-registration contracts under the Corporations Act — 68
        Introduction — 68
        Person contracting on behalf of or for benefit of the company — 69
        Agency — 69
        Types of contracts — 71
    Contract pre-registration — 71
    Registration of the company or reasonably identifiable company — 74
        Registration — 74
        Company or reasonably identifiable company — 74
    Ratified or substituted pre-registration contract — 74
        What amounts to ratification? — 74
        What amounts to a substitution? — 75
        Ultra vires — 75
    Ratification or substitution within time limits — 76
    Effect of ratification — 76
    Effect of no ratification or substitution — 76
    Release from liability — 77
    Trustee's right of indemnity — 77
    Review question — 77
    Further reading — 78
    References Chapter 4 — 78

Chapter 5 Registration of Corporations — 79
Overview — 79
Registration of 'New' Companies — 79
    'Shelf' companies — 79
    Prerequisites to registration — 80
        Membership — 80
        Reservation of company name — 80
        Consent of director/secretary — 81
        Constitution — 81
    Application for registration — 82
    Documents to accompany application for registration — 82
    Registration — 82
    Certificate of registration — 83
    Effect of registration — 83

Post-registration requirements	83
Common seal	83
Appointment of officers and auditors	84
Registers	84
Minute books	85
Share issues	85
Accounting records	85
Annual general meeting	85
Registration of Existing Entities	85
Companies registered under Corporations Law	85
Transfer of registration of companies	86
Transfer of registration by non-companies	86
Registrable Australian Bodies	87
Foreign corporations	87
Review question	88
Further reading	88

Chapter 6 The Corporate Constitution — 89

Overview	89
Identifying the Corporate Constitution	89
Memorandum and articles	89
Mandatory and replaceable rules	90
Adopting/displacing replaceable rules	90
Legal Consequences of Mandatory Rules and Constitution	90
Altering the Constitution	91
Special resolution	91
Precondition in constitution	91
Alterations affecting members	92
Common law requirements	92
Statutory Contract	96
Binding nature of the constitution	96
Alterable contract	96
Separate contract	97
Independent contract	97
Interdependent contract	98
Parties to the statutory contract	99
Outsiders and the statutory contract	99
Members enforcing outsider rights	100
Ultra Vires Doctrine	102
Ultra vires doctrine at common law	102
Ultra vires in the narrow sense: Corporate capacity	103
Ultra vires in the wide sense: Members' and directors' powers	103
Review questions	105
Further reading	106

Chapter 7 Shares and Dividends — 107

Overview	107
Shares	108
Nature of a share	108
Evidence of shareholding	108

Classes of Shares	109
Power to issue different classes of shares	109
Defining a class of shares	109
Deferred shares	110
Ordinary shares	110
Preference shares	110
Governor's shares	112
Employee shares	113
Variation of class rights	113
Defining a variation of class rights	113
Procedure to vary class rights	114
Challenging a variation of class rights	115
Share Capital	116
Description of share capital	116
Altering share capital	117
Maintenance of share capital	117
Prerequisites for a reduction of share capital	117
Procedure for reduction of share capital	118
Challenging a reduction	119
Company purchasing its own shares	124
Prohibition on company purchasing its own shares	124
Buy-backs under Div 2 of Part 2J.1	124
Company lending money on security of its own shares	125
Prohibition on company lending money on security of its own shares	125
Exemptions	127
Company financially assisting purchase of its own shares	127
Prerequisites for financial assistance	127
Procedure for shareholder approval	131
Exemptions	131
Consequences	132
Dividends	132
Procedure for declaring/announcing dividends	132
Effect of declaring a dividend	133
Dividends must be paid out of profits	133
Definition of profits	134
Past years' losses	134
Events after the current financial year	134
Future profits	135
Net profits	136
Capital losses and gains	136
Net profits of the company declaring the dividend	141
Interim dividends	142
Consequences	143
Review questions	143
Further reading	144

Chapter 8 Corporate Fundraising — 146
Overview — 146
Debt Capital — 147
  Pros and cons of debt capital — 147
  Form of debt capital — 147
    Debentures — 147
  Security for debt capital — 148
    Charges — 148
    Fixed and floating charges — 148
    Negative pledges — 149
    Registration of charges — 150
  Definition of securities — 151
  Offers requiring disclosure — 151
  Exceptions to disclosure requirements — 152
    Small scale offerings — 153
    Sophisticated and professional investors — 154
  Disclosure document — 155
    Definition of disclosure document — 155
    Prospectus — 155
    Continuously quoted securities — 156
    Short form prospectus — 157
    Profile statement — 157
    Offer information statement — 158
  Clear, concise and effective disclosure — 159
  Supplementary and replacement disclosure document — 159
    Obligation to correct information — 159
    Supplementary document — 160
    Replacement document — 160
    Stop orders — 161
  Requirements for offering securities — 161
    Preparation of disclosure document — 161
    Lodgement with ASIC — 161
    Exposure period — 162
  Defective disclosure — 162
    Prohibition — 162
    Criminal liability — 162
    Civil liability — 163
  Restrictions on advertising and publicity — 164
    Prohibition — 164
    Exemptions — 165
    Hawking securities — 166
  Financial Services Reform Act — 166
  Review question — 167
  Further reading — 167

Chapter 9 Appointment and Removal of Directors — 169
Overview — 169
Board of Directors — 169
  Role of board of directors — 169
  Division of power between board and general meeting — 170

Directors and Officers	171
Definition of director	171
Definition of officer	175
Validation of appointment	176
Section 129 assumptions	176
Indoor management rule	176
Validation of acts under ss 201M and 204E	177
Court's power to validate acts under s 1322(4)(a)	178
Company Officers	178
Executive and non-executive directors	178
Managing director	178
Chief executive officer	179
Governing director	179
Associate director	179
Chairperson	179
Alternate director	180
Secretary	180
Qualifications	181
Natural persons	181
Number	181
Residence	181
Age	181
Share qualification	181
Consent	181
Disqualification	182
Managing a corporation	182
Automatic disqualification for conviction of certain offences	182
Automatic disqualification of an undischarged bankrupt	183
Court's power to disqualify for breaching civil penalty provisions	184
Court's power to disqualify for managing insolvent companies	188
Court's power to disqualify for repeated breaches of the Corporations Act	188
ASIC's power to disqualify persons subject to liquidator's report	191
Court's power to grant leave to manage a corporation	193
Appointment of Directors	196
First directors	196
Subsequent directors	196
Directors' Remuneration	197
Right to remuneration at common law	197
Right to remuneration under the replaceable rules	197
Single director/shareholder companies	197
Listed entities	197
Managing director	197
Disclosure requirements	197
Listed entities	198
Resignation and Removal of Directors	198
Resignation	198

Vacation of office	199
Retirement by rotation	199
Automatic vacation under the Corporations Act	199
Automatic vacation under constitution	199
Removal of directors	200
Proprietary companies	200
Public companies	200
Payments for loss of office	201
Review questions	203
Further reading	203

Chapter 10 Directors' Duties   204

Overview	204
Duty to Act Honestly/in Good Faith and in the Best Interests of the Company	205
Fiduciary duty	205
What constitutes the company's interests?	205
Company's interests	205
Shareholders	205
Nominee directors	210
Group companies	212
Creditors	212
Employees and other third parties	218
Equitable relief	219
Statutory duty	219
Relationship with other duties	220
Consequences of a breach	220
Civil penalty	220
Disqualification	221
Compensation	227
Criminal offence	227
Duty Not to Fetter Discretion	228
Proper Purpose Doctrine	228
Fiduciary duty	228
Directors' honesty	228
Importance of improper purpose	229
Share issues	229
Registration of share transfers	232
Consequences of breach	234
Generally	234
Share issue	235
Registration of share transfer	235
Statutory duty	235
Duty to Avoid a Conflict of Interests	235
Fiduciary duty	235
Contracting with the company at common law	236
Contracting with the company under the constitution	237
Contracting with the company under the Corporations Act	238

Use of position for personal profit in equity	243
Use of position for personal profit under Corporations Act	249
Duty to Act with Due Care and Diligence	254
Common law	254
Statutory duty of care and diligence	258
Business judgment rule	259
Reliance and delegation	259
Consequences of breach	260
Insolvent Trading	261
Duty to prevent insolvent trading	261
Insolvency	261
Debt	262
'Incurring' a debt	262
Objective test	263
Defences	263
Consequences of breaching s 588G	267
Compensation	267
Civil penalty	267
Criminal offence	267
Review question	268
Further reading	268

Chapter 11 Meetings — 270

Overview	270
What Constitutes a Meeting?	270
More than one person	270
Meeting in person	271
Resolutions and declarations without meetings	271
Board Meetings	272
Convening board meetings	272
Notice	274
Attendance at board meetings	275
Quorum	275
Voting	275
Minutes	276
Annual General Meeting	276
Obligation to convene annual general meeting	276
Convening an annual general meeting	276
Agenda	276
General Meetings	277
Directors' power to convene a general meeting	277
Members requisitioning a general meeting under s 249D	277
Who may requisition a general meeting under s 249D?	277
Basis for requisitioning general meeting	277
Notice	278
Members' right to convene general meeting	278
Members convening a general meeting under s 249F	278

Court's power to order the convening of a general meeting under s 249G	278
Basis for an order convening a general meeting	278
What is 'impracticable'?	279
Notice of general meetings	281
Length of notice	281
Service of notice	281
Content of notice	282
Directors' duty to provide sufficient information	282
Circulation of members' resolution and statement	285
Quorum	285
Resolutions	286
Proxies	286
Appointment of proxies	286
Revocation of proxy's appointment	287
Rights and powers of a proxy	287
Representatives	287
Appointment of representative	287
Rights and powers of representative	288
Voting	288
Show of hands	288
Poll	288
Chairperson's casting vote	289
Minutes of general meeting	289
Validating procedural irregularities	289
Review questions	291
Further reading	291

Chapter 12 Members' Remedies — 293

Outline	293
Rule in *Foss v Harbottle*	293
Proper plaintiff rule	293
Common law exceptions to *Foss v Harbottle*	295
Personal rights	296
Statutory Derivative Action	300
Standing to seek leave to bring a derivative action	300
Grounds for an application	302
Company will not bring proceedings	302
Notice	302
Good faith	303
Best interests of the company	305
Serious question to be tried	306
Substitution of litigant	306
Ratification	307
Court's powers	307
Independent investigator	307
Costs	307
Leave to settle proceedings	308

Oppression	308
Oppressive or unfairly prejudicial or discriminatory conduct	308
Standing under s 234	308
Who may be the oppressor?	311
Scope of s 232	311
Objective test	311
Act or omission	312
Isolated past conduct or continuous course of conduct	312
Ultra vires, illegal or want of probity	312
Discriminatory	312
Oppressive conduct	313
Unfairly prejudicial or discriminatory conduct	314
Contrary to interests of members as a whole	321
Nature of relief under s 233	321
Injunctions	322
Introduction	322
Standing to apply for injunction	322
Nature of relief under s 1324	328
Right to Inspect Books	328
Members' right to inspect books	328
Directors' right to inspect books	329
Review questions	329
Further reading	330
Chapter 13 External Administration	**331**
Overview	331
Receivership	332
Appointment of receiver	332
Appointment by creditor	332
Appointment by a court	332
Impact of appointment on directors' powers	337
Termination of appointment	337
Receiver's powers	338
Receiver's duties	338
Receiver's liability	339
Schemes of Arrangement	340
Defining compromise or arrangement	340
Agreement to scheme	340
Convening meeting to consider proposal	340
Explanatory statement	341
Court's discretion to approve compromise or arrangement	341
Administration of Company	343
Appointment of administrator	343
Impact of appointment on directors' powers	344
Termination of appointment	345
Committee of creditors	345
Administrator's powers	345
Administrator's duties	346
Administrator's liability	347
Moratorium	351

Termination of administration	351
Creditors' meeting	352
Winding Up	352
Types of winding up	352
Appointment of liquidator	353
Impact of appointment on directors' powers	355
Termination of liquidator's appointment	355
Liquidator's powers	356
Liquidator's duties	356
Liquidator's liability	357
Winding up by the court	357
Court's power to wind up a company	357
Winding up in insolvency	357
Winding up on other grounds	359
Voluntary winding up	367
Application by members	367
Application by creditors	368
Court's powers	368
Deregistration	368
Types of deregistration	368
Voluntary deregistration	368
Deregistration initiated by ASIC	369
Reinstatement	369
Review questions	370
Further reading	371
Index	373

Acknowledgments

The author wishes to thank the following for permission to reproduce materials:

CCH Australia, for extracts from cases reported in the *Australian Company Law Cases*.

Commonwealth Copyright Administration, for extracts from the Companies and Securities Law Review Committee Report No 12, *Enforcement of the Duties of Directors and Officers of a Company by Means of a Statutory Directive* (November 1990).

Council of Law Reporting for NSW, for extracts from cases reported in the *New South Wales Law Reports*.

The Federal Court of Australia, for extracts from Federal Court cases.

Incorporated Council of Law Reporting for England and Wales for extracts from cases from the *Law Reports (Appeal Cases)*, *Law Reports (Chancery Division)*.

Lawbook Co, part of Thomson Legal & Regulatory Limited for extracts from cases from the *Commonwealth Law Reports*.

LexisNexis for extracts from cases from the *All England Law Reports*, the *Australian Company Law Reports*, *Australian Corporations and Securities Reports* and the *Victorian Reports*.

Table of Cases

(references in **bold** are to extracts of cases)

Aberdeen Rly Co v Blaikie Brothers (1854) 1 Macq 461: 10.640
ACCC v ASIC [2000] NSWSC 316: 13.780
ACCC v George Weston Foods Ltd (2000) ATPR ¶41-763: 10.220
ACCC v Universal Music Australia Pty Limited (No 2) (2002) ATPR ¶41-862; [2002] FCA 192: 9.480, 10.220
Adams v ASIC [2003] FCA 557: 9.610
Adler v ASIC; Williams v ASIC (2003) 21 ACLC 1810: 7.440, 10.580, 10.670
Adler v DPP [2004] NSWCCA 352: 10.260
Adnot Pty Ltd, Re (1982) 1 ACLC 307; (1982) 7 ACLR 212: 13.420
Advance Bank Australia Ltd (No 2), Re (1997) 22 ACSR 513: 7.160
Advance Bank of Australia v FAI Insurances (1987) 9 NSWLR 464: 10.340
Advent Investors Pty Ltd v Michael Goldhirsch (2001) 19 ACLC 580: 12.50
Agushi and ASC, Re (1996) 19 ACSR 322: 9.580
Ailsa v Watson (1846) 1 Shad 77: 13.30
Airpeak Pty Ltd v Jetstream Aircraft Ltd (1997) 23 ACSR 715: 12.480, 12.490, **12.510**
Alabama New Orleans Texas and Pacific Junction Railway Co, Re [1891] 1 Ch 213: 13.240
Albert Locke (1940) Ltd v Winsford UDC (1973) 71 LGR (Eng) 308: 3.260
Alessi v Original Australian Art Co Pty Ltd (1989) 7 ACLC 595: 13.420
Allen v Atalay (1994) 12 ACLC 7: 12.480, 12.510
Allen v Gold Reefs of West Africa [1900] 1 Ch 656: 6.100, 6.110, 6.140, 6.150, 7.210
Allgas Energy Ltd, Re (1998) 27 ACSR 729: 7.160
Allied Mining and Processing Ltd v Boldbow Pty Ltd [2002] WASC 195: 9.960
Aloridge Pty Ltd (prov liq apptd) v West Australian Gem Explorers Pty Ltd (in liq) (1996) 22 ACSR 484: 9.890, 9.950, 12.440
Altim Pty Ltd, Re [1968] 2 NSWR 762: 9.460, 9.610

AM Spicer & Son Pty Ltd (in liq) v Spicer (1931) 47 CLR 151: 10.430
Ammonia Soda Co Ltd v Chamberlain [1918] 1 Ch D 266: 7.540
Ansett Airlines Ltd and Korda, Re (2002) 20 ACLC 1187: 13.360
Ansett Airlines Ltd and Mentha, Re (2001) 19 ACLC 1678: 13.360
ANZ Executors & Trustee Co Ltd v Qintex Australia Ltd (1990) 8 ACLC 980: 6.230, **6.240**
Arakella v Paton [2004] NSWSC 13: 6.100
ASC v AS Nominees Ltd (1995) 133 ALR 1: 9.70
ASC v Donovan (1998) 28 ACSR 583: 10.220
ASC v Forem-Freeway Enterprises (1999) 17 ACLC 511: 9.480, 10.220
ASC v Forem-Freeway Enterprises Pty Ltd (1999) 30 ACSR 399: 9.490
ASC v Multiple Sclerosis Society of Tasmania (1993) 11 ACLC 461: 12.330
ASC v Roussi (1999) 32 ACSR 568: 9.480, 10.220
ASC v SIB Resources NL (1991) 9 ACLC 1147: 2.160, 5.120
Ascot Investments Pty Ltd v Harper (1981) 148 CLR 337: 3.220
Ashbury Carriage & Iron Co v Riche (1875) LR 7 HL 653: 6.220
ASIC v Adler (2002) 20 ACLC 1146: **9.480**, 9.490, 10.220, 10.580, 10.670
ASIC v Adler (2002) 20 ACLC 576: **7.440**, 7.480, 9.470, 9.540, **10.220, 10.580, 10.670**, 10.700
ASIC v Doyle [2001] WASC 187: 10.670
ASIC v Hutchings (2001) 38 ACSR 387: 9.480, 9.490, 10.220
ASIC v National Exchange Pty Ltd (2003) 21 ACLC 1652: 8.450
ASIC v Parkes (2001) 38 ACSR 355: 9.480, 10.220
ASIC v Pegasus Leveraged Options Group P/L [2002] NSWSC 310: 9.490
ASIC v Starnex Securities Pty Ltd [2003] FCA 1375: **9.530**
ASIC v United Investment Funds Pty Ltd [2003] FCA 674: 3.130
Atherton v Anderson 99 F 2d 883, 889-890 (6 Cir 1938): 10.700

Atherton v Plane Creek Central Mill Co Ltd [1914] St R Qd 73: 12.40
Atkins v Smith (1851) 5 Shad 103: 13.30
Attorney-General's Reference (No 2 of 1982) [1984] QB 624: 10.120
Augold NL, Re [1987] 2 Qd R 297: 12.560
Australasian Oil Exploration Ltd v Lachberg (1958) 101 CLR 119: 7.590, 7.630
Australian Fixed Trusts Pty Ltd v Clyde Industries Ltd [1959] SR (NSW) 33: 6.100
Australian Hydrocarbons NL v Green (1985) 10 ACLR 72: 11.810
Australian Innovation Ltd v Petrovsky (1996) 21 ACSR 218: 10.40, 10.50
Australian Metropolitan Life Assurance Co Ltd v Ure (1923) 33 CLR 199: 10.280, **10.330**, 10.370
Australian Competition and Consumer Commission see ACCC
Australian Securities and Investments Commission see ASIC
Australian Securities Commission see ASC
Automatic Self-Cleansing Filter Syndicate Co Ltd v Cuninghame [1906] 2 Ch 34: 2.280, **9.20**, 10.320
Aztech Science Pty Ltd v Atlanta Aerospace (Woy Woy) Pty Ltd [2004] NSWSC 967: 4.190
Bagnall v Carlton (1877) 6 Ch D 371: 4.10
Bagot Well Pastoral Co Pty Ltd, Re (1992) 9 ACSR 129: 7.500, 8.00
Bagot Well Pastoral Co Pty Ltd, Re (1993) 11 ACLC 1: 12.440
Bailey v Mandala Private Hospital Pty Ltd (1987) 12 ACLR 641: 10.150
Bailey v NSW Medical Defence Union Ltd (1995) 184 CLR 399: 6.150, 6.160, 6.190
Baillie v Oriental Telephone Co [1915] 1 Ch 503: 12.40
Bamford v Bamford [1970] 1 Ch 212: 10.120, 10.340, 10.350, 10.650
Bangor and North Wales Mutual Marine Protection Association, Re [1899] 2 Ch 593: 2.140
Bank of Hindustan China and Japan Ltd v Alison (1871) LR 6 CP 222: 7.240
Bank of New Zealand v Fiberi Pty Ltd (1994) 12 ACLC 48: 9.140
Barnes v Andrews 298 F 614 (SDNY 1924): 10.700
Barrett v Duckett (1996) 14 ACLC 3101: 12.10
Barron v Potter [1914] 1 Ch 895: 11.150

Bay v Illawarra Stationery Supplies Pty Ltd (1986) 4 ACLC 429: **4.110**
Beattie v E & F Beattie Ltd [1938] Ch 708: 6.190
Beckingham v Port Jackson and Manly Steamship Authority [1957] SR (NSW) 403: 2.60
Bell v Burton (1993) 12 ACSR 325: 11.120
Bell v Lever Bros Ltd [1932] AC 161: 10.50
Bell Bros' case (1891) 65 LT 245: 10.330
Bellador Silk Ltd, Re [1965] 1 All ER 667: 12.320
Biala Pty Ltd v Mallina Holdings Ltd (1993) 11 ACLC 751: 12.40
Biggerstaff v Rowatt's Wharf [1896] 2 Ch 93: 9.210
Birch v Cropper (1889) 14 App Cas 525: 7.60, 7.110
BL & GY International Co Ltd v Hypec Electronics Pty Ltd (2003) 171 FLR 268: 12.110
Black v Smallwood [1966] ALR 744: 4.50, 4.60, 4.70
Blackburn v Industrial Equity Ltd [1976] ACLC ¶40-267: 7.610
Bleriot Aircraft Co, Re (1916) 32 TLR 253: 13.630
Blisset v Daniel (1853) 10 Hare 493: 13.640
Blundell v Macrocam Pty Ltd [2004] NSWSC 895: 13.320
Boardman v Phipps [1966] 3 All ER 721: 10.390
Bond Brewing Holdings Ltd v National Australia Bank (1990) 8 ACLC 330: **13.30**
Bond v R (2000) 164 ALR 607: 1.70
Bonelli's Telegraph Co, In re (Collie's Claim) (1871) LR 12 Eq 246: 11.60, 11.100
Borland's Trustee v Steel Bros & Co Ltd [1901] 1 Ch 279: 7.10
Borough Commercial and Building Society, Re [1893] 2 Ch 242: 2.150
Brambles Holdings Ltd v Carey (1976) 2 ACLR 176: 3.90
Brashs Pty Ltd, In re (1994) 15 ACSR 477: 13.270
Breavington v Godleman (1988) 62 ALJR 447; 80 ALR 362: 1.90
Bright Pine Mills Pty Ltd, Re [1969] VR 1002: 12.360
Brighton & Dyke Rwy, Re (1890) 44 Ch D 28: 7.100, 7.110
Brightwell v RFB Holdings [2003] NSWSC 7: 12.120, 12.170
Broadcasting Station 2GB Pty Ltd, Re [1964-1965] NSWR 1648: 10.50

Broken Hill Proprietary Co Pty Ltd v Bell Resources Ltd (1984) 2 ACLC 157: 12.490, 12.510
Brooks v Heritage Hotel Adelaide Pty Ltd (1996) 20 ACSR 61: 10.820
Browne v La Trinidad (1887) 37 Ch D 1: 6.190
Brunninghausen v Glavanics (1999) 17 ACLC 1247: 10.40, **10.50**, 10.160
Brylyn No 2 Pty Ltd, Re (1988) 6 ACLC 505; (1987) 12 ACLR 697: 13.420
Bugle Press Ltd, Re [1961] Ch 270: 3.160
Bulfin v Bebarfalds Ltd (1938) 38 SR (NSW) 423: 11.490
Burland v Earle [1902] AC 83: 10.390
CAC v Bracht (1989) 7 ACLC 40: 9.390
CAC v Drysdale (1978) 141 CLR 236: **9.50**, 9.170
CAC v Ekamper (1988) 6 ACLC 90: 9.540
CAC v Lombard Nash International Pty Ltd (No 3) (1987) 5 ACLC 1020: 13.40
Campaign Holdings Ltd, Re (1990) 8 ACLC 64: 7.320
Campbell v Watson 62 NJ Eq at 416, 50 A 120: 10.700
Canadian Aero Service Ltd v O'Malley (1973) 40 DLR (3d) 371: 10.610
Canadian Land Reclaiming & Colonizing Co, In re (Coventry and Dixon's Case) (1880) 14 Ch D 660: 9.50
Canny Gabriel Castle Jackson Advertising Pty Ltd v Volume Sales (Finance) Pty Ltd (1974) 131 CLR 321: 2.60, **2.90**
Capital Services Ltd, Re (1983) 1 ACLC 1,270: 13.420
Captech Group Ltd v ASIC (2004) 22 ACLC 93: 8.200
Carapark Industries Pty Ltd (in liq), Re [1967] 1 NSWR 337: 13.420
Caratti Holding Co Pty Ltd, Re (1975) 1 ACLR 87: 6.200
Carpenter v Pioneer Park Pty Ltd [2004] NSWSC 1007: 12.100, 12.110, 12.120, 12.170
Carrier Australia Ltd v Hunt (1939) 61 CLR 534: 6.160
Carruth v Imperial Chemical Industries Ltd [1937] AC 707: 12.410
Castlereagh Motels Ltd v Davies-Roe (1966) 67 SR (NSW) 279: 10.500
Central Railway of Venezuela v Kisch (1867) LR 2 HL 99: 4.20
Chan v Zacharia (1984) 154 CLR 178: 10.390
Charles v FCT (1954) 90 CLR 598: 2.40
Charlton v Baber (2003) 21 ACLC 1671: 12.120, 12.170

Charterbridge Corp Ltd v Lloyds Bank Ltd [1970] 1 Ch 62: 10.10
Chew v R (1992) 10 ACLC 816: 10.670
Cinema Plus v ANZ Bank [2000] NSWSC 658: 13.370
Clamp v Fairway Investments Pty Ltd [1973] CLC 27,599: 11.160
Claremont Petroleum NL v Cummings; Claremont Petroleum NL v Fuller (1992) 10 ACLC 1,685, 9 ACSR 1: 9.900, 10.670
Claremont Petroleum NL v Indosuez Nominees Pty Ltd (1986) 4 ACLC 315: 9.900
Claremont Petroleum NL, Re [1990] 2 Qd 31: 12.560
Clements Marshall Consolidated Ltd v ENT Ltd (1988) 6 ACLC 389: 7.60
Club Flotilla (Pacific Palms) Ltd v Isherwood (1987) 12 ACLR 387: 9.290
Club Mediterranean Pty Ltd, Re (1975-1976) CLC ¶40-204; (1975) 11 SASR 481: 13.420
CMPS & F Pty Ltd, Re (1997) 24 ACSR 728: 7.550
Collen v Wright (1857) 120 ER 241: 4.70
Collie Power Co Pty Ltd, Re (1952) 54 WALR 44: 7.100
Colotone Holdings Ltd v Calsil Ltd [1965] VR 129: 12.490
Commissioner for Corporate Affairs v Ekamper (1988) 6 ACLC 90; (1987) 12 ACLR 519: 9.480, 10.220
Commonwealth Bank of Australia v Australian Solar Information Pty Ltd (1987) 5 ACLC 124: **4.130**
Commonwealth Bank of Australia v Friedrich (1991) 9 ACLC 946: 10.700
Compaction Systems Pty Ltd, Re (1976) 2 ACLR 135: 11.360, 11.800
Company, Re a [1983] 1 WLR 927: 13.650
Company, Re a [1985] BCLC 333: 3.150
Company, Re a [1989] BCLC 13: 9.60
Const v Harris (1824) Tur & Rus 496: 13.640
Consul Developments Pty Ltd v DPC Estates Pty Ltd (1975) 132 CLR 373: 7.480
Cook v Deeks [1916] 1 AC 554: 10.390, 10.620
Cooke v Fairbairn [2003] NSWSC 232: 12.440, 13.650
Copal Varnish Co, In re [1917] 2 Ch 349: 10.330
Cope v Butcher (1996) 20 ACSR 37: 10.40
Corsicana Nat'l Bank v Johnson 251 US 68, 71, 40 S Ct 82, 84, 64 L Ed 141 (1919): 10.700

TABLE OF CASES

Costa & Duppe Properties Pty Ltd v Duppe [1986] VR 90: 2.40
Cotman v Broughman [1918] AC 514: 13.630
Cousins v International Brick Co Ltd [1931] 2 Ch 90: 11.630
Cox v Hickman (1860) 8 HL Cas 268: 2.60
Credit Corporation Australia Pty Ltd v Atkins (1999) 17 ACLC 756: 10.870
Crichton's Oil Co, Re [1902] 2 Ch 86: 7.100
Crumpton v Morrine Hall Pty Ltd [1965] NSWR 240: 7.60
Cullen v CAC (1989) 7 ACLC 121: 9.390
Cullen v Wills, Adler and Jooste (1991) 9 ACLC 1450: 12.490
Cumberland Holdings Ltd v Washington H Soul Pattinson & Co Ltd (1977) 13 ALR 561: 12.330
Cumbrian Newspapers Group Ltd v Cumberland & Westmorland Herald Newspapers & Printing Co Ltd [1987] Ch 1: 6.140
Czerwinski v Syrena Royal Pty Ltd (2000) 18 ACLC 337: 12.570
Daimler Co Ltd v Continental Tyre and Rubber Co (Great Britain) Ltd [1916] 2 AC 307: 3.280
Dalkeith Investments Pty Ltd, Re (1984) 9 ACLR 247: 12.440
Dalkeith Investments Pty Ltd, Re (1985) 3 ACLC 74: 13.650
Daniels v Anderson (1995) 13 ACLC 614: **10.700**
Daniels v Daniels [1978] Ch 406: 12.40
Darby, Re; ex p Broughton [1911] 1 KB 95: 3.230
Darvall v North Brick & Tile Co Ltd (1989) 6 ACLC 154; (1989) 7 ACLC 659: 7.420, 10.330
Darvall v North Sydney Brick & Tile Co Ltd (1988) 6 ACLC 154: 10.310
Davidson v Smith (1989) 15 ACLR 732: 10.270
Deloitte Haskins & Sells v National Mutual Life Nominees (1991) 5 NZCLC 67: 10.700
Delonga and ASC, Re (1995) 13 ACLC 246: 9.560
Dennis Wilcox Pty Ltd v FCT (1988) 79 ALR 267: 3.250
Derry v Peek (1889) 14 AC 337: 8.400
Devereaux Holdings Pty Ltd v Pelsart Resources NL (No 2) (1986) 4 ACLC 12: **11.490**
DHN Food Distributors Ltd v London Borough of Tower Hamlets [1976] 1 WLR 852: 3.260
DHN Food Distributors Ltd v Tower Hamlets London Borough Council [1976] 3 All ER 462:1

Dickson v Federal Commissioner of Taxation (1940) 62 CLR 687: 7.630
Diesels & Components Pty Ltd, Re (1985) 3 ACLC 555: 13.170
Dimbulla Valley (Ceylon) Tea Co Ltd v Laurie [1961] Ch 353: 7.110, 7.600, 7.610, 7.630
Ding v Sylvania Waterways Ltd (1999) 17 ACLC 531: 6.80
Dodd v Wilkinson 42 NJ Eq 647, 651, 9 A 685 (E & A 1887): 10.700
Dodge v Ford Motor Co (1919) 170 WN 668: 10.150
Doherty v FCT (1933) 2 ATD 272: 2.40
Dominion Cotton Mills Co v Amyot [1912] AC 546: 10.330
Donnelly v Edelsten (1994) 13 ACSR 196: 3.250
Dorman Long & Co, Re [1934] Ch 635: **13.240**
Dosike Pty Ltd v Johnson (1996) 22 ACSR 752: 12.430
Downey v Crawford [2004] FCA 1264: 13.250
DPP Reference No 1 of 2000 [2001] NTSC 91: 3.50
Duffy v Super Centre Development Corp Ltd [1967] 1 NSWR 382: **13.50**
Duke Group Ltd (in liq) v Pilmer (1999) 17 ACLC 1329: 3.70, 10.700
Duke Group Ltd v Pilmer (1999) 73 SASR 64: 2.60
Dunn v Shapowloff [1978] NSWLR 235: 10.950
Duomatic Limited, In re [1969] 2 Ch 365: 10.120, 11.360
Dwyer v Lippiatt [2004] QSC 281: 10.610
Dynasty Pty Ltd v Coombs (1994) 12 ACLC 915; (1995) 13 ACLC 1290: 12.350
East v Bennett [1911] 1 Ch 163: 11.20
East West Promotions Pty Ltd, Re (1986) 4 ACLC 84: 12.340
Ebrahimi v Westbourne Galleries Ltd [1973] AC 360: 9.950, 12.380, 12.440, 13.630, **13.640**
Edmonds v Foster (1875) 45 LJ MC 41: 9.50
Edwards & Ors v AG (2004) 22 ACLC 1177: 3.190
Edwards v Halliwell [1950] 2 All ER 1064: 12.40
Efstathis v Greek Orthodox Community of St George (1988) 6 ACLC 706; 13 ACLR 691: 12.90
El Sombrero Ltd, In re [1958] Ch 900: 11.360
Elders Executors and Trustee Co v EG Reeves Pty Ltd (1987) 78 ALR 193: 4.10

Elders IXL Ltd, Re (1984) 4 ACLC 736: 7.320
Elderslie Finance Corp Ltd v Australian Securities Commission (1993) 11 ACLC 787: 11.800
Electric Light and Power Supply Corporation Ltd v Cormack (1911) 11 SR (NSW) 350: 3.220
Electro Research v Stec (1996) 20 ACSR 320: 11.120, 11.140, 11.490
Eley v Positive Government Security Life Assurance Co Ltd (1876) 1 Ex D 88: **6.180**, 6.190
Emlen Pty Ltd v St Barbara Mines Ltd (1997) 24 ACSR 303: 10.290, 10.310, 12.510
Emma Silver Mining Co Ltd v Lewis & Son (1879) 4 CPD 396: 4.10
Engineers' case (1920) 28 CLR 129: 1.90
English, Scottish and Australian Chartered Bank, In re [1893] 3 Ch 385: 13.230
Environment Protection Authority v Caltex Refining Co Pty Ltd (1993) 178 CLR 477: 3.130
Equiticorp Financial Services Ltd v Bank of New Zealand (1993) 11 ACLC 952: 10.90
Erlanger v New Sombrero Phosphate Co (1878) 3 App Cas 1218: 4.10, 4.20, 4.30
Ernst & Young (Reg) v Tynski Pty Ltd (CAN 008 162 123) (Receivers and Managers Appointed) [2003] FCAFC 233: 13.30
Eromanga Hydrocarbons NL v Australia Mining NL (1988) 6 ACLC 906: 12.40
Esplanade Developments Ltd v Dinive Holdings Pty Ltd [1980] ACLC 34,232: 10.40
Exchange Banking Co (Flitcroft's case), Re (1882) 21 Ch D 519: 7.520
Expo International Pty Ltd v Chant [1979] 2 NSWLR 820: 13.20
Farrow Finance Company Ltd (in liq) v Farrow Properties Pty Ltd (in liq) (1998) 16 ACLC 897: 10.80
FCT v Everett (1980) 80 ATC 4076: 2.80
FCT v St Helens Farm (ACT) Pty Ltd (1981) 146 CLR 336: 7.30
Federal Commissioner of Taxation v Miller Anderson Ltd (1946) 73 CLR 341: 7.630
Federal Deposit Insurance Corporation v Bierman 2 F 3d 1424 (1993): 10.700
Feher v ASC (1997) 15 ACLC 1774: 9.580
Ferrari Furniture, Re [1972] 2 NSWLR 790: 9.610
Fire Nymph Products Ltd v Heating Centre Pty Ltd (1989) 7 ACLC 90; (1992) 10 ACLC 629: 8.70
Fireproof Doors Ltd, Re [1916] 2 Ch 142: 11.160
Fitzsimmons v R (1997) 15 ACLC 666; (1997) 23 ACSR 355: 10.670
Fitzsimmons v R (1997) 23 ACSR 355: 7.470, 10.80
Fletcher v National Mutual Life Nominees Ltd [1990] 3 NZLR 641: 10.700
Forbes v New South Wales Trotting Club Ltd [1977] 2 NSWLR 515: 6.190
Forge v ASIC [2004] NSWCA 448: 10.210, 10.350, 10.620
Forkserve Pty Ltd v Jack (2001) 19 ACLC 299: 9.70, 10.670
Foss v Harbottle (1843) 2 Hare 461; 67 ER 189: 2.280, 9.30, 10.50, **12.10**, 12.40, 12.80, 12.90, 12.110, 12.120, 12.160, 12.250, 12.500, 12.510
Fowlers Vacola Manufacturing Co Ltd, Re [1966] VR 97: 7.160
Francis v United Jersey Bank 432 A 2d 814 (1981): 10.700
Fraser v NRMA Holdings Ltd (1995) 127 ALR 543: 11.490
Fraser v NRMA Holdings Ltd (1995) 55 FCR 452: 7.320
Fulham Football Club v Cabra Estates plc [1992] BCC 863: 10.270
Furs Ltd v Tomkies (1936) 54 CLR 583: 10.650
G Jeffrey (Mens Store) Pty Ltd, Re (1984) 2 ACLC 421: 7.500, 12.320, 12.440
Gamble v Hoffman (1997) 24 ACSR 369: 10.700
Gambotto v WCP Ltd (1995) 182 CLR 432: 6.100, **6.110**, 6.120, 7.210, 7.330, 9.950
Garden Mews-St Leonards Pty Ltd v Butler Pollnow Pty Ltd (No 4) (1984) 2 ACLC 682: 13.420
Gas Lighting Improvement Co Ltd v IRC [1923] AC 723: 3.140
George Barker (Transport) Ltd v Eyon [1973] 3 All ER 374: 13.70
German Date Coffee Co, Re (1882) 20 Ch D 169: 13.630
Gilford Motor Co Ltd v Horne [1933] Ch 935: 3.210, 3.260
Glenville Pastoral Co (1963) 109 CLR 199: 7.570
Glenville Pastoral Co Pty Ltd (in liq) v Commissioner of Taxation [1894] 2 Ch 239: 7.630
Glover v Willert (1996) 20 ACSR 182: 10.340
Gluckstein v Barnes [1900] AC 240: 4.20, 4.30
Gold Coast Holdings Pty Ltd (in liq), Re; Australian Securities and Investments Commission v Papotto, (2000) 35 ACSR 107: 9.530

TABLE OF CASES

Goozee v Graphic World Group Holdings Pty Ltd (2002) 20 ACLC 1502: 12,140, 12.190
Gould and Birbeck and Bacon v Mount Oxide Mines Ltd (In Liquidation) (1916) 22 CLR 490: 10.700
Gramophone and Typewriter Ltd v Stanley [1908] 2 KB 89: 3.250
Grant v John Grant & Sons Pty Ltd (1950) 82 CLR 1: 9.170
Gray v New Augarita Porcupine Mines Ltd [1952] 3 DLR 1: 10.420
Green & Clara Pty Ltd v Bestobell Industries Pty Ltd [1982] WAR 1: 10.390
Greenhalgh v Arderne Cinemas [1951] Ch 286: 7.160, 7.220, 10.20, 10.30
Greenhalgh v Arderne Cinemas Ltd [1946] 1 All ER 512: 7.160
Greymouth Point Elizabeth Railway and Coal Co Ltd, Re [1904] 1 Ch 32: 11.180
Grove v Flavel (1986) 4 ACLC 654: 10.130
Guerinoni v Argyle Concrete & Quarry Supplies Pty Ltd (unreported, WASC, 1999, Master Sanderson): 13.640
HA Stephenson & Son Ltd v Gillanders Arbuthnot & Co (1931) 45 CLR 476: 5.120
Halt Garage, In re (1964) Ltd [1982] 3 All ER 1016: 10.120
Hamilton v Whitehead (1988) 7 ACLC 34: 3.50, 3.80, 3.100
Hamilton-Irvine, Re (1990) 8 ACLC 1067: 9.610
Hampson v Prices Patent Candle Co (1876) 24 WR 754: 10.140
Hanel v O'Neill (2004) 22 ACLC 274: 3.190
Harlowe's Nominees Pty Ltd v Woodside (Lakes Entrance) Oil Co NL (1968) 121 CLR 483: 10.320, 12.410
Haven Gold Mining Co, Re (1882) 20 Ch D 151: 13.630
Hawcroft General Trading Co Ltd v Edgar (1996) 20 ACSR 541: 10.910
Hawkesbury Development Co Ltd v Landmark Finance Co Pty Ltd [1969] 2 NSWR 782: 12.40
Hawkesbury Development Corp Ltd v Landmark Finance Pty Ltd [1969] 2 NSWR 782: 13.70
Helwig v Jonas [1922] VLR 261: 11.490
Hely-Hutchinson v Brayhead [1968] 1 QB 549: 9.210
Henry v Great Northern Railway (1857) 44 ER 858: 10.30
Heron v Port Huon Fruitgrowers' Co-op Asscn Ltd (1922) 30 CLR 315: 6.190

Heydon v NRMA Ltd (2001) 51 NSWLR 1: 6.100
Hickman v Kent on Romney Marsh Sheepbreeders Association [1915] 1 Ch 881: 6.190, 6.200
Highfield Commodities Ltd, Re [1984] 3 All ER 884: 13.420
HIH Insurance Ltd (in prov liq); Australian Securities and Investments Commission v Adler (2002) 42 ACSR 80: 9.530
Hill v David Hill Electrical Discounts Pty Ltd (in liq) (2001) 19 ACLC 1000: 9.60
Hills Motorway, Re [2002] NSWSC 897: 13.190
Hills Motorway, Re The [2002] NSWSC 897: 7.60, 13.190
Hindle v John Cotton Ltd (1919) 56 Sc LR 625: 10.320
HL Bolton (Engineering) v TJ Graham and Sons Ltd [1956] 3 All ER 624: 3.80
Hobart Bridge Co Ltd v FCT (1951) 82 CLR 372: 3.140
Hogg v Cramphorn Ltd [1967] Ch 254: 10.290
Holders Investment Trust Ltd, Re [1971] 1 WLR 583: 7.130
Holders Investment Trust Ltd, Re [1971] 2 All ER 289: 7.200
Holmes v Life Funds of Australia Ltd (1971-1973) ACLC 27,177: 11.430
Horsley & Weight Ltd, In re [1982] 1 Ch 442: 10.120
Hospital Products Ltd v United States Surgical Corporation (1984) 156 CLR 41: 10.390, 10.670
Host-Plus Pty Ltd v Australian Hotels Association [2003] VSC 145: 13.650
Howard Smith Ltd v Ampol Petroleum Ltd [1974] AC 821: 10.290, 10.310, **10.320**, 12.410
Howard v Patent Ivory Manufacturing Co (1888) 38 Ch D 156: 9.140
HR Harmer Ltd, Re [1958] 3 All ER 689: 12.340, 12.390
Huddart, Parker & Co Proprietary Ltd v Moorehead (1909) 8 CLR 330: 1.90
Humes Ltd v Unity APA Ltd (1987) 5 ACLC 15: 11.300
Hunters Products Group Ltd (in liq) v Kindly Products Pty Ltd (1996) 20 ACSR 412: 7.430, 7.470, 7.480
Hutton v West Cork Railway Co (1883) 23 Ch D 654: 9.700, 10.180
HVAC Construction (Qld) Pty Ltd v Energy Equipment Engineering Pty Ltd [2002] FCA 1638: 13.450
Hypec Electronics Pty Ltd (in liq) v Mead [2004] NSWSC 731: 13.500

Iliopoulos v ASC (1997) 15 ACLC 1512: 9.560, 9.580
Imperial Chemical Industries Ltd, Re [1936] 1 Ch 587: 11.490
Imperial Mercantile Credit Association (Liquidators of) v Coleman (1873) LR 6 HL 189: 4.20
Independent Quarries Pty Ltd, Re (1993) 12 ACLC 159: 12.270
Industrial Equity Ltd v Blackburn (1977) 137 CLR 567: 3.180, 3.250, 3.260, 7.560, 7.610, 7.630, 7.640, 7.650, 10.80
Intagro v ANZ Banking Group (2004) 22 ACLC 1065: 3.190
International Goldfields Ltd, Re [2003] WASC 86: 13.200
Isak Constructions v Faress [2003] NSWSC 784: 12.140, 12.150, 12.160
Ito v Shinko (Australia) Pty Ltd [2004] QSC 268: 12.550, 12.560
Jeda Holdings Pty Ltd, Re (1977) 2 ACLR 438: 11.360
Jenashare Pty Ltd v Lemrib Pty Ltd (unreported, NSWSC, Young J, 1993): 11.120, 11.130, 11.350
Jermyn Street Turkish Baths Ltd, Re [1971] WLR 1042: 12.400
JN Taylor Holdings Ltd, Re (1991) 9 ACLC 1: **13.420**
John J Starr (Real Estate) Pty Ltd v Robert A Andrew (A'Asia) Pty Ltd (1991) 9 ACLC 1372: 12.440
John Shaw & Sons (Salford) Ltd v Shaw [1935] 2 KB 112: 2.280, 9.20, 9.30, 12.30
Johnny Oceans Restaurant Pty Ltd v Page [2003] NSWSC 952: 13.630
Johnson v Gore Wood [2001] 2 WLR 72: 10.40
Jones v Lipman [1962] 1 WLR 832: 3.210, 3.260
Jubilee Cotton Mills Ltd v Lewis [1924] AC 958: 5.120
Kalamazoo (Aust) Pty Ltd v Compact Business Systems Pty Ltd (1984) 84 FLR 101: 3.70
Kang-Kem v Paine [2004] NSWSC 3: **2.60**
Keech v Sandford (1726) Sel Cas T King 61: 10.600, 10.630
Kelner v Baxter (1866) LR 2 CP 174: 4.50, 4.60, 4.80
Killen's case: 11.490 ?
Kinsela v Russell Kinsela Pty Ltd (in liq) (1986) 10 ACLR 395: 10.110, **10.120**, 10.130, 10.160
Knightswood Nominees Pty Ltd v Sherwin Pastoral Co Ltd (1989) 7 ACLC 536: 12.560, 12.570

Kokotovich Constructions Pty Ltd v Wallington (1995) 13 ACLC 1113: 12.440
Kraus v JG Lloyd Pty Ltd [1965] VR 232: 9.30, 12.30
Krstevska v ACN 010505012 Pty Ltd (2002) 20 ACLC 292: 13.770, 13.780
La Monte v Mott 93 NJ Eq 229, 239, 107 A 462 (E & A 1921): 10.700
Lagunas Nitrate Co v Lagunas Syndicate [1899] 2 Ch 392: 4.10, 4.20
Lang v James Morrison & Co Ltd (1911) 13 CLR 1: 2.60
Lee v Lee's Air Farming Ltd [1961] AC 12: 2.210, **3.30**, 3.70
Lee v Neuchatel Asphalte Co (1889) 41 Ch D 1: 7.570, 7.580, 7.630
Leigh-Mardon Pty Ltd v Wawn (1995) 13 ACLC 1244: 10.870
Lennard's Carrying Co Ltd v Asiatic Petroleum Co Ltd [1915] AC 705: 3.80
Licata v Madeddu (Young J, 9 August 1985, unreported): 3.260
Lippitt v Ashley 89 Conn at 457, 94 A: 10.700
Liquorland (Aust) Pty Ltd v Anghie (2002) 20 ACLC 58: 12.520
Little v ASC (1996) 22 ACSR 226: 5.40
Littlewoods Mail Order Stores Ltd v IRC [1969] 1 WLR 1241: 3.270
Liverpool Marine Assurance Co; Greenshield's Case, In re (1852) 5 De G & Sm 599:, 10.330
Lloyd (Pauper) v Grace Smith & Co [1912] AC 716: 3.70
Loch v John Blackwood Ltd [1924] AC 783: 13.630
Lockyer Valley Fresh Foods Cooperative Association Ltd (1980) CLC ¶40-671: 13.420
London, Hamburg & Continental Exchange Bank, Emmerson's Case, Re (1866) LR 2 Eq 231: 13.420
Lubbock v British Bank of South America [1892] 2 Ch 199: 7.590
Luckins (Receiver and Manager of Australian Trailways Pty Ltd) v Highway Motel Carnarvon Pty Ltd (1975) 133 CLR 164: 5.270, 8.70
Lundie Bros Ltd, Re [1965] 1 WLR 1051: 13.630
M Dalley & Co Pty Ltd, Re (1968) 1 ACLR 489: 12.380, 12.400
Macaura v Northern Assurance Co Ltd [1925] AC 619: 2.40, 3.40, 6.240
Macleod v The Queen (2003) 21 ACLC 1601: 3.110
Macquarie Investments Pty Ltd, Re (1975) 1 ACLR 40: 9.620
Magarditch v ANZ Banking Group Ltd (1999) 17 ACLC 424: 12.10

Magna Alloys & Research Pty Ltd (1975) CLC 28,354; 1 ACLR 203: 9.480, 9.610, 10.220
Majestic Resources NL v Caveat Pty Ltd [2004] WASCA 201: 12.550
Manchester & Milford Railway Co, Re (1880) 14 Ch D 645: 13.70
Marks v Commonwealth (1964) 111 CLR 549: 9.820
Marra Developments Ltd v BW Rofe Pty Ltd [1977] 2 NSWLR 616: 7.100, 7.510, 7.550, 7.570, **7.630**, 7.650
Marsden, Re [1981] ACLC 33,210: 9.430, 9.620
Massey v Wales (2003) 21 ACLC 1978: 2.280, 9.20, 12.30
Maxwell Gratton v Carlton Football Club [2004] VSC 379: 11.300, 11.360
McBride v Hudson (1962) 107 CLR 604: 7.630
McLean v Burns Philp Trustee Co Pty Ltd (1985) 9 ACLR 926: 2.50
McLennan Holdings Pty Ltd, Re (1983) 1 ACLC 786; (1983) 7 ACLR 732: 13.420
McLure v Mitchell (1974) 6 ALR 471: 11.480
Meares v Acting Federal Commissioner of Taxation (1918) 24 CLR 369: 7.630
Melcann Ltd v Super John Pty Ltd (1995) 13 ACLC 92: 7.320
Merchants and Shippers ss Co Ltd, Re (1916) 17 SR(NSW) 21: 11.420
Mesenberg v Cord Industrial Recruiters Pty Ltd (1996) 19 ACSR 483: 10.50, 12.40, 12.500, 12.510
Metropolitan Fire Systems Pty Ltd v Miller (1997) 23 ACSR 699: 10.870, 10.920, 10.930, 10.940, **10.950**
Mike Gaffikin Marine Pty Ltd v Princess Street Marina Pty Ltd (1995) 13 ACLC 991: 12.290, 12.300
Milburn v Pivot Ltd (1997) 15 ACLC 1520: 7.460
Milfull v Terranora Lakes Country Club Ltd [2002] FCA 178: 12.100
Mills v Mills (1938) 60 CLR 150: 10.280, 10.310, 10.320, 10.670, 12.410
Minimix Industries Ltd, Re (1982) 1 ACLC 511: 9.430
Mistmorn Pty Ltd (in liq) v Yasseen (1996) 21 ACSR 173: 9.80
Molomby v Whitehead (1985) 63 ALR 282: 10.250
Montgomery Windsor (NSW) Pty Ltd v Ilopa Pty Ltd (1984) 2 ACLC 224: 13.420
Moorgate Mercantile Holdings Ltd, Re [1980] 1 All ER 40: 11.460
Morgan v 45 Flers Avenue Pty Ltd (1986) 10 ACLR 692: 12.350

Morris v Kanssen [1946] AC 459: 6.50, 9.50, 9.130, 9.170
Mudge v Wolstenholme [1965] VR 707: 7.480
Multelink Aust Ltd (Admin Appt), In the Matter of (2003) 21 ACLC 1661: 13.270
Multinational Gas and Petrochemical Co v Multinational Gas and Petrochemical Services Ltd [1983] Ch 258: 10.120
Murray v ASC (1994) 12 ACLC 11: 9.430, 9.610
Myer Retail Investments Pty Ltd, Re (1983) 1 ACLC 990: 7.420
National Australia Bank v Bond Brewing Holdings Ltd (1990) 8 ACLC 365: 13.30
National Bank of Wales, Re [1899] 2 Ch 629: 7.540
National Motor Mail-Coach Co Ltd, Re [1908] 2 Ch 515: 4.50, 4.80
Nece Pty Ltd v Ritek Incorporation (1997) 24 ACSR 38: 12.40
Nell v Longbottom [1894] 1 QB 767: 11.730
Nerang Investments Pty Ltd, Re (1985) 3 ACLC 497; (1985) 9 ACLR 646: 13.420
Nestegg Holdings Pty Ltd v Smith [2001] WASC 227: 10.40, 10.50
New Par Consols Ltd, In re [1898] 1 QB 573: 9.50
New South Wales v Commonwealth (1990) 169 CLR 482: 1.60, **1.90**, 1.100, 1.130
New World Alliance Pty Ltd, Re; Sycotex Pty Ltd v Baseler (1994) 122 ALR 531: 10.130, 10.910
Newborne v Sensolid (Great Britain) Ltd [1954] 1 QB 45: 4.60, 4.70
News Ltd v Australian Rugby Football League Ltd (1996) 21 ACSR 635: 6.180, 6.230
Ngurli Ltd v McCann (1953) 90 CLR 425: 10.320
Nibaldi v RM Fitzroy & Associates Pty Ltd (1996) 23 ACSR 330: 9.890
Nicholson v Permakraft (NZ) Ltd (in liq) (1985) 3 ACLC 453: 10.120
Nilant v Shenton [2001] WASC 421: 9.350, 9.460
Niord Pty Ltd v Adelaide Petroleum NL (1990) 8 ACLC 684: 12.270, 12.290
Norths Ltd v McCaughen Dyson Capel Cure Ltd (1988) 6 ACLC 320: 6.190
Northside Developments Pty Ltd v Registrar-General (1990) 170 CLR 146: 9.140

Northside Developments Pty Ltd v Registrar-General (1990) 93 ALR 385: 9.130, 9.290
North-West Transportation Co Ltd v Beatty (1887) 12 App Cas 589: 10.390, 10.400, 10.420
Norvabron Pty Ltd (No 2), Re (1986) 5 ACLC 184: 12.370
NRMA Ltd (No 1), Re (2000) 156 FLR 349: 13.200
NRMA Ltd v Snodgrass (2001) 19 ACLC 769; 19 ACLC 1675: 6.120, 6.140, 11.280
NRMA Ltd v Spragg [2001] NSWSC 381: **11.800**
Obie Pty Ltd (No 2), Re (1984) 2 ACLC 67; [1984] 1 Qd R 371: 13.420
Octavo Investments Pty Ltd v Knight (1979) 144 CLR 360: 2.40
Omega Estates Pty Ltd v Ganke (1963) 80 WN (NSW) 1218: 11.360
One.Tel Ltd (in liq), Re; Australian Securities and Investments Commission v Rich (2003) 44 ACSR 682: 9.530
Onslow Salt Pty Ltd (ACN 050 159 558) (2003) 21 ACLC 1113: 7.90
Ooregum Gold Mining Co of India v Roper [1892] AC 125: 7.240
Ord Forrest Pty Ltd v FCT (1974) 130 CLR 124: 2.240, 7.20
Oris Funds Management Ltd v National Australia Bank [2003] VSC 315: 6.50
Oswald v Bailey (1987) 11 NSWLR 715: 6.150
Owen v Homan (1853) 4 HL Cas 997: 13.30
Panorama Developments v Fidelis Fabrics [1971] 3 WLR 440: 9.290
Parke v Daily News Ltd [1962] Ch 927: 10.150, 10.160
Parker & Cooper Ltd v Reading [1926] Ch 975: 11.60
Pascoe Ltd (in liq) v Lucas (1998) 16 ACLC 1247: 10.350, 10.650
Patrick Stevedores Operations No 2 Pty Ltd v Maritime Union of Australia (1998) 16 ACLC 1041: 13.320, 13.330, **13.360**
Paul A Davies (Aust) Pty Ltd v Davies (1983) 8 ACLR 1: 10.430
Percival v Wright [1902] 2 Ch 421: **10.40**, 10.50
Perkins v Viney [2001] SASC 362: 9.50, 10.840
Permagon Press Ltd v Maxwell [1970] 1 WLR 1167: 11.250, 11.280
Permanent Building Society (in liq) v McGee (1993) 11 ACLC 761; (1993) 11 ACSR 260: 10.670

Peskin v Anderson (2001) 19 ACLC 3001: 10.40, 10.50
Peso Silver Mines v Cropper (1966) 58 DLR (2d) 1: **10.630**
Peter's American Delicacy Co Ltd v Heath (1939) 61 CLR 457: 6.140, 12.410
Petsch v Kennedy [1971] 1 NSWLR 494: 11.100, 11.110, 11.150
Phillips v Melbourne and Castlemaine Soap and Candle Co Ltd (1890) 16 VLR 111: 7.500, 8.00
Phipps v Boardman [1967] 2 AC 46: 10.640, 10.670
Pine Vale Investments Ltd v McDonnell and East Ltd (1983) 1 ACLC 1294: 10.310
Pioneer Concrete Services Ltd v Yelnah Pty Ltd (1986) 5 NSWLR 254: 3.180, 3.220, **3.260**
Pitt v Bachmann; Re Lockyer Valley Fresh Foods Co-operative Association Ltd (1980) CLC ¶40-671: 13.420
Poliwka v Heven Holdings Pty Ltd (1992) 10 ACLC 641: 11.90, **11.100**
Polyresins Pty Ltd, Re (1998) 16 ACLC 1,674: 12.310
Poole v Middleton (1861) 29 Beav 646: 10.330
Poole v National Bank and China Ltd [1907] AC 229: 7.320, 12.410
Pooley v Driver (1876) 5 Ch D 458: 2.60
Portuguese Consolidated Copper Mines Ltd, Re (1889) 42 Ch D 160: 11.30
Preston Motors Pty Ltd [1957], In re VR 111: 7.320
Prudential Assurance Co Ltd v Newman Industries Ltd (No 2) [1980] 2 All ER 841: 12.40
Prudential Assurance Co Ltd v Newman Industries Ltd (No 2) [1982] Ch 204: **12.80**, 12.100
Pulbrook v Richmond Consolidated Mining Co (1878) 9 Ch D 610: 11.150
Punt v Symons & Co: 10.320
Pyramid Building Society (in liq) v Scorpion Hotels Pty Ltd (1996) 20 ACSR 214: 9.140
QBE Insurance Group v ASC (1992) 10 ACLC 1490: 7.590
Qintex Ltd (No 2), Re (1990) 8 ACLC 811: 9.210
QIW Retailers Ltd v David Holdings Pty Ltd (No 2) (1992) 8 ACSR 333: 12.490, 12.510
Queensland Bacon Pty Ltd v Rees (1966) 115 CLR 266: 10.950
Queensland Mines Ltd v Hudson (1977-1978) CLC ¶40-389; (1978) 18 ALR 1: **10.640,** 10.650, 10.670

Queensland Press Ltd v Academy Investments No 3 Pty Ltd (1987) 5 ACLC 175: 11.300
R v Adler (2004) 22 ACLC 784: 10.260
R v Byrnes (1995) 183 CLR 501: 10.80
R v Byrnes; R v Hopwood; Byrnes v R (1995) 183 CLR 501; 13 ACLC 1,488: 10.670
R v Duncan; Ex p Australian Iron and Steel Pty Ltd (1983) 158 CLR 535: 1.100
R v Gomez [1993] 1 All ER 1: 3.110
R v Hughes (2000) 18 ACLC 394: 1.70, **1.100**
R v Roffel (1984) 9 ACLR 433: 3.110
Ramsay Health Care Ltd v Elkington (1992) 10 ACLC 421: 7.320
Rankin v Cooper (1907) 149 F 1010: 10.700
Rayfield v Hands [1958] 2 All ER 194: 6.200
Read v Astoria Garage (Streatham) Ltd [1952] Ch 637: 6.160
Real Estate Pty Ltd v Valerie Dellow & Wayne Arnold [2003] SASC 318: 10.610
Regal (Hastings) Ltd v Gulliver [1967] 2 AC 134: 10.00, 10.10, 10.390, **10.600**, 10.620, 10.630, 10.640
Reid Murray Holdings v David Murray Holdings (1972) 5 SASR 386: 10.80
Rema Industries & Services Pty Ltd v Coad (1992) 107 ALR 374: 10.910
Residues Treatment and Trading Company Ltd v Southern Resources Ltd (1988) 6 ACLC 1160: 12.40, **12.90**, 12.100
Richard Brady Franks Ltd v Price (1937) 58 CLR 112: 12.410
Roach v Winnote Pty Ltd (in liq) [2001] NSWSC 822: 12.120
Roadmakers Pty Ltd, Re (1985) 3 ACLC 591: 13.420
Roberto v Walter Developments Pty Ltd (1992) 10 ACLC 804: 7.500, 8.00
Roberts v Walter Developments Pty Ltd (1997) 15 ACLC 882: 12.440
Rolled Steel Ltd v British Steel Corporation [1985] 2 WLR 908: 10.120
Rothwells Ltd, Re (1989) 7 ACLC 545; (1989) 15 ACLR 142: 13.420
Royal British Bank v Turquand (1856) 119 ER 886: 9.130
Royal Brunei Airlines Sdn Dnd v Tan Kok Ming [1995] 3 WLR 64: 7.480
Ruralcorp Consulting Pty Ltd v Pynery Pty Ltd (1996) 21 ACSR 161: 12.40, 12.40, 12.300
Russell v Aberdeen Town & Country Bank Ltd (1888) 13 App Cas 418: 7.630

Ryan v Edna May Junction Gold Mine Company NL (1916) 21 CLR 487: 11.490
Salomon v Salomon & Co [1897] AC 22: 2.210, **3.20**, 3.30, 3.110, 3.250, 4.20, 10.50, 10.120, 11.480
Sanford v Sanford Courier Service Pty Ltd (1987) 5 ACLC 394: 7.500, 12.440
Scottish Co-op Wholesale Society Ltd v Meyer [1959] AC 324: **10.50**, 12.360, 12.390, **12.400**, 12.410, 13.630
Scottish Insurance Corporation Ltd v Wilsons and Clyde Coal Co Ltd [1949] AC 462: 7.110
Shaddock and Associates v Parramatta City Council (1981) 150 CLR 225: 8.400
Sharp v Dawes (1876) 2 QBD 26: 11.10, 11.160
Sheahan (as Liq SA Service Stations Pty Ltd) v Verco & Hodge (2001) 19 ACLC 814: 10.700, 10.900
Shears v Phosphate Co-operative Co of Aust Ltd (1988) 14 ACLR 747: 12.440
Sheslow v ASC (1994) 12 ACLC 740: 9.560, 9.580
Shirim v Fesena [2002] NSWSC 10: 12.430, 12.440
Shneider, Re (1996) 22 ACSR 497: 9.430
Shuttleworth v Cox Bros & Co Ltd [1927] 2 KB 9: 12.410
Sidebottom v Kershaw, Leese and Co: 6.110
Smith & Fawcett Ltd, Re [1942] Ch 304: 10.10
Smith v Anderson (1880) 15 Ch D 247: 2.60
Smith v Hancock [1894] 2 Ch 377: 3.260
Smith v Sadler (1997) 15 ACLC 1683: 11.280
Smith, Stone and Knight Ltd v Birmingham Corporation [1939] 4 All ER 116: 3.240, 3.250
South Australia v Marcus Clark (1996) 19 ACSR 606: 10.700
South Downs Packers Pty Ltd v Beaver (1984) 2 ACLC 541: 13.420
Southern Cross Mine Management Pty Ltd v Ensham Resources Pty Ltd (2003) 21 ACLC 1,665: 10.40
Southern Foundries Ltd v Shirlaw [1940] AC 701: 6.150
Southern Resources Ltd, Re (1989) 15 ACLR 770: 11.30
Spanish Prospecting Co Ltd [1911] 1 Ch 92: 7.530, 7.570, 7.630
Spargos Mining NL, Re (1990) 8 ACLC 1218: **12.280**, 12.310
Spies v The Queen (2000) 17 ACLC 727: **10.130**

Spreag v Paeson Pty Ltd (1990) 94 ALR 679: 3.240, **3.250**
Standard Chartered Bank of Australia Ltd v Antico (1995) 13 ACLC 1381: 9.60, 9.70, 9.310, 10.870
Stanham v National Trust of Australia (New South Wales) (1989) 7 ACLC 628: 6.190
Stapp v Surge Holdings Pty Ltd (1999) 17 ACLC 896: 13.630
Steel Improvement Holdings Pty Ltd and the Companies Act [1980] ACLC 34: 7.130
Stein v Blake [1998] 1 All ER 724: 10.40
Stein v Saywell (1969) 121 CLR 529: 8.70
Steinberg v FCT (1975) 134 CLR 640: 3.140
Stevens v Commonwealth General Assurance Corporation Ltd (1938) 55 WN(NSW) 120: 9.350
Stewart v Normandy NFM Ltd [2000] SASC 344: 12.590, 12.600
Stewart v Von Lieven (1988) 6 ACLC 891: 3.60, (1990) 8 ACLC 1014: 3.60
Street Nominees v White Industries Ltd (1980) 5 ACLR 40: 10.360
Strickland v Rocla Concrete Pipes Ltd (1971) 124 CLR 468: 1.90
Strong v J Brough & Son (Strathfield) Pty Ltd (1991) 9 ACLC 1018: 13.630
Summergreene v Parker (1950) 80 CLR 304: 4.60
Super John Pty Ltd v Futuris Rural Pty Ltd (1999) 32 ACSR 398: 11.800
Sutherland v NRMA, In the Matter of [2003] NSWSC 829: 12.460
Swansson v Pratt (2002) 20 ACLC 1594: 12.140, **12.160**, 12.190, 12.230, **12.170**
Swiss Screens (Australia) Pty Ltd v Burgess (1987) 11 ACLR 756: 11.90, 11.100
Symes v Weedow (1892) 14 ALT 197: 11.490
Talisman Technologies Inc v Qld Electronic Switching P/L [2001] QSC 324: 12.160, 12.170
Tanning Research Laboratories Inc v O'Brien (1987) 5 ACLC 820: 13.480
Tasmanian Spastics Association, Re; ASC v Nandan (1997) 23 ACSR 743: 9.490
Tavistock Holdings Pty Ltd v Saulsman (1990) 3 ACSR 502: 10.390
Tavistock Ironworks Co Ltd, Re (Lyster's case) (1867) LR 4 Eq 233: 11.170
Television Broadcasters Ltd v Ashton's Nominees Pty Ltd (1977) 22 SASR 552: 2.60

Tesco Supermarkets Ltd v Nattrass [1972] AC 153: **3.100**
Thomas v D'Arcy [2004] QSC 260: 12.80
Thomas v HW Thomas Ltd (1984) 2 ACLC 610: 7.500, 12.410, **12.420**, 12.440
Thomas v Mackay Investments (1996) 22 ACSR 294: 12.320, 13.630
Thornby v Goldberg (1965) 112 CLR 597: 10.270
Tickle v Crest Insurance Co of Australia Ltd (1984) 2 ACLC 493: 13.420
Tiessen v Henderson [1899] 1 Ch 861: 11.490
Tinios v French Caledonia Travel Services Pty Ltd (1994) 12 ACLC 622: 12.570
Titlow v Intercapital Group (Australia) Pty Ltd (1996) 14 ACLC 1065: 12.270, 12.290
Tivoli Freeholds Ltd, Re [1972] VR 445: **13.630**
TNT Australia Pty Ltd v Normandy Resources NL (1989) 7 ACLC 1090: 7.90
Toole v Flexihire Pty Ltd (1991) 6 ACSR 455: 11.120
Totex-Adon Pty Ltd, Re (1980) ACLC ¶40-617: 11.330, **11.360**, 11.560
Tourprint International Pty Ltd (in liq) v Bott (1999) 17 ACLC 1543: 10.940
Tracy v Mandalay Pty Ltd (1953) 88 CLR 215: **4.10**, 4.20, 4.30
Trade Practices Commission v Simpson Pope Ltd (1980) ATPR ¶40-169; (1980) 30 ALR 544: 10.220
Transvaal Lands Co v New Belgium (Transvaal) Land and Development Co [1914] 2 Ch 488: 10.410
Trevor v Whitworth (1887) 12 App Cas 409: 7.340
Twycross v Grant (1877) 2 CPD 469: 4.10
Ultimate Property Group Pty Ltd v Lord [2004] NSWSC 114: 13.150
Van Reesema, Re (1975) 11 SASR 322: 9.430, 9.610, 9.620
Vector Capital Ltd, Re (1997) 23 ACSR 182: 11.650
Verner v General and Commercial Investment Trust [1894] 2 Ch 239: 7.540, 7.630
Versteeg v R (1988) 14 ACLR 1: 11.90
Vickery v Woods (1952) 85 CLR 336: 4.50
Village Roadshow Broadcasting v Austereo (1997) 15 ACLC 929: 6.120
Village Roadshow Limited, In the Matter of [2003] VSC 440: 7.160
Voli v Inglewood Shire Council (1963) 110 CLR 74: 10.700

TABLE OF CASES

Wakim, Re (1999) 163 ALR 270; 17 ACLC 1055: 1.70, **1.110**
Walker v Wimborne (1976) 137 CLR 1: 10.80, 10.110, 10.120, 10.130
Wall v London & Provincial Trust Ltd [1920] 1 Ch 45;[1920] 2 Ch 582: 7.630
Wayde v New South Wales Rugby League Ltd (1985) 3 ACLC 799: 12.350, **12.410**, 12.430
Webb v Stanfield (1990) 8 ACLC 715: 12.330
Weinberger v Inglis [1919] AC 606: 10.330
Welch v Welch [1971-1973] CLC ¶40-068: 9.240, 9.320
Westburn Sugar Refineries Ltd, Ex p [1951] AC 625: 7.320
Western Counties Steam Bakeries & Milling Co, In re [1897] 1 Ch 617: 9.50
Westgold Resources NL v Precious Metals Australia Ltd (2003) 21 ACLC 102: 7.30
Whaley Bridge Calico Printing Co v Green (1879) 5 QBD 109: 4.10, 4.30
White v Bristol Aeroplane Co Ltd [1953] Ch 65: 7.160
Whitehouse v Capital Radio Network Pty Ltd (2002) 21 ACLC 17: 11.800
Whitehouse v Carlton Hotel Pty Ltd (1987) 162 CLR 285: 9.240, 9.320, 10.310, 10.340
Wilkinson v Dodd 42 NJ Eq 234, 245, 7 A 327 (Ch 1886), affirmed 42 NJ Eq 647, 9 A 685 (E & A 1887: 10.700

Will v United Lankat Plantations Co Ltd [1914] AC 11: 7.100
William Bedford Ltd, Re [1967] VR 490: 7.100
William Kamper v Applied Soli Technology Pty Ltd [2004] NSWSC 891: 12.120
Williams v McKay 46 NJ Eq 25, 36, 18 A 824 (Ch 1889): 10.700
Williams v Riley 34 NJ Eq 398, 401 (Ch 1881): 10.700
Winpar Holdings Ltd v Goldfields Kalgoorlie Ltd (2000) 18 ACLC 665; (2002) 20 ACLC 265: 7.300, **7.320**, 7.330
Winthrop Investments Ltd v Winns Ltd (1975-1976) CLC ¶40-223; [1975] 2 NSWLR 666: 10.120, 10.340, 10.350, 10.650
Wonderflex Textiles Ltd, Re [1951] VLR 458: 13.630, 13.640
Woonda Nominees Pty Ltd v Chng (2000) 18 ACLC 627: 10.310
Wright v Mansell [2001] FCA 1519: 3.20
York Corporation v Henry Leetham and Sons Ltd. [1924] 1 Ch 557: 10.120
York Tramways Co Ltd v Willows (1882) 8 QBD 685: 11.170
Zempilas v JN Taylor Holdings Ltd (in liq) (No 6) (1991) 9 ACLC 835: 12.330
Zim Metal Products Pty Ltd, Re [1977] ACLC 29,556; 2 ACLR 553: 9.430, **9.620**
Zuker v CAC [1980] ACLC 34,334: 9.430

Table of Statutes

Constitution
s 51(i): 1.100
s 51(xx): 1.90
s 51(xxix): 1.100
s 51(xxxvii): 1.80
s 71: 1.110
s 75: 1.110
s 76: 1.110
s 77: 1.110
s 77(iii): 1.110
s 109: 1.100
Ch III: 1.110

Commonwealth
Australian Securities and Investments Commission Act 2001: 1.80
s 1(1): 1.130
s 1(2): 1.130
s 11(1): 1.130
s 11(2)(b): 1.130
s 11(3): 1.130
s 11(6): 1.130
s 49: 1.130
s 50: 1.130
s 241(2): 1.130
s 243: 1.130
s 261: 1.130
Part 3: 1.130
Part 9: 1.130
Part 10: 1.130
Part 14: 1.130
Australian Securities Commission Act 1989: 1.60
Bankruptcy Act 1966
Part X: 9.440
Close Corporations Act 1989: 1.60
Companies Act 1981: 1.40
Companies (Application of Laws) Act 1981: 1.40
Companies Code
s 5(1): 4.130
s 33(1): 4.130
s 65(5): 4.130
s 69(1): 4.130
s 69(8): 4.130
s 70: 4.130
s 70(5): 4.130
s 81: 4.130
s 81(1)(a): 4.130
s 81(1)(a)(i): 4.130
s 81(1)(a)(ii): 4.130
s 81(1)(b): 4.130
s 81(1)(c): 4.130
s 81(1)(c)(i): 4.130
s 81(1)(c)(ii): 4.130
s 81(2): 4.130
s 81(3): 4.130
s 81(4): 4.130
s 81(5): 4.130
s 81(7): 4.130
s 81(10): 4.130
s 81(12): 4.130
Company Law Review Act 1998: 2.140, 6.10, 6.30, 6.230, 6.240, 7.240, 7.250, 7.320
Corporate Law Economic Reform Program Act (CLERP Act): 8.30, 10.180, 12.50, 12.110
Corporate Law Economic Reform Program (Audit and Corporate Disclosure) Act 2004 (CLERP9): 9.110, 9.230, 9.770, 9.780, 9.790, 9.990
s 708A: 8.130
Corporate Law Reform Bill 1992: 13.370
Corporate Law Reform Act 1992: 13.250
Corporations and Securities Industry Bill 1972: 1.40
Corporations Act 1989: 1.60, 1.70, 1.80, 1.90, 1.100, 1.110
s 47: 1.100
s 47(1): 1.100
Corporations Act 2001: 1.80, 1.130, 2.260, 3.160, 7.160, 7.280, 12.530
Part 1.2A: 8.120
Chap 2A: 5.10, 5.20
Part 2A.2: 5.230
Part 2B.3: 4.90, 4.110, 4.160, 4.200, 4.230
Part 2B.7: 6.80, 6.90
Part 2D.1: 10.780
Part 2D.2 Div 2: 9.970
Part 2D.6: 9.370, 9.380, 9.600, 9.860
Chap 2E: 9.800, 9.1010, 10.520, 10.550, 10.580
Part 2F.1A: 12.20, 12.50, 12.110, 12.120, 12.190, 12.200, 12.210
Part 2F.2: 6.90
Chap 2J: 7.320
Part 2J.1: 7.290, 7.320
Part 2J.1 Div 2: 7.290, 7.320, 7.360, 7.470

Corporations Act 2001 (Cth) (cont)
Chap 2K: 8.90
Chap 2L: 8.40
Part 2M.3: 2.290, 5.210
Part 5.1: 8.140, 13.180
Part 5.3A: 13.360
Part 5.4: 13.410, 13.560, 13.730
Part 5.4-5.9: 13.410
Part 5.4A: 13.410, 13.620
Part 5.4B: 13.410
Part 5.4B Div 3: 13.600
Part 5.5: 13.410
Part 5.6: 13.410
Part 5.6 Div 7: 13.410
Part 5.6 Div 6: 13.410
Part 5.7A:5.9: 13.410
Part 5.7B Div 1: 13.410
Part 5.7B Div 2: 13.410
Part 5.7B Div 3-7: 13.410
Part 5A: 13.700
Part 5B.1: 5.250, 5.260, 5.270
Part 5B.2: 5.260
Part 5B.2 Div 1: 5.260
Part 5B.2 Div 2: 5.270
Part 5.3A: 13.250, 13.320
Part 5.4: 13.540
Part 5.4A: 13.540
Part 5.7B: 10.830
Part 5.7B Div 3: 3.170
Part 5.8A: 10.860
Chap 6: 8.140
Chap 6 – 6A: 8.120
Part 6.10 Div 2: 1.130
Chap 6A: 7.320
Chap 6D: 2.300, 3.60, 4.40, 8.40, 8.120, 8.140, 8.170, 8.400, 8.530, 8.570
Part 6D.2: 8.130, 8.160
Part 6D.5: 8.140
Chap 7.2: 8.570
Chap 7.3: 8.570
Chaps 7.6-7.10: 8.570
Part 7.9: 8.590
Part 7.10: 8.430
s 4(6): 1.80
s 4(7): 1.80
s 4(8): 1.80
s 9: 1.80, 2.130, 2.140, 2.150, 2.160, 2.180, 2.220, 3.20, 4.10, 5.80, 5.260, 5.270, 8.30, 8.170. 8.180, 8.230, 8.250, 8.380, 9.40, 9.70, 9.90, 9.110, 9.380, 10.550, 11.580, 13.50
s 9(a): 9.40, 9.50
s 9(a)(i): 9.110
s 9(a)(ii): 9.110
s 9(b): 9.80, 9.90
s 9(b)(i): 9.40, 9.50, 9.90
s 9(b)(ii): 5.270, 9.40, 9.60, 9.70, 9.80, 9.90
s 9(b)(iii): 5.270, 9.90, 9.100
s 9(d): 8.160

s 45A: 2.200
s 45A(2): 2.200
s 45A(3): 2.200
s 50AA: 10.550
s 53: 10.460, 12.250
s 79: 7.440
s 89: 13.530
s 91A(2): 9.390
s 92: 8.120
s 92(1): 8.120
s 92(1)(c): 8.120
s 92(2): 8.120
s 92(2)(c): 8.120
s 92(3): 8.120
s 92(3)(c): 8.120
s 92(4): 8.120
s 95A: 10.810, 13.570
s 95A(1): 3.170
s 100(1): 5.80
s 100(2): 5.80
s 112: 2.110, 2.120, 2.130
s 112(1): 2.140, 2.160, 2.170, 2.180, 2.190, 5.250
s 112(2): 2.160
s 112(2)(b): 2.160
s 112(2)(c): 2.160
s 112(3): 2.160
s 113(1): 2.300
s 113(3) 2.190, 2.300
s 114: 5.30, 9.320
s 115: 2.60
s 115(a): 2.90
s 116: 10.330
s 117: 5.100
s 117(1): 5.80
s 117(2): 5.60, 5.80
s 117(2)(d): 5.60, 9.360
s 117(2)(e): 5.60, 9.360
s 117(2)(f): 5.60, 9.360
s 117(2)(h): 5.80
s 117(2)(l): 5.90
s 117(3): 5.70, 5.90, 6.30
s 117(4): 5.80
s 117(5): 5.60, 9.360
s 118(1)(a): 5.110
s 118(1)(b): 5.100
s 118(1)(c): 5.110
s 118(2): 5.100
s 119: 5.120
s 119A(3): 5.230, 5.240
s 119A(3)(a): 5.240
s 119A(3)(a)(i): 5.240
s 119A(3)(b): 5.240
s 120(1): 5.120, 5.140, 9.640
s 120(2): 5.120, 5.200
s 122: 4.80
s 123(1): 5.50, 5.130
s 124: 4.170, 13.630
s 124(1): 2.110, 3.10, 5.120, 6.230, 8.10
s 124(1)(a): 7.50
s 124(1)(a)-(h): 2.110

s 124(1)(b): 8.30
s 124(2): 6.230
s 125: 4.180, 6.240, 13.630
s 125(1): 6.230
s 125(2): 6.230
s 126: 4.160, 4.170
s 126(1): 4.160
s 127: 4.170
s 127(1): 4.160
s 127(2): 4.160, 5.130
s 128: 6.50, 9.160, 9.300
s 128(1): 9.120
s 128(4): 6.50, 9.120
s 129: 6.50, 9.120, 9.160, 9.300
s 129(1): 6.50, 9.120
s 129(2): 9.120, 9.130
s 129(3): 9.120, 9.130
s 130: 9.160, 9.300
s 130(1): 6.50
s 131: 4.40, 4.50, 4.130, 4.140, 4.220
s 131(1): 4.90, 4.100, 4.110, 4.120, 4.130, 4.140, 4.150, 4.180, 4.190, 4.200, 4.230
s 131(2): 4.90, 4.100, 4.110, 4.130, 4.140, 4.170, 4.190, 4.210
s 131(3): 4.90, 4.160, 4.210
s 131(4): 4.90, 4.200
s 132: 4.50, 4.130
s 132(1): 4.100, 4.200, 4.220
s 132(2): 4.230
s 133: 4.50, 4.110, 4.130, 4.200
s 134: 6.30
s 135(1): 6.20, 6.30
s 135(1)(b): 6.20
s 135(2): 6.30, 6.40, 6.60, 6.140
s 135(3): 6.50
s 136(1): 6.30
s 136(2): 6.30, 6.60, 6.140, 7.180, 7.270
s 136(3): 6.70
s 136(4): 6.70
s 136(5)(a): 6.30
s 137(2): 6.60
s 140(1): 4.180, 6.50, 6.130, 6.140, 6.170, 6.210, 6.240, 7.230, 7.240
s 140(2): 6.80
s 141: 6.20
s 142(1): 5.80
s 144(1): 5.50
s 144(2): 5.50
s 145: 2.290, 5.80
s 147(1)(a): 5.40
s 147(1)(b): 5.40
s 147(1)(c): 5.40
s 147(2): 5.40
s 148(1): 2.130, 2.140, 5.40
s 148(2): 2.130, 2.140, 2.190
s 148(3): 2.150, 2.190
s 148(4): 2.160, 2.190
s 148(5): 2.190
s 149: 2.130, 2.140
s 149(1): 2.160, 2.190

s 149(2): 2.160
s 150: 2.140, 6.90
s 151: 2.130, 2.140
s 152(1): 5.40
s 152(2): 5.40
s 153: 5.50
s 153(2): 5.50
s 154: 5.50
s 155: 5.50
s 157: 6.90
s 157(1): 5.10
s 162: 2.140
s 163: 2.140
s 164: 2.140
s 165(1): 2.190
s 165(3): 2.190
s 168(1): 8.40
s 168(1)(a): 5.170
s 168(1)(b): 5.170
s 169: 5.170
s 170: 5.170
s 171: 8.40
s 172(1): 5.180
s 175(1): 10.360
s 180: 10.200, 10.680, 10.730
s 180(1): 9.520, 10.260, 10.710, 10.730, 10.790, 10.980
s 180(2): 10.730, 10.740
s 180(3): 10.730, 10.740
s 181: 9.520, 10.180, 10.200, 10.210, 10.680, 13.320
s 181(1): 10.210, 10.260, 10.590, 10.690, 10.790, 10.960
s 181(1)(a): 10.180, 10.200, 10.210, 10.380, 10.720, 12.510
s 181(1)(b): 10.380, 10.720
s 181(1)(c): 10.380
s 182: 4.160, 10.200, 10.660, 10.670, 10.680, 10.690
s 182(1): 10.260
s 183: 10.200, 10.660, 10.670, 10.680, 10.690
s 183(1): 10.260, 10.660
s 183(1)(a): 4.120
s 183(2): 4.140
s 183(13): 4.160
s 184: 10.180, 10.200, 10.250, 10.590, 10.680, 10.690
s 184(1): 10.790
s 184(1)(c): 10.180
s 184(1)(d): 10.380
s 184(2): 10.690
s 184(3): 10.690
s 185: 10.200, 10.680, 10.730, 10.740
s 187: 10.70, 10.100, 10.190
s 188(1): 9.300
s 188(2): 9.300
s 188(3): 9.300
s 189: 9.10, 10.750
s 189(a)(i): 10.770
s 189(a)(ii): 10.770

Corporations Act 2001 (Cth) (*cont*)
  s 189(a)(iii): 10.770
  s 189(a)(iv): 10.770
  s 189(b): 10.780
  s 189(c): 10.770, 10.780
  s 190: 9.10, 10.750
  s 190(1): 10.760
  s 190(2): 10.760
  s 191: 9.870, 10.440, 10.450, 10.460, 10.500, 10.520
  s 191(1): 10.490
  s 191(2): 10.460, 10.470
  s 191(2)(a)(i): 10.470
  s 191(2)(a)(ii): 10.470
  s 191(2)(a)(iii): 10.470
  s 191(2)(b): 10.470
  s 191(2)(b): 10.490
  s 191(3): 10.480
  s 191(4): 10.500
  s 192: 10.450, 10.490
  s 192(6): 10.490
  s 192(7): 10.500
  s 193(b): 10.520
  s 194: 10.440, 10.450, 10.500
  s 195: 10.500, 10.520, 10.530
  s 195(1): 10.520, 10.530, 10.540
  s 195(2): 10.530
  s 195(4): 10.530
  s 195(5): 10.540
  s 196: 10.530
  s 197: 2.50, 3.190
  s 198A(1): 2.280, 9.10
  s 198C(1): 9.10, 9.200
  s 198C(2): 9.200
  s 198D: 9.10, 10.730
  s 198D(1): 9.10, 10.730
  s 198D(3): 10.750
  s 198E: 6.20
  s 198F: 12.600, 12.610
  s 198F(1): 12.590
  s 198F(2): 12.590, 12.610
  s 200B: 9.970
  s 200D: 9.970
  s 200E: 9.970
  s 200F(1): 9.990
  s 200F(1)(b): 9.990
  s 200F(2): 9.990
  s 200F(3): 9.990
  s 200F(4): 9.990
  s 200G: 9.970, 9.990
  s 200G(2)(a): 9.980
  s 200G(2)(b): 9.980
  s 200G(5): 9.980
  s 200H: 9.990
  s 200J: 9.970
  s 201A: 2.290, 9.80, 9.240
  s 201A(1): 9.320, 9.330
  s 201A(2): 9.320, 9.330
  s 201B(1): 9.310, 9.340
  s 201C(14): 9.340
  s 201D: 5.60, 5.140

  s 201D(1): 5.60, 9.360
  s 201D(2): 5.60, 9.360
  s 201E: 2.290, 9.660, 9.670
  s 201E(1): 9.660
  s 201E(2): 9.660
  s 201E(3): 9.660
  s 201F: 6.20
  s 201F(1): 9.690
  s 201F(3): 9.450
  s 201G: 9.640, 9.670
  s 201H: 9.680, 10.530
  s 201H(1): 9.680
  s 201H(2): 9.680
  s 201H(3): 9.680
  s 201J: 9.200, 9.740
  s 201K(1): 9.270
  s 201K(3): 9.270
  s 201K(4): 9.270
  s 201M: 9.150, 9.160, 9.300
  s 201M(1): 9.150, 9.160
  s 201M(2): 9.160
  s 202A(1): 9.710
  s 202A(2): 9.710
  s 202B(1): 9.750
  s 202C: 6.20, 9.720
  s 203A: 9.810
  s 203B: 9.370, 9.420, 9.450, 9.480, 9.510, 9.530, 9.570, 9.860
  s 203C: 9.880
  s 203D: 2.300, 9.900, 9.950, 9.960, 11.380
  s 203D(1): 9.900, 9.930, 9.950
  s 203D(2): 9.910, 11.390
  s 203D(3): 9.910
  s 203D(4): 9.920
  s 203D(5): 9.920
  s 203D(5)(b): 9.920
  s 203D(6): 9.920
  s 203E: 2.290, 9.940
  s 203F(1): 9.220
  s 204A(1): 9.280
  s 204A(2): 9.280
  s 204C: 5.60
  s 204C(1): 5.60, 9.360
  s 204C(2): 5.60, 5.140, 9.360
  s 204D: 5.140, 9.280
  s 204E: 9.150, 9.160, 9.300
  s 204E(1): 9.150, 9.160
  s 204R(2): 9.160
  s 205A(1): 9.830
  s 205A(2): 9.830
  s 205B: 5.140, 5.170, 9.80
  s 205B(2): 9.270
  s 205B(4): 9.840
  s 205B(5): 9.840
  s 206A(1): 9.380, 9.390
  s 206A(2): 9.370, 9.420, 9.450, 9.480, 9.510, 9.530, 9.570, 9.860
  s 206B: 9.430, 9.520
  s 206B(1): 9.400, 9.410, 9.620
  s 206B(1)(a): 9.400

s 206B(1)(b): 9.410
s 206B(1)(c): 9.410
s 206B(2): 9.420, 9.450
s 206B(3): 9.440, 9.450
s 206B(4): 9.440, 9.450
s 206BA(1): 9.420
s 206BA(2): 9.420
s 206BA(3): 9.420
s 206BA(5): 9.420
s 206C: 9.470, 10.960
s 206C(1): 10.220
s 206C(2): 10.220
s 206D(1): 9.500, 9.510
s 206D(2): 9.500
s 206D(3): 9.500
s 206E: 9.520, 9.530, 9.540
s 206E(1): 9.520
s 206E(2): 9.520
s 206F: 9.550, 9.580
s 206F(1): 9.550, 9.560, 9.600
s 206F(1)(b)(i): 9.550
s 206F(2): 9.560
s 206F(3): 9.560, 9.570
s 206F(4): 9.570
s 206F(5): 9.570
s 206G: 9.420, 9.450, 9.480, 9.510, 9.530, 9.600
s 206G(1): 9.600
s 206G(3): 9.630
s 206G(5): 9.630
s 208: 10.550, 10.580, 10.590
s 208(1)(a): 10.580
s 208(2)(a): 10.580
s 209(1): 10.590
s 209(2): 10.260, 10.580, 10.590
s 209(3): 10.590
s 210: 10.580
s 211: 10.580
s 212: 10.580
s 213: 10.580
s 214: 10.580
s 215: 10.580
s 216: 10.580
s 226: 9.170
s 228(1): 10.550
s 228(2): 10.560
s 228(3): 10.560
s 228(4): 10.560
s 228(5): 10.560
s 228(6): 10.560
s 228(7): 10.560
s 229: 10.570, 10.580
s 229(1): 10.570
s 229(2): 10.570
s 232: 7.500, 9.950, 12.250, 12.280, 12.290, 12.310, 12.390, 12.400, 12.410, 12.430, 12.450, 13.40, 13.640
s 232(b): 12.360, 12.370, 12.470
s 232(c): 12.370
s 232(d): 12.390

s 232(e): 12.410
s 232(4): 12.510
s 232(6): 12.510
s 233: 7.500, 12.250, 12.260, 12.290, 12.460, 12.470, 12.520, 13.40, 13.560, 13.640
s 233(1): 12.460, 13.260
s 233(1)(a): 13.540
s 233(1)(a)-(j): 12.460
s 233(1)(g): 12.20
s 233(1)(h): 13.40
s 234: 7.500, 12.250, 12.260, 12.290, 12.470, 12.480, 13.40, 13.640
s 234(A)(i): 12.320
s 234(b): 12.290
s 234(c): 12.290
s 235: 7.500, 12.250, 12.290, 12.460, 12.470, 13.40, 13.640
s 236(1)(a): 12.120
s 236(3): 12.50, 12.60
s 237: 12.20, 12.120, 12.560
s 237(1): 12.120, 12.130
s 237(2): 12.130
s 237(2)(b): 12.160
s 237(2)(c): 12.160, 12.170
s 237(3): 12.180
s 237(4): 12.180
s 238(1): 12.120
s 238(2): 12.200
s 239(1): 12.210
s 239(2): 12.210
s 239(2)(a): 12.210
s 239(2)(b): 12.210
s 240: 12.240
s 241: 12.220
s 241(2): 12.220
s 241(3): 12.220
s 242: 12.230
s 246B(1): 7.180, 7.190
s 246B(2): 7.180. 7.190
s 246B(3): 7.190
s 246C: 7.170
s 246C(1)(a): 7.170
s 246C(3): 7.170
s 246C(5): 7.170
s 246C(6): 7.170
s 246D(1): 7.200
s 246D(2): 7.200
s 246D(3)(a): 7.200
s 246D(5): 7.200
s 246F(1): 7.50
s 246F(2): 7.50
s 247A: 12.550, 12.560, 12.580, 12.600
s 247A(1): 12.560
s 247A(2): 12.560
s 247A(4): 12.550
s 247A(5): 12.560
s 247A(5)(b): 12.560
s 247B: 12.570
s 247C: 12.570
s 247D: 12.540, 12.550

Corporations Act 2001 (Cth) *(cont)*
  s 248A: 11.70
  s 248B: 11.20, 11.70, 11.190
  s 248C: 11.80, 11.110
  s 248D: 11.50
  s 248E(1): 9.260
  s 248F: 11.160, 11.170
  s 248G(1): 11.200
  s 248G(2): 11.200
  s 249A: 11.70
  s 249A(2): 11.70
  s 249A(6): 11.70
  s 249B: 11.20, 11.70, 11.520
  s 249C: 9.80, 11.250, 11.280
  s 249CA: 11.250, 11.280
  s 249D: 11.360
  s 249D(1): 11.290
  s 249D(1A): 11.290
  s 249D(5): 11.310
  s 249E: 11.340, 11.360
  s 249E(1): 11.320, 11.330
  s 249E(3): 11.340
  s 249E(4): 11.340
  s 249F: 11.360
  s 249F(1): 11.340
  s 249G: 11.20, 11.40, 11.360, 11.560
  s 249G(1): 11.350, 11.360
  s 249G(2): 11.350
  s 249H(1): 11.370
  s 249H(2)(a): 11.380
  s 249H(2)(b): 11.380
  s 249H(3): 11.380
  s 249H(4): 11.380
  s 249HA(1): 11.370
  s 249J: 11.410
  s 249J(1): 11.370
  s 249J(3): 11.410
  s 249J(3A): 11.410
  s 249L: 11.420
  s 249L(a): 11.440
  s 249L(b): 11.440
  s 249L(c): 11.460
  s 249L(d): 11.470, 11.600
  s 249L(3): 11.440
  s 249LA: 11.440
  s 249N(1): 11.500
  s 249N(1A): 11.500
  s 249O(2): 11.510
  s 249O(4): 11.510
  s 249O(5): 11.510
  s 249P(1): 11.510
  s 249P(8): 11.510
  s 249P(9): 11.510
  s 249Q: 11.250, 11.280
  s 249S: 11.50
  s 249T: 11.520
  s 249T(1): 11.550
  s 249T(2): 11.530, 11.650, 11.690
  s 249T(3): 11.540
  s 249T(4): 11.540
  s 249X : 6.20, 11.40, 11.290, 11.590

  s 249X(1): 11.590
  s 249X(1A): 11.590
  s 249X(3): 11.590
  s 249Y: 11.590
  s 249Y(1): 11.640
  s 249Y(3): 11.630, 11.640
  s 250A: 11.610
  s 250A(1): 11.610
  s 250A(1A): 11.610
  s 250A(2): 11.610
  s 250B: 11.610
  s 250BA: 11.610
  s 250BA(1): 11.600
  s 250C: 11.590
  s 250C(2): 11.620
  s 250D: 11.660
  s 250D(1): 11.660, 11.680
  s 250D(2): 11.680
  s 250D(3): 11.660
  s 250D(4): 11.660, 11.680
  s 250E(1): 11.700, 11.720
  s 250E(2): 11.700, 11.720
  s 250E(3): 11.730
  s 250J(1): 11.700
  s 250K: 11.710
  s 250L(1): 11.710
  s 250L(2): 11.710
  s 250L(3): 11.710
  s 250M(1): 11.710
  s 250N: 2.290, 5.220
  s 250N(1): 5.220, 11.240
  s 250N(2): 11.240
  s 250P: 11.240
  s 250R: 9.790, 11.260
  s 250S: 11.270
  s 250SA: 9.790, 11.270
  s 250T: 11.270
  s 251A: 5.190
  s 251A(1): 5.190, 11.740
  s 251A(1)(b): 11.210
  s 251A(1)(d): 11.210
  s 251A(1)(e): 11.210
  s 251A(2): 11.210, 11.740
  s 251A(3): 9.80, 11.740
  s 251A(4): 11.740
  s 251A(5): 11.220, 11.740
  s 251A(6): 11.230, 11.750
  s 251B: 5.190, 11.220
  s 251B(1): 11.760
  s 251B(2): 11.760
  s 251B(3): 11.760
  s 251B(4): 11.760
  s 254A: 7.50, 7.110
  s 254A(1): 7.90, 7.130
  s 254A(2): 7.60, 7.90, 7.100, 7.110, 7.120, 11.210
  s 254A(3): 7.130
  s 254B: 7.50
  s 254B(1): 7.50
  s 254B (2)(b): 2.160
  s 254C: 7.250

s 254H: 6.90
s 254H(1): 7.260
s 254H(3): 7.260
s 254J(1): 7.130
s 254K: 7.130
s 254L(1): 7.410
s 254L(2): 7.130
s 254M(1): 2.160
s 254M(2): 2.160
s 254Q: 2.160
s 254Q(1): 2.160
s 254Q(2): 2.160
s 254Q(6): 2.160
s 254Q(7): 2.160
s 254R(1): 2.160
s 254T: 7.520, 7.530, 7.640, 7.650, 7.660, 8.10
s 254U: 7.490, 7.510, 7.560
s 254V(1): 7.100, 7.510, 7.550, 7.560, 7.650
s 254V(2): 7.100, 7.510, 7.550
s 254W(2): 7.490
s 254X: 5.200
s 254X(2): 5.90
s 256A: 6.90
s 256A(b): 7.320
s 256B: 6.90, 7.290, 7.320, 7.330
s 256B(1): 7.290, 7.320
s 256B(1)(a): 7.320
s 256B(2): 7.300, 12.260
s 256C: 6.90, 7.290, 7.300, 7.310, 7.320, 7.330
s 256C(1): 7.300
s 256C(2): 7.300
s 256C(3): 7.300
s 256C(4): 7.300, 7.230
s 256C(5): 7.300
s 256D: 6.90
s 256D(2): 7.310
s 256D(3): 7.310
s 256E: 6.90
s 257A: 7.340, 7.360
s 257B(1): 7.370
s 257B(4): 7.370
s 257B(5): 7.370
s 258A: 2.150, 7.290
s 259A: 7.340, 7.350
s 259B: 7.390
s 259B(1): 7.380, 7.390, 7.400
s 259B(2): 7.400
s 259B(3): 7.400
s 259B(6): 7.400
s 259C: 7.340
s 259C(1): 7.340
s 259E(1): 7.340, 7.380
s 259E(2): 7.340
s 259E(2)(b): 7.340
s 259F(1): 7.350, 7.390
s 259F(2): 7.350, 7.390
s 259F(3): 7.350, 7.390
s 260A: 7.410, 7.420, 7.440, 7.480

s 260A(1): 7.410, 7.470
s 260A(1)(a): 7.440
s 260A(1)(b): 7.440
s 260A(1)(c): 7.440
s 260A(2): 7.430
s 260B: 7.410, 7.450
s 260B(1): 7.450
s 260B(2): 7.450
s 260B(3): 7.450
s 260B(4): 7.460
s 260B(5): 7.460
s 260C: 7.410, 7.470, 9.480, 10.220
s 260C(1): 7.470
s 260C(2): 7.470
s 260C(3): 7.470
s 260C(4): 7.150, 7.470
s 260C(5)(a): 7.470
s 260C(5)(b): 7.470
s 260C(5)(c): 7.470
s 260C(5)(d): 7.470
s 260D(1)(a): 7.480
s 260D(1)(b): 7.480
s 260D(2): 7.440, 7.480, 10.260
s 260MA: 8.140
s 262: 8.90
s 263: 8.90
s 263(1): 8.90
s 264: 8.90
s 265: 8.90
s 266: 8.90, 8.100
s 269: 8.90
s 271: 5.170
s 278: 8.110
s 279: 8.110
s 279(2): 8.110
s 279(3): 8.110
s 280: 8.110
s 281: 8.110
s 282: 8.110
s 283AA: 8.40
s 283AB: 8.40
s 283BH: 8.40
s 286: 9.230
s 286(1): 10.830
s 286(2): 10.830
s 290: 12.610
s 290(1): 12.580
s 290(2): 12.580
s 292(2): 2.290, 5.210
s 293: 2.290, 5.210
s 294: 2.290, 5.210
s 294E(2): 9.150
s 295A(1): 9.230
s 295A(2): 9.230
s 295A(3): 9.230
s 295A(5): 9.230
s 295A(7): 9.230
s 300(11)(d): 9.770
s 300A: 9.780
s 300A(1): 9.770, 9.780
s 300A(1)(c): 9.770

Corporations Act 2001 (Cth) (*cont*)
s 320: 12.410
s 324(1)(f): 2.290
s 325: 2.290, 5.160
s 327(1): 2.290, 5.160
s 327(1A): 2.290
s 327(7): 5.160
s 327(8): 5.160
s 327(9): 5.160
s 329: 11.380
s 329(1A): 11.390
s 329(2): 11.390
s 351: 8.380
s 411: 13.210
s 411(1): 13.190
s 411(1a): 13.190
s 411(1B): 13.190
s 411(2): 13.200
s 411(4)(b): 13.220
s 411(10): 13.220
s 412(1): 13.210
s 412(1)(a): 13.210
s 412(2): 13.210
s 413: 13.180
s 413(1): 13.180
s 413(1)(d): 13.750
s 415(2)(a): 13.200
s 418(1): 13.50
s 418(1)(d): 13.60
s 418(3): 13.50
s 418A(1): 13.30
s 418A(2): 13.30
s 419(1): 13.170
s 420: 13.50
s 420(1): 13.100
s 420(2): 13.10, 13.70, 13.100
s 420(3): 13.100
s 420A: 13.150
s 420A(1): 13.150
s 420A(2): 13.150
s 420B: 13.100
s 420C: 13.100
s 421: 13.50
s 421(1): 13.110
s 421A(1): 13.130
s 421A(3)(a): 13.130
s 422(1): 13.130
s 422(2): 13.130
s 422(3): 13.130
s 423: 13.160
s 423(1): 13.80, 13.160
s 423(2): 13.160
s 423(3): 13.160
s 424(1): 13.90
s 427: 13.60
s 427(4): 13.80
s 428(1): 13.60
s 429(2)(a): 13.60
s 429(2)(b): 13.120
s 429(2)(c)(i): 13.120
s 429(2)(c)(ii): 13.120

s 429(2)(c)(iii): 13.120
s 430(1): 13.120
s 432(1): 13.140
s 432(1)(b): 13.80
s 432(1A): 13.140
s 432(2): 13.140
s 432A(b): 13.260
s 435A(a): 13.260
s 435C(1)(b): 13.390
s 435C(2): 13.390
s 435C(3): 13.390
s 435C(3)(b)- 435C(3)(e): 13.400
s 436A: 13.250
s 436B: 13.670
s 436C: 13.250
s 436E(1): 13.310
s 436E(2): 13.310
s 436E(4): 13.310
s 436F(1): 13.310
s 436F(2): 13.310
s 436F(3): 13.310
s 437A(1)(a): 13.280, 13.320
s 437A(1)(b): 13.280, 13.320
s 437A(1)(c): 13.320
s 437A(1)(d): 13.320
s 437C: 13.280
s 437C(1): 13.280
s 437C(2): 13.280
s 437D: 13.280
s 437D(2)(a): 13.320
s 437E: 13.280
s 437F: 13.290
s 438A: 13.330
s 438B(1): 13.330
s 438B(2): 13.330
s 438B(3): 13.330
s 438C(1): 13.330
s 438D(1): 13.340
s 438D(2): 13.340
s 438D(3): 13.340
s 439A: 13.310, 13.390
s 439A(1): 13.400
s 439A(2): 13.300
s 439A(4): 13.400
s 439A(5): 13.400
s 439A(6): 13.390
s 439C: 13.390, 13.400
s 439C(b): 13.390
s 439C(c): 13.390
s 440A(1): 13.380
s 440C: 13.380
s 440D: 13.360, 13.380
s 440F: 13.380
s 440G(2): 13.380
s 440J: 13.380
s 443A-443AA: 13.360
s 443A(2): 13.360
s 443D(a): 13.360
s 444A(2): 13.390
s 444D(2): 13.390
s 446A: 13.370

s 446A(1): 13.270
s 446A(2): 13.390
s 446A(4): 13.390
s 447A(4): 13.390
s 447C(1): 13.270
s 447C(2): 13.270
s 447E: 13.350
s 447E(1): 13.300
s 448A: 13.270
s 448B: 13.270
s 448C: 13.270
s 449B: 13.300
s 449C(1): 13.300
s 449C(2): 13.300
s 450A(1): 13.270
s 450A(2): 13.270
s 450A(3): 13.270
s 450E(1): 13.270
s 459A: 13.560
s 459C(2): 13.580
s 459C(3): 13.580
s 459D: 13.580
s 459P: 13.550
s 459P(1): 13.550
s 459P(2): 13.550
s 461: 13.540, 13.610, 13.620, 13.640
s 461(1): 9.950
s 461(1)(e): 13.620
s 461(1)(f): 13.620
s 461(1)(g): 13.620
s 462: 13.560
s 462(2): 13.610
s 462(2A): 13.610
s 462(3): 13.610
s 462(4): 13.610
s 464: 13.540, 13.560, 13.610
s 467(1): 13.590
s 467A: 13.590
s 471A(1): 13.450
s 472(1): 13.420
s 473: 13.460
s 473(1): 13.460
s 473(3): 13.420
s 474: 13.470
s 475: 13.470, 13.490
s 476: 13.490
s 477(1): 13.470
s 477(2a): 13.470
s 477(2B): 13.470
s 478(1): 13.490
s 478(1A): 13.490
s 480: 13.460
s 481(5)(b): 13.750
s 482(1): 13.600
s 483(1): 13.600
s 483(3): 13.600
s 484: 13.470
s 484(1): 13.600
s 488: 13.470
s 491(1): 13.660
s 494(1); 13.660

s 494(2): 13.660
s 495: 13.420
s 495(1): 13.670
s 496(1): 13.670
s 497(1); 13.680
s 497(5): 13.680
s 497(6): 13.680
s 497(7): 13.680
s 499: 13.420, 13.680
s 502: 13.420
s 503: 13.420, 13.460
s 506: 13.470
s 506(1)(c): 13.490
s 507: 13.470
s 509: 13.470
s 509(6): 13.750
s 511: 13.470
s 511(1): 13.690
s 516: 2.130, 2.220, 3.20
s 517: 2.140, 2.220, 3.20
s 532(1): 2.290, 13.440
s 532(2)(c): 2.290
s 532(4): 2.290, 13.440
s 532(9): 13.440
s 533: 13.490
s 533(1): 9.550
s 535: 13.470, 13.530
s 536(1): 13.460, 13.500
s 536(2): 13.500
s 537: 13.440
s 537(2): 13.460
s 539: 13.490
s 540(1): 13.510
s 541: 13.440
s 548: 13.490
s 563A: 7.100
s 567: 13.470
s 568: 13.470
s 574: 12.470
s 588F(1): 10.850, 10.880
s 588F(2): 10.880
s 588G: 3.170, 3.180, 7.520, 10.800, 10.810, 10.840, 10.860, 10.890, 10.910, 10.950, 10.960, 10.980, 10.990
s 588G(1): 3.170, 10.800
s 588G(1A): 10.850, 10.880
s 588G(2): 3.170, 10.800, 10.900
s 588G(3): 10.960, 10.990
s 588E: 10.830
s 588R(3): 10.830
s 588E(4): 10.830
s 588E(8): 10.830
s 588H: 3.170, 10.800, 10.950
s 588H(2): 3.170, 10.920, 10.950
s 588H(3): 3.170, 10.920, 10.930, 10.950
s 588H(4): 3.170, 10.920, 10.940
s 588H(5): 3.170, 10.920, 10.950
s 588H(6): 10.950
s 588J(1): 10.960

Corporations Act 2001 (Cth) (cont)
  s 588J(2): 10.960
  s 588K(1): 10.960
  s 588M: 10.970
  s 588M(2): 10.960
  s 588M(3): 10.970
  s 588R: 10.970
  s 588S: 10.970
  s 588T: 10.970
  s 588U: 10.970
  s 588V: 3.180
  s 588V(1): 3.180
  s 588W: 3.180
  s 588W(1): 3.180
  s 588Y(1): 10.960
  s 592(2): 10.920
  s 601AA: 13.700
  s 601AA(1): 13.710
  s 601AA(4): 13.720
  s 610AA(5): 13.720
  s 610AB: 13.700
  s 601AB(1): 13.730
  s 601AB(2): 13.730
  s 601AB(3): 13.740
  s 601AB(5): 13.740
  s 601AC(1): 13.750
  s 601AC(2): 13.50
  s 601AD: 2.110, 2.230
  s 601AD(1): 13.700
  s 601AD(2): 13.700
  s 601AE: 13.700
  s 601AH: 13.760
  s 601AH(1): 13.760
  s 601AH(2): 13.760
  s 601AH(3): 13.780
  s 601AH(5): 13.780
  s 601BA(1): 5.250
  s 601BC(1): 5.250
  s 601BC(2): 5.250
  s 601BC(3): 5.250
  s 601BC(4): 5.250
  s 601BC(6): 5.250
  s 601BC(7): 5.250
  s 601BC(8): 5.250
  s 601BC(8)(a): 5.250
  s 601BC(8)(b): 5.250
  s 601BC(8)(d): 5.250
  s 601BC(8)(e): 5.250
  s 601BC(8)(f)(i): 5.250
  s 601BC(8)(f)(ii): 5.250
  s 601BD(1)(a): 5.250
  s 601BD(1)(b): 5.250
  s 601BC(1)(c): 5.250
  s 601BL(1): 5.260, 5.270
  s 601CA: 5.260
  s 601CB: 5.260
  s 601CB(g): 5.260
  s 601CB(h): 5.260
  s 601CD(1): 5.270
  s 601CE: 5.270
  s 601CE(h): 5.270

  s 601CE(j): 5.270
  s 601CF: 5.270
  s 601CG: 5.270
  s 601CJ: 5.270
  s 601CU(1): 5.260, 5.270
  s 601CZB: 8.40
  s 601CZC: 8.40
  s 601CZD: 8.40
  s 667C: 7.320
  s 700(1): 8.120
  s 706: 8.130
  s 707: 8.130
  s 707(1): 8.130
  s 707(2): 8.130
  s 707(3): 8.130, 8.150
  s 707(5): 8.130, 8.150
  s 708: 8.130, 8.140
  s 708(1): 8.150, 8.470
  s 708(2): 8.150
  s 708(2)(b): 8.150
  s 708(3): 8.150
  s 708(3)(a): 8.150
  s 708(3)(b): 8.150
  s 708(4): 8.150
  s 708(4)(a); 8.150
  s 708(4)(b): 8.150
  s 708(5): 8.150
  s 708(7): 8.150
  s 708(8): 8.160, 8.540, 8.560
  s 708(8)(a): 8.160
  s 708(8)(b): 8.160
  s 708(8)(c): 8.160
  s 708(9): 8.160, 8.540
  s 708(9A): 8.160
  s 708(10): 8.160, 8.540, 8.560
  s 708(11): 8.160, 8.450, 8.560
  s 709: 8.250
  s 709(1): 8.370
  s 709(2): 8.230, 8.370
  s 709(3): 8.230
  s 709(4): 8.250, 8.370
  s 710: 8.190, 8.200, 8.280
  s 710(1): 8.190
  s 710(2): 8.190
  s 711: 8.190, 8.280
  s 711(1): 8.190
  s 711(2): 8.190
  s 711(3): 8.190
  s 711(4): 8.190
  s 711(5): 8.190
  s 711(6): 8.190
  s 711(7): 8.190
  s 712: 8.280
  s 712(1)(a): 8.220
  s 712(1)(b): 8.220
  s 712(5): 8.220
  s 713: 8.200, 8.280
  s 713(1): 8.200
  s 713(2): 8.200
  s 713(3): 8.200
  s 713(4): 8.200

s 713(5): 8.200
s 714: 8.240, 8.280
s 714(1)(a): 8.240
s 714(1)(b): 8.240
s 714(1)(c): 8.240
s 714(1)(d): 8.240
s 714(1)(e): 8.240
s 715: 8.260, 8.280
s 715(1): 8.260
s 715(2): 8.260
s 715(3): 8.260
s 715A: 8.270, 8.280, 8.350
s 716(1): 8.190
s 716(2): 8.190
s 718: 8.380
s 719(1): 8.280, 8.290
s 719(1A): 8.290
s 719(2): 8.320
s 719(3): 8.340
s 719(4): 8.310
s 719(5): 8.330
s 720: 8.380
s 721: 8.370
s 724: 8.300
s 724(1)(c): 8.290, 8.300
s 724(1A): 8.300
s 724(3): 8.290
s 727: 8.230, 8.370, 8.380
s 727(3): 8.390
s 728: 8.350, 8.380, 8.410, 8.420, 8.430, 8.450, 8.460
s 728(1): 8.290, 8.410, 8.440
s 728(2): 8.410
s 728(3): 8.290, 8.410
s 729: 8.280, 8.440, 8.460
s 730: 8.280
s 730(1): 8.300
s 730(2): 8.300
s 731: 8.420
s 732: 8.410
s 733(1): 8.420
s 733(3): 8.420
s 734: 8.470
s 734(1): 8.470, 8.530, 8.560
s 734(2): 8.480, 8.490, 8.500, 8.520, 8.530
s 734(3): 8.490
s 734(3)(c): 8.490
s 734(3)(d): 8.490
s 734(3)(e): 8.490
s 734(4): 8.500
s 734(5): 8.500, 8.510
s 734(5)(a): 8.500
s 734(5)(b)(i): 8.500
s 734(5)(b)(ii): 8.500
s 734(5)(b)(iii): 8.500
s 734(6): 8.500, 8.510
s 734(7): 8.500, 8.520
s 734(8): 8.530
s 734(9): 8.540
s 736: 8.550, 8.560

s 736(1): 8.550
s 736(2): 8.560
s 737: 8.300
s 737(1): 8.300
s 737(2): 8.300
s 738: 8.560
s 739: 8.360
s 739(1): 8.350
s 739(2): 8.360
s 739(3): 8.60
s 740: 8.150
s 741(1)(a): 8.140
s 741(2): 8.140
s 741(3): 8.140
s 742: 8.120, 8.140
s 761A: 8.120, 8.580
s 761B: 8.580
s 763A: 8.580
s 763A(1): 8.580
s 763B: 8.580
s 763C: 8.580
s 763D: 8.580
s 766A: 8.600
s 766B: 8.600
s 766C: 8.600
s 766D: 8.600
s 766E: 8.600
s 768A: 7.20
s 913B: 8.600
s 916A: 8.600
s 916B: 8.600
s 1022: 13.40
s 1023: 13.40
s 1041E: 8.430, 8.460
s 1041E(3): 8.430
s 1041F: 8.430, 8.460
s 1041G: 8.430, 8.460
s 1041H: 8.500
s 1041H(1): 8.450
s 1041H(3)(a)(ii): 8.450
s 1041I: 8.460
s 1041I(4): 8.460
s 1047: 5.170
s 1070A(1): 7.20
s 1070C(1): 7.30
s 1070C(2): 7.30
s 1071F: 10.370
s 1071F(2): 10.370
s 1072F(3): 10.330
s 1072G: 10.330
s 1274(7A): 5.110
s 1274(8): 5.100
s 1282(3): 13.440
s 1306: 5.190
s 1317E: 9.470, 10.220
s 1317E(1): 10.210, 10.210, 10.590, 10.980
s 1317G: 10.210, 10.960
s 1317H: 10.230
s 1317H(5): 10.230
s 1317J: 10.230

Corporations Act 2001 (Cth) (*cont*)
  s 1317M: 10.260
  s 1317P: 10.260
  s 1317S: 8.460, 10.240
  s 1317S(3): 10.240
  s 1318: 10.160
  s 1318(1): 10.160
  s 1319: 11.20, 11.40, 11.350, 11.360
  s 1322: 11.140, 11.400, 11.770
  s 1322(1)(b): 11.770
  s 1322(2): 11.770
  s 1322(3): 11.780
  s 1322(3A): 1150, 11.790
  s 1322(4): 11.800, 11.810
  s 1322(4)(a): 9.180, 11.800
  s 1322(4)(a)(i): 11.800
  s 1322(4)(b): 11.800
  s 1322(4)(c): 11.800
  s 1322(4)(d): 11.800
  s 1322(5): 9.180
  s 1322(6)(a): 9.180, 11.800
  s 1322(6)(b): 11.800
  s 1322(6)(c): 9.180, 11.800
  s 1323: 13.40
  s 1323(1): 13.40
  s 1323(3): 13.40
  s 1324: 7.320, 8.410, 12.470, 12.480, 12.490, 12.500, 12.510, 12.520
  s 1324(1): 12.470, 12.520
  s 1323(1)(h): 13.50
  s 1324(1B): 7.440
  s 1324(1B)(a): 7.320
  s 1324(2): 12.470, 12.520
  s 1324(4): 12.470
  s 1324(5): 12.520
  s 1324(6): 12.470
  s 1324(7): 12.470
  s 1324(10): 12.520
  s 1324A: 8.410
  s 1324B: 8.410
  s 1330: 1.130
  s 1344: 5.50
  s 1362CJ(1): 5.260, 5.270
  s 1362CJ(2): 5.260
  s 1362CJ(3): 5.270
  s 1378(1): 5.230
  s 1378(2): 5.230
  s 1378(3): 5.230
  s 1378(4): 5.230
  s 1408: 7.250
  s 1415: 6.10
  s 1446: 7.250
  Sch 1: 6.10
Corporations Regulations
  reg 3(1)(d): 1.100
  reg 4.2.01: 5.40
  reg 4.2.01(1)(a)(ii): 5.40
  reg 4.2.02: 5.40
  reg 65(a): 9.870
  reg 65(c): 9.870
  reg 65(d): 9.870
  reg 65(e): 9.870
  Sch 5 reg 25(2): 9.760
  Sch 5 reg 25(4): 9.760
Corporations (Commonwealth Authorities and Officers) Regulations 1990
  reg 3: 1.100
Corporations Law Amendment (Employee Entitlements) Act 2000: 10.150, 10.860
Criminal Code: 3.60, 3.70, 3.120
Financial Corporations Act 1974: 8.160
Financial Services Reform Act 2001: 8.570, 8.600
Income Tax Assessment Act 1936: 2.40
  s 92: 2.80
  s 215: 13.440
  s 252: 5.150
  s 265-5--272-140: 2.40
Income Tax Assessment Act 1997: 8.10
Insurance Contracts Act 1984
  s 17: 3.40
Jurisdiction of Courts (Cross-vesting) Act 1987: 1.110
Life Insurance Act 1995: 8.140
National Companies and Securities Commission Act 1979: 1.40
National Companies Bill 1972: 1.40
Superannuation Industry (Supervision) Act 1993: 8.160
Trade Practices Act 1974: 8.400
Workplace Relations Act 1996
  s 298K: 13.360

New South Wales
Companies Act 1961
  s 5: 9.50
  s 124(1): 9.50
  s 138: 11.360
  s 142: 11.360
Companies (New South Wales) Code
  s 229(4): 10.120
Corporations (New South Wales) Act 1990: 1.110
Crimes Act 1900
  s 173: 3.110
  s 176A: 10.120

Partnership Act 1892
  s 2(iii): 2.90
  s 44: 2.90
Partnership Act 1898
  s 1: 2.60
Perpetuities Act 1984
  s 7(1): 2.40

Queensland
Partnership Act 1891
  s 5: 2.60

South Australia
Partnership Act 1891
  s 1: 2.60

Tasmania
Partnership Act 1891
  s 6: 2.60

Victoria
Companies Act 1896: 1.40
Mining Companies Act 1871: 1.40
Partnership Act 1958
  s 5: 2.60
  s 9: 2.80
  s 16: 2.80
  s 28.5: 2.80
  s 30(1): 2.80
  s 35: 2.80
  s 36(c): 2.80
  s 37(1): 2.80
  Part 3: 2.70
Supreme Court Rules
  Order 17.01: 2.60

Western Australia
Corporations (Western Australia) Act 1990: 1.100
  s 1064(1): 1.100
Partnership Act 1895
  s 7: 2.60

Australian Capital Territory
Partnership Act 1963: 2.60

Northern Territory
Partnership Act 1997
  s 5: 2.60

United Kingdom
Bubble Act 1720: 1.30
Companies Act 1862: 1.30, 3.280
Companies Act 1948
  s 210: 12.400
Joint Stock Companies Act 1856: 1.30
Joint Stock Companies Registration and Regulation Act 1844: 1.30
Limited Liability Act 1855: 1.30
Trade Description Act 1968: 3.100

1

Introduction to Corporations Law

Overview

This chapter provides a brief discussion of the development of corporations law. It begins with a consideration of the historical development of the company as an entity. It continues with an overview of the development of corporations law in Britain and Australia so as to provide the context for understanding the origins of corporations law in Australia.

The chapter also examines the Australian Federal Parliament's legislative competence in establishing a uniform scheme for the regulation of corporations. The chapter discusses the constitutional crisis stemming from a series of cases in, in particular, 1999 and 2000 that undermined the foundations of the then legal structure regulating corporations under the *Corporations Law*. It outlines the terms of the consequent agreement that saw the referral of the States' legislative power with respect to corporations to the Commonwealth under s 51(xxxvii) of the Constitution.

Finally, the chapter briefly considers the current jurisdictional and administrative arrangements under which the subsequently enacted *Corporations Act* 2001 (Cth) ('*Corporations Act*') and *Australian Securities and Investments Commission Act* 2001 (Cth) ('*ASIC Act*') now operate.

A Select History of Corporations Law

Historical development of the corporate entity

[1.10] The origins of the use and regulation of corporations is unclear. According to Baxt (2003, p 133), under Roman law public institutions were treated as separate entities. It is also suggested that in the 13th century the monastic community was recognised as legally distinct from the monks who constituted it (Baxt, 2003, pp 133-134). By the 15th century, the English Crown was issuing charters of incorporation to monasteries, cities, boroughs and trade guilds (Baxt, 2003, p 134). The benefits of perpetual succession and separate legal personality, enabling these bodies to own assets such as trading licences, made incorporation through Royal Charter crucial. For boroughs, incorporation was often accompanied by the conferral of additional, specific benefits, such as the extension of governmental authority and judicial jurisdictional privileges (Redmond, 1992, p 29).

Initially, the creation of companies was confined to exercises of the English Crown's royal prerogative, through Royal Charters. The East India Company and Hudson's Bay Company are famous examples of companies created under Charters. Parliament did not become involved in incorporating companies until after the Revolution of 1688, when the Crown became less willing to confer the benefits of incorporation. Private Acts of Parliament then provided an expensive way of obtaining the privilege of incorporation.

During this period, the courts only had a limited role in the development of companies, although they did confer on long-standing institutions, such as the Inns of Court and certain university colleges, a 'form of incorporation by prescription' through the notion of a 'lost trust' (Baxt, 2003, p 134).

Hahlo details the expanded use of incorporated bodies with the growth of foreign trade (1982, pp 150-154). Groups of merchants trading with the one country combined forces and sought incorporation and a trading monopoly from the relevant foreign government/sovereign. In colonial situations, the privileges that accompanied incorporation often included quasi-governmental authority. These chartered corporations succeeded the guild in the control of trade.

Joint stock companies

[1.20] As Hahlo details (1982, pp 150-154), these chartered companies could take two forms:
- regulated companies; and
- joint stock companies.

The former involved a more limited type of incorporated trading. Within the confines of the company's by-laws, members traded with their own stock at their own risk. Thus, regulated companies were used to obtain trading privileges, rather than providing a medium through which members' financial resources were combined for entrepreneurial investment. With the growth of trade this objective changed and regulated companies were replaced by joint stock companies.

Unlike regulated companies, the joint stock company traded with jointly contributed 'stock' or capital for the benefit of its members as a whole. Originally each venture was treated as a separate investment, members having a total discretion whether to enter into that particular venture. Profits were consequently distributed to those involved at the end of each venture. In time, however, investment became permanent and profits distributed through dividends.

The joint stock company provided the basis for many of the attributes of the modern day company. Investors subscribed to joint stock through transferable shares akin to modern day share capital. As a matter of practice, voting was based on a proportion of shareholding. The joint stock company was considered a legal entity with the capacity of a natural person for all purposes, rather than simply for trading purposes. Through the use of its common seal, company acts could be authenticated and clearly distinguished from those of its membership (Redmond, 1992, p 34). Finally, shareholders were not personally liable for the company's debts (Hahlo, 1982, p 154). While the company's constitution could require members to pay 'leviations', the payment of which creditors could in turn judicially enforce, generally, personal liability was expressly excluded (Hahlo, 1982, p 154).

Development of corporations law in Britain

[1.30] Initially, the British Parliament attempted to circumscribe the use of joint stock companies as they had led to widespread speculative public trading in the shares of those companies. This period of company law is often characterised by reference to the rise and fall of the notorious South Sea Company. In a bid to reduce competition, the directors of this company procured the passage of the *Bubble Act* 1720 (UK) ('*Bubble Act*'). The Act did not, however, have its intended effect and the directors reacted by bringing legal proceedings to have the charters of rival companies forfeited. This in turn panicked the market place and share values plummeted. The 'bubble' burst, taking with it many of the joint stock enterprises.

Despite these collapses, the poorly drafted *Bubble Act* continued in operation for some time. It was designed to suppress speculation in the shares of unincorporated joint stock companies by prohibiting 'dangerous and mischievous undertakings and projects, wherein the undertakers and subscribers have presumed to act as if they were corporate bodies ... without legal authority, either by Act of Parliament, or by any charter from the Crown'. Such enterprises were declared illegal and void. The Act thereby attempted to confine trading to sales of interests in formally incorporated bodies (Redmond, 1992, p 36). The *Bubble Act* proved ineffective and prosecutions were few (Redmond, 1992, p 37).

With the industrial revolution and the increasing need for structures through which entrepreneurs could invest in trade and commerce, Parliament's attitude to companies changed to one of encouragement. The *Bubble Act* was repealed in 1825 and steps taken towards introducing a general procedure for incorporation. The *Joint Stock Companies Registration and Regulation Act* 1844 (UK) provided a general mechanism through which anyone could establish a company. The Act went beyond mere encouragement and required partnerships with a membership of more than 25 or with transferable shares to incorporate through the registration of an underlying deed of settlement (akin to what is now the corporate constitution). Once registered, the company became a distinct legal entity with perpetual succession.

Whilst the company enjoyed the ability to contract and hold property in its own name under the common seal, members were still personally liable for the company's debts. It was not until the passage of the *Limited Liability Act* 1855 (UK) that even conditional limited liability was extended to shareholders. This protection was premised on the provision of a minimum capital and, *inter alia*, the addition of the word 'Limited' at the end of the company's name to mark the membership's diminished liability. A year later this protection became unconditional with the passage of the *Joint Stock Companies Act* 1856 (UK), marking the beginning of the modern limited liability company. The *fait accompli* was the passage of the first *Companies Act* in 1862.

Development of corporations law in Australia

[1.40] Most Australian States independently enacted corporations legislation based on the English model, with certain modifications. In this respect the Victorian Parliament was the most progressive of the States, introducing 'no liability' companies for mining projects (*Mining Companies Act* 1871 (Vic)), distinguishing between public and proprietary companies and requiring public companies to comply with compulsory audit requirements and annual financial statements: *Companies Act* 1896 (Vic).

Differences in the State corporations statutes proved difficult for companies operating in more than one jurisdiction. In a bid to remove these inconsistencies, attempts were made at co-operative schemes introducing uniform legislation across the States. In 1961 and 1962 the *Uniform Companies Acts*, based on the Victorian model, were passed in all Australian jurisdictions. The Acts were not, however, uniform and, with the passage of time and subsequent amendments to different State legislation, the variations increased. The consequent disparity in legislation was criticised in the *Senate Select Committee on Securities and Exchange (Rae Committee) Report* 1974.

The 1972 Federal (Labor) Government took heed of these criticisms and sought to implement a national scheme for the regulation of corporations. A National Securities Commission and national corporations legislation was to be introduced through the *Corporations and Securities Industry Bill* and the *National Companies Bill*. The government, however, lost office and the Bills were never passed.

In 1974, the then non-Labor States (New South Wales, Victoria, Queensland and later, after a change in government, Western Australia) established the Interstate Corporate Affairs Commission, with the objective of providing a uniform system of corporate regulation in these jurisdictions. Whilst the work of the Commission provided benefits, as it was confined to specific States the difficulties stemming from disparate corporations legislation continued.

Companies Act 1981

[1.50] In 1978 the incoming Federal (Liberal) Government addressed this problem through a negotiated agreement with the States for a uniform national companies code. Each of the States agreed to pass uniform legislation, the Federal Parliament passing the relevant legislation for the Australian Capital Territory. The resultant *Companies Act* 1981 (Cth) was adopted by each of the States through the enactment of a *Companies (Application of Laws) Act* 1981 (Cth). The move towards uniform corporations law was furthered by creating the National Companies and Securities Commission ('NCSC') under the *National Companies and Securities Commission Act* 1979 (Cth). This body was responsible 'for the entire area of policy and administration with respect to company law and the regulation of the securities industry': Clause 32(1). Whilst each State legislatively recognised the NCSC, the existing State Corporate Affairs Commissions ('CAC') continued, exercising delegated authority from the national body.

Corporations Act 1989

[1.60] The system was not without its faults. The NCSC was largely ineffective. Under-funded, it was powerless to act upon most breaches of the Act. The Senate Standing Committee on Constitutional and Legal Affairs recommended 'the Commonwealth Parliament should enact comprehensive legislation covering the field currently regulated by the co-operative scheme' (1987, p 74). In turn, the then Federal (Labor) Government introduced, and the Commonwealth Parliament enacted, legislation embodying, *inter alia*, a national scheme for the regulation of trading, financial and foreign companies. Parliament enacted three key statutes: *Corporations Act* 1989 (Cth), *Australian Securities Commission Act* 1989 (Cth) and *Close Corporations Act* 1989 (Cth). This legislation sought to replace the existing corporations and securities legislation, introduce a national body, the Australian Securities Commission ('ASC') to replace the NCSC and the CACs, and introduce a new form of small company akin to a limited partnership. The legislation also created a separate Corporations and Securities Panel with authority to determine the legitimacy of takeover activities/defences and an advisory body, the Companies and Securities Advisory Committee, to advise the Commonwealth Attorney-General on matters of law reform. As discussed below, however, the High Court held by a 6:1 majority (Mason CJ, Brennan, Dawson, Gaudron, Toohey and McHugh JJ; Deane J dissenting) that the Commonwealth Parliament lacked legislative authority to create a regime for incorporating companies: *New South Wales v Commonwealth* (1990) 169 CLR 482.

Corporations Law

[1.70] The Commonwealth Government's goal was, nevertheless, indirectly implemented. The States and Northern Territory Governments were supportive of a co-operative system and agreed in June 1990 to adopt an amended version of the *Corporations Act* 1989 (Cth). These Acts were collectively known as the *Corporations Law*. The *Corporations Law* was incorporated into the State legislation through s 82 of the respective *Corporations Acts*. The States' adoption of this legislation and recognition of the Commonwealth ASC as solely responsible for the administration of the Act effected in practice a national system for the regulation of companies.

This national corporate law scheme continued to operate for a decade without effective challenge. As discussed below, in 1999 and

2000, however, the foundations of this arrangement were undermined in a series of cases, the outcomes of which left this regime of corporations law and practice in tatters. These cases effectively denied the Federal Court jurisdiction over corporations law matters outside the Territories. Thus, in *Re Wakim* (1999) 163 ALR 270; 17 ACLC 1055, the cross-vesting legislation upon which the administration of the *Corporations Law* was based was held to be invalid by a majority of the High Court in so far as the legislation purported to invest the Federal Court with jurisdiction over State matters. The courts circumscribed the ability of the States to confer authority in relation to corporations law matters on Commonwealth agencies. In *Bond v R* (2000) 164 ALR 607, the court indicated that a conferral of authority by the States upon a Commonwealth officer that exceeded that authorised under Commonwealth legislation would be inoperative pursuant to s 109 of the Constitution. The decisions also significantly limited the Commonwealth's ability to enact enabling legislation allowing its agents to undertake functions pertaining to such State matters. In *R v Hughes* (2000) 18 ACLC 394 the court held that the Commonwealth must be able to identify a legislative head of power that can support the enactment of Commonwealth enabling legislation, facilitating the conferral of authority by the States on Commonwealth officers. The cumulative effect of these cases was to undermine both the validity of the *Corporations Law* and the regime for its administration and enforcement.

Corporations Act 2001

[1.80] In response to urgent calls for comprehensive reforms to rectify this disastrous constitutional position, on 25 August 2000 the Commonwealth Attorney General and the Minister for Financial Services and Regulation announced in a joint press release that the joint Standing Committee of Attorneys General and the Ministerial Council for Corporations had unanimously agreed that the States would refer their corporations law powers to the Commonwealth pursuant to s 51(xxxvii) of the Constitution. Under the agreement the States referred the powers necessary to enact the new Commonwealth *Corporations Act* and *ASIC Act*; effectively re-enacting the prior eight separate *Corporations Acts*.

In addition, the States agreed to refer the power to amend the *Corporations Act* and *ASIC Act* in relation to the formation of corporations, corporate regulation and the regulation of financial services and products. A proposed amendment may be rejected, however, where four or more States agree that it is outside the scope of the referral of power. To this end the State reference legislation provides that the referred powers are not to be used by the Commonwealth for the purposes of regulating, *inter alia*, industrial relations and the environment. The referral of powers was to terminate after five years, unless extended by agreement. If any State terminates its referral of power it ceases being a 'referring State'. See also ss 4(6)-(8) and 9. A State may not terminate the referral of powers to amend the *Corporations Act* and *ASIC Act* by itself. Instead, it is necessary that four States vote to terminate the referral of the amendment power; at which point the referral of the amendment power by all States ceases. In addition, the States are required to put to a vote of the Ministerial Council, discussed below, any amendment to State law significantly overriding the new Commonwealth Acts. On 5 November 2004, Mr Chris Pearce, Parliamentary Secretary to the Treasurer and Chairman of the Ministerial Council, announced that the Council had endorsed a five-year extension of the States' referral of the corporations power to the Commonwealth. The referral was due to expire in 2006.

Commonwealth's Legislative Power to Enact a Federal Corporations Regime

Corporations Act 1989

[1.90] Under the Commonwealth Constitution, the Federal Parliament is accorded enumerated areas of legislative competence. The residue of authority remains in the State and Territory legislatures. One of the Commonwealth's enumerated powers is s 51(xx) of the Constitution, the 'corporations power'. This extends to the Commonwealth the power to legislate with respect to '[f]oreign corporations and trading or financial corporations formed within the limits of the Commonwealth'.

The scope of s 51(xx) is a matter of great controversy. The specificity of the placita's language; that is, being confined to foreign corporations and trading and financial corporations; and the suggestion that it only extends legislative power to regulate corporations once formed, has long undermined the Commonwealth's ability to introduce truly national corporations legislation. As noted above, the validity of crucial aspects of the *Corporations Act* 1989 was successfully challenged as being unconstitutional. A majority of the High Court (Deane J dissenting) held that the Commonwealth Parliament lacked legislative authority to create a regime for incorporating companies (as opposed to regulating corporations that had already been incorporated/formed).

New South Wales v Commonwealth
High Court: Mason CJ, Brennan, Dawson, Gaudron, Toohey,
McHugh and Deane JJ
(1990) 169 CLR 482

The New South Wales, South Australian and Western Australian Governments were concerned over the loss of revenue that would result from the Commonwealth's usurpation of control over corporate affairs. In turn these governments challenged the constitutional validity of the *Corporations Act* 1989 (Cth). The States argued that s 51(xx) of the Constitution did not allow the Commonwealth to regulate the registration of new companies, prohibit the formation of 'outsize partnerships' unless incorporated and prohibit trading corporations from incorporating under State corporations laws. The States asserted that the word 'formed' in s 51(xx) indicated that it presupposed the existence of the corporation that had already been incorporated under State law. In response the Commonwealth asserted that the words 'formed within the limits of the Commonwealth' served merely to distinguish local trading or financial corporations from foreign corporations.

A majority of the High Court held that the Commonwealth lacked legislative authority to regulate the formation and incorporation of companies. Mason CJ, Brennan, Dawson, Gaudron, Toohey and McHugh JJ rejected the Commonwealth's suggestion that the phrasing of s 51(xx) was simply to distinguish local and foreign corporations. The use of the past tense, 'formed', meant that the Commonwealth could only legislate with respect to corporations that had already been formed.

Mason CJ, Brennan, Dawson, Gaudron, Toohey and McHugh JJ: **[497]** The Commonwealth contention is that the words "formed within the limits of the Commonwealth" serve merely to distinguish local trading or financial corporations from foreign corporations. No doubt the words do serve that function but their plain meaning goes beyond the mere drawing of the distinction. The expressions "trading or financial" and "formed within the limits of the Commonwealth" serve to restrict the classes of domestic corporation which can be the subject of Commonwealth power. To fall within one limb of the power, a corporation must satisfy two conditions: it must be formed within the limits of the Commonwealth and it must be a trading or financial corporation. To fall **[498]** within the other limb, a corporation must be a foreign corporation, that is, a corporation formed outside the limits of the Commonwealth. The distinction based on the place of formation is obvious, but the basis of the distinction is formation. The word "formed" is a past participle used adjectivally, and the participial phrase "formed within the limits of the Commonwealth" is used to describe corporations which have been or shall have been created in Australia ... The subject of a valid law is restricted by that phrase to corporations which have undergone or shall have undergone the process of formation in the past, present or future. That is to say, the power is one with respect to "formed corporations". That being so, the words "formed within the limits of the Commonwealth" exclude the process of incorporation itself. ...

Both precedent and history support this construction of the text of s 51(xx). In *Huddart, Parker & Co Pty Ltd v Moorehead* (1909) 8 CLR 330 the five members of the court were unanimously of the opinion that the subject matter of s 51(xx) is confined to corporations already in existence and does not extend to the creation of corporations. That, they said, is the plain meaning of the words 'formed within the limits of the Commonwealth'. ...

[501] Moreover, the history of s 51(xx) confirms that the language of the paragraph was not directed towards the subject of incorporation. ...

The successive drafts of s 51(xx) before it reached the form in which it appears in the Constitution confirm that that paragraph is concerned with existing corporations and was not intended to confer power to legislate for their creation. ...

[503] [I]t may be observed that the limitation imposed upon the reach of s 51(xx) by the requirement that, in the case of domestic corporations, they be of a trading or financial character, would create undeniable difficulties if that paragraph were to be construed as extending to the incorporation of companies. The fact that the character of a corporation may vary, so that it may be at one time a trading or financial corporation and not at another, makes it less likely at least that s 51(xx) was intended to confer power upon the Commonwealth to incorporate companies over which its power of regulation might fluctuate, possibly without knowledge upon either side.

In a vigorous dissent, Deane J rejected the majority justices' reasoning:

Deane J: [505] A plenary legislative power 'with respect to' particular kinds of corporation extends, as a matter of mere language, to laws dealing with both the incorporation and the liquidation of such corporations just as a plenary legislative power with respect to 'copyrights,' 'patents,' 'designs' or 'trademarks' extends to laws dealing with the creation and extinguishment of those particular kinds of industrial property. ...

One might as well say that a legislative power with respect to locally manufactured motor vehicles would not extend to laws governing the local manufacture of motor vehicles or that the legislative power with respect to lighthouses does not [506] extend to laws governing the erection of lighthouses since, until it is manufactured locally or erected, neither the locally manufactured motor vehicle nor the lighthouse exists as such. Another objection is that the argument fails to accord proper scope to the words 'with respect to' in s 51 or to the settled principle which requires that para (xx), which is a constitutional grant of plenary legislative power, be liberally, and not narrowly or technically, construed ... In the context of the use of the phrase 'formed within the limits of the Commonwealth' in contradistinction to 'foreign', the word 'formed' is properly to be understood as representing a use of the past participle as part of an adjectival phrase which is without temporal significance. ... When the word 'formed' is so understood, it affords no basis for excluding the formation or incorporation within the limits of the Commonwealth of trading and financial corporations from the scope of the legislative power granted by the second limb of para (xx). To the contrary, it tends to focus attention upon that aspect of the grant of power. The other main argument in support of the exclusion of incorporation from the ambit of the legislative power was based on the suggested authority of *Huddart, Parker & Co Proprietary Ltd v Moorehead* (1909) 8 CLR 330 ...

[507] That narrow construction of s 51(xx) and the actual decision in *Huddart Parker* were disapproved and authoritatively discarded by the court in *Strickland v Rocla Concrete Pipes Ltd* (1971) 124 CLR 468. As pointed out in *Strickland* (per Barwick CJ at 485), the judgments of Griffith CJ, Barton and O'Connor JJ were all permeated by the doctrine of the reserved powers of the States which was 'exploded and unambiguously rejected' in the *Engineers'* case (1920) 28 CLR 129. ...

[511] Reference should be made to two subsidiary arguments advanced in favour of the view that laws dealing with incorporation were beyond the ambit of para (xx). The first can be shortly disposed of. It was to the effect that that view is supported by what was said in the course of the Convention Debates and by contemporary commentators ... The first answer to that argument is that the few brief references in the Convention Debates are far from compelling ... and one can point to contrary statements in early authority ... The second answer is a more fundamental one. ... It is that it is not permissible to constrict the effect of the words which were adopted by the people as the compact of a nation by reference to the intentions or understandings of those who participated in or observed the Convention Debates: see *Breavington v Godleman* (1988) 62 ALJR 447 at 477; 80 ALR 362 at 412.

The second subsidiary argument was, as I followed it, essentially an appeal to convenience. It was said that the words 'trading or financial' in para (xx) significantly restrict the corporations to which the grant of legislative power extended. That being so, it would be productive of difficulty and inconvenience to construe para (xx) as conferring legislative power with respect to the incorporation of those corporations only. One answer to this argument is that it assumes an unduly restrictive connotation of the phrase 'trading or financial corporations' in para (xx). ... **[512]** In any event, there is a more complete answer to the argument of inconvenience based on the consideration that the grant of legislative power with respect to local trading or financial corporations does not extend to all corporations. It is that, while that consideration might well be seen by the Parliament as calling for restraint in the exercise of the legislative power, it does not provide any legal justification for denying the generality of a plenary grant of legislative power with respect to the designated class of corporation. If even further answer to an argument based upon the alleged inconvenience of uniform companies legislation in relation to trading and financial corporations be needed, it is plain enough. It is the advantages of such national companies legislation with respect to such corporations seem to me overwhelmingly to outweigh the alleged inconvenience.

Corporations Law

[1.100] As noted above, at first, the impact of the decision in *New South Wales v Commonwealth* (1990) 169 CLR 482 was avoided in practical terms by the agreement of the States and Northern Territory Governments to support a co-operative system. These governments agreed in June 1990 to adopt an amended version of the *Corporations Act* 1989 (Cth), the collective of these enactments being known as the *Corporations Law*. As also noted above, this regime was challenged in a series of cases, which, *inter alia*, questioned the constitutional validity of the co-operative system. In the following case the High Court left a question mark hanging over the constitutional validity of, *inter alia*, the States and Commonwealth *Corporations Acts* and thus the *Corporations Law*.

R v Hughes
High Court: Gleeson CJ, Gaudron, McHugh, Gummow,
Hayne, Callinan and Kirby JJ
(2000) 18 ACLC 394

Under *Corporations (Western Australia) Act* 1990 (WA) an offence under this Act was to be taken to be a breach of the *Corporations Act* 1989 (Cth). It was also directed that the Commonwealth Director of Public Prosecutions ('DPP'), rather than the State prosecutors, were to prosecute in regard to such enabling legislation. The complementary Commonwealth legislation was contained in s 47 of the *Corporations Act* 1989 (Cth) and reg 3 of the *Corporations (Commonwealth Authorities and Officers) Regulations* 1990 (Cth). The defendant was prosecuted by the Commonwealth DPP for issuing prescribed interests in Western Australia in breach of s 1064(1) of the *Corporations (Western Australia) Act* 1990 (WA). The defendant sought orders quashing the indictment on the basis that the Commonwealth DPP lacked legislative power to prosecute breaches of the subject offences. In reply the Commonwealth DPP asserted that its legislative authority to prosecute for breaches under the *Corporations (Western Australia) Act* 1990 could be found in the interrelated provisions of that Act and the *Corporations Act* 1989 (Cth). In particular, s 47 of the *Corporations Act* 1989 and reg 3 of the *Corporations (Commonwealth Authorities and Officers) Regulations* 1990 (Cth) supported the conferral of State authority on the Commonwealth DPP. In turn, the defendant asserted this federal legislation was invalid because the offences could not be independently supported by any head of legislative authority under the Constitution.

The High Court held that the States cannot unilaterally confer authority upon Commonwealth officers. For this co-operative regime to be valid the Commonwealth had to pass enabling legislation and this must have the same breadth as the State enactment, otherwise s 109 of the Constitution will render the State Act inoperative to the extent of the inconsistency. Most importantly, the High Court held that the Commonwealth enabling legislation will be unconstitutional unless it is supported by a specific head of legislative power. On the facts, however, the court held the federal legislation to be valid in this case as the subject breach of the *Corporations Law* involved an overseas investment scheme and thus the legislation could be supported by ss 51(i) (trade and commerce with other countries) and 51(xxix) (external affairs) of the Constitution. Once the Commonwealth enabling legislation was held to be valid under ss 51(i) and 51(xxix), s 109 did not render the complementary State enactment to be inoperative.

Gleeson CJ, Gaudron, McHugh, Gummow, Hayne and Callinan JJ: [403]
42. [T]he offences with which the accused is charged relate to the making of investments in the United States and thus to trade and commerce with other countries (s 51(i)). They also relate to matter territorially outside Australia, but touching and concerning Australia, and so would attract s 51(xxix). ...

44. Accordingly, the federal legislation identified above (s 47(1) of the Corporations Act and reg 3(1)(d) of the Regulations) operates to provide such authority as is necessary under federal law to support the prosecution by the DPP of the offences against the law of Western Australia which are specified in the indictment. ...

46. *Duncan* [*R v Duncan; Ex p Australian Iron and Steel Pty Ltd* (1983) 158 CLR 535] is one of a number of decisions which recognise that co-operation on the part of the Commonwealth and States may well achieve objects that could be achieved by neither acting alone. Nothing in these reasons denies that general proposition. The present case emphasises that for the Commonwealth to impose on an officer or instrumentality of the Commonwealth powers coupled with duties adversely to affect the rights of individuals, where no such power is directly conferred on that officer or instrumentality by the Constitution itself, requires a law of the Commonwealth supported by an appropriate head of power.

The necessary implication from this decision was that, but for the overseas nature of the subject breach, the Commonwealth enabling legislation may have been unconstitutional. Kirby J was aware of the significance of the case.

Kirby J: [405] 51. The accused's arguments thus present a challenge to the scheme adopted for the regulation of corporations in Australia, of which the *Corporations Law* is the centrepiece. Unless the offences provided in the *Corporations Law* are valid and may be the subject of prosecutions in Western Australia by the Commonwealth DPP, the legislative and administrative scheme for the regulation of corporations in Australia would collapse. Without enforceability, the *Corporations Law* would be no more than a pious aspiration. The importance of the accused's challenge to the validity of the indictment could therefore not be overstated. ...

[416] 120. It remains to be seen whether, in other factual circumstances, [the absence of an expressly stated head of power supporting the *Corporations Act* 1989 (Cth)] will **[417]** prove fatal to prosecutions. Clearly, it is a fragile foundation for a highly important national law. The present accused fails in his challenge. But the next case may not present circumstances sufficient to attract the essential constitutional support.

Cross-vesting

[1.110] The role of the Federal Court in the co-operative corporations law regime was also dealt a blow by this series of cases. In the following case a majority (Kirby J dissenting) of the High Court held that the corporations law cross-vesting scheme was invalid in so far as it purported to invest the Federal Court with jurisdiction over State matters.

Re Wakim
High Court: Gleeson CJ, Gaudron, McHugh, Gummow,
Hayne, Callinan and Kirby JJ
(1999) 17 ACLC 1055

Three cases were determined concurrently in this decision. Of the three cases the most central to the subject issue was *Re Brown; ex p Amann*. The Federal Court had made orders winding up Amann Aviation Pty Ltd. It also made orders for an examination of the liquidator under ss 596A and 596B of the *Corporations Law*. In making these orders the Federal Court was exercising powers conferred on it under s 42(3) of the *Corporations (New South Wales) Act* 1990 (NSW). The examinees appealed against the orders arguing that the cross-vesting legislation (*Jurisdiction of Courts (Cross-vesting) Act* 1987 (Cth) together with aspects of the *Corporations Act* 1989) that purported to confer on the Federal Court jurisdiction to determine matters arising under the State *Corporations Acts* was constitutionally invalid. It was argued that State Parliaments were unable to confer State judicial power on a federal court established under Chapter III of the Commonwealth Constitution. In reply, it was argued that Chapter III is only concerned with Commonwealth judicial power and does not expressly or impliedly related to other, such as State, judicial authority.

A majority of the High Court (Kirby J dissenting) held the cross-vesting legislation was invalid. The conferral of authority over State matters breached Chapter III as this Chapter exhaustively set out the matters that the federal courts were empowered to consider and this

Chapter did not provide for the investing of State jurisdiction on federal courts, even with the agreement of the Commonwealth.

McHugh J: **[1069]** 55. There is no doubt that, as a result of cooperation between a State and the Commonwealth, the Commonwealth may achieve objects that are beyond the constitutional competence of the Commonwealth. Similarly, as the result of joint legislation, a State and the Commonwealth may achieve an object that neither could achieve by its own legislation. But that is because each political entity has the constitutional power to do what is jointly necessary to achieve the object. Where constitutional power does not exist, no cry of cooperative federalism can supply it. ...

56. Cooperative federalism does not assist those supporting the validity of the present legislation. That is because the legislatures of the States have no power, with or without the consent of the Parliament of the Commonwealth, to invest State jurisdiction or judicial power in federal courts. There is not a word in Ch III which indicates expressly or by implication that it authorises the Parliament of the Commonwealth to create federal courts to exercise State jurisdiction or State judicial power. Nor is there a word in Ch III which indicates that the States can invest such jurisdiction or power in the federal courts. ...

57. But in addition, the settled doctrine of this court is that Ch III exhaustively defines the 'matters' that may be the subject of the judicial power of the Commonwealth and exhaustively defines the 'matters' that the Parliament of the Commonwealth may invest in the federal courts which it creates. The irresistible conclusion from the terms of Ch III is that it authorises the Parliament of the Commonwealth to create federal courts but only for the purpose of exercising jurisdiction with **[1070]** respect to the matters specified in ss 75 and 76 of the Constitution. ...

58. If the terms of ss 71, 75 and 76 of the Constitution impliedly forbid the Parliament of the Commonwealth from adding to the ss 75 and 76 jurisdiction of the federal courts, as everyone accepts they do, those sections must also logically forbid the States from doing so. Certainly, they must at least forbid the States from investing federal jurisdiction in federal courts. Given the terms of ss 71, 75, 76 and 77, which give to the Parliament of the Commonwealth and no other entity the power to create federal courts and to confer upon them the jurisdiction identified in ss 75 and 76, I cannot accept that the States have any power in respect of the matters identified in those sections. ...

59. What prevents a State conferring jurisdiction on a federal court in respect of a matter specified in s 75 or s 76 is not s 109, but the negative implications arising from Ch III of the Constitution. By granting power to the Parliament of the Commonwealth to create federal courts and by expressly stating the matters in respect of which the parliament may confer jurisdiction on those courts, Ch III impliedly forbids the conferring of any other jurisdiction on those courts by the Commonwealth or the States. The express statement of those 'matters' would be pointless if the parliament or the States could disregard them. Moreover, the reasons that show that the States cannot confer jurisdiction on a federal court in respect of ss 75 and 76 matters point just as strongly, perhaps more so because of s 77(iii), to the conclusion that the States cannot confer State jurisdiction on federal courts.

As a result of the finding in *Re Wakim*, those provisions of the States and Commonwealth *Corporations Acts* that purported to vest State judicial authority in the Federal Court were invalid. The Federal Court had no jurisdiction to hear *Corporations Law* matters outside the Territories in all cases except where the court had 'accrued' jurisdiction. 'Accrued' jurisdiction exists where federal and non-federal claims are part of the one controversy, arising out of a common substratum of facts. In such cases, the Federal Court may concurrently determine the non-federal issues provided they form an integral part of the federal issue.

As a result of the constraint of the Federal Court's corporations law jurisdiction, the State Supreme Courts became the appropriate forum for corporations law litigation outside the Territories. This meant that an action that had commenced in the Federal Court before *Re Wakim* had to be recommenced in the State Supreme Courts. Moreover, the validity of past Federal Court decisions could be questioned. In response, the State Governments enacted 'emergency' legislation deeming previous Federal Court decisions dealing with the State *Corporations Acts* to have been determined by the respective State Supreme Courts, thereby validating such determinations, and providing for the transfer of matters that had commenced in the Federal Court to the State Supreme Courts.

[1.120] Such legislation did not, however, rectify the jurisdictional problems flowing from the limitation of the Federal Court's jurisdiction. As discussed above, ultimately, this was addressed by making corporations law a federal matter through the referral of State authority over corporations, agreed to on 25 August 2000.

Current Jurisdictional and Administrative Arrangements

[1.130] As a consequence of the referral of State legislative competence responsibility for, *inter alia*, administering the *Corporations Act* and related legislation now rests with the Australian Securities and Investment Commission ('ASIC'), formerly the ASC: *ASIC Act* ss 1(1) and 11(1) and (6). The aims of ASIC are set out in s 1(2) of the *ASIC Act*.

As ASIC has the responsibility for ensuring that the *Corporations Act* is complied with, it is of course necessary for ASIC to be able to undertake investigations into possible breaches of the Act and instigate civil and criminal prosecutions. Part 3 of the *ASIC Act* extends to ASIC extensive investigatory and information-gathering powers where it has reason to suspect there has been a breach of the Act. These include powers to compel persons to answer questions under oath and/or produce books and records to assist ASIC in its investigations: *ASIC Act* Divs 2 and 3 of Part 3. Where as a result of such investigations ASIC believes it is in the public's interest to initiate civil proceedings, it may do so in the name of a particular company/person: *ASIC Act* s 50. The Commission may also intervene in litigation that has been instigated by others: *Corporations Act* s 1330. As stated above, the ASIC may also instigate criminal proceedings where such investigations indicate that a person has committed an offence under the *Corporations Act*: *ASIC Act* s 49. As this is a concurrent power with the Commonwealth DPP, the ASIC and DPP liase in regard to prosecutions where they have mutual interests.

ASIC advises the minister of necessary changes to the legislative regime to ensure it can carry out its responsibilities: *ASIC Act* s 11(2)(b). ASIC is able to provide corporate law reform advice, either on its own initiative or when requested by the minister: *ASIC Act* s 11(3). ASIC also has a more general educational role. Media releases, information booklets and other publications are designed to educate, *inter alia*, the business community in the operation of the *Corporations Act*. Officers also provide educational seminars on important topics such as recent major reforms to the Act.

The Takeover Panel (previously called the Corporations and Securities Panel) was established under the predecessor to *ASIC Act* and is preserved under the current legislative regime: *ASIC Act* s 261. The Takeover Panel shares ASIC's power to determine whether unacceptable conduct has occurred in relation to the acquisition of shares. See further Part 10 of the *ASIC Act* and Div 2 Part 6.10 of the *Corporations Act*.

Two other bodies with which the ASIC interacts are the Corporations and Markets Advisory Committee ('CAMAC') and Parliamentary Joint Committee on Corporations and Financial Services. Each of the States and Territories is represented on the Advisory Committee, which has the role of advising the Minister on reform of the law and administration of the national companies scheme. See further Part 9 of the *ASIC Act*. The Parliamentary Committee consists of 10 members; five appointed by each House of the Commonwealth Parliament: s 241(2). The Parliamentary Committee inquires into, and reports upon, the operations of the corporations legislation, ASIC and the Takeovers Panel: s 243. In this way it provides a further supervisory role in addition to that of the relevant Minister, the Treasurer. See further Part 14 of the *ASIC Act*.

Review questions

Please read the extracts *New South Wales v Commonwealth* (1990) 169 CLR 482 and answer the following questions:

1. What four bases were suggested by the majority for excluding the power to regulate the incorporation of companies?
2. How did Deane J reply to these suggestions?
3. The Commonwealth Attorney General submitted that the phrase 'formed within the limits of the Commonwealth' merely served to distinguish local from foreign corporations. How did the majority respond to this submission?
4. What is the reserved powers doctrine?
5. According to principles of constitutional interpretation, the Commonwealth's legislative authority is to be interpreted liberally. Does the majority's reasoning accord with this principle?
6. According to the majority, what activities of a trading corporation may be regulated under s 51(xx)?
7. Did Deane J believe inactive trading corporations could be regulated under s 51(xx)? Would a conclusion to the contrary be workable?

8. Did Deane J believe the provisions requiring outsize partnerships to incorporate to be constitutionally valid?
9. Do you believe the Commonwealth can regulate the internal activities of trading corporations under s 51(xx)?
10. Would legislation providing environmental standards to be observed by trading corporations be valid under s 51(xx)?

Further reading

Austin, 'Corporate Confusion: Commonwealth Companies and Securities Regulation after the Constitutional Challenge' (1990) 3 *Aust Corp LB* 27
Cassidy, *Concise Corporations Law* (4th ed, Federation Press, Sydney, 3002) ch 1
Crawford, 'The High Court and the Corporations Power: Incorporation 'Reserved' to the States' (1990) 3 *Aust Corp LB* 32
Ford, Austin and Ramsay, *Ford's Principles of Corporations Law* (11th ed, Butterworths, Sydney, 2003) chs 1-3
McQueen, 'Why High Court Judges Make Poor Historians: The Corporations Act Case and Early Attempts to Establish a National System of Company Regulation in Australia' (1990) 19 *FL Rev* 245
Ramsay, 'The Unravelling of Australia's Federal Corporate Law' *Corporate Law Email Bulletin*, No 31, March 2000

References Chapter 1

Afterman and Baxt, *Cases and Materials on Corporations and Associations* (9th ed, Butterworths, Sydney, 2003)
Hahlo, 'Early Progenitors of the modern company' [1982] *Juridical Review* 139
Redmond, *Companies and Securities Law: Commentary and Materials* (2nd ed, Law Book Co, Sydney, 1992)
Senate Standing Committee on Constitutional and Legal Affairs, *The Role of Parliament in relation to the National Companies Scheme* (1987)

2

Choosing Between Business Organisations

Overview

This chapter provides a brief discussion of the various structures open to a person to use to, *inter alia*, conduct a business. While the primary focus of the text is the regulation and the use of companies, conducting commercial relations through a company will not suit every person's business, financial and family needs. One of the most common issues with respect to which the clients of legal and accountancy advisors will seek advice is as to the best structure for their particular business venture. Providing professional advice on such requires identifying two interrelated matters:

- what are the various business structures available to the client?; and
- what factors, possibly peculiar to the client, suggest one structure to be preferable over others?

As to the first issue, broadly, the possible structures from which an individual may choose include:

- sole proprietorship;
- trust;
- partnership;
- joint venture; and
- company.

As to the second issue, while a whole variety of factors may be pertinent in an individual case, common factors that will be relevant in determining which structure best suits a client's situation will be:

- costs involved in establishing the structure;
- continuing costs stemming from the structure's use;
- demands of applicable regulatory arrangements;
- flexibility of the structure;
- purpose for which the structure is to be used;
- whether control of the structure is to be shared;
- intention to include family members;
- intended size and potential growth;

- whether establishing and using the structure may require obtaining finance;
- whether the business should be conducted through a distinct legal entity;
- considerations of risk and potential liability; and
- taxation.

The chapter begins with a consideration of non-corporate structures. Thus, the pros and cons of using sole proprietorships, trusts, partnerships and joint ventures are considered. It will be seen that these structures are not separate legal entities distinct from, *inter alia*, the controller behind them. In turn there are common positives and negatives entailed in their use as business vehicles. There are also important advantages and disadvantages that are distinct to each of these business structures.

The chapter also examines companies. It begins with a generic consideration of the pros and cons of using a corporate structure to conduct a business. Three of the most important features of a company are its separate legal identity, its perpetual succession and, depending on the nature of the company, limited liability. As the latter comment indicates, there are also relevant considerations that need to be highlighted depending on what type of company is being used. Thus, the chapter considers the different types of companies that may be registered under the *Corporations Act* 2001 (Cth) (*'Corporations Act'*) and identifies their respective positives and negatives.

Sole Proprietorship

Defining a sole proprietorship

[2.10] A 'sole trader' or 'sole proprietorship' exists when an individual personally conducts his or her own business. Whilst that individual may employ staff, he or she owns, and normally manages, the business.

Benefits and shortcomings of a sole proprietorship

[2.20] Sole proprietorships are the simplest form of business organisation. The formalities and costs attributable to creating and using this structure are minimal. Unlike certain companies, there is no need to audit the business finances or to file annual financial reports and other business details with regulatory agencies. The only requirements to be complied with are those provided under general legislation such as taxation laws, registration of business names, occupational health and safety statutes and workers compensation legislation.

The disadvantages, however, can be quite dramatic where any risk attaches to the business being conducted. As a sole proprietorship is not a separate legal entity, debts must be incurred in the individual's name and his or her liability is without limitation. The sole proprietor will be wholly and solely liable for any debts and obligations incurred through the business. In meeting such obligations, recourse is not confined to business assets. Creditors may have recourse to the sole trader's personal assets or interest in assets, whether wholly or jointly owned. Thus, the family car or home can be utilised in satisfaction of business debts.

The size of any business conducted as a sole proprietorship is generally limited. Obtaining finance to expand the business may prove difficult as the sole trader can only provide personal forms of security. If the sole trader introduces new parties consequent to such an expansion, this will dissolve the initial structure and undermine the continuity of business relations. Moreover, the business goodwill may be personal, attaching to the sole trader, making the introduction of new parties difficult.

Mortality dictates that a sole proprietorship will not continue forever. Unlike a company that has perpetual succession in so far as it exists until deregistered, with the death or incapacity of the sole trader the business, in effect, ceases. Whilst goodwill and the business name may be passed on to a spouse or children, there may be taxation consequences attaching to such transfers, for example stamp duty and capital gains tax. Moreover, contractual relations will have to be renegotiated in the new trader's name.

Finally, whilst colloquially sole traders are their 'own boss', strictly they are not employed by anyone. They do not, therefore, enjoy the physical and financial security provided by workers compensation legislation, or the tax benefits provided in the past with respect to employer-contributed superannuation schemes.

Thus, the benefits attaching to a sole proprietorship are few. In essence the benefits provided by the minimal establishment and ongoing costs must outweigh the risks involved in the venture before this can be concluded to be a suitable commercial vehicle.

Trading Trust

Defining a trust

[2.30] A trust exists when one party is obliged to hold or invest property on behalf of another. Unless statutory requirements require evidence in writing because, for example, the trust property includes an interest in land, a trust can arise from a simple declaration by one party that he or she holds property for another. The first party is called the settlor. They are the person who 'settles' the property in the trust. The person for whom the property is held is known as the beneficiary. In this example the settlor is also the trustee. The trustee is the person who holds the trust property on trust for the beneficiary. Alternatively, the settlor may appoint a third party, with their consent, to be trustee. The trustee holds the legal title to the subject property, whilst the beneficial title, the right to enjoy the property or the proceeds therefrom, rests with the beneficiary. This example involves the creation of an express trust. It should be noted that trusts may also be created, for example, by operation of law, where the law deems there to be a constructive trust.

Unlike the registration of a company, a declaration of trust does not create a separate legal entity. The existence of a trust rests on the intangible fiduciary obligations imposed on the trustee to hold and utilise the property for the beneficiary's best interests. Thus, the trust itself cannot hold property or enter into contracts. The trustee must undertake these legal relations.

Trusts may take many forms. They may, for example, be express, implied, constructive, fixed (where the beneficiaries' interests are fixed) or discretionary (where the trustee has a discretion as to who will receive income/capital and/or the amount of that distribution).

Benefits and shortcomings of a trust

[2.40] A trust can be created without great expense or formality; though again the transfer of some forms of property, such as land, require compliance with formalities, such as, being evidenced in writing. Similarly, a trust may be dissolved by either complying with the instructions in any trust deed or simply waiting for the end of its life when the trust automatically dissolves. While stamp duty and capital gains tax implications may arise out of the initial vesting of property, the long-term administration of a trust is comparatively inexpensive and free from the filing and audit costs inherent in the use of most companies. Note, however, that the common practice of combining companies and trusts by appointing a company as trustee, thereby creating what is known as a 'corporate trustee', will negate these benefits as the structure will incur the additional costs involved in creating and maintaining a company. The benefits of a corporate trustee are discussed below.

On a declaration of trust, the beneficiaries enjoy an actual interest in the trust property; that is, the equitable title: *Charles v FCT* (1954) 90 CLR 598 at 609; *Octavo Investments Pty Ltd v Knight* (1979) 144 CLR 360 at 367; *Costa & Duppe Properties Pty Ltd v Duppe* [1986] VR 90 at 95-96. By contrast, shareholders have no legal or equitable interest in company property: *Macaura v Northern Assurance Co Ltd* [1925] AC 619 at 626-627, 630 and 633. The company has absolute ownership of company assets and any rights the shareholder has against the company are merely contractual in nature.

Unlike a partnership, the death of a beneficiary does not dissolve a trust. Depending on the terms of the trust deed, either the beneficiary's estate or other beneficiaries will receive the deceased's interest. While the death of the trustee will also not dissolve the trust, a new trustee must be appointed. The difficulties that may ensue if the original trustee has not appointed a successor may require considering using a corporate trustee.

Trusts are also suited to furthering non-profit sentiments. There is no limitation as to the number of beneficiaries who may benefit under a trust and no requirement to actually name these beneficiaries. As a consequence, the benefits provided under the terms of a trust may extend to large classes of persons falling within the terms of the settlor's intentions.

Distinct benefits attach to different types of trusts. Unit trusts are a form of fixed trust and constitute the primary type of trust utilised in business ventures. Unit trusts resemble companies in so far as beneficial ownership of the trust property is divided up into share-like components called units. Units are acquired by the beneficial owners. One type of unit trust is a 'managed' investment trust. In this type of trust the trustee has power to vary the nature and extent of investments and this allows for risk spreading. Unlike the ownership of shares in a single company, a unit in this form of investment trust indirectly gives the unit holder an interest in a variety of companies. Family businesses are often conducted through discretionary trusts as this allows the trustee to determine who, and to what extent, family member beneficiaries, such as children, should enjoy the 'fruits' of the business depending on, for example, maturity or involvement in any trust business.

There are no longer any real tax incentives for using trading trusts as opposed to companies or partnerships. 'Income splitting', by dividing trust income between beneficiaries for tax reasons, will generally be contrary to the current anti-tax avoidance provisions contained in Part IVA of the *Income Tax Assessment Act* 1936 (Cth). The use of trusts entails the difficulty that while profits may be passed on to beneficiaries through distributions, tax losses cannot be 'distributed' to the beneficiaries and offset against the beneficiaries' personal income: *Doherty v FCT* (1933) 2 ATD 272. Tax losses are accumulated in the trust and carried forward to later tax years. Unlike the position in a partnership, tax losses are in a sense 'trapped' in the trust until the trust makes a profit that may offset losses: *Doherty v FCT*. Income tax legislation also further restricts when these losses may be offset against trust income. See ss 265-5–272-140 of the *Income Tax Assessment Act* 1936 (Cth).

It had been proposed, in accordance with the broad recommendations of the *Review of Business Taxation Report* (known as the *'Ralph Report'*) (July 1999), to tax certain trusts in the same manner as companies. In response to a public backlash, however, the government announced it would not be proceeding with these unified entity taxation measures: *Treasurer's Press Release* 27 February 2001. Nevertheless, the matter has been referred to the Board of Taxation for further consultation and it is far from clear that the government has truly abandoned the idea.

An even more significant problem with the use of trust structures stems from the rule against perpetuities. At common law, with the exception of charitable trusts, the trust property must vest absolutely in the beneficiaries within the life of a nominated person plus 21 years. While the common law has been legislatively modified, generally the relevant Acts nevertheless limit the life of a trust to 80 years. See, for example, s 7(1) of the *Perpetuities Act* 1984 (NSW). Thus, unlike a company, which exists until deregistered, trusts only have a limited life.

A trust structure also often leaves the beneficiaries powerless. Control of the trust, trust property and distributions lies with the trustee. Whilst the trustee is subject to fiduciary duties and any directions in the trust deed, trustees are not subject to the beneficiary's instructions. The beneficiaries have no right to partake in the day-to-day administration of trust property. Thus, a partnership, where members may participate in the management of affairs, may be preferable to a trust arrangement.

The greatest shortcoming underlying the use of trusts lies in the absence of any separate legal identity in the trust. As it is not a legally recognised entity, the trust cannot hold property, contract, sue or be sued. The trustee must undertake such legal relations. When the trustee acts on the beneficiaries' behalf in this manner, despite the representative nature of its actions, the trustee is personally liable for any consequent legal obligations. Unless the creditors agree otherwise, trust creditors may have recourse not only to any trust assets, but also the trustee's personal assets. Whilst, depending on the terms of any trust deed, the trustee may have the right to apply trust property in satisfaction of trust debts and may have a right of indemnity against the beneficiaries, to the extent that such property is insufficient, creditors may look to the trustee's own assets. Thus, the use of a trust in commercial ventures places the trustee in a precarious position.

The potential personal liability of the trustee does not necessarily mean that beneficiaries will always be sheltered from liability. As noted above, depending upon the terms of the trust deed, the trustee may have a right to be indemnified out of trust property and/or the beneficiaries' personal assets. In turn, creditors are entitled to be subrogated to the trustee's right to have recourse to this property.

Corporate trustee

[2.50] The potential for an attack on the trustee's personal assets has spurred the use of corporate trustees. In particular it is common to use a 'two dollar' company (a company with issued share capital of 2 x $1 shares) to act as the trustee. While the company, as trustee, is liable for trust debts, the liability of shareholders in that corporate trustee is generally limited to any unpaid amount on the two $1 shares. If the trust deed does not allow recourse to trust property and/or the beneficiaries' personal assets, creditors will generally not be able to seek recompense from these sources: *McLean v Burns Philp Trustee Co Pty Ltd* (1985) 9 ACLR 926 at 940. Note, however, that the directors of the corporate trustee may be personally liable for such debts under s 197 of the *Corporations Act* if recourse to trust assets is not allowed. See further Chapter 3.

Partnership

Defining a partnership

[2.60] The common law definition of a partnership, echoed in the *Partnership Acts*, provides that a partnership is the relationship which subsists between parties carrying on a business in common with a view to profit: *Pooley v Driver* (1876) 5 Ch D 458 at 472. The requirement that the business be 'in common' implies a mutuality of interests: *Smith v Anderson* (1880) 15 Ch D 247 at 275; *Kang-Kem v Paine* [2004] NSWSC 3 at [41].

Kang-Kem v Paine
New South Wales Supreme Court: Barrett J
[2004] NSWSC 3

The court found that a de facto relationship between the parties commenced in late 1987 or early 1988 and continued until 1998 or possibly 2001. In November 1991 the plaintiff expressed to the defendant an interest in opening a restaurant. The first of two restaurants opened in May 1992. The lease of the premises was in the defendant's name, but the lease did allow for a subletting of the premises to the plaintiff. The plaintiff told the defendant he had no money because of a failed business venture and that as a consequence he had become bankrupt. The defendant 'kept' the plaintiff, paying all his personal expenses. The defendant had also paid into an ANZ bank account (the account into which the proceeds from both restaurants were paid) $100,000 for the fit-out of the first restaurant. The court found that this was a loan to the plaintiff. The registration of business name was initially in both names but in 1998 the plaintiff alone was registered and in 2002 a company of which the plaintiff was a sole director and shareholder became registered. The plaintiff was the holder of the ABN for the restaurant. This same ABN was used to conduct the second restaurant. The second restaurant opened in late 2001. The sublease in this case was again in the defendant's name. She was also sole licensee under the *Liquor Act*. $150,000 was spent on the fit-out of the restaurant. $115,000 of this amount was a loan taken out jointly by the plaintiff and the defendant. The loan was secured by a mortgage over the defendant's home. The remainder of the money came out of the ANZ bank account. The court found that the plaintiff represented that the defendant was the sole owner of the first restaurant until about 1997 at which point proprietorship passed to the plaintiff through, *inter alia*, the sublease. The court found that in various documents after that date the plaintiff represented he was the sole owner of the business. It was also concluded that the plaintiff played the principal role in the operation of both restaurants until he lost interest in the businesses in 2003 when he formed a relationship with his now spouse. While the defendant regularly attended each business, the court believed she did so to support and assist the plaintiff and, later, because she feared for the security of her investment. It was also accepted that the plaintiff had control of the proceeds of the businesses. The plaintiff argued that the business relations between himself and the defendant constituted a partnership and that the proceeds of sale in the case of the first restaurant and the second restaurant itself were partnership assets. The plaintiff sought orders that the said partnership be wound up, that a receiver be appointed, and an account of the partnership assets be taken.

The court held that there was no partnership between the parties due to the absence of a business 'in common'. While each party had interests in the relevant businesses, the rights and obligations arising from the businesses were separate and several. The absence of the requisite agency relationship and mutuality of rights and obligations meant that the arrangement was a joint venture, not a partnership. As a consequence the court refused to declare that a partnership existed between the parties and that the subject assets were partnership assets.

Barrett J: 13. A business was undoubtedly carried on by way of the operation of the two restaurants or each of them. The business (or each business) was obviously carried on "with a view of profit". The central question to be answered by reference to the evidence is whether the business (or each business) was carried on "in common". ...

21. The [plaintiff's] representation [that the defendant was at first sole owner and then later the plaintiff sole owner] is entirely at odds with any assertion that the Junction restaurant business was, or formed part of, a business carried on by the plaintiff and defendant "in common." ...

41. Remembering that it is for the plaintiff to make out the case he asserts, he cannot be successful unless he shows that the business that was undoubtedly conducted was conducted in such a way that the plaintiff and the defendant were "carrying on a business in common". An explanation of the meaning and significance of these words is found at paragraphs 952 to 956 of the joint judgment of Doyle CJ, Duggan and Bleby JJ in *Duke Group Ltd v Pilmer* (1999) 73 SASR 64: "In order to meet this criterion, it is not necessary that each of the alleged partners should take an active part in the direction and management of the firm. The business may well be carried on by or on behalf of the partners by someone else. The person carrying on the business must be doing so as agent for all the other persons who are said to be partners. Lord Wensleydale stressed the need for an agency relationship in *Cox v Hickman* (1860) 8 HL Cas 268; at 312-3; 11 ER 431; at 449: 'A man who allows another to carry on trade, whether in his own name or not, to buy and sell, and to pay over all the profits to him, is undoubtedly the principal, and the person so employed is the agent, and the principal is liable for the agent's contracts in the course of his employment. So if two or more agree that they should carry on a trade, and share the profits of it, each is a principal, and each is an agent for the other, and each is bound by the other's contract in carrying on the trade, as much as a single principal would be by the act of an agent, who was to give the whole of the profits to his employer. Hence it becomes a test of the liability of one for the contract of another, that he is to receive the whole or a part of the profits arising from that contract by virtue of the agreement made at the time of the employment. I believe this is the true principle of partnership liability.' Likewise, Griffith CJ said in *Lang v James Morrison & Co Ltd* (1911) 13 CLR 1; at 11: 'Now in order to establish that there was a partnership it is necessary to prove that JW McFarland carried on the business of Thomas McFarland & Co on behalf of himself, Lang and Keates, in this sense, that he was their agent in what he did under the contract with the plaintiffs – not that they would get the benefit, but that he was their agent.' However, more than mere agency is required. There must be mutuality of rights and obligations. James LJ said in *Smith v Anderson* (1880) 15 Ch D 247; at 275: 'Persons who have no mutual rights and obligations do not, according to my view, constitute an association because they happen to have a common interest

or several interests in something which is to be divided between them.' Those requirements of agency and mutuality are reflected in ss 5 and 6 of the *Partnership Act* as being the consequences of entering into a partnership. ...

42. In the present case, there was no such mutuality. Neither party acted, in the affairs of the business, as the agent of the others and of both together. The rights and obligations arising from the business (with the sole exception of the joint borrowing from Westpac) were not mutual rights and obligations. They were separate or several rights and obligations, even though each party played a part in the totality of activities. The plaintiff and the defendant both had an interest in seeing the restaurants successfully operated. But the interest was not an interest in common. The defendant, as she put it, had an investment to protect. That was the source of her interest. It was the interest of an investor rather than a proprietor or business operator. In addition to that, she had the natural interest of one party to a de facto relationship in seeing the other party achieve personal fulfilment and success in his chosen field.

See further the discussion of *Canny Gabriel Castle Jackson Advertising v Volume Sales (Finance) Pty Ltd* (1974) 131 CLR 321 below. See also *Partnership Act* 1898 (NSW) s 1; *Partnership Act* 1958 (Vic) s 5; *Partnership Act* 1891 (SA) s 1; *Partnership Act* 1891 (Qld) s 5; *Partnership Act* 1895 (WA) s 7; *Partnership Act* 1891 (Tas) s 6; *Partnership Act* 1963 (ACT) s 6; *Partnership Act* 1997 (NT) s 5 for the statutory definition of a partnership.

If the definition of a partnership is met, there are no further common law or statutory requirements for formation. Thus, a partnership can be created orally or by conduct. As the existence of a partnership is dependent upon the contractual/agency relationship between the partners, the parties' intention to create a partnership is the paramount consideration: *Beckingham v Port Jackson and Manly Steamship Authority* [1957] SR (NSW) 403 at 409-410; *Television Broadcasters Ltd v Ashton's Nominees Pty Ltd* (1977) 22 SASR 552 at 565-566.

Partnerships are not separate legal entities. While the Supreme Court Rules in most States and Territories allow a partnership to sue and be sued in the firm's name (eg O 17.01 of the *Supreme Court Rules* (Vic)), these provisions do not purport to effect a change to the substantive nature of partnerships. They do not accord the structure legal identity, but rather introduce a convenient procedural mechanism facilitating the commencement of proceedings by, and against, partners of a firm.

Whilst a partnership is not a separate legal entity, unless ministerial permission is given, a partnership constituted by more than 20 persons must incorporate under s 115 of the *Corporations Act*. Ministerial permission to have more than 20 partners is given where, for example, the partnership is conducting a professional business and the rules of that profession require practitioners to have unlimited liability.

Limited partnerships

[2.70] In certain States, partnerships may be registered as 'limited' partnerships. See, for example, Part 3 of the *Partnership Act* 1958 (Vic).

In limited partnerships the partners are divided into two groups: general partners and limited partners. General partners have the same rights and liabilities as under a normal partnership. Limited partners, however, have no right to participate in the management of the partnership and may limit their liability to a certain amount.

Benefits and shortcomings of a partnership

[2.80] As with a sole proprietorship, creating, maintaining and dissolving a partnership do not involve the formalities and costs attributable to companies. There is no need to publish the partnership accounts, nor have these audited. The only formalities that need to be complied with stem from the general regulatory legislation listed above.

Unlike companies, where the shareholders' ability to partake in, or supervise, the management of the business is limited to exercising their voting rights, unless abrogated by agreement, each partner has a *prima facie* right to take an active part in the conduct of the business/management. See, for example, s 28(5) of the *Partnership Act* 1958 (Vic).

In contrast to companies and trusts, tax losses can be offset against each partner's individual income from other sources. See s 92 of the *Income Tax Assessment Act* 1936. Where a business is expected to make losses in its early years, it may be beneficial to be able to offset these losses against other sources of income.

On the negative side, the absence of separate legal identity means that the conduct of a partnership business rests on the legal personality of the partners. Thus, the partners must personally contract for the partnership. Coupled with the power of each partner to incur debts as the agent for the other partners (eg *Partnership Act* 1958 (Vic) s 9), this characteristic of a partnership renders it ineffective as a means of minimising financial risks. If the other partners are insolvent, a single partner may in certain cases be personally liable for all partnership debts. See, for example, s 16 of the *Partnership Act* 1958 (Vic). While limited partnerships enjoy the benefits of limited liability, the privilege is confined to non-participating partners. Thus, once a partner becomes involved in the management of the partnership the right to limited liability is lost.

Unless the partners otherwise agree, with the death, bankruptcy, retirement or admission of a partner the partnership dissolves and a new partnership is created. See, for example, s 37(1) of the *Partnership Act* 1958 (Vic). This lack of continuity is particularly problematic as partnership assets are not owned by the partnership as such and partnership debts are incurred in the names of the partners personally. While in practice the repercussions of a change in membership are often ignored, with the retirement, for example, of a contracting partner all legal relations should be renegotiated. This uncertainty is multiplied by the ability of any partner to call for the dissolution of the partnership. See, for example, ss 30(1) and 36(c) of the *Partnership Act* 1958 (Vic).

This also limits the flexibility of the partnership structure. While a partner's interest may be assigned to another person, this only gives the latter individual the right to the financial benefits attaching to that interest: *FCT v Everett* (1980) 80 ATC 4076 at 4080. That person does not become a partner, unless the other partners agree: *FCT v Everett* at 4079. See also, for example, s 35 of the *Partnership Act* 1958 (Vic).

The abovementioned prescribed number of partners limits the size of a partnership to 20 partners and hence the growth of the business. Moreover, as finance is again dependent upon the partners' personal guarantees, funding may be difficult to obtain. For this reason it is not uncommon for a business to start as a partnership and then, with time and expansion, to incorporate.

The costs of incorporation often lead people initially to adopt a partnership structure. In many cases, however, the financial risks involved in business suggest that a preferable approach is to incorporate as a small proprietary company, discussed below.

Joint Ventures

Defining a joint venture

[2.90] A joint venture is best described by comparing and contrasting it with a partnership. As with a partnership it is unincorporated and thus not a separate legal entity. The structure is based merely on the parties' contractual relations. While in a joint venture the parties are also operating with a view to profit, the relationship may not be a business in common within the definition of a partnership. The parties' financial input may be determined and their entitlement may be a share of product, rather than profit. As the decision in *Canny Gabriel Castle Jackson Advertising Pty Ltd v Volume Sales (Finance) Pty Ltd* (1974) 131 CLR 321 indicates, the Australian courts have experienced great difficulty in determining whether an arrangement is a partnership or a joint venture. While the parties' intent is a key factor in classifying a partnership, the courts have not always accepted the parties' description of the arrangement as a joint venture.

Canny Gabriel Castle Jackson Advertising Pty Ltd v Volume Sales (Finance) Pty Ltd
High Court: McTiernan, Menzies and Mason JJ
(1974) 131 CLR 321

Fourth Media Management Pty Ltd ('FM Co') and Volume Sales (Finance) Pty Ltd ('VS Co') purported to enter into a joint venture in regard to an Australian tour by two entertainers, Cilla Black and Elton John. VS Co agreed to provide FM Co with a loan of $70,000 and further sums to finance the pre-tour expenses. In consideration of the advance FM Co agreed to assign to VS Co a one-half interest in the management contract for the tours. The contract also included an agreement that the management contracts would be performed 'as a joint venture' and that the loan was to 'the joint venture'. Other relevant clauses of the agreement included that all matters of policy regarding the management and conduct of the purported joint venture were to be 'agreed upon by the parties'. Each party covenanted that they had not had notice of impending liquidation, external administration or outstanding judgments or orders against them. The agreement also provided that after the repayment of the loan and a taking of accounts the net profits from the venture were to be equally divided between the parties. Box office proceeds were to be paid into an account in VS Co's name. FM Co subsequently granted Canny Gabriel Castle Jackson Advertising Pty Ltd ('Canny Gabriel Co') an equitable charge over its business, including its box office receipts. VS Co claimed it had priority over the box office receipts on the basis that the contract between it and FM Co was a partnership, not a joint venture. This partnership gave VS Co an equitable interest in the box office receipts that had priority over the later equitable charge given to Canny Gabriel Co. It was not in issue that if there was a partnership and this created the alleged equitable interests VS Co had priority. FM Co and Canny Gabriel Co suggested to the contrary that VS Co was merely financing the venture and for this purpose it had lent money to FM Co.

Thus, the court had to determine who had first claim on the box office proceeds, VS Co or Canny Gabriel Co. The High Court held that, despite the label of the arrangement as a joint venture, the business was a partnership between FM Co and VS Co. The business arrangement exhibited all the attributes of a partnership except as to the sharing of losses. Even in regard to this matter, the sharing of losses may have been implied. As a consequence VS Co had priority to the box office receipts over Canny Gabriel Co's interest in such.

> **McTiernan, Menzies and Mason JJ**: [326] Our conclusion that the joint venture was a partnership, from which the parties anticipated profits and provided that the advance by Volume Sales to the "Joint venture" should be a first charge upon profits and that upon the repayment of such sum the profits should be divided equally, rests upon the following considerations:
> 1. The parties became joint venturers in a commercial enterprise with a view to profit.
> [327] 2. Profits were to be shared: see Partnership Act 1892, as amended (NSW), s 2(iii).
> 3. The policy of the joint venture was a matter for joint agreement and it was provided that differences relating to the affairs of the joint venture should be settled by arbitration: see cll 7 and 9.
> 4. An assignment of a half interest in the contracts for the appearances of Cilla Black and Elton John was attempted, although, we would have thought, unsuccessfully.
> 5. The parties were concerned with the financial stability of one another in a way which is common with partners: cl 6.
> Against these considerations it was suggested that Volume Sales was merely financing the undertaking and for this purpose it had lent money to Fourth Media. We do not so read the agreement. The advance was made "to the joint venture", not to Fourth Media, and it seems to us that it was intended that it should be paid into the bank account to be opened in accordance with cl 8, and that profits were, in the first instance, to be devoted to its repayment. Furthermore, in the event of the contract "failing", ie not being proceeded with, the advance was to be repaid to Volume Sales from the account but

subject, of course, to the provisions of s 44 of the Partnership Act, 1892 as amended (NSW), in favour of creditors. In short, it seems to us that the contract exhibited all the indicia of a partnership except that it did not describe the parties as partners and did not provide expressly for the sharing of losses, although we venture to think that it did so impliedly. These considerations on the one side are, in our opinion, out-weighed by the considerations upon the other side to which we have already referred.

Again, if the membership extends beyond 20 participants, a joint venture must incorporate: s 115(a) *Corporations Act*. Once incorporated, legally it is no longer a joint venture.

Benefits and shortcomings of a joint venture

[2.100] Joint ventures are inexpensive to create, maintain and dissolve. In contrast to partnerships, a joint venture also provides the benefit of individualising obligations and liabilities. This is particularly suitable when the parties provide differing degrees of financial input. Moreover, unlike partners, in a joint venture the parties are not necessarily agents for one another. This independence has the advantage of enabling one party to distance himself or herself from the other's contractual/legal obligations. Thus, parties to a joint venture are only severally liable, not jointly and severally liable as in a partnership.

The individualisation of profits and losses also provides joint venture parties with the benefit of offsetting joint venture losses against their personal income from other sources, including from other joint ventures. When the venture is likely to incur losses in its earlier years, this aspect of the taxation of joint venture income makes it a suitable business vehicle.

As a joint venture is not incorporated, it suffers the same shortcomings of a partnership, such as the absence of limited liability and perpetual succession. Particularly if the venture is risky, potential unlimited liability will make a joint venture an unsuitable business vehicle. Consequently, this structure will mainly be suited for certain isolated ventures where perpetual succession is not an issue and financial risk is not paramount.

Company

Defining a company

[2.110] A company is an association incorporated, *inter alia,* under the *Corporations Act*. Upon incorporation the company becomes a separate legal entity, distinct from its shareholders and directors, which remains in existence until deregistered: s 601AD. Companies are accorded the powers of an individual and thus can, *inter alia,* hold property, contract, sue and be sued in the company's own name: s 124(1). In addition, a company has all the powers of a body corporate, including those powers specifically listed in s 124(1)(a)-(h). The nature of a company is considered in detail in Chapter 3.

The *Corporations Act* distinguishes between types of companies according to members' liability for company debts and whether it is a proprietary or public company: s 112.

Liability of members

[2.120] In terms of members' liability s 112 identifies four types of companies that may be incorporated:
- a company limited by shares;
- a company limited by guarantee;
- an unlimited company with share capital; and
- a no-liability company.

Company limited by shares

[2.130] The majority of Australian companies are companies limited by shares. In this form of company, members' liability is limited to any unpaid amount on their shares: ss 9 and 516. Thus, if a shareholder acquires 1000 x $1 shares in the company, but only pays $500 (1000 x 50c) when the shares are allotted, he or she will be liable to pay a further $500 or 50c per share at some later date. Such moneys can be recovered while the company is a going concern or when the company goes into liquidation. If, however, the shares are fully paid up there is no risk of future liability. Members cannot be called upon to contribute more than this amount in satisfaction of the company's debts: s 516.

In a bid to warn creditors of this limited liability, the word 'Limited' or its abbreviation, 'Ltd', must be part of the company's name, unless s 151 applies: ss 148(1) and (2) and 149. A further restraint imposed on this type of company in a bid to protect, *inter alia*, creditor interests is the regulation of distributions of the company's capital amongst shareholders. The maintenance of share capital is considered in detail in Chapter 7.

Companies limited by shares may be either public or proprietary companies: s 112.

Company limited by guarantee

[2.140] In this type of company, members agree to be liable for a fixed sum in the event of winding up: ss 9 and 517. The actual transfer of this money under the guarantee does not have to occur until the funds are required on winding up. This gives members the benefit of not having to contribute whilst the company is a going concern.

However, as the amount of the guarantee cannot be varied, this type of company is unsuitable for trading ventures where it is likely that the company's capital needs will increase whilst a going concern. Before the enactment of the *Company Law Review Act* 1998 (Cth), if a company limited by guarantee wanted to change its nature to access share capital it could apply to change to a company limited both by shares and by guarantee: see former s 167. With the passage of this legislation, this type of company is no longer capable of being registered: see s 112(1).

Under ss 162-164 a company limited by guarantee can now apply to convert to a company limited by shares or an unlimited company so that it can access share capital.

The word 'Limited' or its abbreviation, 'Ltd', must again be part of the company's name unless ss 150 or 151 apply: ss 148(1) and (2) and 149. See further ss 150 and 151 as to when a company may apply for a licence to dispense with 'Limited' in its name. Creditors' interests in this type of company are not protected as extensively as in the case of a company limited by shares. As the members' liability under the guarantee ceases on retirement, creditors' interests may be severely undermined if the company's constitution allows members to retire: *Re Bangor and North Wales Mutual Marine Protection Association* [1899] 2 Ch 593.

As proprietary companies are required to have share capital, the absence of such in companies limited by guarantee confines this form of company to public companies: s 112(1).

Unlimited company

[2.150] Section 9 defines an unlimited company as one formed on the basis of having placed no limit on members' liability. Thus, *prima facie*, members are jointly and severally liable for the company's debts without limitation upon winding up. This quality makes this form of company an unsuitable vehicle for trading ventures. It is used primarily by professional associations where its members are required to be liable without limitation.

Under s 258A unlimited companies continue to enjoy an exemption from the restrictions imposed in relation to the reduction of share capital, discussed in Chapter 7. The ability to redeem its own shares without the restrictions applicable to limited companies has been seen by some mutual fund companies as advantageous. See further *Re Borough Commercial and Building Society* [1893] 2 Ch 242 at 253-255.

Note, unlimited companies do not have to include the word 'Unlimited' in the company name: s 148(3).

As unlimited companies are required to have share capital they may be either public or proprietary companies.

No-liability company

[2.160] The use of a no-liability company is confined to mining companies: s 112(2). To be a mining company, the company must have an objects clause in its constitution stating that mining purposes are the company's sole objects: s 112(2)(b). See s 9 for the meaning of 'mining purposes'. If the company's objects clause allows it to undertake activities that are not necessary for, or incidental to, its mining purposes, the company will not meet the definition of a mining company: *ASC v SIB Resources NL* (1991) 9 ACLC 1147 at 1150-1151. This is complemented by the express prohibition in s 112(3) against the company engaging in activities outside its mining objects.

A no-liability company does not have a contractual right under its constitution to recover calls from defaulting shareholders: ss 112(2)(c), 254M(1) and (2). Whilst any amount unpaid for shares is not an enforceable debt, where a call is unpaid at the end of 14 days after it became payable the shares are automatically forfeited: s 254Q(1). A shareholder is not entitled to receive a dividend on any share on which a call is due and unpaid: s 254B(2)(b).

If a share is forfeited, it must be offered for sale by public auction within six weeks from the date on which the call became payable: s 254Q(2). The shares may be offered for sale as paid-up to, *inter alia*, the sum paid on the share at the time of the forfeiture: s 254Q(6). Directors may fix a reserve price not exceeding the amount of calls due and unpaid: s 254Q(7). See further s 254Q. The shareholder may redeem the shares up to the last business day before the sale by paying the amounts due on the shares, plus, if the company requires, a proportion of the expenses stemming from the forfeiture and any related proceedings: s 254R(1).

No-liability companies are expressly excluded from those companies that may be proprietary companies: s 112(1). Consequently, they must be public companies and thus will be subject to all provisions of the *Corporations Act* applicable to public companies.

The words 'No Liability' or the abbreviation, 'NL', must be part of the company's name: ss 148(4), 149(1) and (2).

Public and proprietary companies

[2.170] Companies may be registered as either proprietary or public companies: s 112(1). Whilst proprietary companies are more prevalent, most large companies are public companies. Companies listed on a stock exchange, 'listed companies', must be public companies.

Public companies

[2.180] Section 9 defines a public company in terms of, *inter alia*, a company other than a proprietary company. While companies limited by shares and unlimited companies with shares may be either public or proprietary companies, companies limited by guarantee and no-liability companies may only be public companies: s 112(1).

Proprietary companies

[2.190] Most companies incorporated in Australia are proprietary companies and can be distinguished from public companies by, *inter alia*, the need to include in their names 'Proprietary' or the abbreviation 'Pty': ss 148(2)-(5) and 149(1). Only companies limited by shares or unlimited companies with share capital may be proprietary companies: s 112(1).

Proprietary companies are typically used for self-financing family businesses or small unrelated groups. Under s 113(3), to be incorporated as a proprietary company it must have no more than 50 non-employee shareholders and not engage in any activity that would require the lodging of a disclosure document. In regard to the latter requirement, offers of its shares may, however, be made to existing shareholders of the company or to employees of the company or any subsidiaries: s 113(3). When a company contravenes these requirements ASIC may direct a proprietary company to change to a public company within two months: s 165(1). If the company fails to comply, ASIC may change the company from a proprietary to a public company by altering the details of the company's registration to reflect its change in type: s 165(3).

Small and large proprietary companies

[2.200] Proprietary companies may be 'small proprietary companies' or 'large proprietary companies': s 45A. A proprietary company is a small proprietary company if for a financial year it, and any entities that it controls, satisfy at least two of the following requirements:
- consolidated gross operating revenue is less than $10m;
- value of consolidated gross assets is less than $5m;
- fewer than 50 employees: s 45A(2).

Similarly, a proprietary company will be a large proprietary company if for a financial year it, and any entities that it controls, satisfy at least two of the following requirements:
- consolidated gross operating revenue is $10m or more;
- value of consolidated gross assets is $5m or more;
- 50 or more employees: s 45A(3).

Benefits of registration

Separate legal identity

[2.210] As a company is conferred with separate legal personality, incorporation allows the corporate assets and obligations to remain distinct from the shareholders' and directors' personal assets and obligations: *Salomon v Salomon & Co Ltd* [1897] AC 22. This separation is particularly beneficial if the company fails as, generally, corporate creditors will not be able to have recourse to shareholders' and directors' assets to satisfy corporate debts. The ability to contract in the company's name, rather than in members' or directors' names, also allows for easier identification of company and personal debts and obligations. As the company is a separate legal entity, it can employ its directors and members and thus provide these persons with the benefits of, *inter alia*, workers compensation: *Lee v Lee's Air Farming Ltd* [1961] AC 12. Corporate legal personality is discussed in detail in the next chapter.

Limited liability

[2.220] Related to this first benefit is the ability to confine shareholders' liability for corporate debts to any unpaid amount on their shares and/or guarantee, discussed above: ss 9, 516 and 517. By contrast, partners are jointly and severally liable for all the firm's debts.

Whilst this benefit may be undermined where creditors require a personal guarantee for company debts, not all creditors will be able to demand this protection. In practice, shareholders will be shielded from many of the day-to-day expenses incurred in running a business and any involuntary liabilities, such as those stemming from legal claims.

Perpetual succession

[2.230] As noted above, upon incorporation a company remains in existence until deregistered: s 601AD. This is known as 'perpetual succession'. This has the benefit of providing greater continuity of business relations and prevents disgruntled members from being able to threaten, as a matter of right, the dissolution of the entity.

Flexibility

[2.240] The ability to accommodate differing interests through the drafting of the company's constitution makes this business structure very flexible. This may occur by attaching different rights to certain classes of shares or to different corporate offices.

As a shareholder's interest is limited to the ownership of that individual's shares, as opposed to an interest in company property (*Ord Forrest Pty Ltd v FCT* (1974) 130 CLR 124 at 142), interests in companies are easily transferable. See s 1070A(1). The ease with which a shareholder's capital investment may be realised through the sale of his or her shares, particularly in a listed company, also makes this a very flexible mode of investment.

Finance

[2.250] It is generally easier for companies to obtain finance from outside institutions than other business organisations. The continuity provided by perpetual succession allows financial institutions to enter into long-term financing arrangements with companies with confidence. Companies may also secure loan moneys by way of fixed or floating charges over company assets. The latter form of charge is most beneficial to the company as it continues to be able to deal with the assets in the ordinary course of business despite the charge. Finally, public companies may raise funds from the public through the issue and sale of shares and other forms of securities. This is discussed in detail in Chapter 8. The availability of finance will often be an important factor in determining a suitable business vehicle and may 'tip the balance' in favour of incorporation.

Shortcomings of registration

Formalities

[2.260] To be incorporated, and to continue in operation, a company must comply with particular formalities prescribed by the *Corporations Act*. The extent of these formalities is multiplied in the case of public companies. Compliance with such standards may be onerous and costly

CHOOSING BETWEEN BUSINESS ORGANISATIONS   35

in terms of both time and money. In particular, compliance may depend on an understanding of complex statutory provisions and the case law interpreting their scope.

Costs

[2.270] The expenses involved in complying with these formalities include the direct cost of professional assistance in preparing documents, filing costs, audit and accountancy fees, and the indirect costs stemming from directors and other officers being involved in their preparation.

Whilst rarely in mind when establishing a business, the costs of winding up the company should also be considered. As Ffrench notes, '[l]ike marriage, a company is more easily entered into than dissolved': Ffrench, 1994, p 34.

Participation in management

[2.280] Unless the *Corporations Act* and/or the company's constitution provide otherwise, management powers rest with the board of directors, not the shareholders: *John Shaw and Sons (Salford) Ltd v Shaw* [1935] 2 KB 113; *Automatic Self-Cleansing Filter Syndicate Co Ltd v Cunninghame* [1906] 2 Ch 34; *Massey v Wales* (2003) 21 ACLC 1978. See also replaceable rule, s 198A(1). This is discussed in more detail in Chapter 9. In light of such, the voting power enjoyed by a minority shareholder often proves to be frustratingly ineffective. Moreover, as a general rule, shareholders cannot bring proceedings on behalf of the company, as the company, being a separate legal entity, is regarded in law as the sole, proper plaintiff: *Foss v Harbottle* (1843) 2 Hare 461; 67 ER 189. While common law and statutory exceptions to the 'proper plaintiff' rule exist, unless shareholders initiate costly legal proceedings to establish such a right, they are often at the mercy of the directors. See Chapter 12 regarding the remedies that are open to such shareholders.

Benefits of proprietary companies

[2.290] A proprietary company enjoys a number of advantages over a public company:
- minimum number of directors required is only one, while for a public company at least three directors must be appointed: s 201A;
- unlike the directors of public companies, there are no restrictions upon the ability to appoint more than one director through a single resolution: s 201E;
- while the constitution of a proprietary company may allow the board to remove a director, such a provision is prohibited in the case of a public company: s 203E;
- a person who is an officer of the company or, *inter alia*, a partner, employer or employee of such an officer, may be the company's auditor, while such a person is prohibited holding this office in a public company: s 324(1)(f);

- a person who is not a registered liquidator and is, *inter alia*, an auditor or officer of the company may be appointed as liquidator in the case of a members' voluntary winding up of a proprietary company, while such persons are disqualified from acting as a liquidator of a public company: s 532(1), (2)(c) and (4);
- proprietary companies do not have to appoint an auditor, while public companies are obliged to appoint an auditor: ss 325 and 327(1) and (1A);
- an ordinary resolution may be passed without convening a meeting if all members agree in writing to the resolution, while in the case of a public company a meeting is required: s 249A;
- while public companies are required to hold annual general meetings in accordance with the directives in s 250N unless it has only one member, this obligation does not extend to proprietary companies: s 250N; and
- proprietary companies are also exempt from the obligation to open the company's registered office to the public during certain hours: s 145.

In addition, small proprietary companies enjoy reduced disclosure requirements under Part 2M.3 unless ss 292(2), 293 or 294 apply.

Benefits of public companies

[2.300] Public companies, however, enjoy some advantages over proprietary companies:
- ability to invite the public to subscribe for loan or share capital, while proprietary companies are prohibited from engaging in conduct requiring disclosure under Chap 6D: s 113(3);
- no restriction on the maximum size of its membership, unlike a proprietary company which is limited to 50 non-employee members: s 113(1); and
- shareholders have a statutory right to remove a director: s 203D.

The table opposite lists some of the comparative benefits of public and proprietary companies.

Review question

Susan and Julie wish to conduct a business mining a newly discovered type of radioactive mineral, known as 'uranium plus'. Susan has discovered that extensive deposits exist in land that she owns in outback Victoria. Susan has considerable experience in the mining industry and owns the mining licences etc over the property. Julie's strength lies in her business skills.

Susan is financially secure and has all the funds she needs for her half of the business costs. By contrast, Julie has no extra capital and will need to borrow her funds. She plans to use her home (jointly owned with her husband Fred) as security for the loan.

CHOOSING BETWEEN BUSINESS ORGANISATIONS

TYPE OF COMPANY FEATURES	PUBLIC	PROPRIETARY
Name	N/A	Pty
Maximum number of members	Unlimited	50
Minimum number of directors	3	1
Appointment of directors	Restrictions on appointment of more than one director in one resolution	No restrictions
Removal of directors by board	No	May be provided for in the constitution
Shareholders' statutory right to remove directors	Yes	No
Must have auditor	Yes	No
Must hold an AGM	Yes	No
Must open registered office for prescribed hours	Yes	No
Must have a share capital	No	Yes
Company limited by guarantee	Yes, may be	No
Invitation to public for subscription	Yes	No
No-liability company	Yes, may be	No

Both parties are concerned about the riskiness of the venture; there has been great controversy as to the dangers of mining, and using, 'uranium plus'. Susan does not want to lose her property and Julie does not want to lose her home.

Susan and Julie intend the business will occasionally employ Julie's husband, Fred, on a part-time basis. Both Susan and Julie have high aspirations that, if the business is a success, their children may join them in the business. They both hope that in the future the venture might be successful enough that they might expand and diversify the business.

Susan and Julie have known each other for five years.

Please advise Susan and Julie as to the business structures that they might use.

Further reading

Cassidy, *Concise Corporations Law* (4th ed, Federation Press, Sydney, 2003) ch 2

Chetwin, 'Joint Ventures – A Branch of Partnership Law? (1991) 16 *USQLJ* 256

Fletcher, Higgins and Fletcher, *The Law of Partnership in Australia and New Zealand* (8th ed, Law Book Co, Sydney, 2001) chs 1, 2 and 6

Fletcher, 'Limited Partnership: Getting it together ... eventually' (1989) 19 *QLSJ* 285

Ford, Austin and Ramsay, *Ford's Principles of Corporations Law* (11th ed, Butterworths, Sydney, 2003) ch 5

Graw, *An Outline of the Law of Partnership* (2nd ed, Law Book Co, Sydney, 2001) chs 1, 2 and 4

Jackson, 'Fiduciary Relationships in Australian Joint Ventures' (1986) 14 *ABLR* 107

Milman, 'Partnerships (1): Problems with Identification' (1983) 4(5) *Company Lawyer* 1999

Vann, 'The structuring of project participation arrangements in property developments' (1989) 17 *ABLR* 231

References Chapter 2

Ffrench, *Guide to Company Law* (4th ed, Butterworths, Sydney, 1994)

3

Corporate Personality

Overview

This chapter examines the conferral of separate legal personality on companies. In Australia, upon registration under the *Corporations Act* 2001 (Cth) ('*Corporations Act*'), the company becomes a separate legal person, distinct from, *inter alia*, its directors and membership. This conferral of identity allows the courts to distinguish company debts and liabilities from the debts and liabilities of those persons who control the company: *Salomon v Salomon & Co* [1897] AC 22. In this way the separate legal personality of a company also works alongside the notion of limited liability. As the company is a separate legal person with its own debts and liabilities, shareholders' liability can be confined to any unpaid amount on their shares or guarantee: ss 9 and 516-517. That the company is a separate legal person also allows a natural person to relate to the company in more than one capacity. Thus, a single person might be a majority shareholder, governing director and an employee of the company: *Lee v Lee's Air Farming Limited* [1961] AC 12.

The chapter also considers the limits of this legal fiction, examining the statutory and common law rules that allow courts to lift or 'pierce' the 'corporate veil' and place responsibility with the members or directors of companies.

Corporate Personality

Defining corporate personality

[3.10] Corporations are recognised at law as separate legal entities. In Australia, upon registration under the *Corporations Act*, the company becomes a separate legal person, distinct from, *inter alia*, its directors and membership. This conferral of identity allows companies to operate as if they were natural persons by, for example, holding property, contracting and being able to sue and be sued: s 124(1). In addition, companies enjoy all the powers particular to a body corporate: s 124(1). Such legal personality sets these 'structures' apart from partnerships, unincorporated associations and trusts.

Limited liability

[3.20] This distinction between the company's identity and its members underlies one of the major advantages stemming from incorporating (in particular, a company limited by shares or guarantee); that is, limited liability. As the debts and obligations of the company are its own, not those of its members unless the corporate veil can be pierced, shareholders' liability is limited to any unpaid amount on their shares or guarantee: ss 9 and 516-517. While this means that the member is obligated to pay any unpaid amount on his or her shares when 'called' upon by the company (see, for example, *Wright v Mansell* [2001] FCA 1519) once the shares are fully paid up, there is no further liability to contribute to the company's debts: *Salomon v Salomon & Co* [1897] AC 22. In this way members may limit their contribution to the company to a definite amount.

Salomon v Salomon & Co
House of Lords: Lords Halsbury, Macnaghten, Herschell, Watson, Davey and Morris
[1897] AC 22

Mr Salomon conducted a leather and shoe manufacturing business as a sole trader and had built up a considerable business. Mr Salomon sold the business to a limited company he established. The company's share capital consisted of 40,000 £1 shares. Not all shares were issued upon the formation of the company. Mrs Salomon and five of their grown-up children each held one share, while Mr Salomon received 20,000 fully paid-up shares and debentures to the value of £10,000 effectively for the transfer of the business to the company. Further debentures were issued to an unrelated third party, Mr Broderip, as evidence of a loan to the company of £5000. Mr Salomon and his two elder sons were appointed as directors. The company fell into financial difficulties and when Mr Broderip's interest was not paid he took action and appointed a receiver. The company was subsequently wound up, leaving debts of £77,000. The realisation of the company's assets enabled the payment of Mr Broderip, but not enough to pay the debentures in full or to pay the unsecured creditors. The liquidator, acting on behalf of the unsecured creditors, brought an action against Mr Salomon claiming he was liable to indemnify the liquidator for the unsecured debts of the company. It was argued that the company was a mere agent or alter ego of Mr Salomon and thus Mr Salomon was liable for the company's debts. In addition it was asserted that the debentures issued to Mr Salomon were invalid on the basis of fraud. The transfer of the business was similarly said to be based on fraud. Alternatively, the liquidator claimed £20,000 for Mr Salomon's shares on the basis that he had paid nothing for them.

Initially the courts agreed with the liquidator. Vaughan Williams J held that the company was Mr Salomon's agent and as such Mr Salomon was responsible to indemnify the agent. On appeal the Court of Appeal asserted that limited liability does not extend to what was in effect a one-person company. Mr Salomon appealed to the House of Lords and the decision was reversed. The company was held not to be an alter ego, agent or trustee for Mr Salomon. The House of Lords asserted that, in the absence of fraud, the company was a separate legal entity, distinct from its members, even though one person may have owned most of its shares and controlled the company. Mr Salomon was not, therefore, liable for the company's debts.

> **Lord Halsbury LC**: [29] My Lords, the important question in this case, I am not certain it is the only question, is whether the respondent company was a company at all – whether in truth that artificial creation of the legislature had been validly constituted in this instance; and in order to determine that question it is necessary to look at what the statute itself has determined in that respect. I have no right to add to the requirements of the statute, nor to take from the requirements thus enacted. The sole guide must be the statute itself. Now, that there were seven actual living persons who held shares in the company has not been doubted. As to proportionate amounts held by each I will deal presently; but it is important to observe that this first condition of the statute is satisfied, and it follows as a consequence that it would not [30] be competent to anyone – and certainly not to these persons themselves – to deny that they were shareholders. I must pause here to point out that the statute enacts nothing as to the extent or degree of interests which may be held by each of the seven, or as to the proportion of interest or influence possessed by one or the majority of the shareholders over the others. One share is enough. ... But short of such proof [of fraud by the officer issuing the certificate of registration] it seems to me impossible to dispute that once the company is legally incorporated it must be treated like any other independent person with its rights and liabilities appropriate to itself, and that the motives of those who took part in the promotion of the company are absolutely irrelevant in discussing what those rights and abilities are. ... [31] [In reference to Vaughan Williams J's finding] it seems to me that that very learned judge becomes involved by this argument in a very singular contradiction. Either the limited company was a legal entity or it was not. If it was, the business belonged to it and not to Mr Salomon. If it was not, there was no person and no thing to be an agent at all; and it is impossible to say at the same time that there is a company and there is not. ... [33] If it was a real thing; if it had a legal existence, and if consequently the law attributed to it certain rights and liabilities in its constitution as a company, it appears to me to follow as a consequence that it is impossible to deny the validity of the transactions into which it has entered. ... My Lords, the truth is that the learned judges have never allowed in their own minds the proposition that the company [34] has a real existence. They have been struck by what they have considered the inexpediency of permitting one man to be in influence and authority [sic] the whole company; and, assuming that such a thing could not have been intended by the Legislature, they have sought various grounds upon which they might insert into the Act some prohibition of such a result. Whether such a result be right or wrong, politic or impolitic, I say, with the utmost deference to the judges, that we have nothing to do with that question if this company has been duly constituted by law; and whatever may be the motives of those who constitute it, I must decline to insert into that Act of Parliament limitations which are not to be found there. I have dealt with this matter upon the narrow hypothesis propounded by the learned judges below; but it is, I think, only justice to the appellant to say that I see nothing whatever to justify the impu-

tations which are implied in some of the observations made by more than one of the learned judges. The appellant, in my opinion, is not shewn to have done or to have intended to do anything dishonest or unworthy, but to have suffered a great misfortune without any fault of his own.

Multiple capacities

[3.30] As noted above, separate legal personality is not only relevant from the perspective of limited liability. It is also important in so far as it facilitates one person having concurrently a variety of legal relationships with that company, including majority shareholder, governing director and employee: *Lee v Lee's Air Farming Limited* [1961] AC 12.

Lee v Lee's Air Farming Limited
Privy Council: Lords Morris, Reid, Tucker and Denning and Viscount Simonds
[1961] AC 12

Mr Lee established a company (Lee's Air Farming Ltd) to conduct an aerial top-dressing business. The company's share capital consisted of 3000 £1 shares; 2999 being allotted to Mr Lee, whilst the remaining share was held by his solicitor. Mr Lee was the governing director. He was also employed under a service contract with the company to work as its chief pilot. Mr Lee was killed when an aeroplane engaged in top-dressing crashed. Mr Lee's widow claimed Mr Lee was a servant of the company and thus she was entitled to compensation under the relevant workers compensation legislation. The company at the instance of its insurer defended the claim by Mrs Lee arguing that Mr Lee could not be a 'worker' under the *Workers' Compensation Act* 1922 when he was also the employer.

The New Zealand Court of Appeal recognised that a director may properly enter into a service agreement with his or her company, but they considered that as Mr Lee was the governing director he could not also be a servant of the company. This conclusion was reversed on appeal. The Privy Council held that the decision in *Salomon v Salomon & Co* [1897] AC 22 allowed Mr Lee to act in different capacities, as governing director and employee, distinct from the company. That he was the major shareholder and governing director controlling the company did not undermine the validity of the contract between himself, as an employee, and the company. Thus, Mrs Lee was entitled to claim compensation.

Lord Morris: [24] The substantial question which arises is, as their Lordships think, whether the deceased was a "worker" within the meaning of the *Workers' Compensation Act*, 1922, and its amendments. Was he a person who had entered into or worked under a contract of service with an employer? The Court of Appeal thought that his special position as governing director precluded him from being a servant of the company. On this view it is difficult to know what his status and position was when performing the arduous and skilful duties of piloting an aeroplane [25] which belonged to the company and when he was carrying out the operation of top-dressing farm lands from the air. He was paid wages for so doing. The company kept a wages book in which these were recorded. The work that was being done was being done at the request of farmers whose contractual rights and obligations were with the company alone. It cannot be suggested that when engaged in the activities above referred to the deceased was discharging his duties as governing director. Their Lordships find it impossible to resist the conclusion that the active aerial operations were performed because the deceased was in some contractual relationship with the company. That relationship came about because the deceased as one legal person was willing to work for and to make a contract with the company which was another legal entity. A contractual relationship could only exist on the basis there was consensus between two contracting parties. It was never suggested (nor in their Lordships' view could it reasonably have been suggested) that the company was a sham or a mere simulacrum. It is well established that the mere fact that someone is a director of a company is no impediment to his entering into a contract to serve the company. If, then, it be accepted that the respondent company was a legal entity their Lordships see no reason to challenge the validity of any contractual obligations which were created between the company and the deceased. In this connection, reference may be made to ... *Salomon v Salomon & Co* ...

[26] Nor in their Lordships' view were any contractual obligations invalidated by the circumstance that the deceased was sole governing director in whom was vested the full government and control of the company. Always assuming that the company was not a sham then the capacity of the company to make a contract with the deceased could not be impugned merely because the deceased was the agent of the company in its negotiation. ... The circumstance that in his capacity as a shareholder he could control the course of events would not in itself affect the validity of his contractual relationship with the company. When, therefore, it is said that "one of his first acts was to appoint himself the only pilot of the company," it must be recognised that the appointment was made by the company, and that it was none the less a valid appointment because it was the deceased himself who acted as the agent of the company arranging it. In their Lordships' view it is a logical consequence of the decision in *Salomon's case* that one person may function in dual capacities. ... It is said that therein lies the difficulty, because it is said that the deceased could not both be under the duty of giving orders and also be under the duty of obeying them. But this approach does not give effect to the circumstances that it would be the company and not the deceased that would be giving the orders. ...

[30] The right to control existed in the company, and an application of the principles of *Salomon's case* demonstrates that the company was distinct from the deceased.

Distinguishing company and shareholder property

[3.40] Once a company is incorporated, it is important that the legal effect of that incorporation be appreciated. Shareholders have no proprietary interest in corporate property (*Macaura v Northern Assurance Co Ltd* [1925] AC 619 at 626; *Ord Forrest Pty Ltd v FCT* (1974) 130 CLR 124 at 142) and thus a distinction between private and corporate assets must be strictly maintained. A blurring of corporate and private assets or moneys often leads to unfortunate consequences under insurance, corporations and taxation law. Thus, in *Macaura v Northern Assurance*

Co Ltd [1925] AC 619 Macaura had assigned the right to timber growing on his land to a company. As consideration for the transfer, Macaura and his nominees received shares in the company. The timber was burnt down and Macaura sought to claim for the loss under an insurance policy he had taken out in his own name. The House of Lords held that Macaura could not claim under the insurance policy as it was in his own name rather than the company's name. As shareholder and creditor he had no legal or equitable interest in company property and thus no insurable interest in the timber; the company owned the timber. Whilst since this decision the notion of an insurable interest has been expanded to include a pecuniary and economic interest (see s 17 of the *Insurance Contracts Act* 1984 (Cth)), it is not clear that shareholders have the requisite interest in company property. In any case the decision provides a useful example of the hardship that may stem from failing to regard the company as a separate legal entity.

Company Liability

Difficulties in determining corporate liability

[3.50] As the company is a legal fiction there may be both conceptual and evidential difficulties in trying to identify if a company is liable in law. As the decisions in *Hamilton v Whitehead* (1988) 7 ACLC 43 and *DPP Reference No 1 of 2000* [2001] NTSC 91 indicate, companies are not immune from criminal liability. How is such a company punished when it cannot be sent to prison? How is the necessary *actus reus* determined? How is the *mens rea* established? Similarly in the tortious context, how is any requisite intention determined? How can a company act negligently? The latter issues have been tackled in three ways: (i) strict liability offences, (ii) vicarious liability and (iii) the organic theory.

Strict liability

[3.60] If the offence is a strict liability offence intent, including *mens rea,* is unnecessary. Recent amendments to the Commonwealth *Criminal Code* have made certain offences detailed in more than 50 Commonwealth statutes, including some of those specified in the *Corporations Act,* strict liability offences. See, for example, Chap 6D of the *Corporations Act,* discussed in Chapter 8. As to whether a statute requires *mens rea* or is one of strict liability, see *Stewart v Von Lieven* (1988) 6 ACLC 891; (1990) 8 ACLC 1014.

Vicarious liability

[3.70] Legislation may provide that the company can be convicted for the actions of its agents without any need to impute a guilty intent to the company. Recent amendments to the Commonwealth *Criminal Code* have the effect of making a corporation criminally liable if the board or upper managerial agents intentionally, knowingly or recklessly carry out the relevant conduct or expressly, tacitly or impliedly authorise or permit the commission of the offence.

This method of imposing responsibility is not unlike the civil law's vicarious liability. Under this principle an employer is vicariously liable for the acts of its employees in the course of employment. See, for example, *Lloyd (Pauper) v Grace Smith & Co* [1912] AC 716. The employee's actions automatically make the company liable without imputing any intent to the company. As a company is a separate legal person capable of employing servants (*Lee v Lee's Air Farming Limited* [1961] AC 12) the principles of vicarious liability equally apply to corporate employers. See, for example, *Duke Group Ltd (in liq) v Pilmer* (1999) 17 ACLC 1329. Note, unlike the organic theory, discussed below, generally the seniority of the particular employee is irrelevant to the question of vicarious liability.

Where an employee commits such an act, that individual will also be personally liable. Hence the company's vicarious liability does not relieve the employee of liability. Liability is concurrent: *Kalamazoo (Aust) Pty Ltd v Compact Business Systems Pty Ltd* (1984) 84 FLR 101 at 127.

Primary liability: The organic theory

[3.80] Liability need not be vicarious. Companies can be primarily liable when the acts/intent of a person(s) are taken under the organic theory to be the acts/intent of the company itself: *Lennard's Carrying Co Ltd v Asiatic Petroleum Co Ltd* [1915] AC 705 at 713; *HL Bolton (Engineering) v TJ Graham and Sons Ltd* [1956] 3 All ER 624 at 630.

Under this theory the company is not, however, liable for the acts of every employee. The company will only be liable where the acts of the person are the very acts of the company. Lord Denning in *HL Bolton (Engineering) v TJ Graham and Sons Ltd* at 630 draws a useful analogy between a company and the human body when applying the organic theory:

> A company may in many ways be likened to a human body. It has a brain and a nerve centre which controls what it does. It also has hands which hold the tools and act in accordance with directions from the centre. Some of the people in the company are mere servants and agents who are nothing more than the hands to do the work and cannot be said to represent the mind or will. Others are directors and managers who represent the directing mind and will of the company, and control what it does. The state of mind of these managers is the state of mind of the company and is treated by the law as such.

Thus, the managing director of a company (see, for example, *Hamilton v Whitehead* (1988) 7 ACLC 34) or chief executive officer will commonly constitute the 'mind and will' of the company while 'normal' employees will be the mere 'hands' acting on the directions of others. Care must be taken, however, not to assume that in every given case an employee's acts cannot constitute those of the company and that the actions of all directors and managers equate with that of the company. Whether the acts or intent of such persons can be imputed to the company will 'depend on the nature of the matter under consideration, the relative position of the officer or agent and other relevant factors and the circumstances of the case': *HL Bolton (Engineering) v TJ Graham and Sons Ltd* [1956] 3 All ER 624 at 630. Whether a person constitutes the mind and will of the company must be determined on a case-by-case basis.

[3.90] The organic theory gives rise to a complication in so far as it *prima facie* allows for a multitude of officers' intentions to be simultaneously imputed to the company: *Brambles Holdings Ltd v Carey* (1976) 2 ACLR 176 at 181 and 182. As Bray CJ asserted in this case:

> It is enough to say that, in my view, it is a fallacy to say that any state of mind to be attributed to a corporation must always be the state of mind of one particular officer alone and that the corporation can never know or believe more than that one man knows or believes. This cannot be so when it is a case of successive holders of the office in question or the holder of the office and his deputy or substitute during his absence. ... I hasten to add that although I think a corporation has in a proper case the combined knowledge or belief possessed by more than one of its officers, that does not mean that it can know or believe two contradictory things at once. It is a rational belief, not schizophrenia, which is attributed to it.

[3.100] While the organic theory may be used to make a company primarily liable for the acts of, for example, its managing director (see, for example, *Hamilton v Whitehead* (1988) 7 ACLC 34), it may also be applied to establish that a natural person is not the company and thereby establish a statutory defence based on the relevant acts being that of a third party: *Tesco Supermarkets Ltd v Nattrass* [1972] AC 153.

Tesco Supermarkets Ltd v Nattrass
House of Lords: Lords Reid, Morris, Pearson and Diplock and Viscount Dilhorne
[1972] AC 153

At one of the company's supermarkets a large sign advertised a certain product as being for sale at a reduced price. All reduced items had been sold, but replaced by a shop assistant with the same items at full price. This had not been conveyed to the store manager and the sign remained in the window. The next day a customer tried to buy the product at the reduced price, but was told none was available at that price. An information was laid against the company for a breach of the *Trade Description Act* 1968 for offering goods for sale at a price less than that which they were in fact offered. Under the Act a defence was available if the offence was due to the act or omission of another person. The company argued that the store manager was 'another person'.

The House of Lords held that the store manager lacked sufficient control and responsibility to identify him as the directing mind of the company. Thus, the store manager was 'another person' within the defence and the company was not liable for the actions of the store manager.

Lord Reid: **[167]** My Lords, the appellants own a large number of supermarkets in which they sell a wide variety of goods. ...

[170] I must start by considering the nature of the personality which by a fiction the law attributes to a corporation. A living person has a mind which can have knowledge or intention or be negligent and he has hands to carry out his intentions. A corporation has none of these; it must act through living persons, though not always one or the same person. The person who acts is not speaking or acting for the company. He is acting as the company and his mind which directs his acts is the mind of the company. There is no question of the company being vicariously liable. He is not acting as a servant, representative, agent or delegate. He is an embodiment of the company. If it is a guilty mind then the guilt is the guilt of the company. It must be a question of law whether, once the facts have been ascertained, a person in doing particular things is to be regarded as the company or merely as the company's servant or agent. In that case any liability of the company can only be a statutory or vicarious liability. ...

[171] There have been attempts to apply Denning LJ's words to all servants of a company whose work is brain work, or who exercise some managerial discretion under the direction of superior officers of the company. I do not think that Denning LJ intended to refer to them. He only referred to those who 'represent the directing mind and will of the company, and control what it does.'

I think that is right for this reason. Normally the board of directors, the managing director and perhaps other superior officers of a company carry out the functions of management and speak and act as the company. Their subordinates do not. They carry out orders from above and it can make no difference that they are given some measure of discretion. But the board of directors may delegate some part of their functions of management, giving to their delegate full discretion to act independently of instructions from them. I see no difficulty in holding that they have thereby put such a delegate in their place so that within the scope of the delegation he can act as the company. It may not always be easy to draw the line but there are cases in which the line must be drawn. ...

[174] The Divisional Court decided this case on a theory of delegation. In that they were following some earlier authorities. But they gave far too wide a meaning to delegation. I have said that a board of directors can delegate part of their functions of management so as to make their delegate an **[175]** embodiment of the company within the sphere of the delegation. But here the board never delegated any part of their functions. They set up a chain of command through regional and district supervisors, but they remained in control. The shop managers had to obey their general directions and also to take orders from their supervisors. The acts or omissions of the shop manager were not acts of the company itself.

In my judgment the appellants established the statutory defence.

Note, as stated above, each case must be considered on its specific facts. *Tesco Supermarkets Ltd v Nattrass* [1972] AC 153 involved a public company with a chain of many hundred stores. A different conclusion may have been drawn in the case of the ownership of a single supermarket.

[3.110] The organic theory had also been used in *R v Roffel* (1984) 9 ACLR 433 to provide a director with a defence to charges of stealing by dishonestly appropriating corporate funds with an intention to permanently deprive the company of those funds. Roffel had signed company cheques paying for personal purchases. Roffel was one of two directors and shareholders, and sole controller of the company's affairs. In essence the majority of the court said that stealing involves a unilateral act (ie the taking by Roffel) while a gift involved a bilateral act (the company giving the money to Roffel). The majority of the court said the facts involved a bilateral act as Roffel in his guise as the company gave the money to himself in his capacity as a shareholder/director. It was not a unilateral act by Roffel to deprive the company of its moneys and therefore did not constitute stealing.

The majority view in *R v Roffel* (1984) 9 ACLR 433 was disapproved of by the House of Lords in *R v Gomez* [1993] 1 All ER 1 and more recently by Callinan and McHugh JJ in *Macleod v The Queen* (2003) 21 ACLC 1601. In the latter case the High Court held, contrary to the reasoning in *R v Roffel*, that the self-interested 'consent' of a single shareholder, to perpetuate a crime committed against the company, did not constitute the consent of the company and in turn was not a defence to what otherwise was a breach of s 173 of the *Crimes Act* 1900 (NSW). This section prohibits directors, officers and members of a company fraudulently taking or applying company property for their own use or benefit or any use or purpose other than the use or purpose of the company. In their separate judgments both McHugh and Callinan JJ expressly rejected the reasoning in *R v Roffel*. McHugh J relied on the decision in *Salomon v Salomon* [1897] AC 22 to support his conclusion that the subject company was a separate legal entity from its shareholders even where the shares of the company are closely held. The company's purposes are not, in turn, necessarily those of the person in control of the company. Thus, Macleod's purported consent to the use of company funds for private purposes was no defence to the charge.

[3.120] Recent amendments to the Commonwealth *Criminal Code* have significantly extended the occasions when a corporation will be exposed to primary criminal liability. Under these new measures a corporation can be found criminally liable if it can be established that either a corporate culture existed within the corporation that directed, encouraged, tolerated or led to the non-compliance/offence or the corporation failed to create and maintain a corporate culture that required compliance with the relevant provision.

Privilege against self-incrimination

[3.130] Whether a company can claim the privilege against self-incrimination continues to be controversial. In *Environment Protection Authority v Caltex Refining Co Pty Ltd* (1993) 178 CLR 477, a majority of the High Court held 4:3 that a company was not entitled to the privilege. Brennan J believed that prosecuting companies would be too difficult if the privilege were extended to companies as such investigations are dependent upon access to documents in the company's possession. Mason CJ and Toohey J held that as the privilege was a 'human right' it could not be extended to companies. Brennan and McHugh JJ believed the privilege was designed to protect human dignity and thus similarly decided it should not extend to companies. While the minority justices (Deane, Dawson and Gaudron JJ) agreed that this privilege was a human right, they also believed it had a broader operation, as part of the common law's rejection of the inquisitorial approach to criminal law cases. The majority view in *Environment Protection Authority v Caltex Refining Co Pty Ltd* (1993) 178 CLR 477 was recently reiterated in *ASIC v United Investment Funds Pty Ltd* [2003] FCA 674.

Piercing the Corporate Veil

Piercing the corporate veil

[3.140] When a court looks through a company's separate legal identity it is said to be lifting or piercing the corporate veil. Generally, the corporate veil cannot be pierced to place the corporation's liability upon the shareholders or directors. This principle has been strongly maintained by the courts, stressing that the legally recognised corporate identity is not something that can be lightly ignored: see *Gas Lighting Improvement Co Ltd v IRC* [1923] AC 723 at 740-741; *Hobart Bridge Co Ltd v FCT* (1951) 82 CLR 372; *Steinberg v FCT* (1975) 134 CLR 640 at 682. Nevertheless, there are well defined categories of judicial and legislative triggers for piercing the corporate veil. The key categories are discussed below.

Sham

[3.150] Finding a company to be a 'sham' does not equate with piercing the corporate veil: *Re a Company* [1985] BCLC 333. When a company is a sham it is not recognised as real and thus can be ignored by the courts. By contrast, when the corporate veil is pierced the company's separate legal identity is not denied. The company still exists, but its separate legal personality is penetrated for that particular purpose.

Statutory directives to pierce the corporate veil

[3.160] In certain circumstances the *Corporations Act* allows a company's separate identity to be pierced and liability imposed on the company's officers or members. These legislative directions may be express or implicit: *Re Bugle Press Ltd* [1961] Ch 270.

Insolvent trading

[3.170] The corporate veil may be lifted where the company is involved in insolvent trading. In essence, insolvent trading occurs when the directors of the company fail to prevent the company incurring a debt even though there are reasonable grounds to suspect the company is insolvent or the debt will render it insolvent. A company is considered 'insolvent' when it cannot meet its debts as and when they fall due: s 95A(1). If a defence is not established, in these cases the directors are exposed to personal liability for the corporate debt.

The current provisions governing insolvent trading are contained in Div 3 of Part 5.7B. These provisions prospectively replace, *inter alia*, former s 592, and operate with respect to debts incurred after 25 June 1993. Under s 588G(1) and (2), persons contravene the section if they fail to prevent the company from incurring a debt when:

- they were a director of the company;
- the company was insolvent or incurring the debt rendered it insolvent;
- there were reasonable grounds to suspect the company was insolvent or that the debt would render it insolvent; and
- the director was aware of these grounds or a reasonable person in a like position in a company in the company's circumstances would be aware.

The inclusion of a 'reasonable person' test makes it clear that directors will be adjudged according to the involvement expected under the *Corporations Act*, rather than the actual knowledge of the subject director.

The defences previously detailed in s 592(2) have been replaced by s 588H. Section 588H(2)-(5) provides that directors may invoke as defences to an action under s 588G that they:

- had reasonable grounds to expect, and did expect, when the debt was incurred that the company was solvent and would remain solvent: s 588H(2);
- had reasonable grounds to believe, and did believe, that:
  - a competent and reliable person was responsible for informing the director as to the company's solvency; and
  - that person was fulfilling that responsibility; and

  expected on the basis of such information that the company was solvent and would remain solvent: s 588H(3);
- did not take part in the management of the company at that time because of illness or some other good reason: s 588H(4); or
- took all reasonable steps to prevent the company incurring the debt: s 588H(5).

For a fuller discussion of these provisions, see Chapter 10.

[3.180] While generally the separate legal personality of companies within a group is maintained (*Industrial Equity Ltd v Blackburn* (1977) 137 CLR 567; *Pioneer Concrete Services Ltd v Yelnah Pty Ltd* (1986) 5 NSWLR 254), because a holding company can exercise real control over a wholly-owned subsidiary, in certain cases it will be appropriate to look beyond the legal identity of the subsidiary to the holding company. Sections 588V and 588W detail when a holding company may be liable for certain debts incurred by its subsidiary. To some extent echoing s 588G, the holding company will be liable for the debts of its subsidiary under s 588W(1) when:

- the subsidiary incurs a debt after 25 June 1993;
- at the time the subsidiary is insolvent or incurring the debt renders it insolvent;
- there are reasonable grounds to suspect the subsidiary is insolvent or that the debt would render it insolvent; and
  - the holding company, or one or more of its directors, is aware that there are grounds for so suspecting; or
  - given the holding company's control over the subsidiary, it is reasonable to expect a holding company in the company's circumstances or one of its directors would be so aware: s 588V(1).

As with ss 588G and 588H, the test imposed by s 588V(1) is objective in nature.

Debts incurred as trustee

[3.190] Section 197 allows directors to be held partially or wholly liable for debts incurred by a company, acting as trustee of a trust, where the company is not entitled to be fully indemnified out of trust assets. This is designed to prevent assets being protected from creditors' claims by 'hiding' them in trusts, access to which is denied to the corporate trustee.

Section 197 was recently considered by the Supreme Court of South Australia in *Hanel v O'Neill* (2004) 22 ACLC 274. In this case the trust deed allowed the trustee company, Daroko Pty Ltd, to be indemnified out of the trust assets. However, neither the trustee company nor the trust had any assets. When the trustee failed to pay the subject debt, the creditor obtained a judgment for the debt against the sole director of the trustee company, Hanel. Hanel appealed against the judgment on the basis that s 197 did not apply because the trustee company was entitled to be fully indemnified under the trust deed, irrespective of whether the trust had any assets. The majority of the court (Mullighan and Gray JJ, Debelle J dissenting) disagreed, asserting that the trustee must be entitled to be indemnified as a matter of fact, not just law. If there were no trust assets, there was no entitlement to be indemnified within s 197. Mullighan J stated that it would be contrary to the purpose underlying s 197 if directors of corporate trustees could escape liability by simply ensuring that the relevant trust deed provided for indemnification, even where the directors caused the depletion of trust assets. See further *Intagro v ANZ Banking Group* (2004) 22 ACLC 1065, where the court disagreed with the reasoning in *Hanel* but concluded that as the majority reasoning in that case was not "plainly wrong" it should be followed. However, in *Edwards v AG* (2004) 22 ACLC 1177, while the court found it unnecessary to consider s 197, the court indicated it disagreed with, and would not follow, *Hanel*.

Common law rules regarding piercing the corporate veil

[3.200] Prompted by public interest, courts have at times acted without legislative direction and pierced the corporate veil to impose liability upon, or extend benefits to, the controller of a company. While the Australian courts have been reluctant to lift the corporate veil, the English judiciary has been more inclined to act independently of legislative direction. Despite the Australian courts' reluctance, an examination of the combined practice of Australian and English courts reveals well defined exceptions to the general principle upholding the separate legal identity of companies.

Avoiding a legal obligation

[3.210] The corporate veil will not be allowed to be used to avoid an existing legal obligation. Thus, in *Gilford Motor Co Ltd v Horne* [1933] Ch 935 the court would not allow the defendant, Horne, to use a company to circumvent a pre-existing legal obligation. Horne, while an employee of Gilford Motor Co Ltd, had covenanted not to solicit his previous employer's clients were he to cease employment. To avoid this restrictive covenant Horne established a company to solicit the clients of his former employer. The court pierced the corporate veil and injuncted both Horne and company from soliciting Gilford Motor Co Ltd's clients. Similarly, in *Jones v Lipman* [1962] 1 WLR 832 the court would not allow Lipman to avoid completing a contract for the sale of his house by transferring the land to a company formed for this specific purpose. The court held the company was 'a mask which [the defendant held] before his face in an attempt to avoid recognition by the eye of equity'. The court consequently lifted the corporate veil, ordering specific performance of the contract.

[3.220] These cases were dependent upon a finding that the object underlying the creation of the company was the evasion of a legal obligation. They can be contrasted with *Electric Light and Power Supply Corporation Ltd v Cormack* (1911) 11 SR (NSW) 350; *Pioneer Concrete Services Ltd v Yelnah Pty Ltd* (1986) 5 NSWLR 254; *Ascot Investments Pty Ltd v Harper* (1981) 148 CLR 337 where the courts found this illegitimate object to be absent and consequently refused to lift the corporate veil under this ground.

Fraud

[3.230] A related exception is the ability to lift the corporate veil where the company is used to perpetuate a fraud. Thus, in *Re Darby; ex p Broughton* [1911] 1 KB 95 Darby and another person, Gyde, both undischarged bankrupts, floated a company in the Channel Islands. Darby and Gyde were shareholders and its first and only directors and managers. This 'dummy' company in turn promoted another company, to which it sold property at a vast overvalue. The latter company was funded by public investment. When this company went into liquidation, the liquidator claimed the secret profit from Darby in bankruptcy on the basis he was the true promoter of the second company. Darby had considerable assets, while Gyde had none. It was alleged that, as a promoter, Darby had breached his fiduciary duties and a claim for damages or undisclosed profits was made. The court held that where, as here, a company is used for perpetuating a fraud, the corporate veil may be lifted. While strictly the first company was the promoter of the second company and had made the profit through the non-arm's length sale, once the corporate veil was lifted it was clear that Darby was the true promoter and thus the liquidator could claim against his personal assets.

Agency

[3.240] Sometimes the courts will treat a company and its controller as separate entities in law, but because of the extent of the latter's control, determine the company to be an agent of the controller. Where the company is no more than a 'puppet', the principal (the controller) will be liable for the acts of its agent (the company) (*Spreag v Paeson Pty Ltd* (1990) 94 ALR 679) or entitled to any benefits that may flow from the agent's conduct of a business: *Smith, Stone and Knight Ltd v Birmingham Corporation* [1939] 4 All ER 116.

[3.250] As *Salomon v Salomon & Co Ltd* [1897] AC 22 indicates, that the company is a 'one person company' will not alone allow a court to treat the company as the shareholder's agent. See also *Gramophone and Typewriter Ltd v Stanley* [1908] 2 KB 89; *Dennis Wilcox Pty Ltd v FCT* (1988) 79 ALR 267; *Donnelly v Edelsten* (1994) 13 ACSR 196. An agency relationship will only be implied where the company is a mere 'puppet' to the extent that there is a disregard for the agent company's separate legal identity: *Smith, Stone and Knight Ltd v Birmingham Corporation* [1939] 4 All ER 116; *Spreag v Paeson Pty Ltd* (1990) 94 ALR 679. In *Smith, Stone and Knight Ltd v Birmingham Corporation* at 121 Atkinson J specified six factors indicating whether an agency relationship exists:

1. 'Were the profits treated as the profits of the [parent] company?'
2. '[W]ere the persons conducting the business appointed by the parent company?'
3. '[W]as the [parent] company the head and the brain of the trading venture?'
4. '[D]id the company govern the adventure, decide what should be done and what capital should be embarked on the venture?'
5. '[D]id the [subsidiary] make the profits by [the parent company's] skill and direction?' and
6. 'Was the [parent] company in effectual and constant control [of the subsidiary]?'

These principles were in turn applied in the leading Australian case on this issue, *Spreag v Paeson Pty Ltd*.

Spreag v Paeson Pty Ltd
Federal Court of Australia: Sheppard J
(1990) 94 ALR 679

The Spreags were builders on Norfolk Island who purchased a brickmaker from Paeson Pty Ltd ('Paeson'). The purchase was conditional on Paeson sending staff to Norfolk Island to demonstrate the machinery.

Once delivered, the staff were unable to adjust the machinery to enable it to produce marketable bricks at the stated rate of production, namely 500 to 600 bricks per hour. The Spreags sought damages from, *inter alia*, Componere Systems Pty Ltd ('Componere') which had banked their cheque for the purchase. It was argued that Componere was liable to the Spreags as a principal either because Paeson had allowed Componere to conduct its business or Componere was the undisclosed principal of Paeson. Paeson and Componere argued that the Spreags agreed to buy the brickmaker on the basis of their own examination of the brickmaker rather than any representations made by the seller's agent, Mr Foster. Componere maintained that the vendor of the machines was Paeson and that Componere did not carry on the relevant business.

The court rejected the suggestion the Spreags agreed to buy the brickmaker on the basis of their own examination of the brickmaker. To the contrary, the court found they relied on the representations of Mr Foster, a representative of Componere. Most importantly, the court found Paeson was the agent of Componere and thus the Spreags were entitled to succeed against Componere and Paeson.

Sheppard J: **[707]** The evidence of Mr Smith, Mr Farrow and Ms Bayer establishes the following.
1. At no relevant time did:-
    (a) Paeson have any bank account or other assets.
    (b) Paeson have any premises of its own.
    (c) Paeson keep any books of account, nor prepare any balance sheet or profit and loss account.
2. Componere kept a set of books and balance sheets and profit and loss accounts were prepared for it. There are entries in its books of account **[708]** which suggest that payments were made by Componere on Paeson's behalf for a variety of expenses including wages. Entries relating to these expenditures sometimes, but not always, included notation which would suggest that the moneys were paid on Paeson's behalf.
3. Componere's balance sheet as at 30 June 1987 showed, under the heading "Receivables", loans to Paeson totalling $790,695. The figure as at 30 June 1986 was $144,206. Despite this statement in the balance sheet there is no ledger account in Componere's ledger showing Paeson's indebtedness. There is of course no ledger entry in any of Paeson's records because it kept no books of account.
4. Although Mr MacGrory, Mr Foster and Mr Foster's two sons were either retained or employed by Paeson, the entirety of the moneys to which they were entitled were paid by Componere and the tax deductible from the wages paid to the two Foster sons was paid by Componere.
5. Moneys received by Paeson or on its behalf were paid to Componere and retained by it. Mr Farrow's evidence was that they were applied in reduction of Paeson's indebtedness but there is no book entry which bears this out.
6. The invoices for the brickmaker and the shredder and for the freight paid to secure the delivery of the machines to Norfolk Island were issued under the name of Paeson but a further invoice for hydraulic fluid, air freight and additional sea freight was issued in the name of Componere. In the left hand corner of this invoice is the drawing of a brick and beside it the words, "Componere brickmaker".

7. Mr Foster's business card showed him as a representative, not of Paeson but of Componere. A new brochure which was published in September 1986 but after 9 September 1986 when the critical conversation took place described the brickmaker as the "Componere Brick Maker". It was substantially the same as the earlier brochure except that it showed a brickmaker of the type acquired by the Spreags and claimed a production rate of 350 bricks per hour rather than 500, this notwithstanding that in more prominent print was a claim advising potential purchasers that they could plan production for up to 10 bricks per minute. ...

The question then is where this conclusion leads in relation to the liability of Componere. In the submission of counsel for the Spreags I should conclude that Componere is liable to the Spreags as a principal either because Paeson allowed Componere to conduct its business or delegated its business to Componere or Componere was the undisclosed principal of Paeson. Counsel relied on a number of authorities, the most relevant of which is *Smith, Stone and Knight Limited v City of Birmingham* [1939] 4 All ER 116. ...

[711] The decisions in the *Industrial Equity, Dennis Willcox* and *Sharrment cases* emphasise that *Salomon's case* is still good law. Nevertheless, no case suggests that Atkinson J's decision in the *Smith, Stone and Knight case* was wrong and the question is whether the present case can be said to fall within the principles propounded in it. In other words, what answer should be made, having regard to the facts in this case, to the six questions which Atkinson J asked himself. The first is, who was really carrying on the business? In my opinion, notwithstanding the existence of the loan account in Componere's balance sheet and the references to payments being made on behalf of Paeson in Componere's books of account, the reality was that it was Componere which was carrying on the business. Support for this conclusion is found in the facts that the brickmaker was referred to as the Componere brickmaker and Mr Foster's business card bore the name Componere rather than Paeson.

Atkinson J's second question was whether the persons conducting the business were appointed by the parent company. Plainly they were. The third question was whether the parent company was the head and the brain of the trading venture. Plainly Componere was. Fourthly, did the parent govern the adventure, decide what should be done and what capital should be embarked on the venture? Again, Componere did all these things. The fifth question was whether the subsidiary made profits by the parent's skill and direction. It is doubtful whether there were any profits but certainly any that were made would have been made by Componere's skill and direction. The final question was whether the parent was in effectual and constant control and the answer to this question is again in the affirmative.

There is a further factor which I think must be taken into account. At no relevant time did Paeson ever have any money. It had no bank account. At the most it had a loan account in the books of Componere. If it be right to say that *Salomon's case* prevents a creditor, such as the Spreags, from proceeding against Componere, no such creditor can ever successfully recover moneys owing to it unless Componere is prepared to fund the liability. In that event creditors of Paeson would be paid or not paid at Componere's will. If it were proceeded against and wound up on the ground that it was insolvent, no creditor would have any right to recover a cent from Componere in the winding up (Componere itself would be a substantial creditor) and yet Componere could continue trading exactly as it had previously done. As Atkinson J suggested, in relation to the case which he had to decide, all that would be necessary would be to obliterate any **[712]** reference to Paeson in any documents and in any conduct which was engaged in furthering Paeson's business activities.

In all these circumstances I have decided that I should uphold the submission that Paeson was carrying on such business as it did carry on for Componere and was, at least by analogy, in the position of an agent acting for an undisclosed principal. In those circumstances I have reached the conclusion that the Spreags are entitled to recover not only from Paeson, but also from Componere.

Corporate groups

[3.260] Corporate groups often operate as a single economic unit. Moreover, the management of a holding company will effectively manage each company in the corporate group, including subsidiaries, not just the holding company. This economic reality has not, however, replicated into law. As noted above, the Australian courts have asserted that each company in the corporate group must be treated as a separate legal identity: *Industrial Equity Ltd v Blackburn* (1977) 2 ACLR 421. Most importantly, in the current context, that companies are part of the same corporate group will not provide a basis for piercing the corporate veil so that, for example, a holding company will be liable for the acts of its subsidiary company: *Pioneer Concrete Services Ltd v Yelnah Pty Ltd* (1986) 5 NSWLR 254. Nor will the fact that companies are part of the same corporate group mean that they are necessarily carrying on business in partnership or as agents for one another, as discussed above: *Pioneer Concrete Services Ltd v Yelnah Pty Ltd*.

Pioneer Concrete Services Ltd v Yelnah Pty Ltd
Supreme Court of NSW: Young J
(1986) 5 NSWLR 254

The interrelationship between the relevant companies is complex but the main issue revolved around an agreement between three corporate groups: (i) Hi-Quality Concrete (Holdings) Pty Ltd and its subsidiaries, (ii) Pioneer Concrete Services Ltd and (iii) Ritemix, a joint venture between Trunka Pty Ltd and Yelnah Pty Ltd. Clause 3 of this agreement provided that 'Hi-Quality', defined in the agreement to mean Hi-Quality Concrete (NSW) Pty Ltd, Hi-Quality Concrete (Holdings) Pty Ltd's subsidiary, would at all times act in the best interests of Pioneer Ltd in all matters relating to Trunka and Ritemix. In a separate clause (clause 5.1) Hi-Quality Concrete (Holdings) Pty Ltd guaranteed due performance by 'Hi-Quality' of its obligations under the agreement. Yelnah Pty Ltd subsequently transferred its interest in Ritemix to Hi-Quality Concrete (Holdings) Pty Ltd. Pioneer Ltd alleged Hi-Quality Concrete (Holdings) Pty Ltd, the new controller of Ritemix, had breached clause 3 of the agreement. Pioneer Ltd asserted that it was unrealistic to treat the Hi-Quality companies other than as a single entity, describing the corporate group as a partnership. Thus, the relevant obligation was binding on Hi-Quality Concrete (Holdings) Pty Ltd, not just its subsidiary. Alternatively, Pioneer Ltd sought to invoke the above discussed principle that the corporate veil may be pierced where a company is used to avoid an obligation.

The court held the subject clause was an undertaking made by the subsidiary and could not be treated as binding on the whole corporate group and, in particular, the holding company. As there was no factual basis for the suggestion that the subsidiary was created to avoid a legal obligation and no evidence that the holding company and subsidiary operated in partnership, the corporate veil could not be lifted. Young J expressly disapproved of the approach in *DHN Food Distributors Ltd v London Borough of Tower Hamlets* [1976] 1 WLR 852 where the court went behind the corporate veil and treated the companies in the corporate group as one on the basis that each of the three companies were akin to partners in a partnership.

> **Young J:** **[264]** It is apparent from what has been said above that a major obstacle to the plaintiff's success is the fact that the promises made in cl 3 of the agreement of 16 February 1982 were made by Hi-Quality Concrete (NSW) Pty Ltd and not with the main company in the group Hi-Quality Concrete (Holdings) Pty Ltd. As I have already remarked it is difficult to read cl 3 as applying to the whole group because the Holding company was a party to the deed; it was deliberately separately described and indeed apart from the definition in the description of the parties there is a further definition in cl 12(b) of the deed extending the term 'Hi-Quality' to include its successors and permitted assigns though not to cover other companies in the group. Moreover cl 5.1 is a deliberate guarantee by Holdings of the observance by Hi-Quality of its obligations under the deed. This is significant because it would appear that the parties have deliberately chosen not that there should be a covenant by the Holding company but rather a covenant by the subsidiary which covenant is to be guaranteed by the Holding company, obviously a very different sort of obligation. ...
>
> Even if these difficulties were swept away, there would still be massive problems in performing the exercise commonly called lifting the corporate veil. This expression means that although whenever each individual company is formed a separate legal personality is created courts will on occasions look behind the legal personality to the real controllers. As John H Farrar says in his *Company Law*, Butterworths London (1985) at 57:
>
> "... It is difficult to rationalise the cases except under the broad, rather question-begging heading of policy and by describing the main legal categories under which they fall. These are (1) agency; (2) fraud; (3) group enterprises; (4) trusts; (5) enemy; (6) tax; (7) the Companies Act itself."
>
> ... Of the seven categories mentioned by Farrar only Nos 1, 2 or 3 could be applicable in the instant case. ... Of these headings I **[265]** find it impossible to infer an agency in this case because of the fact that the Holding company was itself a party to the deed of February 1982 and deliberately did not join in the promises in cl 3. That leaves two types of situations to be investigated. ...
>
> **[266]** Thus merely to read the judgments in [*DHN Food Distributors Ltd v Tower Hamlets London Borough Council* [1976] 1 WLR 852; [1976] 3 All ER 462 where the court referred to the relevant corporate group to be a partnership and asserted this provided a justification for lifting the corporate veil]

gives one the impression that it is one of those 'too hard' cases in which judges have for policy reasons justified the lifting of the corporate veil in that particular case rather than the case which lays down any great new principle.
...

Although I am not aware of any relevant Australian authority, unless the **[267]** *DHN case* is confined to its special facts, it gives a result which as Professor Ford points out in the 4th edition of his *Principles of Company Law* (1986) at 139 is inconsistent with the view of the High Court of Australia in *Industrial Equity Ltd v Blackburn* (1977) 137 CLR 567 at 577.

In my view the plaintiff's submissions take the *DHN case* too far and it is only if the court can see that there is in fact or law a partnership between companies in a group or alternatively where there is a mere sham or facade that one lifts the veil. The principle does not apply in the instant case where it would appear that there was a good commercial purpose for having separate companies in the group performing different functions even though the ultimate controllers would very naturally lapse into speaking of the whole group as 'us'.

I thus turn to the alternative approach which might warrant the lifting of the corporate veil that is that it would be inequitable not to. In their submissions plaintiff's counsel referred to the following passage from my judgment in *Licata v Madeddu* (Young J, 9 August 1985, unreported):

"... equity would not permit a person to evade obligations under a restrictive covenant by means of drawing a corporate veil or using a nominee, if that in the eyes of equity would be a cloak for fraud; see also *Smith v Hancock* [1894] 2 Ch 377, *Jones v Lipman* [1962] 1 WLR 832 and *Albert Locke (1940) Ltd v Winsford UDC* (1973) 71 LGR (Eng) 308."

That passage was as its context shows expounding the equity recognised by Lord Hansworth MR in *Gilford Motor Co v Horne* [1933] Ch 935. ...

However it must be realised as Professor Ford points out (at 135) in the 4th edition of his work that the *Gilford Motor Co* decision depends on a finding by unrebutted inference that one of the reasons for the creation of the intervening company was to evade a legal or fiduciary obligation. Where this finding cannot be made then the corporate veil may not be lifted. ...

In the instant case there is no question of a corporation being formed for the sole purpose or for the dominant purpose of evading a contractual or fiduciary obligation and it does not seem to me that the principle of the *Gilford Motor Co case* comes into play at all.

Accordingly it does not seem to me that any of Farrar's heads, of when a court lifts the corporate veil, assists the plaintiff in the instant case. Nor bearing in mind what the High Court has said about courts not being involved with the layman's fallacy of confusing the personalities of members **[268]** of a corporate group can I see any valid reason for lifting the corporate veil in this case ...

Trusts

[3.270] The judiciary has been reluctant to impose a trust relationship between companies and their controllers or companies within a group as a means of lifting the corporate veil. This will only occur in rare cases involving, for example, the use of the company to obtain a tax benefit: *Littlewoods Mail Order Stores Ltd v IRC* [1969] 1 WLR 1241.

Public policy: the enemy

[3.280] Public policy may prompt the courts to lift the corporate veil in some circumstances. One example of this principle relates to the legal principle that contracts with the enemy in times of war are unenforceable. Public policy dictates that the corporate veil may be pierced to determine if a company should be regarded as an enemy alien: *Daimler Co Ltd v Continental Tyre and Rubber Co (Great Britain) Ltd* [1916] 2 AC 307. Thus, in this case the House of Lords held that the doctrine of corporate identity did not dictate 'that the character of its incorporators must be irrelevant to the character of the company ... for the rule against trading with the enemy'. To determine the 'enemy character' of the company the court could lift the corporate veil to consider the nationality of its shareholders. On the subject facts the court pierced the corporate veil of the company registered under the English *Companies Act* to conclude that it was truly an enemy company because its shareholders and directors were nearly all German nationals. The plaintiff/respondent could not, therefore, bring proceedings for recovery of the subject debt.

Review questions

1. What does the 'corporate entity' principle establish?
2. Explain the statement:
   Sometimes as shown by the cases concerning insurable interests ... 'corporate entity' works like a boomerang and hits the man who was trying to use it. (per Kahn-Freud 'Some Reflections on Company Law Reform' (1944) 7 *Mod LR* 54)
3. What limits are there to the corporate entity theory?
4. What limits should be imposed?

Further reading

ALRC Report No 45, *General Insolvency Inquiry* (1988) esp vol 1 paras 336, 857 and Appendix A D 13

Baxt, 'Tensions between commercial reality and legal principle – Should the concept of the corporate entity be re-examined?' (1991) 65 *ALJ* 352

Baxt, 'The Need to Review the Rule in Salomon's Case as it Applies to Groups of Companies' (1991) 9 *C&SLJ* 185

Blumberg, 'Limited Liability and Corporate Groups' (1986) 11 *J of Corp Law* 623

Cassidy, *Concise Corporations Law* (4th ed, Federation Press, Sydney, 2003) ch 3

Cooke, 'Corporate Identity' (1998) 16 *C&SLJ* 160

Duggan, 'The Criminal Liability of Corporations for Contraventions of Part V of the Trade Practices Act 1974' (1977) 5 *ABLR* 22

Duggan, 'Misleading Advertising and The Publishers' Defence' (1978) 6 *ABLR* 309

Farrar, 'Legal Issues Involving Corporate Groups' (1998) 16 *C&SLJ* 184

Fisse, 'Responsibility, Prevention and Corporate Crime' (1973) 5 *NZULR* 250

Fisse, 'The Social Policy of Corporate Criminal Responsibility' (1978) 6 *Adel L Rev* 361

Ford, Austin and Ramsay, *Ford's Principles of Corporations Law* (11th ed, Butterworths, Sydney, 2003) chs 1, 4 and 12

Gates, 'Disregarding the Corporate Entity in Favour of Beneficial Ownership and Control' (1984) 12 *ABLR* 162

Ireland, 'The Rise of the Limited Liability Company' (1984) 12 *Int J of Sociology of Law* 239

Kahn-Freud, 'Some Reflections on Company Law Reform' (1944) 7 *Mod LR* 54

Leigh, 'Criminal Liability of Corporations and Other Groups' (1977) 9 *Ottawa LR* 247

Ottoleghi, 'From Peeping Behind the Corporate Veil to Ignoring it Completely' (1990) 52 *Mod LR* 338

Pickering, 'The Company as a Separate Legal Entity' (1968) 31 *Mod LR* 481

Rixon, 'Lifting the Veil between Holding and Subsidiary Companies' (1986) 102 *LQR* 415

Von Nessen, 'My Body, Myself; Problems of Identity in Corporate Crime' (1985) 3 *C&SLJ* 235

Ziegel, 'Is Incorporation (with Limited Liability) Too Easily Available?' (1990) 31 *Les Cahiers de Droit* 1075

4

Promoters and Pre-registration Contracts

Overview

This chapter considers promoters and pre-registration contracts. It begins by looking at the legal definition of a promoter, observing that to be a promoter it is not necessary for that person be involved in the promotion of the company before its registration. Promoters can become involved in the early conduct of a company. Equally it will be seen that 'dormant' promoters can be promoters despite their inactivity. Once a promoter is identified, equity imposes strict duties on such persons to act in the best interests of the yet to be formed, or newly formed, company.

The chapter continues with a consideration of pre-registration contracts. It will be seen that the common law was unsatisfactory and has been replaced with a legislative regime contained in Part 2B.3 of the *Corporations Act* 2001 (Cth) ('*Corporations Act*'). This legislative regime extends to the courts quite considerable discretion so that liability may be imposed in a given manner depending very much on the facts of the case and thus as fairness requires.

Promoters

Defining a promoter

[4.10] The term promoter is not defined in the *Corporations Act*. The definition that was previously contained in s 9 was of limited utility as its context was confined to the preparation and issuing of a prospectus and the definition was largely exclusionary. In regard to the latter point, the definition served to relieve persons from potential liability where they were only connected with the prospectus through the performance of their professional duties or a business relationship with the company's promoter, for example, solicitors or accountants who prepare documents for the formation of the company in the completion of their professional duties. This aspect of the repealed definition of promoter is equally applicable to the common law definition of a promoter.

At common law there are two aspects to the legal character of a promoter:

- the person is factually involved in the formation and/or initial conduct of the company: *Twycross v Grant* (1877) 2 CPD 469 at 541; *Lagunas Nitrate Co v Lagunas Syndicate* [1899] 2 Ch 392; *Tracy v Mandalay Pty Ltd* (1953) 88 CLR 215 at 241; *Elders Executors and Trustee Co v EG Reeves Pty Ltd* (1987) 78 ALR 193; and
- the person has such a special/fiduciary relationship with the company that it would be contrary to good faith were the individual to retain a secret profit or refuse restitution of a loss inflicted by him or her: *Whaley Bridge Calico Printing Co v Green* (1879) 5 QBD 109 at 111; *Tracy v Mandalay Pty Ltd* at 241-242.

As noted above, the necessary factual involvement in the promotion of the company can occur before or post incorporation: *Tracy v Mandalay Pty Ltd* at 242. Moreover, persons may still be characterised as promoters if they have been inactive, leaving the promotion activities to others on the understanding that they will nevertheless share in the profits stemming from the company's creation: *Tracy v Mandalay Pty Ltd* at 242 and 245.

Tracy v Mandalay Pty Ltd
High Court of Australia: Dixon CJ, Williams and Taylor JJ
(1953) 88 CLR 215

Salon had a scheme for making money through the development of 10-storey flats on certain land. The scheme involved two steps. First, his family company, RSC Co, purchased the block of land. This purchase was assisted by Salon inducing two acquaintances, Griffith and Withy, to buy from Salon and his spouse some of the shares in the company at £10 a share. The par value of the shares was £1. The share acquisitions were based on the promise that Griffith and Withy would benefit financially when the property was on-sold to a second company that was to be formed, M Co. In turn M Co was to be promoted to erect and sell the flats built on the site. Later more shares were sold to another third party, Willard. Again, Willard purchased the shares on the basis of making a profit from the transfer of the land to the second company. Ultimately, the rest of the unissued shares in RSC Co were allotted to Mrs Salon, Willard and the company secretary, Tracy. When M Co was formed (with Salon, Willard and Withy as its initial shareholders, Salon and Willard as its directors and Tracy as company secretary) it entered into contracts to buy the land from RSC Co and to purchase all shares in RSC Co at a premium. These transactions were funded by public acquisitions of flats off the plan and public subscription of shares in M Co. An amendment to the law made it impossible to carry out the intended plans.

An action was brought by the new controllers of M Co against the defendants as promoters. It was asserted that the defendants, as promoters, had not made adequate disclosures to the plaintiff company. As a consequence of this breach of fiduciary duties the contracts for the land and shares were said to be voidable. Action was also taken for the recovery of moneys paid for the land and shares. In reply it was asserted that some of the defendants were not promoters of M Co as they were not involved in the scheme before the company's incorporation and, in the case of Griffith, Willard and Withy, they had not taken an active part in the promotion of the company.

The court at first instance held that all the defendants were promoters and ordered, *inter alia*, that the contracts be rescinded as they had been made without proper disclosure. On appeal, the High Court agreed, finding that a person may be a promoter of an already incorporated company when they are involved it its initial conduct. Moreover, the defendants were all promoters, even those that had taken a passive role, as they did so on the understanding that they would profit from the operation.

Dixon CJ, Williams and Taylor JJ: **[241]** The word "promoter" has been said on many occasions to be a word which has no very definite meaning. It is sufficient to refer to the discussion of its meaning in *Emma Silver Mining Co Ltd v Lewis & Son* (1879) 4 CPD 396. There Lindley J, as he then was, said: "With respect to the word 'promoters', we are of opinion that it has no very definite meaning: see *Twycross v Grant* (1877) 2 CPD 469. As used in connection with companies the term 'promoter' involves the idea of exertion for the purpose of getting up and starting a company (of what is called 'floating' it) and also the idea of some duty towards the company imposed by or arising from the position which the so-called promoter assumes towards it. It is now clearly settled that **[242]** persons who get up and form a company have duties towards it before it comes into existence: see *Bagnall v Carlton* (1877) 6 Ch D 371 and per Lord Cairns LC in *Erlanger v New Sombrero Phosphate Co* (1878) 3 App Cas at p 1236. Moreover, it is in our opinion an entire mistake to suppose that after a company is registered its directors are the only persons who are in such a position towards it as to be under fiduciary relations to it. A person not a director may be a promoter of a company which is already incorporated, *but the capital of which has not been taken up, and which is not yet in a position to perform the obligations imposed upon it by its creators.* The defendants say they owed no duty to this company. But in our opinion this contention cannot be supported. In the first place, the defendants left Park to get up the company upon the understanding that they as well as he were to profit by the operation; they were behind him; they were in the position of undisclosed joint adventures; and in respect of their interest his obligations and theirs are in our opinion undistinguishable. *The defendants in fact were, partly by assisting Park and partly by leaving him to do the best he could for them as well as himself, in the position of promoters of the company*" (1879) 4 CPD, at pp 407, 408. (The italics are ours.)

In the present case Salon was admittedly a promoter of the plaintiff. He was directly responsible for its incorporation. It was on his instructions that the memorandum and articles of association were prepared and registered and incorporation effected. Some of the other defendants also took an active part in the promotion of the plaintiff, and we shall refer shortly to some of these activities. But it is not only the persons who take an active part in the formation of a company and the raising of the necessary share capital to enable it to carry on business who are promoters. It is apparent from the passage cited that persons who leave it to others to get up the company upon the understanding that they also will profit from the operation may become promoters ... Willard, Tracy and Mrs Salon were, in our opinion, all promoters. Willard bought his original parcel of 250 shares from Salon and Mrs Salon with a view to sharing in the profit expected to be made out of the incorporation of the new company. ...

[243] He became chairman of directors of the new company and played a leading part [244] in accepting the new capital and disposing of it. He saw to it that he was paid the purchase money for his own shares and made the intended profit. He was implicated in the scheme up to the hilt.

Tracy assumed the role of secretary throughout, first of the defendant company and later of the plaintiff. ... But the inference was clearly open to his Honour that he was taking an active part in forming and floating the new company. ... Undoubtedly he became a shareholder in the defendant company so that he would have an interest in the profit to be made out of the promotion and formation of the new company. If his activities were merely ministerial he was at least ministering to two boards the members of which were actively engaged on his behalf as well as their own in seeing that the scheme was carried through and he was fully aware and assisted in the means by which that purpose was achieved. Nor can there be any doubt that Salon was acting on behalf of his wife with her knowledge and consent. As for the defendant company, it was a mere puppet in the hands of Salon and Mrs Salon. It was bound by the steps they took on its behalf to sell the land to the new company. In our opinion his Honour was justified in holding that Mrs Salon and the defendant company were promoters of the plaintiff.

The liability of Griffith and Miss Withy requires more consideration. Originally they purchased their shares in the defendant company from Salon and Mrs Salon with a view to making a large profit when the land at Potts Point was sold to the new company. But this scheme was not carried out. A new scheme was substituted for it. Under the new scheme they would have sold their shares to the new company at a loss if they had not been recouped by the promissory notes. They were left out of the distribution of the balance of the capital of the defendant company on 29th December 1948. There is no evidence that either of them took any active part [245] in the formation of the plaintiff or in the attraction and disposition of the new capital. Miss Withy held a minor position in the office of the defendant company, but she only had a hazy idea of what was going on. She does not appear to have realised that, she was taking part in a meeting of shareholders of the plaintiff on 7th January 1949. They were not paid for their shares or on the promissory notes until they resorted to litigation. Even then Griffith only received 500 pounds of his 2,150 pounds. But it is clear that they agreed to participate in the scheme to promote the plaintiff and sell the land and the shares to it provided Mr and Mrs Salon gave them the promissory notes so that they would not lose on their investment by selling their shares at 8 pounds 12s. 0d. In the end they had to be content to get their money back and the only way that they could do so was by accepting the new scheme and standing behind Salon in the operation. They were joint adventurers in the new scheme. As Salon and the other active promoters failed to discharge the fiduciary duties which that operation involved to make it legally binding on the new company, the transaction must be voidable not only against Salon but also those on whose behalf he was acting.

For these reasons we are of opinion that his Honour was right in holding that the plaintiff was entitled to have the contracts of sale of the land and shares set aside.

Promoter's duties

[4.20] By reason of their position of power, promoters stand in a fiduciary relationship with the company: *Erlanger v New Sombrero Phosphate Co* (1878) 3 App Cas 1218 at 1236. They must display the 'utmost candour and honesty' and act in the company's best interests: *Central Railway of Venezuela v Kisch* (1867) LR 2 HL 99 at 113. As a corollary, the promoter may not profit at the expense of the projected enterprise. In dealings with the company, promoters must disclose all material facts, including the nature and extent of any interest they may have in a transaction, to an impartial board where possible or at least to all the shareholders: *Imperial Mercantile Credit Association (Liquidators of) v Coleman* (1873) LR 6 HL 189; *Erlanger v New Sombrero Phosphate Co* at 1236; *Salomon v Salomon & Co* [1897] AC 22; *Lagunas Nitrate Co v Lagunas Syndicate* [1899] 2 Ch 392; *Gluckstein v Barnes* [1900] AC 240; *Tracy v Mandalay Pty Ltd* (1953) 88 CLR 215. Through full disclosure the promoters are to place the company in a position where it can decide in an independent fashion whether to accept the promoter's offer: *Erlanger v New Sombrero Phosphate Co* at 1236; *Tracy v Mandalay Pty Ltd*.

Consequences of a breach of duty

[4.30] Although the company may not as yet exist, the promoter is accountable to it once formed. For example, a contract made by a promoter with the company will be voidable at the company's option in the absence of sufficient disclosure: *Erlanger v New Sombrero Phosphate Co* (1878) 3 App Cas 1218; *Tracy v Mandalay Pty Ltd* (1953) 88 CLR 215. If the company fails, the liquidator will be subrogated the right to set aside the contract and recover any money paid. If the promoter acquired and on-sold property to the company after its formation, the company may retain the property and sue for an account of profits: *Gluckstein v Barnes* [1900] AC 240; *Tracy v Mandalay Pty Ltd*. If, however, the property was acquired by the promoter before the company's creation, the company's remedies are strict alternatives: rescission or retention of the property at the contract price: *Tracy v Mandalay Pty Ltd*. Thus, the company cannot affirm the contract and ask the court for an order, for example, varying the purchase price.

Where the promoter makes an indirect secret profit by, for example, receiving a reward for arranging for a third party to contract with the company, the promoter is again liable to account to the company for the profit: *Whaley Bridge Calico Printing Co v Green* (1880) 5 QBD 109.

[4.40] There are a number of statutory provisions dealing with the liability of promoters. Generally these pertain to false or misleading disclosure documents (Chap 6D of the *Corporations Act*, see further

Chapter 8) or promoters' liability for pre-registration contracts, s 131. The latter topic is discussed below.

Pre-registration Contracts

Pre-registration contracts at common law

Liability of the company

[4.50] Until a company is registered it does not have legal identity and thus cannot contract in its own name. Despite the company's non-existence, promoters often purport to contract on its behalf before registration. This can occur for many legitimate commercial reasons. Business premises, for example, might need to be organised before the company is incorporated. Engaging a solicitor to register the company is itself a pre-registration contract. See *Re National Motor Mail-Coach Co Ltd* [1908] 2 Ch 515. The issue therefore is 'who is liable under such pre-registration contracts?'

It will be seen below that the common law governing liability for pre-registration contracts has been displaced by statutory rules detailed in ss 131-132: s 133. Nevertheless, it is useful to précis the common law position because it assists in understanding the goals sought to be achieved by the statutory regime. At common law, these contracts are not binding on the company once registered because an agent/promoter cannot act for a non-existent principal: *Black v Smallwood* [1966] ALR 744. As the company has not as yet been registered, it cannot act as a principal in an agency relationship. Moreover, the company cannot affirm or ratify the contract once registered: *Kelner v Baxter* (1866) LR 2 CP 174 at 183 and 185. The doctrine of ratification requires the principal to have been able to enter into the contract itself when the agent contracted. Thus, once registered, the company must negotiate afresh or at least substitute the pre-registration contract with a new contract. This is called novating the contract. It is not sufficient that the company act in accordance with the terms of the contract. It must actually renegotiate the contract: *Vickery v Woods* (1952) 85 CLR 336 at 344-345.

Liability of the promoter

[4.60] At common law, the promoter was not necessarily personally liable under the pre-registration contract. The promoter was only liable if the parties intended him or her to be personally liable. As Fullagar J explained in *Summergreene v Parker* (1950) 80 CLR 304 at 323-324, where all parties were aware that the company was not yet in existence and the consideration had been fully executed, there was a strong presumption that the parties intended the promoter to be personally liable:

> Where A, purporting to act as agent for the non-existent principal, purports to make a binding contract with B, and the circumstances are such that B would suppose that a binding contract had been made, there must be a strong

presumption that A meant to bind him personally. Where, as in *Kelner v Baxter*, the consideration on B's part has been fully executed in reliance on the existence of a contract binding on somebody, the presumption could, I should imagine, only be rebutted in very exceptional circumstances. But the fundamental question in every case must be what the parties intended or must be fairly understood to have intended.

In determining whether parties were aware that the company was not yet in existence and whether they intended to contract with the company or the promoter personally, the language used in the contract was often crucial. Thus, in *Kelner v Baxter* (1866) LR 2 CP 174 the plaintiff, a wine merchant, addressed a written offer to the company's promoters 'on behalf of the proposed' company for the purchase of wine. It was held that as a matter of construction, the inclusion of the word 'proposed' in the offer indicated that the plaintiff knew the company was not in existence. For the contract to be effective the parties must have intended the promoters to be personally liable.

By contrast, where the contracting parties believed the company to be in existence, the language in the contract would often reflect an intention to contract with the company and it was more difficult to assume they intended the promoters to be personally liable. Thus, in the leading Australian case, *Black v Smallwood* [1966] ALR 744, the appellants had purported to contract for the sale of land to Western Suburbs Holdings Pty Ltd. The contract was signed in the company's name. Under the company's name the promoters signed their own names, purportedly as directors. It was subsequently found that Western Suburbs Holdings Pty Ltd was not incorporated at the time of the contracting, but all parties believed that it had been. The court held the promoters were not liable to complete the contract. In light of the facts that both parties believed the company was incorporated, as a matter of construction the contract was not intended to make the promoters liable. The contract was in the company's name and the promoters had signed as directors of that company in the belief that the company had been formed and they were directors of that company. The purported contract was consequently held to be a nullity as the supposed purchaser did not exist when it was made. See also *Newborne v Sensolid (Great Britain) Ltd* [1954] 1 QB 45.

Breach of warranty of authority

[4.70] In *Black v Smallwood* [1966] ALR 744, Windeyer J suggested that persons who entered into a pre-registration contract might be able to sue the promoters for a breach of the warranty that the company existed and that the promoters were authorised agents of the company. Contra Parker J in *Newborne v Sensolid (Great Britain) Ltd* [1954] 1 QB 45. If this remedy was available there was also an issue as to the measure of damages for such a breach. It had been suggested that the measure of damages was the amount that the third party would have received if they had been successful against the principal, that is, the company. If the company was insolvent, the damages available from the agent would, therefore, only be nominal. A contrary view was, however, adopted by the court in *Collen v Wright* (1857) 120 ER 241. In that case the court considered a claim for breach of warranty of authority, but it should be noted the case did not involve a pre-registration contract, nor for that matter a company. The court held the measure of damages was the amount which equated with the substantive damages stemming from the failure to execute the subject lease, rather than focusing on the solvency of the purported principal, Mr Gardner.

Note, at common law, the only other possible remedies available to innocent third parties included the tortious remedies of deceit and negligent misstatement.

Reimbursement of promoter's costs

[4.80] Before turning to pre-registration contracts under the *Corporations Act*, one further related issued should be addressed. If the promoter incurs expenses before the company is registered, can that person require the company to reimburse him or her once it is incorporated? At common law, a promoter cannot require the newly formed company to reimburse any costs incurred in the company's initial promotion: *Re National Motor Mail-Coach Co Ltd* [1908] 2 Ch 515; *Kelner v Baxter* (1866) LR 2 CP 174. Essentially the payments are treated by the courts as a gift to the unformed company: *Re National Motor Mail-Coach Co Ltd*. While this is generally not a problem in practice as the promoters are normally the founding shareholders and directors and thus can ensure reimbursement, if the company, through its board, refuses to do so, the promoter has no remedy.

While s 122 of the *Corporations Act* allows these expenses to be paid out of the company's assets, the section only confers a discretion ('may be paid') and thus does not purport to confer a right on the promoter.

Pre-registration contracts under the Corporations Act

Introduction

[4.90] Part 2B.3 of the *Corporations Act* attempts to deal with the practical difficulties stemming from the inability of companies to ratify pre-registration contracts and the unfairness that may stem from an application of the above common law rules. Section 131(1) reverses the common law position by allowing companies in certain cases to ratify pre-registration contracts and thereby become bound by the contract. Perhaps even more importantly, the legislation also provides that the promoter should share responsibility for any loss to the third party if the company is not formed or does not subsequently ratify the contract (s 131(2)) or the company fails to meet its obligations under a ratified pre-registration contract: s 131(4). Where the company is registered, but does not ratify the contract or enter into a substitute contract, the courts also have a residuary discretion to make such orders as they consider appropriate in the circumstances: s 131(3). These include orders requiring the company to pay all, or part, of the damages payable by the promoter, transfer property received under the contract to the third party to the contract and/or pay an amount to the third party to the contract: s 131(3).

[4.100] A useful way of approaching a pre-registration contract under the Act is to consider the following issues in turn:

- Has a person entered into, or purported to enter into, a contract on behalf of, or for the benefit of, the company?: s 131(1);
- Was the contract entered into before the company was registered?: s 131(1);
- Was the company subsequently registered?: s 131(2);
- Is this registered company the unregistered company or is it reasonably identifiable with the unregistered company?: s 131(1);
- Has that company ratified or substituted the pre-registration contract?: s 131(1) and (2);
- Was any ratification within the time agreed to by the parties to the contract or if there is no time agreed, within a reasonable time of the contract?: s 131(1) and (2); and
- Has the third party released the promoter from personal liability?: s 132(1).

Person contracting on behalf of or for the benefit of the company

Agency

[4.110] This element of s 131(1) requires consideration of two sub-issues. First, the 'person' who enters into the contract within s 131(1) is the person who faces potential liability for the pre-registration contract under s 131(2). Technically, under the legislation it is this person, and not the promoters as a whole, who faces liability under the pre-registration contract: *Bay v Illawarra Stationery Supplies Pty Ltd* (1986) 4 ACLC 429 at 430. While, as noted above, s 133 provides that Part 2B.3 replaces any rights and liabilities anyone would otherwise have under the pre-registration contract, the court in *Bay v Illawarra Stationery Supplies Pty Ltd* at 430 asserted that a predecessor to the current provisions did not exclude the law of agency. Consequently, if the 'person' who is liable under s 131(2) is acting as an agent for the promoters, that liability will be passed to the principals under that contract – the promoters: *Bay v Illawarra Stationery Supplies Pty Ltd* at 430-431.

Bay v Illawarra Stationery Supplies Pty Ltd
Supreme Court of New South Wales: Grove J
(1986) 4 ACLC 429

The respondent brought an action against the four defendants, the 'promoters', for payment of goods sold and delivered. Stationery was acquired from the respondent by Dyke, allegedly the defendants' agent, through a credit account in the name of Australian Sports and Health Pty Ltd, a non-existent company. The promoters acquired, and were appointed as directors to, a pre-existing shelf company. They intended to change its name to Australian Sports and Health Pty Ltd, but were prevented from making the change. One of the defendants, Bay, challenged the first instance court's finding for the respondent on the basis that the legislation only authorised imposing liability on Dyke, the person who had actually executed the contract.

The court noted that the Act did not extend liability beyond the person(s) who entered into the pre-registration contract, but concluded there to be nothing in the terms of the legislation that purported to exclude the law of agency. Thus, the Act could impose liability on the person who entered into the pre-registration contract, but that liability may in turn flow to any principal. On the facts, however, the court found that Dyke was not acting as an authorised agent for the appellant and thus the appeal was allowed.

Grove J: **[430]** At various times, Osborn, Bay, Hughes and Pack became interested in a proposal for an enterprise which they intended to conduct through a company to be styled Australian Sports and Health Pty Ltd. I shall refer to these four men collectively as 'the venturers'. The services of a man named Dyke were acquired for the purpose of utilising his reputed skills in budget and cash flow controls. Stationery and like requisites were acquired from the respondent which on 27 August 1982 opened a credit account in the name Australian Sports and Health Pty Limited, a non-existent company. The person who made this arrangement was Mr Dyke. Subsequent to the establishment of this account, which was in essence the entry of a contract to supply goods, the venturers were appointed directors of a company called Scrivuhud Pty Limited. This was I gather, in existence as a shelf company and the venturers intended applying for a change of name to Australian Sports and Health Pty Limited. This was never achieved because the Corporate Affairs Commission withheld approval. The appointment as directors took place on 9 September 1982. The appellant resigned as a director of Scrivuhud Pty Limited on 14 October 1982. ...

[431] Section 81 does not declare liability beyond the person or persons who execute on behalf of the non-existent company but nothing in its terms purports to exclude any rights or obligations flowing between that person or those persons and any principal nor does it otherwise impugn the doctrines of agency ...

[I]t does not seem incompatible with the Code provision that, on the one hand s 81 imposes liability upon the person who executes as agent of the non-existent company and, contemporaneously on the other, it is established that the person who executed was the agent of a real person or corporation. Hypotheticals may usefully demonstrate. A contractor seeking a remedy can sue the person who executed (s 81). That person can, either in a separate action or by cross-claim, institute proceedings against his principal in a conventional action by an agent seeking indemnity from his principal. The availability of this 'two-step' procedure was conceded by counsel for the appellant. The law to be applied can be no different if the plaintiff seeks a remedy directly against the principal: what the plaintiff assumes is an additional evidentiary burden of establishing in his own case the existence of the agency between the defendant sued and the person who executed the contract on behalf of the non-existent company.

It is unnecessary for me to express a concluded view about the submission. If my provisional view is wrong the appellant is entitled to succeed. If it is correct he will succeed by reason of the absence of any evidence upon which a finding could be made that on 27 August 1982 Dyke was the agent of the appellant. ...

[432] In summary, I hold that the appellant did not purport to execute a contract on behalf of a non-existent company within the meaning of s 81 of the Companies Code and there is no evidence to support a finding that at the time Dyke did so he was an agent of the appellant. The appellant was therefore not liable to have judgment entered against him.

There is no reason to doubt that *Bay v Illawarra Stationery Supplies Pty Ltd* (1986) 4 ACLC 429 will also be applicable to the current provision.

Types of contracts

[4.120] The second sub-issue regarding this element of s 131(1) is that the section applies where the person 'enters into, or purports to enter into, a contract on behalf of, or for the benefit of, a company before it is registered'. The language used in s 131(1) to identify the contractual relations within the legislation's scope is more general than that used by its predecessor, s 183(1)(a). The phrase 'on behalf of, or for the benefit of, a company' would appear to extend to all contractual capacities in which a promoter might act, including that of purported principal.

Contract pre-registration

[4.130] Under s 131(1) the contract must be entered into on behalf of the 'company before it is registered'. Similarly, the liability imposed under s 131(2) pertains to the 'pre-registration contract'. Thus, s 131 and its predecessors are technically confined to situations where the company did not exist when the pre-registration contract was executed: *Commonwealth Bank of Australia v Australian Solar Information Pty Ltd* (1987) 5 ACLC 124.

This issue may arise in three contexts. First, where persons believe the company is yet to be incorporated and purport to enter into a pre-registration contract, yet in fact the company is incorporated. As the precedent in *Commonwealth Bank of Australia v Australian Solar Information Pty Ltd* indicates, ss 131-133 do not apply to such situations as the contract is not a pre-registration contract. Second, and similarly, it may be thought by lay persons that by changing a company's name they are thereby creating a new corporate entity and thus any contractual relations entered into before the change in name are pre-registration contracts. This was specifically in issue in *Commonwealth Bank of Australia v Australian Solar Information Pty Ltd* where the court confirmed that a change of name does not create a new corporate entity. This is a logical conclusion because when a company is registered it is designated an Australian Company Number ('ACN') and that number does not change with a registration of change of name. Third, the courts have yet to exhaustively consider the application of the statutory regime governing pre-registration contracts to shelf companies. While the court in *Commonwealth Bank of Australia v Australian Solar Information Pty Ltd* acknowledged that the Act may apply to a shelf company that was both formed and acquired after the pre-registration contract, the courts are yet to consider the difficult question of a contract entered into before a shelf company was acquired, but after its formation. To date the most extensive discussion of these issues can be found in *Commonwealth Bank of Australia v Australian Solar Information Pty Ltd*.

Commonwealth Bank of Australia v Australian Solar Information Pty Ltd
Supreme Court of Queensland: Master Weld
(1987) 5 ACLC 124

The defendant's promoters had acquired a shelf company, Towrang Pty Ltd. On 4 March 1986 the promoters changed the company's name to Australian Solar Information Pty Ltd. Before the name change, the company incurred debts due to the plaintiff. The plaintiff sought to enforce these debts through, *inter alia*, a predecessor to s 131. The plaintiff asserted that from 4 March 1986, with the change in name, the company, Australian Solar Information Pty Ltd, was a duly incorporated company capable of being sued, and thus the alleged contract of approximately 15 January 1986 was a pre-registration contract. The defendant brought an application to strike out this part of the plaintiff's statement of claim on the basis the company was incorporated at the time of the contract in January 1986.

The court rejected the plaintiff's suggestion that the defendant company was a 'proposed company' that had not been duly incorporated until 4 March 1986. The court held that for the predecessor to ss 131-133 to apply there must be an absence of formation at the time and a subsequent formation of a company after the contract. Contrary to the plaintiff's suggestion, the change of name did not create a new entity within the terms required under the equivalent to ss 131-133. Thus, if Towrang Pty Ltd was in existence before the contract, these provisions were *prima facie* inapplicable. The court added, however, that these provisions mighty apply where the promoter executes the contract in the name of, or as an agent for, a then non-existent company, intending to form that company, where that intention is 'fulfilled by the acquisition of a "shelf" company formed subsequently (and acquired subsequently) to the contract'. As Towrang Pty Ltd may have satisfied these prerequisites, the application to strike out this part of the statement of claim was dismissed.

> **Master Weld:** **[125]** [O]n 4 March 1986, Towrang Pty Ltd changed its name to Australian Solar Information Pty Ltd ...
>
> **[126]** I should be inclined to conclude that s 81 is not intended to refer to the situation where an existing company has changed its name to the name in question, at least, where the company has been incorporated at the time at which it is alleged that a person has executed a contract in the name of the company or has purported to enter into a contract as agent or trustee of the

company. It will be noted that s 81 commences with a series of definitions directing how various expressions in the section shall be construed. It, in fact, uses two terms, 'a non-existent company' and a 'proposed company.' It is, however, clear from sub-s (1) that a proposed company must be a non-existent company, for example, s 81(1)((b) covers both of the bases referred to in ss 81(1)(a)(i) and (ii), and s 81(1)(c) speaks of formation of the company in relation to both of the cases which appear in s 81(1)(a) and deals with them in the sub paras designated, s 81(1)(c)(i) and (ii) respectively. Subsequent subss (2), (3), (4), (5), (7), (10) and (12) contain indications of that construction. See also C Gerrard, "Stamps Duty Implications of Pre-Incorporation Contracts" (1984) 12 ABLR 266 at pp 275 and 277, particularly the passages on those pages referring to 'future formation' and 'subsequent formation.' It would appear, therefore, that for s 81 to apply, the absence of formation at the time and the subsequent formation of a company is essential after the events in question.

The idea of formation is consistent through the Code. See, for example, the definitions in s 5(1) of the 'company limited by guarantee', 'company limited by shares" and 'corporation' and see the use of that term in s 33(1). It is clear that under s 65(5) on a change of name, a new company or a company is not formed. Similarly it is clear under s 69(1) that conversion by change of status does not bring into existence a company or a new company; and similarly, s 70, see ss 69(8) and 70(5).

It appears to me therefore that the change in name ... is of no significance in determining the application of s 81 to the material facts. If that, however, is put aside s 81 may apply because the person who executed the contract in the name Australian Solar Information Pty Ltd or who entered into the contract as an agent or trustee for a company by that name which was a non-existent company as alleged, may have intended formation of a company. It is arguable that that intention may be fulfilled by the acquisition of a 'shelf' company formed subsequently (and acquired subsequently) to the 'contract' in question. Therefore, the material facts alleged in this part may be capable of establishment by evidence and give rise to the reliefs sought, not because of the change of name but because of the facts alleged to which change of name may be entirely irrelevant. The application, therefore, to strike out this part of the statement of claim is dismissed.

Again, the reasoning in *Commonwealth Bank of Australia v Australian Solar Information Pty Ltd* is equally applicable to the current provisions. One aspect of the decision that has yet to be considered by the courts relates to its addendum that the subsequent purchase of a shelf company may satisfy the requirements of the statutory regime. Moreover, if the focus is on the intent of the person at the time of executing the pre-registration contract, this comment could be taken further and the subsequent acquisition of a shelf company that was formed before the pre-registration contract could satisfy s 131. If the focus is upon the person purporting to enter into a contract when he or she has not as yet registered a company, the subsequent purchase of even a pre-registered shelf company would not be contrary to the intended scope of the legislation.

Registration of the company or reasonably identifiable company

Registration

[4.140] It is necessary to note whether the company was subsequently registered for two reasons. First, and obviously, to ratify the contract under s 131(1) the proposed company must be registered. Perhaps more importantly, under s 131(2) the person who entered into the pre-registration contract is liable under that contract if the company is not registered.

Note in regard to this latter point the prior requirement that the company be formed within a reasonable time (s 183(2)) has not been replicated in s 131. The only reference in s 131(1) to a reasonable time is the requirement that the contract be ratified in a reasonable time from the date of the pre-registration contract. From a practical point of view this will also necessitate a timely formation of the company.

Company or reasonably identifiable company

[4.150] Under s 131(1), in order for the company to be able to ratify the contract, it must either be 'the' proposed company or reasonably identifiable with that company. The use of the words 'reasonably identifiable' raises difficult questions of fact. While the intention underlying s 131(1) was presumably not to exclude companies that differ in some non-essential way, such as the companies' names, no guidance is given as to the importance of differences in:

- companies' objects;
- type of company, that is, public or proprietary;
- directors; or
- members' liability, for example, no-liability or unlimited liability.

The change would probably have to be quite material – such as a change in members' liability, prejudicing the third party's rights under the contract – before it will be held to prevent an effective ratification of the contract.

On a practical level, in the absence of some form of description of the company in the pre-registration contract or the negotiations surrounding such, it may be difficult to establish the necessary correspondence of identity.

Ratified or substituted pre-registration contract

What amounts to ratification?

[4.160] Once registered the company has the option of ratifying the contract. Unlike its predecessor (ss 182 and 183(13)), Part 2B.3 does not specify how a company may ratify a contract. Thus, how a company may ratify a contract will be determined by its general powers to enter into contractual relations. Under s 126 the company's power to 'make, vary, ratify or discharge a contract' may be exercised by an individual with express or implied authority to act on the company's behalf. Depending on the terms of the company's constitution which may specify it is necessary to execute contracts using the company seal, this authority may be invoked with or without the use of the common seal: s 126(1). Again, depending on the terms of the company's constitution, the company may execute a document without using a common seal if the document is signed by:

- two directors;
- a director and a company secretary; or
- in the case of a sole director/company secretary of a proprietary company, that director: s 127(1).

Similarly, the company may execute a document by affixing the common seal and such being witnessed by the person(s) specified in s 127(1): s 127(2).

It has been suggested that a contract might be ratified by part performance of the contract: Tomasic, 2002, p 205; Cassidy, 2003, p 67. At first glance this is plausible given s 124(1) provides that companies have the legal capacity and powers of an individual. As an individual can incur contractual responsibilities through part performance, it would appear logical that a company could equally be liable in contract through part performance. However, the legislative framework of Part 2B.3 may suggest otherwise. It will be seen that when the company has not ratified the contract the court has a discretion to order the company to return property it may have received under the pre-registration contract: s 131(3). This would suggest that a partly performed contract does not imply a ratification of the pre-registration contract and only formal ratification under ss 126 and 127 is sufficient. Alternatively, this provision may be intended to apply where the third party, but not the company, has partly performed the contract through the delivery of property. The matter continues to be unclear.

What amounts to a substitution?

[4.170] Under s 131(2) a promoter escapes 'primary' liability (see below) under a pre-registration contract when the contract is either ratified or substituted within the time limits specified by the parties or a reasonable time. A contract which substitutes the pre-registration contract may be entered into in the same manner as any other contract in accordance with the principles delineated in ss 124, 126 and 127. Whether a new contract sufficiently 'substitutes' the pre-registration contract to satisfy s 131(2) may, however, be a difficult question unless the contracts are very similar or the new contract expressly states that it is in substitution of the original contract.

Ultra vires

[4.180] The abolition of the *ultra vires* doctrine under s 125 ensures that a company may ratify or substitute a contract outside its objects. A variation in the objects of the proposed company and the ratifying company may, however, prevent the company being considered 'reasonably identifiable' as required by s 131(1). Moreover, under s 140(1), a ratification or substituted contract that is contrary to an objects clause would contravene the statutory contract. See further the discussion of these issues in Chapter 6.

Ratification or substitution within time limits

[4.190] For the company to be *prima facie* bound by the contract under s 131(1), the contract must be ratified within the time agreed to by the parties to the contract or, if there is no agreed time, within a reasonable time of the contract being entered into. Similarly, a promoter will not be liable to pay damages under s 131(2) if the company has ratified or substituted the contract within these temporal requirements. The notion of 'reasonable time' is not defined and will be a question of fact to be determined on a case-by-case basis. It would be thought, however, that the ratification of pre-registration contracts would be a matter of priority upon the registration of the company. For a recent case when a pre-registration contract was not ratified within the time agreed to by the parties, see *Aztech Science Pty Ltd v Atlanta Aerospace (Woy Woy) Pty Ltd* [2004] NSWSC 967.

Effect of ratification

[4.200] If ratification occurs in time, the company becomes bound by, and entitled to the benefits under, the contract: s 131(1). As noted above, s 133 provides that these rights and liabilities are in substitution for any rights the parties may have apart from Part 2B.3.

While the company has what may be referred to as 'primary' liability under the ratified contract (s 131(1)), if the company fails to fulfil all or part of its obligations under the contract and the person has not been released from liability under s 132(1), the court may order the person who entered into the pre-registration contract to pay all or part of the damages the company is ordered to pay for the breach: s 131(4). The extension of what may be called 'secondary' liability to this person is designed to ensure that the innocent third party will not be left without a remedy where, *inter alia*, the person ensures that the company ratifies the contract, but with no intention of actually meeting its contractual obligations.

Effect of no ratification or substitution

[4.210] If the company is not registered, or the contract is not ratified or substituted in time, the person who entered into the pre-registration contract is liable to pay the third party damages: s 131(2). The person does not, however, become the principal under the contract and thus is not entitled to the benefits of the contract. The person is only subjected to the negative aspects of the contract. The quantum of damages is tied to the amount that the company would be liable to pay, rather than the amount obtainable from the company. The distinction is crucial for if the latter criterion were applicable, the person's liability would be nominal were the company insolvent or with little capital backing.

If proceedings are brought against the person for damages under s 131(2) because a registered company has not ratified or substituted the pre-registration contract, the court may make such orders against the company that it thinks appropriate, including that the company:

- pay the whole or part of any damages for which the promoter is liable;
- transfer any property it has received as a result of the contract; and/or
- pay an amount to a party to the contract: s 131(3).

Thus, where it would be unfair for a company that refuses to ratify or substitute a contract to be able to retain any benefits it has received under the contract, the court may order it to return property or contribute to the damages payable under the pre-registration contract.

Release from liability

[4.220] The person who entered into the pre-registration contract will be released from liability where a party to the contract releases the promoter from liability under s 131 by signing a release: s 132(1). The person may release the promoter from part or all of their liability: s 132(1). The use of singular language in s 132(1), namely 'A party', indicates one party to the contract may release a promoter with or without the agreement of any other contracting parties. Section 132(1) does not specify any particular point when the release must occur. Thus, it may be included in the original contract or stem from subsequent negotiations/events.

Note, a release does not make the company liable. The company will only be liable in accordance with s 131.

Trustee's right of indemnity

[4.230] As noted above, s 131(1) extends to contracts entered into by a person on behalf of, or for the benefit of, the proposed company. This would include a person acting as a trustee of a pre-registration company. At common law, a person who contracts as a trustee for an unidentifiable beneficiary is personally liable under that contract, but enjoys in certain cases a right to be indemnified by the beneficiary once ascertained. Section 132(2) provides that, even where a person purports to contract as a trustee of a proposed company, a promoter's liability under Part 2B.3 cannot be avoided by seeking an indemnity from the company.

Review question

Fred, Gertie and David have decided to incorporate a company to manufacture sparkling wine. It is proposed the company's name will be 'Champers Pty Ltd'. Fred enters into a contract on behalf of the proposed company for the purchase and delivery of a grape-picking machine. Two weeks later a shelf company is purchased. The company's name is

Grog Ltd. David, Gertie, Fred and Fred's spouse, Cheryl, are appointed directors.

Soon after the purchase of the shelf company, a meeting is held at which Fred proposes the grape-picking machinery contract should be ratified by Grog Ltd. Gertie asserts that:
- the company cannot ratify the contract; and
- Fred should not have entered into the contract, so he should bear all the liability under its terms.

Advise Fred as to who is liable under the contract for the purchase of the grape-picking machinery and as to the correctness of Gertie's statements.

Further reading

Cassidy, *Concise Corporations Law* (4th ed, Federation Press, Sydney, 2003) ch 4
Ford, Austin and Ramsay, *Ford's Principles of Corporations Law* (11th ed, Butterworths, Sydney, 2003) ch 5
Gross, 'Who is a Company Promoter' (1970) 86 *LQR* 493
Hambrook, 'Pre-incorporation contracts and the National Companies Code: What does section 81 really mean?' (1982) 8 *Adel L Rev* 119
McKenzie, 'Legal Status of the Unborn Company' (1973) 5 *NZULR* 211

References Chapter 4

Cassidy, *Concise Corporations Law* (4th ed, Federation Press, Sydney, 2003)
Tomasic, Jackson and Woellner *Corporations Law: Principles, Policy and Process* (4th ed, Butterworths, Sydney, 2002)

5

Registration of Corporations

Overview

The factors relevant to the decision to conduct a business through, *inter alia*, a company have been examined in Chapter 2. Similarly, the consequences of registering of a company have been considered in Chapter 3. This chapter examines the process of registration under the *Corporations Act* 2001 (Cth) ('*Corporations Act*'). While the primary focus of this chapter is the registration of new companies, the chapter also briefly considers transfers of registration to the *Corporations Act* and the registration of 'non-companies' under the Act. More specifically, this includes an examination of the registration of:

- companies on their initial registration under Chap 2A;
- companies registered under the *Corporation Act's* predecessors under s 1378;
- companies wishing to transfer their registration to another State or Territory under s 119A(3);
- non-companies wishing to transfer the source of their incorporation to the *Corporations Act* under Part 5B.1;
- registrable Australian bodies under Div 1 of Part 5B.2; and
- foreign companies under Div 2 of Part 5B.2.

In regard to the registration of 'new' companies under Chap 2A, the chapter considers the prerequisites to registration, the application for registration, the process of registration and post-registration requirements. It will be seen that this entails primarily a consideration of the *Corporations Act*, rather than case law.

Registration of 'New' Companies

'Shelf' companies

[5.10] Before the process of registering a new company under Chap 2A is considered, the notion of a 'shelf' company requires brief mention. In practice, clients often purchase a 'shelf' company, rather than instruct their advisors to incorporate a new company. Shelf companies are companies that have been registered but are inactive. Generally, the existence of a shelf company can arise in two ways. First, lawyers and accountants often keep a stock of newly registered companies available for purchase by clients that have not been previously used to conduct a business. Second, lawyers and accountants sometimes buy defunct companies from clients who no longer need that corporate vehicle. In both cases purchasing a shelf company allows clients to avoid the delays involved in the registration process. Care must be taken, however, where the company has been previously used to ensure that it has no actual or potential liabilities for which the company may subsequently have to be paid.

Note that the name of the shelf company may be changed under s 157(1) if the company passes a special resolution and lodges with ASIC a copy of the resolution and the prescribed application form (Form 410), discussed below.

Prerequisites to registration

[5.20] Where a client's needs are more specific, it may be necessary to register a new company through the process outlined in Chap 2A of the *Corporations Act*. There are a number of prerequisites that must be met before the application form for registration may be lodged with ASIC.

Membership

[5.30] Any person(s), whether natural or corporate, can incorporate to pursue a lawful purpose. As noted in Chapter 2, today a single person may register a company: s 114.

Reservation of company name

[5.40] While reserving the company's name is not an essential prerequisite to registration (s 152(1)), if the incorporators wish the company to be registered under a particular name, it is best practice to reserve the name under s 152(1) before registration by completing Form 410. (See <www.asic.gov.au> – 'Download ASIC forms'.) Instead of reserving a company name, the company may simply adopt its Australian Company Number ('ACN') as its name: s 148(1). The ACN is a nine-digit number that is unique to each company and obtained on registration.

Under s 152(1) and (2), if a person has lodged an application to reserve a name and that name is available, ASIC must reserve the proposed name for two months from the date of the lodgment. ASIC will confirm the reservation by letter, advising the expiry date of the reservation and the reservation number that needs to be stated on the application for registration, Form 201. Form 410 may also be used to obtain an extension of the period for which the name is reserved. The request must be made before the lapsing of the first period of reservation: s 152(2). ASIC may then extend the period of reservation by a further two months: s 152(2).

A name may not be reserved in the absence of the Minister's written consent (s 147(2)) if another company has already reserved the identical name or another person has registered such under the national business names register: s 147(1)(a) and (b). In addition, the name may not be reserved if the name has been declared by the regulations (see *Cor-*

porations Regulations regs 4.2.01 and 4.2.02) to be unacceptable for registration: s 147(1)(c). Thus, in *Little v ASC* (1996) 22 ACSR 226 the name 'Virgin Mary's Pty Ltd' was held to unacceptable under reg 4.2.01(1)(a)(ii) as it was likely to cause offence to members of the Anglican, Roman Catholic and Islamic faiths who hold the Virgin Mary in high veneration.

[5.50] Under s 123(1), if the company has a common seal, this must display the company's name and ACN. If the last nine digits of a company's Australian Business Number ('ABN') are the same as its ACN, from 1 July 2003 the company has a choice of using either its ABN or ACN on its common seal: s 123(1).

Subject to ss 154 and 155, under s 153 the company's name and ACN must be set out on all public documents and negotiable instruments. Again, if the last nine digits of a company's ABN are the same as its ACN, from 1 July 2003 the company has a choice of using either its ABN or ACN with the company name on all public documents and negotiable instruments: s 153(2).

More generally, under s 1344, if the last nine digits of a company's ABN are the same as its ACN, from 1 July 2003 the company has a choice of using either its ABN or ACN when required/permitted by any Commonwealth law administered by ASIC.

In addition, s 144(1) requires the name of the company to be prominently displayed at every place where its business is carried on that is accessible to the public. In the case of public companies, it must also be displayed at its registered office: s 144(2).

Consent of director/secretary

[5.60] The written, signed consent of each director and secretary whom it is proposed that the members will appoint must be obtained before applying for registration: ss 117(2) and (5), 201D and 204C. The company breaches the Act if it fails to receive such consent before the appointment: ss 201D(1) and 204C(1). Once the company is registered, these consents must be retained with the company's records: ss 117(5), 201D(2) and 204C(2). The details of those persons who have consented to be directors and/or secretary are also included in the application for registration, discussed below: s 117(2)(d), (e) and (f).

Constitution

[5.70] As will be seen in the next chapter, generally a company no longer needs a constitution. Instead, the company can simply use the model rules prescribed in the *Corporations Act*, known as 'replaceable rules'. If, however, it is intended to displace, modify or add to the replaceable rules, a constitution will need to be drafted. This document must be retained with the company's records. Only a public company that wishes to be governed by a written constitution on its registration must lodge that constitution with their application for registration, discussed below: s 117(3). The corporate constitution is discussed in more detail in the next chapter.

Application for registration

[5.80] To register a company, the prescribed form, Form 201, Application for registration as an Australian company, must be lodged: s 117(1) and (4). (See <www.asic.gov.au> – 'Download ASIC forms'.) Section 117(2) prescribes the information that must be included in the application. This includes the type of company, the company's proposed name (unless it is to be the ACN), the reservation number for any reserved company name, the details of the proposed members, directors and company secretary, details of share capital or guarantee and the address of the proposed registered office and principal place of business.

As noted in Chapter 2, while all companies are required to have a registered office (s 142(1)), proprietary companies are no longer required to open the company's registered office to the public during certain hours: s 145. For this reason, only public companies are required to state in the application their proposed opening hours, unless they are the standard opening hours of 10 am – 12 noon and 2 – 4 pm each business day: ss 9 and 117(2)(h). If the registered office is not occupied by the company, but rather a third party, such as the company's accountant or solicitor, the company must have the written consent of that person to use that address as its registered office: s 100(1). This consent document does not have to accompany the application, but should be retained with the company's records so that it may be produced to ASIC if required: s 100(2).

The applicant must sign the application or where there is no separate applicant, a member, director or secretary must sign as applicant.

Documents to accompany application for registration

[5.90] As noted above, where the application is to register a public company and the incorporators wish to be governed by a written constitution on the company's registration, a copy of the constitution must be lodged with the application for registration: s 117(3).

A public company that is limited by shares or an unlimited company must lodge additional documentation where it is proposed that shares be issued for non-cash consideration. The company must lodge either Form 208, Notification of details of shares allotted other than for cash, or, where issued pursuant to a written contract, a copy of that contract and Form 207Z, Certification of compliance with stamp duty law: ss 117(2)(l) and 254X(2).

All annexures must be signed and dated by the applicant.

Registration

[5.100] If the application is lodged in accordance with s 117, ASIC may register the company: s 118(1)(b). This involves the registration of the application and, where necessary, the company's constitution (if any). Under s 118(2) ASIC must keep a record of the registration.

Under s 1274(8) ASIC may refuse to register a company where, for example, Form 201 contains false or misleading information, errors or omissions. In turn, ASIC may then also request that, *inter alia*, the form be appropriately amended and resubmitted or a fresh document be submitted in its place: s 1274(8). ASIC may also require the applicant to provide further information to assist it in determining whether to refuse to receive or register a form.

Certificate of registration

[5.110] On registration, ASIC allots to the company its ACN (s 118(1)(a)) and issues a certificate of registration: s 118(1)(c). The certificate states the company's name and ACN, the type of company, that it is a company registered under the *Corporations Act* and the date of its registration: s 118(1)(c). This certificate provides conclusive evidence that all requirements for registration have been complied with and that the company was registered on the date specified: s 1274(7A); *Jubilee Cotton Mills Ltd v Lewis* [1924] AC 958; *HA Stephenson & Son Ltd v Gillanders Arbuthnot & Co* (1931) 45 CLR 476 at 498 and 500. Persons dealing with the company do not, therefore, have to inquire into the validity of the registration process and can deal with the company in confidence: *HA Stephenson & Son Ltd v Gillanders Arbuthnot & Co* at 498-501. Where facts cast doubt on the validity of the registration process, ASIC may, however, review the validity of the registration: *ASC v SIB Resources NL* (1991) 9 ACLC 1147 at 1153.

Effect of registration

[5.120] On and from the date of registration the company becomes a body corporate with the name specified in its certificate of registration: s 119. The company acquires the legal capacity of a natural person and can, for example, hold property, contract and sue and be sued: s 124(1). In addition, the company enjoys all the powers peculiar to a body corporate, such as the power to issue shares: s 124(1). A company's separate legal identity is considered in detail in Chapter 3.

Upon registration the persons specified in the application for registration as having consented to being a member, director and/or secretary become a member, director and/or secretary of the company: s 120(1). The shares to be taken up by the members specified in the application are taken to be issued to the members on registration: s 120(2).

Post-registration requirements

Common seal

[5.130] Under s 123(1), the company may have a common seal. It is common for companies to have a common seal and equally common that the company constitution (if any) provides that it may contract through the affixing of the common seal. See further s 127(2) in this regard. If the company is to have a common seal, this should be prepared immediately upon registration. As noted above, this must state the company's name and ACN: s 123(1).

Appointment of officers and auditors

[5.140] Post registration it is important to hold meetings of members and/or directors to pass any resolutions necessary to appoint company officers. As noted above, upon registration the persons specified in the application for registration as having consented to being a director and/or secretary become a director and/or secretary of the company: s 120(1). However, if this method has not been adopted, one of the first post-registration tasks is to appoint the company's directors/company secretary. To this end, once the certificate of registration has been received the subscribers should meet to appoint the directors. Again note that the written consent of the director(s) must be given before appointment and retained by the company: s 201D. In turn the directors should meet to appoint a company secretary: s 204D. Again, as noted above, the written consent of that person must be obtained before appointment and retained with the company's records: s 204C. See further Chapter 9 as to the appointment of directors and the company secretary. Notice of the personal details of a director or secretary must be lodged with ASIC within 28 days of appointment: s 205B. See Form 484 Change of Company Details (<www.asic.gov.au> – 'Download ASIC forms'.)

[5.150] Under s 252 of the *Income Tax Assessment Act* 1936 (Cth), every company carrying on business in Australia is required to appoint a public officer. This officer is responsible for ensuring that the company complies with its taxation obligations.

[5.160] Section 327(1) of the *Corporations Act* requires the directors of a public company to appoint an auditor within one month of registration if the general meeting has not made such an appointment. Where, however, the company is a proprietary company, the directors may, but are not required to, appoint an auditor if the general meeting has not made an appointment: s 325. Once again a signed consent to act as auditor must be obtained by the company before appointments: s 327(7)-(9).

Registers

[5.170] Once registered, the *Corporations Act* requires the company to maintain certain registers. The company is required to keep a register of its directors and secretary. ASIC must be notified of a change of officeholders within 28 days: s 205B. See again Form 484 Change of Company Details (<www.asic.gov.au> – 'Download ASIC forms'.) The company is also required to establish registers of:

- members: ss 168(1)(a) and 169;
- options granted to take up unissued shares: ss 168(1)(b) and 170;
- charges: s 271; and
- debenture-holders: s 1047.

Other documents that should be kept on the company's register include:

- certificate of registration;
- original executed copy of Constitution (if any) plus two photocopies;

- original consents; and
- common seal.

[5.180] A company's registers must be kept at:
- the company's registered office;
- the company's principal place of business;
- the place where the work involved in maintaining the register is conducted; or
- another place approved by ASIC: s 172(1).

Minute books

[5.190] Companies must create and maintain minute books in which the minutes of general meetings and directors meetings are to be entered: s 251A(1). As to the manner in which the minute books are to be kept and access to these records, see ss 251A-251B and 1306.

Share issues

[5.200] Where the company is limited by shares, shares are deemed to have been issued to the original subscribers at the date of incorporation: s 120(2). Where the company is deemed to have allotted shares under s 120(2) or has otherwise allotted shares, under s 254X the company must lodge a notice regarding the allotment within 28 days of issuing the shares. See again Form 484 'Change of Company Details' (<www.asic.gov.au> – 'Download ASIC forms').

Accounting records

[5.210] The *Corporations Act* requires companies to maintain specified records and make certain disclosures of financial matters. As noted in Chapter 2, these requirements are reduced in the case of small proprietary companies under Part 2M.3 unless ss 292(2), 293 or 294 apply.

Annual general meeting

[5.220] Only public companies are required to hold annual general meetings (AGM): s 250N. Section 250N(1) provides that a public company's first AGM must be held within 18 months of being registered. See further Chapter 11 regarding meetings, including AGMs.

Registration of Existing Entities

Companies registered under *Corporations Law*

[5.230] Under s 1378(1) all companies registered under the previous *Corporations Law* continue to be registered after the commencement of the *Corporations Act* as if they were duly registered under Part 2A.2 of the Act. Section 1378(1) does not have the effect of creating a new company, but rather facilitates the continuation of the company with the same characteristics and attributes it had before the commencement of the Act: s 1378(3). Thus, the company's classification according to the nature of its members' liability and its status as proprietary or public are preserved: s 1378(1) and (2). Similarly, its constitution, membership, ownership of property, rights and obligations before registration are not affected.

The company is taken to have been registered in the relevant State or Territory of the old *Corporations Law* under which the company was previously registered: s 1378(4). This is, however, subject to s 119A(3). Section 119A(3) provides that a company continues to be registered under the *Corporations Act* even if the State in which it was registered ceases to be a referring State, discussed in Chapter 1.

Transfer of registration of companies

[5.240] The members of a company may seek to transfer the company's registration to another State or Territory jurisdiction under s 119A(3). Under the *Corporations Act* such a transfer may occur with the consent of the Minister of the jurisdiction in which the company is currently registered: s 119A(3)(a)(i). Such consent is, however, unnecessary if the State in which the company was registered ceases to be a referring State: s 119A(3)(a). See again Chapter 1. In addition, a change in registration may be affected by complying with the procedure specified in the Regulations: s 119A(3)(b).

Transfer of registration by non-companies

[5.250] Part 5B.1 facilitates the registration under the *Corporations Act* of a body corporate that is not a company. The entity may be registered as one of the types of companies listed in s 601BA(1). This provision echoes the types of companies listed in s 112(1), discussed in Chapter 2. As a consequence, to be registered the entity must be of a class that is the same or substantially the same as the proposed type of company: s 601BC(8)(a). If members' liability is to be limited, the extent and manner in which it is limited must be detailed in the entity's constitution: s 601BC(8)(b).

A non-company is not eligible to be registered under the *Corporations Act* if it is an externally administered body corporate or a body corporate with respect to which an application has been made to wind up the company or for the approval of an arrangement or compromise. Evidence that the body does not fall into any of these categories must accompany the application: s 601BC(7).

A non-company may only apply to register under the *Corporations Act* if the law of its place of origin allows this and any requirements under that law have been satisfied: s 601BC(8)(d) and (e). If that law does not require the members, or a percentage of them, to consent to the transfer, s 601BC(8)(f)(i) requires the consent of 75% of the membership entitled to vote. Twenty-one days' notice of the meeting is required: s 601BC(8)(f)(ii).

To register the body as a company under Part 5B.1, the prescribed form must be lodged with ASIC: s 601BC(1) and (4). The application must state the details specified in s 601BC(2) and be accompanied by the documents required by s 601BC(3), (6), (7) and (8).

If the application is successful, ASIC registers the body as a company of the proposed type specified in the application and allots the company an ACN: s 601BD(1)(a) and (b). On registration, ASIC issues a certificate of registration under s 601BD(1)(c).

Registrable Australian Bodies

[5.260] Non-companies that transfer their registration under Part 5B.1 are to be contrasted with 'registrable Australian bodies' which must be registered under Div 1 of Part 5B.2 if they wish to carry on business in an Australian jurisdiction other than their place of formation: s 601CA. Registration under Part 5B.2 does not effect a transfer of registration. Moreover, if a transfer is effected under Part 5B.1, there is no need to comply with Div 1 of Part 5B.2 and any registration under that Part ceases: s 601BL(1).

Registrable Australian bodies include associations that have been incorporated or registered under statutes other than the *Corporations Act* or its predecessors. The definition in s 9 extends beyond body corporates and includes unincorporated bodies that under the law of their place of formation may sue or be sued, or hold property in the name of their secretary or an officer duly appointed for that purpose. The definition continues by excluding foreign companies, which must be registered under Div 2 of Part 5B.2, discussed below.

As noted above, registrable Australian bodies cannot carry on business outside their place of formation unless they transfer their registration to the *Corporations Act* or register under Div 1 of Part 5B.2: s 601CA. Subject to any legislative guidance, whether a company is carrying on business in a particular jurisdiction is a question of fact to be determined in light of all the circumstances of the case: *Luckins v Highway Motel (Carnarvon) Pty Ltd* (1975) 133 CLR 164 at 178 and 186. See further s 21.

If an application for registration under Div 1 of Part 5B.2 is lodged in the prescribed form and is accompanied by the documents listed in s 601CB, ASIC will register the body, issue a certificate of registration and allot the body an Australian Registered Body Number ('ARBN'): ss 601CB(g) and (h), 601CU(1).

Registrable Australian bodies registered under previous company legislation are deemed to be registered under the *Corporations Act*: s 1362CJ(1) and (2).

Foreign corporations

[5.270] As discussed above, foreign non-companies may transfer their registration to an Australian jurisdiction under Part 5B.1. If a body's registration is so transferred, there is no need to be registered under

Div 2 of Part 5B.2, discussed below, and any pre-existing registration under that Division will cease: s 601BL(1).

As noted above, s 9 excludes a foreign company from the notion of registrable Australian bodies. A foreign company is defined in s 9 to include both incorporated and unincorporated bodies formed outside Australia. To be a foreign company the unincorporated body must not have its head office or principal place of business in Australia and, again, must under the law of its place of formation be able to sue or be sued, or hold property in the name of its secretary or an officer duly appointed for that purpose: s 9(b)(ii) and (iii).

Such foreign companies are prohibited from carrying on business in Australia unless registered by ASIC under Div 2 of Part 5B.2 or an application for registration has been made and is still pending: s 601CD(1).

The procedure for registration is set out in s 601CE. If the appropriate form is lodged and the requirements of s 601CE satisfied, ASIC must enter the foreign company's name in a register of foreign companies, issue a certificate of registration and allot the company an ARBN: ss 601CE(h) and (j), 601CU(1). Before registration, however, the foreign company must appoint a local agent to be responsible for the company's obligations under the Act: ss 601CF, 601CG and 601CJ.

Foreign companies registered under previous company legislation are deemed to be registered under the *Corporations Act*: s 1362CJ(1) and (3).

Review question

In light of earlier advice you have given, a client has decided to register a small proprietary company to conduct the subject business. The proposed name of the company is 'Champers Pty Ltd'. You have checked the registers of company and business names and this name has not been adopted by another business/company. Nor in your view are any names similar enough to be misleading. You suggest that your business address be the company's registered office. You also suggest that in the initial stages of conducting the business the replaceable rules will suit the nature of the business so no separate constitution needs to be adopted at this stage.

Identify those documents that need to be completed and lodged with ASIC, identifying relevant statutory authorities. Indicate the order of lodgement where this is a relevant consideration. Also identify those documents that do not need to be lodged with ASIC, but need to be maintained with the company's records, again identifying relevant statutory authorities.

Further reading

<www.asic.gov.au> – 'Info for Companies: How to Form a Company' and 'Download ASIC forms'

Cassidy, *Concise Corporations Law* (4th ed, Federation Press, Sydney, 2003) ch 5

Ford, Austin and Ramsay, *Ford's Principles of Corporations Law* (11th ed, Butterworths, Sydney, 2003) ch 5

6

The Corporate Constitution

Overview

This chapter considers the corporate constitution. Before 1 July 1998, the corporate constitution usually comprised two documents: the memorandum of association and the articles of association. It will be seen, however, that with the enactment of the *Company Law Review Act* 1998 (Cth) companies no longer need a separate written constitution. Instead the company can simply use the basic set of rules prescribed in the *Corporations Act* 2001 (Cth) ('*Corporations Act*') known as the 'replaceable rules'. If, however, it is intended to displace, modify or add to these replaceable rules, a separate written constitution will need to be drafted.

This chapter considers the nature and effect of the corporate constitution (whether it be the replaceable rules or a separate written constitution displacing those rules). The chapter considers how the constitution may be altered. It will be seen that there are both statutory and common law constraints that must be complied with before an amendment will be effective. It also examines how the constitution works as a statutory contract between the persons detailed in s 140(1) of the *Corporations Act* and finally considers the doctrine of *ultra vires*.

Identifying the Corporate Constitution

Memorandum and articles

[6.10] As a consequence of the changes effected by the *Company Law Review Act* 1998 (Cth), in identifying the constitution of a particular company it is necessary to distinguish between companies that were registered before and after 1 July 1998. If the company was registered before this date its original constitutional documents (the memorandum of association and articles of association) will continue to constitute the company's constitution unless they have been validly repealed: s 1415. The memorandum of association defines the nature of the company, specifying matters such as whether it has share capital and the nature of members' liability. The articles of association set out the rules governing its internal management, such as the conduct of meetings, the issuing of shares and declaring dividends. While every company was required to have a memorandum (formerly s 114), not all companies were required to have their own articles. Companies limited by shares (Table A) and no-liability companies (Table B) could adopt model articles contained in

Sch 1 to the Act: former s 175(1). There was, however, no model memorandum of association in the Act.

Mandatory and replaceable rules

[6.20] As noted above, companies are no longer required to have a constitution. Instead they can simply use the rules of internal management specified in the *Corporations Act*. Some rules are mandatory for all companies, while others are only applicable to one shareholder/director companies. Other rules are not, however, mandatory. These are known as 'replaceable rules'. Provisions that apply as replaceable rules are identified in s 141. Some rules are mandatory rules for public companies, while replaceable rules for proprietary companies. See ss 135(1)(b) and 249X. Replaceable rules are also inapplicable to one shareholder/ director companies: s 135(1). See ss 198E, 201F and 202C (formerly s 224B) for special provisions applying to this type of company.

Adopting /displacing replaceable rules

[6.30] Replaceable rules are applicable to companies registered after the commencement of the *Company Law Review Act* 1998 (Cth) on 1 July 1998: s 135(1). Such companies have a choice. They can simply adopt the replaceable rules or adopt a constitution that displaces the replaceable rules: s 135(2). Thus, a company's internal management may be governed by the replaceable rules, its constitution or a combination of both: s 134.

A constitution may be adopted either on or after registration: s 136(1). A company adopts a constitution on registration where every person specified on the application for registration as consenting to being a member agrees in writing to the terms of the constitution before the application is lodged: s 136(1). As noted in the previous chapter, only public companies must lodge their constitution with their application for registration: s 117(3). A constitution may be adopted after registration through the passage of a special resolution by the company: s 136(2). Public companies must lodge a copy of the special resolution and constitution with ASIC within 14 days of the resolution: s 136(5)(a). The constitution may in turn be altered through the passage of a special resolution: s 136(2).

[6.40] The replaceable rules also apply to companies registered before 1 July 1998 that have repealed their prior constitutional documents: s 135(2). The position of companies that retain their constitutional documents is discussed above.

Legal Consequences of Mandatory Rules and Constitution

[6.50] A breach of a mandatory rule will constitute a breach of the *Corporations Act* and will attract the relevant criminal and/or civil liability prescribed by the Act. By contrast, a failure to comply with a replaceable rule does not in itself constitute a breach of the law: s 135(3). However, as discussed in more detail below, the corporate constitution (including the replaceable rules) applies as if it constituted a contract between the company, its members, the directors and the company secretary: s 140(1). The consequences of breaching this 'statutory contract' and the possible application of the *ultra vires* doctrine are discussed in detail below.

Moreover, under ss 128(4) and 129(1), unless a person knew or suspected that the assumption was incorrect, he or she may assume, *inter alia*, that any constitutional requirements applicable to the company have been complied with. See further the assumptions provided for in ss 128 and 129. These assumptions are cumulative in the sense that a third party may rely on more than one assumption: *Oris Funds Management Ltd v National Australia Bank* [2003] VSC 315.

Sections 128 and 129 statutorily entrench a modified form of the common law 'indoor management rule'. Under this rule a third party dealing with a company is entitled to 'assume that acts within [the company's] constitution and powers have been properly and duly performed, and are not bound to inquire whether acts of internal management have been regular': *Morris v Kanssen* [1946] AC 459.

Moreover, s 130(1) statutorily abolishes the doctrine of constructive notice by declaring that persons are not deemed to have constructive knowledge of, *inter alia*, a company's constitution simply because it is available from ASIC.

Altering the Constitution

Special resolution

[6.60] As noted above, companies that are *prima facie* subject to the replaceable rules may displace, modify or add to them by adopting a constitution: s 135(2). More generally, a company may modify or repeal its constitution or a provision(s) in the constitution through the passage of a special resolution: s 136(2). The alteration takes effect from the date on which the resolution was passed or any such later date specified in, or determined in accordance with, the resolution: s 137(2).

Precondition in constitution

[6.70] A provision of the constitution may not, however, be changed through the mere passage of a special resolution if the constitution has specified a further precondition before the alteration will be effective: s 136(3). This section's predecessor, s 172, detailed examples of such preconditions:

- the resolution be passed by a percentage of members higher than that required under a special resolution;
- the consent of a specified person be obtained; or
- 'that a particular condition be fulfilled'.

Unless the constitution otherwise provides, a precondition cannot itself be modified or repealed unless the further requirement is satisfied: s 136(4).

Alterations affecting members

[6.80] Members are not bound by an alteration of the constitution unless they consent in writing where the change:
- requires members to take up additional shares;
- increases members' liability to contribute to share capital or otherwise pay money to the company (see, for example, *Ding v Sylvania Waterways Ltd* (1999) 17 ACLC 531); or
- imposes or increases restrictions on the right to transfer shares; except where the modification is made in relation to a change from a public company to a proprietary company or in the course of inserting takeover provisions under Part 2B.7: s 140(2).

[6.90] Specific provision is also made for the alteration of the constitution to affect:
- the company's name: s 157;
- the type of company: Part 2B.7;
- class rights (considered in Chapter 7): Part 2F.2;
- the company's ability to dispense with the inclusion of 'Limited' in its name: s 150; and
- the company's capital: ss 254H and 256A-256E.

Common law requirements

[6.100] The power to alter the constitution must be exercised *bona fide* for the benefit of the company as a whole: *Allen v Gold Reefs of West Africa* [1900] 1 Ch 656 at 671. See also *Australian Fixed Trusts Pty Ltd v Clyde Industries Ltd* [1959] SR (NSW) 33. Where the alteration affects all members equally, this test must be applied. The test espoused in *Gambotto v WCP Ltd* (1995) 182 CLR 432, discussed below, is not applied. It will be seen that *Gambotto* is concerned with amendments that involve a conflict between interests and advantages amongst different groups of shareholders. Where the alteration applies equally to all members *Gambotto v WCP Ltd* has no application. Thus, in *Arakella v Paton* [2004] NSWSC 13, one of the issues before the court was whether the *Gambotto* principles could apply to an amendment of the subject trust deed to implement a scheme of arrangement so that all unit holders would have their interests replaced with shares in a newly formed company. Austin J rejected the applicability of *Gambotto v WCP Ltd* on these facts because, *inter alia*, the proposed amendment applied equally and uniformly to all unit holders. Following the earlier decision in *Heydon v NRMA Ltd* (2001) 51 NSWLR 1, Austin J declared 'the ratio in *Gambotto* ... has no application where the proposed amendment will replace all interests with another species of property in a manner that treats the interest-holders equally, at any rate (as here) there is no "majority" voting bloc' (at [148]).

[6.110] Where, however, the alteration of the constitution affects different shareholders differently, thereby involving a conflict of shareholders' interests, it is not possible to apply the *Allen v Gold Reefs of West Africa* [1900] 1 Ch 656 test: *Gambotto v WCP Ltd* (1995) 182 CLR 432 at 444. In such a case it will not be possible to identify the 'company's interests' as required by this test: *Gambotto* at 444. The interests of a majority shareholder, for example, do not equate with the interests of the company as a whole and thus an alternative test must be applied. In *Gambotto* the High Court formulated two tests dealing with alterations that (i) give rise to a conflict of interests and advantages amongst different groups of shareholders and/or (ii) involve an expropriation of shares.

Gambotto v WCP Ltd
High Court of Australia: Mason CJ, Brennan, Deane,
Dawson and McHugh JJ
(1995) 182 CLR 432

WCP Ltd held a meeting of its shareholders at which an amendment of its constitution was approved. The effect of the alteration was to allow the holder of 90% or more of the issued shares to compulsorily acquire the residual shares. The purchase price was to be $1.80 per share. An expert report valued the shares at $1.365. The majority shareholders held approximately 99.7% of the issued share capital of WCP Ltd. The majority shareholders were in turn wholly owned subsidiaries of IEL. Minority shareholders, including the appellant, Gambotto, held the remaining shares in WCP Ltd. The appellant did not want to sell his shares. Gambotto objected to the alteration on the basis that it was, *inter alia*, oppressive. The majority shareholders asserted the amount to be paid for the shares was fair.

The High Court held the alteration was invalid. The Court held that the test in *Allen v Gold Reefs of West Africa* [1900] 1 Ch 656 could not be applied because the interests of the company as a whole were not determinable on the facts as the alteration involved a conflict between the interests and advantages of the majority and minority shareholders. In such a case the High Court held that the alteration will be valid unless it is (i) *ultra vires*, (ii) beyond any purpose contemplated by the corporate constitution or (iii) oppressive. As the particular facts involved an expropriation of shares, the court held that a more specific test also applied. Such an alteration can only be valid if it is (i) for a proper purpose and (ii) not oppressive. On the facts the alteration was held to breach these tests.

Mason CJ, Brennan, Deane and Dawson JJ: **[444]** In the context of a special resolution altering the articles and giving rise to a conflict of interests and advantages, whether or not it involves an expropriation of shares, we would reject as inappropriate the "bona fide for the benefit of the company as a whole" test of Lindley MR in *Allen v Gold Reefs of West Africa Limited*. The application of the test in such a context has been criticized on grounds which, in our view, are unanswerable. It seems to us that, in such a case not involving an actual or effective expropriation of shares or of valuable proprietary rights attaching to shares, an alteration of the articles by special resolution regularly passed will be valid unless it is *ultra vires*, beyond any purpose contemplated by the articles or oppressive as that expression is understood in the law relating to corporations. Somewhat different considerations apply, however, in a case such as the present where what is involved is an alteration of the articles to allow an expropriation by the majority of [445] the shares, or of valuable proprietary rights attaching to the shares, of a minority. In such a case, the immediate purpose of the resolution is to confer upon the majority shareholder or shareholders power to acquire compulsorily the property of the minority shareholder or shareholders. Of itself, the conferral of such a power does not lie within the "contemplated objects of the power" to amend the articles.

The exercise of a power conferred by a company's constitution enabling the majority shareholders to expropriate the minority's shareholding for the purpose of aggrandizing the majority is valid if and only to the extent that the relevant provisions of the company's constitution so provide. The inclusion of such a power in a company's constitution at its incorporation is one thing. But it is another thing when a company's constitution is sought to be amended by an alteration of articles of association so as to confer upon the majority power to expropriate the shares of a minority. Such a power could not be taken or exercised simply for the purpose of aggrandizing the majority. In our view, such a power can be taken only if (i) it is exercisable for a proper purpose and (ii) its exercise will not operate oppressively in relation to minority shareholders. In other words, an expropriation may be justified where it is reasonably apprehended that the continued shareholding of the minority is detrimental to the company, its undertaking or the conduct of its affairs – resulting in detriment to the interests of the existing shareholders generally – and expropriation is a reasonable means of eliminating or mitigating that detriment.

Accordingly, if it appears that the substantial purpose of the alteration is to secure the company from significant detriment or harm, the alteration would be valid if it is not oppressive to the minority shareholders. So, expropriation would be justified in the case of a shareholder who is competing with the company, as was the case in *Sidebottom v Kershaw, Leese and Co*, so long as the terms of expropriation are not oppressive. Again, expropriation of a minority shareholder could be justified if it were necessary in order to ensure that the company could continue to comply with a regulatory regime governing the principal business which it carries on. To take a hypothetical example: if the conduct of a TV station were the undertaking of a company and a renewal of a television licence under a statute depended upon the licensee's [446] entire share capital being held by Australian residents, the expropriation of foreign shareholders who are unwilling to sell their shares to Australian residents might be justified assuming it is fair in all the circumstances. But that is not to say that the majority can expropriate the minority merely in order to secure for themselves the benefit of a corporate structure that can derive some new commercial advantage by virtue of the expropriation.

Notwithstanding that a shareholder's membership of a company is subject to alterations of the articles which may affect the rights attaching to the shareholder's shares and the value of those shares, we do not consider that, in the case of an alteration to the articles authorizing the expropriation of shares, it is a sufficient justification of an expropriation that the expropriation, being fair, will advance the interests of the company as a legal and commercial entity or those of the majority, albeit the great majority, of corporators. This approach does not attach sufficient weight to the proprietary nature of a share and, to the extent that English authority might appear to support such an approach, we do not agree with it. It is only right that exceptional circumstances should be required to justify an amendment to the articles authorizing the compulsory expropriation by the majority of the minority's interests in a company. To allow expropriation where it would advance the interests of the company as a legal and commercial entity or those of the general body of corporators would, in our view, be tantamount to permitting expropriation by the majority for the purpose of some personal gain and thus be made for an improper purpose. It would open the way to circumventing the protection which the *Corporations Law* gives to minorities who resist compromises, amalgamations and reconstructions, schemes of arrangement and takeover offers.

As noted in the preceding paragraphs, an alteration to the company's articles permitting the expropriation of shares will not be valid simply because it was made for a proper purpose; it must also be fair in the circumstances. Fairness in this context has both procedural and substantive elements. The first element, that the process used to expropriate must be fair, requires the majority shareholders to disclose all relevant information leading up to the alteration and it presumably requires the shares to be valued by an independent expert. Whether it also requires the majority shareholders to refrain from voting on the proposed amendment is a question that is best left open at this stage.

[447] The second element, that the terms of the expropriation itself must be fair, is largely concerned with the price offered for the shares. Thus, an expropriation at less than market value is prima facie unfair, and it would be unusual for a court to be satisfied that a price substantially above market value was not a fair value. That said, it is important to emphasize that a shareholder's interest cannot be valued solely by the current market value of the shares. Whether the price offered is fair depends on a variety of factors, including assets, market value, dividends, and the nature of the corporation and its likely future. ...

[I]n the case of expropriation, we consider that the onus lies on those supporting expropriation to show that the power is validly exercised.

It is for the majority to prove that the alteration is valid because it was made for a proper purpose and is fair in all the circumstances. This approach ensures that the application of the relevant principle does not unduly favour the majority and it largely alleviates the sting of practical difficulties, such as poor access to information, that would otherwise confront minority shareholders. ...

[448] As the appellants did not contend that the expropriation was not fair in the sense explained above, the validity of Art 20A hinges on whether the respondents have proved that the amendment was not made for a proper purpose. The immediate purpose of the amendment was to allow the expropriation by the majority shareholder of the shares held by the minority, including the shares held by the appellants. There is no suggestion that the appellants' continued presence as members puts WCP's business activities at risk or that the appellants have in some way acted to WCP's detriment. Nor is there any suggestion that WCP sought 100 per cent ownership in order to comply with a regulatory regime. All that is suggested is that taxation advantages and administrative benefits would flow to WCP if minority shareholdings were expropriated and WCP were to become a wholly-owned subsidiary of IEL. In our view, however, that cannot by itself constitute a proper purpose for a resolution altering the articles to allow for the expro-

priation of a minority shareholder's shares. In that regard, it is not irrelevant to note that it is difficult to conceive of circumstances in which financial and administrative benefits would not be a consequence of the expropriation of minority shareholdings by a majority shareholder.

Accordingly, we would hold Art 20A invalid and ineffective on the basis that it was not made for a proper purpose.

[6.120] As *Gambotto v WCP Ltd* (1995) 182 CLR 432 has been distinguished in subsequent cases (see, for example, *Village Roadshow Broadcasting v Austereo* (1997) 15 ACLC 929 and *Arakella v Paton* [2004] NSWSC 13) it appears the case will not be too broadly applied. In this regard it is also relevant to note the court's treatment of *Gambotto* in *NRMA Ltd v Snodgrass* (2001) 19 ACLC 769 where the applicability of these principles to an alteration of the constitution that would introduce a new disqualification provision for the directors was in issue. NRMA Ltd argued that the proposed alteration was oppressive to the directors in their capacity as members and oppressive to the members who had voted for the directors when they were elected. The court held there was no oppression within the *Gambotto* principles. First, as to the *Gambotto* test for an expropriation of minority shareholders' shares, Windeyer J held that no member had any proprietary right in a director and thus the alteration did not involve a taking of shareholders' property. Second, in regard to the more general *Gambotto* test, Windeyer J found that the proposed resolution was not beyond any purpose contemplated in the company's constitution and that it was not oppressive as it did not involve any fraud on, or unfairness to, the minority shareholders. On appeal, the Court of Appeal agreed that the proposed amendment was not oppressive, adding that the mere alteration of the constitution did not remove a director; disqualification would only occur if a director chose not to comply with the new rule: *NRMA Ltd v Snodgrass* (2001) 19 ACLC 1675.

Statutory Contract

Binding nature of the constitution

[6.130] Section 140(1) provides that the company's constitution and any applicable replaceable rules have the effect of a contract under which each person agrees to observe and perform their provisions in so far as they are applicable to that person.

Alterable contract

[6.140] The binding nature of the statutory contract is, however, qualified by the ability to alter these replaceable rules and/or provisions of the constitution under ss 135(2) and 136(2). Section 140(1) does not render, *inter alia*, the constitution unalterable. In fact, a constitution cannot state that it is unalterable. Any such statement is ineffective in law: *Allen v Gold Reefs of West Africa* [1900] 1 Ch 656 at 671, 673 and 676; *Peter's American Delicacy Co Ltd v Heath* (1939) 61 CLR 457 at 479;

Cumbrian Newspapers Group Ltd v Cumberland & Westmorland Herald Newspapers & Printing Co Ltd [1987] Ch 1 at 23.

Unlike ordinary contracts, the statutory contract may be altered unilaterally through the passage of a special resolution even though that change may prejudice members' or directors' interests, subject to any applicable common law and statutory protections: *Allen v Gold Reefs of West Africa* at 671. The effect of an alteration of the constitution is not confined to prospective rights. As Lord Lindley MR stressed in *Allen v Gold Reefs of West Africa* at 671, existing 'rights are in truth limited as to their duration by the duration of the articles which confer them'. See also *Shuttleworth v Cox Bros & Co Ltd* [1927] 2 KB 9; *Gambotto v WCP Ltd* (1995) 182 CLR 432; *NRMA Ltd v Snodgrass* (2001) 19 ACLC 769; 19 ACLC 1675. In the absence of a separate contract, discussed below, the alteration will not constitute an enforceable breach of contract unless the alteration is constrained by the principles espoused in, *inter alia*, *Gambotto*.

The interplay between s 140(1) and the ability to alter the constitution means that, if a clause in the statutory contract has not been amended to derogate from any rights it provides, a breach of that clause through acts or omissions contrary to its terms will *prima facie* be actionable by a party to the statutory contract. By contrast, if the clause is amended before the contrary acts or omissions, the aggrieved shareholder, for example, will no longer be able to source their rights in the statutory contract. They will need to find an alternative source of rights.

Separate contract

Independent contract

[6.150] As recognised in *Allen v Gold Reefs of West Africa* [1900] 1 Ch 656 at 671, 673 and 676, members, for example, may protect their rights under the constitution by including them in a separate contract. While this will not prevent the constitution being altered to affect such rights, the contract will provide the member with an independent, enforceable source of rights: *Oswald v Bailey* (1987) 11 NSWLR 715 at 741; *Bailey v NSW Medical Defence Union Ltd* (1995) 184 CLR 399 at 410-412. Where this separate contract clearly provides that an alteration of the company's constitution will not affect the rights under that contract, the latter will provide an effective means of protecting the contracting parties' rights: *Southern Foundries Ltd v Shirlaw* [1940] AC 701; *Bailey v NSW Medical Defence Union Ltd* at 411. That the contract is such an independent contract may be indicated by statements in the constitution itself that indicate that the former is to prevail over the latter. Thus, in *Southern Foundries Ltd v Shirlaw* [1940] AC 701 the managing director's contract of service for 10 years was held to be a separate contract in light of the statement in the constitution that the managing director was entitled to the benefit of the provisions of any contract between himself and the company. Alternatively, the purpose of the contract may indicate that the parties did not intend the company to be able to amend the contract by unilaterally altering the constitution.

Thus, in *Bailey v NSW Medical Defence Union Ltd* at 414-415 the court found that the parties would not have intended that a contract for insurance could have the terms of that insurance policy diminished by a subsequent alteration of the articles.

Interdependent contract

[6.160] Where, however, the independence of the contract and the company's constitution is less clear, the contract will not always prevent an alteration of the constitution contemporaneously denying the parties' rights under the contract: *Read v Astoria Garage (Streatham) Ltd* [1952] Ch 637; *Carrier Australia Ltd v Hunt* (1939) 61 CLR 534. Thus, the interdependency of the contract and the constitution may indicate that an amendment of the constitution also automatically changes the terms of the contract. In such a case the contract will not provide a separate independent source of contractual rights. For example, a contract may import a clause(s) of the constitution on the basis that an alteration of the constitution will also alter the contract. See the discussion in *Bailey v NSW Medical Defence Union Ltd* (1995) 184 CLR 399 at 410-411 and 414. Alternatively, a statement in the contract that the contract is subject to the constitution will indicate the contract is not an independent contract and that it will be subject to any constitutional amendment. More subtle perhaps was the statement in the constitution in *Read v Astoria Garage (Streatham) Ltd* [1952] Ch 637 that provided that the board's power to appoint a managing director was 'subject to determination ... if he ceases for any cause to be a director or if the company in general meeting resolve that his tenure of office of managing director ... be determined'. As the managing director's contract of service contained no provision for the termination of office, the power to terminate his office under the terms of the constitution were found to prevail and the exercise of this power was held not to breach the contract of service.

The matter becomes even more complicated when both the contract and constitution refer to the other and each appears to defer to the other. This occurred in *Carrier Australia Ltd v Hunt* (1939) 61 CLR 534. Hunt's contract of service as managing director for five years was stated as being, *inter alia*, 'subject to the company's articles of association and the provisions hereinafter contained'. In turn, however, the dismissal power in the company's constitution was stated as being subject to any contract between the company and the director. By special resolution the company deleted this qualification and proceeded to remove Hunt. Hunt sued for damages for wrongful dismissal. The High Court was divided 2:2 as to whether the alteration allowed the company to dismiss Hunt without breaching the contract. Rich and Starke JJ asserted that as the contract had been made subject to an alterable document, the company's constitution, Hunt had been validly removed. By contrast, Evatt and McTiernan JJ asserted that to give business efficacy to agreements existing outside the constitution, it was necessary to conclude that the power to dismiss under the constitution was subject to the terms of the contract of service. If an alteration of the constitution could be relied upon to remove the director it would be nugatory to enter into a contract for a fixed term, here five years. As the High Court was divided, the prior decision of the Supreme Court in favour of the plaintiff was upheld. Nevertheless, in light of the division amongst the members of the court, the matter cannot be considered resolved.

Parties to the statutory contract

[6.170] Section 140(1) provides that any applicable replaceable rules and/or the company's constitution operate as a statutory contract between:
- the company and each member;
- the company and each director and company secretary; and
- a member and each other member.

The section does not extend the benefits of the statutory contract to the relations between members and directors and company secretary, nor does it safeguard the rights of third party 'outsiders'.

Outsiders and the statutory contract

[6.180] As third party outsiders have no rights under the statutory contract, they cannot bring an action for a breach of its terms: *Eley v Positive Government Security Life Assurance Co Ltd* (1876) 1 Ex D 88.

Eley v Positive Government Security Life Assurance Co Ltd
Court of Appeal: Kelly CB and Cleasby and Amphlett BB
(1876) 1 Ex D 88

The company's constitution provided that Eley was to be the company's solicitor, who would conduct all the company's legal business and that he could not be removed from office except for misconduct. From the time of incorporation Eley was employed as the company solicitor and, until 1871, transacted all of the company's legal business. In 1871, however, another firm of solicitors performed some of the company's legal business. This transaction was the basis of the dispute between Eley and the company. From this date onwards the company ceased to employ Eley for its legal services, using several other legal firms instead.

Eley insisted that under the terms of the constitution he had a right to be employed as the sole solicitor of the company and that he had to transact all the company's legal business unless there had been misconduct. Eley sued the company for breach of contract, relying on the constitution. In reply, the directors of the company asserted Eley had no such rights under the constitution and no 'special' contract independent of the constitution, pointing out that he had never been appointed solicitor by the directors, the general meeting or under any company instrument. The Court of Appeal held Eley had no rights under the statutory contract as he was not a party to the contract. Nor was there any special contract. Thus, Eley had no claim for breach of contract.

Amphlett B: **[26]** The articles, taken by themselves, are simply a contract between the shareholders inter se, and cannot ... give a right of action to a person like the plaintiff, not a party to the articles, although named therein ... **[27]** All that appears is that the directors allowed the plaintiff to attend their first meeting **[28]** and afterwards employed him as the solicitor of the company, which, as between themselves and the company, though not as between themselves and the plaintiff, they were bound by the articles to do. But how does that show that they entered into a special contract with him, that he should not only receive the ordinary remuneration for his services, but transact all future business of the company, and not be removed from his office unless for misconduct? [It is] highly probable that ... the plaintiff, who prepared the articles and inserted the 118th clause in his own favour, thought he was safe under the clause itself, and therefore did not think it necessary, and, it may be, for many reasons, not for his own interest, to ask the directors to enter into any such strange and special contract with him. He was, however, in my judgment, mistaken in that respect; but of course, such mistake cannot create any special contract between him and the company, or between him and the directors. All that can be said is that he intended that the company should be bound hand and foot to himself, but from a mistaken view of the law he has, most fortunately for the company, failed to carry such intention into effect. The act of the directors in employing another solicitor was, no doubt, as between themselves and the company, a violation of the 118th clause; but that might have been condoned by the company, and if the plaintiff, as a member of the company, had called that act into question at a general meeting, I do not think it difficult to guess what the result would have been. For these reasons, I think there was no contract at all between the plaintiff and the company to the effect stated in the declaration.

This principle was reaffirmed in *News Ltd v Australian Rugby Football League Ltd* (1996) 21 ACSR 635. Here an action against certain rugby league clubs for breach of the statutory contract failed. As the subject clubs were not members of the League – rather two representatives of each club were members – the clubs were not privy to, and thus not bound by, the League's constitution.

Members enforcing outsider rights

[6.190] Two interrelated points flow from the above discussion in *Eley v Positive Government Security Life Assurance Co Ltd* (1876) 1 Ex D 88. First, could the conclusion in *Eley* have been avoided if a shareholder of the company sought to enforce the subject clause of the company constitution thereby indirectly allowing the outsider to enforce the statutory contract? The courts have rejected the suggestion that members have a right to demand that all terms of the company's constitution be complied with, including when the subject term does not affect them personally: *Stanham v National Trust of Australia (New South Wales)* (1989) 7 ACLC 628 at 631. Second, can an outsider enforce such rights if they subsequently become a member and thus a party to the statutory contract? In *Eley*, shares were subsequently allotted to Eley in return for advances he had made, yet this did not affect the Court of Appeal's conclusion that he had no contract with the company. This is because a person privy to the statutory contract, for example a member, can only enforce their rights under the constitution in that capacity, ie as a member: *Browne v La Trinidad* (1887) 37 Ch D 1; *Hickman v Kent on Romney Marsh Sheepbreeders Association* [1915] 1 Ch 881 at 897 and 900; *Heron v Port Huon Fruitgrowers' Co-op Asscn Ltd* (1922) 30 CLR 315 at 338; *Beattie v E & F Beattie Ltd* [1938] Ch 708; *Bailey v NSW Medical Defence Union Ltd* (1995) 184 CLR 399 at 437. They cannot enforce their rights in their capacity as an outsider: *Hickman v Kent on Romney Marsh Sheepbreeders Association* at 897-897; *Forbes v New South Wales Trotting Club Ltd* [1977] 2 NSWLR 515 at 520; *Bailey v NSW Medical Defence Union Ltd* at 437. Thus, as Astbury J stated in *Hickman v Kent on Romney Marsh Sheepbreeders Association* at 897-897 and 100:

> The actual decisions amount to this, that an outsider to whom rights purport to be given by the articles in his capacity as such outsider, whether he subsequently becomes a member or not, cannot sue on such articles treating them as contracts between himself and the company to enforce such rights. Such rights are not part of the general regulations of the company applicable alike to all shareholders and can only exist by virtue of some contract between such non-member and the company, and the subsequent allotment of shares to an outsider in whose favour such an article is inserted does not enable him to sue the company on such an article to enforce rights which are res inter alios acta and not part of the general rights of the corporators as such ... I think this much is clear – first, that no article can constitute a contract between the company and a third person; second, that no right merely purported to be given by an article to a person, whether a member or not, in a capacity other than that of a member, as for instance, as solicitor, promoter, or director can be enforced against the company; and, third, articles regulating the rights and obligations of the members generally as such do create rights and obligations between them and the company respectively.

Thus, in cases such as *Hickman v Kent on Romney Marsh Sheepbreeders Association* at 897 and 900; *Norths Ltd v McCaughen Dyson Capel Cure Ltd* (1988) 6 ACLC 320 at 325-326 and *Bailey v NSW Medical Defence Union Ltd* at 437-440 it has been suggested that the rights enforceable by members in their capacity as member are confined to those matters pertaining to the internal administration of the company or rights enjoyed by all shareholders alike.

[6.200] There are two cases, however, that must be briefly mentioned because, while following this line of authority, factually they are difficult to reconcile with this legal principle. In *Rayfield v Hands* [1958] 2 All ER 194 the company's constitution required the directors to buy any outgoing member's shares at fair value. The directors of the company were required to conform with a share qualification and were therefore also shareholders. The plaintiff argued that as the directors were members they were bound by this article to buy his shares. The court asserted that the clause was enforceable 'between the plaintiff as a member and the defendants not as directors but as members'. Thus, the court echoed the principle that the clause must be binding on the (director) member in his or her capacity as a member. However, the subject clause of the constitution was not 'applicable alike to all shareholders' under the above *Hickman v Kent on Romney Marsh Sheepbreeders Association* [1915] 1 Ch 881 test as it only affected certain members in their capacity as directors. Factually, the case can only be reconciled with this aspect of *Hickman* if the focus is on the outgoing members and it is asserted that the clause is applicable alike to all members because, if they wish to leave the company, all have a right to demand the directors buy their shares.

Similarly, in *Re Caratti Holding Co Pty Ltd* (1975) 1 ACLR 87, one clause in the company's constitution provided the 'founder', Caratti, with the right to compel the sale of shares by other members for a sum equal to the paid-up value of the shares. Caratti gave notice pursuant to this article requiring Zampatti, the holder of 10% of the issued shares, to transfer his shares for $3000. On this particular issue, the court agreed with Caratti that Zampatti was bound by the clause. Again the court echoed the above principles, asserting that the statutory contract can only confer rights upon a shareholder in his or her capacity as a shareholder, concluding that the rights conferred on Caratti were in his 'capacity of shareholder or member'. Yet the clause was not 'applicable alike to all shareholders' as it only conferred the power to compel the sale of the shares on Caratti in his capacity of founder. Again, the clause could only be said to have general import if the focus is on the fact that all shareholders were equally subject to the potential compulsory acquisition of their shares.

[6.210] The case law that provides that the statutory contract can only be enforced in the member's relevant capacity must also be read in light of the terms of s 140(1) which suggest that a broader array of rights may be enforced under the statutory contract. First, s 140(1) makes no reference to capacity. It merely identifies the parties to the statutory contract. The mere identification of a member, for example, as a party to the statutory contract does not deny that a member may also deal with the company in another 'outsider' capacity. Thus, a member may have rights in that outsider capacity that could purportedly be protected by the constitution. Second, and most importantly, s 140(1) provides that the provisions of the statutory contract are binding 'so far as they apply to that person'. This would appear to extend the ability to enforce the statutory contract to provisions specifically dealing with that member, not just matters that affect the members as a whole. The scope of this aspect of s 140(1) remains, therefore, uncertain.

Ultra Vires Doctrine

Ultra vires doctrine at common law

[6.220] Until 1983, a company's constitution had to state the objects for which it was formed. The company's capacity to act was in turn limited to furthering those objects. Acts outside those objects were void for being beyond power or *ultra vires*: *Ashbury Carriage & Iron Co v Riche* (1875) LR 7 HL 653. Not even a unanimous resolution of its members could rectify an *ultra vires* act: *Ashbury Carriage & Iron Co v Riche*. Moreover, under the doctrine of constructive notice, all persons were deemed to know the contents of the company's constitutional documents as these were lodged with the appropriate regulatory authority and accessible by the public. The combination of this rule and the *ultra vires* doctrine meant that contracting parties needed to inspect the company's constitution to ensure it was acting within its objects.

Ultra vires in the narrow sense: Corporate capacity

[6.230] This course of practice was commercially unrealistic. As a consequence, provisions were included in the *Corporations Law* with the express object of abolishing the *ultra vires* doctrine. See, *inter alia*, former s 160. While these provisions were repealed by the *Company Law Review Act* 1998 (Cth) and not re-enacted in the *Corporations Act*, the current legislation still impacts on the *ultra vires* doctrine. First, companies generally no longer have to state their objects. Second, if an objects clause or some other restriction is included in the company's constitution, this no longer confines the company's legal capacity to the pursuit of such objects. The impact the *ultra vires* doctrine had on corporate capacity is known as *ultra vires* in the narrow sense: *ANZ Executors & Trustee Co Ltd v Qintex Australia Ltd* (1990) 8 ACLC 980 at 988. This is abolished under the *Corporations Act*. As noted in Chapter 5, s 124(1) declares a company to have, *inter alia*, the legal capacity of an individual. Most importantly, this capacity is not limited by any prohibition or restriction or statement of objects included in the company's constitution: s 125(1) and (2). Any act contrary to any such prohibition, restriction or object is not thereby invalidated: s 125(1) and (2). See also *News Ltd v Australian Rugby Football League Ltd* (1996) 21 ACSR 635. Even if the act is contrary to the company's best interests the restriction will not undermine the company's legal capacity: s 124(2). A company's powers are now only limited to the extent that they are constrained by the *Corporations Act*.

Ultra vires in the wide sense: Members' and directors' powers

[6.240] The abovementioned provisions that were designed to abolish the *ultra vires* doctrine also provided that acting contrary to a company's objects constituted a breach of the Act and could be relied on in, for example, proceedings against directors for breaches of their duties. See former s 162. The impact the *ultra vires* doctrine has on the exercise of powers by members and directors is known as *ultra vires* in the wide sense: *ANZ Executors & Trustee Co Ltd v Qintex Australia Ltd* (1990) 8 ACLC 980 at 988. As noted above, these provisions were repealed by the *Company Law Review Act* 1998 (Cth) and not re-enacted in the *Corporations Act*. Nevertheless, acting contrary to a company's objects continues to be relevant under the current legislation for two reasons. First, as noted above, a breach of the corporate constitution will constitute a breach of the statutory contact under s 140(1). Second, as s 125 is only concerned with corporate capacity, *ultra vires* in the narrow sense, no provision of the Act has repealed *ultra vires* in the wide sense. Thus, *ultra vires* still has relevance in the wide sense of affecting the powers of the directors and shareholders: *ANZ Executors & Trustee Co Ltd v Qintex Australia Ltd*. Hence, the *ultra vires* doctrine may still operate internally, effectively confining company officers' authority.

ANZ Executors & Trustee Co Ltd v Qintex Australia Ltd
Supreme Court of Queensland: McPherson, Lee and Mackenzie JJ
(1990) 8 ACLC 980

Qintex raised $185 million by issuing unsecured debentures. To facilitate this Qintex executed a deed in favour of ANZ, the terms of which included an undertaking to have its subsidiaries guarantee the indebtedness. Qintex failed before the subsidiaries executed these guarantees. ANZ sought specific performance of the undertaking by the subsidiaries. By the time of the hearing the subsidiaries were insolvent.

ANZ argued that the directors and members of each of the subsidiaries could validly make, and the court could validly order them to make, the voluntary disposition that was envisaged by the guarantees. It was argued that the case law that said that companies could not so dispose of their assets was based on the *ultra vires* doctrine and that doctrine had been abolished. Moreover, when determining if such a voluntary disposition was proper the time that the matter should be considered was when the deed was first entered into. At that time, it was said, the capital raised by the debentures benefited the whole corporate group. Qintex asserted that the members and directors were not free to deal with company assets without restriction and could not gift company property by entering into the guarantees.

The court refused to order specific performance. While *ultra vires* in the narrow sense had been abolished, this did not free members and directors from ensuring that the rules of the company are complied with. *Ultra vires* in this wide sense had not been abolished and prevented the members and directors of the subsidiaries gifting the company's property, which would be the effect of the guarantees. The courts would not order the members and directors to do such an illegal act.

McPherson J (Lee and Mackenzie JJ concurring): **[984]** This to my mind raises a question, fundamental to the law relating to companies, which is whether a company that is insolvent or verging on insolvency may properly make a gift of its assets to some other person. I say "gift of assets" ... [because for] a person to submit to a liability that must be satisfied at once by payment is, actually and really, to require him to make payment to the extent at least of available assets. If the payment is made or the commitment that precedes it is assumed for no consideration, it is, by any standard, nothing but a gift. Applied to an insolvent company, this means that directors or shareholders, or all of them acting together, may validly make a voluntary **[985]** disposition of assets that serves no corporate purpose whatever; and that they may do so in derogation of the interests of creditors, for whom the assets, disposed of present the only prospect of receiving payment of their debts. ...

[I]t does not follow that the holder **[986]** may always do whatever he pleases with the corporate assets. For they are the property of the company and not of the shareholder, who has no legal or equitable interest in them: *Macaura v Northern Insurance Co* [1925] AC 619 at p 626. That is the inescapable consequence of treating the company in law as an entity distinct from its members.

For this reason there are some things that shareholders cannot do. ...

[987] Mr Keane QC submits that the judgments in the forgoing cases [restricting the ability of shareholders of insolvent companies to gift property] resort to the *ultra vires* doctrine in support of the decisions. That is so **[988]** in some but not all of them. ... The thrust of the submission is that in Australia the doctrine has been abolished "in its application to companies": see Companies (Queensland) Code sec 67, 68 ...

The purposes of sec 67 and 68 are sufficiently achieved if, despite deficiencies in corporate capacity, the validity of corporate dealings with outsiders is made unimpeachable. Beyond that point the legislation does not affect or abrogate restrictions, explicit or implicit, on the exercise of directors' or shareholders' powers ... Another limitation also identifiable in that way is that corporate property may be applied only for corporate purposes. No one can doubt that this is implicit in the structure of the legislation regulating the formation, management and winding up of corporate traders with limited liability ...

[A] distinction is made between corporate capacity (*ultra vires* in the narrow sense), and abuse of power by directors or shareholders (*ultra vires* in the wide sense). It is ultra vires in this second sense that is directly relevant in answering the question "whether a disposition of property of the company was made for the benefit and to promote the prosperity of the company." ...

[989] [The legislation] does not free directors or shareholders from ensuring that 'rules of the company are given effect to by the company's officers and members' ... Except in relation to the validity of corporate dealings with outsiders, it therefore does not disturb the fundamental rule that the powers or funds of a company may be used only for company purposes. ...

The present case is not one in which the validity of company dealings with outsiders comes into question. None of the subsidiary companies dealt with ANZ. ... Our order cannot compel QAL to do something that, apart from the order, the law does not permit. We cannot order a shareholder to require the company to execute the instrument of guarantee if to do so would involve infringing the "essential principle" that corporate powers and funds may be used only for corporate purposes. For a commercial or trading company confronting insolvency to make a gift of its assets in derogation of the interests of creditors is not to use powers or purposes for their corporate but to do so for a non-corporate purpose.

Review questions

1. Fred has entered into a contract with Champagne Pty Ltd. The contract was clearly contrary to the company's objects.
   (a) Can Fred enforce the contract?
   (b) What rights do members have as a result of this action?
2. Is the doctrine of *ultra vires* still important under the *Corporations Act*?

3. Is the constitution akin to a contract?
4. Critically evaluate the decision in *Rayfield v Hands* and *Re Caratti Holding Co Pty Ltd*.
5. Champagne Pty Ltd's constitution specifies that all company liquor supplies are to be purchased from Bourbon Ltd. What rights does Bourbon Ltd have if:
   (a) Champagne Pty Ltd purchases liquor from Grog Pty Ltd?
   (b) Champagne Pty Ltd alters the constitution to remove this clause?
   (c) Would your answer to (b) be different if Champagne Pty Ltd and Bourbon Ltd also had a separate contract echoing the terms of the subject clause?

Further reading

Baxt, 'Company Law Reform – the future and fixing up the past – the doctrine of *ultra vires*' (1991) 19 *ABLR* 147

Baxt, 'Ultra Vires – Has it Been Revived?' (1991) 9 *C&SLJ* 101

Cassidy, *Concise Corporations Law* (4th ed, Federation Press, Sydney, 2003) ch 6

Ford, Austin and Ramsay, *Ford's Principles of Corporations Law* (11th ed, Butterworths, Sydney, 2003) chs 6 and 12, paras 11.060-11.110

O'Donovan, 'Corporate Benefit and Guarantees in Relation to Third Party Mortgages' (1994) 24 *ABLR* 126

Prentice, 'Ultra vires – Review of Law' [1986] *L Soc Gaz* 338

Ramsay (ed), *Gambotto v WCP Ltd: Its Implication for Corporate Regulation* (Centre for Corporate Law and Securities Regulations, Melbourne,1996)

Watson, 'Corporate Collapses – Time to Reintroduce the Ultra Vires Rule' (1990) 8 *C&SLJ* 240

7

Shares and Dividends

Overview

This chapter considers shares and dividends. As with the corporate constitution, discussed in the previous chapter, this area of the law has been dramatically changed by the *Company Law Review Act* 1998 (Cth). As noted in Chapter 2, while companies may take many forms, the most common is the proprietary company limited by shares. This chapter begins by considering the nature of shares. It will be seen that shares are transferable property that are distinct from the company's assets: *Ord Forrest Pty Ltd v FCT* (1974) 130 CLR 124 at 143-144. Shares are often classified into different types of shares, such as ordinary shares, preference shares etc. These different types of shares are known as 'classes' of shares. Different classes of shares enjoy different rights and restrictions. It will be seen that s 246B of the *Corporations Act* 2001 (Cth) ('*Corporations Act*') seeks to protect these class rights by prescribing certain procedures that must be complied with before the rights attaching to a class of shares may be validly altered.

The second part of the chapter considers the maintenance of share capital doctrine. In return for enjoying the benefits of limited liability, the common law and the *Corporations Act* place restrictions on the ability of the company to return to its members the amounts they have paid for their shares. These restrictions are founded upon the fact that often the only money creditors of a company may resort to when seeking the payment of debts is this share capital: *Re Exchange Banking Co (Flitcroft's case)* (1882) 21 Ch D 519 at 533. The discussion begins with a consideration of the general prohibitions against the company reducing its share capital (s 256B) and buying its own shares (ss 259A and 259C) and then considers more specific provisions, such as s 260A's restriction on a company's ability to provide financial assistance to another to buy shares in that company.

The third part of the chapter considers the most common mechanism through which corporate profits are returned to investors, the payment of dividends. It will be seen this is also linked to the maintenance of share capital doctrine. Dividends can only be paid out of profits, not out of the share capital, as the latter would effect a reduction of share capital: s 254T.

Shares

Nature of a share

[7.10] At common law a share is defined in terms of the rights and liabilities stemming from the ownership of the shares. Thus, a share is defined as 'the interest of a shareholder in the company measured by a sum of money, for the purpose of limited liability in the first place, and of interest in the second, but also consisting of a series of mutual covenants entered into by all the shareholders inter se': *Borland's Trustee v Steel Bros & Co Ltd* [1901] 1 Ch 279 at 288.

[7.20] While, in accordance with this definition, a share corresponds with an interest in the company that confers on the shareholder certain rights such as voting rights, it does not give members an immediate interest in company property: *Ord Forrest Pty Ltd v FCT* (1974) 130 CLR 124 at 142. It is not until the company is wound up and its debts and liabilities paid that any entitlement to the surplus value of the assets arises. Moreover, as stated in s 1070A(1) of the *Corporations Act*, a share is personal property that is physically independent from the company's assets: *Ord Forrest Pty Ltd v FCT* at 143-144. It is personalty that is transmissible in accordance with any prescriptions detailed in the company's constitution or, if applicable, the operating rules of a Clearing and Settlement Facility ('CS Facility') as defined in s 768A: s 1070A(1). A CS Facility is in essence an organisation that provides a mechanism for the settlement of share transfers. See the discussion below and in Chapter 8.

Evidence of shareholding

[7.30] Until recently, shareholding was generally evidenced by a share certificate issued by the company specifying the shares held by a member, the company name, class of shares and any unpaid amount: s 1070C(1). A share certificate, however, only provides *prima facie* evidence of the member's title to the share: s 1070C(2). It is the registration of the member's holding in the register of members which actually confers upon a subscriber the status of shareholder: *FCT v St Helens Farm (ACT) Pty Ltd* (1981) 146 CLR 336 at 427. Section 169 specifies the matters that a company must detail in its share register. See *Westgold Resources NL v Precious Metals Australia Ltd* (2003) 21 ACLC 102.

[7.40] In recent times the Australian securities industry has adopted a new practice in relation to evidencing shareholdings. The Clearing House Electronic Sub-register System ('CHESS') enables securities in companies to be held in an uncertificated mode by entering into an agreement with a broker or under the Issuer Sponsorship of the Company. Replacing the share certificate are statements akin to bank statements. These will identify the shareholder's Security Reference Number ('SRN'). If a shareholder's security holdings change, a new statement is issued, detailing the number of securities held and the changes since the previous statement. Unlike share certificates, these statements do not have to be settled with a stockbroker to complete a transfer of shares.

Classes of Shares

Power to issue different classes of shares

[7.50] Under s 124(1)(a) companies enjoy the power to issue shares. Section 254B(1) provides that a company may determine the terms on which shares are issued and the rights and restrictions attaching to the shares. Thus, shares may be issued 'with such preferred, deferred or other special rights or such restrictions, whether with regard to dividend, voting, return of capital or otherwise' as the directors determine: see former reg 2 of Table A. Using the power contained in s 254B, the directors may create many types of shares. Note, s 254A, discussed below, complements s 254B by providing for the issuing of a particular class of shares, preference shares.

The Australian Securities and Investment Commission ('ASIC') must be notified of the creation of classes of shares or the conversion of shares in a class into shares of another class within 14 days of the creation/conversion: s 246F(1). Section 246F(2) details additional documents related to the creation/conversion of classes of shares that must be lodged with ASIC.

Defining a class of shares

[7.60] Where a category of shares enjoys rights, benefits, disabilities or other incidents sufficiently distinct from other categories of shares, these shares will be taken as constituting a 'class' of shares: *Clements Marshall Consolidated Ltd v ENT Ltd* (1988) 6 ACLC 389 at 393. Correspondingly, the rights and entitlements under the shares must not be 'so dissimilar as to make it impossible for [the members] to consult together': *Re Hills Motorway* [2002] NSWSC 897. From this definition it will be apparent that shares need not be expressly categorised into classes. Even in the absence of such formal delineation, classes may exist: *Crumpton v Morrine Hall Pty Ltd* [1965] NSWR 240. At common law, all shares issued with the same nominal value are presumed to enjoy the same rights and thus be part of the same class: *Birch v Cropper* (1889) 14 App Cas 525. It will be seen that today this will not apply to preference shares, as none of their rights may be presumed – they need to be specified in accordance with s 254A(2).

The classification of shares into classes is particularly important where the company seeks to vary the rights attached to those shares. Such a change is governed by specific rules, considered later in this chapter.

Deferred shares

[7.70] Deferred shares are so called because the right to dividends is deferred until dividends of a particular amount have been paid to other shareholders. This type of share may be adopted by the founders of a company as an indication of their faith in the company's profitability.

Ordinary shares

[7.80] Ordinary shares make up the majority of shares held by members of companies. These shareholders are usually entitled to dividends before deferred shareholders, but after preference shareholders, discussed below. These shareholders normally enjoy full voting rights and, because of their combined numbers, can usually exercise a great degree of control over company affairs.

Preference shares

[7.90] As noted above, the power to issue shares may be used to issue preference shares: s 254A(1). As noted above, establishing that shares are preference shares requires that certain rights be specified in accordance with s 254A(2). This subsection provides that the company's constitution (if any) or a special resolution passed by the general meeting must specify the rights attached to the preference shares with respect to:

- repayment of capital;
- participation in surplus assets and profits;
- cumulative or non-cumulative dividends;
- voting; and
- priority of payment of capital and dividends.

It is not necessary to set out in the constitution/resolution the full detail of the rights enjoyed by the shareholder: *TNT Australia Pty Ltd v Normandy Resources NL* (1989) 7 ACLC 1090 at 1099. Thus, it suffices if the constitution/resolution cross-refers to another document where that detail can be ascertained: *TNT Australia* at 1099.

A failure to specify these matters renders the allotment invalid. For a recent case where the company failed to specify the matters required by s 254A(2) (formerly s 200 of the *Corporations Law*) and had to seek from the court validation orders, see *Onslow Salt Pty Ltd (ACN 050 159 558)* (2003) 21 ACLC 1113.

[7.100] Preference shares normally enjoy preferential rights to the payment of dividends over, for example, ordinary shareholders: *Re Brighton & Dyke Rwy* (1890) 44 Ch D 28 at 38. Such rights do not, however, assure shareholders automatic dividends each year. Unless the company makes a profit and a dividend is announced in accordance with the proper procedure, discussed below, preference shareholders have no right to demand the payment of a dividend: *Marra Developments Ltd v BW Rofe Pty Ltd* [1977] 2 NSWLR 618.

The extent of a preference shareholder's entitlement to any declared dividends will also depend on whether they are cumulative or non-cumulative preference shareholders. As noted above, s 254A(2) requires the company's constitution, or a special resolution, to state whether preference shares are cumulative or non-cumulative. Non-cumulative preference shareholders are only entitled to a share of any declared dividends for that particular year. By contrast, cumulative preference shareholders' entitlement to dividends accumulates year to year, whether or not a dividend has actually been declared. Any undeclared dividends are in a sense carried forward and added to future years' entitlements. These accumulated profits have priority over any other dividend payments. When payable, all the accumulated profits are paid to the present holder of the share. This is because the right to the dividend only arises when it becomes a debt which, depending on the company's constitution, is either when the dividend is declared (s 254V(2) and *Marra Developments Ltd v BW Rofe Pty Ltd* [1977] 2 NSWLR 616) or when the time fixed for payment arises: s 254V(1). The procedure for, and effect of, declaring a dividend is discussed in detail below.

As dividends may not be declared after the company has started to be wound up (*Re Crichton's Oil Co* [1902] 2 Ch 86; *Re Collie Power Co Pty Ltd* (1952) 54 WALR 44), the right to such accumulated profits can be lost if the company is liquidated: *Re William Bedford Ltd* [1967] VR 490. 'The fact is that there are no true arrears when the winding-up occurs, because there are no arrears until preference dividends' become a debt owing to the preference shareholder: *Re William Bedford Ltd* at 497. If before winding up the accumulated dividend has been declared and becomes a debt, but is not paid, the shareholder can prove the debt in liquidation. Payment of this debt is, however, postponed until all debts owed to non-members are paid: s 563A. Thus, while not ranking equally with other creditors, accumulated dividends owed to preference shareholders will normally be paid before any return on capital to other shareholders.

If preference shareholders have been paid their preference dividend for a particular year, their entitlement to participate in any further company profits will be confined to cases where that additional right is proved under s 254A(2): *Will v United Lankat Plantations Co Ltd* [1914] AC 11. Shares that enjoy this additional right are called participating preference shares.

[7.110] It is also usual for preference shareholders to have priority over ordinary shareholders in the return of share capital: *Re Brighton & Dyke Rwy* (1890) 44 Ch D 28 at 38. Again, however, this right and/or the right to share in surplus assets must be established in accordance with s 254A(2). If s 254A is complied with, but preference shareholders are not accorded preferential rights to capital, at common law they will rank equally with other shareholders: *Scottish Insurance Corporation Ltd v Wilsons and Clyde Coal Co Ltd* [1949] AC 462; *Dimbulla Valley (Ceylon) Tea Co Ltd v Laurie* [1961] Ch 353; *Birch v Cropper* (1889) 14 App Cas 525.

[7.120] Whilst preference shareholders' voting rights may *prima facie* equate with those of ordinary shareholders, usually they are restricted.

Generally, the right to vote is confined to specified situations, such as the reduction in capital, the winding up of the company or an alteration of their class rights. Where the right to vote is expressly confined, these occasions will be taken to be the only time when these shareholders can vote. Again, preference shareholders' voting rights must be specified in the constitution or a special resolution in accordance with s 254A(2).

[7.130] The power to issue shares may be used to issue redeemable preference shares: s 254A(1). Section 254A(3) defines redeemable preference shares as preference shares that are liable to be redeemed:

- at a fixed time or upon the happening of an event;
- at the company's option; or
- at the shareholder's option.

The ability to redeem shares provides the company with greater flexibility, allowing the company to react to changes in the market place by buying back shares entitled to a high percentage of dividends and replacing them with either shares entitling the holder to a lesser rate of return or loan capital.

The shares may only be redeemed in accordance with the terms of issue: s 254J(1). On redemption, the shares are cancelled: s 254J(1). The redemption must be paid out of either profits otherwise available for distribution as dividends or the proceeds of a fresh share issue made for the purpose of the redemption: s 254K. Thus, the redemption cannot be paid out of the company's capital: *Steel Improvement Holdings Pty Ltd and the Companies Act* [1980] ACLC 34,274. Under the terms of the issue, the company may also be liable to pay a premium as 'compensation' for the redemption. The compensation must also be paid out of either profits otherwise available for distribution as dividends or the proceeds of a fresh share issue made for the purpose of the redemption: s 254K. A person involved in a company's failure to comply with the restrictions contained in ss 254J and 254K contravenes s 254L(2). Section 254L(2) is a civil penalty provision. The consequences of breaching such a provision are detailed in Chapter 10. The breach does not, however, impact on the validity of the redemption or a related contract/transaction, nor render the company to have committed an offence: s 254L(1).

If the company fails to redeem the shares on any specified due date, the shareholder may seek an injunction restraining the payment of dividends to ordinary shareholders until redeemed: *Re Holders Investment Trust Ltd* [1971] 1 WLR 583.

Governor's shares

[7.140] Small proprietary companies may sometimes issue governor's shares to the company's founder/governing director. These shares will usually enjoy special voting rights, enabling that shareholder to control the company.

Employee shares

[7.150] Some companies' constitutions provide for the issuing of shares to employees. Such shares normally confer limited rights, ensuring that too much control is not conceded to the employees. It is usual for no voting rights to be attached to the shares. It is also common that the shares are not transferable and/or that they have to be forfeited if the shareholder is no longer an employee. The purchase of these shares can be financed by the company through an employee acquisition scheme, approved by the company in general meeting: s 260C(4).

Variation of class rights

Defining a variation of class rights

[7.160] It will be seen below that the *Corporations Act*, and often the corporate constitution, prescribe procedures for the variation of class rights. Certain actions clearly involve a variation of class rights. Thus, a reduction in the dividend rights of the holders of certain shares clearly denies a right peculiar to that class of shareholders. In more difficult cases, however, the courts have drawn a distinction between alterations that affect the substance, as opposed to the mere enjoyment, of a class right. Only those alterations which affect the substance of the class right need comply with the procedures detailed below: *White v Bristol Aeroplane Co Ltd* [1953] Ch 65; *Re Fowlers Vacola Manufacturing Co Ltd* [1966] VR 97; *Greenhalgh v Arderne Cinemas Ltd* [1946] 1 All ER 512; *Re Advance Bank Australia Ltd (No 2)* (1997) 22 ACSR 513; *In the Matter of Village Roadshow Limited* [2003] VSC 440. Thus, in *White v Bristol Aeroplane Co Ltd*, while a bonus issue to the ordinary shareholders had the effect of diluting the preference shareholders' voting power, as a matter of substance the preference shareholders' voting rights had not been affected. They still had their voting power. It was just the enjoyment of that voting power that had been practically affected by the share issue. Hence, the court held there was no need to comply with the relevant variation of class rights procedure specified in the company's constitution.

Similarly, unless the constitution provides otherwise, a reduction in share capital, discussed below, is not usually considered a variation of class rights: *Re Fowlers Vacola Manufacturing Co Ltd*. Thus, in that case a special resolution was passed by the general meeting to reduce its share capital by returning to the ordinary shareholders 7s 6D on each 10s share and by reducing the nominal value of those shares to 2s 6D. The reduction was opposed by certain preference shareholders on the basis that their priority in the return of capital in a winding up had been abrogated by the reduction in capital. While the court recognised there had been a '*pro tanto* destruction' of the right because on a winding up the capital available for distribution to the preference shareholders would have been reduced, the right to priority in the return of capital remained unimpaired. It was only the value of that right that had been affected.

Note, *Re Fowlers Vacola Manufacturing Co Ltd* was recently distinguished in *In the Matter of Village Roadshow Limited* [2003] VSC 440. The latter case involved a share buy-back scheme. However, unlike the former case, the resolution would have entitled the company to buy-back all preference shares. Mandie J held that, unlike *Re Fowlers Vacola Manufacturing Co Ltd*, this resolution affected more than the mere enjoyment of the preference shareholders rights. The legal rights of the preference shareholders would have been abrogated as a matter of substance. See also *Re Allgas Energy Ltd* (1998) 27 ACSR 729.

[7.170] If there is no actual variation of class rights, it is necessary to determine if there is a deemed variation of class rights. A deemed variation may be provided for in the Act or the company's constitution. Section 246C deems divisions of shares/classes of shares or membership rights (in companies with no shareholding) into further classes of shares/rights to be deemed variations of class rights. The relevant conduct in most cases has the effect of creating new classes of shares/membership interests and thus would constitute an actual variation of class rights. See, for example, ss 246C(1)(a) and 246C(3). There are exceptions where the deeming provisions make important extensions to the common law. Section 246C(5) deems there to be a variation of class rights where a company that has one class of shares issues new shares that have rights that differ from those attached to the existing shares. This will be a deemed variation of the class rights of the shares in the original class of shares unless provided for in the company's constitution or a notice, document or resolution lodged with ASIC. In addition, s 246C(6) (former s 197(8)) deems the allotment of preference shares ranking equally with existing preference shares to be a variation of the latter's class rights, unless the new allotment was authorised under the terms of the existing allotment or the terms of any constitution existing when the existing preference shares were issued. Similarly, former reg 4(3) of Table A deems the creation or issuing of shares ranking equally with pre-existing shares to which rights are attached to be a variation of the latter's class rights unless the contrary is provided for in the terms of the initial issue. The latter provision is not confined to preference shares.

Procedure to vary class rights

[7.180] If there is a variation of class rights, the procedure with which the company must comply will depend on whether provision is made in the constitution for altering class rights. Where the company has a constitution it will usually provide a mechanism for varying the rights attached to shares. This normally requires the written consent of 75% of the class or the passage of a special resolution by the affected class in a class meeting. See, for example, former reg 4 of Table A. Where the company's constitution provides for the alteration of class rights, s 246B(1) declares that these rights shall only be altered in accordance with the specified procedure. Note, unlike its predecessors, s 246B(1) does not specify any minimum standard by which the procedure in the constitution must comply. The subsection allows companies to use a procedure much less stringent than that which s 246B(2) applies to companies which have no provision in their constitution governing a variation in class rights. Thus, the procedure may deny the affected class any right to participate in the decision, yet still satisfy s 246B(1).

Note that the clause specifying the procedure may be varied, but only if the procedure specified in that clause is complied with: s 246B(1).

Where the affected class rights are stated in the company's constitution it would be assumed that it would be necessary to also amend the constitution to so vary the class rights. While s 246B(1) does not expressly provide that, in addition to complying with the procedure specified in the constitution for varying the class rights, there must be a special resolution passed at a general meeting, it would seem logical the constitution must be formally amended in accordance with s 136(2), as detailed in Chapter 6. A contrary view would mean that s 246B(1) would allow a class to change their rights without the agreement of the rest of the company members.

[7.190] Where the constitution is silent as to how class rights may be altered, as long as these rights are not declared to be unalterable, s 246B(2) specifies how they may be altered. Echoing reg 4 of Table A, this subsection provides that class rights may only be altered by the passage of a special resolution at a meeting of the affected class or with the written consent of 75% of that class. The company must give written notice of a variation or cancellation to the members of the class within seven days after the variation or cancellation: s 246B(3).

In contrast to s 246B(1), s 246B(2) specifically requires, in addition to the consent of the affected class, the passage of a special resolution by the company in general meeting.

Challenging a variation of class rights

[7.200] Section 246D(1) allows members with at least 10% of the votes in the affected class to apply to the court within one month (s 246D(2)) of the variation to have it set aside. If an application is made, the alteration has no effect until the application is withdrawn or determined by the court: s 246D(3)(a). If the court believes the variation unfairly prejudices the members of the class represented by the applicant, it may set aside the alteration: s 246D(5). Equally, if the court is not so satisfied, the alteration must be confirmed: s 246D(5). By providing this mechanism for challenging an alteration, the Act ensures that persons holding 75% or more of votes in the affected class cannot sacrifice the rights of their class to further their own interests in another capacity ie as holders of another class of shares: *Re Holders Investment Trust Ltd* [1971] 2 All ER 289.

[7.210] Even where the consent of the affected class is received in accordance with the applicable variation procedure, if, as discussed above, the constitution must also be altered, that alteration may be set aside if it is not *bona fide* and in the best interest of the company (*Allen v Gold Reefs of West Africa* [1900] 1 Ch 656 at 671) or is *ultra vires*, for improper purposes or oppressive (*Gambotto v WCP Ltd* (1995) 182 CLR 432). These cases are discussed in more detail in Chapter 6.

[7.220] Similarly, the alteration must not be designed to perpetuate a fraud on minority shareholders: *Greenhalgh v Arderne Cinemas* [1951] Ch 286. If an alteration is oppressive, unfairly discriminatory or prejudicial, the court may also set the alteration aside pursuant to the powers conferred by ss 232-235 (formerly s 246AA), discussed in Chapter 12.

[7.230] Where the procedure for varying class rights is incorporated into the constitution, a failure to comply with its terms would enable an aggrieved shareholder to seek a remedy for breach of the statutory contract under s 140(1), discussed in Chapter 6.

Share Capital

Description of share capital

[7.240] Before the enactment of the *Company Law Review Act* 1998 (Cth), most companies limited by shares were required to specify in their constitution the amount of their authorised share capital and the division of such into shares of a fixed amount, known as the share's par value. See former s 117(1)(b). If shares were acquired for less than the par value they were issued at a 'discount' and the shareholder remained liable to pay for the share's full par value, otherwise there would be an unauthorised reduction in share capital: *Ooregum Gold Mining Co of India v Roper* [1892] AC 125. By contrast, if the shares were acquired for more than the par value they were acquired at a 'premium'. This premium was held in a separate account, the premium share account.

Until varied according to the procedures detailed in former s 193 and the company's constitution, the statement of authorised share capital set out the maximum number of shares that the company could allot. Any allotment in excess of the authorised share capital was void: *Bank of Hindustan China and Japan Ltd v Alison* (1871) LR 6 CP 222. Moreover, as this was merely the maximum number of shares that could be issued, this numerical amount did not necessarily correspond with the actual issued shares. Thus, it was common in the case of proprietary companies that their authorised share capital was one million x $1 shares, yet only two x $1 shares had been issued.

[7.250] As the statement of authorised share capital was not tied to issued share capital and as the par value was a historical amount set in the constitution when first incorporated and thus might not reflect the market or asset value of a share, both were abolished by the *Company Law Review Act* 1998. Under this Act par value was abolished and the provisions in the corporate constitution complying with former s 193 were automatically deleted. See ss 254C and 1408 of the *Corporations Act*. Any amount in the premium share account at the commencement of the *Company Law Review Act* 1998 was transferred to the company's share capital account: s 1446.

These changes did not mean that shares no longer had a value and companies would no longer have any underlying capital. Consideration is still paid for the 'nominal' value of shares and the proceeds are held in a capital account that continues to be subject to common law and statutory restrictions upon its reduction. Shares will continue to have 'paid' and (where not fully paid for) 'unpaid' components. See s 1408.

Note, companies can still prevent directors issuing shares over a set number by including in their constitution a provision setting a numerical limit on the number of shares that may be issued. Such clauses will be binding under the statutory contract (s 140(1)) and can only be amended in accordance with the *Corporations Act* and any common law requirements.

Altering share capital

[7.260] Under s 254H(1), a company may convert all or any of its shares into a larger or smaller number of shares through the passage of an ordinary resolution. Note, a conversion under s 254H(1) must not alter the proportion between the paid and unpaid amounts on issued shares: s 254H(3). If it did have such an effect, it would be a reduction of share capital as discussed below.

[7.270] As noted above, any statement in the corporate constitution setting a numerical limit on the number of shares which the directors may issue may be amended in the same manner as any other provision in the constitution, through, *inter alia*, the passage of a special resolution: s 136(2).

Maintenance of share capital

Prerequisites for a reduction of share capital

[7.280] As noted above, in return for enjoying the benefits of limited liability, the common law and the *Corporations Act* place restrictions on the ability of the company to return to its members the amounts they have paid for their shares. These restrictions are founded upon the fact that often the only money creditors of a company may have resort to when seeking the payment of debts is this share capital: *Re Exchange Banking Co (Flitcroft's case)* (1882) 21 Ch D 519 at 533. See also Lord Herschell in *Trevor v Whitworth* (1887) 12 App Cas 409 at 415.

[7.290] Reflecting common law concerns for the preservation of a company's share capital, generally, share capital may not be reduced unless the company complies with s 256B(1) or effects a permissible buyback under Div 2 of Part 2J.1, discussed below. Section 256B allows a company to reduce its share capital if the reduction:

- is fair and reasonable to the company's shareholders as a whole; and
- does not materially prejudice the company's ability to pay its creditors; and
- is approved by the shareholders under s 256C.

Unlimited companies do not need to comply with Part 2J.1: s 258A.

Procedure for reduction of share capital

[7.300] As to shareholder agreement under s 256C, an 'equal reduction' must be approved by an ordinary resolution passed at a general meeting of the company: s 256C(1). A reduction is an equal reduction if it (i) relates only to ordinary shares, (ii) applies to each ordinary shareholder in proportion to the number of ordinary shares held and (iii) the terms are the same for each shareholder: s 256B(2). Other reductions of capital are referred to as 'selective reductions': s 256B(2). Selective reductions must be approved by either a special resolution passed at a general meeting of the company or a resolution agreed to by all ordinary shareholders at a general meeting: s 256C(2). These special requirements are prescribed because selective reductions have the capacity to advantage some shareholders over others. If the reduction is approved by a special resolution, a vote may not be cast in favour of the resolution by a person to whom capital is proposed to be paid or whose liability in respect of amounts unpaid on shares is to be reduced. This ensures that disinterested shareholders approve the resolution and is consistent with the approach taken in relation to selective share buy-backs, briefly detailed below.

If the reduction involves a cancellation of shares, it must also be approved by a special resolution passed at a meeting of the shareholders whose shares are to be cancelled: s 256C(2). A separate class meeting must be held without the presence of shareholders not affected by the reduction. Thus, it is necessary to hold two separate meetings – one to approve the selective reduction and one to approve the cancellation of shares: *Winpar Holdings Ltd v Goldfields Kalgoorlie Ltd* (2002) 20 ACLC 265.

To ensure shareholders are properly informed, the company is required to include with the notice of the meeting at which shareholder approval for a capital reduction is to be sought a statement setting out all information known to the company that is material to the decision to vote in favour of the resolution: s 256C(4). The company will not be required to disclose information if it would be unreasonable to require the company to do so because the company had previously disclosed the information to its shareholders: s 256C(4). These rules are the same as those required for shareholder approval under the share buy-back provisions, discussed below. Under s 256C(5), before the notice of the meeting is sent to shareholders, the company must lodge with ASIC a copy of the notice and any document relating to the reduction that is to accompany the notice.

Any resolution required by s 256C(2) must be lodged with ASIC within 14 days of its passage: s 256C(3). The reduction can only be made after a further 14 days has lapsed: s 256C(3).

[7.310] A person involved in a company's failure to comply with s 256C contravenes s 256D(3). Section 256D(3) is a civil penalty provision. The consequences of breaching such a provision are detailed in Chapter 10.

The breach does not, however, impact on the validity of the reduction or related contract/transaction, nor render the company to have committed an offence: s 256D(2).

Challenging a reduction

[7.320] While Div 1 of Part 2J.1 does not make express provision for shareholders or creditors to object to a reduction of capital on the basis that s 256B(1) has not been satisfied, the general injunction provision, s 1324, indirectly facilitates this: *Winpar Holdings Ltd v Goldfields Kalgoorlie Ltd* (2000) 18 ACLC 665 at 675. Section 1324 allows interested persons to make an application to the courts injuncting a breach of the Act. Thus, s 1324 would allow creditors to assert that the reduction prejudices the company's ability to pay its debts and/or shareholders to claim that the reduction is not fair and reasonable to the company's shareholders as required by s 256B. In this sense the previous case law governing when a court will confirm a capital reduction will remain relevant. According to this case law, a reduction would not be confirmed if it unfairly prejudiced the interests of, *inter alia*, present and future shareholders and creditors and the public: *Poole v National Bank and China Ltd* [1907] AC 229 at 239; *Ex p Westburn Sugar Refineries Ltd* [1951] AC 625 at 629; *In re Preston Motors Pty Ltd* [1957] VR 111 at 111-112; *Re Elders IXL Ltd* (1984) 4 ACLC 736 at 738-739. Moreover, in determining the fairness of a reduction it was necessary to consider the impact on each kind of shareholder, not merely each class: *Re Campaign Holdings Ltd* (1990) 8 ACLC 64. For example, within a class of shareholders it was necessary to consider the fairness of the reduction to the holders of both fully paid and party paid shares: *Re Campaign Holdings Ltd*. The fairness of any compensation payments consequent to the reduction is to be determined as at the date of the shareholders' meeting, not in light of subsequent events that may render that compensation insufficient: *Ramsay Health Care Ltd v Elkington* (1992) 10 ACLC 421.

The current provisions were considered for the first time in *Winpar Holdings Ltd v Goldfields Kalgoorlie Ltd*.

Winpar Holdings Ltd v Goldfields Kalgoorlie Ltd
Supreme Court of New South Wales: Santow J
(2000) 18 ACLC 665

The Goldfields shareholders held 87.7% of the issued shares in Goldfields Kalgoorlie Ltd. Winpar Holdings Ltd held 12,373 ordinary shares in Goldfields Kalgoorlie Ltd. This shareholding represented 0.005% of the issued ordinary shares of the latter company. This in turn represented 0.5% of the shares that it was proposed to cancel. A further 11.4% of the issued ordinary shares were held by the QBE Group. This represented 92.7% of the shares that it was proposed to cancel.

Goldfields Kalgoorlie Ltd was a publicly listed company that conducted a business involving gold mining and acquiring and exploring for gold resources. Goldfields Kalgoorlie Ltd held an extraordinary general meeting of shareholders to consider a proposal for a selective reduction of its capital under s 256B. The proposal was that all shares held by non-Goldfields shareholders be cancelled and paid consideration of 55 cents per share held. If this occurred Goldfields Kalgoorlie Ltd would be a wholly owned subsidiary of Goldfields Ltd. The notice of the meeting was accompanied by, *inter alia*, an independent expert's report that the shares were valued between 45.7 and 46.9 cents and that the proposed selective capital reduction at a price of 55 cents per share was fair and reasonable. A majority numerically exceeding the requirements under s 256C passed the relevant resolutions, including for the cancellation of the affected shares.

Winpar Holdings Ltd challenged the acquisition of their shares under the selective reduction of capital on various grounds relating to the legal efficacy of the steps taken in passing the relevant resolutions. It was asserted that the financial benefits Goldfields Ltd received through Goldfields Kalgoorlie Ltd becoming a wholly owned subsidiary should have been allocated to the minority shareholders whose shares were cancelled and thus the compensation offered was too low. Further it was argued that the statutory disclosure requirements had not been met, including in regard to these 'special benefits' Goldfields Ltd received from the cancellation of the shares. Winpar Holdings Ltd consequently sought an injunction on the basis that Goldfields Kalgoorlie Ltd had breached ss 256B and 256C. In reply, Goldfields Kalgoorlie Ltd asserted that while the special benefits that accrued to its parent company had not been totally allocated to the minority shareholders, they had been *pro rata* allocated to all shareholders and were included in part in the minority shareholders' compensation. Moreover, it asserted that the value of such 'special benefits' had been adequately detailed in the independent expert's report.

> **Santow J:** **[667]** 1. This is the first challenge to a minority takeover by selective reduction of capital, since court approval ceased two years ago to be a requirement for reductions of capital, selective or otherwise. Court approval for reductions cancelling minority capital used to be a trade off for a much lower acceptance requirement for compulsory acquisition so achieved. But, as emerges, the court, at the behest of an aggrieved shareholder, still retains a supervisory jurisdiction. So the trade off partially remains.
>
> 2. The Plaintiff, Winpar Holdings Limited, ("Winpar") challenges the acquisition of its minority shareholding in Goldfields Kalgoorlie Limited ("GKL") pursuant to a selective reduction of capital. It does so on various grounds. They are essentially grounds going to the legal efficacy of the steps taken. Winpar brings its challenge at the conclusion of those corporate steps but before payment has been effected. It does so by way of an injunction pursuant to s 1324 of the *Corporations Law* on the ground that the conduct or proposed conduct of GKL would contravene ss 256B and C of the *Corporations Law* under which the selective reduction of capital is sought to be effected. However, that challenge, with its associated grounds relating to lack of sufficient disclosure of material information, takes place against the background of a radical series of changes in 1998 affecting share capital reductions under the *Corporations Law*, which have eliminated the need for court approval. But first some history. ...

4. ... [U]ntil 1998, reductions of capital, selective or otherwise, required not only the affirmative vote of three-quarters of the total shareholder votes cast at the meeting but also court approval. That latter safeguard was primarily directed at the interest of creditors. But because of the prevalence of selective reductions of capital to effect takeovers, it necessarily had to accommodate shareholder interests as well. In particular there had to be adequate safeguards against unfair [668] expropriation for the minority shareholder. ...

5. By the reforms effected under the *Company Law Review Act* 1998 statute finally caught up with the commercial world. It was recognised for the first time that there is a distinct functional difference between a conventional return of capital on an equal basis and a selective reduction of capital. The latter, despite use of the term "reduction", really amounts to takeover by another name; cancelling for cash or shares, all the external shareholdings save that of the intended new corporate holding company. However, if minority shareholdings were to be so cancelled, the new Part 2J.1 required there be not only a special resolution of all shareholders save those who were to receive consideration as part of the reduction but also a special resolution passed at a meeting of shareholders whose shares are to be cancelled; see s 256C of the *Corporations Law*. The new s 256B imposed only three conditions for a reduction of capital under Part 2J.1 when eliminating the need for court *approval* but retaining the capacity for court *challenge*. The first of these conditions, that creditors not be materially prejudiced, is not in issue here. However, what is in issue is whether the necessary special resolutions have been passed in accordance with the requirements of s 256C of the *Corporations Law* and whether, as required by s 256B(1)(a), the reduction "is fair and reasonable to the company's shareholders as a whole". ...

[674] 51. That the terms of the expropriation be fair is clearly reflected in s 256B(1)(a) in requiring that the reduction must be "fair and reasonable to the company's shareholders as a whole". Nonetheless as emerges in answering question 3 below, how fairness is determined is more prescriptive under the statute, though that difference should not be overstated.

52. Though Court appraisal as such is no longer *initially* required, s 1324 in providing for injunctive relief expressly contemplates in s 1324(1B)(a) that a selective reduction of capital may be challenged in court on grounds including its fairness and reasonableness. That brings the Court directly into consideration of any fairness grounds of challenge. Moreover s 1324(1B)(a) reverses the onus such that "the court must assume that the conduct constitutes, or would constitute, a contravention of that paragraph, section or provision unless the company or person proves otherwise." The cited provisions include paragraph 256B(1)(a) or (b) thus emphasising the centrality of fairness and reasonableness. ...

53. I should add that sub-s 256C(4) contains an express regime of disclosure, further emphasising that the legislature has created its own comprehensive, protective code. *Gambotto* principles of general law are left with no further work to do. I agree with ASIC's submission that properly informed minority shareholder approval can be taken to express a view about the substantive fairness of the terms offered to the minority. That is a view to which courts ordinarily give considerable weight, as with schemes of arrangement, on the basis that shareholders, properly informed, are the best judge of what is in their interests. However, the Court must still, in the case of a challenge, reach its own view. ...

[676] 61. The Plaintiff then relies upon the decision of McLelland CJ in Eq in *Melcann Ltd v Super John Pty Ltd* (1995) 13 ACLC 92. In that case, the relevant valuation and the price consequently paid for the minority failed altogether to take into account the value to the acquiring company of "the synergies involved in its ability after cancellation of the minority shareholders to merge substantial elements of the company's activities with those of ACH itself." (at 93). ...

63. ... In determining the fair value of the shares the expert had unfairly failed to take into account the special benefits to the acquiring company. What McLelland CJ in Eq did not decide is whether the whole of such special benefits should be attributable to the minority or merely the pro rata portion represented by their shareholding as a proportion of the total issued share capital, or indeed, whether that depends on other relevant circumstances embraced by what is fair or unfair. The pro rata alternative would share the benefit pro rata between the acquiring company and the minority shareholders who were eliminated by the selective reduction. The Defendant contends that the pro rata allocation here allowed was, in the overall context, "fair and reasonable to the company's shareholders as a whole". ASIC adopt the submission that a pro rata allocation is not intrinsically unfair or unreasonable. That conclusion is based on the construction of that requirement in the context of Pt 2J.1. It is said also to find support in the parallel provision covering, *inter alia*, conventional takeovers under Ch 6, which is to be found in s 667C of Ch 6A. ... Rather pro rata allocation reflects the nature of a reduction of capital. ...

[678] 71. The harmonious and mutually supportive operation for Ch 6A and Ch 2J is ordinarily achieved in transactions within Ch 2J by the allocation of special benefits as reflected in any premium pro rata between the shareholders as a whole. However, that is not to say that some other allocation may not in unusual circumstances be required as "fair and reasonable to the company's shareholders as a whole". This is in order to achieve the stated purpose of Pt 2J.1 in s 256A(b) namely "seeking to ensure fairness *between* the company's shareholders" and taking into account what is *both* fair *and* reasonable for shareholders "as a whole". An example would be where the special value derives not only from 100% ownership, but also extraordinary efforts on the part of the 100% parent, such as to exploit a particular resource. There is also the converse case where 100% ownership is of such unique value to the 100% parent, that it may be arguable that more should be attributed to the minority than the pro rata amount. Even so, one would not expect 100% to go to the minority. Here there is an extra loading in favour of the minority in the 8 cents above value.

72. Indeed the words "as a whole" in s 256B reinforce that interpretation. Those words require fairness and reasonableness as between majority and minority, not some one-sided allocation. ...

74. ... The decision in *Melcann* is simply authority in the present context that special benefits to the acquiring company must be taken into account in a manner that is "fair and reasonable to the company's shareholders as a whole". It would prima facie be unfair to deny minority shareholders *any* attribution of that value to their shares. This is more especially under the new regime for capital reduction, where no longer is it primarily a matter of whether the proposal has been "fairly" presented to members for their commercial judgment, though this Court retains a residual discretion. Now the Court must be positively satisfied, in the event of challenge, that "the reduction" –not the

consideration – is "fair and reasonable to the company's shareholders as a whole", with the onus on the company doing the reduction, though members' commercial judgment on that is certainly not irrelevant. ...

[679] 81. My answer to the previous question means that there is no failure to disclose any supposed inequity from such benefits being allocated pro rata, as there is no intrinsic inequity in that allocation. ...

[680] 84. ... I agree with the Defendant that it is not necessary to have descended to the level of detail where the capitalised saving is actually stated. Here the information is given from whence it can be worked out by anyone sufficiently interested and the allocation has been fair and reasonable. In those circumstances actually stating the end calculation is not of material importance; compare *Fraser v NRMA Holdings Ltd* (1995) 55 FCR 452 at 468. ...

[681] 91. Summing up, I consider that the evidentiary onus has passed to the Plaintiff to establish the method, or methodology of valuation is not fair and reasonable, and the Plaintiff has failed to do so. ...

95. It follows that in answering question 4, I do not consider that there has been any substantiated non-disclosure or misleading or deceptive conduct as regards the various matters including of economic upside identified by the Plaintiff. ...

[682] 102. I am satisfied that the Court can conclude that the selective capital reduction was fair and reasonable, notwithstanding that QBE as a single shareholder could determine the outcome of the vote. While that shareholders' decision was influenced as a result of a general corporate strategy to reduce its exposure to the Australian market, it does not follow that the overall vote is vitiated. To take the analogy of a scheme of arrangement, it could not be said that the interest of QBE was so divergent from that of the other members who voted that it would have been treated as a separate class under a scheme of arrangement. Closer scrutiny gives no cause for concern here. In any event, QBE indicated that it has obtained its own valuations. It would be unreasonable to suppose that QBE would not have considered its commercial corporate interest including matters of value ...

103. In any event, only 224,546 proxy votes were cast against the proposal. Out of the [683] minority, non-QBE shareholders comprised 2,233,807 shares representing 7.3% of the shares to be cancelled. Whereas, QBE's holding of 27,801,342 shares represented 92.7% of the shares to be cancelled. Winpar Holdings 12,373 shares represented 0.5% of the non-QBE shares to be cancelled. That indicates that there were a very substantial number of other shareholders whose shares were cancelled who were satisfied either not to vote at all or to vote for the resolution. That certainly does not point to major opposition.

104. The other contention is that the consideration for the reduction being at a substantial discount to the long-term average weighted Stock Market price for the shares being cancelled should, for that reason, lead to a conclusion that the selective reduction was not fair and reasonable. However, the PWC report at paras 113-115 concluded that having regard to the level of trading in the shares, share trading was not a reliable indicator. While the Stock Market price is often an important indicator of value, it is not determinative in every case as to what is or is not a fair and reasonable price. It may be sometimes too high and sometimes too low; see generally *Holt v Cox* (supra). Here there is nothing to indicate that PWC were mistaken in rejecting the stock market price as the determinant of what was fair and reasonable.

[7.330] Note, the courts in *Winpar Holdings Ltd v Goldfields Kalgoorlie Ltd* (2000) 18 ACLC 665; (2002) 20 ACLC 265 also held that ss 256B and 256C provide a comprehensive, protective code and thus the principles espoused in *Gambotto v WCP Ltd* (1995) 182 CLR 432, discussed in Chapter 6, are inapplicable in this context. Thus, *Gambotto* will not provide an alternative way of challenging a reduction in capital.

Company purchasing its own shares

Prohibition on company purchasing its own shares

[7.340] Even in the absence of a statutory prohibition, the House of Lords in *Trevor v Whitworth* (1887) 12 App Cas 409 held that the use of company assets to repurchase shares fell within the scope of the general prohibition against the reduction of share capital. Today, ss 259A and 259C incorporate the House of Lord's sentiments by prohibiting a company acquiring shares or units of shares in itself or issuing or transferring shares to an entity it controls. The prohibition extends to the purchase of the shares of an entity it controls as this would indirectly reduce the company's assets. The notion of control is not confined to legal control, but rather extends to actual control: s 259E(2)(a). In this regard control is defined in terms of AASB 1024; that is, the company's capacity to determine the other company's financial and operating policies: s 259E(1). Acting in a manner consistent with the controlling company's interests or being economically dependent may also indicate control: see s 259E(2)(b).

Both ss 259A and 259C(1) incorporate a number of exemptions to this general principle. In relation to the acquisition of shares in itself, the most exception is a buy-back under s 257A, discussed below.

[7.350] Section 259F(2) provides that a person involved in a company's failure to comply with s 259A contravenes s 259F(2). Section 259F(2) is a civil penalty provision. The consequences of breaching such a provision are detailed in Chapter 10. Moreover, where a person's involvement in the breach of s 259A is dishonest, that person will also commit an offence: s 259F(3). The breach does not, however, impact on the validity of the acquisition or a related contract or transaction: s 259F(1). Nor does the breach mean that the company has committed an offence: s 259F(1).

Buy-backs under Div 2 of Part 2J.1

[7.360] As noted above, the most important exception to the prohibition against the company buying its own shares is contained in Div 2 of Part 2J.1. Section 257A provides that a company may buy-back its own shares if the buy-back does not materially prejudice the company's ability to pay its creditors and the company follows the procedures in Div 2. These buy-back schemes include:

- equal access buy-backs;[1]
- selective buy-backs;[2]
- on-market buy-backs;[3]
- employee share scheme buy-back;[4] and
- minimum holding buy-backs.[5]

[7.370] Section 257B(1) provides a table (*see over*) governing these different types of buy-backs. Under s 257B(4) the 10/12 limit for a company proposing to make a buy-back is 10% of the smallest number, at any time over a 12-month period, of votes attaching to voting shares in the company. This limit is exceeded if the number of votes attaching to all voting shares bought in the past 12 months and the voting shares that will be bought back if the proposed buy-back is made, exceed the 10/12 limit: s 257B(5). See the sections specified in the s 257B(1) table (*see over*) for a more detailed discussion of the relevant prerequisites.

Company lending money on security of its own shares

Prohibition on company lending money on security of its own shares

[7.380] Section 259B(1) prohibits a company taking security over shares or units of shares in itself or a company it controls. See the above discussion of s 259E, defining when a company controls an entity. The reason for this prohibition is twofold. First, if the share capital is used to fund a loan, if the loan is not repaid there will be a reduction in share capital. Second, and most relevantly, if the borrower defaults on the loan the company will call upon the security, its own shares, and will have acquired its own shares contrary to the above prohibition.

[7.390] Section 259F(2) provides that any person involved in a company's failure to comply with s 259B(1) contravenes s 259F(2). As noted above, s 259F(2) is a civil penalty provision, the consequences of such

---

1 An equal access scheme involves:
   - an offer of ordinary shares;
   - a *pari passu* offer;
   - all persons have a reasonable opportunity to accept the offer;
   - a specified time after offers close governs when agreements may be entered into;
   - the terms of all offers are the same: s 257B(2). See also s 257B(3).
2 Section 9 defines a selective buy-back as a buy-back other than:
   - an equal access buy-back;
   - a minimum holding buy-back;
   - an on-market buy-back;
   - an employee share buy-back scheme.
3 Section 257B(6) defines this as a buy-back that results from an offer made by a listed corporation at an official meeting of a securities exchange in Australia in the ordinary course of trading on a stock market of that exchange. See also s 257B(7)-(8).
4 Section 9 defines such a scheme as:
   - having its purpose the acquisition of shares in a company by or on behalf of participating employees (including salaried directors) of the company or related corporation; and
   - having been approved by the general meeting.
5 Section 9 defines these as a buy-back of shares in a listed corporation where the parcel of shares bought back is less than a marketable parcel.

Table from Section 257B(1) – Different Types of Buy-back

Procedures [and sections applied]	minimum holding	employee share scheme		on-market		equal access scheme		selective buy-back
		within 10/12 limit	over 10/12 limit	within 10/12 limit	over 10/12 limit	within 10/12 limit	over 10/12 limit	
ordinary resolution [257C]	–	–	yes	–	yes	–	yes	–
SPECIAL/unanimous resolution [257D]	–	–	–	–	–	–	–	yes
lodge offer documents with ASIC [257E]	–	–	–	–	–	yes	yes	yes
14 days notice [257F]	–	yes	yes	yes	yes	yes	yes	yes
disclose relevant information when offer made [257G]	–	–	–	–	–	yes	yes	yes
cancel shares [257H]	yes	yes	yes	yes	yes	yes	yes	yes
notify cancellation to ASC [254Y]	yes	yes	yes	yes	yes	yes	yes	yes
notify cancellation to ASIC [254Y] +	yes	yes	yes	yes	yes	yes	yes	yes

being detailed in Chapter 10. Moreover, where a person's involvement in the breach of s 259B is dishonest, that person will also commit an offence: s 259F(3). The breach does not, however, impact on the validity of the security or related contract/transaction, nor render the company as having committed an offence: s 259F(1).

Exemptions

[7.400] The prohibition contained in s 259B(1) does not apply to approved employee share schemes (s 259B(2)) and certain transactions with finance companies (s 259B(3)). If, however, a company acquires shares or units of shares in itself because it exercises rights under a security exempted by s 259B(2) or (3), the company must within 12 months cease to hold the shares: s 259B(3). ASIC may extend this 12-month period on the application of the company: s 259B(3). If at the end of the 12 months the company still holds the shares or units of shares, the company commits an offence for each day the situation continues: s 259B(6).

Company financially assisting purchase of its own shares

Prerequisites for financial assistance

[7.410] Section 260A (former s 205(1)(a)) provides that a company may only financially assist a person to acquire shares or units of shares in the company or its holding company if certain conditions, detailed below, are met. Again, the rationale for this proscription lies in the maintenance of capital theory. First, if the company's assets are used to finance the purchase of its own shares, a failure to repay that finance gives effect to a reduction in the company's overall capital. Second, and less direct, if the borrower defaults on the loan the company will call upon whatever property/security the borrower might have, including its own shares, to source the repayment of the loan.

Whilst the basic rationale underlying both s 260A and its predecessor remain the same, this doctrine is severely undermined by changes introduced by s 260A. This section differs from s 205(1)(a) by allowing financial assistance to be given as long as it:
- does not materially prejudice the interests of the company or its shareholders or the company's ability to pay its creditors; or
- is approved by the shareholders under s 260B; or
- is exempted under s 260C.

The use of the word 'or' dictates that these requirements are not cumulative. The introduction of these conditions means that financial assistance that materially prejudices the company's ability to pay its creditors will not breach s 260A(1) where, for example, the shareholders have approved the measure under s 260B. As a result, whether conduct amounts to financial assistance need only be considered where there is a material financial deterioration of the company as a result of the assistance. It is only in these cases that shareholders' approval under s 260B or a s 260C exemption needs to be invoked.

[7.420] 'Financial assistance' is not defined in s 260A so it will be accorded its ordinary meaning. While s 205(1) defined 'financial assistance' and expressly provided that the financial assistance may be given 'directly or indirectly', the absence of such express statements in s 260A would provide no reason to read s 260A down to require that the assistance be given directly to the purchaser of the shares. See the earlier cases of *Re Myer Retail Investments Pty Ltd* (1983) 1 ACLC 990 at 996; *Darvall v North Sydney Brick & Tile Co Ltd* (1988) 6 ACLC 154 at 181. Thus, in the latter case the financial assistance was indirect, the company requiring a joint venture partner to guarantee the loan used by the former company's managing director to acquire shares in that company.

[7.430] Section 260A(2) provides that the financial assistance may be given before or after the acquisition. See also *Hunters Products Group Ltd (in liq) v Kindly Products Pty Ltd* (1996) 20 ACSR 412 at 429. In this case the financial assistance was given some time after the relevant acquisition of shares.

[7.440] The financial assistance provisions and, in particular, the issue whether the company has suffered material prejudice from such financial assistance was recently considered in *ASIC v Adler* (2002) 20 ACLC 576. The court held this is determined by not only looking at the actual transaction providing the financial assistance, but also other, interlocking factual elements that led to the financial assistance. Moreover, the court affirmed that the onus of proving that there was no material prejudice lies with the person seeking to defend the transaction.

ASIC v Adler
Supreme Court of New South Wales: Santow J
(2002) 20 ACLC 576

Adler was a non-executive director of HIH Insurance Ltd ('HIH'). Williams was a director and the CEO of HIH. Fodera was a director and the finance controller of HIH. HIH Casualty and General Insurance Ltd ('HIHC') was a wholly owned subsidiary of HIH. Adler requested, and Williams and Fodera arranged, for HIHC to advance $10 million to Pacific Eagle Equity Pty Ltd ('PEE'), a company controlled by Adler. The $10 million payment was arranged so that no other directors of HIH would be aware of the advance. During the next two weeks PEE used some of these funds to purchase HIH shares to the value of approximately $4 million. Through these share purchases Adler sought to support HIH's share price for the benefit of his substantial personal shareholding in the company. Williams was aware of the intended use of the $10 million to acquire HIH shares. Soon after a unit trust was established with PEE as trustee. Units were issued to HIHC at a price of $10 million; representing the $10 million advance. Units were also issued to another corporation controlled by Adler, Adler Corporation ('A

Co'). The $10 million advance and the HIH shares purchased with such funds became part of the trust property. The HIH shares were subsequently sold at a loss of more than $2.1 million. Adler caused the unit trust to use a further part of the $10 million to buy certain unlisted technology/ communications investments from A Co at cost. The purchases were made without any independent analysis of their worth and after the collapse of the stock market for technology and communication stocks. The unit trust suffered a loss of more than $3.8 million on these investments. Adler also caused PEE to make three unsecured loans totalling more than $2 million to companies and funds associated with Adler.

ASIC brought proceedings against Adler, Williams, Fodera and A Co for breaches of, *inter alia*, s 260A. It was contended that HIHC had contravened s 260A by providing financial assistance to PEE to acquire shares in its holding company, HIH. The defendants asserted that the financial assistance did not materially prejudice the interests of the company or its shareholders or its ability to pay its creditors within s 260A(1)(a). Adler asserted that the rights HIHC acquired through the transaction meant that its interests had not been materially prejudiced.

The court held that s 260A had been contravened as HIHC had suffered material prejudice as a result of financially assisting PEE to acquire shares in HIH. The rights HIHC acquired through the transaction, whether as an unsecured creditor or through a resulting trust, were of a materially lesser value than the advance of $10 million that had been made. Adler, Williams, Fodera and A Co were sufficiently involved in the contravention to breach s 260D(2).

Santow J: [646] 345. I would adopt what Ford says as to onus being on the party seeking to demonstrate lack of material prejudice (at 24.710):

The notion that the onus is on those seeking to defend the transactions to show that there is no material prejudice is reinforced by s 1324(1B) which says that in proceedings for relief under that section based on the alleged contravention of s 260A(1)(a), the Court must assume that the transaction constitutes a contravention unless the Defendant proves otherwise.

346. That contention is reinforced by the presence of the "material prejudice" provisions (s 260A(1)(a)) immediately alongside what in earlier versions of the prohibition on financial assistance was the other gateway out of that prohibition, namely shareholder approval (see s 260A(1)(b)) and note the final gateway added in the contiguous s 260A(1)(c).

347. I turn now to the potential application of s 260A in the present circumstances. ...

349. ... As I earlier conclude, one assesses material prejudice by reference to the transaction with its interlocking elements giving rise to the financial assistance, taking into account its financial consequences for the interests of the company or its shareholders. This is in order to determine where the net balance of financial advantage lies from the giving of the financial assistance.

...

[648] 355. HIHC suffered material prejudice as a result of its financial assistance, so contravening s 260A of the *Corporations Act*. It did so by exchanging cash for either unsecured indebtedness owed to it, or alternatively in the first instance equitable rights by way of resulting or other trust in respect of the HIH shares being contemporaneously bought. Such rights against PEE were from the start of materially lesser value than the cash handed over. This is because such equitable rights would be likely to be contentious and to require expensive litigation to enforce in Court. Thereafter material prejudice also resulted from the other elements of the transaction, that is, the lack of safeguards in, and disadvantageous terms of, the AEUT Trust documentation and the circumstances which, from its inception, rendered the investment in HIH shares inherently likely to give rise to the loss that in fact occurred. These included Mr Adler's intention, not to make a quick profit, but to support the HIH share price. A loss was inherently likely from the inception, and did in fact eventuate, both in HIH's carrying value as an investment and when the shares were realised at a loss. Either would constitute "material prejudice" both to HIHC and HIH within the meaning of s 260A(1)(a) and in terms of the pleaded Particulars. That completes the elements for such contravention by HIH and HIHC to have occurred. It leads to the conclusion that both HIH and HIHC contravened s 260A of the *Corporations Act*. ...

356. I turn now to consider whether Mr Adler, Mr Williams or Mr Fodera were *involved* in HIHC's contravention of s 260A so as to be liable under s 260D(2) of the *Corporations Act*. Similarly as to Adler Corporation. I shall deal with each of them in turn. But before doing so I need to deal with a preliminary question, namely, whether *"involved"* as defined by s 79 requires that there be actual knowledge on the part of the person concerned, not only of financial assistance to acquire shares, but also that the assistance did materially prejudice, in this case, "the interests of the company or its shareholder", as the First and Fourth Defendants contend. ...

[649] 360. A powerful argument in favour of a more limited requirement for actual knowledge is that the contravention is made out *unless* the company satisfies the onus upon it to show that one or other of the potential defences or gateways apply. That gateway relevantly here is that the assistance does not materially prejudice the interests of the company or its shareholders. To convert what is thereby expressed in the negative to an affirmative element of the contravention when it comes to the aiding and abetting provisions of s 260D(2) would be incongruous in terms of the primary position of the company as principal offender. It proceeds by denying that the contravention is made out by the proof of each of the elements which precede the words "only if", with thereafter the onus passing to the company concerned. Clearly the company knows best the consequences in terms of material prejudice to it, and in consequence its shareholders and its creditors. ...

[651] 369. Each of Mr Adler and Mr Williams were "involved" in the contravention by HIHC of s 260A of the *Corporations Act*, in giving financial assistance to HIHC to acquire shares in its holding company HIH, being assistance which did materially prejudice the interests of the company or its shareholders. However, if it be the case that for Mr Fodera to be so involved, he had to have knowledge not only of the financial assistance but also of the essential facts pertaining to material prejudice (though it be a defence rather than an element of the contravention) then I could not be positively satisfied that at the time Mr Fodera had that knowledge of material prejudice. As I do not consider that there need be knowledge of what is essentially a defence rather than an ingredient of the contravention, I conclude that he too was sufficiently involved, though to a lesser degree than Messrs Williams and Adler. The result is that each contravened s 260D(2) of the *Corporations Act* as did Adler Corporation, with the above qualification concerning Mr Fodera.

The decision in *ASIC v Adler* (2002) 20 ACLC 576 was upheld on appeal: *Adler v ASIC; Williams v ASIC* (2003) 21 ACLC 1810.

Procedure for shareholder approval

[7.450] As noted above, the financial assistance may be provided even though it involves a material deterioration in the company's finances etc if it is approved by the shareholders within s 260B. Section 260B(1) provides that the approval may be through:

- a special resolution passed by the company at general meeting (no votes being cast in favour of the resolution by the person acquiring the shares or by any associates); or
- a resolution agreed to at a general meeting by all ordinary shareholders.

If the company will be a subsidiary of a listed domestic company immediately after the acquisition, the financial assistance must also be approved by a special resolution passed by that company in general meeting: s 260B(2). Similar provision is made in s 260B(3) where the holding company is not listed and is not itself a subsidiary of a domestic corporation.

[7.460] To ensure shareholders are fully informed, s 260B(4) requires the notice of the meeting to be accompanied by a statement setting out all information known to the company that is material to the resolution. Again, the company is not required to disclose information if it would be unreasonable to require the company to do so because the company had previously disclosed the information to its shareholders: s 260B(4). Under s 260B(5), before the notice of the meeting is sent to shareholders, the company must lodge with ASIC a copy of the notice and any document relating to the financial assistance that is to accompany the notice. See *Milburn v Pivot Ltd* (1997) 15 ACLC 1520 for a discussion of the adequacy of information given to shareholders under the predecessor to s 260B(4), s 205(1).

Exemptions

[7.470] As noted above, s 260A(1) does not apply if one of the exemptions detailed in s 260C are operative. These include:

- the creation of a lien over partly paid shares or an agreement for shares to be paid by instalments where the financial assistance is given by the company in the ordinary course of commercial dealing: s 260C(1);
- where the company is a financial institution and the financial assistance is given in the ordinary course of that business and on ordinary commercial terms: s 260C(2);
- where the company is a subsidiary of a borrowing corporation and the financial assistance is a guarantee or other security given by the subsidiary for repayment by the borrowing corporation of money that it is or will be liable to repay and is given in the ordinary course of commercial dealing: s 260C(3);

- financial assistance under an approved employee share scheme: s 260C(4);
- a reduction of capital authorised under Div 2 of Part 2J.1: s 260C(5)(a);
- a share buy-back in accordance with Div 2 of Part 2J.1: s 260C(5)(b);
- assistance given pursuant to a court order: s 260C(5)(c); and
- the discharge on ordinary commercial terms of a liability that the company incurred as a result of a transaction entered into on ordinary commercial terms: s 260C(5)(d).

See *Hunters Products Group Ltd (in liq) v Kindly Products Pty Ltd* (1996) 20 ACSR 412 at 430-431 and *Fitzsimmons v R* (1997) 23 ACSR 355 at 375-376 for a discussion of those transactions which are in the ordinary course of business.

Consequences

[7.480] Any person involved in a company's contravention of s 260A contravenes s 260D(2). The person need only be aware of the acts that affect the breach before they contravene s 260D(2). There is no requirement that he or she appreciate that they constitute an offence: *Mudge v Wolstenholme* [1965] VR 707 at 718; *Consul Developments Pty Ltd v DPC Estates Pty Ltd* (1975) 132 CLR 373 at 398; *Royal Brunei Airlines Sdn Dnd v Tan Kok Ming* [1995] 3 WLR 64; *Hunters Products Group Ltd (in liq) v Kindly Products Pty Ltd* (1996) 20 ACSR 412 at 431. Also, as noted above, in *ASIC v Adler* (2002) 20 ACLC 576 the court adopted an objective test in this regard, noting that while Fodera may not have had knowledge that the financial assistance would materially prejudice HIHC, the onus of proving such was on the defendant and 'a combination of suspicious circumstances and the failure to make appropriate enquiry when confronted with the obvious, makes it possible to infer knowledge of the relevant essential matters'.

Again, this section is stated as being a civil penalty provision, the consequences of which are detailed in Chapter 10. Moreover, if the person's involvement in the breach was dishonest, the contravention also constitutes a criminal breach of the Act. The breach does not, however, impact on the validity of the financial assistance or related contract/ transaction: s 260D(1)(a). Nor does the breach render the company as having committed an offence: s 260D(1)(b).

Dividends

Procedure for declaring/announcing dividends

[7.490] The most common method by which corporate net profits are returned to investors is through the payment of dividends. The company's constitution will usually specify the procedure by which dividends are to be paid. Generally, this will provide that the general meeting has the authority to declare a dividend, but only upon the directors' recommendation. Under replaceable rule s 254U, directors may determine that a dividend is payable and fix the amount, the time for payment and method of payment. See also replaceable rule, s 254W(2), in relation to proprietary companies. Dividends may be paid in cash or in the form of shares/options: s 245U.

[7.500] In this context it is important to note at the outset that a company is not required to pay a dividend. This is so even though it may be making substantial profits: *Phillips v Melbourne and Castlemaine Soap and Candle Co Ltd* (1890) 16 VLR 111 at 113. See also *Re Bagot Well Pastoral Co Pty Ltd* (1992) 9 ACSR 129; *Roberto v Walter Developments Pty Ltd* (1992) 10 ACLC 804. Such action may, however, amount to oppression where the directors continually refuse to recommend dividends. As discussed in Chapter 12, under ss 232-235 aggrieved members may seek an order of the court directing the payment of dividends or another suitable remedy. However, this will only be granted in rare cases such as in *Sanford v Sanford Courier Service Pty Ltd* (1987) 5 ACLC 394 where unreasonable emoluments were paid to the directors at the expense of dividends. That the directors have adopted a conservative policy in regard to the payment of dividends will not suffice to satisfy ss 232-235: *Thomas v HW Thomas Pty Ltd* (1984) 2 ACLC 610 and *Re G Jeffrey (Mens Store) Pty Ltd* (1984) 2 ACLC 421.

Effect of declaring a dividend

[7.510] At common law, once a dividend is declared it becomes a debt owed to the subject member: *Marra Developments Ltd v BW Rofe Pty Ltd* [1977] 2 NSWLR 616; *Re CMPS & F Pty Ltd* (1997) 24 ACSR 728 at 730-731. While the common law rule continues to apply where the company has a constitution that provides for the declaration of a dividend (s 254V(2)), in other cases the company does not incur a debt merely by fixing an amount or time for payment under s 254U: s 254V(1). The debt will only be incurred in such cases when the time fixed for payment arrives: s 254V(1). As a consequence, in such cases the decision to pay the dividend may be revoked at any time before the date fixed for payment, without a debt being incurred: s 254V(1).

Dividends must be paid out of profits

[7.520] Both the common law and the *Corporations Act* have intervened to ensure, *inter alia*, that the payment of dividends is not used as a means of returning capital to shareholders contrary to the maintenance of share capital doctrine. Central to combating this practice is the principle that dividends may only be paid out of profits: *Re Exchange Banking Co (Flitcroft's case)* (1882) 21 Ch D 519. This common law rule is now statutorily entrenched in s 254T that provides that dividends are only payable out of profits.

It may be obvious from the concept that dividends may only be paid out of profits that dividends cannot be declared if this would prevent the company paying its debts as and when they fall due. Hence, an insolvent company may not declare/pay a dividend. See further the discussion of the insolvent trading provisions, particularly s 588G, in Chapter 10.

Definition of profits

[7.530] Application of s 254T necessitates an understanding of the meaning of the term 'profits'. As the term is not defined in the legislation, regard must be had to commercial practice as echoed in the common law: *Re Spanish Prospecting Co Ltd* [1911] 1 Ch 92 at 98:

> "Profits" implies a comparison between the state of a business at two specific dates usually separated by an interval of a year. The fundamental meaning is the amount of gain made by the business during the year.

Past years' losses

[7.540] A dividend may be paid if the company has a net trading profit in an accounting period. In regard to the latter point, as the focus is simply on a particular financial year, as long as a net profit exists in that year, earlier years' losses do not have to be made good before dividends can be declared: *Ammonia Soda Co Ltd v Chamberlain* [1918] 1 Ch D 266 at 283; *Re National Bank of Wales* [1899] 2 Ch 629 at 699-671. This is so whether or not the past years' losses have resulted in a reduction in capital: *Verner v General and Commercial Investment Trust* [1894] 2 Ch 239 at 266-267; *Ammonia Soda Co Ltd v Chamberlain* [1918] 1 Ch D 266 at 283-285.

Events after the current financial year

[7.550] Similarly, as long as the accounts for the relevant financial year revealed a profit, events occurring after the financial year do not need to be taken into account unless they indicate the former year's accounts were false: *Marra Developments Ltd v BW Rofe Pty Ltd* [1977] 2 NSWLR 616 at 624, 625, 640 and 641. Thus, in *Marra Developments*, extracted in more detail below, the company's accounts disclosed a trading profit, on the basis of which a dividend was declared. Subsequently, the company's assets were revalued and their value written down, revealing a $20m loss to the company. The court held the shareholders were entitled to payment of their dividends despite these subsequent events, Hutley JA asserting at 624 and 625:

> [I]n determining whether a dividend is payable out of profits, events between the end of the financial year and the declaration of the dividend, unless they are of a nature to demonstrate that the accounts which disclosed the profits were false ... cannot be regarded. ... Any other approach makes the right of a shareholder to a dividend which has been declared entirely capricious and involves conferring a power upon individual directors and managers which is contrary to one of the fundamental understandings of company law.

See further the extracts below. It will be apparent that the conclusion in *Marra Developments* was tied to the fact that at common law once a dividend is declared it is a debt due to shareholders: s 254V(2). See also

Re CMPS & F Pty Ltd (1997) 24 ACSR 728 at 731. While under s 254V(1) the debt does not arise until the date for payment, and up until that date the dividend might be revoked, once the date for payment arises the dividend will again be a debt and subsequent events cannot change its character.

Future profits

[7.560] Similarly, dividends cannot be based on future profits. Thus, the profits providing the basis of a dividend must have accrued before the dividend is declared: *Industrial Equity Ltd v Blackburn* (1977) 137 CLR 567 at 578-579; *Re CMPS & F Pty Ltd* (1997) 24 ACSR 728 at 730. In *Industrial Equity* this meant that a dividend that was based upon the profits of the company's subsidiaries was invalid. That such profits would in time be passed to the parent company did not suffice as the dividend could only be supported by existing profits. As Mason J explained in *Industrial Equity Ltd* at 578-579:

> Underlying the rule that dividends are payable out of profits is the notion that the profits in question have already accrued in the company and that upon the declaration of a dividend by the directors or the company in the general meeting there immediately springs into existence, fully armed so to speak, a debt owing by the company to each shareholder ... However, it is accepted that a company may declare a dividend which is to be paid or payable to shareholders at some future date. This has evidently inspired the thought that the requirement as to the existence of profits is satisfied if they exist at the time stipulated for payment. It is incorrect. Both the article and the section are to be understood as stipulating that the profits in an amount necessary to sustain the dividend are in existence in the company itself at the time of the declaration of the dividend ... The rule has been expressed in the United States in these terms: "corporations can only declare dividends from earnings, which must be present when the dividend is declared. They cannot be declared in anticipation of earnings" ... "The theory of a dividend is that it shall be payable only from ... earnings which are or will be ready for actual distribution at a definite date provided for in the resolution declaring the dividend. Generally, the earnings or profits from which dividends are properly payable must be present when the dividend is declared; it cannot ordinarily be declared in anticipation of earnings or on a mere hope or expectation of profits". It would be productive of confusion and uncertainty if companies were to declare dividends against the possibility that profits not in existence at the time of declaration would or might be earned or received by the time the dividend was paid.

While, as noted above, a company that uses the s 254U replaceable rule enjoys the benefit of being able to revoke the dividend up until the time fixed for payment arrives (s 254V(1)), the rationale for the decision in *Industrial Equity Ltd v Blackburn* (namely the uncertainty that would stem from declaring dividends on the basis of anticipated profits) would appear equally applicable to such situations.

Net profits

[7.570] The definition of 'profit' in *Re Spanish Prospecting Co Ltd* [1911] 1 Ch 92 at 98 also requires an understanding of what amounts and expenses need or may be taken into account when identifying if there is such a net profit. In determining the net trading profit, expenses incurred in gaining revenue must be deducted from the gross trading profit and any difference in the value of the company's trading stock must be taken into account: *Lee v Neuchatel Asphelte Co* (1889) 41 Ch D 1. Profits might include profits from previous trading periods that have been earmarked for the payment of dividends in later years: *Marra Developments Ltd v BW Rofe Pty Ltd* [1977] 2 NSWLR 616 at 622. This is not contrary to the principle that a profit is determined on the basis of the current financial year only because the past profits are carried over into the new financial year and are in essence treated as current year profits. If, however, the company has capitalised these profits, this may limit their availability for the payment of dividends: *Glenville Pastoral Co* (1963) 109 CLR 199 at 207-208.

Capital losses and gains

[7.580] In determining the net profit, losses on fixed capital do not have to be adjusted against any trading profit: *Lee v Neuchatel Asphelte Co* (1889) 41 Ch D 1. Thus, in calculating a net profit the court in *Lee v Neuchatel Asphelte Co* held that the depreciating value of the 'concession', under which the company conducted its business, did not have to be taken into account.

[7.590] By contrast, capital gains are treated as profits and may *prima facie* support the declaration of a dividend. Unless prohibited by the company's constitution, dividends may be paid out of capital accretions realised on the sale of capital assets: *Lubbock v British Bank of South America* [1892] 2 Ch 199 at 201. In *Lubbock* the court held that the capital gain made when the company sold its 'undertaking' (ie business) could be used to support the declaration of a dividend. The company's capital must, however, remain intact and thus it is only the increase in value that is treated as profit and may be used for the payment of the dividend: *Australasian Oil Exploration Ltd v Lachberg* (1958) 101 CLR 119 at 133; *Lubbock v British Bank of South America* at 201; *QBE Insurance Group v ASC* (1992) 10 ACLC 1490 at 1503.

[7.600] More controversial is the use of capital profits from unrealised capital gains that arise from the revaluation of an asset. Whilst not authoritatively determined in Australia, it appears that unrealised profits stemming from the revaluation of capital assets may in certain circumstances be used for the payment of a dividend: *Dimbulla Valley (Ceylon) Tea Co Ltd v Laurie* [1961] Ch 353 at 372-373. Thus, as Buckley LJ stated in *Dimbulla Valley* at 372-373:

> It has, I think, long been the generally accepted view of the law of this country (though not established by judicial authority) that, if the surplus on capital account results from a valuation made in good faith by competent valuers, and is not likely to be liable to short-term fluctuations, it may properly be

capitalised ... I can see no reason why, if the valuation is not open to criticism, this should not be so, or even why, in any case in which the regulations of the company permit the distribution by way of dividend of profit on capital account, a surplus so ascertained should not be distributed in that manner. After all, every profit and loss account of a trading concern which opens and closes with a stock figure necessarily embodies an element of estimate ... I do not say that in many cases such a course of action would be a wise commercial practice, but for myself I see no ground for saying that it is illegal.

[7.610] While not totally clear, it appears *Dimbulla Valley* is applicable in Australia. In *Blackburn v Industrial Equity Ltd* [1976] ACLC ¶40-267 at 28,719, Needham J indicated at first instance that he would follow *Dimbulla Valley*, adding that he would leave open, however, the question whether such was permissible where the profit 'arose from a selective or incomplete revaluation of a company's assets'. In these circumstances it may be necessary to offset the increase in value of some assets against any devaluation of other assets. On appeal, the New South Wales Court of Appeal appeared to accept *Dimbulla Valley* as applicable: *Industrial Equity Ltd v Blackburn* (1977) 2 ACLR 421 at 426. Glass JA added, however, that '[e]ven greater circumspection' is required before directors may transfer 'a surplus resulting from an appreciation of assets ... to the profit and loss account and pay dividends from the fund thereby created'. On further appeal to the High Court, Jacobs J declared that 'if a revaluation of assets had taken place, there would have been disclosed capital profits with the result that such capital profits could be taken into account even without a realisation. It was accepted before the court that the reasoning of Buckley J in *Dimbulla Valley (Ceylon) Tea Co Ltd v Laurie* correctly stated the law': *Industrial Equity Ltd v Blackburn* (1977) 137 CLR 567 at 580. As there was no revaluation on the facts of this case, counsel before the High Court did not argue the issue. Hence the matter has not been authoritatively determined.

[7.620] The problem with using unrealised capital accretions as the basis for a declaration of dividends is that these profits may never be realised; they are no more than 'paper' profits. For this reason the Jenkins Committee recommended that unrealised capital profits should not be used for the payment of dividends.

[7.630] *Marra Developments Ltd v BW Rofe Pty Ltd* [1977] 2 NSWLR 616 provides a useful discussion of the notion of 'net profit' and the requirement that dividends be paid out of profits.

Marra Developments Ltd v BW Rofe Pty Ltd
New South Wales Court of Appeal: Moffitt P and Hutley and Mahoney JJA
[1977] 2 NSWLR 616

The company's accounts disclosed a trading profit, on the basis of which a dividend of $170,000 was declared. After the declaration, but before the dividend had been paid, a revaluation of assets held by its subsidiaries led to the company writing down its shares in such subsidiaries by approximately $21m. As a consequence, after the application of accumulated unappropriated profits (but not the retained earning reserve) the accounts now revealed a $20m loss to the company. A shareholder sought an order that he was entitled to the dividend despite the revelation of the loss. The court held that the dividend had been validly declared and that at the point of declaration it was a debt owed to the shareholder. It consequently made the order sought by the shareholder for the payment of the dividend.

Mahoney JA: [628] *(a) The general law as to dividends:*
Under the general law, the payment of a dividend normally involves two steps: the declaration of the dividend by the competent authority (in the present case, the company: art 116); and the payment over of money in satisfaction of the dividend. It was early said that a dividend may not be (to use the term in a neutral sense) paid except out of profits ...

It is not necessary for present purposes to consider whether the principle is more accurately stated in terms of the existence of available profits or as a proscription upon payments of dividends out of capital or paid-up capital. ... Whichever formulation be adopted, it is then necessary to enter upon an examination of the terms involved in it to establish, for the purposes of the application of that formulation of the principle, what is an available profit or what is or represents capital or paid-up capital. ...

[I]t is necessary to consider, first, the meaning in this context of 'profits' and, second, the significance of the requirement that, at the relevant time, profits be 'available'.

The term 'profits' in general is one having a wide meaning and it has been given different meanings according to the context in which it has been used. In its widest sense, it includes all the advantageous variations between the financial position of a person at a given earlier and later date: *Re Spanish Prospecting Co Ltd* [[1911] 1 Ch 92 at 98] ... **[629]** In particular contexts, the term has been given a more restricted meaning, eg in determining the competing rights of the life tenants and remaindermen: *McBride v Hudson* [(1962) 107 CLR 604 at 623]. In the income tax context, it has been narrowed to exclude, in substance, profits arising merely from an increase in value of fixed capital assets and has been limited to revenue profits: *Russell v Aberdeen Town & Country Bank Ltd* [(1888) 13 App Cas 418 at 424] ('annual' profits').

For the purposes of the present aspect of company law, the term has not been given the restricted meaning which generally has been applied to it in the income tax field. In company law, revenue profits are of course, profits for this purpose. Whether a revenue profit has been derived must be determined by reference to a particular period: *Meares v Acting Federal Commissioner of Taxation* [(1918) 24 CLR 369 at 372]. ... What matters, by way of incomings or outgoings, actual or accrued, may or must be taken into account in determining the revenue profit for that particular period, has been the subject of consideration in many cases ... It has been said that this is to be determined by 'men of business' and, presumably, those advising them in the keeping of their accounts: *Lee v Neuchatel Asphalte Co* [(1889) 41 Ch D 1 at 21] per Lindley LJ; but this does not depend upon eg, the whim or idiosyncrasy of the persons concerned and no doubt the court will, in an appropriate case, hold that particular items should have been brought to account in determining whether a revenue profit has been earned or earned in a particular period: *Verner v General and Commercial Investment Trust* [[1894] 2 Ch 239 at 266].

SHARES AND DIVIDENDS 139

It is not in question in the present case that (subject to matters to which I shall hereinafter refer) what in the accounts are shown as revenue profits were properly determined to be such.

It is also established that capital profits may, in appropriate circumstances, be relied upon for dividend purposes. It is the generally accepted view that, subject to qualifications not here relevant, and subject to the terms of the memorandum and articles of association of the company: cf *Verner v General and Commercial Investment Trust* [at 258], an accretion to the fixed or capital assets of a company, when realised, may be brought to account as available profits ... It has also been held that unrealised accretions of this kind may, at least after being dealt with in the appropriate way, be relied upon in this regard: *Dimbulla Valley (Ceylon) Tea Co Ltd v Laurie* [[1961] Ch 353 at 371] ... In *Industrial Equity Ltd v Blackburn* it was accepted before the Court that the reasoning of Buckley J in the *Dimbulla* case, correctly stated the law: per Jacobs J; and a similar view appears to underlie or to have been assumed in cases concerned with s 44(2) of the *Income Tax Assessment Act* 1936 (Cth) and its statutory predecessors; eg *Dickson v Federal Commissioner of Taxation* [(1940) 62 CLR 687] ... **[630]** However, there can be no capital profits for this purpose unless the company has its paid up capital intact; 'capital profits' for this purpose implies that, upon a balance of account there must be seen to be an accretion to the paid up capital: *Australasian Oil Exploration Ltd v Lachberg* [(1958) 101 CLR 119 at 133].

In some cases, what are 'profits' for dividend purposes may be restricted by the articles of association of the particular company, eg to 'business profits': see *Wall v London & Provincial Trust Ltd* [[1920] 1 Ch 45;[1920] 2 Ch 582], or otherwise so as to exclude capital profits. It has not been argued that, in the present case, and such restriction existed. ...

A dividend may of course, be based upon the revenue profits of a then current (or last concluded) period, and this is so even though the company has previously lost and not replaced its fixed capital: *Lee v Neuchatel Asphalte Co Ltd* [(1889) 41 Ch D 1]; and even where it has lost all of its subscribed capital: *Verner v General and Commercial Investment Trust; Glenville Pastoral Co Pty Ltd (in liq) v Commissioner of Taxation* [[1894] 2 Ch 239 at 264]. It is not necessary that capital losses be recouped before such revenue profits can be used to base dividends. It is, as I have said, different in the case of capital profits; a capital profit cannot exist unless there be, on a balance of the capital account, an excess over the paid up capital; this in my opinion, is the purport of the observation of the court in *Lachberg's* case [at 123] ...

[631] The availability of profits from previous trading periods as a basis for dividend may be affected by the way in which the company has elected to treat them. For example, a company may elect to distribute the profits, derived in its current trading period, it may carry them to a reserve, or it may so treat them as, in effect, to capitalize them: *Federal Commissioner of Taxation v Miller Anderson Ltd* [(1946) 73 CLR 341 at 373]; and see also the *Glenville Pastoral Co* case [at 207]. By so applying or capitalizing profits, a company may restrict the extent to which they are available subsequently to base a dividend. Thus it may apply profits so as to replace capital previously lost ... Profits so dealt with may cease to be available as such, either at all or until the company has elected to write them back into its revenue accounts. In the present case, it is not necessary to consider in detail when and subject to what restrictions profits so dealt with can later be relied upon to base a dividend. On the other hand, a company may retain revenue profits from past periods in such a form as will leave them immediately available to base a dividend.

In the *Miller Anderson* case, Dixon J referred to the phrase 'accumulated profits' and, at 373-4 said '... [A]lthough a profit and loss account **[632]** should be confined to the transactions of a single accounting period, sometimes the profit of the previous year is carried to the actual profit and loss account itself, of the subsequent period. ...

(b) Did the company have 'available profits' in April 1976?
[636] As to the [company's] retained earnings reserve ... The use of them to base a dividend might, in particular circumstances, be imprudent, or might even provide evidence of the lack of bona fides on the part of those so using them; but that does not, in my opinion, mean that, at least if bona fides be granted, the availability of these as profits for dividend purposes can be questioned. ...

[638] For these reasons, I accept the defendant's submission that, if profits must be available at the time when a dividend is to be satisfied, revenue profits were available for that purpose in the present case. ...

(c) The need at general law to have available profits when a dividend is to be satisfied ...
[639] I do not read his [Mason J's judgment in *Industrial Equity Ltd v Blackburn*] as deciding the present question. His Honour held that it was necessary for the profits to be available at the date of the declaration of the dividend, and that it was not sufficient to declare a dividend payable out of such profits as might be available at the future date specified for its payment. ...

[640] I do not think that profits must be seen to be available at the date for satisfaction of the dividend.

It has been argued that to satisfy a dividend, without there being available profits, would be to pay the dividend out of capital, contrary to the basic principles in company law. But this, in my opinion, is to mistake the significance of this principle. ... The rule does not prevent the company paying debts due by it, even though in so doing, it employs money which (in default of other moneys) must be debited, in its accounts, against its paid up capital. ...

In my opinion, the obligation which the company owes in respect of its unsatisfied dividends is to be assimilated to that it owes to its ordinary creditors. When a dividend is properly declared, "there immediately springs into existence, fully armed so to speak, a debt owing by the company to each shareholder": *Industrial Equity Ltd v Blackburn*. These are debts for which a shareholder may sue the company. ... This being the nature of a declared but unsatisfied dividend, there is, in my opinion, no reason in principle why it should not be paid or recovered as an ordinary debt of the company. ...

[641] The contrary view would, in my opinion, be productive of anomaly and inconvenience. It would, as counsel pointed out, mean that before satisfaction of any part of any dividend, albeit properly declared, the directors would be required to satisfy themselves that the position of the company had not deteriorated or changed so that the fund of available assets relied on by them when the dividend was declared, or any other available funds, had not ceased to be available. ... [I]n determining the validity for any claim for a dividend, it was [not] relevant to inquire what was the position of the company qua available profits at any time after the declaration of the dividend. In my opinion, therefore, the company fails on this point.

Hutley JA: [623] What a director or manager must do if, subsequently to a declaration of a dividend but before payment, he discovers that the dividend, if paid, will not be out of profits, was not explored in argument. A shareholder may apply by injunction to restrain the payment of a dividend: *Lee v Neuchatel Asphalte Co* [(1889) 41 Ch D 1]; ... or to have a declaration declared void: *Blackburn v Industrial Equity Ltd.* ... Its board has no power to declare its own private moratorium.

Any construction of the section which would require a director or manager to have regard to what has occurred after the period of the accounts in **[624]** respect of which a dividend is declared in deciding whether to pay it would, in my opinion lead to chaotic administration in a company. ...

I am of the opinion, in determining whether a dividend is payable out of profits, events between the end of the financial year and the declaration of the dividend, unless they are of a nature to demonstrate that the accounts which disclosed the profits were false ... cannot be regarded. ... The declaration, in the most literal sense, would have been a declaration of a dividend payable out of profits, and it did not cease to be a declaration payable out of profits because, in respect of an entirely different period, there were crippling losses. ... [I]n my opinion, it is in respect of the period of account, and that period alone, that the question whether there are profits to enable a dividend to be declared has to be determined. ... **[625]** If from the profit and loss account, or from other accounts created out of the profit and loss account, there is sufficient to permit the declaration of the dividend, the losses between the end of the financial year in which these accounts are produced cannot be used to prevent, on legal grounds, the declaration and payment of a dividend, unless the subsequent revealed losses invalidate the accounts themselves. Any other approach makes the right of a shareholder to a dividend which has been declared entirely capricious and involves conferring a power upon individual directors and managers which is contrary to one of the fundamental understandings of company law.

Net profits of the company declaring the dividend

[7.640] The net profits which provide the basis for the dividend must be the profits of the company declaring the dividend: *Industrial Equity Ltd v Blackburn* (1977) 137 CLR 567. They cannot, for example, constitute the profits of a corporate group or another company within a corporate group: *Industrial Equity*. Thus, until such profits are distributed to the company declaring the dividend, and thus become the latter company's profits, the undistributed profits of another company cannot be used as a basis for paying a dividend: *Industrial Equity*. As noted above, this was an issue in *Industrial Equity Ltd* as the board of the parent company had declared a dividend of just under $1m even though it had only made a profit of $300,000. The dividend had been declared on the basis of a group profit of $1m. As noted above, the dividend was successfully challenged by a shareholder on the basis that a dividend could not be declared on the basis of future profits (ie that the group profits would in time be distributed to the parent company). Interrelated with this finding was the court's conclusion that the profits that supported the declaration of the dividend had to be the profits of the declaring company, not the corporate group. As Mason J declared at 578-579:

> The *Companies Act* does not, in the case of holding companies, substitute the requirement for group accounts for the old requirement of accounts of the holding company itself. Group accounts are an additional requirement; the holding company is still obliged to lay before its shareholders in general meeting its profit and loss account and balance sheets ... Indeed [the legislation] draws a distinction between the 'profit or loss of the company' and 'the profit or loss of the company and its subsidiaries', thereby indicating, to my mind, that [s 254T] refers to the profits of the company, not those of the group. ... Underlying the rule that dividends are payable out of profits is the notion that the profits in question have already accrued in the company and that upon the declaration of a dividend by the directors or the company in the general meeting there immediately springs into existence, fully armed so to speak, a debt owing by the company to each shareholder ... Both the article and the section are to be understood as stipulating that the profits in an amount necessary to sustain the dividend are in existence in the company itself at the time of the declaration of the dividend.

Interim dividends

[7.650] The law draws a distinction between final and interim dividends. The latter are estimated, provisional dividends, the declaration of which does not give rise to an enforceable debt: *Marra Developments Ltd v BW Rofe Pty Ltd* [1977] 2 NSWLR 616. As the declaration of an interim dividend does not give rise to a debt, it may be revoked before payment. As Hutley JA explained in *Marra Developments* at 622:

> The profits out of which [an interim dividend] is paid may be estimated, not disclosed in a formal balance sheet or profit and loss account ... The dividend is wholly provisional and anticipates the profits to be disclosed in the final accounts. Its declaration requires that the directors form opinions that there are profits from which it can be paid. The profits from which an interim dividend is paid are profits which the directors anticipate would be disclosed when the final accounts are produced. The profits out of which it is to be paid are profits which the directors believe will be disclosed in anticipated accounts. In my opinion s [254T] can also be applied to interim dividends, with this difference – the profits only have to be disclosed in such accounts as enable the directors to form a genuine opinion that the profits out of which they will be paid will actually exist. In the case of interim dividends, there is no distinction between "payable" and "paid", as only on payment does the shareholder acquire a right.

The distinction between final and interim dividends is inapplicable to companies governed by s 254V(1) as even final dividends in such cases only become a debt when the time fixed for payment arrives. As with interim dividends at common law, under s 254V(1) all types of dividends may be revoked before the date fixed for payment.

Consequences

[7.660] The statutory consequences of breaching these principles were not restated in the legislation when amended in 1998. However, if the dividends are not paid out of profits in accordance with s 254T, but rather share capital, this would be an unauthorised reduction of share capital as discussed earlier in this chapter. Thus, all the consequences of breaching s 256B, discussed above, would be applicable.

Even apart from these statutory principles, at common law if the directors breach these principles they are liable to repay the company the amount with interest: *Blackburn v Industrial Equity Ltd* [1980] ACLC ¶40-604. The conduct could also constitute a breach of the directors' general duties discussed in Chapter 10. Further, a shareholder who receives a dividend, knowing that it is not paid out of profits, holds that amount on constructive trust for the company. The shareholder may also be liable to indemnify a director who has been required to repay the amount of the dividend to the company: *Blackburn v Industrial Equity Ltd*.

Review questions

1. Bourbon Ltd's issued capital consists of 5000 fully paid $2 ordinary shares and 5000 partly paid $2 ordinary shares, $1 being paid up in respect of each share.

    In 2000 the company also decided to raise some capital by, *inter alia*, issuing 500 x $5 preference shares with an annual dividend right of 5%. No dividends have ever been declared / paid.

    In 2003 the company sought to maintain the services of Fred, the managing director of Bourbon Ltd, by offering him a further 500 preference shares.

    Advise the Board as to whether:
    (a) the issue of 500 preference shares to Fred amounted to a variation of the preference shareholders' class rights?
    (b) Fred enjoys the right to a 5% annual dividend?
    (c) the preference shareholders may demand a dividend representing a 5% return?
    (d) the preference shareholders would be entitled to be back-paid for past years when no dividend was paid were a dividend to be declared this year?
    (e) the preference shareholders would be able to participate in any further company profits if they had already been paid their preference dividend for that particular year?
    (f) the preference shares may be consolidated and then redivided into shares with a $10 par value?
    (g) the ordinary shares may be subdivided into 20,000 x $1 shares?

2. As a result of your brilliant performance at university you have been asked to be a director of Champagne Enterprises Ltd. Prior to the first board meeting you learn the following facts about Champagne Enterprises Ltd.

Champagne Enterprises Ltd was formed to produce an inexpensive Australian pinot noir sparkling wine. The company's issued share capital consists of 5000 fully paid $1 ordinary shares and 5000 partly paid $1 ordinary shares paid to 50c each.

During 2000 the business began to deteriorate as cheaper sparkling wines of poorer quality took hold of the domestic market. In light of this downturn, in 2003 the managing director threatened to leave the company. The board persuaded the managing director to stay with the company and, in order to give the managing director an added incentive to turn the company around, the board decided to issue 500 preference shares to the managing director. To enable the managing director to finance the purchase of these shares the company agreed to guarantee a bank loan to the managing director. Business did not improve.

Advise your colleagues on the board of directors on the legal issues raised by these facts.

3. Champagne Pty Ltd was incorporated in 1995. Its main asset was a shack purchased for $30,000 and some computer equipment purchased for $5000. The company did not do well in its first five years and ended the 2000-2001 financial year with net assets of $5000. During the 2001-2002 financial year, however, the company's business began to turn around. At the end of 2003 the company accounts show a profit of $1 million. In addition, the company has revalued the shack at $100,000 because of its prime location. A dividend of $30 per share is immediately declared.

Before the dividend is paid the company is sued by its competitor, Grog Pty Ltd, for $2 million. Despite this potential liability, Champagne Pty Ltd pays the dividend.

Comment on the above dividend.

Further reading

Austin and Vann (eds), *The Law of Public Company Finance* (Law Book Co, Sydney, 1986)
Baxt, 'The Group Entity and the Law of Company Dividends – A Puzzle?' (1978) 6 *ABLR* 325
Cassidy, *Concise Corporations Law* (4th ed, Federation Press, Sydney, 2003) ch 7
Dharmawan and Mitchell, 'Australian Buy-Back Regulations: A Cross Country Comparison' (2001) 12 *AJCL* 246
Dharmawan and Mitchell, 'The Legislative Framework of Share Buy-Backs: A Comparison of the 'old' and existing requirements' (1999) 18 *U Tas LR* 283
Fletcher, 'Re-baiting the Financial Assistance Trap' (2000) 11 *AJCL* 119
Ford, Austin and Ramsay, *Ford's Principles of Corporations Law* (11th ed, Butterworths, Sydney, 2003) chs 17 and 18
Harris and Ramsay, 'An Empirical Investigation of Australian Share Buy-Backs' (1995) 4 *AJCL* 393
Magner, 'The Power of a Company to Purchase its Own Shares: A Comparative Approach' (1984) 2 *C&SLJ* 79
Mason and Fletcher, 'Company Dividends: Towards a Counter-Revolution' (1982) 1 *C&SLJ* 16

Partlett and Burton, 'The Share Repurchase Albatross and Corporation Law Theory' (1988) 62 *ALJ* 139

Yamey, 'Aspects of the Law Relating to Company Dividends' (1941) 4 *Mod LR* 273

8

Corporate Fundraising

Overview

Companies may need to obtain funds to provide the capital to start a business or subsequently to finance an expansion of their operations. This fundraising may take the form of equity capital by way of shareholder contribution or debt capital secured, for example, against corporate assets. As noted in the previous chapter, under s 124(1)(a) of the *Corporations Act* 2001 (Cth) (*'Corporations Act'*) companies may issue shares. See also ss 254A and 254B. Equally, s 124(1) empowers a company to borrow funds.

Deciding whether to raise capital through equity or debt is important as the legal consequences of each differ dramatically. Interest paid on loan arrangements connected with the production of assessable income may be tax deductible under *Income Tax Assessment Act* 1997 (Cth). Dividends, by contrast, are not tax deductible. Unlike shares, loan arrangements do not extend membership rights to the lender and thus control of the company is not put at risk through debt capital. Companies will usually have no choice whether to make repayments under a loan arrangement. Interest and principal must be paid whether or not the company makes a profit in a given financial year. By contrast, as seen in the previous chapter, a company is not required to pay a dividend even though it may be making substantial profits: *Phillips v Melbourne and Castlemaine Soap and Candle Co Ltd* (1890) 16 VLR 111 at 113; *Re Bagot Well Pastoral Co Pty Ltd* (1992) 9 ACSR 129; *Roberto v Walter Developments Pty Ltd* (1992) 10 ACLC 804. Moreover, dividends must only be paid out of profits: s 254T.

The issuing of shares and the payment of dividends have been discussed in the previous chapter. This chapter begins with a consideration of debt capital and charges that may be used by a lender to secure its loan.

The chapter also discusses the provisions of the *Corporations Act* that regulate corporate fundraising through the offering of securities, such as shares and debentures, to investors. Chapter 6D of the *Corporations Act* protects these investors by imposing stringent rules governing the offering of securities. In particular, the legislation seeks to ensure the disclosure document, through which the securities are offered, provides potential investors with accurate and adequate information about the investment. To encourage compliance, Chap 6D imposes civil and criminal liability for, *inter alia*, misleading or deceptive statements pertaining to these securities. The general law consequences of misstatements and misleading conduct contained in, or relating to,

CORPORATE FUNDRAISING   147

disclosure documents, such as breach of contract and actions in tort, are not canvassed in this text.

The regulation of financial services and markets has been subject to considerable change as a consequence of the enactment of the *Financial Services Reform Act* 2001 (Cth) ('*FSR Act*'). It will be seen that the *FSR Act* repealed Chaps 7 and 8 of the *Corporations Act*, which regulated the securities and futures industries. The regulation of such industries is outside the scope of this text. Nevertheless, because the *FSR Act* has had what is largely a consequential impact upon Chap 6D of the *Corporations Act,* a brief summary of the *FSR Act* is also provided in this chapter. It will be seen that the *FSR Act* builds on Chap 6D and extends the Act's disclosure requirements to a broad range of financial products including derivatives, general insurance and life insurance, superannuation, deposit accounts and payment facilities, not just securities. As this text focuses on the regulation of companies, the regulation of this broader category of products, 'financial products', is beyond the scope of this text.

Debt Capital

Pros and cons of debt capital

[8.10] As noted above, under s 124(1) of the *Corporations Act* a company may borrow funds. There are a number of positive features to the use of debt capital. First, the interest paid on a loan arrangement connected with the production of assessable income, such as business income, may be tax deductible if the requirements stated in *Income Tax Assessment Act* 1997 (Cth) are met. Dividends, by contrast, are not tax deductible. Second, unlike shares, loan arrangements do not extend membership rights to the lender. This may be important to ensure that control of the company is retained. However, repayments under a loan will have to be made whether or not the company makes a profit in a given financial year. By contrast, dividends do not have to be paid and can only be paid out of profits: s 254T.

Form of debt capital

[8.20] Debt capital may take a number of forms. The loan may be from banks or other financial institutions or another member within an intra-corporate group. The loan itself may take a number of forms, including promissory notes or debentures.

Debentures

[8.30] Issuing debentures is a common way corporations raise debt capital. Section 124(1)(b) specifically provides that companies may issue debentures. The definition of debenture in s 9 of the *Corporations Act* was amended by the *Corporate Law Economic Reform Program Act* 1999 ('*CLERP Act*') and now states that a debenture 'means' a chose in action that includes an undertaking by the company to repay money that has been deposited with, or lent to, the company. The definition no longer refers to a debenture as being a document, but rather focuses on the legal obligation to repay money. Section 9 excludes from this definition such an undertaking where:

- the person deposits or lends the money in the ordinary course of that person's business and the body receives the money as part of a business other than the business of borrowing money and providing finance;
- it is by an Australian ADI ('authorised deposit-taking institutions': s 9) and the undertaking is for money deposited with, or lent to, it in the ordinary course of its banking business;
- it is under a cheque;
- it is under an order for the payment of money;
- it is under a bill of exchange;
- it is under a promissory note with a face value of at least $50,000;
- it is by a body corporate to pay money to a related body corporate; or
- it is excluded by the Regulations.

[8.40] It will be seen that a debenture is a form of 'security' and issuing securities is highly regulated under Chap 6D of the *Corporations Act*. This is discussed in detail below. In addition to the requirements set out in Chap 6D with which the offering of all securities must comply, there are further prerequisites for the offering of debentures. These require, *inter alia*, that the debentures be described in the disclosure document in the manner detailed in s 283BH, the maintenance of a register of debenture holders (ss 168(1), 171 and 601CZB-601CZD), the appointment of a trustee for debenture holders (s 283AA) and the inclusion of specified limitations and covenants pertaining to borrowings in the required trust deed: s 283AB. See further Chap 2L of the *Corporations Act*.

Security for debt capital

Charges

[8.50] A loan to a company may be secured in the same manner in which a loan to a natural person is secured. For example, the loan might be secured by a mortgage over company property. A charge is an alternative way that a lender might secure the repayment of money lent to a company. While a charge is similar to a mortgage in so far as it provides the lender with the right to seize and sell the property charged, unlike a mortgage, the creation of a charge does not involve the transfer of title to the property.

Fixed and floating charges

[8.60] Charges may be legal or equitable in nature. A fixed charge is a legal charge that attaches to specific property. As it can only attach to specified property, a fixed charge cannot attach to property that the company is yet to acquire. If the company wishes to dispose of property that is the subject of a fixed charge it must obtain the consent of the chargee, so that a clear title might pass to the transferee.

[8.70] A floating charge is an equitable charge. As its name suggests, a floating charge 'floats' above the assets that are being used as security and only becomes fixed on the happening of certain events discussed below, such as a breach of the loan arrangement. It will be seen that this allows the company to continue to be able to deal with property the subject of a floating charge. Moreover, as a floating charge does not have to be fixed to specified property, a floating charge may affect property acquired by the company after the creation of the charge. Generally, a floating charge will secure the whole of the company's business. Alternatively it could relate to a specific class of property, such as the company's trading stock.

Property the subject of a floating charge may be sold or otherwise dealt with (including having a fixed charge created over it) in the ordinary course of business: *Stein v Saywell* (1969) 121 CLR 529 at 556; *Fire Nymph Products Ltd v Heating Centre Pty Ltd* (1989) 7 ACLC 90 at 95; (1992) 10 ACLC 629 at 639 and 640. There is no need to receive the consent of the chargee in these circumstances. Thus, the benefit of a floating charge is that the company can continue to deal with the property despite the existence of the charge: *Fire Nymph Products Ltd v Heating Centre Pty Ltd* (1989) 7 ACLC 90 at 95; (1992) 10 ACLC 629 at 634. A floating charge becomes a fixed charge (and thus the property can no longer be dealt with without the consent of the chargee) when it crystallises: *Luckins (Receiver and Manager of Australian Trailways Pty Ltd) v Highway Motel Carnarvon Pty Ltd* (1975) 133 CLR 164 at 173; *Fire Nymph Products Ltd v Heating Centre Pty Ltd* (1992) 10 ACLC 629 at 635 and 636. A floating charge may crystallise as a consequence of:

- the winding up of the company; or
- the company ceasing business; or
- the appointment of a receiver over any of the charged property; or
- a breach of a condition in the floating charge.

A loan arrangement may provide a creditor with the authority to appoint a receiver who in turn seizes and sells property to satisfy the debt owed to the creditor. Receivers are discussed in more detail in Chapter 13.

Negative pledges

[8.80] Negative pledges are contractual promises by the borrower that it will not grant a charge in favour of another creditor without the consent of the lender. Alternatively, the promise may be that it will not grant any prior or equally ranking charge without the consent of the lender. The existence of a negative pledge should be noted in the form of registration, discussed below. A breach of a negative pledge usually gives the lender the right to demand repayment. It will be seen that if such a pledge is breached, priority of charges will depend on a number of factors including the nature of the charges, whether and when they were registered and notice of the earlier charge.

Registration of charges

[8.90] Under Chap 2K of the *Corporations Act*, registrable charges must be registered with ASIC. Section 262 sets out what charges are registrable. These include a floating charge on the whole or part of the company's property or business. See further s 262. The company must lodge the details of a charge with ASIC within 45 days of creating the charge: s 263(1). Section 263 details the information that must be specified. Equally, if a company acquires property that is subject to a charge, the details must be reported to ASIC under s 264. See s 266 for the ability to apply to a court for an extension of time for registration. When a charge is discharged the holder of the charge is also required to provide written notice and that information is also entered into the register: s 269.

In turn ASIC maintains the Australian Register of Company Charges: s 265. This register of charges allows persons dealing with a company to find out if another person has rights over company property. It will be seen below that it is also a key factor in determining the validity of charges and the priority of competing charges.

[8.100] A charge that is registrable, but is not registered, is generally enforceable against a company. Where, however, the company is in administration or being wound up, an unregistered charge or late registered charge may be unenforceable. An unregistered charge or one that is registered both more than 45 days after its creation and within six months of voluntary administration being commenced is void against the administrator and against the administrator of any subsequent deed of company administration: s 266. It is also void against the liquidator if the company is wound up: s 266.

[8.110] Sometimes lenders might be competing to enforce charges over the same assets. In such cases this system of registering charges takes on considerable importance in determining the priority between registrable charges. Sections 278-282 set out the rules determining priority. In essence they specify that:

- registered charges take priority over unregistered charges and over charges registered later (even if earlier created), unless the first registered chargee had notice of an earlier created charge when it took its charge; and
- unregistered charges have priority over later created unregistered charges and over later charges that are registered when the latter chargee had notice of the earlier created unregistered charge.

These rules apply unless a chargee has consented (expressly or implicitly) to give up priority: s 279(2). A holder of a floating charge is deemed to have consented to giving priority to a later fixed charge unless the contract creating the floating charge contains a 'negative pledge' and the pledge is registered: s 279(3). By registering the negative pledge later chargees will have constructive notice that there is an existing floating charge over the property and that floating charge has priority over later charges. If the negative pledge is not registered, it will not bind later chargees.

Definition of securities

[8.120] As noted above, Chap 6D of the *Corporations Act* applies to offers of 'securities'. As a consequence of the *FSR Act* there are now four definitions of 'securities'. For the purposes of Chap 6D, the definition of 'securities', previously contained in s 92(3), is now contained s 761A. See ss 92(4) and 700(1). Section 761A defines 'security' as:

(a) a share in a body; or
(b) a debenture of a body; or
(c) a legal or equitable right or interest in a security covered by paragraph (a) or (b); or
(d) an option to acquire, by way of issue, a security covered by paragraph (a), (b) or (c);
but does not include an excluded security.

'Excluded securities' are defined in s 9 as, in essence, any share, debenture or interest in a managed investment scheme entitling the holder to participate in a retirement scheme. Note also that new s 742 allows the Regulations, *inter alia*, to further exempt securities from the operation of Chap 6D. See further s 742.

The definition of securities for the purposes of Chap 6D differs from the general definition of 'securities' in s 92(1) and (2) and the definition of 'securities' for the purposes of Chaps 6–6CA and Part 1.2A in s 92(3). These continue to include interests in managed investment schemes (see s 92(1)(c), (2)(c) and (3)(c)) and exclude a derivative and an excluded security in the case of s 92(1) and (2) and a derivative and a market traded option in the case of s 92(3). See further s 92.

Offers requiring disclosure

[8.130] The offer of securities for issue needs to comply with the disclosure requirements of Part 6D.2 unless they are excluded offers under s 708, discussed below: s 706.

The position, however, is slightly different for offers of securities for sale that have already been issued. Only certain sales of such securities, specified in s 707(2), (3) or (5), must comply with the disclosure requirements: s 707(1). Section 707(2) concerns offers of sales of securities by a controller of the issuing body when the securities are not quoted or are off-market sales of quoted securities. Section 707(3) relates to what is essentially an indirect share issue by the company: s 707(3). Section 707(3) applies to a sale of shares within 12 months of the shares' issue when the shares were originally issued without a disclosure document and either the issuing body or the person to whom the shares were issued intended to on-sell or transfer the shares or intended to grant, issue or transfer options or warrants over the shares. The *Corporate Law Economic Reform Program (Audit Reform and Corporate Disclosure) Act* 2004 (Cth) ('*CLERP 9*'), effective from 1 July 2004, introduced three new exceptions to s 707(3): s 708A. Effectively this exempts the requirement to prepare a disclosure document in relation to secondary sales of securities where:

- the securities are in a class of securities that were quoted securities at all times in the 12 months before the day the securities were issued and the ASX has been given the required notice;
- the securities are in a class of securities that were quoted securities and either a prospectus in relation to the same class of securities has been lodged with ASIC; or
- the securities are issued to an underwriter named in the prospectus as being an underwriter of the issue.

See further s 708A.

Section 707(5) is also concerned with indirect share issues. This section applies to the sale of unquoted securities or an off-market sale of quoted securities by the controller of the company where the sale occurs within 12 months of the shares' issue and the share issue was without a disclosure document. Again, the controller or the person to whom the shares were sold must have intended to on-sell or transfer the shares or intended to grant, issue or transfer options or warrants over the shares.

Section 707 does not apply, however, if the offer is excluded under s 708, discussed below.

Exceptions to disclosure requirements

[8.140] The disclosure requirements discussed below are not applicable to certain excluded offers: s 708. These include offers that are:

- small scale offerings;
- made to sophisticated or professional investors;
- to an executive officer (or his or her spouse, parent, child, brother or sister) of the body or related body;
- to a body corporate controlled by an executive officer (or his or her spouse, parent, child, brother or sister) of the body or related body;
- part of certain dividend reinvestment schemes, bonus share plans, distribution reinvestment plans or switching facilities;
- offers of a debenture to existing debenture holders;
- for securities for which no consideration is to be provided for the issue or transfer;
- under a scheme of compromise or arrangement under Part 5.1;
- made as consideration for an offer to acquire securities under a takeover bid under Chap 6;
- offers of debentures in an Australian ADI or body registered under the *Life Insurance Act* 1995 (Cth); or
- by exempt bodies or exempt public authorities.

The notion of a small scale offering and who are sophisticated or professional investors is discussed in more detail below.

In addition, under s 741(1)(a), ASIC may exempt persons from complying with Chap 6D. The exemption may be conditional: s 741(3). Moreover, the exemption may extend to particular persons or classes of persons, to particular securities or classes of securities and/or may specify those provisions which are to be inapplicable: s 741(2) and (3). See also s 260MA in regard to ASIC's powers to exempt requirements in relation to debentures.

New Part 6D.5 has been inserted at the end of Chap 6D. New s 742 allows the Regulations to exempt persons or securities from the operation of Chap 6D or modify how the Chapter operates in regard to such persons or securities. See further s 742.

Small scale offerings

[8.150] Section 708(1) exempts offers of securities where:
- the offers are personal offers of the body's securities (s 708(2));
- none of the offers breaches the 20 investors ceiling (s 708(3) and (4)); and
- none of the offers breaches the $2 million ceiling (s 708(3) and (4)).

It is an offence under s 727(4) to issue or transfer securities without a disclosure document once the 20 investors or $2 million ceiling has been met.

A personal offer may only be accepted by the person to whom it is made and the offer must be made to a person who is likely to be interested in the offer: s 708(2). The person must be likely to be interested in the offer by reason of some previous contact between the parties, some professional or other connection between the parties or statements or actions by that person indicating that they are interested in offers of that kind: s 708(2)(b).

The 20 investors ceiling is breached if the offer by a body to issue securities results in the number of persons to whom securities of the body have been issued exceeds 20 in any 12 months: s 708(3)(a). Similarly, the ceiling is breached if the offer by a person to transfer a body's securities results in the number of persons to whom the person has sold securities of the body exceeds 20 in any 12 months: s 708(4)(a). In counting issues and sales, those stemming from offers that do not need a disclosure document because of some other section, that were not received in Australia or were made under a disclosure document are disregarded: s 708(5).

The $2 million ceiling is breached if the offer by the body would result in the amount raised through securities exceeding $2 million in any 12 months: s 708(3)(b). Similarly, the ceiling is breached if the offer by a person to transfer securities would result in the amount raised by that person from selling the body's securities exceeding $2 million in any 12 months: s 708(4)(b). In calculating the amount raised, it is necessary to include:
- the amount payable at the time when the securities are issued;
- any amount payable in the future on partly paid shares;
- any amount payable on the exercise of an option; and
- any amount payable upon the conversion of convertible securities: s 708(7).

Again, in counting the amount raised from issues and sales, those stemming from offers that do not need a disclosure document because of some other section, that were not received in Australia or were made under a disclosure document are disregarded: s 708(5).

Thus, with respect to the 20 investors ceiling and $2 million ceiling requirements, the legislation specifies two separate rules, one for offers of securities by the body itself and the second for sales by another person of securities in the body. Moreover, separate ceilings apply to each separate body and to each individual seller. Under s 740 ASIC may, however, aggregate transactions of related bodies and transactions of a body and a person controlling the body.

This exemption is not applicable to an offer of securities that had been issued for on-sale within s 707(3) or off-market sales of securities by the controller of the issuing body where the securities were acquired for the purpose of on-sale within s 707(5): s 708(1).

Sophisticated and professional investors

[8.160] Section 708(8)-(11) exempts from the disclosure requirements offers made to 'sophisticated investors' and 'professional investors'.

Section 708(8) exempts from the disclosure requirements offers made to 'sophisticated investors'. The subsection contains three alternative limbs.

Under the first limb, contained in s 708(8)(a), the offer is exempt if the minimum amount payable for the securities on acceptance of the offer by the person to whom it is made is at least $500,000. This differs from its predecessor in so far as it is the amount payable on acceptance, ie the initial instalment, rather than the subscription amount, that is relevant.

Under the second limb, s 708(8)(b), the exemption is extended to cases where the amount payable for the subject securities plus the amounts previously paid by that person for the same class of securities in the body is at least $500,000. In calculating the amount payable and/or paid, any amounts payable/paid out of money lent by the body offering the securities, or an associate, are to be disregarded: s 708(9).

The third limb exempts the body from disclosure where it appears from a certificate provided by a certified accountant no more than six months before the offer that the person to whom the offer is made has net assets of at least an amount specified in the Regulations (to date $2.5 million) *or* gross income for each of the last two financial years of at least an amount specified in the Regulations (to date $250,000 per year): s 708(8)(c). New s 708(9A) provides that the Regulations may also deal with how the net assets and/or gross income in s 708(8)(c) may be determined.

These exemptions are complemented by s 708(10). This provides that an offer of securities is exempt from the disclosure requirements if:

- the offer is made through an AFS licensee;
- the licensee is satisfied on reasonable grounds that the person to whom the offer is made has previous experience in investing in securities that allows them to assess for themselves, *inter alia*, the risks and merits of the offer and adequacy of information provided by the offering body;
- the licensee provides the person with a written statement as to the reasons for being satisfied as to these matters; and

- the person signs a written acknowledgement that the licensee has not given him or her a disclosure document under Part 6D.2.

The licensee's statement of reasons and the acknowledgment made by the person to whom the offer is made must be provided before, or at the time of, the offer.

Under s 708(11), the exemption extends to 'professional investors'. These include:

- an AFS licensee;
- a body regulated by APRA (other than a trustee of a fund or trust under s 9(d));
- a body registered under the *Financial Corporations Act* 1974 (Cth);
- a trustee of a regulated superannuation fund, ADF, pooled superannuation trust or public sector superannuation scheme within the *Superannuation Industry (Supervision) Act* 1993 (Cth) if the fund, trust or scheme has net assets of at least $10 million;
- a person who controls at least $10 million for the purpose of investment in securities;
- a listed entity;
- an exempt public authority;
- a body corporate or unincorporated body that carries on a business of investment in financial products, interests in land or other investments and invests funds for those purposes;
- a foreign entity that conducts the above.

Disclosure document

Definition of disclosure document

[8.170] As noted above, Chap 6D of the *Corporations Act* seeks to protect investors by ensuring the disclosure document through which the securities are offered provides potential investors with accurate and adequate information about the investment. Under s 9 there are three types of disclosure documents:

- a prospectus;
- a profile statement; or
- an offer information statement.

In addition the legislation recognises a form of prospectus known as a 'short form prospectus'.

Prospectus

[8.180] In what may be perceived as unhelpful definition, s 9 provides that a prospectus 'means a prospectus that is lodged with the ASIC'. Apart from reinforcing the need to lodge a prospectus with ASIC, the significance of this definition lies in what it does not require. A prospectus had previously been defined in terms of a written notice or other instrument. The deletion of any requirement that the prospectus be in writing facilitates electronic prospectuses.

[8.190] Of the disclosure documents listed above, a prospectus must comply with the most comprehensive disclosure requirements. Under ss 710 and 711, the prospectus must contain certain information/disclosures designed to protect investors. Section 711 provides a list of specific material that must be included in the prospectus. This includes the terms and conditions of the offer and information regarding the interests of, and fees and benefits payable to, persons such as a director, proposed director, a person named in the prospectus as performing a function in the preparation or distribution of the prospectus, a promoter, an AFS licensee and underwriter: s 711(1)-(4). Where the prospectus states or implies that the securities are to be quoted on a stock exchange, additional information must be included as the status of the admission of the securities to quotation: s 711(5). The prospectus must state that a copy of the prospectus has been lodged with ASIC and that ASIC takes no responsibility for the content of the prospectus: s 711(7). The prospectus must also provide that no securities will be issued on the basis of the document after the expiry date and that date must be no more than 13 months from the date of the prospectus: s 711(6). See further s 711.

All disclosure documents must be dated: s 716(1). The date is the date the document is lodged with ASIC: s 716(1). In addition, all disclosure documents may only contain statements attributed to persons if they have consented, the document must state that they have consented and the consent must not have been withdrawn before the document was lodged with ASIC: s 716(2).

The list of contents prescribed by, *inter alia*, s 711 is supplemented by a general obligation imposed on the company by s 710(1) to include 'all the information that investors and their professional advisers would reasonably require to make an informed assessment' of the matters detailed in the table set out in s 710(1). Section 710(2) details some of the factors that should be borne in mind in determining what information should be included in the prospectus by virtue of s 710(1). Through s 710 the *Corporations Act* shifts the burden of ascertaining what information should be disclosed in the prospectus from ASIC to the issuing body. In turn, s 710 has the advantage of allowing the body to tailor the prospectus to the needs of the class of investors targeted. See further s 710.

Continuously quoted securities

[8.200] Special rules pertaining to the content of prospectuses for continuously quoted securities are specified in s 713. In September 1994 a regime was introduced requiring disclosing entities to comply with continuous disclosure requirements. In turn s 713 reduces the content requirements for disclosing entities that have complied with the continuous disclosure obligations where the prospectus pertains to the offer of continuously quoted securities. The rationale underlying this approach lies in a belief that it is unnecessary for a new issue of securities in the same class as existing quoted securities to be subject to the above detailed prospectus requirements.

The specific content that must be included in a prospectus for continuously quoted securities is detailed in s 713(3)-(5). Under s 713(3), the prospectus must include a statement that, as a disclosing entity, the body is subject to regular reporting and disclosure obligations and that copies of documents lodged with ASIC may be obtained from, or inspected at, an ASIC office. This is supported by s 713(4) which adds that the prospectus must also either inform persons of their right to obtain a copy of the most recent annual financial report, any half-year report or continuous disclosure notice lodged after that report or include a copy of such document with the prospectus.

Rather than require the prospectus to comply with the 'reasonable investor' standard of s 710, s 713(1) deems this standard to be met where the prerequisites of s 713(2)-(4) are met. Under s 713(2) the prospectus must contain all the information investors and their professional advisers would reasonably require to make an informed assessment.

ASIC may determine that any body may not rely on s 713 if it is satisfied that it has failed to comply with its continuous disclosure requirements during the past 12 months. Note, such a decision is reviewable. See, for example, *Captech Group Ltd v ASIC* (2004) 22 ACLC 93.

Short form prospectus

[8.210] As noted above, the Act also recognises a 'short form prospectus'. Instead of replicating in the prospectus information that has been lodged with ASIC, this type of prospectus allows this information to be deemed part of the prospectus by simply referring to the document. This type of prospectus is designed to reduce the length and complexity of prospectuses.

[8.220] The content provided in this type of prospectus is specified in s 712. As noted above, this allows material lodged with ASIC to be deemed to be included in the prospectus. To effectively include material in this manner, the disclosure document must identify the document or the part to which the prospectus refers: s 712(1)(a). In addition, under s 712(2)(a), if the referenced information is primarily of interest to professional analysts/advisers or investors with similar specialist needs, there must be included in the prospectus a description of the document's content and a statement to the effect that the document is primarily of interest to these people. In any other case, the prospectus must give sufficient information about the contents of the document to allow a person to whom an offer is made to decide whether to obtain a copy of the document: s 712(2)(b). The document must also inform people of their right to obtain a free copy of the document from the issuing body: s 712(1)(b) and (5).

Profile statement

[8.230] Another mechanism designed to simplify disclosure requirements is a profile statement. Again, the s 9 definition of this term provides no great assistance as it simply provides that a profile statement is a profile statement lodged with ASIC. Thus, the definition does no more than reinforce the obligation to lodge the document under s 727.

The notion behind a profile statement is that this document may be prepared in addition to the prospectus and is designed to facilitate investors making comparisons of securities within particular industries. Under this arrangement the information needed to make this comparison will be in the profile statement, though the investor may also request a copy of the prospectus.

Under s 709(2) a profile statement may only be prepared if ASIC has approved the use of a profile statement for that type of offer. In turn, under s 709(3), ASIC may approve the use of profile statements for offers of securities of a particular kind. This approval may specify the matters to be included in the profile statement.

[8.240] The contents of a profile statement are specified under s 714. Under s 714(1)(a)-(e), the statement must:

- identify the body and the nature of the securities;
- state the nature of the risk involved in investing in the securities;
- give details of all amounts payable in respect of the securities, including fees, commissions or charges;
- state that the person given the statement is entitled to a copy of the prospectus free of charge; and
- state that a copy of the statement has been lodged with ASIC and that ASIC takes no responsibility for the content of the statement.

The profile statement must also provide that no securities will be issued on the basis of the statement after the expiry date and that date must be no more than 13 months from the date of the prospectus.

Offer information statement

[8.250] The introduction of an offer information statement was a further step designed to reduce the disclosure requirements under the Act. Again, the s 9 definition provides no great assistance. It simply provides that an offer information statement is an offer information statement lodged with ASIC.

An offer information statement is a simplified disclosure document that may be used instead of a prospectus where the amount of money to be raised by the company through the issuing of securities is less than $5m: s 709(4). In determining if the $5m ceiling is met, all previous amounts raised by the issuing body, a related body or an entity controlled by a person who controls the issuing body or an associate of that person, must be aggregated together: s 709(4). See further s 709.

[8.260] The contents of an offer information statement are specified under s 715. Under s 715(1)-(3), the statement must include information about the nature of the issuing body's business, how the funds are to be used and the risk involved in the investment. In particular the offer information statement must provide that it is not a prospectus and that it has a lower level of disclosure requirements than a prospectus and

CORPORATE FUNDRAISING   159

that investors should obtain professional investment advice before accepting the offer. Again it must provide that no securities will be issued on the basis of the statement after the expiry date and that that date must be no more than 13 months from the date of the statement. The statement must also include an audited 12-month financial report of the body with a balance date within the last six months of the securities being first offered under the statement.

Clear, concise and effective disclosure

[8.270] The specific disclosure requirements detailed above have been complemented by a new provision, s 715A, incorporated through *CLERP 9*, effective from 1 July 2004. Section 715A requires that disclosure documents be worded and presented in a 'clear, concise and effective manner'. As the Explanatory Memorandum explains, in this way the Act recognises that a disclosure document may be misleading, not only though the absence of information, but by being presented in an ambiguous, vague or unclear manner.

Supplementary and replacement disclosure document

Obligation to correct information

[8.280] Under s 730, those persons referred to in the table in s 729, including directors and proposed directors, who become aware of a deficiency in the disclosure document must notify the issuing body. The document may be deficient because it contains a material false or misleading statement, a material omission of that required under ss 710-715 or a new circumstance has occurred and, had it occurred before the document was lodged, it should have been included in the disclosure document. Within the introduction of new s 715A such a deficiency might also include the failure to word or present the disclosure document in a 'clear concise and effective manner'. The person must give the issuing body written notice as soon as practicable after becoming aware of the matter.

In determining if a disclosure document is deficient, it is important to remember that if a short form prospectus has been used under s 712, then any material included in the prospectus by reference must also not be deficient. See Note 2 to s 719(1).

[8.290] In turn, if during the application period the issuing body becomes aware of such a deficiency in a lodged disclosure document, under ss 719(1), 719(1A) and 724(1)(c) and (3), the company may lodge a supplementary or replacement document correcting the matter. Under s 724(1)(c) and (3), where the issuing body has used a prospectus and a profile statement, instead of issuing a supplementary or replacement prospectus the company may provide a statement that sets out the changes needed to the prospectus to correct the deficiency.

These provisions are supported by s 728(1) that prohibits making offers after the person becomes aware of the deficiency in a disclosure document. This constitutes an offence if the misleading or deceptive statement or omission is materially adverse from the point of view of an investor: s 728(3).

[8.300] If persons have already applied for shares pursuant to the disclosure document, the company can repay the money received from applicants or, with or without issuing the shares, provide the applicants with a supplementary or replacement disclosure document and give them one month to withdraw their application: s 724. This provision is complemented by s 737 which provides that, where securities have been issued in breach of s 724, the investor may provide written notice to the company within one month of the issue, returning the securities and asking for repayment: s 737(1) and (2). If the money is not repaid, the directors of the body or seller are personally liable to repay the money.

Note, ss 724(1) and 730(1) are now strict liability offences: ss 724(1A) and 730(2).

Supplementary document

[8.310] A supplementary document corrects a false or misleading statement or material omission in the original disclosure document or provides particulars of matters that have occurred since the document was prepared. The information contained in the supplementary document is taken as being included in the original disclosure document under s 719(4).

[8.320] Section 719(2) provides that at the beginning of the document there must be (i) a statement that it is a supplementary document, (ii) an identification of the disclosure document it supplements and any previous supplementary documents, and (iii) a statement that it is to be read in conjunction with the disclosure document it supplements and any other identified supplementary documents. The supplementary document must be dated, the relevant date being the date on which it was lodged with ASIC: s 719(2).

Replacement document

[8.330] A replacement document replaces the original disclosure document so far as it corrects a false or misleading statement or material omission in the document or provides particulars as to matters that have occurred since the original document was prepared. The replacement document is taken as being the relevant disclosure document for all events that occur after it is lodged with ASIC: s 719(5). Thus, all subsequent offers of securities must be accompanied by the replacement document, not the original document.

[8.340] Section 719(3) provides that at the beginning of the document there must be a statement that it is a replacement document and the disclosure document it replaces must be identified. The replacement document must be dated, the relevant date being the date on which it was lodged with ASIC: s 719(3).

CORPORATE FUNDRAISING   161

Stop orders

[8.350] The supplementary or replacement document may be lodged in response to an ASIC stop order. Section 739(1) empowers ASIC to order that no offers, issues, sales or transfers of securities be made while the order is in force where ASIC is satisfied the disclosure document lodged with it is contrary to s 715A or would contravene s 728. Section 715A requires that disclosure documents be worded and presented in a 'clear, concise and effective manner'. Section 728 prohibits the making of offers after the issuing body becomes aware of the deficiencies in the disclosure document discussed above.

[8.360] ASIC must conduct a hearing before the stop order is issued to determine whether a contravention has occurred: s 739(2). At this hearing, ASIC must provide 'a reasonable opportunity to any interested people to make oral or written submissions': s 739(2). Nevertheless, where ASIC believes that any delay may be prejudicial to the public interest, it may issue an interim stop order: s 739(3). Such an order may be made before a hearing and is effective for 21 days unless revoked earlier: s 739(3). See further s 739.

Requirements for offering securities

Preparation of disclosure document

[8.370] Under s 709(1) and (4), if the offer needs disclosure to investors then a prospectus, short form prospectus or offer information statement must be prepared for the offer. In addition, a profile statement may be prepared: s 709(2). These disclosure documents have been discussed in more detail above. Under ss 721 and 727 the offer must be made in, or accompanied by, the prospectus, offer information statement and/or profile statement. In turn, the securities may only be issued or transferred in response to an application form where there are reasonable grounds to believe the form was included in, or accompanied by, the prospectus, offer information statement and/or profile statement or was copied or directly derived from such a form by the person making the application.

Lodgement with ASIC

[8.380] If an offer requires a disclosure document, then the offer must not be made unless the disclosure document is lodged with ASIC: ss 718 and 727. See also the s 9 definitions of 'prospectus', 'offer information statement' and 'profile statement' which require these disclosure documents to be lodged with ASIC. The document may not be lodged unless duly signed and all required consents have been obtained: ss 720 and 351. These requirements are complemented by the prohibition in s 728 against offering securities under a disclosure document that, *inter alia*, contains, or is accompanied by, a misleading or deceptive statement or omits materials required under the Act.

Exposure period

[8.390] In addition to these requirements, once the disclosure document is lodged with ASIC, an application may not be accepted or shares issued or transferred for a further seven days: s 727(3). This may be extended by ASIC for a further seven days. The Explanatory Memorandum states that this cooling-off period, known as the 'exposure period', is designed to provide a period during which the disclosure document can be looked at before securities are issued pursuant to its terms. To facilitate this process ASIC has developed OFFERlist. Under this facility, the public can access disclosure documents during the exposure period via ASIC's website.

Defective disclosure

Prohibition

[8.400] As noted above, criminal and civil liability may result from a disclosure document containing a false or misleading statement. Such conduct may lead to remedies for breach of contract (that is, rescission or damages), tort (that is, damages for fraudulent misrepresentation: *Derry v Peek* (1889) 14 AC 337) or negligence (negligent misrepresentation: *Shaddock and Associates v Parramatta City Council* (1981) 150 CLR 225). Chapter 6D also prohibits persons from engaging in misleading and deceptive conduct in relation to securities and imposes additional criminal and civil liability for such conduct. Note, *Trade Practices Act 1974* (Cth) and the States' *Fair Trading Acts* no longer apply to dealings with securities.

Criminal liability

[8.410] As noted above, s 728(1) prohibits making offers after the person becomes aware of the deficiency in a disclosure document. This constitutes an offence if the misleading or deceptive statement or omission is materially adverse from the point of view of an investor: s 728(3). Section 728(2) provides that a statement about a future matter will constitute a misleading statement if the person does not have reasonable grounds for making the statement. Where there is a contravention of, *inter alia*, s 728, the court has power to grant injunctions, order a disclosure of information or order the publication of corrective advertising: ss 1324, 1324A and 1324B.

[8.420] There are five defences to a criminal breach of s 728:

- after making such inquiries as were reasonable, the person believed on reasonable grounds that the statement in the prospectus was true and not misleading or that there was no omission: s 731;
- the person did not know that a statement in an offer information statement or profile statement was misleading or deceptive or that there was an omission from the statement: s 732;

- the person placed reasonable reliance on information given to them by someone other than a director, employee or agent of the person: s 733(1);
- the person publicly withdrew their consent to be named in the disclosure document as (i) a proposed director or underwriter, (ii) making a statement in the document, or (iii) having made a statement upon which a statement in the disclosure document was based: s 733(3); or
- the person was unaware of the new circumstance that has arisen.

[8.430] Section 728 is complemented by Part 7.10 that specifies that certain misconduct pertaining to financial products and financial services, not merely disclosure documents, constitutes an offence. Under s 1041E, for example, it is an offence to knowingly, recklessly or negligently make a false or misleading statement or disseminate such information where it is likely, *inter alia*, to induce a person to acquire financial products. This is a strict liability offence: s 1041E(3). Under s 1041F it is an offence to induce a person to deal in financial products by, *inter alia*, knowingly or recklessly making a misleading, false or deceptive statement. It is also an offence under s 1041G to engage in dishonest conduct in regard to a financial product or service in the course of carrying on a financial services business. See further ss 1041E-1041G.

Civil liability

[8.440] Under s 729, a person who suffers loss or damage because of an offer of securities under a disclosure document that contravenes s 728(1), discussed above, may recover the amount of loss or damage from a person listed in the table in s 729 if that table makes him or her liable for the loss or damage. The table in s 729 makes the person making the offer, each director of that body and each person who has consented to being named as a proposed director of the body or as underwriter, liable for any loss or damage caused by a contravention of s 728(1). See further s 729. The defences to s 729 are the same as those detailed above in regard to s 728.

[8.450] If a breach falls outside the scope of s 728, civil liability may nevertheless be imposed under s 1041H(1): s 1041H(3)(a)(ii). Section 1041H(1) prohibits persons engaging in misleading and deceptive conduct or conduct likely to mislead or deceive in connection with a financial service or financial product, which includes, but extends beyond, securities.

In *ASIC v National Exchange Pty Ltd* (2003) 21 ACLC 1652, Finkelstein J detailed the principles to consider when applying s 1041H. First, objectively viewed, the conduct under scrutiny must amount to a false representation. In this regard Finkelstein J later noted that an offer that is factually true in all respects might still be misleading. Moreover, it is not to be expected that each shareholder would weigh each word in an offer in an analytical or educated manner. Thus, whether the conduct was misleading was determined by the offer's overall impression on the general shareholding public. Second, and flowing on from the first point, the defendant's intention will not determine if the conduct is false. Thus, a defendant with innocent intentions might nevertheless be guilty of conduct that amounted to a false representation. Correspondingly though, later in the judgment Finkelstein J added it was relevant in that case that the offer had been purposely composed in a manner designed to mislead shareholders. Third, the conduct is only misleading if there is a 'sufficient nexus' between the conduct and the alleged erroneous assumption created by the conduct. In this regard Finkelstein J later noted that as the test is an objective one, proof that actual shareholders were misled is not essential. Even in the absence of actual proof of deception, the necessary nexus may be established by objectively viewing the conduct.

[8.460] Unlike ss 728 and 729, there are no specific defences to liability under this section. Only the general provision s 1317S, which allows a court to excuse a person from liability where they acted honestly, and Div 4, which, in certain circumstances, extends relief to publishers of advertisements that breach the Act, may be applicable: s 1041I(4). Civil liability under s 1041I may also arise from a breach of ss 1041E-1041G, discussed above.

Restrictions on advertising and publicity

Prohibition

[8.470] Section 734 contains two prohibitions pertaining to the advertising of offers of securities. The first is confined to offers, or intended offers, that would need a disclosure document but for the exemption in s 708(1). It will be recalled this exempts small scale offerings. Where the offer is exempt under this provision, s 734(1) provides that a person must not advertise or publish a statement that directly or indirectly refers to that offer or intended offer.

[8.480] The second, and more general, prohibition is found in s 734(2). Under this provision, where an offer or intended offer requires a disclosure document, a person must not advertise the offer or intended offer, nor publish a statement that directly or indirectly refers to the offer or intended offer and is reasonably likely to induce people to apply for the securities.

[8.490] Section 734(3) specifically deals with the problem of applying this prohibition to image advertising. At times, corporations have engaged in advertising campaigns promoting either their products or, more blatantly, the company itself, either before or contemporaneously with public fundraising. Section 734(3) assists in determining whether this constitutes an indirect referral to the offer that is likely to induce public subscriptions within s 734(2). For example, the section directs that regard is to be had, *inter alia*, to whether the statement forms part of the 'normal advertising' of a body's products that is 'genuinely' designed to maintain existing customers or attract new customers (s 734(3)(c)) and whether the advertising materially pertains to the body (ie rather than its products): s 734(3)(d). Finally, regard is to be had to whether the statement is likely to encourage investment decisions being made on the basis of the statement rather than the information in the disclosure document: s 734(3)(e).

Exemptions

[8.500] The prohibition provided in s 734(2) is stated as being subject to s 734(4)-(7). Note from the outset, however, that none of these exemptions provides defences to s 1041H, discussed above.

These exemptions, particularly in regard to quoted securities, are so extensive that they essentially 'gobble up the rule'. For example, s 734(4) authorises the dissemination of a disclosure document lodged with ASIC. Moreover, as long as certain statements are included in an advertisement or publication pertaining to already quoted securities, s 734(2) will not be breached. Thus, where the offer is of already quoted securities, an advertisement or publication can be effected before the lodgement of the disclosure document as long as it contains a statement that a disclosure document will be made available when the securities are offered and anyone wishing to acquire the shares will need to fill in the application form in, or accompanying, the document: s 734(5)(a). For non-quoted securities, the advertisement/publication must include a statement identifying the offeror and the securities, a statement that a disclosure document will be made available when the securities are offered and that anyone wishing to acquire the shares will need to fill in the application form in, or accompanying, the document: s 734(5)(b)(i)-(iii).

[8.510] Strangely, the exemption for advertisements and publicity occurring after the lodgment of the disclosure document is broader than s 734(5). It does not distinguish between quoted and non-quoted securities. Under s 734(6), the advertisement or publication need only include a statement that the offers of securities will be made in, or accompanied by, a copy of the disclosure document and anyone wishing to acquire the shares will need to fill in the application form in, or accompanying, the document: s 734(6).

[8.520] Further, general exceptions to s 734(2) are provided in s 734(7). These include advertisements or publications that consist solely of a notice or report of a general meeting and genuine comments regarding the disclosure document or its contents made by persons who have not been paid for the publication of the document. See further s 734(7).

[8.530] Section 734(8) provides an exemption to both s 734(1) and (2) where the person publishes the advertisement or statement in the ordinary course of a business of publishing a newspaper or magazine or broadcasting by radio or television and the person did not know, and had no reason to suspect, the publication would breach Chap 6D.

[8.540] Section 734(9) exempts sending a draft disclosure document to a person where the offer of the securities would not require a disclosure document because the person is a sophisticated or professional investor under s 708(8)-(11). As indicated in the heading to s 734(9), these documents are known as 'pathfinder documents'.

Hawking securities

[8.550] Section 736 (formerly ss 1078 and 1081) is designed to protect the public from door-to-door share salespersons. Section 736(1) prohibits persons from offering securities for issue or sale in the course of, or because of, an unsolicited meeting or telephone call. Note, it is unclear if this extends to forms of electronic communications, such as faxes and emails.

[8.560] Section 736(2) exempts from the operation of s 734(1) offers of securities if:
- the offer does not need a disclosure document because it is made to a sophisticated or professional investor within s 708(8), (10) or (11);
- the securities are listed securities and the offer is made by telephone by a licensed securities dealer;
- the offer is made to a client by a licensed securities dealer through whom the client has bought or sold securities in the last 12 months.

If securities are issued or transferred to a person as a result of an offer that contravenes s 736, the person may return the securities within one month of the issue or transfer and is entitled to be repaid the amount they paid for the securities: s 738.

Financial Services Reform Act

[8.570] The *FSR Act* introduced a new regime for the licensing and regulation of financial markets (Chap 7.2), the licensing and regulation of clearing and settlement facilities ('CS Facilities') (Chap 7.3) and the licensing and regulation of providers of financial services, including disclosure requirements for licensees and their representatives (Chaps 7.6–7.10). It is in regard to the latter point that the *FSR Act* builds on Chap 6D of the *Corporations Act* and, as noted above, extends the Act's disclosure requirements to a broad range of financial products, not just securities.

[8.580] 'Financial products' is broadly defined in s 763A. This focuses on three key functions provided by such products. Section 763A(1) provides that a financial product is a 'facility' through which a person:
- makes a financial investment;
- manages financial risk; or
- makes non-cash payments.

See further s 763A in regard to this definition. Each of these three functions is in turn separately defined in ss 763B-763D. These three functions of financial products are acquired through a 'facility': s 763A. Section 762C defines a facility as including 'intangible property', 'an arrangement or a term of an arrangement' or a combination of both. See also ss 761A and 761B regarding what is an 'arrangement'.

Note that in addition to this general definition of financial product, the Act provides further specific inclusions (Subdiv 3-C) and exclusions

(Subdiv 3-D). It is intended that further inclusions/exclusions will be introduced through Regulations.

[8.590] Offers, issues or sales of such financial products must be through a new type of disclosure document, a product disclosure statement, rather than a prospectus. See further Part 7.9.

[8.600] As noted above, the *FSR Act* also provides for the licensing of financial services providers. A person provides a financial service if they:

- provide financial product advice;
- deal in a financial product;
- make a market for a financial product;
- operate a registered scheme;
- provide a custodial or depository service; or
- engage in conduct of a kind prescribed in the Regulations: s 766A.

See further, *inter alia*, ss 766B-766E for definitions of these concepts. Unless otherwise exempt, a person must hold an AFS licence if they carry on a financial service business otherwise than as a representative of a licensee: s 913B. A person who provides financial services as a representative of a financial services licensee must be authorised under ss 916A or 916B of the *Corporations Act*.

Review question

The board members of Champers Pty Ltd were discussing the company's need to raise more capital to take up business opportunities. Fred suggested the company include in its usual weekly sales advertisement (published in local newspapers) that it would welcome five-year loans from readers at an interest rate of 10% per annum. Jessica responded with a proposal that the company offer 15 of its current shareholders the chance to buy $100,000 worth of new shares each. She explains that this would certainly bolster the $500,000 invested by 10 existing shareholders earlier in the year.

Discuss the legality of the suggestions of Fred and Jessica.

Further reading

Austin and Vann (eds), *The Law of Public Company Finance* (Law Book, Sydney, 1986)

Cameron, 'Company Charges and the Australian Law Reform Commission: Scrutinising 'The Department of Utter Confusion" (1994) 12 *C&SLJ* 357

Cassidy, *Concise Corporations Law* (4th ed, Federation Press, Sydney, 2003) ch 8

Dean, 'Crystallisation of a Floating Charge' (1983) 1 *C&SLJ* 185

Everett, *The Nature of Fixed and Floating Charges as Security Devices* (LawPress, Centre for Commercial Law & Applied Legal Research, Faculty of Law, Monash University, Melbourne, 1988)

Ford, Austin and Ramsay, *Ford's Principles of Corporations Law* (11th ed, Butterworths, Sydney, 2003) Part V

Grose, 'Will the Small Business Fundraising Reforms Proposed by CLERP Really Make it Easier for SMEs to Raise Capital in Australia' (1998) 16 *C&SLJ* 297

Hart, 'The Deterrent Effect of Civil Liability in Investor Protection' (1987) 5 *C&SLJ* 162

Hone, 'Fundraising and Prospectuses – the CLERP Proposals' (1998) 16 *C&SLJ* 311

Kyrwood, 'Disclosure Forecasts in Prospectuses' (1998) 16 *C&SLJ* 350

McConvill, *An Introduction to CLERP 9* (LexisNexis, Sydney, 2004)

McLauchlan, 'Automatic Crystallisation of a Floating Charge' [1972] *NZLJ* 330

Nkala, 'Some Aspects of the Jurisprudence of the Floating Charge' (1993) 11 *C&SLJ* 301

Pennington, 'The Genesis of the Floating Charge' (1960) 23 *Mod LR* 630

Sykes and Walker, *The Law of Securities* (5th ed, Law Book Co, Sydney, 1993)

9

Appointment and Removal of Directors

Overview

In this chapter the role of the board of directors is considered. It will be seen that this body is usually empowered with the management of the company. In turn this means it is this body, rather than the general meeting, that usually enjoys decision-making powers.

The chapter then considers the definition of director and officer and the different types of directors. The appointment and removal of persons from such offices is also considered. This involves a discussion of qualification requirements and disqualifying events. In regard to the latter, some events automatically disqualify a person from acting, *inter alia*, as a director, while others require the intervention of the courts or ASIC to eventuate in a disqualification. In this context the factors for leave being granted for disqualified persons to continue to manage a corporation(s) will also be considered. Interrelated with the appointment and removal of directors is the remuneration, including termination payments, of such persons. The final part of the chapter considers this issue. It will be seen that this area of the law has been dramatically impacted upon by the *Corporate Law Economic Reform Program (Audit Reform and Corporate Disclosure) Act* 2004 (Cth) ('*CLERP 9*').

Board of Directors

Role of board of directors

[9.10] The company directors are collectively known as the board of directors. This body is often regarded as representing the mind and will of the company and is usually empowered under any constitution to manage the company's affairs. Thus, under replaceable rule, s 198A(1), the 'business of the company is to be managed by or under the direction of the directors'. Usually such powers of management may be further delegated to, or conferred upon, a committee of directors, director, employee of the company, any other person (s 198D(1)) or the managing director: replaceable rule, s 198C(1). See further ss 189, 190 and 198D discussed in Chapter 10.

Division of power between board and general meeting

[9.20] Unless the *Corporations Act* 2001 (Cth) (*'Corporations Act'*) and/or the company's constitution expressly requires that certain matters be approved by the company in general meeting, where the powers of management are vested in the directors, they alone may exercise these powers: *Automatic Self-Cleansing Filter Syndicate Co Ltd v Cunninghame* [1906] 2 Ch 34; *John Shaw and Sons (Salford) Ltd v Shaw* [1935] 2 KB 113; *Massey v Wales* (2003) 21 ACLC 1978. See also replaceable rule, s 198(2), and in relation to single director/shareholder companies, s 198E(1). While the general meeting may displace a replaceable rule, alter the corporate constitution or refuse to re-elect the directors, unless the *Corporations Act* or the company's constitution otherwise provides, this body may not simply usurp those powers conferred on the board: *Automatic Self-Cleansing Filter Syndicate Co Ltd v Cunninghame*.

Automatic Self-Cleansing Filter Syndicate Co Ltd v Cunninghame
Court of Appeal: Collins MR, Cozens-Hardy LJ
[1906] 2 Ch 34

The company's constitution conferred on the board the powers of management and the specific power to sell company property on such terms as it thought fit. Relying on these provisions, the board refused to comply with a general meeting resolution that certain property be sold, asserting that the sale was not in the company's best interests. It was argued that the directors were the agents of the members and thus were bound to comply with the general meeting resolution.

The Court of Appeal agreed with the first instance decision of Warrington J that the 'management article' in the company's constitution constituted an agreement on the part of the membership to confer the powers of management solely on the board. The general meeting's resolution was, therefore, a nullity and could be ignored by the board. The Court of Appeal rejected the suggestion that the directors were agents who had to obey the directions of their principal, the company.

Cozens-Hardy LJ: **[44]** I am of the same opinion. It is somewhat remarkable that in the year 1906 this interesting and important question of company law should for the first time arise for decision, and it is perhaps necessary to go back to the root principle which governs these cases under the Companies Act, 1862. It has been decided that the articles of association are a contract between the members of the company inter se. ... I will not again read articles 96 and 97, but it seems to me that the shareholders have by their express contract mutually stipulated that their common affairs should be managed by certain directors to be appointed by the shareholders in the manner described by other articles, such being liable to be removed only by special resolution. If you once get a stipulation of that kind in a contract made between the parties, what right is there to interfere with the contract, apart, of course, from any misconduct on the part of the directors? There is no such misconduct in the present case. ... **[45]** [I]t is a fallacy to say that the relation is that of simple principal and agent. The person who is managing is managing for himself as well as for others. It is not in the least a case where you have a master on the one side and a mere servant on the other. You are dealing here ... with parties having individual rights as to which there are mutual stipulations for their common benefit, and when you once get that, it seems to me that there is no grounds for saying that the mere majority can put an end to the express stipulations contained in the bargain which they have made. Still less can that be so when you find in the contract itself provisions which shew an intention that the powers conferred upon the directors can only be varied by extraordinary resolution, that is to say, by a three-fourths majority at one meeting, and that the directors themselves when appointed shall only be removed by special resolution, that is to say, by three-fourths majority at one meeting and a simple majority at a confirmatory meeting. That being so, if you once get clear of the view that the directors are mere agents of the company, I cannot see anything in principle to justify the contention that the directors are bound to comply with the votes or the resolutions of a simple majority at an ordinary meeting of the shareholders. I do not think it true to say that the directors are agents. I think it is more nearly true that they are in a position of managing partners appointed to fill that post by a mutual arrangement between all the shareholders.

See also *John Shaw and Sons (Salford) Ltd v Shaw* [1935] 2 KB 113; *Massey v Wales* (2003) 21 ACLC 1978.

[9.30] This division of power between the board and the general meeting is particularly significant in the context of corporate litigation. As directors owe their fiduciary duties, discussed in the next chapter, to the company, if there is a breach of these duties the company is the entity which must initiate any litigation seeking redress: *Foss v Harbottle* (1843) 2 Hare 461; 67 ER 189. This is called the 'proper plaintiff' rule. As the decision to commence litigation is considered a management decision (*Kraus v JG Lloyd Pty Ltd* [1965] VR 232 at 236-237; *Massey v Wales* (2003) 21 ACLC 1978), where replaceable rule, s 198A(1), is not displaced or the corporate constitution confers the powers of management on the board, it will be for the board to determine whether the company should bring such proceedings: *John Shaw and Sons (Salford) Ltd v Shaw* [1935] 2 KB 113. Naturally this rule can be problematic where the board is hesitant about bringing proceedings against an offender who is one of the board. In light of this possibility, exceptions to the rule in *Foss v Harbottle* developed. Nevertheless, unless leave to bring a derivative action is granted, the basic principle underlying the 'proper plaintiff' rule remains applicable in law today. See further the discussion of these principles in Chapter 12.

Directors and Officers

Definition of director

[9.40] Section 9 of the *Corporations Act* 2001 (Cth) ('*Corporations Act*') defines a director as meaning:

- a person who is appointed to the position of director or alternate director regardless of the name given to their position: s 9(a);
- unless a contrary intention appears, a person who is not validly appointed if they act in the position of director: s 9(b)(i); or
- unless a contrary intention appears, a person who is not validly appointed if the directors of the company/body are accustomed to act in accordance with the person's instructions or wishes: s 9(b)(ii).

[9.50] Section 9(a) is intended to include directors who may be called by some other title, such as 'Governor' or 'President'. Section 9(b)(i) includes 'de facto directors' who may, for example:
- not have been validly appointed initially as they failed to satisfy a prerequisite;
- no longer validly hold office as a result of a supervening disqualification;
- have resigned as director, but not notified ASIC; or
- have assumed greater authority than that attaching to their office.

Thus, in *Perkins v Viney* [2001] SASC 362, the court held the defendant to be a director even though he asserted that he had not been properly appointed as he had not signed a consent to act as a director. The court found that the defendant had acted as chairman of the board, had signed minutes of directors' meetings, had instructed solicitors and engaged in financial dealings on the company's behalf and had been held out as a director in various notices lodged with ASIC. *CAC v Drysdale* (1978) 141 CLR 236 provides a further examination of the notion of de facto director.

CAC v Drysdale
High Court of Australia: Gibbs, Mason, Murphy and Aickin JJ
(1978) 141 CLR 236

The issue whether the defendant was a director was central to this case because he had been charged and convicted of breaching s 124(1) *Companies Act* 1961 (NSW). This required directors at all times to 'act honestly and use reasonable diligence in the discharge of the duties of his office'.

The defendant appealed to the New South Wales Court of Criminal Appeal on the basis that as he was not a director within s 5 of the *Companies Act* 1961 (NSW) as his previous position as a director had been terminated. In reply the Crown asserted that s 5 should not be interpreted in a manner that would allow a person whose conduct was proven to breach s 124(1) to go free. The Court of Criminal Appeal rejected the Crown's submission asserting that s 124(1) was confined to directors, rather than persons who have been held out as directors. As the defendant was not a director *per se* he was acquitted.

The Crown appealed to the High Court. The High Court allowed the appeal adopting the expanded definition of director that included de facto directors.

Mason J: So much of the applicant's case as was based on what was said to be the natural and ordinary meaning of "director", as it appears in s 124(1), drew heavily on a series of English cases in which persons who were de facto directors or de facto officers were held to be directors or officers of companies within the meaning of various sections of the statutes relating to companies. Of these cases *In re Canadian Land Reclaiming & Colonizing Co (Coventry and Dixon's Case)* (1880) 14 Ch D 660 is perhaps the most important. There two persons who were appointed directors without possessing the necessary share qualification and who continued thereafter to act as directors were held by Jessel MR to be guilty of misfeasance under s 165 of the Companies Act **[241]** 1862 in that they participated in the management of the company without authority so to do. ...

Jessel MR said (at 665) "... the de facto director is a director for the purposes of the section", observing that by virtue of s 67 and Art 104 a disqualified director "has the power to manage the company, and by his acts to bind the company". The Master of the Rolls went on to say: "In what capacity except as officer of some kind? Whether, therefore, they can be properly described as directors or not (and I think they can be so properly described) I am satisfied they can be included under the term 'officer'." The Court of Appeal appears to have accepted that the appellant was a director. Indeed, Bramwell J (at 673) indicated that a de facto director fell within s 165. To the like effect were the comments of Lord Russell of Killowen CJ in *In re New Par Consols Ltd* [1898] 1 QB 573 at 576 where a person who had ceased to be a director by reason of bankruptcy but continued to act as such was held to be a director for the purposes of s 7 of the Companies (Winding up) Act, 1890. The observations of Lord Coleridge CJ and Amphlett B in *Edmonds v Foster* (1875) 45 LJ MC 41 at 45 point in the same direction.

In two of the three cases to which I have referred the de facto director was one whose appointment was or became defective, in particular because he did not possess or acquire a share qualification. As his appointment was defective his acts and the acts of the directors in which he participated were validated by statutory provisions similar to s 119 of the Companies Act and Art 89 of Table A. Here, however, there was no defect in the appointment of the respondent; what happened was that his appointment terminated. The stated case does not reveal whether Art 89 of Table A or a similar article formed part of the **[242]** constitution of the company. But this is of no consequence because both s 119 and Art 89 apply to defects in appointment. They are not expressed to apply to acts done after a director has ceased to hold office in other circumstances pursuant to the articles. And it is authoritatively established that neither the section nor the article applies when there has been no appointment at all: *Morris v Kanssen* [1946] AC 459. As Kitto J said in *Grant v John Grant and Sons Pty Ltd* (1950) 82 CLR 1 at 53:

> The proposition which I think is justified by *Morris v Kanssen* is that where a person acts as a director, either without being appointed or in pursuance of a purported appointment made by a person or body not authorized to make an appointment, neither the section nor the article operates to validate his actions.

But this does not dispose of the question, for *In re New Par Consols Ltd* [1898] 1 QB 573 shows that a director who holds over after his appointment has terminated may be held to be a director, though he is de facto only. As Lindley LJ said in *In re Western Counties Steam Bakeries & Milling Co* [1897] 1 Ch 617 at 627 "to be an officer there must be an office". He went on to say, "an office imports a recognised position with rights and duties annexed to it" and came close to acknowledging, if he did not actually acknowledge, that a person may fill an office de jure or de facto.

The words of s 124(1) assume that the person in question occupies an office ("his office") and that there are functions ("duties") attaching to that office which he is discharging. I say "occupies" rather than "holds" because the first part of the definition of "director" makes it clear that a director is a person who occupies rather than holds an office. Even if the function of that part of the definition is not to include a de facto director and is only to include a director of a foreign corporation described by a different name, it proceeds on the footing that one who occupies the position of director is a director. To say that a person occupies a position or office is to say something more than that he holds the position or office. The first statement denotes one who acts in the position, with or without lawful authority; the second denotes one who is the lawful holder of the office.

This view of the meaning of "director" in s 124(1) finds support in s 119. That section describes the person whose appointment as a director is defective as a "director" and validates his acts notwithstanding that he does not lawfully hold that office. The section has many ancestors the first of which was s 67 of the Companies Act 1862.

[243] The case of the de facto director who holds over after his appointment as a director has terminated, accords with the assumptions which s 124(1) makes. He continues to occupy the office of director, albeit now without lawful authority, and discharge the duties attaching to that office. It is not incongruous that, although he is a de facto director, he is commanded to "act honestly and use reasonable diligence" in the discharge of those duties. There is no inconsistency in acknowledging that he should not attempt to discharge the duties of an office to which he has no title and in going on to say, as the sub-section does, that if he does set about discharging those duties he shall do so in the manner described by the sub-section.

Accordingly, in my view s 124(1) applies to the respondent without recourse to the first part of the definition of "director". That part of the definition speaks of a person "occupying the position of director of a corporation by whatever name called". It is possible that it supplies an alternative ground for reaching the same result.

[9.60] Section 9(b)(ii) also includes in the definition of directors persons known as 'shadow directors'. The use of the plural, 'directors', in s 9(b)(ii) suggests that the board, rather than a single director, must be accustomed to acting in accordance with the shadow director's instructions or wishes before the subsection will be satisfied. Such an interpretation has been adopted with respect to the English equivalent of s 9(b)(ii): *Re a Company* [1989] BCLC 13.

In *Standard Chartered Bank of Australia Ltd v Antico* (1995) 13 ACLC 1381 the court held that a body corporate could be a shadow director where it controlled another company. In *Hill v David Hill Electrical Discounts Pty Ltd (in liq)* (2001) 19 ACLC 1000, Santow J held that, in light of the powers of a Deed administrator, the subject administrator was *prima facie* a shadow director within s 9(b)(ii).

[9.70] Section 9 clarifies the scope of s 9(b)(ii) by excluding from its parameters those persons in accordance with whose directions the directors usually act where that advice is given in the person's professional capacity (for example, as a solicitor) or because of their business relationship with the directors or company (for example, as a consultant). A consultant is someone 'engaged to perform specific functions whilst [a director] is engaged in the affairs of the company generally': *Mistmorn Pty Ltd (in liq) v Yasseen* (1996) 21 ACSR 173 at 183. As a consequence of this definition the manager of the business in that case was held to be a director even though he had not been appointed as such.

Particularly in light of this qualification to s 9(b), the distinction between an employee, consultant and director is important. In *Forkserve Pty Ltd v Jack* (2001) 19 ACLC 299, in distinguishing between an employee and a director, Santow J asserted that the impression in the minds of third parties was important. Thus, the court held the subject employee to also be a de facto director as he had on a number of occasions signed documents as a director of the company and had, therefore, knowingly represented to third parties that he was a director. See also *ASC v AS Nominees Ltd* (1995) 133 ALR 1 at 53; *Standard Chartered Bank of Australia Ltd v Antico* (1995) 13 ACLC 1381.

[9.80] The s 9(b) definition is not operative for all purposes under the *Corporations Act*. Where the Act evidences an intention to exclude the operation of s 9(b), a narrow definition of director (ie one properly appointed to the position) will be applicable. Thus, while the extended definition will mean that de facto and shadow directors will be liable for breaches of directors' duties under the Act, as if they formally held office, it will not be applicable, for example, when determining whether the company has satisfied any prescribed minimum number of directors specified in s 201A. The Note to s 9(b) identifies ss 249C (power to call a meeting of a company's members), 251A(3) (signing minutes of meetings) and 205B (notice to ASIC of change of address) as examples of provisions for which the extended definition of director in s 9(b) would not be applicable.

Definition of officer

[9.90] Under s 9, an officer includes a director, secretary, receiver, administrator, liquidator or trustee administering a compromise scheme. Section 9(b) also includes in the definition of officer:

- a person who makes, or participates in making, decisions that affect the whole, or a substantial part, of the corporation's business: s 9(b)(i);
- a person who has the capacity to affect significantly the corporation's financial standing: s 9(b)(ii); or
- a person in accordance with whose instructions or wishes the directors of the corporation are accustomed to act: s 9(b)(iii).

[9.100] As with shadow directors, s 9(b)(iii) does not extend to persons in accordance with whose directions the directors usually act where that advice is given in the person's professional capacity (for example, as a solicitor) or because of their business relationship with the directors or company (for example, as a consultant).

[9.110] Note *CLERP 9* inserted a new related definition, that being 'senior manager'. Section 9 defines such a person in regard to a corporation as:
- a person who makes, or participates in making, decisions that affect the whole, or a substantial part, of the corporation's business: s 9(a)(i); or
- a person who has the capacity to affect significantly the corporation's financial standing: s 9(a)(ii).

Validation of appointment

Section 129 assumptions

[9.120] Related to the definition of director is the ability of third parties to make certain assumptions as to, *inter alia*, the validity of the appointment of persons who appear to be directors. Thus, under s 129, where a person is found not to have been validly appointed, a third party dealing with the company through the de facto director may be entitled to assume that that person has been properly appointed. If the defect stems from the de facto director's failure to comply with a replaceable rule or the company's constitution by, for example, not satisfying a prescribed share qualification, s 129(1) allows the third party to assume that this requirement has been satisfied. No matter how the defect arises, if the de facto director appears from public information provided by the company to ASIC, such as the company's annual return, to be a director or company secretary (s 129(2)) or has been held out by the company as an officer or agent of the company (s 129(3)), the third party will again be entitled to assume that the de facto director 'has been duly appointed and ... has authority to exercise the powers and perform the duties customarily exercised or performed' by an officer of the kind concerned. See also s 128(1).

Under the s 128(4) the third party will be prevented from relying on s 129 where that party knew or suspected that the assumption was incorrect.

Indoor management rule

[9.130] If the defect does not stem from a failure to comply with a replaceable rule or the corporate constitution and there has been no relevant public document within s 129(2) or a holding out under s 129(3), the third party may nevertheless be able to rely on the common law 'indoor management rule'. Under this rule, persons acting in good faith 'may assume that acts within its constitution and powers have been properly and duly performed, and are not bound to inquire whether acts of internal management have been regular': *Morris v Kanssen* [1946] AC 459. This covers, *inter alia*, the appointment of directors, the conferral of authority on such persons and the satisfaction of conditions governing the exercise of that authority: *Northside Developments Pty Ltd v Registrar-General* (1990) 93 ALR 385 at 406. This principle is sometimes referred to as the rule in *Turquand's* case as it was first developed in *Royal British Bank v Turquand* (1856) 119 ER 886.

[9.140] At common law, these protections will not apply where the third party knows or ought to know that the de facto director had not been properly appointed or lacked authority: *Howard v Patent Ivory Manufacturing Co* (1888) 38 Ch D 156; *Northside Developments Pty Ltd v Registrar-General* (1990) 170 CLR 146. These disqualifying events are often referred to as the 'due inquiry' defence. Where the third party is suspicious as to whether the assumption is correct, they are expected to make further inquiries that would, in turn, have revealed the absence of an appointment or lack of authority. See *Northside Developments Pty Ltd v Registrar-General* (1990) 170 CLR 146; *Bank of New Zealand v Fiberi Pty Ltd* (1994) 12 ACLC 48; *Pyramid Building Society (in liq) v Scorpion Hotels Pty Ltd* (1996) 20 ACSR 214.

Validation of acts under ss 201M and 204E

[9.150] Sections 201M and 204E validate the acts of company directors and secretaries, respectively, in certain cases where their appointment or continuance of appointment is invalid. The defect must arise out of a failure by either the company or the director/secretary (ie not a third party) to comply with the company's constitution or the *Corporations Act*: ss 201M(1) and 204E(1).

The Notes to ss 201M and 294E(2) provide that these sections validate only those acts which would be legally effective if the person doing them is a director or secretary, respectively. Note also in this regard that these sections only validate the acts of such persons, not their actual appointment to the subject office.

[9.160] Sections 201M(2) and 204E(2) specify that ss 201M(1) and 204E(1) are not concerned with whether an effective act by a director/secretary binds, or makes the company liable to, third parties. These matters are governed by ss 128-130 and the indoor management rule, discussed above. Thus, ss 201M and 204E are confined to internal matters, rather than dealings with third parties.

[9.170] The predecessor to these provisions, s 226, had been interpreted by courts as only being applicable where there had been an actual or purported appointment. The acts of a person who merely assumed the office of director were not validated by the section: *Morris v Kanssen* [1946] AC 459; *CAC v Drysdale* (1978) 141 CLR 236. This would also appear to be implicit under ss 201M(1) and 204E(1) given these sections refer to an 'appointment, or the continuance of their appointment'. Moreover, under s 226 the purported appointment had to be by a person who had power to make the appointment: *Grant v John Grant & Sons Pty Ltd* (1950) 82 CLR 1. See further the above case extracts from *CAC v Drysdale* (1978) 141 CLR 236.

Court's power to validate acts under s 1322(4)(a)

[9.180] Under s 1322(4)(a), on application by any interested person, a court has a broad discretion to order that an act purportedly done under the *Corporations Act* or in relation to the company is not invalid by reason of a contravention of the Act or the company's constitution. The court may make an order even if the act constitutes an offence: s 1322(5). An order may only be made, however, where the act is essentially procedural in nature, the parties involved in the failure acted honestly or it is in the public interest to make the order: s 1322(6)(a). In addition, the order must not cause, or be likely to cause, substantial injustice to any person: s 1322(6)(c).

Company Officers

Executive and non-executive directors

[9.190] The board of directors may be constituted by:
- executive directors, who are full-time employees of the company; and
- non-executive directors, who are not so employed.

To fall within the former category, the director's responsibilities must extend beyond that ordinarily expected of such an office holder. While not necessary, executive directors will usually hold office under a contract for service, rather than simply under the corporate constitution.

Managing director

[9.200] The most well known executive director is the managing director. Under replaceable rule, s 201J, the board may appoint one or more of the directors as managing director(s). Under replaceable rule, s 198C(1), the directors may then confer upon this person(s), either concurrently with the board or exclusively, any of their powers. Thus, it is usual for the board to confer on the managing director the power to manage the company's daily affairs. These powers may, however, be withdrawn or varied by the directors at any time: s 198C(2).

[9.210] In addition to the authority expressly conferred on the managing director, this officer enjoys broad ostensible and implied authority to act for the company: *Biggerstaff v Rowatt's Wharf* [1896] 2 Ch 93; *Hely-Hutchinson v Brayhead* [1968] 1 QB 549 at 583. This authority does not, however, extend to 'critical decisions' (*Re Qintex Ltd (No 2)* (1990) 8 ACLC 811 at 815) as fundamental as the sale of the company's undertaking/business.

[9.220] To promote continuity in the company's management, the managing director is generally not subject to the rules providing for the rotation of directors, discussed below. This does not mean, however, that the managing director cannot be removed from office. Under replaceable rule, s 203F(1), the managing director will automatically cease to be managing director if he or she ceases to be a director. Thus, managing directors will generally be subject to the same removal provisions as the other directors and, if any are activated, they will automatically be removed from the office of managing director. Moreover, under replaceable rule, s 203F(2), the directors may revoke or vary an appointment of a managing director.

Chief executive officer

[9.230] The chief executive officer will often be the managing director. This officer need not, however, be a director and may merely be a manager of the company. If the officer is not a director, he or she will lack the decision-making authority enjoyed by directors; though the officer may be invited to attend board meetings.

Pursuant to the enactment of *CLERP 9*, effective from 1 July 2004, the chief executive officer of listed entities must make a written declaration to the board of directors that the financial records of the company have been properly maintained pursuant to s 286, the annual financial statements are in accordance with the accounting standards and the statements present a true and fair view of the company's financial position: s 295A(1)-(3). Where no one person, but rather a group of persons, performs the function of chief executive officer each person is required to make the declaration: s 295A(5) and (7).

Governing director

[9.240] Particularly in the past, the constitution of proprietary companies often accorded to the 'founder' of the company the status of governing director. This individual usually enjoys extensive powers enabling him or her to retain control of the company.

Note, while this may have the effect of concentrating real power in just one director, this will not result in the company failing to satisfy any minimum number of directors prescribed by s 201A: *Welch v Welch* [1971-1973] CLC ¶40-068; *Whitehouse v Carlton Hotel Pty Ltd* (1987) 162 CLR 285.

Associate director

[9.250] The board usually enjoys the power to appoint junior executives as associate directors to act in an advisory capacity. Such associate directors are not usually required to satisfy any directors' share qualification. In accordance with their junior status, the corporate constitution usually limits the associate directors' ability to attend and vote at board meetings.

Chairperson

[9.260] Under replaceable rule, s 248E(1), the board may appoint one director as chairperson. Apart from any other powers that may be delegated to this director, he or she will chair board and general meetings and generally act as the company spokesperson in public affairs.

Alternate director

[9.270] Under replaceable rule, s 201K(1), a director may appoint, with the approval of the board, a person to be an alternate director for a specified period. ASIC must be notified of any such appointment: s 205B(2). This power is useful when a director is to be absent from board meetings. Generally, the constitution provides that the alternate director need not be a member of the company and thus need not comply with any share qualification. The appointing director may terminate the alternate director's appointment at any time: s 201K(4). Again, ASIC must be notified of the termination: s 205B(5).

Under replaceable rule, s 201K(1), the alternate director may be appointed to exercise some or all of the director's powers. If a general conferral of power is made, in the absence of the appointing director, the alternate director may attend meetings and vote in the appointing director's stead. See also s 201K(3). Correspondingly, alternate directors are bound by the same duties and face the same potential liabilities as ordinary directors.

Secretary

[9.280] Proprietary companies are no longer required to have a company secretary, but may appoint such an officer: s 204A(1). Public companies continue to be required to have at least one secretary: s 204A(2). In both cases, at least one secretary must ordinarily reside in Australia: s 204A(1) and (2). The power to appoint a company secretary rests with the board: s 204D. ASIC must be notified of the appointment under s 205B(1).

[9.290] While this officer usually has extensive express authority over administrative matters, the courts have recognised the extent that the secretary enjoys implied and ostensible authority to act on the company's behalf: *Panorama Developments v Fidelis Fabrics* [1971] 3 WLR 440. A secretary's implied authority includes the power to make contracts (*Panorama Developments v Fidelis Fabrics*), but does not extend to management decisions such as commencing litigation: *Club Flotilla (Pacific Palms) Ltd v Isherwood* (1987) 12 ACLR 387; *Northside Developments Pty Ltd v Registrar-General* (1990) 93 ALR 385.

[9.300] The company secretary has responsibility for ensuring the company meets its obligations in relation to its registered office and lodging certain information with ASIC: s 188(1). In a proprietary company with no secretary, this responsibility is instead placed on the director(s): s 188(2). Under s 188(3), a secretary/director does not breach the legislation, however, if they show that they took all reasonable steps to ensure the company complied with its obligations.

Note, under s 204E, acts by a company secretary are effective even though that person's appointment is invalid. In this regard, see the above discussion of, *inter alia*, ss 201M and 204E. See also the above discussion of ss 128-130 and the indoor management rule.

Qualifications

Natural persons

[9.310] Only an 'individual', that is, a natural person, may be a director: s 201B(1). As noted above, however, in *Standard Chartered Bank of Australia Ltd v Antico* (1995) 13 ACLC 1381, the court held that a body corporate could be a shadow director where it controlled another company. Similarly, only natural persons may be a company secretary: s 204B(1).

Number

[9.320] Proprietary companies are required to have at least one director, while public companies must have at least three directors: s 201A(1) and (2). The latter requirement is a little strange given that public companies are now only required to have one member: s 114. Thus, even one-member public companies must continue to have three directors. As noted above, s 201A will be satisfied even where one director is invested with such powers that he or she is effectively a sole director: *Welch v Welch* [1971-1973] CLC ¶40-068; *Whitehouse v Carlton Hotel Pty Ltd* (1987) 162 CLR 285.

Residence

[9.330] At least one of the proprietary company's directors, and two of a public company's directors, must ordinarily reside in Australia: s 201A(1) and (2).

Age

[9.340] The minimum age for a director is 18 years: s 201B(1). Similarly, the minimum age for the company secretary is 18 years: s 204B(1). There is no longer any maximum age for directors specified in the *Corporations Act*. The company's constitution may, however, include such an age restriction. See s 201C(14).

Share qualification

[9.350] There is no statutory requirement that a director hold shares in the company. The corporate constitution may, however, prescribe a share qualification. If the constitution specifies that obtaining the share qualification is a prerequisite to the director's actual appointment, the purported appointment of a person who has not so satisfied the requirement will be void: *Stevens v Commonwealth General Assurance Corporation Ltd* (1938) 55 WN(NSW) 120.

Consent

[9.360] As noted in Chapter 5, the written, signed consent of each director and secretary whom it is proposed that the members will appoint must be obtained before applying for registration: ss 117(5), 201D(1) and 204C(1). The company breaches the Act if it fails to receive such consent before the appointment: ss 201D(1) and 204C(1). Once the company is registered, these consents must be retained with the company's records: ss 117(5), 201D(2) and 204C(2). The details of those persons who have consented to be directors and/or secretary are also included in the application for registration: s 117(2)(d), (e) and (f).

Disqualification

Managing a corporation

[9.370] A number of provisions of the *Corporations Act* prohibit, or allow a court or ASIC to prohibit, a person from managing a company if certain events have occurred. Under ss 203B and 206A(2), a person ceases to be a director of a company if they become disqualified from managing a corporation under Part 2D.6, discussed below, unless ASIC or the court allows them to manage a corporation.

[9.380] Section 206A(1) provides that a person who is disqualified from 'managing a corporation' under Part 2D.6 commits an offence if:

- they make, or participate in making, decisions that affect the whole, or a substantial part, of the business of the corporation;
- they exercise the capacity to affect significantly the corporation's financial standing; or
- they are, in essence, shadow directors, discussed above.

It will be apparent that 206A(1) echoes the definitions of directors and officer in s 9, discussed above.

[9.390] Section 206A(1) also largely codifies the courts' interpretation of its predecessor, s 91A(2). In determining whether a person was involved in the management of a company under s 91A(2), the courts drew a distinction between those who merely carried out predetermined corporate policies and those involved in the central direction of the company: *CAC v Bracht* (1989) 7 ACLC 40; *Cullen v CAC* (1989) 7 ACLC 121; *Nilant v Shenton* [2001] WASC 421. The latter, but not the former, was considered to be involved in the management of the company.

Automatic disqualification for conviction of certain offences

[9.400] Section 206B(1) disqualifies persons from managing corporations if they are convicted of an indictable offence that either concerns decisions affecting the whole or a substantial part of the business of the corporation or has the capacity to affect significantly the corporation's financial standing: s 206B(1)(a). Note, there is no reference in s 206B(1)(a) as to the punishment for such breaches.

[9.410] A person is also automatically disqualified under s 206B(1) if they are convicted of an offence under the *Corporations Act* that is punishable by imprisonment for a period greater than 12 months or involves dishonesty and is punishable by imprisonment for at least three months: s 206B(1)(b). The disqualification also extends to persons convicted under the laws of a foreign country that are punishable by imprisonment for a period greater than 12 months: s 206B(1)(c).

[9.420] The period of disqualification begins the day the person is convicted and lasts for five years if the person does not serve a term of imprisonment or, if they serve a term of imprisonment, five years after the date of their release: s 206B(2). Under new s 206BA(1) and (2) ASIC may apply to the court to increase the penalty up to a further 15 years. ASIC must apply before the period of disqualification begins or before the end of the first year of disqualification: s 206BA(3). The court has a total discretion and may have regard to any matters it considers appropriate: s 206BA(5).

If the person was appointed as a director before the breach, once he or she has fallen foul of a disqualifying conviction, the person's office is automatically vacated for the prescribed period unless permission to manage the corporation is given under s 206G: ss 203B and 206A(2).

[9.430] Section 206B is not punitive in nature, but rather is designed to protect the public by preventing persons convicted of indictable offences relating to corporate affairs, or offences involving dishonesty in general, having control over corporate funds: *Re Magna Alloys* (1975) 1 ACLR 203 at 205. See also *Re Van Reesema* (1975) 11 SASR 322 at 332; *Re Zim Metal Products* (1977) 2 ACLR 553 at 558; *Zuker v CAC* [1980] ACLC 34,334 at 34,338; *Re Marsden* [1981] ACLC 33,210 at 33,215; *Re Minimix Industries Ltd* (1982) 1 ACLC 511 at 512; *Murray v ASC* (1994) 12 ACLC 11 at 13; *Re Shneider* (1996) 22 ACSR 497 at 501.

Automatic disqualification of an undischarged bankrupt

[9.440] Persons who are undischarged bankrupts or who have entered into a Part X arrangement under the *Bankruptcy Act* 1966 (Cth)[1] but have not fulfilled all the obligations entailed in the arrangement are also automatically disqualified: s 206B(3) and (4).

[9.450] Unlike s 206B(2), s 206B(3) and (4) do not specify a fixed period of disqualification. Thus, the prohibition against managing corporations continues until the person is no longer disqualified under s 206B(3) and (4) or permission to manage the corporation is given under s 206G, discussed below: s 206A(2).

Again, if the person was appointed as a director before becoming bankrupt, the person's office is automatically vacated unless permission to manage the corporation is given under s 206G: ss 203B and 206A(2).

Under s 201F(3), in the case of a sole shareholder/director company, where the office of director is vacated under s 206B(3) or (4), if a trustee in bankruptcy is appointed to that person's property, the trustee may appoint a person as director of the company.

---

1 This is a 'private' arrangement between the debtor and his or her creditor(s) outside bankruptcy. This may be by (i) a composition arrangement, or (ii) a deed of arrangement.

[9.460] Again, these provisions are not punitive in nature, but rather designed to prevent people with a history of bankruptcy from managing corporations and thereby subjecting further creditors to financial loss: *Re Altim Pty Ltd* [1968] 2 NSWR 762 at 764; *Nilant v Shenton* [2001] WASC 421.

Court's power to disqualify for breaching civil penalty provisions

[9.470] Section 206C allows a court, on the application of ASIC, to disqualify a person from managing corporations if a declaration is made under s 1317E that the person has breached a civil penalty provision. See s 1317E for those provisions that constitute civil penalty provisions.

[9.480] The period of disqualification is a matter for the court's discretion. The most recent extensive discussion of the relevant factors for consideration in a s 260C application is found in *ASIC v Adler* (2002) 20 ACLC 1146. The court applied the above principles and held that one director, Adler, should be banned for 20 years and another director, Williams, for 10 years as a consequence of breaching a number of civil penalty provisions. The factual basis for the s 260C application (ie the numerous breaches of directors duties established in *ASIC v Adler* (2002) 20 ACLC 576) is detailed in Chapters 7 and 10. The judgment of Santow J also provides a summary of these breaches.

ASIC v Adler
Supreme Court of New South Wales: Santow J
(2002) 20 ACLC 1146

Santow J: **[1159]** 55. It is useful if, at the outset, I identify the propositions, by way of guiding principles or relevant factors that can be derived from the cases which have dealt with these provisions or their predecessors.

56. The cases on disqualification gave orders ranging from life disqualification to 3 years. The propositions that may be derived from these cases include:

(i) Disqualification orders are designed to protect the public from the harmful use of the corporate structure or from use that is contrary to proper commercial standards. ...

(ii) The banning order is designed to protect the public by seeking to safeguard the public interest in the transparency and accountability of companies and in the suitability of directors to hold office: ...

(iii) Protection of the public also envisages protection of individuals that deal with companies, including consumers, creditors, shareholders and investors ...

(iv) The banning order is protective against present and future misuse of the corporate structure ...

(v) The order has a motive of personal deterrence, though it is not punitive ...

(vi) The objects of general deterrence are also sought to be achieved ...

(vii) In assessing the fitness of an individual to manage a company, it is necessary that they have an understanding of the proper role of the company director and the duty of due diligence that is owed to the company ...
(viii) Longer periods of disqualification are reserved for cases where contraventions have been of a serious nature such as those involving dishonesty: (ix) In assessing an appropriate length of prohibition, consideration has been given to the degree of seriousness of the contraventions, the propensity that the defendant may engage in similar conduct in the future and the likely harm that may be caused to the public ...
(x) It is necessary to balance the personal hardship to the defendant against the public interest and the need for protection of the public from any repeat of the conduct ...
(xi) A mitigating factor in considering a period of disqualification is the likelihood of the defendant reforming ...
(xii) The eight criteria to govern the exercise of the court's powers of disqualification set out in *Commissioner for Corporate Affairs v Ekamper* (1988) 6 ACLC 90; (1987) 12 ACLR 519 have been influential. It was held **[1160]** that in making such an order it is necessary to assess:
- Character of the offenders
- Nature of the breaches
- Structure of the companies and the nature of their business
- Interests of shareholders, creditors and employees
- Risks to others from the continuation of offenders as company directors
- Honesty and competence of offenders
- Hardship to offenders and their personal and commercial interests; and
- Offenders' appreciation that future breaches could result in future proceedings.

(xiii) Factors which lead to the imposition of the longest periods of disqualification (that is disqualifications of 25 years or more) were:
- Large financial losses
- High propensity that defendants may engage in similar activities or conduct
- Activities undertaken in fields in which there was potential to do great financial damage such as in management and financial consultancy.
- Lack of contrition or remorse
- Disregard for law and compliance with corporate regulations.
- Dishonesty and intent to defraud
- Previous convictions and contraventions for similar activities

(xiv) In cases in which the period of disqualification ranged from 7 years to 12 years, the factors evident and which lead to the conclusion that these cases were serious though not "worst cases", included:
- Serious incompetence and irresponsibility
- Substantial loss

- Defendants had engaged in deliberate courses of conduct to enrich themselves at others' expense, but with lesser degrees of dishonesty
- Continued, knowing and wilful contraventions of the law and disregard for legal obligations
- Lack of contrition or acceptance of responsibility, but as against that, the prospect that the individual may reform

The difficulty with *Roussi's* case [*ASC v Roussi* (1999) 32 ACSR 568] is that disqualification for 10 years was ordered, as this was the period of disqualification that the ASC had sought. Had a longer period been applied for, Einfeld J may have considered giving a longer period: *ASC v Roussi* at 571;

(xv) The factors leading to the shortest disqualifications, that is disqualifications for up to 3 years were:
- Although the defendants had personally gained from the conduct, they had endeavoured to repay or partially repay the amounts misappropriated
- The defendants had no immediate or discernible future intention to hold a position as manager of a company
- In *Donovan's* case, the respondent had expressed remorse and contrition, acted on advice of professionals and had not contested the proceedings ...

[1162] 60. It is well settled (see [56(i) to (iii)] above) that the primary purpose of the disqualification power is the protection of the public; see, for example, *ASC v Forem-Freeway Enterprises Pty Ltd* at ACLC 521; ACSR 349. That its object is the need to protect the public, with its corollary of personal deterrence, does not mean that its aim should be punitive though personal deterrence is relevant. That is explained in the judgment of Bowen CJ in *Re Magna Alloys & Research Pty Ltd* (supra) at CLC 28,354; ACLR 205: "The policy to which s 122 [the predecessor to s 206C and s 206E of the *Corporations Act*] gives effect is that a person convicted of an offence of any of the type specified in that section is not to be permitted to act as a director or take part in the management of a company. The section is not punitive. It is designed to protect the public and to prevent the corporate structure from being used in the financial detriment of investors, shareholders, creditors and persons dealing with the company. In its operation, it is calculated to act as a safeguard against the corporate structure being used by individuals in a manner which is contrary to proper commercial standards." ... The discretion of the Court is still directed to the nature of the relevant person's conduct in relation to the management, business or property of any corporation. It is also directed, more broadly, to any other matters that the Court considers appropriate, once the Court is satisfied that the disqualification is justified.

62. In any event, we are here dealing with a repeated series of contraventions though that needs to be put in proper perspective. ... I would agree that the most that could be said is that a multiplicity of contraventions by reference to breaches of not just one but several provisions of the *Corporations Law* (or *Corporations Act*) may give a broad indication of the seriousness of the contravention, but much more to the point is to look at the contraventions themselves. ... We are moreover here dealing with disqualification with its paramount protective purpose. Highly relevant is thus the number of companies suffering dereliction of duty by Mr Adler (HIH, HIHC and PEE) *and* the fact that there were nine instances of misconduct by Mr Adler. That the conduct in question was repeated and followed a pattern,

simply makes it more serious in terms of dereliction, with consequently greater risk to the public if Mr Adler were allowed to continue to manage companies. ... **[1163]** [I]n applying s 206E of the *Corporations Act*, not only has there been at least two contraventions of the Act by HIH and at least two contraventions of the Act by HIHC, but the relevant person, here Mr Adler, did not merely fail to take reasonable steps to prevent the contravention but was himself directly involved in it so as himself to contravene the Act. That clearly reinforces the basis for applying s 206E with a substantial disqualification order.

69. Indeed the gravity of the contraventions as well as their repetition in distinct transactions, numbering nine in all, make a powerful case for the lengthiest disqualification period.

70. The principles of parity which guide the exercise of judicial discretion do not produce any neat arithmetic algorithm from other cases though the earlier propositions ([56] above) give some guidance. I would adopt what is said by Hill J in *ACCC v Universal Music Australia Pty Limited (No 2)* (2002) ATPR ¶41-862; [2002] FCA 192 at [34] where, in the analogous context of the *Trade Practices Act* he says: "Hence, while pecuniary penalties imposed in one case provide a guide, that guide will seldom if ever be able to be used mechanically."

71. Austin J, while making similar observation, in *ASIC v Parkes* (2001) 38 ACSR 355 at 386 refers to a number of factors which are directly applicable to the present case and its circumstances: "In reaching this conclusion [disqualification for 25 years], I take into account the following factors:

- the contraventions that I have found include some very serious contraventions;
- those contraventions have led to loss and damage on the part of companies and investors, contrary to the protective purpose of the relevant provisions of the Corporations Law;
- the defendant's field of activity, management and financial consultancy, is an area where the potential to do damage is especially high, compared, say, with a defendant whose expertise is in making cement;
- the defendant's contraventions have been recurrent, arising in the context of three different sets of companies;
- until the end, the defendant asserted explanations for what he had done which I found to be implausible, and this suggests to me that he has no contrition;
- all of these facts lead me to believe that there is a high propensity that the defendant will engage in similar conduct if only a short period of prohibition is imposed;
- **[1164]** I am conscious of the fact that a prohibition for 25 years will effectively prevent the defendant from managing a corporation for the rest of his life, it will not prevent him from earning income as an employee, using his undoubted financial skills under proper supervision.

72. In the present case each of those factors are present, though it should be noted that Mr Adler himself did not assert any personal explanation for what he had done. Rather, through his legal advisers, he denied that there was any contravention in the circumstances, a denial which is at odds with the findings of the Judgment and thus cannot stand.

73. A review of the cases demonstrates that a wide range of banning periods have been imposed by the courts. For the most serious, there is

prohibition for life, though in one case with a right to apply for variation after five years; *ASIC v Hutchings*.

Again, if the person was appointed as a director before breaching the civil penalty provision, the person's office is automatically vacated unless permission to manage the corporation is given under s 206G, discussed below: ss 203B and 206A(2).

[9.490] As noted above, these provisions are not punitive in nature, but rather designed to protect the public: *Re Tasmanian Spastics Association; ASC v Nandan* (1997) 23 ACSR 743 at 751-752; *ASC v Forem-Freeway Enterprises* (1999) 17 ACLC 511; *ASIC v Hutchings* (2001) 38 ACSR 387 at 395; *ASIC v Pegasus Leveraged Options Group P/L* [2002] NSWSC 310; *ASIC v Adler* (2002) 20 ACLC 1146.

Court's power to disqualify for managing insolvent companies

[9.500] Under s 206D(1) and (3), a person may be prevented from managing a company for up to 20 years where, on the application of ASIC, the court finds:
- within the last seven years the person was an officer of two or more companies when they failed;
- the management of the companies was wholly or partly responsible for the corporation failing; and
- the disqualification is justified having regard to the person's conduct in relation to the management, business or property of the corporation and any other matters the court considers appropriate.

See s 206D(2) as to when a corporation is taken to have failed.

[9.510] As noted above, the period of disqualification is a maximum of 20 years.

If the person is presently acting as a director, that office will be automatically vacated when the s 206D order is made unless permission to manage the corporation is given under s 206G: ss 203B and 206A(2).

Court's power to disqualify for repeated breaches of the Corporations Act

[9.520] Section 206E complements s 206B by allowing a court to disqualify a person from taking part in the management of a company for such period as the court prescribes if he or she has:
- at least twice been an officer of a body corporate that has contravened the *Corporations Act* while they were an officer and each time the person has failed to take steps to prevent the contravention;
- at least twice contravened the *Corporations Act* while they were an officer of a body corporate; or
- been an officer of a body corporate and has done something that would have contravened ss 180(1) or 181 if the body corporate had been a corporation.

Again, the court may determine whether disqualification is justified having regard to the person's conduct in relation to the management, business or property of the corporation and any other matters the court considers appropriate: s 206E(1) and (2).

[9.530] The period of the prohibition is a matter for the court's discretion and the court must believe the period of disqualification is justified: *ASIC v Starnex Securities Pty Ltd* [2003] FCA 1375.

ASIC v Starnex Securities Pty Ltd
Federal Court of Australia: Finkelstein J
[2003] FCA 1375

This case concerned an application by ASIC to have a defendant, Mr Camiolo, disqualified from managing corporations for a period of two years under s 206E. Initially, ASIC and the defendant asked that a disqualification order be made by consent. The court decided against that course, determining the matter under the legislative and judicial contexts of s 206E.

Finkelstein J: 2. Initially ASIC and Mr Camiolo asked that a disqualification order be made by consent. I declined to take that course. Section 206E(1)(b) provides that the court may make a disqualification order if it is "satisfied that the disqualification is justified." It is not possible to be satisfied that an order is justified simply because the person to be disqualified agrees to that course. A similar view of the provision seems to have been taken by Bryson J in R*e One.Tel Ltd (in liq); Australian Securities and Investments Commission v Rich* (2003) 44 ACSR 682. There the parties submitted a consent order for a disqualification but the judge examined the facts for himself and only made the order when he was satisfied that, in all the circumstances, it should be made.

3. What then are the facts? They appear principally in the affidavit of Mr Grant, an investigator with ASIC. Mr Grant conducted an investigation into the affairs of Icorp Technologies Ltd, Contech Australia Ltd (Contech), Starnex Capital Ltd and Starnex Securities Pty Ltd (Starnex Securities). Mr Camiolo was a director of each company. The companies were incorporated in May 2000, April 2001, May 2002 and August 2002 respectively. The principal business of Starnex Securities was to act as a broker to arrange loans for its clients. The remaining companies did not appear to actively transact business.

4. Mr Grant instituted his investigation following a complaint received from one of Starnex Securities' clients, Northwest Earthmoving Pty Ltd (Northwest), who had paid a commitment fee of $36,300 for a credit facility of $9,000,000. Although the facility was not provided the commitment fee was not repaid.

5. During the course of the investigation Mr Camiolo was required to attend at the offices of ASIC on several occasions to be examined about the affairs of Starnex Securities. He did not attend at the appointed times, causing the examinations to be rescheduled. Mr Camiolo had no valid reason for failing to attend. He was simply being uncooperative. I eventually made an order that Mr Camiolo appear for examination. Only then did Mr Camiolo attend.

6. As the investigation proceeded ASIC obtained documents about the affairs of the companies. They disclosed a number of things, none of which were to Mr Camiolo's credit. First and foremost it was discovered that the companies were insolvent. Most of the money which had come into the Starnex Securities accounts (usually by way of a brokerage fee) was paid to meet the debts of another company, channelled into unrelated ventures and applied to discharge Mr Camiolo's personal expenses or expenses of his family. The money in the Contech account was treated in an equally irregular manner.

7. Second, aside from Northwest there were other clients who had requested Starnex Securities to procure a loan but, when that loan was not forthcoming, were not repaid their commitment fee. Thousands of dollars were withheld from clients in this way.

8. Third, on at least one occasion, and perhaps more, Starnex Securities advertised that it would arrange commercial mortgages for "no brokerage fees". Despite this statement a brokerage fee was charged, albeit under a different guise.

9. Fourth, Mr Camiolo and Starnex Securities may have engaged in misleading conduct in contravention of ss 12DA(1) and 12DB(1) of the Australian Securities and Investments Commission Act 2001 (Cth). ...

10. Fifth, the companies have committed many offences. As regards the public companies, the following offences were committed by at least one and often all of the companies – contrary to s 201A they did not have at least three directors; contrary to s 201D the appointed directors had not signed consents to act prior to their appointment; contrary to s 327 there was a failure to appoint an auditor within one month of incorporation; contrary to s 292 the companies did not prepare annual financial reports and directors' reports; contrary to s 301 the companies did not have their financial reports audited; contrary to s 314 the companies did not send annual reports to members; contrary to s 319 the companies did not lodge annual financial reports with ASIC; contrary to s 345 the companies failed to lodge an annual return with ASIC by 31 January each year; contrary to s 146 the companies did not notify ASIC of changes of their principal places of business; contrary to ss 168 and 169 there was a failure to maintain registers of members; contrary to s 251A there was a failure to keep minute books; contrary to s 205B the companies did not notify ASIC of changes in details of directors and secretaries within twenty-eight days; contrary to s 250N there was a failure to hold an annual general meeting within eighteen months of registration; and contrary to s 286 there was a failure to keep appropriate financial records which would enable true and fair financial statements to be prepared and audited. The private company, Starnex Securities, also contravened ss 345, 146, 251A, 205B and 286.

11. The foregoing establishes that Mr Camiolo failed to act responsibly as a director of the companies. He appears to have little or no knowledge of how a company should be managed. He certainly has little appreciation of the legal obligations imposed on a corporation in relation to its administration and record keeping.

12. In *Re Gold Coast Holdings Pty Ltd (in liq); Australian Securities and Investments Commission v Papotto* (2000) 35 ACSR 107 Anderson J said (at 111) that:

"The factors to be considered which govern the exercise of the court's powers of disqualification are the character of the offender, nature of the breaches, structure of the company and nature of its business, interests of shareholders, creditors and employees, risks to others from continuation of offenders as company directors, honesty and competence of the offender, hardship to the offender and his personal and commercial interests, and the offender's appreciation that future breaches could result in future proceedings ..."

See also *HIH Insurance Ltd (in prov liq); Australian Securities and Investments Commission v Adler* (2002) 42 ACSR 80. The following factors are also relevant considerations: whether or not a disqualification order is needed to protect the public; whether or not the disqualification order will adversely affect the interests of shareholders, creditors or employees; and whether or not the errant director is conducting the company's affairs to secure his own interests at the expense of the interests of others: see HIH Insurance Ltd (2002) 42 ACSR at 96-99.

13. ASIC has established that an order should be made against Mr Camiolo. It is in the public interest that he be quarantined from the management of any company for some period. A two year disqualification is warranted and an order to that effect will be made. If, after the period of disqualification, Mr Camiolo intends to re-enter the world of corporate commerce, he must amend his ways.

Once again, if the order is made in the course of the person's office as director, that office will be automatically vacated unless permission to manage the corporation is given under s 206G: ss 203B and 206A(2).

[9.540] Again, s 206E is not punitive in nature, but rather is designed to protect the public from persons who recklessly or incompetently manage corporations: *CAC v Ekamper* (1988) 6 ACLC 90 at 95-96; *ASIC v Adler* (2002) 20 ACLC 576.

ASIC's power to disqualify persons subject to liquidator's report

[9.550] Section 206F allows ASIC, without a court order, to prohibit a person from managing a company for up to five years. An order may be made where ASIC determines:

- within seven years immediately before the notice under s 206F(1)(b)(i) is given, the person was an officer of two or more corporations;
- while the person was an officer, or within 12 months after the person ceased to be an officer, of those corporations, each of the corporations was wound up;
- the liquidator lodged a s 533(1) report regarding the corporation's inability to pay its debts;
- notice has been served on the person to demonstrate why they should not be disqualified; and
- the person has been given an opportunity to be heard on the question: s 206F(1).

[9.560] In determining whether disqualification is justified under s 206F(1), ASIC *must* have regard to whether any of the two corporations were related, and *may* have regard to the person's conduct in regard to the management, business or property of any corporation and any other matters ASIC considers appropriate: s 206F(2) (emphasis added). If a person is so disqualified, they must be notified under s 206F(3).

In *Sheslow v ASC* (1994) 12 ACLC 740 at 743, Deputy President McMahon asserted that the section is directed at persons who have 'displayed a cynical disregard for the trading advantages of limited liability' and who have been 'dishonest, unscrupulous, untrustworthy or irresponsible'. If to the contrary the director has been honest and not guilty of gross incompetence, the court suggested that an order should not be made: *Sheslow* at 743. These factors were also addressed in *Re Delonga and ASC* (1995) 13 ACLC 246 at 254:

> Looking at these provisions in a general sense, their emphasis is upon a director's being open and frank in carrying out his or her duties and functions as a director of the company, upon his or her personal interests in dealing with the company, and upon his or her taking reasonable steps to ensure compliance with the accounting and reporting provisions of the *Corporations Law* and to ensure that the company only incurs debts when it is able to pay its debts as they fall due. Distilling the general principles yet further, the *Corporations Law* focuses upon the actions of directors in light of the need to protect the shareholders, actual and prospective, of the company and to protect the general public in so far as it attempts to ensure that the information which is given to the general public is adequate and accurate and that the general public does not deal with an insolvent company.

In *Iliopoulos v ASC* (1997) 15 ACLC 1512 at 1519, the court held that the background of the particular director, the type of activities in which the companies were involved, the subsequent behaviour of the director in respect to the companies and any involvement with other companies were additional factors to consider.

[9.570] As noted above, the maximum period for disqualification is five years. The period of disqualification starts from the date the notice required under s 206F(3) is served on the person: s 206F(4).

If the person is a director when he or she becomes subject to a s 206F order, that office is automatically vacated under ss 203B and 206A(2), unless permission to manage the corporation is given under ss 206F(5).

[9.580] The courts have asserted that a s 206F notice should not be issued for punitive reasons as the overall function of s 206F is to protect the public: *Sheslow v ASC* (1994) 12 ACLC 740 at 743; *Re Agushi and ASC* (1996) 19 ACSR 322 at 324 and 331; *Iliopoulos v ASC* (1997) 15 ACLC 1512 at 1518; *Feher v ASC* (1997) 15 ACLC 1774 at 1782.

[9.590] Under s 206F(5), ASIC has power to grant a person who has been disqualified under s 206F(1) permission to manage a particular corporation or corporations. The permission may be expressed to be conditional or subject to exceptions: s 206F(5). The section does not extend to persons the subject of automatic disqualification under s 206B or disqualification pursuant to a court order.

Court's power to grant leave to manage a corporation

[9.600] As noted above, under s 206G the courts have a general discretion to allow a person who has been disqualified under Part 2D.6 to take part in the management of a corporation(s). Section 206G(1) does not, however, extend to persons who have been disqualified by ASIC under s 206F(1): s 206G(1). The section expressly confers on the court a power to grant leave to manage, not only 'a particular corporation' or 'a particular class of corporations', but simply 'corporations'.

[9.610] The onus of proving grounds for an exercise of this discretion rests with the applicant: *Re Altim Pty Ltd and Companies Act 1961* [1968] 2 NSWR 762; *Re Ferrari Furniture* [1972] 2 NSWLR 790 at 792; *Re Van Reesema* (1975) 11 SASR 322 at 331; *Re Magna Alloys & Research Pty Ltd* (1975) 1 ACLR 203 at 205; *Re Hamilton-Irvine* (1990) 8 ACLC 1067 at 1071; *Murray v ASC* (1994) 12 ACLC 11 at 13; *Adams v ASIC* [2003] FCA 557.

[9.620] In *Re Marsden* (1981) 5 ACLR 694 at 699, the court identified five primary factors for consideration in assessing an application for leave to manage a company:

- the nature of the applicant's offence;
- the nature of his involvement;
- his or her general character;
- the structure of the companies in which the applicant may be a director;
- the assessment of the risk to those connected with the company and the public involved if the applicant assumed a position on the Board.

In addition, the courts have considered as relevant the hardship that would be brought to bear on, *inter alia*, the company and the applicant were the latter refused leave to participate in the management of the company (*Re Zim Metal Products Pty Ltd* [1977] ACLC 29,556 at 29,559), the applicant's appearance in court (*Re Van Reesema* (1975) 11 SASR 322 at 326 and *Re Macquarie Investments Pty Ltd* (1975) 1 ACLR 40 at 46) and, to a small extent, ASIC's attitude to the application, ie any lack of opposition. These principles were applied in *Re Zim Metal Products Pty Ltd*.

Re Zim Metal Products Pty Ltd
Supreme Court of Victoria: McInerney J
[1977] ACLC 29,556

One of the applicants, McKissack, was approached by an unidentified stranger while driving a fork lift near the entrance to the factory premises. McKissack purchased from this person two stolen amplifiers. He in turn persuaded the other applicant, Paxton, to purchase an amplifier. Both were convicted of dishonestly receiving stolen goods. In accordance with a predecessor to s 206B(1)(b), they resigned from their positions as directors and sought leave to be a director or to take part in the management of the family company, Zim Metal Products Pty Ltd.

They asserted that their participation in the company was essential for the company's preservation.

McInerney J took into account the nature of the offence, the applicants' general character, the structure of the company, the risk of injury to the public and the shareholders and stressed that the offences did not arise out of or in relation to the management of the company, but rather in McKissack's guise as an employee. In light of these factors the court concluded that leave should be granted to both applicants to take part in the management of the company, but not leave to act as a director.

McInerney J: **[29,558]** The case made for the applicants is that their participation, at least in management, is essential for the preservation of the company and I think it likely enough that that is so. I have regard, as Sir Nigel *Bowen* suggests a court should have, to the nature of the offence of which each of the applicants has been convicted. It was an offence involving dishonesty. It was an offence committed in circumstances which, in my view, show that the applicants deliberately committed an offence of dishonesty for the sake of a very small saving in money in the cost of the article purchased. The fact that they took that course troubles me somewhat as it indicates that each was prepared to sacrifice his reputation of honesty and his reputation for being law-abiding citizens, which on the affidavits filed in this case, each appears to have held, for the sake of a very small monetary gain.

Looking at the nature of the involvement of each of them, McKissack would seem to have been more culpable than Paxton in that he tempted Paxton into becoming involved in the offence. This did not appear from his own affidavit, and I was troubled by this omission, suggesting as it did that he was being far from candid with the court. The story of McKissack's involvement emerged only from Paxton's affidavit which, as I pointed out to Mr Beaumont, was not strictly admissible against McKissack. Mr Beaumont, however, who appears for both applicants, has assured me, and I accept his assurance, that McKissack's part in Paxton's offence was at all times known to him, that he himself drafted the affidavits and drafted them on the footing that both cases would come on at the same time and that there was no intention of misleading the court. McKissack has filed a further affidavit substantially to the same effect, although it does not, perhaps, go as far as I suggested yesterday it ought to go. However, I acquit McKissack of any intention to suppress his own participation in Paxton's offence or of any intention to mislead the court. Had I been satisfied that he had sought to mislead the court, it is difficult to conceive of circumstances which would warrant the court granting him the leave he now seeks.

Looking at the general character of each applicant, including his conduct in the intervening period since he was removed from the board and from management, it has to be said that, so far as is known, each applicant had borne himself honestly up to the time of the commission of this offence. Nothing can really be made of the conduct of either applicant in the period from the time of the conviction for the offence to the present time, having regard to the fact that it is so short. Mr Beaumont has urged that I should take into account, in the case of each applicant, the fact that a thorough search was made by the police of the home of each applicant and the only article which could not honestly be accounted **[29,559]** for was the amplifier. I think each applicant is entitled to have that fact taken into account in his favour. It does not, of course, negative the possibility that he may have engaged in this kind of dealing before without detection. On the other hand, it is equally consistent with this having been the first occasion on which he had succumbed to the temptation.

What strikes me about the offences is that they do not really arise out of or relate to the management or conduct of the company. They occurred on the premises of the company. They occurred in circumstances which, in my view, related more to the fact that the applicant was doing work at the company than to the fact that he was a director of or manager of the company. The applicant, McKissack, was, at the time of the approach to him by the unidentified stranger, driving a forklift near the entrance to the factory premises. Whether the unidentified stranger knew what McKissack's identity was or what his position was in the company does not appear. But for all that appears in the material it may well have appeared that McKissack was merely an ordinary workman in the company. In those circumstances, the commission of the offences does not appear to me to threaten commercial morality or to threaten the welfare of shareholders and creditors of the company, the persons investing in or dealing with the company, to anything like the same extent as would have been the case had the offences involved falsification of company accounts or the like.

Looking at the structure of the companies, that structure will remain much the same if leave is granted, as it will if leave is denied. It is possible that if the leave is denied, the company may not be able to continue to operate satisfactorily and may have to be wound up. That circumstance will apparently impose some hardship on the applicants because they apparently derived their income substantially from their salaries, rather than from the dividends.

It is not likely, I suppose, that the same salaries would be paid to the applicants if they were performing ordinary work, not involving work of management or directorships if they were permitted to take part in the management or directorship. I do not think that there is any significant risk of injury to the public or the shareholders if I grant the leave sought to permit the applicants to take part in the management of the company. That result is all that is presently pressed for.

I have considered whether I should grant leave to the applicants to become directors. I have come to the conclusion I should not. The policy of the legislation is that, prima facie, the persons convicted, the applicants, should be excluded from being directors. The possible harm which might occur to the company and to the applicants if they are excluded from management is, in my view, much more real than any harm that may flow if they are not allowed to become directors. There is something to be said, I think, for the view that public morality is better vindicated if the applicants continue to be excluded from being directors. Creditors and persons dealing with the company who now know or may hereafter come to know of the convictions of the applicants, may take the view that the court views the convictions as matters of no concern, if the court allows an applicant to be reinstated as director in a case where, in my view, there is no real need for that appointment. Consequently, I grant leave to each of the applicants to take part in the management of the company, but I do not grant either of them leave to act as or to be a director of the company.

[9.630] If the court grants leave for a person to manage a corporation, it may do so with such conditions or restrictions as it thinks fit: s 206G(3).

Moreover, if leave is granted the court may at any time, on application of ASIC, revoke such leave: s 206G(5).

Appointment of Directors

First directors

[9.640] The first company directors may be appointed in a number of ways. Upon registration, the person specified in the application for registration as having consented to being a director and/or secretary becomes a director and/or secretary of the company: s 120(1).

[9.650] The first directors may also be appointed by a person(s) authorised under the constitution or by the members in general meeting. Replaceable rule, s 201G, provides that the company may appoint a director through the passage of a resolution at a general meeting.

[9.660] The appointment of directors of public companies must be voted on individually unless:

- the company passes without dissent a resolution that more than one director may be voted on per motion;
- the resolution to appoint the directors is by an amendment to the company's constitution; or
- the election by poll or ballot does not require members voting for one candidate to also vote for another candidate: s 201E(1) and (2). See also s 201E(3).

Any purported appointment in contravention of s 201E is void: s 201E(1).

Subsequent directors

[9.670] The corporate constitution may make special provision for the appointment of subsequent directors. Generally, however, this power is conferred on the general meeting. Thus, as noted above, under replaceable rule, s 201G, the company may appoint a director through the passage of a resolution at a general meeting. See the above discussion of the restrictions on the appointment of directors of public companies under s 201E.

[9.680] Under replaceable rule, s 201H, the directors of a company are also conferred the power to appoint a person as director. This power of appointment may be used, *inter alia*, to fill a casual vacancy. The appointment can be made to make up a quorum for a directors' meeting even if the total number of directors does not constitute a quorum: s 201H(1). If the director is appointed to a proprietary company, the company must confirm the appointment within two months of the appointment: s 201H(2). In the case of public companies, the appointment must be confirmed at the next AGM: s 201H(3). If it is not so confirmed, the appointment ceases at that point: s 201H(2) and (3).

[9.690] Under s 201F(1), the director of a single director/ shareholder company may appoint another director by recording the appointment and signing the record.

Directors' Remuneration

Right to remuneration at common law

[9.700] At common law, in the absence of an express provision in any constitution, non-executive directors are not entitled to remuneration for holding their office: *Hutton v West Cork Railway Co* (1883) 23 Ch D 654 at 686. Executive officers, as employees of the company, have the normal contractual right to remuneration even in the absence of any provision in the corporate constitution or a service contract.

Right to remuneration under the replaceable rules

[9.710] Under replaceable rule, s 202A(1), the company may determine by way of resolution the extent of both executive and non-executive directors' remuneration. Under replaceable rule, s 202A(2), the company may also pay travelling and other expenses properly incurred in attending board meetings, meetings of committees of directors, general meetings and otherwise in connection with the company's business.

Single director/shareholder companies

[9.720] In the case of a one director/shareholder company, the director's remuneration is determined by resolution of the company and again the director's travelling and other expenses may be paid by the company: s 202C.

Listed entities

[9.730] Under ASX Rule 3L(7), the general meeting of listed corporations must approve any fees payable to directors. See further the discussion below of the extended disclosure requirements for listed entities.

Managing director

[9.740] For the managing director, the amount of remuneration usually rests with the board to determine. Thus, under replaceable rule, s 201J, the board may appoint the managing director on such terms, including as to remuneration, as they see fit.

Disclosure requirements

[9.750] If the members of a company wish to obtain information as to the directors' remuneration, under s 202B(1), members with at least 5% of the votes that may be cast at a general meeting, or at least 100 members entitled to vote, may require the company to disclose the remuneration of its directors. This also extends to the directors of the company's subsidiaries or an entity controlled by the company: s 202B(1). The company must disclose all remuneration paid to the director, whether in his or her capacity of director or some other capacity: s 202B(1). The company is required to comply with s 202B(1) by sending to each member an audited statement of the remuneration of each director for the last financial year: s 202B(1).

[9.760] Under the *Corporations Regulations*, Sch 5, reg 25(2) and (4), companies, other than small proprietary companies, are required to append to their financial statement details of the total income received by the directors from the company and related corporations and the number of directors whose income falls within bands of $10,000.

Listed entities

[9.770] Additional disclosure provisions apply to listed entities. Under s 300(11)(d), the annual report of all listed corporations must include details of all contracts in which each director or senior executive is a party or under which a director is entitled to a benefit. This would, of course, extend to contracts of remuneration. More specifically, s 300A(1)(c), as amended by *CLERP 9*, requires the annual directors' report of such corporations to include a remuneration report detailing the nature and amount of each element of emoluments of each director of the listed company, the five highest paid executives of the listed company and the five highest paid executives in other members of a consolidated corporate group. If a person is an executive in more than one member of the corporate group, the total of that person's remuneration must be disclosed: s 300A(1).

[9.780] The directors' report must include a discussion of the board's policy in regard to determining the nature and amount of executive remuneration: s 300A(1). In particular, the report must disclose the link between executive remuneration and corporate performance. See further s 300A as amended /extended by *CLERP 9*.

[9.790] Pursuant to the enactment of *CLERP 9*, effective from 1 July 2004, directors are required to hold a non-binding shareholder vote to adopt the remuneration disclosures within the remuneration report: s 250R. This is complemented by s 250SA that requires the chair of the Annual General Meeting to afford shareholders reasonable opportunity to discuss the remuneration report.

[9.800] The payment of directors' fees is also governed by, *inter alia*, Chap 2E, discussed in Chapter 10.

Resignation and Removal of Directors

Resignation

[9.810] Unless otherwise provided in the constitution or the director's contract of service, a director may resign from office at any time with proper notice. Under replaceable rule, s 203A, a director may resign by giving written notice to the company at its registered office.

[9.820] The resignation does not have to be accepted by the company before it will be effective, unless the constitution states acceptance to be a prerequisite: *Marks v Commonwealth* (1964) 111 CLR 549 at 571. If the office is held under a service contract, the resignation may, however, give rise to an actionable breach of that contract.

[9.830] Notice of resignation may be given to ASIC under s 205A(1). To be effective, the notice must be accompanied by a copy of the letter of resignation given to the company: s 205A(2).

[9.840] The company must also notify ASIC of the resignation in accordance with its general obligations to notify ASIC of any change of directors under s 205B(4) and (5).

Vacation of office

Retirement by rotation

[9.850] The constitution will normally provide that the first directors are to retire at the first AGM. See, for example, regs 58 and 59 of Table A. Thereafter, the constitution will normally prescribe that a percentage of the directors, for example one third, retire from office each year at the AGM. The longest serving directors since their last appointment will usually retire according to the prescribed rotation. Retiring members are, however, usually eligible for reappointment.

Automatic vacation under the Corporations Act

[9.860] As noted above, in addition, the *Corporations Act* prescribes circumstances when the office of director is automatically vacated. As discussed above, under ss 203B and 206A(2), a person ceases to be a director if they become disqualified under Part 2D.6, unless they are granted permission to manage the corporation.

Automatic vacation under constitution

[9.870] It is also common for the constitution to provide grounds for automatic vacation from office. Table A, for example, details a number of supervening disqualifying events that are typically found in corporate constitutions:

- mental incapacity: reg 65(a);
- absence from board meetings without permission for a six-month period: reg 65(c);
- holding any office of profit under the company other than managing director or principal executive officer without the consent of the company in general meeting: reg 65(d); and
- failure to disclose in accordance with s 231 (now s 191) an interest in a contract with the company: reg 65(e).

Removal of directors

Proprietary companies

[9.880] Under replaceable rule, s 203C, a proprietary company may by resolution remove a director from office. The constitution of a proprietary company will, however, often confer on the board of directors the right to remove a director.

[9.890] Where a procedure for the removal of a director is specified in the corporate constitution, these terms must be strictly adhered to. See *Nibaldi v RM Fitzroy & Associates Pty Ltd* (1996) 23 ACSR 330 and *Aloridge Pty Ltd (prov liq apptd) v West Australian Gem Explorers Pty Ltd (in liq)* (1996) 22 ACSR 484 for instances where a purported removal was held to be invalid for failing to meet the requirements specified in the constitution.

Public companies

[9.900] Section 203D provides a mechanism for the removal of directors by the general meeting of public companies. Notwithstanding anything in the company's constitution or any agreement between the director and the company or all/any of its members, a public company may by the passage of an ordinary resolution remove any director before the expiration of his or her term of office: s 203D(1). There is no requirement to show cause for dismissal. Unlike the power of appointment, a single resolution may be passed under s 203D(1) to remove several directors: *Claremont Petroleum NL v Indosuez Nominees Pty Ltd* (1986) 4 ACLC 315.

[9.910] While a director may be so removed, s 203D(2) requires that 'special' notice of the removal be given. As noted in Chapter 11, notice of the intention to move the resolution must be given to the company at least two months before the meeting is to be held: s 203D(2). As soon as practicable after receiving the notice the company is required to send a copy of the notice to the relevant director: s 203D(3). Strangely, s 203D(2) continues by providing that, if the company calls a meeting after the notice of intention is given, the resolution may be passed even though the meeting is held less than two months after the notice of intention is given.

[9.920] Directors who may be removed under the section have a right to defend their position. They may:
- give the company written representations, of a reasonable length;
- request the representations be circulated to each member; and
- speak to the motion at the meeting: s 203D(4), (5) and (6).

The director's statement does not have to be circulated if it is more than 1000 words long or considered defamatory: s 203D(6). If there is no time to comply with the requirement to send a copy of the statement to members, s 203D(5)(b) provides that the statement may be distributed to the members attending the meeting and read out at the meeting before the resolution is voted on.

[9.930] If the director was a nominee director, appointed to represent the interests of a particular class of members or debenture holders, the resolution to remove him or her will not be effective until he or she has been replaced by a successor: s 203D(1).

[9.940] A resolution, request or notice of all or any of the directors of a public company is void to the extent that it purports to remove a director from office or require that a director vacate his or her office: s 203E. This confines the ability to remove a director of a public company to the company's members.

[9.950] While s 203D may authorise the removal of a director, *prima facie* this could amount to an actionable breach of the director's independent contract of service, if any. However, as s 203D(1) is stated as being effective despite any contract with the director this would suggest that s 203D excludes any contractual remedies otherwise available to the director. The matter remains unclear.

As discussed in Chapters 12 and 13, the removal of a director may be regarded as oppressive or unjust within ss 232 and/or 461(1) where he or she had a legitimate expectation that he or she would continue in the management of the company: *Ebrahimi v Westbourne Galleries Ltd* [1973] AC 360 (see the case extracts in Chapter 13); *Aloridge Pty Ltd (prov liq apptd) v West Australian Gem Explorers Pty Ltd (in liq)* (1996) 22 ACSR 484 at 490. Moreover, where the director is removed through an alteration of the corporate constitution, it may be that the principles espoused in *Gambotto v WCP Ltd* (1995) 182 CLR 432, discussed in Chapter 6, could also apply. If applicable, the removal may be held to be oppressive and the alteration of the constitution ineffective.

[9.960] When examining the predecessor to s 203D, s 227, the courts had held that a director could be removed without, in essence, complying with s 227 where the company's constitution, for example, allowed directors to be removed without complying with the rigidity of s 227, now s 203D. While s 227 differed significantly from s 203D, in *Allied Mining and Processing Ltd v Boldbow Pty Ltd* [2002] WASC 195 Roberts-Smith J held that this reasoning is equally applicable to s 203D. The court stated that, while s 203D could not be excluded, it could be 'supplemented by constitutional articles providing alternative ways, whether more or less rigorous than s 203D, by which shareholders may remove directors'.

Payments for loss of office

[9.970] In a bid to safeguard members from the dissipation of company funds through the payment of large amounts to retiring directors, Div 2 of Part 2D.2 restricts the payment of benefits by the company, an associate or a prescribed superannuation fund in connection with the retirement of a person from, *inter alia*, the office of director. Payments beyond that permitted under the prescribed formulae in s 200G cannot be made without the approval of the company in general meeting within s 200E: ss 200B and 200D. If they are made without the members' approval, the recipient will be deemed to hold such money or money value of the benefit on trust for the company and is thereby held accountable for the payments: s 200J.

[9.980] For a full-time executive director who has been employed for at least three years, s 200G(2)(a) and (5) allow payment without member approval where the amount is no more than the average of the total remuneration received in the last three years of service, multiplied by the number of years of service or seven, whichever is the lesser. For full-time executive directors who have held office for less than three years and non-executive officers, the maximum amount is the total emoluments during the last three years: s 200G(2)(b).

[9.990] Section 200F(1) and (2), as amended by *CLERP 9*, exempt benefits paid:

- pursuant to agreements entered into before 1 January 1991 where they would have been lawful if given at that time;
- in respect of leave of absence pursuant to an industrial instrument;
- pursuant to a court order;
- as genuine damages for a breach of contract and do not exceed the formulae stated in new s 200F(3) and (4);
- pursuant to an agreement made by the company with the director before the commencement of the position as part of the consideration for holding that office and do not exceed the formulae stated in new s 200F(3) and (4).

Pursuant to *CLERP 9* new s 200F(3) and (4) specify the same formulae as that prescribed in s 200G. Thus, effectively, unless such payments meet the prescribed formulae they must be approved by the general meeting.

Section 200F(1)(b) exempts benefits given in 'prescribed circumstances'. 'Prescribed circumstances' for the purposes of s 200F(1)(b) are not defined. Section 200H also exempts benefits that are required to be paid by law (other than the law of contract and trusts).

[9.1000] The ASX Listing Rules provide additional constraints on the payment of termination payments to officers of listed companies. Under ASX Listing Rule 3C(2), the corporation's annual reports must disclose the extent of the corporation's, and its subsidiaries', contingent liability for termination payments under existing contracts with officers. ASX Listing Rule 3J(16)(a) prohibits listed corporations or their subsidiaries including in a contract of service entitlements to termination payments on a change in the corporations shareholding through, for example, a takeover. ASX Listing Rule 3J(16)(b) further provides that the general meeting must approve any service agreement where the termination benefits exceed 5% of share capital and reserves.

[9.1010] Note, termination payments are included in the concept of remuneration within Chap 2E and must be either reasonable or approved by the general meeting to be valid. See further the discussion of Chap 2E in Chapter 10.

Review questions

1. Last week Doug was convicted of offences under the *Traffic Act 1925*. The convictions stemmed from his representing to the traffic authority, by putting a fictitious signature on four applications for registration, that certain trailers were roadworthy. He purported the signature to be that of a transport inspector. At the time of the conviction Doug was a director of five proprietary companies and two public companies. The group employs 2000 employees and a further 20 subcontractors. Doug is worried that he may be prevented from continuing in this position. Advise Doug.
2. Betty was employed by a firm of accountants to assist in the development of tax minimisation schemes. She was appointed director of a number of client's companies to enable these schemes to be implemented. Each of these companies was wound up when legislation was passed declaring the schemes to be illegal. Each company's creditors received only 10 cents in the dollar. Since these events Betty has become they key operating director in another group of companies. Betty is worried that she may be prevented from continuing in this position. Advise her.
3. Fred is managing director of Bourbon Ltd and an executive director of Champagne Pty Ltd. Under the constitution of both companies it is provided that Fred is to be appointed as managing director and executive director, respectively, for a period of five years. Fred has no independent contract of service. He was appointed pursuant to these constitutions in 2003. The majority shareholder of each company, Gertie, wishes to remove Fred and put in a director sympathetic to her interests. There is no suggestion that Fred has conducted himself other than with due diligence and honesty.

Further reading

Cassidy, 'Disqualification of Directors under the Corporations Law' (1995) 13 *C&SLJ* 3 Cassidy, *Concise Corporations Law* (4th ed, Federation Press, Sydney, 2003) ch 9

Companies and Securities Law Review Committee's Report No 8, *Nominee Directors and Alternate Directors*

Corkery, 'Convicted Offenders and Section 227 of the National Companies Code: Restrictions on Certain Persons Managing Companies' (1983) 1 *C&SLJ* 153

Ford, Austin and Ramsay, *Ford's Principles of Corporations Law* (11th ed, Butterworths, Sydney, 2003) ch 7

Ford, Austin and Ramsay, *An Introduction to the CLERP Act 1999* (Butterworths, Sydney, 2000)

Lipton, 'Holding out that a person is an officer of a company' (1991) *C&SLJ* 404

Lipton, 'The Inquiry Exception to the Rule in Turquand's case: Past or Present?' (1991) 9 *C&SLJ* 37

McConvill, *An Introduction to CLERP 9* (LexisNexis, Sydney, 2004)

Mourell, 'Northside' (1991) 19 *ABLR* 36

Russell, 'The Companies Amendment Act 1980: Protecting the Company Against Its Directors' [1981] *NZLJ* 131

Travers, 'Removal of the Corporate Director During his Term of Office' (1967) 53 *Iowa LR* 389

10

Directors' Duties

Overview

As noted in the previous chapter, directors are usually conferred with extensive express and implied powers that may be used in managing a company. As these powers leave the fate of the company largely in the directors' hands, the common law and *Corporations Act* 2001 (Cth) ('*Corporations Act*') impose certain duties on these directors. These duties are designed to ensure that they will use their powers with a reasonable degree of care and for the company's best interests.

This chapter considers these director's duties and the extent to which an offender may be held liable when these duties are breached. It will be seen that in most cases there are parallel common law and statutory duties. As directors enjoy this ability to control the company's conduct, directors are considered to stand in a fiduciary relationship with their company and are subject to the duties that stem from that relationship: *Regal (Hastings) Ltd v Gulliver* [1967] 2 AC 134. As a consequence of this fiduciary relationship, equity imposes duties on directors requiring them:

- to act honestly and in the company's best interests;
- not to fetter their discretions;
- to exercise their powers for their proper purposes; and
- to avoid conflicts of interest.

In addition, the common law requires directors to act with due care and diligence. The Act in turn imposes further duties on directors requiring them to:

- act in good faith and in the company's best interests: s 181(1)(a);
- exercise their powers for their proper purposes: s 181(1)(b);
- avoid conflicts of interest: ss 182, 183, 191 and Chap 2E;
- act with due care and diligence: s 180; and
- prevent the company engaging in insolvent trading: s 588G.

Express statutory provisions such as ss 185 and 193 confirm the continued relevance of the common law duties. The one exception to this approach relates to the business judgment rule that provides a defence to a breach of the duty of care. Sections 180(2) and 185 provide that this defence is equally applicable to the common law duty of care and thus to this degree has qualified the common law duty. In turn there are also complementary common law and statutory remedies that may be imposed when such duties are breached.

Duty to Act Honestly/in Good Faith and in the Best Interests of the Company

Fiduciary duty

[10.10] As noted above, as directors stand in a fiduciary relationship with their company (*Regal (Hastings) Ltd v Gulliver* [1967] 2 AC 134) directors must do what they honestly believe to be in the company's best interests. The courts have held that it is for the directors to determine what is in the company's best interests and the courts cannot substitute their own view, formulated with the benefit of hindsight: *Re Smith & Fawcett Ltd* [1942] Ch 304 at 306. The law has, nevertheless, inserted a degree of objectivity into this *prima facie* subjective test. As Pennycuick J asserted in *Charterbridge Corp Ltd v Lloyds Bank Ltd* [1970] 1 Ch 62 at 74, the test is 'whether an intelligent and honest man in the position of a director of the company concerned, could, in the whole of the existing circumstances, have reasonably believed that the transactions were for the benefit of the company'. Thus, the law requires directors to act:

- honestly (a subjective test); and
- in a manner motivated by the company's best interests as would be determined by an intelligent director in this director's position (a quasi-objective test).

What constitutes the company's interests?

Company's interests

[10.20] Strictly, the duty is owed to the company; the separate legal entity created by law through incorporation. As noted below, the duty to safeguard the interests of a legal fiction entails some difficulty and, as a consequence, generally the interests of the company whilst solvent are those of the 'corporators as a whole': *Greenhalgh v Arderne Cinemas* [1951] Ch 286 at 291.

Shareholders

[10.30] While the duty to act in the company's interests entails a consideration of the interests of the 'corporators as a whole' (*Greenhalgh v Arderne Cinemas* [1951] Ch 286 at 291), care must be taken, however, not to equate this notion with the majority shareholders' interests: *Henry v Great Northern Railway* (1857) 44 ER 858 at 872. The directors must consider the interests of existing and future shareholders as a whole.

[10.40] Moreover, this does not mean that the directors owe a duty to individual shareholders: *Percival v Wright* [1902] 2 Ch 421.

Percival v Wright
Chancery Division: Swinfen Eady J
[1902] 2 Ch 421

Certain shareholders' solicitor approached the company secretary with a view to finding a purchaser for their shares. Unknown to these shareholders, the chairman of the directors had entered into negotiations for the sale of the company's undertaking. With this knowledge, the chairman bought the shareholders' shares.

These shareholders brought an action, seeking to have the share transaction set aside on the basis that, had the negotiations been public, the value of their shares, and hence the purchase price, would have been greater. The court rejected the suggestion that the directors stood in a fiduciary position in regard to individual shareholders. As the directors owed no duty to the shareholders, the chairman had no duty to disclose the subject negotiations to the shareholders.

Swinfen Eady J: **[425]** It is urged that the directors hold a fiduciary position as trustees for the individual shareholders, and that, where negotiations for sale of the undertaking are on foot, they are **[426]** in the position of trustees for sale. The plaintiffs admitted that this fiduciary position did not stand in the way of any dealing between a director and a shareholder before the question of sale of an undertaking had arisen, but contended that as soon as that question arose the position was altered. No authority was cited for that proposition, and I am unable to adopt the view that any line should be drawn as that point. It is contended that a shareholder knows that the directors are managing the business of the company in the ordinary course of management, and implicitly releases them from any obligation to disclose any information so acquired. That is to say, a director purchasing shares need not disclose a large casual profit, the discovery of a new vein, or the prospect of a good dividend in the immediate future, and similarly a director selling shares need not disclose losses, these being merely incidents in the ordinary course of management. But it is urged that, as soon as negotiations for the sale of the undertaking are on foot, the position is altered. Why? The true rule is that a shareholder is fixed with knowledge of all the directors' powers, and has no more reason to assume that they are not negotiating a sale of the undertaking than to assume that they are nor exercising any other power. It was strenuously urged that, though incorporation affected the relations of the shareholders to the external world, the company thereby becoming a distinct entity, the position of the shareholders inter se was not affected, and was the same as that of partners or shareholders in an unincorporated company. I am unable to adopt that view. I am therefore of opinion that the purchasing directors were under no obligation to disclose to their vendor shareholders the negotiations which ultimately proved abortive. The contrary view would place directors in a most invidious position, as they could not buy or sell shares without disclosing negotiations, a premature disclosure of which might well be against the best interests of the company. I am of opinion that directors are not in that position. There is no question of unfair dealing in this case. The directors did not approach the shareholders with the view **[427]** of obtaining their shares. The shareholders approached the directors, and named the price at which they were desirous of selling. The plaintiff's case wholly fails, and must be dismissed with costs.

While this case has been criticised, it has been adopted in both Australia and England: *Esplanade Developments Ltd v Dinive Holdings Pty Ltd* [1980] ACLC 34,232; *Cope v Butcher* (1996) 20 ACSR 37; *Australian Innovation Ltd v Petrovsky* (1996) 21 ACSR 218 at 222; *Stein v Blake* [1998] 1 All ER 724; *Brunninghausen v Glavanics* (1999) 17 ACLC 1247 at 1254; *Peskin v Anderson* (2001) 19 ACLC 3001; *Johnson v Gore Wood* [2001] 2 WLR 72; *Nestegg Holdings Pty Ltd v Smith* [2001] WASC 227; *Southern Cross Mine Management Pty Ltd v Ensham Resources Pty Ltd* (2003) 21 ACLC 1,665.

[10.50] In certain circumstances, however, there may be a special factual relationship between the directors and the shareholder(s) that is capable in itself of giving rise to a fiduciary relationship: *Australian Innovation Ltd v Petrovsky* (1996) 21 ACSR 218 at 222; *Brunninghausen v Glavanics* (1999) 17 ACLC 1247; *Peskin v Anderson* (2001) 19 ACLC 3001; *Nestegg Holdings Pty Ltd v Smith* [2001] WASC 227. In *Peskin v Anderson*, the English Court of Appeal noted that such a special relationship will only arise where the directors are brought into close contact with the shareholder(s) in a manner capable of giving rise to a fiduciary duty. Thus, it requires 'dealings, negotiations, communications or other contact directly between the directors and the members'. On the facts in that case such contact had not occurred and, therefore, the directors owed no duty to disclose information regarding the demutualisation of the subject company to the individual shareholder claimants.

Where, however, the company is a 'two-person' company, such a special relationship exists. Thus, the courts have in recent years recognised that in such companies a director owes a fiduciary duty to the other shareholder/director as much as the company: *Mesenberg v Cord Industrial Recruiters Pty Ltd* (1996) 14 ACLC 519; *Brunninghausen v Glavanics* (1996) 14 ACLC 345; (1999) 17 ACLC 1247.

Brunninghausen v Glavanics
New South Wales Court of Appeal: Handley, Priestley and Stein JJA
(1999) 17 ACLC 1247

Five thousand of the shares in S Co were held by Brunninghausen ('Mr B') and 1000 by Glavanics ('Mr G'). Both Mr B and Mr G were directors of the company. Relations between the two men broke down and they no longer trusted each other. Mr G commenced a business that competed with S Co. While Mr G remained a director this was a mere formality and he took no part in the conduct of the company's affairs. In the course of negotiations designed to resolve the dispute, Mr G indicated that he was willing to sell his shares and resign as a director provided he received a fair price. While these negotiations were proceeding, Mr B received an unexpected offer from a third party to buy the assets of the company. Mr B had extensive negotiations to this end without informing

Mr G. Mr G agreed to sell his shares to Mr B for a price well below the equivalent price paid by the third party for the assets.

Mr G brought an action against Mr B for failing to disclose the existence of the other negotiations, asserting this was in breach of his fiduciary duties. Bryson J at first instance agreed and ultimately awarded Mr G $300,000 compensation.

Mr B appealed, arguing that there existed an oral binding contract between the parties for the sale of Mr G's shares before any negotiations as to the price for the sale of the business had begun. Mr B contended that the existence of that contract terminated any possible fiduciary duty owed to Mr G.

The Court of Appeal dismissed Mr B's argument as to the absence of any fiduciary obligations. While the court accepted that generally directors' fiduciary duties are owed to the company and not to the shareholders, they found that the nature of a transaction may have given rise to a fiduciary duty owed by the directors to the shareholders. In this case Mr B had special knowledge that placed him in an advantageous position. In the circumstances it was held that Mr B, as a director, owed a fiduciary duty to Mr G as a shareholder. That duty had been breached by Mr B's non-disclosure of the negotiations for the sale of the company's business before the purchase of Mr G's shares.

Handley J: **[1254]** 39. In my opinion therefore if the defendant owed a fiduciary duty to the plaintiff the question of breach must be determined by reference to the facts as they existed when the oral contract was made on the afternoon of 8 December. However the Judge's findings in the passage quoted above establish that by that time the negotiations with Gardner and Austen had radically transformed the situation. The defendant's approach in the morning, and the speed with which the negotiations with the plaintiff were concluded that day, present a stark contrast with the absence of progress until then since the plaintiff's approach in September. If the defendant had a fiduciary duty to the plaintiff he could not contract to purchase his shares that day without disclosing the existence of the other negotiations.

40. A director occupies a fiduciary position in the company and owes fiduciary duties to it. The general principle established for well over 100 years is that a director's fiduciary duties in relation to the company's affairs are owed to the company. This reflects the distinction between the company and its members established in *Salomon v Salomon & Co* [1897] AC 22. It is reinforced by the rule in *Foss v Harbottle* (1843) 2 Hare 461 which denies shareholders standing to sue directors and others for wrongs done to the company. The breach of a fiduciary duty owed by a director to the company attracts an accounting, or an award of compensation or damages in favour of the company alone, the losses of individual shareholders being derivative not personal. ...

41. If fiduciary duties owed by directors to their companies were also owed to the shareholders, directors would be liable to harassing actions brought by minority shareholders. Since in that event each shareholder would have a personal right, directors would also be exposed to a multiplicity of actions. There are therefore good reasons behind the established rule that in general a director's fiduciary duties are owed only to the company.

42. The general rule was applied in *Percival v Wright* [1902] 2 Ch 421 where Swinfen-Eady J held that directors who purchased shares in their

company owed no fiduciary duty to their vendors to disclose the existence of takeover negotiations then in progress. ...

[1256] 54. If a fiduciary duty exists here it must arise from the bare facts of the relationship. These include the position of the defendant as the sole effective director, the existence of only one other shareholder, their close family association, the intervention of the mother-in- law to secure a family reconciliation, and the exclusive advantage or opportunity which the defendant's position conferred on him to receive any offers to purchase the company's business from third parties.

55. Any fiduciary duty arising from these facts must be one imposed by law. The defendant did nothing which could be construed as a voluntary assumption of such a duty. The Judge held that the relationship between the parties did not create a comprehensive fiduciary duty but one which was limited to the disclosure of the unexpected offer by third parties to purchase the entire business. The existence of such a duty was denied in *Percival v Wright* and that case cannot be distinguished from the present. We can only hold that the defendant owed the fiduciary duty found by the Judge if we decline to follow *Percival v Wright*.

56. The decision is not binding on this Court ... It has not been followed in Australia in circumstances comparable with the present.

57. The general principle that a director's fiduciary duties are owed to the company and not to shareholders is undoubtedly correct, and its validity is undiminished. The question is whether the principle applies in a case, such as the present, where the transaction did not concern the company, but only another shareholder.

58. Any statement that the defendant owed a duty to the company in relation to his dealings with the plaintiff over his shares is meaningless. Such a duty would lack all practical content. The company could not suffer any loss from the breach of such a duty, and had no interest in its loyal and disinterested performance. Where a director's fiduciary duties are owed to the company this prevents the recognition of concurrent and identical duties to its shareholders covering the same subject matter. However this should not preclude the recognition of a fiduciary duty to shareholders in relation to dealings in their shares where this would not compete with any duty owed to the company. ...

[1263] 102. In the present case there was a factual basis for some expectation on the part of the plaintiff. ...

103. The plaintiff had no idea of the real value of his shares to the defendant while the latter continued to operate the company, and made no attempt to find out. He would have had no reason to be unhappy if the company had continued to operate the business because he could not compare the true value of his shares with the value he received. In that event the transaction would probably have restored harmony in the family.

104. The sale to Gardner and Austen was bound to come to the plaintiff's notice. When it did its terms would demonstrate in a moment the gross disparity in price and the quick profit the defendant made from his purchase of the plaintiff's shares. The plaintiff's knowledge that in layman's terms he had been cheated by his brother-in-law was bound to destroy family harmony forever, even if it did not lead to litigation. In my view, although this finding is not necessary in this case, the family relationship, and the initiative taken by Mrs Lloyd, created a situation in which the plaintiff was "entitled to expect"

that he would not be cheated by non-disclosure of negotiations such as those held with Messrs Gardner and Austen.

105. The sale of the plaintiff's shares to the defendant required a reconciliation of their competing interests in the transaction. A sale to outsiders in which both participated involved no such conflict. It would have enabled both plaintiff and defendant to receive full value for their shares without any conflict of interest necessarily arising between them.

106. A fiduciary duty owed by directors to the shareholders where there are negotiations for a takeover or an acquisition of the company's undertaking would require the directors to loyally promote the joint interests of all shareholders. A conflict could only arise if they sought to prefer their personal interests [1264] to the joint interest. That is the very conduct which would be proscribed by the duty.

107. In my judgment the decision of a single Judge in *Percival v Wright* should not stand in the way of the recognition of such a duty at this time.

Nominee directors

[10.60] The duty to place the company's interests first is particularly problematic for nominee directors who must grapple with their duty to the company and their loyalty to the class of shareholders whom they represent. As long as directors may in good faith assert that there is a coincidence of these interests, the directors will be able to do their duty by both their patron and the company without difficulty: *Scottish Co-operative Society v Meyer* [1959] AC 324; *Re Broadcasting Station 2GB Pty Ltd* [1964-1965] NSWR 1648; *Molomby v Whitehead* (1985) 63 ALR 282. Where, however, these interests conflict, the nominee director is in an impossible position and is bound to place the company's interests over those of their patron: *Scottish Co-operative Society v Meyer* [1959] AC 324.

Scottish Co-operative Society v Meyer
House of Lords: Viscount Simonds, Lords Morton of Henryton, Keith of Avonholm and Denning
[1959] AC 324

The board of directors was constituted by the two respondents and three nominee directors of the appellant society. As a result of the rejection of a share offer made by the appellant, seeking to buy further shares in the company, relations on the board became hostile. The appellant established within itself a new department that competed with the company and diverted the produce from its mills to this body, rather than the company. The appellant declined to supply the company the cloth it needed, except at non-competitive prices. The effect of creating the new department and passive policy of non-supply was to take business from the company and starve it of the materials it needed to conduct its business. With the downturn in business, the value of the company's shares plummeted. While the nominee directors were aware of the appellant's policy, they did nothing to remedy the situation.

The respondents sought relief under the s 210 of the *Companies Act* 1948 (UK) on the ground that the affairs of the company were being conducted in an oppressive manner. The court at first instance agreed and ordered the appellants to purchase the respondents' shares. On appeal the House of Lords agreed that by adopting this passive policy the directors had subordinated the interests of the company to those of the Society and in turn acted in an oppressive manner.

Lord Denning: [366] So long as the interests of all concerned were in harmony, there was no difficulty. The nominee directors could do their duty by both companies without embarrassment. But, as soon as the interests of the two companies were in conflict, the nominee directors were placed in an impossible position. Thus, when the realignment of shareholding was under discussion, the duty of the three directors was to get the best possible price for any new issue of its shares ... whereas their duty to the society was to obtain the new shares at the lowest possible price – at par, if they could. Again, when the society determined to set up its own rayon department, [367] competing with the business of the company, the duty of the three directors to the company was to do their best to promote its business and to act with complete good faith towards it; and, in consequence, not to disclose their knowledge of its affairs to a competitor, and not even to work for a competitor, when to do so might operate to the disadvantage of the company ... whereas they were under the self-same duties to the society. It is plain that, in the circumstances, these three gentlemen could not do their duty by both companies, and they did not do so. They put their duty to the society above their duty to the company in this sense, at least, that they did nothing to defend the interests of the company against the conduct of the society. They probably thought that 'as nominees' of the co-operative society their first duty was to the co-operative society. In this they were wrong. By subordinating the interest of the company to those of the society, they conducted the affairs of the company in a manner oppressive to other shareholders. It is said that these three directors were, at most, only guilty of inaction – of doing nothing to protect the company. But the affairs of a company can, in my opinion, be conducted oppressively by the directors doing nothing to defend its interests when they ought to do something – just as they can conduct its affairs oppressively by doing something injurious to its interests when they ought not to do it. The question was asked: What could these directors have done? They could, I suggest, at least on behalf of the company, have protested against the setting up of a competing business. But then it was said: What good would that have done? Any protest by them would be sure to have been unavailing, seeing that they were in a minority on the board of the society. The answer is that no one knows whether it would have done any good. They never did protest. And it does not lie in their mouths to say it would have done no good, when they never put it to the test ... [368] Even if they had protested, it might have been a formal gesture, ostensibly correct, but not to be taken seriously. Your Lordships were referred to *Bell v Lever Bros Ltd* [1932] AC 161 at 195, where Lord Blanesburgh said that a director of one company was at liberty to become a director also of a rival company. That may have been so at that time. But it is at the risk now of an application under s 210 if he subordinates the interests of the one company to those of the other.

[10.70] Note, however, that s 187, discussed below, allows the director of a wholly-owned subsidiary to act in the best interests of the holding company if certain prerequisites are met. Thus, a nominee of a holding company may act in accordance with this company's interests whilst on the board of the subsidiary if the prerequisites detailed in s 187 are met.

Group companies

[10.80] The duty to promote a company's interests is also problematic where the person is a director of several companies, particularly companies within the one group. As each company is a separate legal entity, the director must consider each company's individual interests, not those of the group as a whole: *Reid Murray Holdings v David Murray Holdings* (1972) 5 SASR 386 at 402-403; *Industrial Equity Ltd v Blackburn* (1977) 137 CLR 567. If directors place one company's interests, or those of the group as a whole, over the interests of another company in the group, they will be breaching their duty to act in the latter company's best interests: *Reid Murray Holdings v David Murray Holdings*, above; *Walker v Wimborne* (1976) 137 CLR 1 at 7; *Industrial Equity Ltd v Blackburn*, above; *R v Byrnes* (1995) 183 CLR 501 at 517; *Fitzsimmons v R* (1997) 23 ACSR 355 at 359; *Farrow Finance Company Ltd (in liq) v Farrow Properties Pty Ltd (in liq)* (1998) 16 ACLC 897.

[10.90] A possible exception to this rule is where acting in the interests of the other company also benefits the company to which the duty is owed: *Equiticorp Financial Services Ltd v Bank of New Zealand* (1993) 11 ACLC 952. This may occur where, for example, the company to which the duty is owed has a major shareholding in that other company.

[10.100] Section 187 provides a statutory exception to this principle by allowing the director of a wholly-owned subsidiary to act in the best interests of the holding company if:

- the constitution of the subsidiary expressly authorises the director to act in the best interests of the holding company;
- the director acts in good faith in the best interests of the holding company; and
- the subsidiary is not insolvent at the time the director acts and does not become insolvent because of the director's act.

Creditors

[10.110] Clearly, where the interests of the company and creditors coincide, it is legitimate for the director to consider the creditors' position: *Walker v Wimborne* (1976) 137 CLR 1 at 6-7:

> [T]he directors of a company in discharging their duty to the company must take account of the interest of its shareholders and creditors. Any failure by the director to take into account the interests of creditors will have adverse consequences for the company as well as for them. The creditor of a company ... must look to that company for payment. His interests may be prejudiced by

the movement of funds between companies in the event that the companies become insolvent.

While the company is solvent, a failure to consider creditors' interests will only amount to a breach of a director's duty where it also involves a failure to act in the company's best interests: *Kinsela v Russell Kinsela Pty Ltd (in liq)* (1986) 10 ACLR 395.

[10.120] Where the company is insolvent or of doubtful solvency, however, the creditors' interests displace those of the shareholders/ company and the directors must have regard to creditors' interests: *Kinsela v Russell Kinsela Pty Ltd (in liq)* (1986) 2 ACLC 215.

Kinsela v Russell Kinsela Pty Ltd (in liq)
New South Wales Court of Appeal: Street CJ, Hope and McHugh JJA
(1986) 2 ACLC 215

When the company was in a financially precarious position, it entered into a three-year lease of premises it owned at a fixed rent substantially below current market rents. The lease also included a three-year lease option and a further option to purchase it at a price that was again likely to be substantially below the market value. Shortly after entering into the lease, the company went into liquidation.

The liquidator sought a declaration that the lease was voidable for being contrary to the company's best interests. In response the directors asserted that given the lease was granted with the unanimous knowledge and approval of all the shareholders there could be no question of its not being in the best interests of the company.

The Court of Appeal agreed with Powell J at first instance. The court held that in a solvent company the shareholders are properly regarded as the company when questions of directors' duty arise. Where, however, a company is insolvent, the interests of the creditors supplant those of the shareholders. Through the process of liquidation the creditors displace the power of the shareholders and directors to deal with the company's assets and thus the shareholders had no ability to absolve the directors from liability for a breach of their duties.

Street J: **[220]** The learned Judge at first instance held, as I have noted, that he was bound by authority to **[221]** hold that the approval by all of the shareholders validated an action which would otherwise be beyond the powers of the directors provided that there had been a full and frank disclosure to the shareholders of all of the circumstances relevant to the proposed transaction (*Bamford v Bamford* [1970] 1 Ch 212 at 238-242; *Winthrop Investments Ltd v Winns Ltd* (1975-1976) CLC ¶40-223; [1975] 2 NSWLR 666 at 679-689). He added, however, an express reservation of his own in accepting that such a statement of principle could have been intended to exclude a challenge based upon an allegation of misuse of a director's power deliberately to prejudice or encumber creditors. This reservation in my view was well founded.

The authorities to which his Honour submitted, notwithstanding the generality of their enunciations of principle, were not intended to, and do not, apply in a situation in which the interests of the company as a whole involve the rights of creditors as distinct from the rights of shareholders. In a solvent company the proprietary interests of the shareholders entitle them as a general body to be regarded as the company when questions of the duty of directors arise. If, as a general body, they authorise or ratify a particular action of the directors, there can be no challenge to the validity of what the directors have done. But where a company is insolvent the interests of the creditors intrude. They become prospectively entitled, through the mechanism of liquidation, to displace the power of the shareholders and directors to deal with the company's assets. It is in a practical sense their assets and not the shareholders assets that, through the medium of the company, are under the management of the directors pending either liquidation, return to solvency, or the imposition of some alternative administration.

In a later part of his judgment in *Rolled Steel Ltd v British Steel Corporation* [[1985] 2 WLR 908] at 947-948 Slade LJ acknowledged that the principle of a company's action being validated by the unanimous consent of all the shareholders "is not an unqualified one". Generally expressed statements of principle regarding the validating effect of shareholder approval are directed to solvent companies:

"First, if an act is beyond the corporate capacity of a company it is clear that it cannot be ratified. As against the company itself 'an *ultra vires* agreement cannot become *intra vires* by means of estoppel, lapse of time, ratification, acquiescence, or delay': *York Corporation v Henry Leetham and Sons Ltd* [1924] 1 Ch 557, 573 per Russell J. However, the clear general principle is that any act that falls within the corporate capacity of a company will bind it if it is done with the unanimous consents of all the shareholders or is subsequently ratified by such consents: see, for example, *Salomon v A Salomon & Co Ltd* [1897] AC 22, 57 per Lord Davey; *In re Horsley & Weight Ltd* [1982] 1 Ch 442, 454 per Buckley LJ and *Multinational Gas and Petrochemical Co v Multinational Gas and Petrochemical Services Ltd* [1983] Ch 258. This last-mentioned principle certainly is not an unqualified one. In particular, it will not enable the shareholders of a company to bind the company itself to a transaction which constitutes a fraud on its creditors: see, for example, *In re Halt Garage (1964) Ltd* [1982] 3 All ER 1016, 1037, per Oliver J. But none of the authorities which have been cited to us have convinced me that a transaction which (i) falls within the letter of the express or implied powers of a company conferred by its memorandum, and (ii) does not involve a fraud on its creditors, and (iii) is assented to by all the shareholders, will not bind a fully solvent company merely because the intention of the directors, or the shareholders, is to effect a purpose not authorised by the memorandum. The recent decision of this Court in the *Multinational case* [1983] Ch 258 seems to me to point to a contrary conclusion: see also *Attorney-General's Reference (No 2 of 1982)* [1984] QB 624, 640 per Kerr LJ."

There has been a recent comprehensive and authoritative analysis in New Zealand by Cooke J of the principles of law to be applied in a case such as that presently under consideration (*Nicholson v Permakraft (NZ) Ltd (in liq)* (1985) 3 ACLC 453). In that case the directors of a manufacturing company which was facing liquidity problems adopted a reconstruction scheme which had the effect of prejudicing the creditors of the company. The informed assent of all of the shareholders to the reconstruction was established and this was relied upon by the directors as a defence to a **[222]** claim brought by the company on the initiation of its liquidator seeking to have the transaction set aside. The case was not so straightforward as is the present: the degree of the company's financial stability was open to some debate; also, the directly prejudicial effect on creditors was not so plainly apparent at the time the transaction was entered into.

Cooke J drew upon English, Australian and New Zealand case law as well as upon other learned writings in formulating a series of principles that provide valuable and illuminating guidance in resolving problems within this area. He stated those principles at 457-460 of his judgment. That entire passage could well be cited in full as pointing to the fate of the present litigation but I shall quote only a few brief extracts:

"(i) A company is bound in a matter *intra vires* by the unanimous agreement of its members ...

(ii) The principle about assent has a particular application in matters of procedure. As Buckley J put it in *In re Duomatic Limited* [1969] 2 Ch 365 at 373: '... where it can be shown that all shareholders who have a right to attend and vote at a general meeting of the company assent to some matter which a general meeting of the company could carry into effect, that assent is as binding as a resolution in general meeting would be ...'. A fortiori the creditors in the present case, who of course had no right to attend general meetings of the company or directors' meetings, cannot take advantage – directly or indirectly through an action by the liquidator in the name of the company – of the informality in the declaration of the dividend. It is cured by the unanimous assent of the shareholders.

(iii) The duties of directors are owed to the company. On the facts of particular cases this may require the directors to consider inter alia the interests of creditors. For instance, creditors are entitled to consideration, in my opinion, if the company is insolvent, or near insolvent, or of doubtful solvency, or if a contemplated payment or other course of action would jeopardise its solvency ...

To translate this into legal obligation accords with the now pervasive concepts of duty to a neighbour and the linking of power with obligation. It is also consistent with the spirit of what Lord Haldane said. In a situation of marginal commercial solvency such creditors may fairly be seen as beneficially interested in the company or contingently so. ...

in such cases the unanimous assent of the shareholders is not enough to justify the breach of duty to the creditors. The situation is really one where those conducting the affairs of the company owe a duty to creditors. Concurrence by the shareholders prevents any complaint by them, but compounds rather than excuses the breach as against the creditors.

(vi) The foregoing principles relate to actions by the company against directors, whether or not in truth brought by the liquidator."

Richardson J expressed his agreement with the conclusion reached by Cooke J but stated his preference to reserve to another day what he described as "the controversial question of the nature and scope of the duties owed by directors and shareholders to creditors of the company". His concern, however, to leave open this point stemmed rather from the far more difficult state of facts which were under consideration in that case. He made this plain in a passage at 463:

"If a company is solvent in the sense of its assets exceeding its liabilities there can, I think, be no question of a separate duty to creditors: they have their ordinary remedies if their accounts are not paid. If it is insolvent the creditors have an interest in the company and the directors might be said to have a duty to them for creditors' money is then at stake. It is in the intermediate situation of near insolvency or doubtful insolvency that greater difficulties of legal principle arise."

The third member of the Bench in that case, Somers J, was likewise conscious of the difficulties presented by the particular facts under consideration. He said at 464: **[223]**

"In the case of an insolvent company, at least in the sense that its liabilities exceed its assets, directors in the management of a company must have regard to the interests of creditors. That is because according to the order of application of assets on a winding up they are trading with the creditors' money. It has been suggested that when the solvency of a company is doubtful or marginal it will be a misfeasance (probably not capable of being ratified or exonerated by shareholders) to enter into a transaction which directors ought to know is likely to cause a loss to creditors – see, eg, *In re Horsley & Weight Ltd* [1982] 1 Ch 442 at 455 per Cumming-Bruce LJ and Templeman LJ. Whether that is so does not in my view fall to be decided now for in the instant case I am satisfied the company was solvent at the material times."

The obligation by directors to consider, in appropriate cases, the interests of creditors has been recognised also in the High Court of Australia. In *Walker v Wimborne* (1975-1976) CLC ¶40-251 at 28,537; (1975-1976) 137 CLR 1 at 6-7 Mason J said:

"... it should be emphasized that the directors of a company in discharging their duty to the company must take account of the interests of its shareholders and its creditors. Any failure by the directors to take into account the interests of creditors will have adverse consequences for the company as well as for them."

Barwick CJ concurred in the judgment of Mason J.

It is, to my mind, legally and logically acceptable to recognise that, where directors are involved in a breach of their duty to the company affecting the interests of shareholders, then shareholders can either authorise that breach in prospect or ratify it in retrospect. Where, however, the interests at risk are those of creditors I see no reason in law or in logic to recognise that the shareholders can authorise the breach. Once it is accepted, as in my view it must be, that the directors' duty to a company as a whole extends in an insolvency context to not prejudicing the interests of creditors (*Nicholson v Permakraft (NZ) Ltd* and *Walker v Wimborne*) the shareholders do not have the power or authority to absolve the directors from that breach.

I hesitate to attempt to formulate a general test of the degree of financial instability which would impose upon directors an obligation to consider the interests of creditors. For present purposes, it is not necessary to draw upon *Nicholson v Permakraft* as authority for any more than the proposition that the duty arises when a company is insolvent inasmuch as it is the creditors' money which is at risk, in contrast to the shareholders' proprietary interests. It needs to be borne in mind that to some extent the degree of financial instability and the degree of risk to the creditors are interrelated. Courts have traditionally and properly been cautious indeed in entering boardrooms and pronouncing upon the commercial justification of particular executive decisions. Wholly differing value considerations might enter into an adjudication upon the justification for a particular decision by a speculative mining company of doubtful stability on the one hand, and, on the other hand, by a company engaged in a more conservative business in a state of comparable financial instability. Moreover, the plainer it is that it is the creditors' money that is at risk, the lower may be the risk to which the directors, regardless of the unanimous support of all of the shareholders, can justifiably expose the company.

[10.130] Under this view, the duty is still owed to the company, not the creditors: *Re New World Alliance Pty Ltd; Sycotex Pty Ltd v Baseler* (1994) 122 ALR 531; *Spies v The Queen* (2000) 17 ACLC 727.

Spies v The Queen
High Court of Australia: Gaudron, McHugh, Gummow, Hayne and Callinan JJ
(2000) 17 ACLC 727

Sterling Nicholas Duty Free Pty Ltd was in financial difficulties. Spies and McPherson were directors of this company. They resolved that this company would purchase all of the issued shares in another company of which they were directors and shareholders, Holdings Co. Spies held 9999 shares, with the remaining share being held by McPherson. As Sterling Nicholas Duty Free Pty Ltd had no capacity to pay for these shares, an equitable charge was granted over all the assets of Sterling Nicholas Duty Free Pty Ltd in favour of Spies until he was repaid. In addition, that director's loan account with the company was credited with $500,000 being the purchase price of all the shares in Holdings Co. Through these transactions Spies had sold shares in an otherwise worthless company (Holdings Co) for $500,000 and had gone from a substantial debtor of Sterling Nicholas Duty Free Pty Ltd to a secured creditor.

Spies was charged under s 229(4) of the *Companies (New South Wales) Code* and s 176A of the *Crimes Act* 1900 (NSW) for, in essence, defrauding Sterling Nicholas Duty Free Pty Ltd's creditors and improperly using his position to gain a financial advantage. As the charges were laid in the alternative, at trial the accused was convicted under s 176A, but no verdict was taken in regard to s 229(4). The accused appealed to the Court of Criminal Appeal. However, this court entered a conviction against the accused under s 229(4).

Spies appealed to the High Court. The High Court allowed the appeal, setting aside the conviction under s 176A and ordering a new trial under s 229(4). In the course of the judgment the court made significant comments on the duty to have regard to creditors' interests. The court held that cases such as *Walker v Wimborne* (1975-1976) CLC ¶40-251; *Kinsela v Russell Kinsela Pty Ltd* (1986) 4 ACLC 215 were not authority that directors owed an independent duty to creditors. As a consequence, while there was a duty in certain cases to take into account the interests of creditors, this did not confer upon creditors any general law right against directors of the company to recover losses.

Gaudron, McHugh, Gummow and Hayne JJ: [730] 93. It is true that there are statements in the authorities, beginning with that of Mason J in *Walker v Wimborne*, which would suggest that because of the insolvency of Sterling Nicholas, the appellant, as one of its directors, owed a duty to that company to consider the interests of the creditors and potential creditors of the company in entering into transactions on **[731]** behalf of the company. *Walker v Wimborne* was an appeal by a liquidator against the dismissal of his misfeasance summons brought against former directors under s 367B of the Companies Act 1961 (NSW). Statements in this and other cases came within Professor Sealy's description of: "words of censure directed at conduct which anyway comes within some well-established rule of law, such as the law imposing liability for misfeasance, the expropriation of corporate assets or fraudulent preference." Hence the view that it is "extremely doubtful" whether Mason J "intended to suggest that directors owe an independent duty directly to creditors." To give some unsecured creditors remedies in an insolvency which are denied to others would undermine the basic principle of pari passu participation by creditors.

94. In *Re New World Alliance Pty Ltd; Sycotex Pty Ltd v Baseler* [(1994) 51 FCR 420], Gummow J pointed out: "It is clear that the duty to take into account the interests of creditors is merely a restriction on the right of shareholders to ratify breaches of the duty owed to the company. The restriction is similar to that found in cases involving fraud on the minority. Where a company is insolvent or nearing insolvency, the creditors are to be seen as having a direct interest in the company and that interest cannot be overridden by the shareholders. This restriction does not, in the absence of any conferral of such a right by statute, confer upon creditors any general law right against former directors of the company to recover losses suffered by those creditors … the result is that there is a duty of imperfect obligation owed to creditors, one which the creditors cannot enforce save to the extent that the company acts on its own motion or through a liquidator."

95. In so far as remarks in *Grove v Flavel* [(1986) 4 ACLC 654] suggest that the directors owe an independent duty to, and enforceable by, the creditors by reason of their position as directors, they are contrary to principle and later authority and do not correctly state the law.

96. The appellant had no legal relationship with the creditors such that his conduct in selling the shares to Sterling Nicholas constituted a defrauding of the creditors of that company.

97. Furthermore, the mere fact that a transaction with a company may have adverse consequences for the creditors of the company does not constitute a defrauding of those creditors even if it is done dishonestly. A person who induces a company to buy land by means of a false misrepresentation defrauds the company but for legal purposes he or she does not defraud its shareholders, creditors or employees although their interests are or may be detrimentally affected by the fraud. Nor does such a transaction constitute a defrauding of the creditors because the person implementing it intends it to be to the detriment of the creditors.

Employees and other third parties

[10.140] Once again, where the interests of third parties, such as employees, coincide with those of the company, the directors can act in the best interests of the employees. Thus, in *Hampson v Prices Patent Candle Co* (1876) 24 WR 754, the court held that bonus payments could be made to employees to encourage greater productivity as this would benefit the company.

[10.150] However, directors owe no direct fiduciary duty to third parties, whether they be consumers, employees, directors or associates of these persons: *Dodge v Ford Motor Co* (1919) 170 WN 668; *Parke v Daily News Ltd* [1962] Ch 927; *Re W & M Roith Ltd* [1967] 1 WLR 432; *Bailey v Mandala Private Hospital Pty Ltd* (1987) 12 ACLR 641. Thus, in *Parke v Daily News Ltd* [1962] Ch 927 the court held that the directors wrongly proposed to distribute the proceeds from the sale of the company's undertaking/business to its employees who were retrenched as a result of the sale. In the absence of specific statutory provisions, such as the employee entitlements provisions introduced by the *Corporations Law Amendment (Employee Entitlements) Act* 2000 (Cth), discussed below, directors owe no duty to have regard to employee interests.

Equitable relief

[10.160] In addition to the statutory remedies discussed below, a breach of the duty to act honestly will give rise to equitable relief. Such may involve injuncting actions in breach of the duty (*Parke v Daily News Ltd* [1962] Ch 927), declaring such actions to be voidable at the company's option (*Kinsela v Russell Kinsela Pty Ltd (in liq)* (1986) 2 ACLC 215) or orders for equitable damages (*Brunninghausen v Glavanics* (1996) 14 ACLC 345; (1999) 17 ACLC 1247).

Under s 1318(1), the court has power to relieve a director or other officer from liability for a breach of trust or duty where the person acted honestly and, having regard to all the circumstances, the person ought fairly be excused. See further s 1318.

Statutory duty

[10.170] Section 181(1)(a) of the *Corporations Act* requires a director to exercise his or her powers and discharge his or her office in good faith in the corporation's best interests. Section 184(1)(c) similarly provides that it is an offence if directors are reckless or intentionally dishonest and fail to exercise their powers and discharge their duties in good faith in the corporation's best interests.

[10.180] There was some uncertainty as to whether the predecessors to s 181(1)(a) imposed a subjective or constructive standard of honesty. If the latter is correct, the section may be breached when in the director's mind he or she is acting honestly (subjective honesty), but his or her actions do not accord with community standards of conduct (constructive dishonesty). The Explanatory Memorandum to the *Corporate Law Economic Reform Program Act* 1999 (Cth) ('*CLERP Act*') indicates that this controversy was to be resolved through the separation of civil and criminal breaches between ss 181(1)(a) and 184(1)(c). In para 6.79 it states that a criminal breach (s 184) will only arise where the fault element exists, while a civil breach (s 181) may occur without fault. This view was adopted by Santow J in *ASIC v Adler* (2002) 20 ACLC 576 at 705:

Objective standard for duty to act in good faith and proper purpose under s 181

738. I also agree broadly with the submissions of the Plaintiff regarding the proper principles to apply in relation to the requirement of s 181(1) to act in good faith for a proper purpose. ... In particular, I consider that the standard of behaviour required by s 181(1) is not complied with by subjective good faith or by a mere subjective belief by a director that his purpose was proper, certainly if no reasonable director could have reached that conclusion. This is made clear by the new provisions in s 184(1) which by contrast imposes the additional elements of being "intentionally dishonest" or "reckless" for the purpose of criminal sanctions. Thus, as was said by Bowen LJ in *Hutton v West Cork Railway Co* (1883) 23 Ch D 654 at 671: "Bona fides cannot be the sole test, otherwise you might have a lunatic conducting the affairs of the company, and paying its money with both hands in a manner perfectly bona fide yet perfectly irrational."

739. Where, as my findings indicate apply here, no reasonable board could consider a decision to be within the interests of the company, the making of the decision will be a breach of duty (Ford 6th Ed, para 8.060 at p 313).

[10.190] Note again the above discussion of s 187 and when a director of a wholly owned subsidiary will be taken to have acted in good faith and in the best interests of the subsidiary even though the director acts in the best interests of the holding company.

Relationship with other duties

[10.200] Section 185 provides that ss 180-184 are not in derogation of any rule of law relating to the duty or liability of directors. Thus, an action under s 181(1)(a) may coincide with an action for a breach of contract, breach of common law duties or breach of other statutory duties.

Consequences of a breach

Civil penalty

[10.210] Section 181 is a civil penalty provision: s 1317E(1). If a court is satisfied a person has breached s 181(1)(a), it must make a declaration of contravention under s 1317E(1). In turn, once the declaration is made, in the case of a breach that materially prejudices the interests of the corporation or its members or the corporation's ability to pay its creditors or constitutes a serious breach of s 181(1), a court may order the payment of a pecuniary penalty of up to $200,000: s 1317G (former s 1317EA). In *ASIC v Forge* [2002] NSWSC 760, Foster AJ identified as relevant to the decision to order civil penalties that the breach had caused a considerable loss (over $3m) to a public company, the breach had been deliberate and for the personal gain of the defendant directors, the defendants had shown no contrition, general deterrence and the need to punish the defendants. Note that ratification by the company shareholders is ineffective to cure a breach of statutory duty: *Forge v ASIC*

[2004] NSWCA 448. If a court makes a declaration of contravention, it must hold a separate hearing on the issue of penalty: *Forge v ASIC*.

Disqualification

[10.220] Under s 206C(1) and (2), where a declaration of contravention has been made under s 1317E, on the application of ASIC, the court may disqualify a person in light of, *inter alia*, the person's conduct in relation to the management, business or property of the corporation. The period of disqualification is a matter for the court's discretion. The most recent extensive discussion of the relevant factors for concern in a s 260C application is found in *ASIC v Adler* (2002) 20 ACLC 1146. The court applied the above principles and held that one director, Adler, should be banned for 20 years and another director, Williams, for 10 years as a consequence of breaching a number of civil penalty provisions. The factual basis for the s 260C application (ie the numerous breaches of directors' duties) is specified in *ASIC v Adler* (2002) 20 ACLC 576 in Chapter 7 and later in this chapter. The judgment of Santow J also provides a summary of these breaches.

ASIC v Adler
Supreme Court of New South Wales: Santow J
(2002) 20 ACLC 1146

Santow J: [1152] 13. In the Judgment, HIH and HIHC (who were not parties to the proceedings) were held in the circumstances found to have contravened (a) s 208 (related party financial benefits without shareholder approval) of the *Corporations Law* by the payment of $10 million to AEUT in the circumstances; and (b) s 260A (financial assistance for the purchase of shares) of the *Corporations Law* by such payment of $10 million followed by the purchase of shares by AEUT from part of the $10 million; paras [182], [183] and [355].

14. Mr Adler and Adler Corporation, as well as the Second Defendant ("Mr Williams") and Third Defendant ("Mr Fodera"), were also found to have been relevantly "involved" in those contraventions, so as to place themselves in breach of (respectively) ss 209(2) and 260D(2) of the *Corporations Law*; [199], [217] & [369].

15. Mr Adler was held to have contravened his directorial duties, or duties as an officer, that were owed to HIH and HIHC and (save in relation to s 183) PEE, under ss 180, 181, 182 and 183 of the *Corporations Law*, by reason of the transactions, described above: [387], [577], [694], [706] & [730]. Adler Corporation was found to have been "involved" in these contraventions, so as to be liable itself under ss 181(2), 182(2) and 183(2) of the *Corporations Law*: [578]. Mr Adler was also relevantly involved in Williams' contravention of his duty **[1153]** under s 182 so as to be liable himself under s 182(2): [731].

16. Mr Williams was held to have contravened his directorial duties, or duties as an officer, owed to HIH and HIHC, under ss 180 and 182 of the *Corporations Law*, through his involvement with the payment of $10 million by HIHC to PEE: [453], [461].

17. Mr Fodera was also held to have contravened his directorial duties, or duties as an officer, owed to HIH and HIHC under s 180(1) of the

Corporations Law, through his involvement with the payment of $10 million by HIHC to PEE: [512(a)].

18. In submissions on relief, ASIC pointed out that it was found or derived from the Judgment that there were 101 contraventions of the *Corporations Law* by Mr Adler; 84 by Adler Corporation; seven by Mr Williams and five by Mr Fodera; see T, 31.20 and the attachment A to this judgment. This multiplicity was put by ASIC not so much as having significance as to pecuniary penalty, but of some general relevance in relation to disqualification as a director.

RELIEF SOUGHT BY ASIC:

Declarations

19. Following publication of the Judgment, declarations were made in respect to these contraventions, pursuant to s 1317E(1) of the *Corporations Act* 2001 (Cth) on 27 March 2002, with brief reasons accompanying, as to their formulation.

20. Apart from these declarations, ASIC sought disqualification orders, compensation orders and pecuniary penalties against Messrs Adler, Williams and Fodera pursuant to ss 206C, 1317H and 1317G of the *Corporations Act* respectively, as well as compensation orders and pecuniary penalties against Adler Corporation. ASIC submitted that the disqualification orders for Mr Adler and Mr Williams should be significantly longer than for Mr Fodera. It also submitted that it should be borne in mind that s 206G of the *Corporations Act* retains in the Court the discretion, should future application be made, to give leave in appropriate circumstances to disqualified persons again to manage corporations; also to impose exceptions and conditions on that leave; (s 206G(3)). That should be contrasted with the "all or nothing" character of a disqualification order, save as to period; s 206C. ...

[1159] 54. ... 206C "(2) In determining whether the disqualification is justified, the Court may have regard to: (a) the person's conduct in relation to the management, business or property of any corporation; and (b) any other matters that the Court considers appropriate."

55. It is useful if, at the outset, I identify the propositions, by way of guiding principles or relevant factors that can be derived from the cases which have dealt with these provisions or their predecessors.

56. The cases on disqualification gave orders ranging from life disqualification to 3 years. The propositions that may be derived from these cases include:

(i) Disqualification orders are designed to protect the public from the harmful use of the corporate structure or from use that is contrary to proper commercial standards. ...

(ii) The banning order is designed to protect the public by seeking to safeguard the public interest in the transparency and accountability of companies and in the suitability of directors to hold office: ...

(iii) Protection of the public also envisages protection of individuals that deal with companies, including consumers, creditors, shareholders and investors ...

(iv) The banning order is protective against present and future misuse of the corporate structure ...

(v) The order has a motive of personal deterrence, though it is not punitive ...

(vi) The objects of general deterrence are also sought to be achieved ...

(vii) In assessing the fitness of an individual to manage a company, it is necessary that they have an understanding of the proper role of the company director and the duty of due diligence that is owed to the company ...

(viii) Longer periods of disqualification are reserved for cases where contraventions have been of a serious nature such as those involving dishonesty

(ix) In assessing an appropriate length of prohibition, consideration has been given to the degree of seriousness of the contraventions, the propensity that the defendant may engage in similar conduct in the future and the likely harm that may be caused to the public ...

(x) It is necessary to balance the personal hardship to the defendant against the public interest and the need for protection of the public from any repeat of the conduct ...

(xi) A mitigating factor in considering a period of disqualification is the likelihood of the defendant reforming ...

(xii) The eight criteria to govern the exercise of the court's powers of disqualification set out in *Commissioner for Corporate Affairs v Ekamper* (1988) 6 ACLC 90; (1987) 12 ACLR 519 have been influential. It was held **[1160]** that in making such an order it is necessary to assess:
  - Character of the offenders
  - Nature of the breaches
  - Structure of the companies and the nature of their business
  - Interests of shareholders, creditors and employees
  - Risks to others from the continuation of offenders as company directors
  - Honesty and competence of offenders
  - Hardship to offenders and their personal and commercial interests; and
  - Offenders' appreciation that future breaches could result in future proceedings.

(xiii) Factors which lead to the imposition of the longest periods of disqualification (that is disqualifications of 25 years or more) were:
  - Large financial losses
  - High propensity that defendants may engage in similar activities or conduct
  - Activities undertaken in fields in which there was potential to do great financial damage such as in management and financial consultancy.
  - Lack of contrition or remorse
  - Disregard for law and compliance with corporate regulations.
  - Dishonesty and intent to defraud
  - Previous convictions and contraventions for similar activities

(xiv) In cases in which the period of disqualification ranged from 7 years to 12 years, the factors evident and which lead to the conclusion that these cases were serious though not 'worst cases' included:
  - Serious incompetence and irresponsibility
  - Substantial loss
  - Defendants had engaged in deliberate courses of conduct to enrich themselves at others' expense, but with lesser degrees of dishonesty

- Continued, knowing and wilful contraventions of the law and disregard for legal obligations
- Lack of contrition or acceptance of responsibility, but as against that, the prospect that the individual may reform

The difficulty with *Roussi's* case [*ASC v Roussi* (1999) 32 ACSR 568] is that disqualification for 10 years was ordered, as this was the period of disqualification that the ASC had sought. Had a longer period been applied for, Einfeld J may have considered giving a longer period: *ASC v Roussi* at 571;

(xv) The factors leading to the shortest disqualifications, that is disqualifications for up to 3 years were:
- Although the defendants had personally gained from the conduct, they had endeavoured to repay or partially repay the amounts misappropriated
- The defendants had no immediate or discernible future intention to hold a position as manager of a company
- In *Donovan's* case, the respondent had expressed remorse and contrition, acted on advice of professionals and had not contested the proceedings ...

[1162] 60. It is well settled (see [56(i) to (iii)] above) that the primary purpose of the disqualification power is the protection of the public; see, for example, *ASC v Forem-Freeway Enterprises Pty Ltd* [(1999) 17 ACLC 511] at 521; ACSR 349. That its object is the need to protect the public, with its corollary of personal deterrence, does not mean that its aim should be punitive though personal deterrence is relevant. That is explained in the judgment of Bowen CJ in *Re Magna Alloys & Research Pty Ltd* [(1975) CLC 28,354] at 28,354: "The policy to which s 122 [the predecessor to s 206C and s 206E of the *Corporations Act*] gives effect is that a person convicted of an offence of any of the type specified in that section is not to be permitted to act as a director or take part in the management of a company. The section is not punitive. It is designed to protect the public and to prevent the corporate structure from being used in the financial detriment of investors, shareholders, creditors and persons dealing with the company. In its operation, it is calculated to act as a safeguard against the corporate structure being used by individuals in a manner which is contrary to proper commercial standards."

61. Here, of course, the occasion for considering disqualification does not arise after the conviction by indictment for a criminal offence; compare s 206B which provides for automatic disqualification in the circumstances there delineated. That of itself does not mean that because these proceedings have been by way of civil penalty, the Court is thereby constrained in the exercise of its discretion to apply a lesser period of disqualification than the mandatory five years under s 206B. The discretion of the Court is still directed to the nature of the relevant person's conduct in relation to the management, business or property of any corporation. It is also directed, more broadly, to any other matters that the Court considers appropriate, once the Court is satisfied that the disqualification is justified.

62. In any event, we are here dealing with a repeated series of contraventions though that needs to be put in proper perspective. While in arithmetic terms, the declarations made on 27 March 2002 produced 101 contraventions by Mr Adler and a further 84 by Adler Corporation, that simply represents the result of multiplying the nine episodes or transactions giving rise to a contravention by the number of corporate entities involved and the number of

sections of the *Corporations Law* contravened by that same conduct. I would agree that the most that could be said is that a multiplicity of contraventions by reference to breaches of not just one but several provisions of the *Corporations Law* (or *Corporations Act*) may give a broad indication of the seriousness of the contravention, but much more to the point is to look at the contraventions themselves. Thus two factors should be considered. First, the number of episodes or transactions. These are themselves numerous, nine in all for Mr Adler and the same number for Adler Corporation.

63. To this, the First and Fourth Defendants contend that the correct characterisation, having regard to findings in the judgment, are that all of these pieces of conduct in substance constituted a single transaction, reference being made to para [141] of the judgment, especially subparas (c) and (f) thereof, and paras [191] and [193]. It is therefore submitted that a single penalty only should be imposed.

64. I should say at the outset that the judgments provide no basis for such contention as I explain below. We are moreover here dealing with disqualification with its paramount protective purpose. Highly relevant is thus the number of companies suffering dereliction of duty by Mr Adler (HIH, HIHC and PEE) *and* the fact that there were nine instances of misconduct by Mr Adler. That the conduct in question was repeated and followed a pattern, simply makes it more serious in terms of dereliction, with consequently greater risk to the public if Mr Adler were allowed to continue to manage companies.

65. The specific references in the earlier judgment of 14 March 2002 provide on analysis no basis for treating the nine transactions or episodes as in substance a single transaction. It is one thing to treat the purchase of shares in HIH over some two weeks as a single transaction (para [141(f)], quite another to treat each of the other transactions as in substance one transaction when they are distinct though not unrelated. Thus, clearly, the provision of $10 million payment to AEUT is a discrete transaction from its subsequent application in purchasing shares in HIH. These likewise represent distinct contraventions, namely of **[1163]** s 208 and s 260A of the *Corporations Act* by HIH and HIHC, with Mr Adler and Adler Corporation being "involved" so as to contravene the s 209(2) and s 260D respectively.

66. Then there are three separate investments by AEUT in purchasing from Adler interests the three entities, dstore Limited, Planet Soccer International Limited and Nomad Telecommunications Limited. Then there are the further four loan transactions occurring when Mr Adler caused AEUT to make four separate unsecured loans to associated entities. There is nothing in the Judgment which justifies treating these transactions as one single transaction, though of similar motivation.

67. By way of analogy, whilst in *ACCC v George Weston Foods Ltd* (2000) ATPR ¶41-763 the ACCC was unsuccessful in arguing that conduct in which the respondent had attempted to involve two retailers in price- fixing amounted to separate contraventions, in *Trade Practices Commission v Simpson Pope Ltd* (1980) ATPR ¶40-169; (1980) 30 ALR 544 Franki J said, appositely to the present context: "[D]ifferent acts of a supplier, each of which is a contravention of s 48 because it falls within or more of the categories of acts set out in s 96(3), which take place at different times and in relation to three different customers, are not to be regarded as 'the same conduct' within s 76(3). The words 'the same conduct' in s 76(3) must be more limited in

scope than the words 'any similar conduct' which appear at the end of s 76(1)." [these references are of course to the *Trade Practices Act* 1974 Cth.]

68. In considering the effect of the multiple contraventions, for purposes of determining whether or not to make a disqualification order, the relevant transactions are to be judged individually as well for their cumulative effect. Thus in applying s 206E of the *Corporations Act*, not only has there been at least two contraventions of the Act by HIH and at least two contraventions of the Act by HIHC, but the relevant person, here Mr Adler, did not merely fail to take reasonable steps to prevent the contravention but was himself directly involved in it so as himself to contravene the Act. That clearly reinforces the basis for applying s 206E with a substantial disqualification order.

69. Indeed the gravity of the contraventions as well as their repetition in distinct transactions, numbering nine in all, make a powerful case for the lengthiest disqualification period.

70. The principles of parity which guide the exercise of judicial discretion do not produce any neat arithmetic algorithm from other cases though the earlier propositions ([56] above) give some guidance. I would adopt what is said by Hill J in *ACCC v Universal Music Australia Pty Limited (No 2)* (2002) ATPR ¶41-862; [2002] FCA 192 at [34] where, in the analogous context of the *Trade Practices Act* he says: "Hence, while pecuniary penalties imposed in one case provide a guide, that guide will seldom if ever be able to be used mechanically."

71. Austin J, while making similar observation, in *ASIC v Parkes* (2001) 38 ACSR 355 at 386 refers to a number of factors which are directly applicable to the present case and its circumstances: "In reaching this conclusion [disqualification for 25 years], I take into account the following factors:
- the contraventions that I have found include some very serious contraventions;
- those contraventions have led to loss and damage on the part of companies and investors, contrary to the protective purpose of the relevant provisions of the *Corporations Law*;
- the defendant's field of activity, management and financial consultancy, is an area where the potential to do damage is especially high, compared, say, with a defendant whose expertise is in making cement;
- the defendant's contraventions have been recurrent, arising in the context of three different sets of companies;
- until the end, the defendant asserted explanations for what he had done which I found to be implausible, and this suggests to me that he has no contrition;
- all of these facts lead me to believe that there is a high propensity that the defendant will engage in similar conduct if only a short period of prohibition is imposed;
- **[1164]** I am conscious of the fact that a prohibition for 25 years will effectively prevent the defendant from managing a corporation for the rest of his life, it will not prevent him from earning income as an employee, using his undoubted financial skills under proper supervision.

72. In the present case each of those factors are present, though it should be noted that Mr Adler himself did not assert any personal explanation for what he had done. Rather, through his legal advisers, he denied that there was any contravention in the circumstances, a denial which is at odds with the findings of the Judgment and thus cannot stand.

DIRECTORS' DUTIES   227

73. A review of the cases demonstrates that a wide range of banning periods have been imposed by the courts. For the most serious, there is prohibition for life, though in one case with a right to apply for variation after five years; *ASIC v Hutchings* [(2001) 38 ACSR 387].
See further Chapter 9.

Compensation

[10.230] In addition, the company may initiate an action, or intervene in civil penalty proceedings, seeking compensation for the damage suffered by the company, including any profits made by the director, as a consequence of the contravention: ss 1317H and 1317J. Any order to pay compensation is enforceable as if it were a judgment of the court: s 1317H(5).

[10.240] Under s 1317S a court can excuse a director partially or wholly from liability for a breach of a civil penalty provision. Relief may only be provided where the person has acted honestly and, having regard to all the circumstances, the person ought fairly be excused: s 1317S(3). See further s 1317S.

Criminal offence

[10.250] As noted earlier, under s 184, the breach will only constitute an offence where the director contravened the provision recklessly or with intentional dishonesty. The court has no power under the *Corporations Act* to relieve a director from criminal liability.

[10.260] In *R v Adler* (2004) 22 ACLC 784, Adler made an unsuccessful application to stay criminal proceedings against him on the basis that the proceedings exposed him to double jeopardy. Adler argued that the criminal proceedings were an abuse of process as he had already been punished for the same conduct pursuant to earlier civil proceedings brought by ASIC. In these earlier proceedings Santow J found that Adler had breached ss 209(2) (financial benefit to a related party), 260D(2) (financial assistance to acquire shares), 180(1), 181(1), 182(1) and 183(1) (director's duties). On the basis of the same conduct Adler was indicted on five counts. Briefly, the charges related to stock market manipulation and knowingly disseminating false information to induce people to purchase HIH shares. The facts are more comprehensively set out in Chapter 7 and later in this chapter.

James J rejected Adler's application for a number of reasons. The court found the criminal and civil proceedings were different in a number of ways. The court accepted the submission that the elements of the criminal proceedings were different from the requisite elements for the causes of actions considered in the earlier civil proceedings. The purposes underlying the civil and criminal proceedings also differed. The former was concerned with enforcing the director's obligations to provide a remedy for wrongs done to the company or its shareholders while the purpose of the criminal proceedings pertaining to the manipulation of the stock market was to protect the integrity of the market and to punish for the wrongs done to potential share purchasers. A consideration of ss 1317M and 1317P reinforced James J's conclusion that the criminal proceedings should not be stayed as an abuse of process. While s 1317M states that a pecuniary penalty should not be ordered for breach of a civil penalty provision if the person had already been convicted of an offence for essentially the same conduct, s 1317P states that criminal proceedings may be instigated in regard to essentially the same conduct with respect to which a pecuniary penalty ordered had already been made. James J reiterated, however, that for the reasons detailed above, the proceedings would not be stayed, independently of s 1317P. In *Adler v DPP* [2004] NSWCCA 352 the court agreed with James J that there was no abuse of process in bringing the subject criminal proceedings against Adler as the criminal offences were different in important respects from the civil proceedings.

Duty Not to Fetter Discretion

[10.270] As directors are bound to act for the company, their decision-making authority cannot be limited to accommodate another's interests. Hence directors cannot agree to exercise their discretion in a particular manner: *Thornby v Goldberg* (1965) 112 CLR 597; *Davidson v Smith* (1989) 15 ACLR 732; *Fulham Football Club v Cabra Estates plc* [1992] BCC 863. Any contract or resolution purporting to so fetter a director's discretion will be ineffective.

Proper Purpose Doctrine

Fiduciary duty

[10.280] In accordance with the duty to act in the company's best interests, directors must exercise their powers for their proper corporate purposes. Thus, directors' powers must be exercised for the purpose for which they were conferred and in a manner which promotes the interests of the shareholders as a whole: *Australian Metropolitan Life Assurance Co Ltd v Ure* (1923) 33 CLR 199 at 217; *Mills v Mills* (1938) 60 CLR 150 at 169.

Directors' honesty

[10.290] Traditionally, this duty may be breached even though the director is acting honestly. Thus, while directors may think that they are acting in the company's best interests by, for example, exercising powers so as to 'protect' the company from a hostile takeover, if they use their powers for improper purposes in achieving that goal, they will be in breach of their fiduciary duties: *Hogg v Cramphorn Ltd* [1967] Ch 254; *Emlen Pty Ltd v St Barbara Mines Ltd* (1997) 24 ACSR 303 at 306. Correspondingly, the mere fact that the power is not being exercised for reasons of self-interest will not place the act outside the scope of the doctrine: *Howard Smith Ltd v Ampol Petroleum Ltd* [1974] AC 821.

[10.300] It has been suggested, however, that directors may weigh up whether a current takeover offer is in the company's best interests or whether a higher offer may be made in the future. Thus, even in the face of a hostile takeover, if the directors make an honest, commercial decision that the takeover is not in the company's best interests, under this approach, they will not be in breach of their duties: *Darvall v North Brick & Tile Co Ltd* (1989) 6 ACLC 154; (1989) 7 ACLC 659. This approach is clearly contrary to the general principle that this duty may be breached even though the director is acting honestly and thus is contrary to the weight of authority.

Importance of improper purpose

[10.310] In *Howard Smith Ltd v Ampol Petroleum Ltd* [1974] AC 821 at 831 Lord Wilberforce declared that it is the 'substantial purpose for which [the power] is exercised' that must be analysed to determine whether the power was improperly used. Cases such as *Pine Vale Investments Ltd v McDonnell and East Ltd* (1983) 1 ACLC 1294 at 1304 and *Woonda Nominees Pty Ltd v Chng* (2000) 18 ACLC 627 at 631 affirm that a secondary improper purpose or incidental effect will not suffice to render the act a breach. Thus, where an act is prompted by several purposes, one of which is improper, whether there is a breach will depend on which of those factors was the 'trigger' for the director's actions and whether that purpose is a proper or improper purpose: *Mills v Mills* (1938) 60 CLR 150 at 185-186; *Whitehouse v Carlton Hotel Pty Ltd* (1987) 162 CLR 285 at 293 and 294; *Darvall v North Sydney Brick and Tile Co* (1988) 6 ACLC 154; *Emlen Pty Ltd v St Barbara Mines Ltd* (1997) 24 ACSR 303 at 306 and 307.

Share issues

[10.320] The most common context for the discussion of the proper purpose doctrine is the issuing of shares. The power to issue shares may be properly used to, *inter alia*, raise capital: *Howard Smith Ltd v Ampol Petroleum Ltd* [1974] AC 821. Other legitimate uses of this power include, in appropriate circumstances, the issuing of shares to employees as incentives and fostering business relations. Improper uses of the power include defeating a takeover, facilitating a takeover by weakening majority shareholders' voting power, entrenching control of the company in oneself, family members or associates (*Ngurli Ltd v McCann* (1953) 90 CLR 425) or benefiting one group of shareholders at the expense of others: *Howard Smith Ltd v Ampol Petroleum Ltd* [1974] AC 821.

Howard Smith Ltd v Ampol Petroleum Ltd
Privy Council: Lords Wilberforce, Diplock, Simon of Glaisdale,
Cross of Chelsea and Kilbrandon
[1974] AC 821

RW Millers (Holdings) Ltd ('Millers') was subject to a takeover offer by Ampol Petroleum Ltd ('Ampol'). Howard Smith Ltd ('Howard Smith') made a rival offer. Ampol and its associated company, Bulkships Ltd ('Bulkships'), who in combination already held 55% of shares in Millers, rejected the offer and in a press statement declared that they intended to 'act jointly in relation to the future operation' of Millers. The majority of Millers' board were in favour of the Howard Smith takeover bid. To facilitate the bid they agreed to issue enough shares to Howard Smith to reduce Ampol and Bulkships to minority shareholders. Millers did at the time need to raise some capital.

Ampol sought to have the share issue set aside. Street J at first instance found that the directors had used their powers for an improper purpose. Howard Smith appealed to the Privy Council. Two polaristic views as to the proper purpose doctrine were put to the Board. The directors argued that once it was determined that they had not acted for reasons of self-interest there could be no breach of the duty. At the other extreme Ampol asserted that raising capital was the only proper purpose for issuing shares.

The Privy Council rejected both extreme views, asserting there could be an honest breach of the duty where the directors were not acting for self-interest, but also noting that raising capital was not the only proper use of the power. The Privy Council agreed with Street J that the directors had improperly used the power to issue shares to dilute the majority voting power held by Ampol and Bulkships. This was to enable Howard Smith, a then minority shareholder, to sell their shares more advantageously. As an issue of shares purely for the purpose of creating voting power had repeatedly been condemned, the court found that the duty had been breached. The Privy Council ordered the share issue be set aside and the share register rectified.

Lord Wilberforce: [834] In their Lordships' opinion neither of the extreme positions can be maintained. ...

Self interest is only one, though no doubt the commonest, instance of improper motive; and, before one can say that a fiduciary power has been exercised for the purpose for which it was conferred, a wider investigation may have to be made. This is recognised in several well-known statements [835] of the law. Their Lordships quote the clearest which has so often been cited:

"Where the question is one of abuse of powers, the state of mind of those who acted, and the motive on which they acted, are all important, and you may go into the question of what their intention was, collecting from the surrounding circumstances all the material which genuinely throw light upon that question of the state of mind of the directors so as to show whether they were honestly acting in discharge of their powers in the interests of the company or were acting from some bye-motive, possibly of personal advantage, or for any other reason: *Hindle v John Cotton Ltd* (1919) 56 Sc LR 625 at 630, 631 per Viscount Finlay.

On the other had, taking Ampol's contention, it is, in their Lordship's opinion, too narrow an approach to say that the only valid purpose for which shares may be issued is to raise capital for the company. The discretion is not in terms limited in this way: the law should not impose such a limitation on directors' powers. To define in exact limits beyond which directors must not pass is, in their Lordships' view, impossible. This clearly cannot be done by enumeration, since the variety of situations facing directors of different types of companies in different situations cannot be anticipated. No more, in their Lordships' view, can this be done by the use of a phrase – such as "bona fide in the interests of the company as a whole" or "for some corporate purpose." Such phrases, if they do anything more than restate the general principle applicable to fiduciary powers, at best serve, negatively, to exclude from the area of validity cases where the directors are acting sectionally, or partially, ie improperly favouring one section of the shareholders against another. Of such cases it has been said:

"The question which arises is sometimes not a question of the interests of the company at all, but a question of what is fair as between different classes of shareholders. Where such a case arises some other test that that of the 'interests of the company' must be applied …": *Mills v Mills* (1938) 60 CLR at 168 per Latham CJ.

In their Lordships' opinion it is necessary to start with a consideration of the power whose exercise is in question, in this case a power to issue shares. Having ascertained, on a fair view, the nature of this power, and having defined as can best be done in the light of modern conditions the, or some, limits within which it may be exercised, it is then necessary for the court, if a particular exercise of it is challenged, to examine the substantial purpose for which it was exercised, and to reach a conclusion whether that purpose was proper or not. In doing so it will necessarily give credit to the bona fide opinion of the directors, if such is found to exist, and will respect their judgment as to matters of management; having done this, the ultimate conclusion has to be as to the side of a fairly broad line on which the case falls.

"The application of the general equitable principle to the acts of directors managing the affairs of a company cannot be as nice as it is **[836]** in the case of a trustee exercising a special power of appointment": *Mills v Mills* (1938) 60 CLR at 185-186 per Dixon J.

The main stream of authority in the Lordships' opinion, supports this approach. In *Punt v Symons & Co*, Byrne J expressly accepted that there may be reasons other than to raise capital for which shares may be issued. In the High Court case of *Harlowe's Nominees Pty Ltd v Woodside (Lakes Entrance) Oil Co NL* (1968) 121 CLR 483, an issue of shares was made to a large oil company in order, as was found, to secure the financial stability of the company. This was upheld as being within power although it had the effect of defeating the attempt of the plaintiff to secure control by buying up the company's shares. …

[837] [T]he present case, on the evidence, does not, on the findings of the trial judge, involve any considerations of management, within the proper sphere of the directors. The purpose found by the judge is simply and solely to dilute the majority voting power held by Ampol and Bulkships so as to enable a then minority of shareholders to sell their shares more advantageously. So far as authority goes, an issue of shares purely for the purpose of creating power has repeatedly been condemned. … In the leading Australian case of *Mills v Mills*, it was accepted in the High Court that if the purpose of issuing shares was solely to alter the voting power the issue would be invalid. The constitution of a limited company normally provides for directors, with powers of management, and shareholders, with defined voting powers having power to appoint the directors, and to take, in general meeting, by majority vote, decisions on matters not reserved for management. Just as it is established that directors, within their management powers, may take decisions against the wishes of the majority shareholders, and indeed that the majority of shareholders cannot control them in the exercise of these powers while they remain in office (*Automatic Self-Cleansing Filter Syndicate Co Ltd v Cuninghame* [1906] 2 Ch 34), so it must be unconstitutional for directors to use their fiduciary powers over the shares in the company purely for the purpose of destroying an existing majority, or creating a new majority which did not previously exist. To do so is to interfere with that element of the company's constitution which is separate from and set against their powers. If there is added, moreover, to this immediate purpose, an ulterior purpose to enable an offer for shares to proceed which the existing majority was in a position to block, the departure from the legitimate use of the fiduciary power becomes not less, but all the greater.

Registration of share transfers

[10.330] The use of powers for improper purposes has also arisen in the context of the directors' discretion to register share transfers. Previously, proprietary companies were required to restrict the transfer of their shares: see former s 116. Giving the directors a discretion whether to register share transfers commonly facilitated this. Even with the repeal of s 116, companies may chose to continue to restrict the transfer of shares in this way. To this end, *inter alia*, replaceable rule, s 1072F(3), allows directors of both public and proprietary companies to refuse to register shares that are not fully paid-up shares or shares subject to a lien. Directors of proprietary companies may be afforded an additional discretion under replaceable rule, s 1072G, to refuse the registration for 'any reason'.

Directors may abuse this power by refusing to register a transfer of shares to unfriendly interests thereby entrenching their own position in the company. The proper and improper use of this power was discussed in *Australian Metropolitan Life Assurance Co Ltd v Ure* (1923) 33 CLR 199, the court reiterating that the onus of proof lies with the person asserting a breach of directors' duties.

Australian Metropolitan Life Assurance Co Ltd v Ure
High Court of Australia: Knox CJ, Isaac and Starke JJ
(1923) 33 CLR 199

Pursuant to the company's constitution, the directors refused to register a transfer of shares without providing any reasons for their actions. Were the transfers registered, one faction of the company, opposed by all but one director, would have gained voting control. This voting power would in turn ensure the election of the respondent's husband as director. The respondent's husband was once a solicitor of the Supreme Court of Queensland who had been struck off the roll.

The Supreme Court of Queensland had found against the directors and ordered the share transfers be registered. The company appealed to the High Court. The High Court allowed the appeal, finding that it had not been proven that the directors had been motivated by extraneous or unworthy considerations. The directors' silence was held not to be sufficient to base an inference of impropriety.

Isaacs J: **[216]** The right to challenge the decision of directors in such cases as this is a very important matter. A share in a limited company is personal property, and the right to deal with it, to sell and to buy it is absolute, except so far as that right is lawfully restricted by the regulations of the Company. Sec 21 of the Queensland Act is typical of the statutory enactments as to this. Judicial authority is clear – as *Poole v Middleton* [(1861) 29 Beav 646]; *In re Liverpool Marine Assurance Co; Greenshield's Case* [(1852) 5 De G & Sm 599], and *In re Copal Varnish Co* [[1917] 2 Ch 349 at 353].

[217] A regulation such as art 21 entrusts to the directors a corporate power, which is exercisable by them as agents of the Company. But, although it is a power which necessarily involves some discretion, it must be exercised, as all such powers must be, bona fide – that is, for the purpose for which it was conferred, not arbitrarily or at the absolute will of the directors, but honestly in the interest of the shareholders as a whole. ... The general character of such a regulation is clear, but the ambit of the purpose of the power of course varies with the circumstances of each particular case. The nature of the company, its constitution and the scheme of its regulations as a whole must all be taken into account in determining whether a given factor comes within its range. Solvency of a transferee is, of course, important; for otherwise the mutual undertaking to contribute would be ineffectual, and creditors would be unjustly dealt with. But his solvency is not necessarily the only consideration. The reputation of the company may be an essential element of success, and where, as in the present case, the corporation is one appealing to the public for its confidence and transfers are presented which are of such magnitude as to control the whole administration of the company, the maintenance of a board of directors against whom not even a suggestion of reproach can be made is manifestly a high business consideration, which no person charged with the beneficial administration of the corporate affairs would be likely to overlook, in the interests of the shareholders as a whole. It is necessary to notice here an argument very strenuously pressed by Mr **[218]** *Macrossan*. He urged that directors had no right to refuse a transfer to prevent a majority from carrying its way. That is true, but not completely true. The accuracy of the statement has its limits. A majority has not the right to destroy or injure the common property or otherwise deprive the minority of their rights (see *Dominion Cotton Mills Co v Amyot* [[1912] AC 546]). If directors, possessing by the regulations the power of protecting and guiding the company's affairs that the regulations of this Company provide, honestly come to the conclusion that general destruction or injury will ensue by reason of a proposed transfer of shares, it cannot be said that, because the transfer if effected by registration would enable a majority to effect its will, they are bound to register. ... It follows that if the directors honestly acted upon the business consideration mentioned, it was within their power, even though a transient majority thought differently or desired differently. It is possible, of course, that the directors were not really moved by that legitimate consideration, but acted upon some extraneous reason, perhaps some unworthy reason. If they did, then their power is gone, and **[219]** the Court would, as in *Bell Bros' case* [(1891) 65 LT 245], hold that the right had become absolute and would direct registration. That depends on the facts, and the first thing to ascertain is the proper approach to them.

It is well established that the onus of showing that a power has not been properly exercised is on the party complaining ...

[220] It is provided by art 21 that the directors need not assign any reason for their refusal to register. They have preserved silence in this case. The authorities just cited establish that their silence is not a sufficient circumstance in itself on which to base an inference of impropriety. Indeed, it is part of the basic contract that no reason need be assigned. (See per Lord Wrenbury in *Weinberger v Inglis* [[1919] AC 606 at 641].) But an applicant is not helpless; nor is the Court deprived of its power to do justice in a proper case. The Court will judge of circumstances, and form its conclusions on reasonable probabilities. It is for the applicant to place, if he can, such circumstances before the Court as will reasonably lead to the conclusion that in some way an improper use has been made of the power, so that the discretion committed to the directors has not been exercised. ...

[221] While silence *per se* is no starting-point from which to infer impropriety, silence preserved when once a prima facie case of impropriety is presented may be entirely different. There is no initial duty to speak created by the mere refusal to register, but such a duty may arise from proof of circumstances pointing in themselves, if unexplained, either affirmatively to the existence of an unjustifiable reason or negatively to the absence of any legitimate reason. Applying those rules of guidance to the circumstances of this case, I am clear that the applicant has not discharged the required onus. On the contrary, I am morally clear, notwithstanding the official silence of the directorate as to their reasons, that the basic ground of objection was the genuine apprehension of, humanly speaking, the certain results that would follow upon registration, namely, first the election of Mrs Ure's husband to the directorate through the commanding voting power that she, moved by her husband, would exert through her agents, and then the disruption of the directorate, a want of harmonious co-operation, and possibly a general prejudicial effect on the Company as a whole. That being so, the matter was one which by the terms of the social compact rested within the uncontrolled discretion of the directors. Acting entirely within the scope of their power, honestly basing their action on their own business opinion, they were exercising a function with [222] which no Court can interfere, and over which no Court has any jurisdiction of review or appeal.

The applicants failed to sustain the onus resting upon them, and this appeal should be allowed.

Consequences of breach

Generally

[10.340] A transaction stemming from an improper use of power is voidable at the company's option: *Bamford v Bamford* [1970] Ch 212; *Winthrop Investments Ltd v Winns Ltd* [1975] 2 NSWLR 666 at 679-680 and 689; *Whitehouse v Carlton Hotel Pty Ltd* (1987) 162 CLR 285 at 294; *Glover v Willert* (1996) 20 ACSR 182 at 186 and 188. The company may not, however, avoid a transaction where it would prejudice the rights of an innocent third party that had no notice of the breach: *Whitehouse v Carlton Hotel Pty Ltd*. If the breach causes loss to the company, the guilty directors are jointly and severally liable to compensate the company: *Advance Bank of Australia v FAI Insurances* (1987) 9 NSWLR 464. Again, shareholders may apply for injunctive relief to stop an actual or threatened breach.

[10.350] The company in general meeting may elect to ratify the breach. For a ratification to be effective, full and proper disclosure of the underlying facts must be made to the general meeting, thereby enabling shareholders to make an informed decision whether to ratify: *Bamford v Bamford* [1970] Ch 212; *Winthrop Investments Ltd v Winns Ltd* [1975] 2 NSWLR 666; *Pascoe Ltd (in liq) v Lucas* (1998) 16 ACLC 1247; *Forge v ASIC* [2004] NSWCA 448. This requires the directors to inform the general meeting that there was a breach and the nature of such: *Winthrop Investments Ltd v Winns Ltd*.

Share issue

[10.360] If the breach involves an improper share issue that has not been ratified, an action may be brought by the company or an aggrieved person to have the share issue disallowed and the share register rectified under s 175(1). This may not occur, however, when the allottee has taken the shares for value and without notice of the breach: *Street Nominees v White Industries Ltd* (1980) 5 ACLR 40.

Registration of share transfer

[10.370] Where the breach involves an improper refusal to register a share transfer, the transferee is entitled to be registered: *Australian Metropolitan Life Assurance Co Ltd v Ure* (1923) 33 CLR 199 at 218. The common law remedies are now supplemented by s 1071F. Where a court finds that the refusal/failure to register shares is 'without just cause' the court may order the registration or make such other orders it thinks just and reasonable: s 1071F(2).

Statutory duty

[10.380] Section 181(1)(b) provides that a director must exercise his or her powers 'for a proper purpose'. Also, s 184(1)(d) specifies that a breach of this duty will have criminal consequences if the director contravened the provision recklessly or with a dishonest intent. Section 181(1)(b) is a civil penalty provision. Thus, a breach of this duty will have the same consequences as those detailed above in relation to ss 181(1)(a) and 184(1)(c).

Duty to Avoid a Conflict of Interests

Fiduciary duty

[10.390] Under both the common law and the *Corporations Act*, directors are bound to avoid any conflict between their personal interests and those of the company. This duty extends to avoiding being placed in a position where such a conflict is even possible: *North-West Transportation Co Ltd v Beatty* (1887) 12 App Cas 589; *Boardman v Phipps* [1966] 3 All ER 721; *Regal (Hastings) Ltd v Gulliver* [1967] 2 AC 14; *Green & Clara Pty Ltd v Bestobell Industries Pty Ltd* [1982] WAR 1; *Chan v Zacharia* (1984) 154 CLR 178 at 199; *Hospital Products Ltd v United States Surgical Corp* (1984) 156 CLR 41 at 103. This duty prevents directors:

- contracting with the company without making full and proper disclosure of their interest in the contract; and
- making 'secret profits' through the director's position in the company.

Contracting with the company at common law

[10.400] The conferral of management power on the directors brings with it the potential for abuse. Directors could use their management powers to have the company contract in terms that would directly or indirectly extend a profit to themselves. The courts have consequently declared that 'a director of a company is precluded from dealing, on behalf of the company, with himself, and from entering into engagements in which he has a personal interest conflicting, or which possibly may conflict, with the interests of those whom he is bound by fiduciary duty to protect': *North-West Transportation Co Ltd v Beatty* (1887) 12 App Cas 589.

[10.410] The director's interest in the contract need only be small for the contract to fall within the rigours of this rule. The director may merely be one of many shareholders with an interest in the contracting company: *Transvaal Lands Co v New Belgium (Transvaal) Land and Development Co* [1914] 2 Ch 488.

[10.420] At common law, directors directly or indirectly interested in a contract with the company must disclose to the general meeting the nature of their interest and the extent to which they stand to profit: *Gray v New Augarita Porcupine Mines Ltd* [1952] 3 DLR 1. Disclosure to the board alone is ineffective. Even if the interested director does not vote on the matter, a resolution by independent members of the board will not validate the transaction. The contract can only be validated by the general meeting after the director has made full and proper disclosure of his or her interest in the contract.

The extent to which the general meeting may ratify a contract and the director's ability to participate in that voting was discussed in *North-West Transport Co Ltd v Beatty* (1877) 12 App Cas 589 at 593-594:

> Unless some provision to the contrary is to be found in the charter or other instrument by which the company is incorporated, the resolution of a majority of the shareholders, duly convened, upon any question with which the company is legally competent to deal, is binding upon the minority, and consequently upon the company, and every shareholder has a perfect right to vote upon any such question, although he may have a personal interest in the subject matter opposed to, or different from, the general or particular interests of the company. ... [A] director is precluded from dealing, on behalf of the

company with himself, and from entering into engagements in which he has a personal interest conflicting, or which possibly may conflict, with the interests of those whom he is bound by fiduciary duty to protect; and this rule is as applicable to the case of one of several directors as to a managing director or sole director. Any such dealing or engagement may, however, be affirmed or adopted by the company, provided such affirmance or adoption is not brought about by unfair or improper means, and is not illegal or fraudulent or oppressive towards those shareholders who oppose it.

[10.430] If the contract is not ratified, it is voidable at the company's option: *AM Spicer & Son Pty Ltd (in liq) v Spicer* (1931) 47 CLR 151 at 175. Any moneys or property received by the directors under such a voidable transaction are held on constructive trust for the company: *Paul A Davies (Aust) Pty Ltd v Davies* (1983) 8 ACLR 1. The company may not, however, affirm the contract for less than the initial contract price and seek an account for any profit made by the director: *Burland v Earle* [1902] AC 83 at 99. The company must choose between affirming the contract or avoiding it and seeking an account for profits: *Cook v Deeks* [1916] 1 AC 554 at 564. Where the breach causes a loss to the company, the company may seek compensation from the director: *Tavistock Holdings Pty Ltd v Saulsman* (1990) 3 ACSR 502 at 510.

Contracting with the company under the constitution

[10.440] At general law it is possible to modify the common law requirements through the company's constitution. A constitution will typically modify the common law duty by expressly providing that directors may contract with the company despite any consequent conflict of interests. In addition, contrary to the common law, the constitution usually prescribes that the conflict of interest must be disclosed to the board, rather than the general meeting. Thus, under replaceable rule, s 194, directors of proprietary companies may, *inter alia*, contract with the company where they have disclosed the nature and extent of their interest in the matter to the board in accordance with s 191, discussed below. The director may also retain the benefits of that contract as long as the disclosure is made before the contract was entered into: s 194. This provision confirms that the contract may not be avoided by the company merely because of the conflict of interest, but again this only applies where the disclosure is made before the transaction is entered into: s 194.

[10.450] The consequences of failing to meet these disclosure requirements are also normally specified in the constitution. Obviously the benefits of the contract cannot be retained without proper disclosure. See in this regard replaceable rule s 194. Regulation 65(e) of Table A also specified that the position of a director who failed to comply with the predecessor to ss 191-194, s 231, was automatically vacated.

Contracting with the company under the Corporations Act

[10.460] The widespread use of the corporate constitution to modify the common law rules, detailed above, led to the introduction of a statutory disclosure rule now found in s 191 that is applicable to both public and proprietary companies. Under s 191, a director who has a 'material personal interest in a matter that relates to the company's affairs' must give the other directors notice of his or her interest unless one of the exemptions in s 191(2) applies. The notion 'company's affairs' is broadly defined in s 53.

[10.470] Exemptions from disclosure are stated in s 191(2). These disclosure requirements do not extend to directors whose interest, *inter alia*, arises because the director is a member of the company and that interest is held in common with the other members: s 191(2)(a)(i). Disclosure is also not required where the director's material interest relates to the director's remuneration (s 191(2)(a)(ii)) or the director has merely guaranteed the repayment of part or all of a loan to the company: s 191(2)(a)(iii). Where the board of a proprietary company is already aware of the director's interest, disclosure is again not required: s 191(2)(b). See further s 191(2).

[10.480] Section 191(3) requires the nature of the director's conflicting interest to be disclosed as soon as practicable after the director becomes aware of his or her interest in the matter. The details must be recorded in the minutes of the meeting: s 191(3).

[10.490] The notice required under s 191(1) may be satisfied by the provision of a standing notice to the other directors specifying the nature and extent of the director's interest: s 192. Thus, the director may, for example, notify the board that he or she is an officer or member of a company or firm and is to be regarded as interested in any contract made with that company or firm. As long as the notice is given in accordance with the procedure specified in s 192 and that interest has not increased since the notice, there will be no need for further disclosure: ss 191(2)(d) and 192(6).

[10.500] A breach of s 191 does not affect the validity of any act, transaction, agreement, instrument, resolution 'or other thing': ss 191(4) and 192(7). Equally, a breach of s 191 will not give the company a statutory right to recover damages in addition to any rights at common law: *Castlereagh Motels Ltd v Davies-Roe* (1966) 67 SR (NSW) 279 at 284 and 286-287. The key relevance of this section lies in replaceable rule, s 194 (discussed above) for proprietary companies and s 195 (discussed below) for public companies.

[10.510] Section 193 states that these requirements are in addition to any general law duty regarding conflict of interests. They are also in addition to any provision in the company's constitution that restricts a director's ability to have a material interest in a matter or from holding an office or possessing property: s 193.

[10.520] Where directors of public companies have an interest in a transaction, in addition to the requirements specified in s 191 and any restrictions contained in the corporate constitution (see s 193(b)), regard must also be had to s 195 and Chap 2E. Under s 195(1), directors of public companies that have a 'material personal interest' (within s 191) in a matter being considered by the board must not vote on such or be present while the matter is being discussed.

[10.530] The effect of s 195 may be that a board meeting is inquorate. This difficulty may be addressed in a number of ways. First, s 195(4) provides that where, as a result of s 195(1), an absence of a quorum prevents the board dealing with an issue, one or more of the directors (including those with a material interest) may call a general meeting which may in turn determine the matter. However, having the matter referred to the general meeting might not provide a solution where, for example, the matter needs to be considered urgently. A second option is for the board to resolve that the director's interest should not disqualify the director from considering or voting on the matter: s 195(2). See further s 195(2). Third, under s 196 ASIC has a discretion to declare that a director with a material interest within s 195(1) may nevertheless be present and/or vote on a matter. ASIC may only make such a declaration if because of s 195(1) a quorum would not exist and the urgency of the matter, or some other compelling reason, dictates that it should be dealt with by the board, rather than the general meeting, despite the board's conflict of interest. Finally, replaceable rule, s 201H, allows the directors to appoint a person as a director in order to make up a quorum for a directors' meeting.

[10.540] A breach of s 195(1) will not invalidate any resolution: s 195(5). Thus, the consequences will depend on whether the common law has been modified and the terms of the company's constitution.

[10.550] The basic prohibition around which Chap 2E revolves is contained in s 208. This prevents a public company, or an entity that it controls, giving a financial benefit to a related party of the public company unless the conferral has the general meeting's approval or the benefit is exempt. Sections 9 and 50AA respectively define the notions of 'entity' and 'control'.

[10.560] Section 228(1)-(4) defines 'related parties'. This section identifies related parties as including entities that the public company controls, directors of the public company or entities its controls and parents, spouses and children of such directors. The reach of this section is extended by s 228(5) and (6) to those persons who have been a related party within the preceding six months or have reasonable grounds to believe that they will become a related party in the future. Section 228(7) provides a further extension by including unrelated parties who have acted in concert with a related party on the understanding that, if the public company gives the unrelated entity a financial benefit, the related party will also receive a financial benefit.

[10.570] Section 229 provides a non-exhaustive list of guidelines to assist in determining what is to be considered a 'financial benefit'. The financial benefit may be made indirectly to the party and may be non-monetary in nature: s 229(2). A wide interpretation of this notion is further ensured by an express statement that the definition is to be interpreted broadly despite any possible criminal or civil consequences and that transactions are to be adjudged by their commercial substance, rather than legal form: s 229(1).

[10.580] Chapter 2E expressly exempts from s 208 financial benefits that are:
- given on arm's length terms or terms that are less favourable than arm's length terms: s 210;
- reasonable remuneration, which includes superannuation contributions and termination payments, for company officers: s 211;
- certain indemnities, insurance premiums or payments of legal costs in respect of a liability incurred as a company officer: s 212;
- advances up to $2000 to directors or their spouses: s 213;
- given to, or by, a 'closely held subsidiary': s 214;
- given to members in that capacity as long as they do not discriminate unfairly against the other members: s 215; or
- given to another entity pursuant to an order of the court: s 216.

See each of these sections for a more detailed discussion of the prerequisites to their operation. Unless these exemptions apply, the financial benefit must be approved by a fully informed general meeting within Div 3 and the benefit must be provided within 15 months after the approval: s 208(1)(a) and (2)(a).

The application of Chap 2E was recently considered in *ASIC v Adler* (2002) 20 ACLC 576.

ASIC v Adler
Supreme Court of New South Wales: Santow J
(2002) 20 ACLC 576

Adler was a non-executive director of HIH Insurance Ltd ('HIH'). Williams was a director and the CEO of HIH. Fodera was a director and the finance controller of HIH. HIH Casualty and General Insurance Ltd ('HIHC') was a wholly owned subsidiary of HIH. Adler requested, and Williams and Fodera arranged, for HIHC to advance $10 million to Pacific Eagle Equity Pty Ltd ('PEE'), a company controlled by Adler. The $10 million payment was arranged so that no other directors of HIH would be aware of the advance. During the next two weeks PEE used some of these funds to purchase HIH shares to the value of approximately $4 million. Through these share purchases Adler sought to support HIH's share price for the benefit of his substantial personal shareholding in the company. Williams was aware of the intended use of the $10 million to acquire HIH shares. Soon after a unit trust was established with PEE as trustee. Units were issued to HIHC at a price of $10 million; representing the $10 million advance. Units were also issued to another corporation controlled by Adler, Adler Corporation ('A Co'). The $10 million advance and the HIH shares purchased with such funds became part of the trust property. The HIH shares were subsequently sold at a loss of more than $2.1 million. Adler caused the unit trust to use a further part of the $10 million to buy certain unlisted technology/communications investments from A Co at cost. The purchases were made without any independent analysis of their worth and after the collapse of the stock market for technology and communication stocks. The unit trust suffered a loss of more than $3.8 million on these investments. Adler also caused PEE to make three unsecured loans totalling more than $2 million to companies and funds associated with Adler.

ASIC brought proceedings against Adler, Williams, Fodera and A Co for breaches of, *inter alia*, Chap 2E. It was contended that HIH, as a public company, and HIHC, as an entity controlled by that public company, had provided Adler, PEE and A Co a financial benefit without shareholder approval in breach of s 208. The defendants disputed that 'financial assistance' had been given. Adler asserted that $10m was not a loan, but rather constituted a trust. He also asserted that the transactions were at arm's length within s 210.

The court held HIH and HIHC had contravened s 208. The payment of the $10 million advance by HIHC contravened s 208 as it amounted to the giving of a 'financial benefit' within s 229 to PEE, A Co and Adler. It was irrelevant whether the advance was an unsecured loan or resulting trust, neither was arm's length within s 210. Adler, Williams, Fodera and A Co were all involved in HIH's and HIHC's breach of s 208 and thus had contravened s 209(2).

> **Santow J**: **[617]** 176. ... [S]uch a transaction hardly meets the description in s 210 of "arms length terms". That is to say it is hardly on terms that "would be reasonable in the circumstances if **[618]** the public company or entity and the related party were dealing at arm's length". Even assuming the propriety of the overall transaction and accepting that a financial benefit is given, one would not consider it "reasonable" (within s 210) for the transaction to involve a purchase of shares in the parent HIH, to be paid for by its wholly owned subsidiary HIHC, without any legal documentation whatsoever nor any prospect of security. If (as the Defendants say) the general law of trusts may be invoked to confer remedial protection in this unsatisfactory state of affairs, from HIH/HIHC's viewpoint, that is hardly to render the terms of any financial benefit "reasonable" in any arm's length sense. In particular, HIHC could never have obtained a valid transfer of the shares, (see s 259C). Moreover s 259B would preclude taking security over the relevant shares further to protect its interest.
>
> 177. None of this analysis depends upon a contravention of s 260A of the Corporations Act where the issue is whether "giving the assistance does not materially prejudice" the interests of the company or its shareholders, or the company's ability to pay its creditors. But even if there were no contravention, the fact that financial assistance was thereby provided goes to the reasonableness of the terms and thus whether arm's length within s 210(a).
>
> 178. Finally, I should add that s 210(b) could hardly apply, since the actual terms here are self-evidently not "less favourable" to the related party (PEE) than the arm's length terms of s 210(a).
>
> 179. That still leaves further argument that the First and Fourth Defendants mount, namely that no "financial benefit" was in fact provided, having regard to the definition in s 229 of the Corporations Act and the characterisation of

the relevant payment. In short, the argument put by the Defendants is that as the HIH shares purchased by PEE were at the time of each purchase held absolutely on trust for HIHC, then HIHC ex hypothesi gets an asset worth no less than was paid for it, judged as at the date of each purchase. ...

181. Clearly enough, "financial benefit" is to be given the broadest of interpretation. Importantly, "economic and commercial substance of conduct is to prevail over its legal form". Any consideration for the financial benefit must be disregarded, even if adequate. The strictures of Pt 2E.1, in requiring member approval for related party benefits, requires therefore a wide meaning to "financial benefit" with s 210 providing the gateway out.

[619] 182. The Defendants argue that from 15 June 2000 it was only the bare legal title to the sum of $10 million and the shares bought with part of that sum, which were held by PEE. The entire beneficial interest was held by HIHC. They say there cannot therefore be any financial benefit conferred on PEE, Adler Corporation or Mr Adler on 15 June 2000 by reason of the $10 million payment made that day. But that cannot be right. First, it was intended from the outset, before any purchases took place, that Mr Adler or interests associated with him, would have a 10% interest. That this started with Drenmex, subsequently replaced by PEE, is nothing to the point. Clearly Mr Adler never forewent that 10% interest. Second, where is the financial benefit in a practical sense of PEE having control over the sum of $10 million and legal title, even if bare, to the shares. That must be a real benefit looking, as s 229 directs, to economic and commercial substance, even if as the Defendants' contend the beneficial interest resides with HIHC. Remember even on that hypothesis, this is in circumstances where a transfer to HIHC of the HIH shares would have been precluded, as would any protective charge. Clearly the terms of s 229 are wide enough to embrace these kind of benefits as "financial benefits".

183. ... As a result both HIH, and HIHC being an entity which it controlled, contravened s 208 of the Corporations Law (with equivalent result under the Corporations Act). That result follows even on the Defendants' characterisation of the relevant payment as giving rise to a trust over the shares in HIH acquired out of the A$10 million, as well as over the balance of the A$10 million. It would clearly arise if the payment of $10 million were characterised as an (undocumented) unsecured borrowing with no provision for interest.

See also *ASIC v Adler* (2002) 20 ACLC 1146 regarding the penalties imposed for the breach. In *Adler v ASIC; Williams v ASIC* (2003) 21 ACLC 1810, the court upheld Santow J's findings in *ASIC v Adler* (2002) 20 ACLC 576 that Chap 2E had been breached.

[10.590] A contravention of s 208 does not invalidate the transaction (s 209(1)), but will constitute a breach of the section by those persons involved in the transaction: s 209(1) and (2) (formerly s 243ZE(2) and (3)). If the involvement is dishonest, the person will commit an offence: s 209(3). The company, however, is not guilty of an offence: s 209(1). As s 209(2) is a civil penalty provision (s 1317E(1)), a breach by the persons involved in the transaction will give rise to the same civil and criminal consequences as detailed above with respect to ss 181(1) and 184.

Use of position for personal profit in equity

[10.600] Under both the common law and the *Corporations Act*, directors are prohibited from using company property, company information, corporate opportunities or their positions in the company or inside information for personal profit: *Regal (Hastings) Ltd v Gulliver* [1967] 2 AC 134. Under the strict *Regal (Hastings) Ltd v Gulliver* approach, directors may breach this duty even though:

- the directors were acting bona fide;
- the company suffered no corresponding loss;
- the transaction benefited the company; or
- the company was unable to make the profit itself.

Regal (Hastings) Ltd v Gulliver
House of Lords: Viscount Sankey, Lords Russell of Killowen, Macmillan, Wright and Porter
[1967] 2 AC 134

The appellant company owned a cinema. To facilitate its sale as a going concern, the company sought to acquire the leases over two other cinemas. A subsidiary company was formed to purchase the leases. The company had, however, insufficient paid-up capital to guarantee the purchase of the leases. This was rectified by five of the directors of the appellant company taking up 500 £1 shares in the subsidiary. Three weeks later the sale of the three leases was effected through the sale of the shares in the appellant company and the subsidiary. The directors made a profit on the sale of their shares in the subsidiary.

The new board of directors of Regal (Hastings) Ltd brought an action against the former directors for the profits they had made on the sale of the shares. The court at first instance, Wrottesley J, and the Court of Appeal found in favour of the directors. The company appealed to the House of Lords. The House of Lords unanimously reversed the finding in favour of the directors, finding that they were liable to account for the profits. This was so even though the court concluded that the directors had acted *bona fide* and caused no damage to the company.

> **Lord Russell of Killowen: [144]** The rule of equity which insists on those, who by use of a fiduciary position make a profit, being liable to account for that profit, in no way depends on fraud, or absence of bona fides; or upon such questions or considerations as to whether the profit would or should otherwise have gone to the plaintiff, or whether the profiteer was under a duty to obtain the source of the profit for the plaintiff, or whether he took a risk or acted as he did for the benefit of the plaintiff, or whether the plaintiff has in fact been damaged or benefited by his action. **[145]** The liability arises from the mere fact of a profit having, in the stated circumstances, been made. The profiteer, however honest and well-intentioned, cannot escape the risk of being called upon to account.
>
> The leading case of *Keech v Sandford* [(1726) Sel Cas T King 61] is an illustration of the strictness of this rule of equity in this regard, and of how far the rule is independent of these outside considerations. A lease of the profits of a market had been devised to a trustee for the benefit of an infant. A renewal on behalf of the infant was refused. It was absolutely unobtainable.

The trustee, finding that it was impossible to get a renewal for the benefit of the infant, took a lease for his own benefit. Though his duty to obtain it for the infant was incapable of performance, nevertheless he was ordered to assign the lease to the infant, upon the bare ground that, if a trustee on the refusal to renew might have a lease for himself, few renewals would be made for the benefit of *cestui que trust*. Lord King said at 62:

"This may seem hard, that the trustee is the only person of all mankind who might not have the lease; but it is very proper that the rule should be strictly pursued, and not in the least relaxed." ...

[149] I am of opinion that the directors standing in a fiduciary relationship to Regal in regard to the exercise of their powers as directors, and having obtained these shares by reason and only by reason of the fact that they were directors of Regal and in the course of the execution of that office, are accountable for the profits which they have made out of them. ... [150] The suggestion that the directors were applying simply as members of the public is a travesty of the facts. They could, had they wished, have protected themselves by a resolution (either antecedent or subsequent) of the Regal shareholders in meeting. In default of such approval, the liability to account must remain.

[10.610] This fiduciary duty continues to operate even though the director's position may have terminated: *Canadian Aero Service Ltd v O'Malley* (1973) 40 DLR (3d) 371; *Real Estate Pty Ltd v Valerie Dellow & Wayne Arnold* [2003] SASC 318. Thus, in *Canadian Aero Service Ltd v O'Malley* (1973) 40 DLR (3d) 371, two executive directors had conducted negotiations on behalf of their company for an aerial mapping contract. The directors resigned their positions and established a company that tendered in competition with their former company and won the subject project. The court held that they had breached their fiduciary duties despite the resignations. The resignation did not change the fact that the opportunity had come to the directors whilst acting for the company. See also *Dwyer v Lippiatt* [2004] QSC 281.

[10.620] While, as noted in *Regal (Hastings) Ltd v Gulliver*, generally breaches may be ratified by the company in general meeting, ratification will be ineffective if it involves an expropriation of corporate property or fraud on the minority shareholders: *Cook v Deeks* [1916] 1 AC 554; *Forge v ASIC* [2004] NSWCA 448.

[10.630] The strict *Regal (Hastings) Ltd v Gulliver* approach has in two cases been significantly undermined. The first of these cases suggests that a director may usurp a corporate opportunity where the company has rejected the proposal and the director is approached in a private capacity: *Peso Silver Mines v Cropper* (1966) 58 DLR (2d) 1.

Peso Silver Mines v Cropper
Supreme Court of Canada: Cartwright, Martland, Judson, Ritchie and Hall JJ
(1966) 58 DLR (2d) 1

The respondent was the managing director of Peso Silver Mines ('Peso'). In 1962 Peso was offered certain mining claims. As they were speculative and unproven, Peso's board, including the respondent, rejected the offer. The respondent was approached to form, with two other persons, a company to purchase the claims. In time a public company was incorporated to take over the claims. In 1963 the respondent disclosed his interest in these companies, but refused to transfer his interest in such to Peso at cost.

Peso sought a declaration that Cropper's shares were held on trust for the company and should be delivered to Peso or that he be made to account for the proceeds from such. Peso argued that the shares had been acquired as a result of Cropper's position as director without shareholder approval. The court at first instance, Gregory J, and the Court of Appeal of British Columbia rejected the company's claims. The company appealed to the Supreme Court where again the company's claims were rejected. The court held that Cropper had been approached as a member of the public and as the information was public information there had been no breach of his fiduciary duties and thus no liability to account for the shares/profits.

> **Cartwright J**: [7] The difference of opinion in this court was not as to the principles of law stated in *Regal* but as to whether the facts of the case fell within those principles. ... [8] On the facts of the case at Bar I find it impossible to say that the respondent obtained the interests he holds in Cross Bow and Mayo by reason of the fact that he was a director of the appellant and in the course of the execution of that office. When Dickson, at Dr Aho's suggestion, offered his claims to the appellant it was the duty of the respondent as director to take part in the decision of the board as to whether that offer should be accepted or rejected. At that point he stood in a fiduciary relationship to the appellant. There are affirmative findings of fact that he and his co-directors acted in good faith, solely in the interests of the appellant and with sound business reasons in rejecting the offer. There is no suggestion in the evidence that the offer to the appellant was accompanied by any confidential information unavailable to any prospective purchaser, or that the respondent as director had access to any such information by reason of his office. When later, Dr Aho approached the appellant it was not in his capacity as a director of the appellant, but as an individual member of the public whom Dr Aho was seeking to interest as a co-adventurer.

This decision is clearly contrary to the reasoning in *Regal (Hastings) Ltd v Gulliver* and fails to heed the warning expressed in that case in its discussion of *Keech v Sandford*.

[10.640] The second case goes further and suggests, contrary to *Regal (Hastings) Ltd v Gulliver*, that the company's inability to make the profit does serve to place the transaction outside the realm of a conflict of interests: *Queensland Mines Ltd v Hudson* (1977-1978) ACLC ¶40-389. Further, the decision suggests that if the company has acquiesced in the usurpation there will be no breach: *Queensland Mines*.

Queensland Mines Ltd v Hudson
Privy Council: Viscount Dilhorne, Lords Hailsham, Simon and
Edmund Davies
(1977-1978) CLC ¶40-389

Hudson and another person formed Queensland Mines Ltd for the purpose of exploiting a particular uranium mining operation. Hudson was appointed managing director. When the company ran out of funds, it was 'mothballed', pending an expression of interest by a third party. Hudson turned his interest to the possibility of mining iron ore in Tasmania. He used Queensland Mines Ltd's resources and good name to secure title to two exploration licences. The licences were issued in Hudson's name. Hudson's co-adventurer fell into severe financial difficulties and could not proceed with the project. Without such funding, Queensland Mines Ltd was also prevented from proceeding. Hudson resigned as managing director, formed another company and successfully devoted his efforts to the exploration project, proving the existence of certain valuable deposits. Under an arrangement with another company, mining leases over these areas were granted to its subsidiary, in return for which Hudson obtained the right to royalties upon the ore mined.

An application was brought seeking Hudson to account to Queensland Mines Ltd for the profits made from the venture. Wooten J at first instance applied *Regal (Hastings) Ltd v Gulliver* [1967] 2 AC 134 to the facts and held that Hudson had breached his duties. The court stressed that the duty was a strict one and a mere possibility of a conflict sufficed. The action was, however, held to be statute barred.

Queensland Mines Ltd appealed to the Privy Council. It sought to have the finding of breach of duties maintained, but the decision that the action was statute barred dismissed. The Privy Council agreed with Wooten J's ultimate conclusion but disagreed with his statements as to the breach of duty. The Privy Council stated that no breach of duty had occurred as there was no real sensible possibility of conflict and Hudson had acted with the informed consent of the board.

> **Lord Scarman:** [29,774] The law governing the liability to account of one who is in a special fiduciary relationship with another has been authoritatively declared by the House of Lords in *Phipps v Boardman* [1967] 2 AC 46. Though their Lordships in that case differed in their analysis of the facts, they were agreed on the law. The accepted (see Lord Hodson at 106) that the general principle was as stated by Lord Cranworth LC in *Aberdeen Rly Co v Blaikie Brothers* (1854) 1 Macq 461 at 471:
>
>> "And it is rule of universal application, that no one, having such duties to discharge, shall be allowed to enter into engagements in which he has, or can have, a personal interest conflicting, or which possibly may conflict, with the interests of those whom he is bound to protect."
>
> Lord Upjohn, who dissented on the facts but [29,775] not on the law, commented upon this dictum that the phrase "possibly may conflict" required consideration. He said, at 124B-C:
>
>> "In my view it means that the reasonable man looking at the relevant facts and circumstances of the particular case would think that there was a real

sensible possibility of conflict; not that you could imagine some situation arising which might, in some conceivable possibility in events not contemplated as real sensible possibilities by any reasonable person, result in a conflict."

All their Lordships recognised that a limit has to be set to the liability to account of one who is in a special relationship with another whose interests he is bound to protect. Lord Cohen, at 102G, said:

"... it does not necessarily follow that because an agent acquired information and opportunity while acting in a fiduciary capacity he is accountable to his principals for any profit that comes his way as the result of the use he makes of that information and opportunity. His liability to account must depend on the facts of the case."

The limit was described in varying terms. Viscount Dilhorne, who (with Lord Upjohn) also dissented on the facts, emphasised the need to define the scope of the trust and the scope of the agency (at 91). Lord Cohen, in the passage to which reference has already been made (at 103), said that liability to account must depend on the facts of the case. Lord Hodson put the limit in words, which the Board accepts as an authoritative formulation of a real limitation upon the liability:

"Nothing short of fully informed consent which the learned judge found not to have been obtained could enable the appellants in the position which they occupied having taken the opportunity provided by that position to make profit for themselves (at 109D)."

Lord Guest (at 117G) said:

"In the present case the knowledge and information obtained by Boardman was obtained in the course of the fiduciary position in which he had placed himself. The only defence available to a person in such a fiduciary position is that he made the profits with the knowledge and assent of the trustees. It is not contended that the trustees had such knowledge or gave such consent."

Lord Upjohn thought it necessary to examine the facts to determine whether a person in a fiduciary relationship with another had placed himself in a position where there was any possibility of a conflict between duty and interest (124B and 133B).

All their Lordships attached importance to the case of *Regal (Hastings) Ltd v Gulliver* [1942] 1 All ER 378, a decision of the House of Lords in 1942 but not reported until 1967, when it appears as a note to *Phipps v Boardman* [1967] 2 AC 134. In the *Regal* case Lord Wright said that an agent, a director, a trustee or other person in an analogous fiduciary position cannot defeat a claim to account for profits acquired by reason of his fiduciary position upon any ground "save that he made profits with the knowledge and assent of the other person" (at 154B-C). In the course of the judgment under appeal, Wootten J examined the case law in great detail and reached a conclusion from which their Lordships would in no way dissent. He said (at 711 of the Record):

"That obligation [ie the duty owed by Mr Hudson as managing director to Queensland Mines] was twofold, namely that he should not make a profit or take a benefit through his position as fiduciary without the informed consent of his principal, and that he should not act in a way in which there was a possible conflict between his own interest and that of his principal."

In their Lordships' opinion, therefore, the facts have to be examined to determine whether Mr Hudson acted in a way in which "there was a real

sensible possibility of conflict" between his interest and the interest of Queensland Mines, and whether in exploiting for himself the opportunity provided by the mining exploration licence obtained by him while managing director he did so with the informed consent of Queensland Mines. The learned trial judge found against Mr Hudson on both these questions. ...
[29,776] In the present case, after a full examination of the relevant facts – a task in which their Lordships have been greatly assisted by learned counsel –, their Lordships have reached the clear conclusion that in the circumstances there was after the 13th February 1962 no real, sensible possibility of a conflict of interest between Mr Hudson and Queensland Mines, and that Queensland Mines were fully informed as to the facts and assented to Mr Hudson's exploitation of the mining exploration licence in his own name, for his own gain, and at his own risk and expense. ...

[29,777] Mr Hudson was ... in a position of the utmost difficulty. ... That source of finance having dried up, Mr Hudson was left with nothing save only his personal resources and a company which it had already been decided to "mothball"'.

Mr Hudson responded to the situation with energy, and also with openness. Nothing was now, or hereafter, concealed. Mr Hudson never sought to hide anything that he did. On the 15th March he resigned as managing director of Queensland Mines – no doubt so that he could devote all his energy to the iron ore venture. His cliff-hanging but ultimately successful endeavour to exploit the iron ore licence was widely known and followed in Australian mining circles and in the press. On the 21st March he told the Tasmanian Director of Mines that Mr Korman had withdrawn. He also told him that he, Mr Hudson, intended to honour his own obligations and to seek finance to enable him to do so. On the 30th May he was able to inform the Tasmanian Government that he had formed a company (the second defendant) which was to be "capitalised by myself and which will bear all expenses up to the date of the formation" of a public company. Certainly, Mr Hudson conducted correspondence with overseas interests and others under the name of Queensland Mines until the 1st May 1961, but not thereafter.

[29,778] From that date until success ultimately crowned his efforts he was on his own, running all the risks and meeting all the expense. In June 1963 he succeeded in interesting an American company. By this time he had proved the existence of valuable deposits. In 1964 application was made for a mining lease of part of the land covered by the exploration licence (EL4/61). On the 3rd June 1966 a mining lease of this land was granted to subsidiaries of the American company. Mr Hudson's reward was a right under his contract with the American company to royalties upon the ore mined.

Their Lordships agree with the learned trial judge's conclusion that the opportunity to earn these royalties arose initially from the use made by Mr Hudson of his position as managing director of Queensland Mines. He must, therefore, account to that company unless he can show that, fully informed as to the circumstances, Queensland Mines renounced its interest and assented to Mr Hudson "going it alone" ie at his own risk and expense and for his own benefit.

Their Lordships have reached the conclusion that by February 1962 at the latest, and possibly much earlier, the board of Queensland Mines, fully informed as to all relevant facts, had reached a firm decision to renounce all interest in the exploitation of the licence and had assented to Mr Hudson taking over the venture for his own account. The learned trial judge, however, has found that Mr Hudson deliberately refrained from revealing to Queensland Mines the fact of its interest in the licence. He said that:

"in my view, Mr Hudson has not established any informed consent to his appropriation of the opportunity on the part of Queensland Mines, whether by directors, general meeting or shareholders, or any rejection of the opportunity which was not tainted by Mr Hudson's non-disclosure to the company of relevant facts."

The basis of the finding appears to be the lack of evidence that Mr Hudson ever informed Kathleen Investments Ltd or its subsidiary, AOE, that through his activities as managing director Queensland Mines had an interest in the licence.

The judge's finding that Queensland Mines was not informed as to the existence of its interest in the licence, in their Lordships' opinion, cannot stand. The board of Queensland Mines knew of the company's interest at all times.

[10.650] The correctness of *Queensland Mines Ltd v Hudson* must be doubted as it is well established that disclosure of a conflict to the board of directors is insufficient: *Furs Ltd v Tomkies* (1936) 54 CLR 583. Only a fully informed general meeting can ratify such a breach: *Bamford v Bamford* [1970] Ch 212; *Winthrop Investments Ltd v Winns Ltd* [1975] 2 NSWLR 666; *Pascoe Ltd (in liq) v Lucas* (1998) 16 ACLC 1247.

Use of position for personal profit under Corporations Act

[10.660] Sections 182 and 183 complement these common law remedies by prohibiting officers and employees from improperly using their positions (s 182) or corporate information (s 183) to directly or indirectly gain an advantage for themselves or third parties or to cause detriment to the company. The prohibition against the improper use of information extends to present and former officers and employees of the company: s 183(1).

[10.670] Whether the officer has acted 'improperly' is determined objectively: *Chew v R* (1992) 10 ACLC 816 at 647; *ASIC v Adler* (2002) 20 ACLC 576. Hence, the officer's actual *bona fides* are irrelevant unless they correspond with an objective appraisal of the situation: *Forkserve Pty Ltd v Jack* (2001) 19 ACLC 299. The key is whether there has been impropriety from the viewpoint of a reasonable person with relevant knowledge and hence does not require a subjective intent to obtain an advantage or cause detriment to the company: *Forkserve Pty Ltd v Jack*. Thus, in *ASIC v Doyle* [2001] WASC 187, the director was held to breach the duty even though he had a reasonable, but mistaken, belief that the subject conduct would benefit the company. To establish a breach it is not necessary that an actual advantage accrue or the company suffer damage. It suffices that the improper conduct was done for the purpose of gaining an advantage or causing detriment to the company: *ASIC v Doyle*. Again *ASIC v Adler* (2002) 20 ACLC 576 provides a recent extensive consideration of these principles.

ASIC v Adler
Supreme Court of New South Wales: Santow J
(2002) 20 ACLC 576

Adler was a non-executive director of HIH Insurance Ltd ('HIH'). Williams was a director and the CEO of HIH. Fodera was a director and the finance controller of HIH. HIH Casualty and General Insurance Ltd ('HIHC') was a wholly owned subsidiary of HIH. Adler requested, and Williams and Fodera arranged, for HIHC to advance $10 million to Pacific Eagle Equity Pty Ltd ('PEE'), a company controlled by Adler. The $10 million payment was arranged so that no other directors of HIH would be aware of the advance. During the next two weeks PEE used some of these funds to purchase HIH shares to the value of approximately $4 million. Through these share purchases Adler sought to support HIH's share price for the benefit of his substantial personal shareholding in the company. Williams was aware of the intended use of the $10 million to acquire HIH shares. Soon after a unit trust was established with PEE as trustee. Units were issued to HIHC at a price of $10 million; representing the $10 million advance. Units were also issued to another corporation controlled by Adler, Adler Corporation ('A Co'). The $10 million advance and the HIH shares purchased with such funds became part of the trust property. The HIH shares were subsequently sold at a loss of more than $2.1 million. Adler caused the unit trust to use a further part of the $10 million to buy certain unlisted technology/communications investments from A Co at cost. The purchases were made without any independent analysis of their worth and after the collapse of the stock market for technology and communication stocks. The unit trust suffered a loss of more than $3.8 million on these investments. Adler also caused PEE to make three unsecured loans totalling more than $2 million to companies and funds associated with Adler.

ASIC brought proceedings against Adler and A Co for breaches of, *inter alia*, ss 182 and 183 and Williams for breaches of, *inter alia*, s 182. It was asserted that Adler had improperly used his position to gain an advantage for himself, PEE and/or A Co in breach of s 182. Williams was said to have breached the section through his accessory involvement in Adler's misconduct. Adler was said to have breached s 183 through the use of his knowledge concerning the HIH Investment Committee procedures and the Investment Guidelines, the HIH investment portfolio and the susceptibility of Williams to a proposal whereby HIH would invest money in less conservative ways.

The court held Adler had improperly used his position within s 182 and had improperly used information within s 183. In regard to s 182, Adler had organised the $10 million advance by HIHC to purchase the shares in HIH for the improper purpose of supporting HIH's share price for the benefit of his own personal shareholding. In regard to s 183, Adler had improperly used corporate information to make a gain for himself when requiring the unit trust to acquire the technology investments and in causing PEE to make the three unsecured loans to companies and funds associated with Adler. A Co was involved in these contraventions and thus was also liable under ss 182 and 183. Williams had also breached s 182 when he authorised the $10 million advance from HIHC to PEE without ensuring that proper safeguards were in place and without the knowledge or approval of the HIH Investment Committee.

Santow J: [666] 458. I should commence by a brief statement of the effect of the case law on the application of s 182 in the present context.
(1) Causing a company to enter into an agreement which confers unreasonable personal benefits on a director is a breach of ss 180, 181 and 182.
(2) Failing to end an agreement that pays reasonable benefits to a related consultant after the director should realise that the company is insolvent breaches s 182: *Simar Transit Mixers Pty Ltd v Baryczka* (1998) 28 ACSR 238 [CL s 232 1992].
(3) Obtaining the agreement in a manner which keeps any independent director "in the dark" is strong evidence that the benefits are unreasonable, as is the lack of any evidence as to what the director did for the company in return: *Claremont Petroleum NL v Cummings; Claremont Petroleum NL v Fuller* (1992) 10 ACLC 1,685, 9 ACSR 1; on appeal *Cummings v Claremont Petroleum NL; Fuller v Claremont Petroleum NL* (1993) 11 ACLC 125, 9 ACSR 583 [CC s 229 1989].
(4) Moreover it is sufficient to establish that the conduct of a company was carried out in order to gain an advantage for that director or someone else without also having to establish that an advantage was actually achieved: *Chew v R* (1992) 10 ACLC 816; (1992) 173 CLR 626 per Mason CJ, Brennan, Gaudron and McHugh JJ at ACLC 819; CLR 633.
(5) Where a director acts in relation to a transaction in which he or a party to whom the director owes a fiduciary duty stands to gain a benefit without making adequate disclosure of his interest, that director acts "improperly" within the meaning of s 182(1): *R v Byrnes; R v Hopwood; Byrnes v R* (1995) 13 ACLC 1,488 at 1,497; (1995) 183 CLR 501 at 516-17. That is likely to lead also to a conclusion of lack of good faith for s 181 purposes. There could be no adequate disclosure here, or the essential fully informed consent, where there was neither disclosure to HIH's or HIHC's board or even to the Investment Committee. It does not suffice that Mr Williams or Mr Fodera knew (or Mr Howard as a non-director knew) of the transactions, or for that matter Mr Cassidy, his knowledge being in any event limited. [667]
(6) Finally, impropriety for the purposes of s 182(1) is to be determined objectively and does not depend upon the director's consciousness of impropriety. It consists in a breach of the standards of conduct that would be expected of a person in the position of the alleged offender by reasonable persons with knowledge of the duties, powers and authority of the position and the circumstances of the case: *R v Byrnes* (supra) at ACLC 1,496; CLR 514-15 per Brennan, Deane, Toohey and Gaudron JJ.
...

Conclusion
461. Mr Williams breached his statutory obligation under s 182 not to improperly use his position as a director of HIH and HIHC to gain an advantage for Mr Adler. He likewise improperly used his position to cause detriment to HIH and HIHC, in authorising the relevant payment without

proper safeguards and without having the relevant mandate to Mr Adler and PEE submitted for approval to the Investment Committee and for the relevant investment to be ratified by the Investment Committee, in accordance with the Investment Guidelines. ...

[685] 577. Mr Adler breached his obligation ... (c) not to improperly use his position to gain an advantage for himself or to cause detriment to each of HIH, HIHC and PEE, so breaching s 182 of the Corporations Act, and (d) not to improperly use information obtained by him to gain an advantage for himself or to gain an advantage for Adler Corporation, so contravening s 183 of the Corporations Law, being information concerning the Investment Committee procedures and Investment Guidelines, the HIH Investment Portfolio and the susceptibility of Mr Williams to a proposal whereby HIH invest money in less conservative ways, such as in unlisted equities and venture capital; see para 95 of the Plaintiff's Statement of Claim (no s 183 claim is made in relation to PEE). ...

[703] 735. It is useful if I now set out in summary form the principles applicable to s 181 of the *Corporations Act* as applicable to the relevant transactions, in ascribing the statutory duty to act in good faith and for a proper purpose (as to the latter see also para 458 above). Some of these, insofar as dealing with impropriety, or lack of good faith, are common to both s 181 and s 182. I have set out those principles below (and see also paras 738-40) with reference where noted to the present circumstances.

(1) A director (as a fiduciary) is under an obligation not to promote his personal interest by making or pursuing a gain in circumstances where there is a conflict or a real or substantial possibility of a conflict between his personal interests and those of the company: *Hospital Products Ltd v United States Surgical Corporation* (1984) 156 CLR 41 per Mason J at 103. This is both at general law and by statute (s 181 and as applicable ss 182 and 183). ... If the director has improperly used his position or information to gain such advantage ss 182 and 183 respectively are breached.

(2) In order to assess whether or not there is a real sensible possibility of conflict one must adopt the position of the reasonable person looking at the relevant facts and circumstances of the particular case: *Phipps v Boardman* [1967] 2 AC 46 per Lord Upjohn (at 124); *Queensland Mines Ltd v* [704] *Hudson* (1977-1978) CLC ¶40-389; (1978) 18 ALR 1.

(3) Nonetheless, a director may act with a personal interest even though the director has not freed his or her mind of that personal interest when acting provided that this personal interest was not the actuating motive rather than some bona fide concern for the benefit of the company as a whole or for fairness as between members: *Mills v Mills* (1938) 60 CLR 150 per Latham CJ (at 164-65).

(4) In certain circumstances, such as a director in "a position of power and influence" over the board, mere disclosure of a conflict between interest and duty and abstaining from voting is insufficient to satisfy a director's fiduciary duty. The director may also be under a positive duty to take steps to protect the company's interest such as by using such power and influence as he had to prevent the transaction going ahead: *Permanent Building Society (in liq) v McGee* (1993) 11 ACLC 761; (1993) 11 ACSR 260 per Anderson J (at ACSR 289). Here neither Mr Adler nor Mr Williams, and failing them Mr Fodera did anything to have the following reach the Investment Committee or the Board; that is, payment

of the $10 million, the formation of AEUT and its investment in HIH. This allowed the subsequent unlisted investments and loans to be made with no properly approved mandate permitting this and no specific approval or ratification within a reasonable time thereafter.

(5) What action, beyond disclosure, the director must take will depend on matters such as the degree to which the director has been involved in the transaction, and the gravity of possible outcomes for the company: *Fitzsimmons v R* (1997) 15 ACLC 666; (1997) 23 ACSR 355 per Owen J (at ACLC 669; ACSR 358). Here Mr Adler was intimately involved in all aspects of the transactions, while Messrs Williams and Fodera were involved to the lesser degrees earlier identified, with Mr Fodera least involved and the outcomes for HIH and HIHC were clearly adverse, in terms of ultimate loss.

(6) A director of a company (here Mr Adler) who is also a director of another company (here Adler Corporation) must not exercise his or her powers for the benefit or the gain of the second company without clearly disclosing the second company's interests to the first company and obtaining the first company's consent: *R v Byrnes* (1995) 13 ACLC 1,488; (1995) 183 CLR 501 per Brennan, Deane, Toohey and Gaudron JJ at ACLC 1,497; CLR 517 (which here was never effectively given by HIH or HIHC).

736. The manifest failure of AEUT and the fact that the HIH share price did fall despite AEUT's buying, in no way obviates the intended advantage to Mr Adler and Adler Corporation. Thus to establish liability under s 182(1) it is sufficient to establish that the conduct of the director was carried out in order to gain an advantage. It is not necessary to establish that advantage was actually achieved; *Chew v R* (1992) 10 ACLC 816; (1992) 173 CLR 626 per Mason CJ, Brennan, Gaudron and McHugh JJ at ACLC 819; CLR 633. Nor does that failure obviate the actual advantages earlier identified, as were in fact achieved by Mr Adler and Adler Corporation from the transactions. These include selling off at original cost Adler corporation's three unlisted investments, with their (by then) manifest difficulties raising the capital that they needed. They also included the advantages associated entities of Mr Adler achieved from the loans to them by AEUT. That failure thus affords no defence to each of the allegations of impropriety under ss 181-3.

See also *ASIC v Adler* (2002) 20 ACLC 1146 regarding the penalties imposed for the breach. In *Adler v ASIC*; *Williams v ASIC* (2003) 21 ACLC 1810, the court upheld Santow J's findings in *ASIC v Adler* (2002) 20 ACLC 576 that s 182 had been breached, but upheld the appeal in regard to s 183. The key issue was whether the disregarding of HIH's Investment Committee guidelines and procedures could be an improper use of information. The Court of Appeal held that this did not amount to an improper use of information. Similarly, disregard of known information regarding the HIH investment portfolio was held not to amount to a misuse of that information. Even Adler's knowledge that Williams was susceptible to less than conservative investments did not amount to information under s 183.

[10.680] As noted above, the duties prescribed in ss 180-184 are in addition to, and not in derogation of, any other law relating to these officers' duties or liability: s 185.

[10.690] Sections 182 and 183 are civil penalty provisions. In addition, a breach of these provisions will constitute a criminal offence where the director dishonestly used the position or information with the intention of directly or indirectly gaining an advantage for themselves or third parties or to cause detriment to the company or was reckless as to whether this may result: s 184(2) and (3). Thus, a breach of ss 182 or 183 will give rise to the same civil and criminal consequences as outlined above with respect to ss 181(1) and 184.

Duty to Act with Due Care and Diligence

Common law

[10.700] The leading case on the duty of care at common law is *Daniels v Anderson* (1995) 13 ACLC 614. In that case the court held that an objective standard of care was applicable to both executive and non-executive directors.

Daniels v Anderson
New South Wales Court of Appeal: Clarke, Sheller and Powell JJA
(1995) 13 ACLC 614

AWA Ltd had decided to hedge against currency fluctuations by making forward purchases of foreign currency against contracts for imported goods. While it appeared to the board of directors that AWA Ltd had made substantial profits from the foreign exchange dealings, it had in fact lost over $49m. The company's failure to establish adequate internal controls and record-keeping systems for the foreign exchange dealings had allowed the loss to be concealed. The company's auditors were, to some extent, aware of these weaknesses, but failed to report them to the board of directors.

When the company knew the true position, AWA Ltd commenced proceedings against the auditors for breach of contract and negligence. The auditors alleged in defence that the chief executive officer and three non-executive directors had been contributorily negligent. Rogers J at first instance found that the auditors were negligent and that their negligence had caused the loss. It was also agreed that the chief executive officer and the management of AWA Ltd had been negligent, but that the non-executive directors had not been negligent.

The Court of Appeal agreed with the findings of Rogers J. Clarke and Sheller JJA rejected, however, Rogers J's approach to the directors' duty of care, especially in regard to directors' delegation of responsibility. They believed there was no basis for suggesting that directors' duties fell outside the scope of general law notions of negligence. In turn they adopted an objective standard of care that was held applicable to both executive and non-executive directors.

Clarke and Sheller JJA: [662] The insolvent trading cases demonstrate that ignorance is no longer necessarily a defence to proceedings brought against a director. In some respects, at least, the director must inform himself or herself about the affairs of the company.

There is no doubt reason for establishing a board which enjoys the varied wisdom of persons drawn from different commercial backgrounds. Even so a director, whatever his or her background, has a duty greater than that of simply representing a particular field of experience. That duty involves becoming familiar with the business of the company and how it is run and ensuring that the board has available means to audit the management of the company so that it can satisfy itself that the company is being properly run. The board may be assisted by sub-committees consisting of its members, including non-executive directors; see generally Sievers, "Farewell to the Sleeping Director," (1993) 21 Australian Business Law Review 111 at 115-7.

In our opinion the responsibilities of directors require that they take reasonable steps to place themselves in a position to guide and monitor the management of the company. The board of AWA met only once a month for half a day. But to our mind the board should meet as often as it deems necessary to carry out its functions properly. The question is what in the particular case are the duties and responsibilities of the directors and then what time is required of them as a board to carry out these duties and responsibilities. It is not a matter of tailoring the extent of the duty or function to pre-fixed intervals between board meetings.

To be balanced against calls that the modern public company director has acquired and now asserts a professional status together with professional skills (which should carry a requirement that the director conform to professional standards and the imposition of an objective standard of care which would not yield to considerations such as lack of knowledge or lack of experience) are the difficulties deriving from the variety of businesses with which companies may be concerned and from the highly diversified activities of a large and complex company. In such circumstances it would be unreasonable to expect every director to have equal knowledge and experience of every aspect of the company's activities. Furthermore traditionally non-executive directors have been appointed for perceived commercial advantage such as attracting customers or adding to the prestige and status of the company; Mitchell, "Directors' Duties and Insider Dealing" (1982) 49. But in *Deloitte Haskins & Sells v National Mutual Life Nominees* (1991) 5 NZCLC 67,418 at 67,442-3 (on appeal from Henry J sub nom *Fletcher v National Mutual Life Nominees Ltd* [1990] 3 NZLR 641) Gault J, with whom McGechan J agreed, rejected the argument that a lower standard of care should be applied to a non executive director than to the executive directors and that a non executive director should be entitled to rely on information provided to him. ...

[663] The law of negligence can accommodate different degrees of duty owed by people with different skills but that does not mean that a director can safely proceed on the basis that ignorance and a failure to inquire are a protection against liability for negligence. Section 1318 of the Corporations Law provides such protection as the legislature considers necessary.

A matter of particular significance in these appeals is the extent to which directors are justified in trusting and relying upon officers of the company. Rogers J said that a director is justified in trusting such officers to perform all duties that, having regard to the exigencies of business, the intelligent devolution of labour and the articles of association, may properly be left to them. He said that a director is entitled to rely without verification on the judgment, information and advice of the officers so entrusted and on management to go through relevant financial and other information of the corporation and draw to the board's attention any matter requiring their consideration. ... In our respectful opinion it does not accurately state the extent of the duty of directors whether non-executive or not in modern company law.

Federal Deposit Insurance Corporation v Bierman 2 F 3d 1424 (1993), a decision of the United States Court of Appeals (Seventh Circuit), concerned an action brought against bank directors to recover for losses suffered by the bank on loan transactions. At 1432-3 Circuit Judge Ripple said:

"Directors are charged with keeping abreast of the bank's business and exercising reasonable supervision and control over the activities of the bank ... A director may not rely on the judgment of others, especially when there is notice of mismanagement. Certainly, when an investment poses an obvious risk, a director cannot rely blindly on the judgment of others ..."

Rankin v Cooper (1907) 149 F 1010 at 1013 was cited: **[664]**

"If nothing has come to the knowledge to awaken suspicion that something is going wrong, ordinary attention to the affairs of the institution is sufficient. If, upon the other hand, directors know, or by the exercise of ordinary care should have known, any facts which would awaken suspicion and put a prudent man on his guard, then a degree of care commensurate with the evil to be avoided is required, and a want of that care makes them responsible. Directors cannot, in justice to those who deal with the bank, shut their eyes to what is going on around them."

See also *Commonwealth Bank of Australia v Friedrich* [(1991) 9 ACLC 946] at 955-956; ACSR 126.

The modern cases to which we have referred, set in the context of a legislative pattern of imposing greater responsibility upon directors, demonstrate that the director's duty of care is not merely subjective, limited by the director's knowledge and experience or ignorance or inaction. The duties of a director are eloquently explained in the judgment of Pollock J, giving the opinion of the Supreme Court of New Jersey, in *Francis v United Jersey Bank* 432 A 2d 814 (1981). The relevant legislative context was different. The description of the duties of directors spoke of "skill". The New Jersey Business Corporation Act (1969) required directors to:

"discharge their duties in good faith and with that degree of diligence, care and skill which ordinarily prudent men would exercise under similar circumstances in like positions."

But the judgment exposes by reference to other cases what is generally expected of directors not only in the United States but in Australia and elsewhere. In our opinion, this has become what the law requires of directors.

At 821-3 Pollock J said:

"As a general rule, a director should acquire at least a rudimentary understanding of the business of the corporation. Accordingly, a director should become familiar with the fundamentals of the business in which the corporation is engaged. *Campbell v Watson* 62 NJ Eq at 416, 50 A 120. Because directors are bound to exercise ordinary care, they cannot set up as a defence lack of the knowledge needed to exercise the requisite degree of care. If one 'feels that he has not had sufficient business experience to qualify him to perform the duties of a director, he should either acquire the knowledge by inquiry, or refuse to act.'

Directors are under a continuing obligation to keep informed about the activities of the corporation. Otherwise, they may not be able to participate in the overall management of corporate affairs. *Barnes v Andrews* 298 F 614 (SDNY 1924) (director guilty of misprision of office for not keeping himself informed about the details of corporate business); *Atherton v Anderson* 99 F 2d 883, 889-890 (6 Cir 1938) (ignorance no defense to director liability because of director's 'duty to know the facts); Campbell at 409, 50 A 120 (directors 'bound to acquaint themselves with ... extent ... of supervision exercised by officers'); *Williams v McKay* 46 NJ Eq 25, 36, 18 A 824 (Ch 1889) (director under duty to supervise managers and practices to determine whether business methods were safe and proper). Directors may not shut their eyes to corporate misconduct and then claim that because they did not see the misconduct, they did not have a duty to look. The sentinel asleep at his post contributes nothing to the enterprise he is charged to protect. *Wilkinson v Dodd* 42 NJ Eq 234, 245, 7 A 327 (Ch 1886), affirmed 42 NJ Eq 647, 9 A 685 (E & A 1887).

Directorial management does not require a detailed inspection of day-to-day activities, but rather a general monitoring of corporate affairs and policies. *Williams v McKay* at 37, 18 A 824. Accordingly, a director is well advised to attend board meetings regularly. ...

While directors are not required to audit corporate books, they should maintain familiarity with the financial status of the corporation by a regular review of financial statements. ...

The review of financial statements, however, may give rise to a duty to inquire further into matters revealed by those statements. *Corsicana Nat'l Bank v Johnson* 251 US 68, 71, 40 S Ct 82, 84, 64 L Ed 141 (1919); *Atherton* 99 F2d at 890; *La Monte v Mott* 93 NJ Eq 229, 239, 107 A 462 (E & A 1921); *see Lippitt v Ashley* 89 Conn at 457, 94 A at 998. Upon discovery of an illegal **[665]** course of action, a director has a duty to object and, if the corporation does not correct the conduct, to resign. See *Dodd v Wilkinson* 42 NJ Eq 647, 651, 9 A 685 (E & A 1887); *Williams v Riley* 34 NJ Eq 398, 401 (Ch 1881) ...

A director is not an ornament, but an essential component of corporate governance. Consequently, a director cannot protect himself behind a paper shield bearing the motto 'dummy director'. *Campbell* at 443, 50 A 120 ('The directors were not intended to be mere figure-heads without duty or responsibility'); *Williams v McKay* at 57-58, 18 A 824 (director voluntarily assuming position also assumes duties of ordinary care, skill and judgment). The New Jersey Business Corporation Act, in imposing a standard of ordinary care on all directors, confirms that dummy, figurehead and accommodation directors are anachronisms with no place in New Jersey law. See NJSA 14A: 6-14. Similarly, in interpreting section 717, the New York courts have not exonerated a director who acts as an 'accommodation." ...

Although there was no reference to skill in s 229(2) of the Code – nor is there in s 232(4) of the Corporations Law – Malcolm CJ in *Vrisakis* at 172 thought that the duties imposed by the section reflected the general concept of negligence at common law. This means conduct ordinarily measured by reference to what the reasonable man of ordinary prudence would do in the circumstances. Skill is that special competence which is not part of the ordinary equipment of the reasonable man but the result of aptitude developed by special training and experience which requires those who undertake work calling for special skill not only to exercise reasonable care but measure up to the standard of proficiency that can be expected from persons undertaking such work; *Voli v Inglewood Shire Council* [(1963) 110 CLR 74] at 84 per Windeyer J. A director may be appointed because of a particular or special skill and may take up the appointment on the basis that he or she will bring that skill to the performance of the office. In *Gould and Birbeck and Bacon v Mount Oxide Mines Ltd (In Liquidation)* (1916) 22 CLR 490 at 531 Isaacs and Rich JJ said:

"No rule of universal application can be formulated as to a director's obligation in all circumstances. The extent of his duty must depend on the particular function he is performing, the circumstances of the specific case, and the terms on which he has undertaken to act as a director."

But, as we have said, DHS' cross-claims against Hooke and the NED were not based upon an alleged failure to exercise any particular or special skill.

We are of opinion that a director owes to the company a duty to take reasonable care in the performance of the office. As the law of negligence has developed no satisfactory policy ground survives for excluding directors from the general requirement that they exercise reasonable care in the performance of their office. A director's fiduciary obligations do not preclude the common law duty of care. Modern statutory company law points to the existence of the duty. In some circumstances the duty will require action. The concept of a sleeping or passive director has not survived and is inconsistent with the requirements of current company legislation such as, at the relevant time, ss 229 and 269 of the Code. ...

A person who accepts the office of director of a particular company undertakes the responsibility of ensuring that he or she understands the nature of the duty a director is called upon to perform. That duty will vary according to the size and business of the particular company and the experience or skills that the director held himself or herself out to have in support of appointment to the office. None of this is novel. It turns upon the natural **[666]** expectations and reliance placed by shareholders on the experience and skill of a particular director. The duty is a common law duty to take reasonable care owed severally by persons who are fiduciary agents bound not to exercise the powers conferred upon them for private purpose or for any purpose foreign to the power and placed, in the words of Ford and Austin, *Principles of Corporations Law*, 6th ed at 429, at the apex of the structure of direction and management. The duty includes that of acting collectively to manage the company. Breach of the duty will found an action for negligence at the suit of the company. Negligent directors are tortfeasors within the meaning of s 5(1)(c) of the *Law Reform (Miscellaneous Provisions) Act* 1946.

The court's finding in *Daniels v Anderson* (1995) 13 ACLC 614 that the duty of care imposes an objective standard of care was subsequently accepted in *South Australia v Marcus Clark* (1996) 19 ACSR 606 at 627-628; *Gamble v Hoffman* (1997) 24 ACSR 369 at 372-373; *Duke Group Ltd (in liq) v Pilmer* (1999) 17 ACLC 1329; *Sheahan (as Liq SA Service Stations Pty Ltd) v Verco & Hodge* (2001) 19 ACLC 814; *ASIC v Adler* (2002) 20 ACLC 576.

Statutory duty of care and diligence

[10.710] Section 180(1) provides that a director or other officer of a corporation 'must exercise their powers and discharge their duties with the degree of care and diligence that a reasonable person would exercise'. Thus, s 180(1) incorporates an objective 'reasonable director' test. In accordance with the current common law position, under s 180(1) the director may not plead personal idiosyncrasies in defence of a claim that he or she has breached the duty of due care and diligence.

[10.720] The relevant standard of care is determined in light of the 'corporation's circumstances' and the office held by the director and the responsibilities attaching to that position within the corporation: s 180(1)(a) and (b). This will ensure 'the composition of its board ... the distribution of work between the board and other officers' and 'the type of company, the size and nature of its enterprise [and] the provisions of its articles of association' will continue to be relevant in determining whether sufficient care has been exercised. See *Commonwealth Bank of Australia v Friedrich* (1991) 9 ACLC 946 at 955

[10.730] As noted above, s 185 provides that the duty imposed by s 180 is in addition to any other common law or statutory duties. Section 185 does not, however, apply to s 180(2) and (3) in so far as these provisions apply to the duty of care. It will be seen below that these provisions introduce a business judgment rule that may be relied upon in defence to a claim of breach of the duty of care whether that be under s 180(1) or the common law duty of care: ss 180(2) and 185.

Business judgment rule

[10.740] The business judgment rule allows a director who has otherwise breached the duty of care, whether at common law or under s 180(1), to plead this rule in defence: ss 180(2) and 185. Under s 180(2), a director is taken to have satisfied the duty of care if they have made a business judgment:

- in good faith for a proper purpose;
- they do not have a material personal interest in the subject matter of the judgment;
- they have informed themselves about the subject matter 'to the extent they reasonably believe to be appropriate'; and
- they 'rationally believe' that the judgment is in the best interests of the corporation.

A business judgment is defined in s 180(3) as any 'decision to take or not take action' in respect to a matter relevant to the company's business operations. Thus, a business judgment may be a decision to act or not to act. The director's belief that the judgment is in the company's best interests is taken to be rational unless the belief is one that no reasonable person in their position would hold: s 180(2).

Reliance and delegation

[10.750] Also relevant to the duty of care are ss 189, 190 and 198D, designed to clarify when a director may delegate his or her responsibilities and the ability to rely on the advice of others when making decisions. Section 198D(1) provides that, unless the company's

constitution provides otherwise, the directors may delegate any of their powers to:
- a committee of directors;
- a director;
- an employee of the company;
- any other person.

The acts of the delegate are as effective as if the director had acted: s 198D(3).

[10.760] Under s 190(1) directors are responsible for the acts of the delegate, as if the director had exercised the power himself or herself. However, under s 190(2), the director is not responsible for the acts of the delegate where the director believed on reasonable grounds that the delegate would exercise the powers in accordance with the duties of directors and that the delegate was reliable and competent. The belief must be based on reasonable grounds, arrived at in good faith and, where circumstances indicated a need for, on the basis of proper inquiry.

[10.770] Under s 189(a)(i)-(iv), a director may rely on the advice of:
- an employee where the director has reasonable grounds to believe the employee is reliable and competent to give that advice;
- professional advisers or experts where the director has reasonable grounds to believe that the matters are within that person's professional or expert competence;
- another director or officer in relation to matters within that person's designated authority; or
- a committee of directors, where the director did not serve on that committee, in relation to matters within that committee's designated authority.

Take careful note of the different requirements depending on the category of persons upon whom reliance is placed.

[10.780] Under s 189(b) and (c), reliance on these persons is presumed to be reasonable for the purposes of determining if the director has breached his or her duties (under either Part 2D.1 or the general law) where the director has acted in good faith and has made an independent assessment of the information or advice. This assessment is made having regard to the 'director's knowledge of the corporation and the complexity of the structure and operations of the corporation': s 189(c).

Consequences of breach

[10.790] Section 180(1) is stated as giving rise to only civil obligations. Thus, while the section is a civil penalty provision and thus has the civil consequences detailed above with respect to s 181(1), not even an intentionally dishonest breach of s 180(1) will have criminal consequences. In practice, however, this may not be significant as a dishonest breach of s 180(1) is likely to constitute a criminal breach of another provision of the *Corporations Act* such as ss 181(1) and 184(1).

Insolvent Trading

Duty to prevent insolvent trading

[10.800] The Corporations Act places liability on company officers in certain cases where they allow the company to incur debts when either the company is insolvent or the debt will render the company insolvent. This is known as insolvent trading and is governed by ss 588G and 588H. Replacing s 592(1), s 588G(1) and (2) provide that directors contravene the section if they fail to prevent the company from incurring a debt when:

- they were a director of the company;
- the company was insolvent or incurring the debt rendered the company insolvent;
- there were reasonable grounds to suspect the company was insolvent or would become insolvent; and
- the director was aware of these grounds or a reasonable director in a like position in a company in the company's circumstances would be aware.

Insolvency

[10.810] Section 588G requires the company to have incurred a debt and that the company was either insolvent or the debt rendered it insolvent. A company is insolvent if it cannot meet its debts as and when they fall due: s 95A. In determining a company's solvency under s 95A regard must be had to:

- the company's existing debts; and
- debts it will incur in the near future.

[10.820] The legislation is not, however, concerned with temporary problems with cash flow. As the court asserted in *Brooks v Heritage Hotel Adelaide Pty Ltd* (1996) 20 ACSR 61 at 64, 'it should not be forgotten that the statutory focus is on solvency and not liquidity'. To this end the courts have taken a very practical approach to the concept of insolvency and will have regard to:

- the company's ability to borrow money;
- the company's ability to realise assets;
- promises of injections of capital;
- whether the creditor would extend credit to the company.

[10.830] Proof of the company's insolvency is assisted in civil proceedings by s 588E which introduces rebuttable presumptions of insolvency. Under s 588E(3), where it is proved that the company was insolvent during the 12 months ending on the 'relation-back day',[1] it will be presumed that the company was insolvent throughout the entire period. Under s 588E(4) where a company has failed to maintain accounting records in the manner prescribed by s 286(1) or (2), the com-

---

1   Defined in s 9, which includes the date of filing the application for winding up.

pany will be presumed to have been insolvent throughout the relevant period. Finally, if in earlier proceedings under Part 5.7B it was proved that the company was insolvent at a particular time, s 588E(8) provides that it may be presumed that the company was insolvent at that time for the purpose of other proceedings.

Debt

[10.840] It will be apparent s 588G requires the incurring of a debt. In the absence of a debt, s 558G does not apply. Thus, in *Perkins v Viney* [2001] SASC 362, the court accepted that some of the amounts claimed by the liquidator in that case, such as donations and voluntary payments, were not debts.

[10.850] However, in determining the debts that may be taken into account, s 588G(1A) assists by deeming certain actions to be, in essence, 'deemed debts'. These acts include the paying of a dividend, a reduction in share capital and the provision of financial assistance for the acquisition of shares. Section 588F(1) has a similar effect by clarifying the previous position and ensuring that a company's liability to remit certain taxes is considered a debt once the deduction of that tax has been made.

[10.860] Note, under the *Corporations Law Amendment (Employee Entitlements) Act* 2000 (Cth), the operation of s 588G is extended to certain 'non-debt' transactions in a bid to increase the protection of employee entitlements. The *Corporations Law Amendment (Employee Entitlements) Act* 2000 (Cth) also seeks to increase the protection of employee entitlements by introducing new Part 5.8A into the *Corporations Act*. This new Part introduces a prohibition against entering into agreements or transactions with the intention (or part intention) of avoiding the payment of employee entitlements. A breach of the section gives rise to criminal liability and, if the company is being wound up and the employees suffer a loss because of the breach, the person is also liable to pay compensation.

'Incurring' a debt

[10.870] Another prerequisite to the operation of the legislation is the 'incurring' of the relevant debt(s). When a debt is incurred is important to the operation of the legislation because the company must either be insolvent when the debt was incurred or the debt(s) rendered the company insolvent. A company incurs a debt 'when by its choice, it does or omits something which, as a matter of substance and commercial reality, renders it liable for a debt for which it would not otherwise have been liable': *Leigh-Mardon Pty Ltd v Wawn* (1995) 13 ACLC 1244; *Standard Chartered Bank of Australia Ltd v Antico* (1995) 13 ACLC 1381 at 1429; *Credit Corporation Australia Pty Ltd v Atkins* (1999) 17 ACLC 756. While the matter has not been definitively determined, it appears a debt may be incurred even though it is contingent and the amount involved is uncertain; *Metropolitan Fire Systems Pty Ltd v Miller* (1997) 23 ACSR 699 at 705.

[10.880] In determining when a debt was incurred, the 'deemed debt' provisions again assist. Section 588G(1A) not only deems certain acts by a company to be a debt, but also specifies when the debt was incurred. For example, the section states that a reduction in share capital is a debt and it occurs when the reduction takes effect. Similarly, as noted above, s 588F(1) provides that a company incurs a debt when it deducts an amount which it is liable to remit under the legislation specified in s 588F(2).

Objective test

[10.890] Directors do not contravene s 588G, however, just because the company is insolvent. There must also be reasonable grounds to suspect that the company is insolvent when the debt was incurred: s 588G(1)(c). Moreover, the director must be aware of these grounds of suspicion, or a reasonable director would be aware of the grounds: s 588G(2). Directors will be adjudged according to the diligence and involvement expected under the *Corporations Act*, rather than the actual knowledge of the subject director: *Metropolitan Fire Systems Pty Ltd v Miller* (1997) 23 ACSR 699 at 702-703.

[10.900] The inclusion in s 588G(2) of the phrase 'in a like position in a company in the company's circumstances' ensures, however, that the particular circumstances of the company and the director's particular position will continue to be relevant in determining what is reasonable. Cf *Sheahan (as Liq SA Service Stations Pty Ltd) v Verco & Hodge* (2001) 19 ACLC 814.

[10.910] The language used in s 588G makes it clear that the director need not actually be involved in the incurring of the debt before s 588G will be triggered: *Rema Industries & Services Pty Ltd v Coad* (1992) 107 ALR 374 at 381-382; *Re New World Alliance Pty Ltd; Sycotex Pty Ltd v Baseler (No 2)* (1994) 122 ALR 531; *Hawcroft General Trading Co Ltd v Edgar* (1996) 20 ACSR 541 at 548. It is the director's failure to prevent the company incurring the debt that is the crux for the attraction of liability.

Defences

[10.920] The defences previously detailed in s 592(2) have been replaced by more specific defences provided for in s 588H(2)-(5). Under s 588H(2), if the director had reasonable grounds to expect, and did expect, when the debt was incurred that the company was solvent and would remain solvent, such expectation will provide a defence. The defence will only be available where the director has taken steps to monitor the company's finances and can point to objectively reasonable grounds that indicate that the company was solvent. See the extracts of *Metropolitan Fire Systems Pty Ltd v Miller* (1997) 23 ACSR 699 at 711-713 below.

[10.930] Section 588H(3) accords a defence where directors believed the company to be solvent on the basis of information provided by third parties to whom they had delegated responsibility for monitoring the company's solvency, as long it was reasonable for them to believe that that person was competent and reliable and that the responsibility was being fulfilled by that person. See again the extracts of *Metropolitan Fire Systems Pty Ltd v Miller* (1997) 23 ACSR 699 below.

[10.940] If the director did not take part in the management of the corporation at that time because of illness or some other good reason, a defence is accorded by s 588H(4). This defence will not allow a director who has failed to meet the standard of care expected of directors to hide behind his or her ignorance by claiming they did not take part in the management of the corporation: *Metropolitan Fire Systems Pty Ltd v Miller* (1997) 23 ACSR 699; *Tourprint International Pty Ltd (in liq) v Bott* (1999) 17 ACLC 1543 at 1556.

[10.950] Finally, if the director took all reasonable steps to prevent the company incurring the debt, s 588H(5) provides a defence to an action under s 588G. To rely on this defence, the director must have taken unequivocal action either to prevent the debt being incurred or to bring the matter to the attention of those who have authority to prevent the debt being incurred. In considering the availability of this defence, s 588H(6) provides that regard is to be had, *inter alia*, to:

- any action the director took with a view to appointing an administrator;
- when that action was taken; and
- the results of that action.

The most detailed discussion of these defences is contained in *Metropolitan Fire Systems Pty Ltd v Miller* (1997) 23 ACSR 699.

Metropolitan Fire Systems Pty Ltd v Miller
Federal Court of Australia: Einfeld J
(1997) 23 ACSR 699

The respondents were directors of a company, Raydar. In December 1993 another company, Reed, subcontracted work to Raydar. At this point Raydar's creditors had been demanding payment of money. A director of Raydar, Miller, arranged for the applicant company, Metropolitan, to do some of the work for Reed as a subcontractor. The contract was entered into on 22 December 1993. Metropolitan completed the work. On 24 February 1994 Miller assured Metropolitan that it would be paid soon because it expected payment from Reed shortly. A supplier, Turk, served a statutory demand for payment of a debt and a winding-up application on the company. Raydar owed this company over $100,000.

Metropolitan thereafter commenced proceedings against the directors of Raydar with the permission of the liquidators. Miller was the first respondent. The second respondent was Miller's wife. She was also employed by the company as a casual clerk. The third respondent was Mr Ewins. He was also employed by the company as a full-time electrician. All three respondents asserted that there were reasonable grounds to expect the company was solvent within s 588H(2) and Mrs Miller and Mr Ewins asserted they had delegated their responsibilities to Mr Miller within s 588H(3).

Einfeld J held that none of the defences under s 588H was established. In the subject case there were no reasonable grounds to expect that the company was solvent. The court also rejected the second and third respondents' submission that they relied on Miller with respect to the company's affairs, including informing them as to the state of the company's finances, within s 588H(3). Mrs Miller must have known that the company was, at best, in trouble. Moreover, both respondents' evidence was that their belief that the company was solvent was not based on the information put to them by Miller. Mrs Miller's belief as to the company's solvency was based on her own impressions. Most importantly, both had failed to inquire of Miller as to the financial state of the company. Moreover, there were no reasonable grounds to believe that Mr Miller was fulfilling the responsibility of providing Mrs Miller and Mr Ewins with adequate information.

Einfeld J: **[711]** The onus of proof for these defences is on the director seeking to rely on them who must establish the elements of the defences on the balance of probabilities. The grounds on which the director forms the view as to the company's solvency or otherwise must be reasonable. This implies an objective consideration of the grounds viewed against all circumstances and not whether, when looked at from the point of view of the director in question, the grounds appear reasonable.

The defences under section 588H require that there be reasonable grounds to 'expect', as opposed to 'suspect', solvency as provided in section 588G. From the cases in which the meaning of these words has been considered, it would appear that to 'suspect' something requires a lower threshold of knowledge or awareness than to 'expect' it: see a discussion on 'to suspect' by Kitto J in *Queensland Bacon Pty Ltd v Rees* (1966) 115 CLR 266 at 303; and *3M Australia* at 192. The expectation must be differentiated from mere hope in order to satisfy this defence: *Dunn v Shapowloff* [1978] NSWLR 235. It implies a measure of confidence that the company is solvent. The directors must have reasonable grounds for regarding it as likely that the company would at the relevant date have been able to pay its debts as and when they fall due.

The respondents claimed under subsection (2) that at the time Raydar incurred the debt to Metropolitan, they had reasonable grounds to expect, and did expect, that the company was solvent and would remain solvent even if it incurred that particular debt. In light of the evidence, however, it cannot be said objectively that there were reasonable grounds to expect that this would be the case. There was no reason to believe that Reed would pay Raydar any money in the short term, and Raydar's creditors had already begun to take an ominous and aggressive attitude towards the company's persistent disputation of accounts. These factors, in addition to the situation brought about by the actions of Turks, and the unlikelihood that either the company or the directors could raise further significant funds, show that at the time Raydar incurred the debt to Metropolitan, there were no reasonable grounds to expect that Raydar would be able to pay this or any other debts as and when they fell due. Any optimism regarding the company's future was based on hope rather than reasonable expectations. Therefore, I reject the defence raised under section 588H(2) in respect to all three defendants.

The second and third respondents also raised defences under section 588H(3). It is now settled that directors have a positive duty to take an active part in the affairs **[712]** of the company to the extent that they should be aware of what is going on in the company ...

Patricia Miller and Leonard Ewins asserted that they had relied on Raymond Miller with respect to the running of Raydar's affairs, including informing them on the state of the company's finances. They said that he was responsible for the day to day running of the company and for providing them with all necessary information about its affairs. They asserted that, as far as they were aware, he was fulfilling those responsibilities and that, on the basis of the information he provided, they expected that the company would remain solvent if and when it incurred the debt to Metropolitan.

Patricia Miller, as well as being a director, was employed by the company as a full time casual clerk performing banking, some invoicing and general banking duties from home. She typed the invoices but claimed that she did not take in the details. Mrs Miller also sometimes made phone calls regarding debt collection, but she claimed not to be aware of the details of these debts or the difficulties being experienced in recovering them. She claimed to be unaware of the dispute with Turks or the company's liability to the Tax Office, although she was aware of the mortgages granted over the family home and the factory unit. Mrs Miller also admitted that she was aware that the company was reducing its staff although this apparently caused her no concern. More importantly, there is no evidence of her inquiring of her husband, the director of the company on whom she relied for information about the company, as to the state of the company's finances.

Contrary to her assertion, required for her defence to succeed, and to some of her own statements, the evidence leads to the conclusion that Mrs Miller's opinion that the company was trading profitably and was solvent was not based on information provided by her husband at all but on her own observations as part of her duties: she saw "plenty of banking and invoices going out". She may have believed that her husband would inform her if the company was in trouble but as a director she had a duty to take an interest in and demand information on the financial state of the company, especially as she undoubtedly knew that it was at best "in trouble". As a working director, she had a duty to observe and draw reasonable and obvious conclusions from facts coming to her attention.

I accept that Mrs Miller lacked detailed knowledge of the financial situation of Raydar, but I cannot find that there were and that she had reasonable grounds to believe that Mr Miller was fulfilling the responsibility of providing adequate information to his co-director. I therefore reject her defence raised under section 588H(3). In respect to Leonard Ewins, the reasons for rejecting this defence are even stronger. ...

[713] As a person working on Raydar projects and having contact with suppliers, Mr Ewins could reasonably have been expected to know of the attitudes of some of the suppliers towards Raydar's slow payment of debts and also of the difficulties Raydar was having in obtaining payment for jobs. There did not exist reasonable grounds on which Mr Ewins could rely to support a belief that Raymond Miller was providing adequate information on Raydar's solvency at the time of the Metropolitan contract. As a director, he had an obligation to inquire as to the financial health of Raydar, yet so far as the evidence goes, he failed to make any demands for information at a time when his suspicions about the company's financial viability and survival should and would have been aroused. I therefore reject the defence raised by him under section 588H(3).

There is, in my view, no doubt that on 22 December 1993 when Raydar incurred the debt to Metropolitan, it was insolvent. It is my further opinion that on the same date reasonable grounds existed on which to base a suspicion, within the meaning of section 588G of the Corporations Law, that Raydar was insolvent, and that a reasonable director would have been aware of these grounds. I do not accept the defences on which the respondents relied. All other conditions precedent to an order as sought by Metropolitan pursuant to sections 588M and 588R have been satisfied. I therefore find that the respondents contravened section 588G and that Metropolitan has established its entitlement to recover the debt owed by Raydar from the respondents, being directors of the company, under section 588M.

Consequences of breaching s 588G

Compensation

[10.960] In a manner similar to the consequences of a breach of s 181(1) detailed above, where a company is being wound up, a liquidator may initiate an action under s 588M(2) or under s 588J(2) join in an application for a civil penalty order brought by ASIC, seeking an order that the director compensate the company an amount that equates with the loss or damage suffered by a partly or wholly unsecured creditor. Even without the intervention of a liquidator, the court can make such an order against the guilty director where ASIC has brought civil penalty proceedings: s 588J(1). Such an order may be made whether or not the court imposes a penalty under s 1317G or makes a disqualifying order under s 206C: s 588J(1). If a criminal breach of s 588G has occurred within s 588G(3), the court may also order that the guilty director pay the company compensation under s 588K(1). Such an order may be made whether or not the court imposes some other penalty on the director: s 588K(1). See also s 588Y(1).

[10.970] Creditors have a limited right to personally bring an action under s 588M(3). The availability of this right is governed by Subdiv B which provides, in essence, that this may only occur where the liquidator fails to act under s 588M or the liquidator consents to the creditor's proceedings: ss 588R-588U.

Civil penalty

[10.980] As s 588G is a civil penalty provision (s 1317E(1)), the consequences detailed above with respect to s 181(1) are equally applicable.

Criminal offence

[10.990] As with the other statutory duties detailed above, a breach of s 588G will not give rise to a criminal penalty unless the director actually suspected the company was, or would be as a result of the debt, insolvent and the failure to prevent the debt being incurred was dishonest: s 588G(3).

Review question

Bourbon Ltd is an investment company, its primary activity being investment in real estate on the outskirts of Sydney. In 2000 Fred and Gertie, directors of Bourbon Ltd, on behalf of the company approached Yellow Ltd, a large national company interested in land development, with a view to the two companies entering into a joint venture to acquire and develop land in the vicinity of Sydney. After preliminary negotiations Yellow Ltd indicated that it was unwilling to deal with Bourbon Ltd and that it would deal only with Fred and Gertie personally. Fred and Gertie incorporated a company, Whisky Ltd, which acquired land in the vicinity of Sydney for development purposes and entered into a joint venture with Yellow Ltd. In 2001 Gertie decided she was too busy with Whisky Ltd and determined that she would become less involved in the affairs of Bourbon Ltd, leaving the management of the company to Fred. Last week she received a phone call from an angry creditor, demanding Bourbon Ltd pay money owed to him. After a little investigation, Gertie discovered that the solvency of Bourbon Ltd is now questionable.

Advise Fred and Gertie as to whether they will be liable to account for any profits made from the joint venture and any course of action they may take to prevent such. Advise Gertie as to any potential liability she faces for Bourbon Ltd's debts and any other breaches of directors' duties.

Further reading

Afterman, *Company Directors and Controllers* (LawBook Company, Sydney, 1970)
Baxt, 'Taking Up A Corporate Opportunity Without Proper Authority and Getting Some Reward For It!' (1997) 25 *ABLR* 369
Baxt, *The Corporate Law Economic Reform Program Act 1999; 'CLERP' Explained* (CCH Australia, Sydney, 2000)
Beck, 'The Saga of Peso Silver Mines: Corporate Opportunity Reconsidered' (1971) 49 *Can Bar Rev* 80
Cassidy, *Concise Corporations Law* (4th ed, Federation Press, Sydney, 2003) ch 10
Cassidy, 'An evaluation of s 232(4) and the Directors' Duty of Due Care, Skill and Diligence' (1995) 23 *ABLR* 201
Cassidy, 'Has the 'Sleeping' Director Finally Been Laid to Rest?' (1997) 25 *ABLR* 102
Cassidy, 'Standards of Conduct and Standards of Review: Divergence of the Duty of Care in the United States and Australia' (2000) 28(3) *ABLR* 180
Cassidy, '"Sexually Transmitted Debts': The Scope of Defences to Directors' Liability for Insolvent Trading' (2002) 20(7) *C&SLJ* 372
Clarke, 'The Business Judgment Rule: Good Corporate Governance or Not?' (2000) 12 *AJCL* 85
Corkery, *Directors' Powers and Duties* (Longman Cheshire, Melbourne, 1987)
De Mott, 'Directors' Duty of Care Under the Business Judgment Rule: American Precedents, Australian Cases' (1992) 16 *C&SLJ* 575
Farrar, 'Legal Issues Involving Corporate Groups' (1998) 16 *C&SLJ* 184

Farrar, 'Business Judgment and Defensive Tactics in Hostile Takeover Bids' (1989) 15 *Can Bus LJ* 15
Finn (ed), Equity in Commercial Relationships (1987)
Ford, Austin and Ramsay, *Ford's Principles of Corporations Law* (11th ed, Butterworths, Sydney, 2003) chs 8 and 9
Fridman, 'An Analysis of the Proper Purpose Rule' (1998) 10 *Bond LR* 164
Gillooly (ed), *The Law Relating to Corporate Groups* (Federation Press, Sydney, 1993)
Hammond, 'Insolvent Companies and Employees: The Government's Year 2000 Solutions' (2000) 8 *ILJ* 86
Heath, 'The Corporations Law, Section 181: A Two-Edged Sword' (2000) 18 *C&SLJ* 377
Langton and Trotman, 'Defining the 'Best Interest of the Corporation': Some Australian Reform Proposals' (1999) 3 *Flinders Journal of Law Reform* 163
McConvill, 'Directors' Duties to Creditors in Australia after Spies v The Queen' (2002) 20 *C&SLJ* 4
Mitchell, 'The Concept of Honesty under s 232(2) of the Corporations Law' (1994) 12 *C&SLJ* 231
Ramsay (ed), *Corporate Governance and the Duties of Company Directors* (Centre for Corporate Law and Securities Regulation, Melbourne, 1997)
Ramsay and Stapledon, 'Corporate Groups in Australia' (2001) 29 *ABLR* 7
Senate Standing Committee on Legal and Constitutional Affairs, *Company Directors' Duties – Report on the Social and Fiduciary Responsibilities and Obligations of Company Directors* (AGPS, Canberra, 1989)

11

Meetings

Overview

Corporate decision-making generally occurs in two main forums, board meetings and general meetings. Circumstances, however, may require the convening of other types of meetings, such as meetings of classes of shareholders. This chapter concentrates on board meetings and general meetings, although many of the principles governing these meetings will be equally applicable to other types of meetings.

The *Corporations Act* 2001 (Cth) (*'Corporations Act'*) and any corporate constitution will require that certain matters be sanctioned in particular types of meeting. The Act and the constitution will also regulate the conduct of these meetings. Compliance with these rules is crucial to ensuring the validity of meetings and the resolutions passed therein. This chapter examines the relevant provisions of the *Corporations Act* governing the convening of meetings and the procedural requirements underlying the conduct of these meetings.

The chapter begins by examining what constitutes a meeting and how members/directors may attend such meetings. It will be seen that while at common law meetings must be attended in person (*Re Southern Resources Ltd* (1989) 15 ACLR 770 at 793-794), the *Corporations Act* reflects the technological advances of today and facilitates the conduct of meetings in modes other than face to face.

The chapter then considers directors' meetings and general meetings in turn, examining matters such as how they are convened and the prerequisites for the valid passage of resolutions.

What Constitutes a Meeting?

More than one person

[11.10] At common law, the notion of a meeting implies 'a coming together of more than one person': *Sharp v Dawes* (1876) 2 QBD 26 at 29.

[11.20] There are some exceptions/modifications to this rule. First, where a single person can hold all of a class of shares, a single shareholder may constitute a class meeting: *East v Bennett* [1911] 1 Ch 163 at 169. Second, as discussed below, under ss 249G and 1319 the courts may direct, *inter alia*, that a meeting attended by one person constitutes a valid meeting. Third, as noted below, in the case of single shareholder/director companies, under ss 248B and 249B resolutions may be passed without a meeting by recording the resolution and signing the record.

Meeting in person

[11.30] At common law, unless the corporate constitution otherwise provides, a meeting must be attended in person. Thus, an absent director or member may not appoint another as his or her proxy (*Re Portuguese Consolidated Copper Mines Ltd* (1889) 42 Ch D 160 at 165-166), nor attend by telephone: *Re Southern Resources Ltd* (1989) 15 ACLR 770 at 793-794.

[11.40] Section 249X, however, provides for the appointment of proxies to represent members' interests at general meetings. This is a replaceable rule for proprietary companies and a mandatory rule for public companies. In addition, the courts have power under ss 249G and 1319 to direct, *inter alia*, that a meeting attended by a proxy constitutes a valid meeting. Proxies are discussed in more detail below.

[11.50] Section 248D facilitates the conduct of board meetings other than in person. This section provides that a directors' meeting may be called or held using any technology consented to by all directors. The consent may be a standing one that may only be withdrawn within a reasonable period before the meeting: s 248D. Similarly, s 249S allows the use of technology in holding a meeting of members at two or more venues. This is, however, dependent upon the technology providing the members as a whole with a reasonable opportunity to participate in the meeting. Section 1322(3A), discussed below, details the consequences when a member has not been given a reasonable opportunity to participate in a meeting held at two or more venues.

Resolutions and declarations without meetings

[11.60] In *Parker & Cooper Ltd v Reading* [1926] Ch 975 at 982-983, Astbury J held that a general meeting of shareholders is not necessary if all members assent to the transaction providing that the action was *intra vires* (within power) and honest. Similarly, at common law the unanimous, but informal, agreement of all directors may be deemed equivalent to the passage of such a resolution in a board meeting: *In re Bonelli's Telegraph Co (Collie's Claim)* (1871) LR 12 Eq 246. Section 249A(7) preserves the abovementioned common law principles allowing for informal assent of matters by members.

[11.70] To some extent these common law rules are now embodied in the *Corporations Act*. If all members of a proprietary company entitled to vote agree in writing to a resolution, the resolution will be deemed to have been passed without holding a general meeting: s 249A(2) and (6). See further s 249A. Under replaceable rule, s 248A(1), directors may pass a resolution without a directors' meeting being held if all directors entitled to vote sign a document stating that they are in favour of the resolution set out in the document. See further s 248A. Also, as noted above, resolutions may be passed by single director/ member companies under ss 248B and 249B by that person recording the resolution and signing the record.

Board Meetings

Convening board meetings

[11.80] Under replaceable rule, s 248C, any director may convene a board meeting by giving reasonable notice to every other director.

[11.90] Meetings do not need to be conducted at the company's registered office. If all directors are in attendance and in agreement, they may turn an informal gathering elsewhere into a board meeting: *Swiss Screens (Australia) Pty Ltd v Burgess* (1987) 11 ACLR 756 at 758; *Versteeg v R* (1988) 14 ACLR 1 at 14; *Poliwka v Heven Holdings Pty Ltd* (1992) 10 ACLC 641 at 646. Thus, board meetings do not have to be conducted with any degree of formality: *Swiss Screens* at 758; *Poliwka* at 646.

[11.100] However, the directors must be aware that the discussions constitute a meeting: *Petsch v Kennedy* [1971] 1 NSWLR 494; *Poliwka* at 646.

Poliwka v Heven Holdings Pty Ltd
Supreme Court of Western Australia: Anderson J
(1992) 10 ACLC 641

Mr Boccamazzo ('B') and his spouse became bankrupt on their own petitions in 1991. Through the agency of his bookkeeper, Mrs Mamouney ('M'), B acquired a shelf company, Heven Holdings Pty Ltd ('Heven') in 1989. B and M held the two issued shares in the company and were appointed directors of the company. M was appointed secretary. M was to stand in as shareholder and director until B found a purpose for the company. In mid-1989, B was advised to set up a corporate entity to act as trustee for a family trust. B approached his sister and a business associate, Mr Poliwka ('P'), to become directors of the proposed trustee company. B intended to use Heven as the trustee company. To make suitable arrangements, B met M, at a cafe, with a blank transfer form that he wished her to sign to transfer her share in Heven. B also signed another transfer form later on that day. The details on the transfer forms were filled in after all the signatures were gathered. A minute was prepared which purported to record a meeting between B and M that was allegedly held at the registered office of the company at which the prospective trustees were also present. The transfers were never registered. In late 1989 Heven acquired a controlling interest in another company, Golden Park Pty Ltd ('Golden'), that B used to conduct his business activities. Creditors appointed P as trustee of the bankrupt estates. P held B's share in Heven in his capacity as trustee of B's bankrupt estate. M also signed a share transfer concerning Heven in P's favour as trustee for B's spouse's bankrupt estate and resigned as a director. Consequently, the company was without directors. P considered himself sole shareholder and in that capacity purported to convene a meeting appointing other directors. At a later directors' meeting, the new directors petitioned for the winding up of Golden. P was appointed provisional liquidator.

A question arose about the legal and beneficial ownership of the two shares issued by Golden. B contended that P did not have any right to wind up the company. This in turn raised the question as to whether the meeting in the cafe had constituted a directors' meeting between M and B approving the transfer of the shares.

The court held that the luncheon conversation between B and M did not constitute a meeting of the directors of Heven. While a meeting may be conducted without great formality, there must at least be an intention that the occasion be a directors' meeting and an awareness by the persons present that they are concurring in their capacity as directors in the management of the affairs of their company. In this case that intention was found to be absent. As the transfers were never registered there had been no transfer of shares to the prospective trustees.

Anderson J: **[645]** I do not believe there was anything in the nature of a directors' meeting at the North Road Cafe. It would be wholly unreal to characterise **[646]** the luncheon conversation between these two people as a meeting whereby the directors of Heven Holdings Pty Ltd met to transact the business of the company. It may be accepted that much latitude is given to directors of private companies in regard to the formalities that should attend their corporate activities. *Swiss Screens (Australia) Pty Ltd v Burgess* (1987) 5 ACLC 1,076; *Petsch v Kennedy* [1971] 1 NSWLR 494; *Collie's Claim* (1871) LR 12 Eq 246. But I think there must at least be an intention that the occasion be a directors' meeting and an awareness by the persons present that they are concurring, in their capacity as directors, in the management of the affairs of their company. I do not consider those elements to have been present in the meeting between Mr Boccamazzo and Mrs Mamouney at the cafe. There was not that kind of animus. If anything, it was a meeting between a cestui que trust and his bare trustee, at which the former called for a transfer of the trust property. I think that Mr Boccamazzo's intention was to do no more than request and obtain a blank transfer and Mrs Mamouney's intention was to do no more than comply with that request, as she was indeed bound to do. That, I think, is all that happened at the North Road Cafe. I do not believe she was asked to or intended to do anything in her capacity as a director of Heven Holdings Pty Ltd. I do not believe their evidence to the contrary. If Mr Boccamazzo discussed the proposed structure of his family trust with Mrs Mamouney and if the names of Mrs Padula and Mr Poliwka were mentioned by him, it was not with the object of obtaining anything in the nature of agreement or consent.

The conclusion I have reached that the meeting between these two people at the North Road Cafe was not a directors' meeting is partly based on the nature of the relationship between them. I have reached the firm conclusion that neither Mrs Mamouney nor Mr Boccamazzo regarded Mrs Mamouney as anything but a nominee or, in the language of equity, a bare trustee of her entire interest in the company. However there is other evidence. There is the false minute of 10 July 1989. That minute, although unsigned purports to record a meeting between Mr Boccamazzo and Mrs Mamouney at the registered office of the company at which Mr Poliwka and Mrs Padula were in attendance. ...

The minute purports to record that the meeting commenced at 1:30 pm and concluded 2:00 pm. It is common ground that no such meeting took place. However the existence of the minute is not altogether without significance on the question whether there had been a directors' meeting on 29 July, at which the same business is claimed to have been transacted. The minute tells against there having been any earlier meeting with respect to those matters. If there had been, there was simply no need to type up a bogus minute, false from beginning to end.

In my opinion, nothing happened on 29 June to work any change in the structure or affairs of Heven Holdings Pty Ltd. Mr Boccamazzo and Mrs Mamouney remained as the shareholders and directors of the company and Mrs Mamouney continued to hold her legal estate in the share in her name in trust for Mr Boccamazzo. The signing by Mrs Mamouney of the blank transfer did not of itself have any effect in law. It was a step in an incomplete transfer of the legal estate in the share, the beneficial interest in which she already held in trust for him.

Notice

[11.110] As noted above, reasonable notice must be given of a directors' meeting under replaceable rule, s 248C. What is reasonable, however, is determined in light of the company's particular 'structure, practice and affairs': *Petsch v Kennedy* [1971] 1 NSWLR 494. Moreover, if a director does not object to a lack of notice, but rather participates in a meeting, he/she will be taken to have impliedly waived the need for such notice: *Petsch v Kennedy*.

[11.120] While it has been considered unnecessary to include an agenda with the notice (*Toole v Flexihire Pty Ltd* (1991) 6 ACSR 455 at 461; *Bell v Burton* (1993) 12 ACSR 325 at 329; *Electro Research v Stec* (1996) 20 ACSR 320 at 351), in *Jenashare Pty Ltd v Lemrib Pty Ltd* (unreported, NSWSC, Young J, 1993), Young J asserted that a notice 'must contain in clear language a full summary of the business with which the meeting is convened to deal'.

[11.130] The manner in which notice of board meetings is to be served on directors is usually determined by the constitution. Thus, in *Jenashare Pty Ltd v Lemrib Pty Ltd* (unreported, NSWSC, Young J, 1993) Young J held that where the constitution requires that notice of a board meeting be served personally or by post, it is insufficient to give notice by facsimile.

[11.140] Note, where a meeting is invalid by reason of lack of notice, yet the meeting is deliberately held despite the lack of notice, this is not a 'procedural irregularity' which can be rectified under s 1322, as discussed below: *Electro Research v Stec* (1996) 20 ACSR 320 at 351.

Attendance at board meetings

[11.150] Every director has a right to attend board meetings and an improper exclusion may be injuncted: *Pulbrook v Richmond Consolidated Mining Co* (1878) 9 Ch D 610 at 612, 613 and 616. Equally, a director may not be forced to participate in a meeting held in inappropriate circumstances, such as a railway station platform: *Barron v Potter* [1914] 1 Ch 895. As noted above, however, if the director fails to object, the gathering may constitute a valid meeting: *Petsch v Kennedy* [1971] 1 NSWLR 494.

Quorum

[11.160] For a board meeting to be valid a minimum number of directors, a quorum, must be present: *Clamp v Fairway Investments Pty Ltd* [1973] CLC 27,599 at 27,613. The quorum for board meetings is specified in replaceable rule, s 248F, as two directors, unless the directors otherwise determine. It is unclear whether the directors may prescribe the quorum to be one director, as suggested in *Re Fireproof Doors Ltd* [1916] 2 Ch 142 at 149, given the common law definition of a meeting requires at least two persons: *Sharp v Dawes* (1876) 2 QBD 26 at 29.

[11.170] If s 248F was displaced by a constitution that did not prescribe a quorum or how it was to be determined, a majority of board members (*York Tramways Co Ltd v Willows* (1882) 8 QBD 685 at 695 and 698) or the number of directors who usually conducted meetings (*Re Tavistock Ironworks Co Ltd* (*Lyster's* case) (1867) LR 4 Eq 233 at 237) may constitute a quorum.

[11.180] In determining whether a quorum exists only those directors 'capable of voting on the business before the board' may be counted: *Re Greymouth Point Elizabeth Railway and Coal Co Ltd* [1904] 1 Ch 32 at 34-35. As discussed in Chapter 10, a director may be prevented from voting because of a conflict of interest. See further the discussion in Chapter 10 as to the steps that may be taken when because of these principles a quorum does not exist.

[11.190] Note again that in single director companies, board resolutions may be made by a single director under s 248B without a meeting.

Voting

[11.200] Under the constitution, the directors are usually accorded one vote each at board meetings. Matters are determined by a majority of votes of directors present and voting: replaceable rule, s 248G(1). Where the voting result is equal, the chairperson is also usually given a casting vote: replaceable rule, s 248G(2).

Again, see Chapter 10 for a discussion of the constraints imposed on directors' voting power where there is a conflict of interest.

Minutes

[11.210] Under s 251A(1)(b) and (2) (former s 258(1)), minutes of board meetings must be recorded in a book, signed by the chairperson of the meeting or the chairperson of the next succeeding meeting, within one month of the meeting. Resolutions passed by directors without a meeting and declarations by single director proprietary companies must be similarly recorded: s 251A(1)(d) and (e).

[11.220] These books must be kept at the company's registered office, principal place of business or such other place approved by ASIC: s 251A(5) (former s 259(1)). The minute books of board meetings do not appear to be open to inspection by members as s 251B (former s 259(1)) confines the right of access to the minutes of members' meetings.

[11.230] The minutes provide evidence of the business transacted at the meeting to which they relate, unless the contrary is proved: s 251A(6) (former s 258(2)).

Annual General Meeting

Obligation to convene annual general meeting

[11.240] The requirement to hold an Annual General Meeting ('AGM') is confined to public companies. A public company's first AGM must be held within 18 months of being incorporated: s 250N(1). Subsequent AGMs must be held at least once each calendar year and within five months of the end of the financial year: s 250N(2). On application of the company, ASIC has authority under s 250P to grant an extension of time to hold such meetings.

Convening an annual general meeting

[11.250] As noted above, the directors are usually conferred with the authority to convene any meeting, including the AGM. Under replaceable rule, s 249C, a single director of a company may convene a meeting of the company's members. Under s 249CA, a director of a listed company has such power notwithstanding anything to the contrary in the company's constitution. As with all the board's powers, the power to convene a meeting must be exercised in good faith for the benefit of the company and for a proper purpose: *Permagon Press Ltd v Maxwell* [1970] 1 WLR 1167 at 1172. See also s 249Q.

Agenda

[11.260] The business to be conducted at the AGM is ordinarily determined by the constitution. Under s 250R, this may include a consideration of the annual financial report, directors' and auditor's reports, election of directors, appointment of auditor and fixing of the auditor's remuneration even if these matters are not referred to in the notice of meeting. These matters are called 'ordinary business'. Other matters are called 'special business'.

[11.270] In addition, the chairperson will usually make a general statement at the meeting as to the company's affairs. Under ss 250S, 250SA and 250T the chairperson must also allow the members a reasonable opportunity to ask questions or make comment upon the management of the company, the remuneration report (discussed further in Chapter 9) and the conduct of the audit and preparation of the auditor's report.

General Meetings

Directors' power to convene a general meeting

[11.280] General meetings of members, other than an AGM, are known as extraordinary meetings. The directors' general power to convene meetings, specified in ss 249C and 249CA, provides the board or a single director with authority to call a meeting of the company's members. Again this power must be exercised in good faith for the benefit of the company and for a proper purpose: *Permagon Press Ltd v Maxwell* [1970] 1 WLR 1167 at 1172; *NRMA Ltd v Snodgrass* (2001) 19 ACLC 769; 19 ACLC 1675. See also s 249Q. To this end it should be noted that the directors must not nominate a time or place that will prevent a particular member attending: *Smith v Sadler* (1997) 15 ACLC 1683.

Members requisitioning a general meeting under s 249D

Who may requisition a general meeting under s 249D?

[11.290] Pursuant to s 249D(1), the directors must comply with a request for a general meeting when presented with a written requisition by members who either:

- hold 5% or more of the votes that may be cast at a general meeting; or
- number 100 or more and are entitled to vote at the general meeting.

Importantly, as this is not a replaceable rule, this provision operates notwithstanding anything in the corporate constitution. Under s 249D(1A), however, the Regulations may vary the number of members entitled to requisition such a meeting. To date no Regulations have been passed modifying s 249D(1).

Basis for requisitioning general meeting

[11.300] A meeting of a company must be held for a proper purpose: s 249Q. Thus, the requisition's objective must be 'to have the resolutions passed and not simply to harass the company and its directors': *Humes Ltd v Unity APA Ltd* (1987) 5 ACLC 15 at 19, Moreover, 'if the sole object of a requisition is to do something which cannot be lawfully effectuated at a meeting' because it is in the realm of the directors' management powers, as discussed in Chapter 9, the board is entitled to refuse to convene the meeting: *Queensland Press Ltd v Academy Investments No 3 Pty Ltd* (1987) 5 ACLC 175 at 178. Similarly, the court may on this basis refuse to convene a meeting under s 249G, discussed below: *Maxwell Gratton v Carlton Football Club* [2004] VSC 379.

Notice

[11.310] The directors must call the meeting within 21 days after the request is given to the company: s 249D(5). The meeting must be held not later than two months after the request: s 249D(5).

Members' right to convene general meeting

[11.320] If the directors do not comply with the members' requisition within 21 days, members with more than 50% of the total voting rights of all the members that made the request may proceed to convene the meeting themselves: s 249E(1). Such members must convene the meeting, however, within three months of the requisition: s 249E(1). See further s 249E(1).

[11.330] To activate s 249E(1), there must be a failure on the part of the directors. Section 249E(1) will not, therefore, facilitate shareholders convening a meeting where the company has no directors: *Re Totex-Adon Pty Ltd* (1980) ACLC ¶40-617.

Members convening a general meeting under s 249F

[11.340] Section 249E is supplemented by s 249F(1). This provides that members holding no less than 5% of the votes that may be cast at a meeting may convene a general meeting. Unlike s 249E(3) and (4), under s 249F(1) the members calling the meeting must pay the expenses of calling and holding the meeting.

Court's power to order the convening of a general meeting under s 249G

Basis for an order convening a general meeting

[11.350] If it is impracticable to convene a meeting in any other way, a court may on the application of any director or voting member, order a meeting to be convened: s 249G(1) and (2). In exercising this power the court may give such ancillary or consequential directions as it thinks fit: s 1319. The power is discretionary and the court will only exercise this power where 'there is evidence that there is good reason to do so': *Jenashare Pty Ltd v Lemrib Pty Ltd* (unreported, NSWSC, Young J, 1993).

What is 'impracticable'?

[11.360] Section 249G(1) may be important where, for example, all members, or all but one member, are deceased. The courts' ancillary power under s 1319 allows a meeting to be held by a single remaining member, if any, or the legal personal representatives of the deceased members. The word impracticable is not synonymous with the word 'impossible': *In re El Sombrero Ltd* [1958] Ch 900 at 904. It does, however, require more than mere inconvenience; it must be genuinely impracticable to convene a meeting: *Omega Estates Pty Ltd v Ganke* (1963) 80 WN (NSW) 1218 at 1223. Moreover, s 249G may not be invoked simply because it is impracticable to convene a meeting in one of the usual ways: *Re Jeda Holdings Pty Ltd* (1977) 2 ACLR 438 at 442. Every normal or permitted method must be shown to be impracticable. Thus, in *Re Totex-Adon Pty Ltd* (1980) ACLC ¶40-617, it was not until the court determined that neither the predecessor to s 249E nor s 249F could be invoked that it exercised its power to order a meeting under the predecessor to s 249G.

Re Totex-Adon Pty Ltd
Supreme Court of New South Wales: Needham J
(1980) ACLC ¶40-617

Manly held three shares, while Marco held one share in the company. The company had failed to hold an AGM as was then required by the law and as a consequence the directors (Manly and Marco) ceased to hold office by operation of law. Marco refused to attend a meeting to re-establish the management of the company.

Manly consequently applied to the court seeking an order calling a meeting of the company pursuant to s 142 of the *Companies Act* (NSW) (now s 249G). The respondent (Marco) opposed the application on the ground that a meeting could be called by virtue of the power given by s 138 of the Act (now s 249F). The applicant argued that s 138 was inapplicable to the facts of the case as that section applied only where the articles made no provision at all for the calling of meetings. The company was a Table A company and the articles provided machinery for calling meetings.

The court agreed that s 138 did not apply as the articles of the company made provision for the calling of a meeting of the company. As it was 'impracticable' to call a meeting because the respondent refused to co-operate with the applicant in calling a meeting of the company the court made the order sought.

> **Needham J: [34,135]** The substantial question, therefore, is whether sec 138(1) applies to the present circumstances. The articles do make provision for the calling of meetings – art 44 – but those provisions cannot be effective to permit the calling of an extraordinary general meeting (nor, for that matter, can an annual general meeting be called – art 43). The respondent, however, submitted that "other provision in that behalf" means a provision inconsistent with the terms of sec 138(1). ...

[34,137] In my opinion, sec 138(1) should be construed in the following manner. One should look at the articles of the company and ascertain whether they make provision for the calling of a meeting of the company other than the provision made by sec 138(1). If they do, then sec 138 does not apply. If the provisions made by the articles are frustrated by the facts of the case, then one cannot resort to sec 138(1), but must resort to sec 142 (or, in the case of default in calling an annual general meeting, sec 136(4)).

Where there is no power, either in the Act or in the articles, which can be used in order to call a meeting of the company, the calling of such a meeting is, in my opinion, "impracticable". To adapt the words of Wynn-Parry J in *In re El Sombrero Ltd* [1958] Ch 900 at 904, one must "examine the circumstances of the particular case and answer the question whether, as a practical matter, the desired meeting of the company can be (convened)." The respondent has declined to act on the suggestion of the applicant, based on an interpretation of *In re Duomatic Ltd* [1969] 2 Ch 365, that a meeting of Class "A" shareholders should be held, and has put forward no alternative suggestion for regularising the company's activities, and there is no means whereby the applicant (or for that matter any shareholder) can secure the calling of the meeting. In such circumstances, it seems to me to be plain that the calling of the meeting is "impracticable".

Section 142 is couched in terms which appear to give the Court a discretion to make the order sought. The respondent, by cross-examination of the applicant, established that the blame for the failure to appoint directors in a proper manner and to call annual general meetings should be laid more at the applicant's door, as he was in charge (through his accountant) of the books of the company, than at the respondent's. While this may be so, I do not think that that fact disentitles the applicant to relief. It was further established, by the same procedure, that the applicant's purpose in making the application was to enable the election of directors and the ratification of the legal proceedings against the respondent. Again, I do not think that this fact disentitles the applicant to an order. The respondent called no evidence. ...

There is no evidence that the respondent will not attend a meeting ordered by the Court to be called, but, as the applicant has a majority of 3 to 1 in voting shares, it is likely that the respondent will not attend. I think there is substance in the applicant's submission that a quorum must consist of [34,138] members entitled to vote – if it were not so, validly convened meetings could be impotent if the members who attended were not entitled to vote. For this reason, I think it proper to make an order that, at the meeting to be called, the presence of one member holding "A" class shares shall constitute a quorum.

I do not think I should order the calling of a meeting of "A" class shareholders only. The members not entitled to vote are entitled to notice of the meeting and to attend the meeting – art 111, and *Re Compaction Systems Pty Ltd and the Companies Act* [1976] 2 NSWLR 477 at 485 ... Where a meeting is called pursuant to an order of the Court, that order can include directions as to its calling and conduct. In the present case, I think a direction should be given that the meeting should appoint an auditor unless all the members agree that it is not necessary for the company to do so.

See also *Maxwell Gratton v Carlton Football Club* [2004] VSC 379. The court refused to order a meeting under s 249G because there had been no valid request of the directors under s 249D. Thus, it was not impracticable to hold a meeting. The members could have requisitioned the meeting under s 249D and if the directors subsequently refused to hold the meeting, the members could have convened it under s 249E.

Notice of general meetings

Length of notice

[11.370] Written notice of not less than 21 days, or such longer period as is provided in the company's constitution, must be provided: ss 249H(1) and 249J(1). For listed companies 28 days' notice must be given of a meeting of its members: s 249HA(1).

[11.380] An AGM may be called on shorter notice if all members entitled to attend and vote agree beforehand: s 249H(2)(a). Similarly, any other general meeting may be called with shorter notice if members with at least 95% of the votes that may be cast agree beforehand: s 249H(2)(b). As noted in Chapter 9, shorter notice is not allowed where it is proposed to remove a director of a public company under s 203D, to appoint a director in place of a director removed under s 203D or to remove an auditor under s 329: s 249H(3) and (4).

[11.390] As also noted in Chapter 9, special notice must be given to remove a director of a public company under s 203D(2) or to remove an auditor under s 329(1A). Notice of the intention to move the resolution must be given to the company at least two months before the meeting is to be held: ss 203D(2) and 329(1A). As soon as practicable after receiving the notice the company is required to send a copy of the notice to the relevant director or auditor: ss 203D(3) and 329(2). Strangely, under ss 203D(2) and 329(2), these sections continue by providing that if the company calls a meeting after the notice of intention is given, the resolution may be passed even though the meeting is held less than two months after the notice of intention is given.

[11.400] Note that under s 1322, discussed below, procedural irregularities, such as the lack of appropriate notice, may be validated by the courts.

Service of notice

[11.410] Written notice of a meeting must be given to every member entitled to attend and vote at the meeting and to each director: s 249J(1). Notice may be served on a member:

- personally;
- by posting it to the member's address as shown in the register of members or an alternative address nominated by the member;
- by faxing it to the fax number or sending it to an electronic address nominated by the member; or
- by any other means permitted under the company's constitution: s 249J(3) and (3A).

[11.420] Under replaceable rule, s 249J(4), notice by post shall be deemed to have been effected three days after it was posted, while notice given by fax or other electronic means is taken to be given on the business day after it was sent.

[11.430] Failure to serve every member entitled to notice will, *prima facie*, render void any resolutions passed at the meeting. The constitution may provide, however, that a failure to serve members will not invalidate the proceedings. Such a clause will only validate an accidental omission to notify members: *Re Merchants and Shippers ss Co Ltd* (1916) 17 SR(NSW) 21 at 28-29. Section 1322, discussed below, may also be utilised to validate honest, accidental omissions: *Holmes v Life Funds of Australia Ltd* (1971-1973) ACLC 27,177 at 27,181.

Content of notice

[11.440] Under s 249L(a), notice of a general meeting must specify the place, date and time of the meeting and, where the meeting is to be held in two or more places, the technology that will be used to facilitate such. The notice must state the general nature of the business to be transacted at the meeting: s 249L(b). Under new s 249L(3) the notice must also be worded and presented in a 'clear, concise and effective manner'. New s 249LA provides that the contents otherwise required by s 249L may be excluded by the Regulations. To date no such Regulations have been passed.

[11.450] Note, the company's constitution will normally provide that it is not necessary for a notice of an annual general meeting to state that the business to be transacted at the meeting includes matters which fall into the category of 'ordinary business', discussed above. In such a case only detail of 'special business' need be included.

[11.460] If it is proposed that a special resolution will be passed at the meeting, the notice must set out an intention to propose a special resolution and state the resolution: s 249L(c). See also *Re Moorgate Mercantile Holdings Ltd* [1980] 1 All ER 40.

[11.470] If a member is entitled to appoint a proxy, the notice must contain a statement informing the member of the right, whether the proxy needs to be a member and that a member entitled to cast two or more votes may appoint two proxies and may specify the proportion or number of votes each proxy is appointed to exercise: s 249L(d).

[11.480] If a matter is not detailed in the notice (other than 'ordinary business') the members 'cannot proceed to any other matter without the unanimous consent of the whole body': *McLure v Mitchell* (1974) 6 ALR 471 at 494. A purported resolution on such a matter will be invalid unless all the shareholders of a company are present and agree to waive the formality: *Salomon v Salomon & Co* [1897] AC 22 at 57; *McLure v Mitchell* (1974) 6 ALR 471 at 494.

Directors' duty to provide sufficient information

[11.490] Notice of a meeting should contain sufficient accurate information as to the purpose of the meeting and proposed resolutions to enable a reasonable member to determine whether he or she should attend or appoint a proxy: *Fraser v NRMA Holdings Ltd* (1995) 127 ALR 543 at 554; *Electro Research v Stec* (1996) 20 ACSR 320 at 354-355. The directors are bound by their fiduciary duties not to mislead shareholders 'by providing them with material that is other than substantially full and true': *Devereaux Holdings Pty Ltd v Pelsart Resources NL (No 2)* (1986) 4 ACLC 12 at 14.

Devereaux Holdings Pty Ltd v Pelsart Resources NL
Supreme Court of New South Wales: Young J
(1986) 4 ACLC 12

Devereaux Holdings Pty Ltd ('Devereaux') was a shareholder in Pelsart Resources NL ('Pelsart'). Devereaux sought to have an allotment of shares by Pelsart to the Parry Corporation set aside. The allotment had been authorised by a resolution passed at a general meeting of Pelsart. Devereaux attacked the resolution on the basis that the notice convening the meeting contained inaccuracies which meant that the shareholders had not been properly informed.

The application was dismissed. While the court recognised that the directors had a fiduciary duty not to mislead the members by providing them with material that is other than substantially full and true, on the facts the notice was not misleading.

> **Young J: [14]** It is important to realise at the outset that a resolution of a company may be attacked in relation to a defect in the notice convening a meeting in two completely separate ways, though not all the authorities clearly make this distinction.
>
> First, at common law unless all corporators are present or otherwise consent, a meeting is only competent to deal with special business which is properly notified to all members in a notice convening the meeting. See for example *Symes v Weedow* (1892) 14 ALT 197; *Helwig v Jonas* [1922] VLR 261 and perhaps *Ryan v Edna May Junction Gold Mine Company NL* (1916) 21 CLR 487.
>
> Secondly, there is an equitable principle that it is the fiduciary duty of directors not to mislead the corporators who are to consider whether to pass a resolution by providing them with material that is other than substantially full and true and this is especially so where the directors themselves may benefit from the passing of a resolution.
>
> In considering this equitable rule one does not adopt the legalistic approach of a 19th century examiner of titles searching for a base fee nor does one approach the question in what counsel aptly described as a nitpicking way, but one asks what effect will the information provided have on the ordinary shareholder who scans or reads the document quickly, not as a lawyer, but as an ordinary man or woman in commerce or as an ordinary investor. One asks, viewed in such a way, will the information fully and fairly inform and instruct the shareholder about the matter upon which he or she will have to vote.
>
> There is no conflict in the case law on this point though some cases enlighten the point from different aspects.

In *Bulfin v Bebarfalds Ltd* (1938) 38 SR (NSW) 423, Long-Innes J at 432-438 reviewed the cases and held that directors are under a duty to make full disclosure of all facts within their knowledge which are material to enable the members to determine upon their action. As was pointed out in one of the cases referred to by his Honour, namely *Tiessen v Henderson* [1899] 1 Ch 861 at 870 the person to be protected by the rules is "not the dissentient, but the absent shareholder – the man who is absent because, having received and with more or less care looked at the circular" considers that he can leave the matter to the majority. ...

I think it is only necessary to quote two passages to further illumine the point for the purposes of the current case. First there is the well known and oft cited passage from the judgment of Clauson J in *Re Imperial Chemical Industries Ltd* [1936] 1 Ch 587 at 618, a passage which was expressly approved by Lord Maugham in the appeal to the House of Lords in that case which is reported as *Carruth v Imperial Chemical Industries Ltd* [1937] AC 707 at 768. Clauson J said:

"The question is not whether the circular might not have been differently framed, but whether there is any reasonable ground for supposing that such imperfections as may be [15] found in the circular have had, with or without other circumstances, the result that the majority (who have approved the proposal placed before them) have done so under some serious misapprehension of the position."

Secondly, I should cite what Kearney J said in *Killen's case*. The case is unreported but the note in the Australian Current Law Digest quotes Kearney J.

"The relevant duty with respect to directors informing shareholders of the business of meetings has been put in a variety of ways, but can be summarised in the terms that the directors seeking the passage of a resolution at a meeting of shareholders should provide shareholders with sufficient information concerning the business to be brought forward at the meeting. The shareholders must be enabled to have an understanding and form a judgment upon such business. A further obligation requires the information to be propounded for the consideration of shareholders in terms enabling the man in the street 'on the run' to absorb and understand the substance of what it is that the shareholders are being called upon to determine at the meeting ... I don't think that the shareholders would be assisted in their consideration of their business to be brought forward at the proposed meetings by being subjected to what would amount to an intolerable burden of information, most of which, if not all, would be unlikely to assist their judgment and would be more likely to confuse than assist the recipient of such information."

On this basis I turn to consider the four objections raised before dealing with them seriatim. However, I should make some general observations.

First, it seems to me that in a complex matter such as the present it is virtually impossible by a circular to tell the shareholders the truth, the whole truth and nothing but the truth and still have a commercially informative document. The more one steers clear of the Scylla of the whole truth the more one veers towards the Charybdis of confusion.

Secondly, whilst it would be very helpful if people got tenses of the verbs they use correct, such imperfections would not usually have more than a trivial significance.

Thirdly, it seems to me that the natural way of reading the word "presently" and at looking at the tenses of verbs in the circular is to read them with respect to the date of the circular, namely 17 May 1985. ...

[17] It does not seem to me that it is necessary to go into the other matters which were raised by counsel because I am firmly of the view that the plaintiff's case fails and the proceedings should be dismissed.

Circulation of members' resolution and statement

[11.500] Pursuant to s 249N(1), members who either:

- have the right to cast 5% or more of the total votes that may be cast on the resolution; or
- number at least 100 and are entitled to vote at a general meeting;

may give notice to the company that they wish to move a resolution at a general meeting. Section 249N(1A) provides that the number of members entitled to move such a resolution may be varied by the Regulations. To date, no such Regulations have been passed.

[11.510] The company is in turn required to give the members notice of the resolution to be moved at the meeting: s 249O(2). These members may also request that the company give all members a statement with respect to the proposed resolution or another matter that may be properly considered at a general meeting: s 249P(1). The company does not have to give notice of the resolution or circulate the statement if it is more than 1000 words long or defamatory: ss 249O(5) and 249P(9). Where the request is not made in time for the notice or statement to be sent out with the notice of the meeting, the members making the request are liable for the costs involved: ss 249O(4) and 249P(8). In such a case, the company does not have to give notice of the resolution or circulate the statement unless the members give the company a sum reasonably sufficient to meet the expenses: ss 249O(5) and 249P(9).

Quorum

[11.520] A quorum is a minimum number of members who must be present before a meeting can proceed. Under replaceable rule, s 249T(1), the quorum for a meeting of a company's members is two members. See above for a discussion of quorum requirements in board meetings. As noted above, s 249B makes provision for resolutions passed by single member companies.

[11.530] In determining whether a quorum exists, under replaceable rule, s 249T(2), proxies and corporate representatives (discussed below) are taken into account for the purpose of determining whether a quorum is present. Where a member appoints more than one proxy or representative, only one may be counted for the purposes of constituting a quorum: s 249T(2).

[11.540] At common law no business may be transacted in the absence of a quorum. Under replaceable rule, s 249T(3), if the quorum is not present within 30 minutes, the meeting must be adjourned to another day, time and place as determined by the directors. If the directors do not so determine, the meeting is adjourned for exactly a week at the same time and place: s 249T(3). If the quorum is not present at the adjourned meeting within 30 minutes, the meeting automatically dissolves: s 249T(4).

[11.550] Replaceable rule, s 249T(1), provides that the quorum must be present at all times during the meeting.

[11.560] As noted above, if it is impracticable to have a quorum at a meeting, a director or member may apply to the court under s 249G for an order to overcome the problem. Thus, as in *Re Totex-Adon Pty Ltd* (1980) ACLC ¶40-617, the court may direct that one member shall be deemed to constitute a meeting.

Resolutions

[11.570] Unless a special resolution is required under the *Corporations Act* or the company's constitution, a resolution put to a meeting will be an ordinary resolution, requiring a simple majority. A simple majority is a majority of those members present and voting at a meeting. This is to be contrasted with an absolute majority that is a majority of all those entitled to vote, whether or not present.

[11.580] A special resolution requires the support of 75% of the members entitled to vote on the resolution: s 9.

Proxies

Appointment of proxies

[11.590] A proxy is a person who is appointed by a member as an agent to attend and vote at a meeting on his or her behalf. Section 249X(1), (1A) and (3) provide that a member of a company who is entitled to attend and vote at a meeting of a company may appoint a person(s) or body corporate(s) as his or her proxy(s) to attend and vote instead of the member at the meeting. If a member is entitled to cast two or more votes at the meeting, they may appoint two proxies: s 249X(3). Section 249X is a replaceable rule for proprietary companies and a mandatory rule for public companies. See further ss 249X, 249Y and 250C

[11.600] Under s 249L(d) (i) the right to appoint a proxy, (ii) whether the proxy needs to be a member, (iii) that a member entitled to cast two or more votes may appoint two proxies and (iv) that the member may specify the proportion or number of votes each proxy is appointed to exercise, must be specified in the notice of a meeting. Under s 250BA(1), listed companies must also detail in the notice of the meeting a place and fax number, and may specify an electronic address, for the receipt of proxy appointments.

[11.610] Section 250A(1) provides that an appointment of a proxy is valid if it is signed (or otherwise authenticated in accordance with any Regulations) by the member making the appointment and specifies the member's name and address, the company's name, the proxy's name or office held by the proxy and the meeting at which the appointment may be used. The constitution may provide that an appointment is valid even if it contains only some of the information prescribed in s 250A(1): s 250A(2). Moreover, under new s 250A(1A), the Regulations may modify the requirements for the authentication of appointment. To date no Regulations have been passed. See further ss 250A, 250B and 250BA.

Revocation of proxy's appointment

[11.620] A member may revoke the power of a proxy at any time. The power will be automatically revoked upon the death of the member. The revocation will only be effective as against the company if written notice is given to the company before the commencement of the meeting: replaceable rule, s 250C(2).

[11.630] The proxy's appointment is not necessarily revoked by the member's attendance or even participation in the meeting: *Cousins v International Brick Co Ltd* [1931] 2 Ch 90 at 103. However, unless the company constitution specifies the effect of a member's presence at a meeting, the proxy's authority to speak and vote is suspended while the member is present at the meeting: s 249Y(3).

Rights and powers of a proxy

[11.640] A proxy has the same right as the member to speak at a meeting, vote and join in a demand for a poll: s 249Y(1). The company's constitution often specifies that a proxy is not entitled to vote on a show of hands. See, for example, reg 49(b) of Table A. As noted above, unless the company constitution specifies the effect of a member's presence at a meeting, the proxy's authority to speak and vote is suspended while the member is present at the meeting: s 249Y(3).

[11.650] As noted above, under replaceable rule, s 249T(2), proxies are taken into account for the purpose of determining whether a quorum is present. Where a member appoints more than one proxy, only one may be counted for the purposes of constituting a quorum: s 249T(2). Where the same individual is proxy for more than one person, the proxy may enable a quorum to be established through his or her numerous representations even though physically there are less than the required number of persons present to constitute a quorum: *Re Vector Capital Ltd* (1997) 23 ACSR 182 at 183.

Representatives

Appointment of representative

[11.660] Section 250D(1) and (4) provide that a body corporate may authorise a person to act as its representative at a meeting and such a person is entitled to exercise the same powers as the body corporate. More than one representative may be appointed, but only one representative may exercise the body corporate's powers at any one time: s 250D(3). See further s 250D.

[11.670] The constitution may make provision for shareholders other than body corporates to also be so represented. For example, reg 51 of Table A also permits the manager of the estate of a member who is of unsound mind to exercise any rights of the member in relation to a general meeting as if the manager were a member.

Rights and powers of representative

[11.680] As noted above, a corporate representative is entitled to exercise the same powers as the body corporate: s 250D(1) and (4). The appointment may, however, set out restrictions on the representative's powers: s 250D(2). Again, the constitution may confine the voting rights of a representative. For example, under Table A, although representatives of bodies corporate and members of unsound mind have full membership rights at meetings, other representatives are limited to voting on a show of hands: reg 49 of Table A.

[11.690] As noted above, under replaceable rule, s 249T(2), corporate representatives are taken into account for the purpose of determining whether a quorum is present. Where a member appoints more than one representative, only one may be counted for the purposes of constituting a quorum: s 249T(2).

Voting

Show of hands

[11.700] At common law, unless the constitution provides otherwise, a resolution is to be determined on a show of hands. This principle is echoed in replaceable rule, s 250J(1). Unless a poll is demanded, resolutions are decided on a show of hands: s 250J(1). Under replaceable rule, s 250E(1) and (2), subject to any restrictions attached to any shares, on a show of hands each member has one vote. *Prima facie* this rule would include within its scope corporate representative and proxies. As noted above, however, it is common for a company's constitution to provide that a proxy is not entitled to vote on a show of hands.

Poll

[11.710] A poll may be demanded by five or more members entitled to vote on the resolution, members with at least 5% of the votes that may be cast on the resolution on a poll, or the chair: s 250L(1). The constitution may, however, modify this principle by providing that fewer members or members holding a lesser percentage of votes may demand a poll: s 250L(2). See, for example, reg 46(a) of Table A. Section 250L(1) would generally include within its scope corporate representative and proxies. Note, however, that under reg 49(b) of Table A other types of representatives cannot vote on a poll.

The poll may be demanded before a vote is taken, before the voting results on a show of hands are declared or immediately after such results are declared: s 250L(3). When a poll is duly demanded, the vote on the show of hands is deprived of any force. See also ss 250K and 250M(1).

[11.720] The right to demand a poll is important because the number of shares held by the member is irrelevant to his or her voting power where the resolution is determined on a show of hands. While each member only has one vote on a show of hands, where the company has share capital and a vote is on a poll, each member has one vote for each share: s 250E(1). Note, where the company does not have share capital, each member has one vote on both a show of hands and on a poll: s 250E(2).

Chairperson's casting vote

[11.730] Where the votes are equal, at common law the chairperson will not have a casting vote in the absence of a provision conferring such in the constitution: *Nell v Longbottom* [1894] 1 QB 767 at 771. It is usual, however, for the constitution to confer on the chairperson a right to a casting vote. Thus, under replaceable rule, s 250E(3), where the votes on either a show of hands or on a poll are equal, the chairperson will have a casting vote in addition to his or her deliberative vote as a member.

Minutes of general meeting

[11.740] Under s 251A(1) and (2), minutes of meetings must be recorded in a book, signed by the chairperson of the meeting or the chairperson of the next succeeding meeting, within one month of the meeting. These requirements extend to resolutions passed without a meeting and single director/member company declarations: s 251A(1). In such cases the minutes must be signed within a reasonable time: s 251A(3) and (4). The minute books must be kept at the company's registered office, principal place of business or such other place approved by ASIC: s 251A(5).

[11.750] The minutes provide evidence of the business transacted at the meeting to which they relate, unless the contrary is proved: s 251A(6).

[11.760] Unlike the minute books of board meetings, those pertaining to general meetings must be open to inspection by members without charge: s 251B(1). In addition, under s 251B(2) a member may request the company to furnish a copy of any minutes of a general meeting or an extract of the minutes or any minutes of a resolution passed by members without a meeting. Upon such a request, the company must send copies to the member within 14 days of the request, or the receipt of payment where payment is required, or such longer period approved by ASIC: s 251B(3) and (4).

Validating procedural irregularities

[11.770] Under s 1322(2), procedural irregularities, such as the absence of a quorum or a defect in the notice of a meeting (s 1322(1)(b)), will not invalidate proceedings under the *Corporations Act*, unless the court is of the opinion that the irregularity has caused or may cause substantial injustice that cannot be remedied by any order of the court, and the court declares the proceedings to be invalid. In light of the remedial nature of s 1322, the term 'procedural irregularity' has been broadly interpreted.

[11.780] Under s 1322(3), neither a meeting, notice of a meeting, nor any proceedings at the meeting will be invalidated by reason of the accidental omission to give notice or the non-receipt of notice by any person, unless the court declares proceedings at the meeting to be void.

[11.790] Similarly, a meeting or resolution will only be invalid by reason of the inability of a member to reasonably participate in a meeting held in two or more venues because there was, for example, a failure of the technology being used, where the court is of the opinion that substantial injustice has occurred and that it cannot be remedied by any order of the court: s 1322(3A).

[11.800] The court is also empowered under s 1322(4) to:
- validate an act, matter, thing or proceeding purporting to have been done under the *Corporations Act* or in relation to a company that would be invalid by reason of any contravention of the Act or the company's constitution: s 1322(4)(a);
- order the rectification of any register kept by ASIC: s 1322(4)(b);
- relieve persons of civil liability stemming from failing to comply with the Act or the company's constitutional documents: s 1322(4)(c); or
- extend or abridge the period for doing various things under the Act or in relation to the company: s 1322(4)(d).

The power to make an order under s 1322(4)(a)(i) is only to be exercised where the matter is procedural in nature, the person acted honestly or it is in the public interest to exercise the power: s 1322(6)(a). An order under s 1322(4)(c) may only be made if the person acted honestly: s 1322(6)(b). In addition, in all cases the order may only be made if no substantial injustice has been or is likely to be caused to any person: s 1322(6)(c). In *Whitehouse v Capital Radio Network Pty Ltd* (2002) 21 ACLC 17, Underwood J stressed that the question is whether validation of the meeting, as opposed to the business conducted at the meeting, would cause a substantial injustice. What constitutes substantial injustice was discussed in *NRMA Ltd v Spragg* [2001] NSWSC 381 at [27]:

> In that regard I should note that the cases have determined that "injustice" within s 1322(b)(c) requires "the Court to consider real, and not merely insubstantial or theoretical prejudice" (*Elderslie Finance Corp Ltd v Australian Securities Commission* (1993) 11 ACLC 787 at 790); and that a degree of prejudice to a person or persons may be outweighed by the "overwhelming weight of justice" (*Re Compaction Systems Pty Ltd* (1976) 2 ACLR 135 at 150). Moreover, as I said in *Super John Pty Ltd v Futuris Rural Pty Ltd* (1999) 32 ACSR 398 at 402 (paragraph 14): "detriment per se is not the same as substantial injustice; that must depend on whether the remedial order in giving

rise to that detriment is unjust in the sense of causing such prejudice overall as to be unfair or inequitable, taking into account the interests of all of those directly affected by such dispensation."

The court may make an order subject to such conditions as it thinks fit: s 1322(4).

[11.810] The person seeking a declaration of validity under s 1322(4) bears the onus of showing that no substantial injustice has been or is likely to be caused to any person if the irregularity is validated: *Australian Hydrocarbons NL v Green* (1985) 10 ACLR 72 at 83.

Review questions

1. Advise the directors of ABC Ltd as to the requirements that must be met if they wish to call a meeting where they propose to pass the following resolutions:
   (a) remove two of the company's directors;
   (b) change the company's auditors;
   (c) vary the class rights of preference shareholders; or
   (d) alter the constitution.
2. How may a failure to provide the appropriate notice of a meeting be validated?
3. Jeff and Liz conduct the family business through a small proprietary company. They are the sole shareholders and directors of the company. Jeff and Liz make most of their decisions regarding the business over breakfast. Are these decisions regarded as resolutions of the company?
4. Jeff has been killed in a car accident. Can Liz convene and conduct an extraordinary meeting of the company?

Further reading

Baxt, 'A Fair Chair' (1989) *Chartered Accountant* 26
Cassidy, *Concise Corporations Law* (4th ed, Federation Press, Sydney, 2003) ch 11
Corcoran, 'The Fiduciary Duty of Directors to Give Adequate Notice of Company Meetings' (1987) 5 *ABLR* 7
Ford, Austin and Ramsay, *Ford's Principles of Corporations Law* (11th ed, Butterworths, Sydney, 2003) ch 7
Lang, *Horsley's Meetings: Procedure, Law and Practice* (4th ed, Butterworths, Sydney, 1998)
Magner, 'Convocation of General Meetings in Company Law: Reflections on *Totex-Adon* and Companies Act' (1981) 9 *ABLR* 79
Magner, 'Notice of Purpose of Company General Meetings: The Common Law Requirements, The Fiduciary Duty' (1987) 5 *C&SLJ* 92
Magner, *Joske's Law and Procedure at Meetings in Australia* (8th ed, LawBook Co, Sydney, 2001)
McConvill, *An Introduction to CLERP 9* (LexisNexis, Sydney, 2004)
Nash, 'Meetings Valid and Invalid' (1991) *Australian Accountant* 82
Simmonds, 'Why must we meet? Thinking about why shareholders meetings are required' (2001) 19 *C&SLJ* 506

Woellner, 'Preserving Order at Company Meetings – Oppression of the Majority' (1981) 13 *CLAB* 69

Zakrewski, 'The Law Relating to Single Director and Single Shareholder Companies' (1999) 17 *C&SLJ* 156

12

Members' Remedies

Outline

This chapter considers a member's ability to initiate proceedings against offending directors/majority shareholders. At common law, this power is limited by the 'proper plaintiff' rule which confines the ability to commence proceedings for a breach of directors' duties owed to the company to the company itself. In time the common law position was weakened by judicial exceptions to the 'proper plaintiff' rule and the introduction of statutory remedies. It will be seen, however, that these common law exceptions to the 'proper plaintiff' rule were abolished by the *Corporate Law Economic Reform Program Act* 1999 (*'CLERP Act'*). The company continues to be the proper plaintiff in proceedings for wrongs against it and it will only be where a member's personal rights have been affected by the breach that the member can litigate in his or her own right.

The *CLERP Act* also introduced Part 2F.1A which enables, *inter alia*, members to apply to court for leave to bring, or intervene in, proceedings on behalf of a company. This statutory derivative action is complemented by other statutory forms of relief for, *inter alia*, minority shareholders. To this end this chapter discusses what is known as the oppression remedy, now found in ss 232-235, and the general injunction provision, s 1324. These provisions are also complemented by s 461 which empowers a court to order a company be wound up because it is, *inter alia*, just and equitable. Section 461 is discussed in Chapter 13.

Rule in *Foss v Harbottle*

Proper plaintiff rule

[12.10] The *Corporations Act* 2001 (Cth) (*'Corporations Act'*) may on occasion specify that a member may bring an action to remedy a breach of a specific section. Generally, however, the breach will be of a director's duty with respect to which there is no express right in individual members to initiate proceedings against the offending director. As directors' duties are owed to the company, the company has the right to bring the proceedings. The company is the 'proper plaintiff': *Foss v Harbottle* (1843) 2 Hare 461; 67 ER 189.

Foss v Harbottle
Court of Chancery: Wigram VC
(1843) 2 Hare 461; 67 ER 189

Foss and Turton initiated proceedings on behalf of themselves and all other shareholders against the defendants (five directors, a solicitor and an architect of the company) seeking damages to be paid to the company for an alleged loss of the company's property. They also asserted that no properly constituted board existed and sought the appointment of a receiver.

The court held that the action did not lie at the suit of the shareholders. The injury was to the company as a whole, not to the plaintiffs exclusively. The plaintiffs consequently had no ability to sue in the name of the corporation.

> **Wigram VC: [490]** The Victoria Park Co is an incorporate body, and the conduct with which the defendants are charged in this suit is an injury not to the plaintiffs exclusively; it is an injury to the whole corporation by individuals whom the corporation entrusted with powers to be exercised only for the good of the corporation. ... [T]he plaintiffs [have assumed] to themselves the right and power in that manner to sue on behalf of and represent the corporation. It was not, nor could it successfully be argued, that it was a matter of course for any individual members of a corporation thus to assume to themselves the right of suing in the name of the corporation. In law, the corporation, and the aggregate members of the corporation, are not the same thing for purposes like this; and the **[491]** only question can be whether the facts alleged in this case justify a departure from the rule which prima facie would require that the corporation should sue in its own name and in its corporate character, or in the name of someone whom the law has appointed to be its representative. ... **[493]** [I]t is only necessary to refer to the clauses of the Act to shew that, whilst the supreme governing body, the proprietors at a special general meeting assembled, retain the power of exercising the functions conferred upon them by the Act of Incorporation, it cannot be competent to individual corporators to sue in the manner proposed by the plaintiffs on the present record. ... **[494]** In order then that this suit may be sustained it must be shown either that there is no such power [for the general meeting to ratify the breach] or, at least, that all means have been resorted to and found ineffectual to set that body in motion; this latter point is nowhere suggested in the bill: there is no suggestion that an attempt has been made by any proprietor to set the body of proprietors in **[495]** motion, or to procure a meeting to be convened for the purpose of revoking the acts complained of.

The sentiments expressed in this passage from *Foss v Harbottle* have been reiterated by the Australian courts. See, for example, *Barrett v Duckett* (1996) 14 ACLC 3101 at 3106; *Magarditch v ANZ Banking Group Ltd* (1999) 17 ACLC 424.

[12.20] While Part 2F.1A, discussed below, has introduced a statutory derivative action, the proper plaintiff rule continues to be relevant as the legislation does not purport to abolish the proper plaintiff rule, but rather, only its judicial exceptions. Thus, unless leave to bring a derivative action is granted under ss 237 or 233(1)(g), the company continues to be the proper plaintiff in proceedings for wrongs against it.

[12.30] The proper plaintiff rule is interrelated with the principle that the decision to initiate proceedings on the company's behalf is a management decision that therefore generally rests with the board of directors: *Kraus v JG Lloyd Pty Ltd* [1965] VR 232 at 236-237; *Massey v Wales* (2003) 21 ACLC 1978. Exercises of this discretion cannot be overruled by the general meeting: *John Shaw & Sons (Salford) Ltd v Shaw* [1935] 2 KB 112; *Massey v Wales* (2003) 21 ACLC 1978. In practice, the board may be disinclined to initiate proceedings against another officer.

Common law exceptions to *Foss v Harbottle*

[12.40] As noted above, the courts recognised that justice requires that in certain cases minority shareholders should be allowed to initiate corporate litigation. In *Foss v Harbottle* (1843) 2 Hare 461; 67 ER 189 itself, the court recognised that there may be circumstances requiring the rule to be relaxed. As a consequence, the courts developed four well established exceptions to the proper plaintiff rule:

- ultra vires or illegal acts: *Atherton v Plane Creek Central Mill Co Ltd* [1914] St R Qd 73 at 93;
- the absence of any necessary authorisation by a special majority of the company in general meeting or class of shareholders: *Baillie v Oriental Telephone Co* [1915] 1 Ch 503; *Edwards v Halliwell* [1950] 2 All ER 1064;
- fraud on the minority: *Daniels v Daniels* [1978] Ch 406; *Prudential Assurance Co Ltd v Newman Industries Ltd (No 2)* [1980] 2 All ER 841; *Eromanga Hydrocarbons NL v Australia Mining NL* (1988) 6 ACLC 906; *Biala Pty Ltd v Mallina Holdings Ltd* (1993) 11 ACLC 751; *Ruralcorp Consulting Pty Ltd v Pynery Pty Ltd* (1996) 21 ACSR 161; and
- breaches of members' personal rights: *Residues Treatment and Trading Company Ltd v Southern Resources Ltd* (1988) 6 ACLC 1160.

In addition, in recent years a fifth, more controversial, general exception has been accepted by the Australian courts, 'where justice so requires': *Hawkesbury Development Corp Ltd v Landmark Finance Pty Ltd* [1969] 2 NSWR 782 at 789; *Biala Pty Ltd v Mallina Holdings Ltd* (1993) 11 ACLC 751; *Mesenberg v Cord Industrial Recruiters Pty Ltd* (1996) 19 ACSR 483; *Ruralcorp Consulting Pty Ltd v Pynery Pty Ltd* (1996) 21 ACSR 161 at 168; *Nece Pty Ltd v Ritek Incorporation* (1997) 24 ACSR 38 at 44.

[12.50] As noted above, the *CLERP Act* abolished the ability of members to bring derivative actions on behalf of the company under the common law exceptions to the proper plaintiff rule: s 236(3). In *Advent Investors Pty Ltd v Michael Goldhirsch* (2001) 19 ACLC 580, Warren J held that Part 2F.1A is a procedural law that operates both retrospectively and prospectively. Thus, Warren J held that the common law exceptions were retrospectively abolished by the *CLERP Act*.

Personal rights

[12.60] However, as also noted above, s 236(3) does not abolish the 'personal rights' exception to the proper plaintiff rule because, in fact, this does not entail a derivative action being brought by the applicant. See also Note 3. A derivative action entails bringing an action on behalf of the company. By contrast, where the rights affected are personal to a member the member brings an action for a breach of that personal right in their own name rather than the company's.

[12.70] Personal rights are particular 'membership' rights that may accrue in individuals by reason of rights attached to their shares, provisions in a separate contract or pursuant to the company's constitution. They are membership rights in so far as they must be conferred on the shareholder in his or her capacity as a member.

[12.80] The courts have had difficulty determining when a shareholder has an actionable personal right. The decision in *Prudential Assurance Co Ltd v Newman Industries Ltd (No 2)* [1982] Ch 204 evidences a narrow conception of personal rights.

Prudential Assurance Co Ltd v Newman Industries Ltd (No 2)
Court of Appeal: Cumming-Bruce, Templeman and Brightman LJJ
[1982] Ch 204

Bartlett and Laughton were directors of two companies, Thomas Poole and Gladston China Ltd ('TPGC') and Newman Industries Ltd ('NI'). Both directors directly or indirectly held shares in TPGC. When TPGC came to be in serious financial difficulties, the directors organised NI to purchase certain of TPGC's assets at a gross over-value. In accordance with Stock Exchange Regulations, the transaction was approved by NI's general meeting, but only on the basis of a deceitful circular.

The plaintiff company, a minority shareholder in NI, brought a representative claim on behalf of the shareholders of NI seeking a declaration that the circular was misleading and tricky, and both a representative and a personal action against Bartlett and Laughton for common law damages for conspiring together to benefit TPGC at the expense of NI's shareholders.

At first instance, Vinelott J found that the claims of misconduct to be made out and that by conspiring to hurt NI, the directors had indirectly hurt its shareholders. In the interests of justice the court held that the plaintiff's personal claim should be permitted. On appeal, the Court of Appeal reversed this finding. The Court of Appeal reiterated that, where a fraud is brought to bear on a company, it was the company that should bring that action. Moreover, it was held that a person's shareholding in a company that was damaged by conduct did not suffice for a claim of breach of a personal right.

> **Cumming-Bruce, Templeman and Brightman LJJ: [222]** In our judgment the personal claim is misconceived. ... [What a shareholder] cannot do is to recover damages merely because the company in which he is interested has

suffered damage. He cannot recover a sum equal to the diminution in the [223] market value of his share, or equal to the likely diminution in dividend, because such a "loss" is merely a reflection of the loss suffered by the company. The shareholder does not suffer any personal loss. His only "loss" is through the company ... The plaintiff's shares are merely a right of participation in the company on the terms of the articles of association. The shares themselves, his right of participation, are not directly affected by the wrongdoing. The plaintiff still holds all the shares as his own absolutely unencumbered property. The deceit practised on the plaintiff does not affect the shares; it merely enables the defendant to rob the company. ...

[224] A personal action would subvert the rule in *Foss v Harbottle* and that rule is not merely a tiresome procedural obstacle placed in the path of the shareholder by a legalistic judiciary. The rule is a consequence of the fact that a corporation is a separate legal entity.

In a slightly different context (a claim against solicitors for negligence) this view was echoed in *Thomas v D'Arcy* [2004] QSC 260. The plaintiff shareholder's claim for the loss of value of his shareholdings was struck out as it was held that his loss was not separate to that suffered by the two respective companies in which he had shares.

[12.90] A much broader definition of personal rights was adopted in *Residues Treatment and Trading Company Ltd v Southern Resources Ltd* (1988) 6 ACLC 1160 where the court was at pains to ensure the plaintiff had standing to proceed with the litigation.

Residues Treatment and Trading Company Ltd v Southern Resources Ltd
Supreme Court of South Australia: King CJ, Matheson and Bollen JJ
(1988) 6 ACLC 1160

The plaintiffs were minority shareholders in Southern Resources Ltd ('SR'). In response to a takeover bid, the board proposed to allot shares that would have the effect of giving one of the defendants, MacDougall, a shareholder/director of the company, and his associates a majority of voting shares. The plaintiffs challenged the share issue as being for improper purposes, namely to ensure control of the company in the hands of friendly interests and not in the company's best interests. The plaintiffs argued that they had standing to bring the action as their personal rights had been infringed. SR asserted that the plaintiffs did not have standing to bring the action as the alleged breach by the directors was a matter that could be ratified by the general meeting.

Perry J at first instance agreed with SR's submission and struck out the plaintiffs' claim. On appeal the Supreme Court reversed this decision and reinstated the plaintiffs' statement of claim. The court held that the plaintiffs, as shareholders, had a personal right to prevent the diminution of their voting rights by an improper allotment of shares by directors.

King CJ: [1161] This appeal raises for decision the important question whether a shareholder in a limited liability company has locus standi to prosecute an action to challenge an allotment of shares made by the directors

for an improper purpose. The appellants have appealed to this Court against an order of a single judge striking out their statement of claim on the ground that they lacked standing to prosecute the claims made in the statement of claim.
...

[1162] An allotment of shares by the directors for an improper purpose is a breach of their fiduciary duty to the company for which they are liable to the company. It is not open to an individual shareholder, generally speaking, to sue to enforce the company's rights. The proper plaintiff in an action for that purpose is the company itself, *Foss v Harbottle* (1843) 2 Hare 461; 67 ER 189. Even where the company should properly be the plaintiff, a shareholder may sue, in certain circumstances however, for remedies for the benefit of the company in what is often called a derivative action if the company is under the control of persons who refuse to institute proceedings.

I have qualified the rule in *Foss v Harbottle* stated above by the phrase "generally speaking" because there are well recognised exceptions to the rule. One such exception exists where the actions for which a remedy is sought amount to an infringement of a shareholder's personal rights. In such a situation the shareholder has locus standi to sue to enforce those personal rights. The statement of claim which has been struck out does not plead the plaintiffs' claim as a derivative action to enforce the company's rights or to obtain a remedy for the directors' alleged breach of duty to the company ... If there is locus standi it must be because the statement of claim raises a cause or causes of action based upon the infringement of the plaintiff's personal rights. Mr Bathurst QC, who appeared on the appeal for the plaintiffs, based his argument firmly upon that ground. ... It is necessary to consider whether the causes of action pleaded in the statement of claim which has been struck out, are based, properly understood, not upon the wrong which has undoubtedly been done to the company, if the allegations are true, but upon a wrong done to the plaintiffs as shareholders amounting to an infringement of their personal rights. ...

[1165] If there is a personal right in a shareholder not to have a majority of which he is a member converted into a minority by an improper allotment of shares, I can see no reason in principle or logic why that right should not extend to protection against improper dilution of his voting rights the effect of which does not go so far.

The personal right of a shareholder to which I refer is founded, in my opinion, upon general equitable considerations referred to in the cases cited above arising out of membership of a body whose management is in the hands of directors having fiduciary obligations. It is fortified by the nature of the contract between the company and the members constituted by the memorandum and articles of association and given statutory force by s 78(1) of the *Companies Code*. I do not mean that the relevant right of a shareholder is founded in contract or that his remedies for infringement are remedies for breach of contract. The shareholder's right is founded in equity and is a right to have the say in the company which accrues to him by virtue of the voting rights which are attached to his shares by his contract with the company, preserved against improper actions by the company or the directors who manage its affairs. It is true, as the learned Judge appealed from observed, that a person taking shares in a company must be taken to have agreed to suffer such effects as may flow from the allotment of further shares made by the company, but that is not to say that he is without rights in relation to such further allotment as may be made by the directors for improper purposes.

The rule in *Foss v Harbottle* (supra) clearly operates to preclude a shareholder from suing in his personal capacity in respect of a detriment which he suffers in common with other shareholders in consequence of a wrong done to the company. There is a clear distinction, however, between such a detriment and the diminution of a shareholder's effective voting power by an improper allotment of shares by directors acting on behalf of the company. The latter is not merely a breach of duty by the directors to the company, it is also a wrong done to the shareholder by the company acting through its agents. To make that distinction is not necessarily to subscribe to the view that a shareholder has a personal right not to be affected detrimentally by any breach of what is said to be an implied term in the contract between the member and the company that the affairs of the company will be managed without impropriety on the part of the directors. Diminution of voting power stands on a fundamentally different footing from other detriments resulting from abuse of power by directors. A member's voting rights and the rights of participation which they provide in the decision-making of the company are a fundamental attribute of membership and are rights which the member should be able to protect by legal action against improper diminution. The rule in *Foss v Harbottle* has no application where individual membership rights as opposed to corporate rights are involved: *Efstathis v Greek Orthodox Community of St George* (1988) 6 ACLC 706; 13 ACLR 691 esp per Ryan J at ACLC p 711; ACLR p 696.

It must be acknowledged that there has often been a lack of clear differentiation in the cases between the situations in which the company is the only proper plaintiff, the situations in which a shareholder may prosecute a derivative action for a remedy in favour of the company and situations in which a shareholder may bring an action on his own behalf for a personal remedy. There is also a lack of clarity as to the basis upon which individual shareholders have been allowed to sue to have allotments of shares made for improper purposes set aside. I think, however, that there is a clear trend in cases of the highest authority tending to indicate the existence of a personal right in a shareholder, grounded upon equitable principles, to have the voting power of his shares undiminished by improper actions on the part of the directors and of his locus standi to institute and prosecute proceedings to protect that right. I think that the time has come for the courts to give unequivocal recognition to such a right.

[12.100] While the two cases reflect a difference in approach, in both cases the courts accepted that a shareholder may bring an action for a personal loss where he or she suffered a loss which was separate and distinct from the loss suffered by the company. A diminution in the market value of shares, as in, *inter alia, Prudential Assurance Co Ltd v Newman Industries Ltd (No 2)* [1982] Ch 204 will not suffice as such a loss is merely a reflection of the loss suffered by the company. By contrast, the diminution of voting powers, as in *Residues Treatment and Trading Company Ltd v Southern Resources Ltd* (1988) 6 ACLC 1160, affects a membership right that is distinct from any loss to the company. Similarly, in *Milfull v Terranora Lakes Country Club Ltd* [2002] FCA 178, the Timeshare Rights held by members were held not to be a mere incident of the members' shareholding and thus the diminution of the value of these rights was distinct from the diminution of their shareholding value and the company's assets.

Statutory Derivative Action

Standing to seek leave to bring a derivative action

[12.110] As noted above, the *CLERP Act* introduced a statutory derivative action, contained in Part 2F.1A. The legislation extends beyond derivative actions. It also allows a successful applicant to intervene in proceedings to which the company is a party so as to take on the responsibility for the conduct of the proceedings or a particular step, such as settlement. The rationale for introducing such measures were outlined in Companies and Securities Law Review Committee Report No 12, *Enforcement of the Duties of Directors and Officers of a Company By Means of a Statutory Derivative Action* (November 1990):

CONTROL OVER INITIATION OF PROCEEDINGS BY COMPANIES

[1] In the majority of companies, the powers of management are expressly vested in the board of directors by the constituent documents of the company. By subscribing for shares or otherwise becoming a member (in the case of a company not limited by shares), a member is taken to have agreed that, with a number of exceptions concerning matters that are the exclusive province of the company in general meeting, the conduct of the company's affairs ordinarily will be at the discretion of the board of directors or, through delegation by the board, at the discretion of the executive officers of the company.

[2] The discretion reposed in both directors and officers is subject to an overriding requirement that in all cases they act in the best interests of the company. That requirement has influenced the formulation of the recognized duties that directors and officers owe to a company. Those duties, which in many instances involve onerous standards of loyalty and fidelity, are imposed by statute, established by the general law or arise out of the terms of contracts of employment with a company.

[3] Directors and officers who breach [some] duty owed to a company are in theory as vulnerable to have proceedings taken against them in relation to that breach as are outsiders who have caused loss to the company through failure to observe the terms of some contract with the company or by way of tortious act or omission.

[4] The power to initiate, prosecute, settle or otherwise deal with legal proceedings by any [company] ordinarily resides in the board of directors as the primary organ of management. Apart from any power of review or direction which my be expressly reserved to the general meeting or which may be made necessary by the circumstances of the case, a member of a company has little control over the initiation or conduct of litigation which is founded on a cause of action which belongs exclusively to the company, whether that cause of action involves breach of duty by any corporate insider or is one which can be pursued against a third party.

INADEQUACY OF THE PRESENT LAW CONCERNING ENFORCEMENT WHERE A COMPANY FAILS OR REFUSES TO ENFORCE A CAUSE OF ACTION

[5] There is likely to be little criticism of that part of the rule in *Foss v Harbottle*, which states that a company is the only proper plaintiff in respect of wrongs done to the company, in a case where there is a readiness on the

part of the company to pursue causes of action that belong to it, regardless of the identity of the party or parties against whom proceedings are contemplated.

[6] The proposition upon which Discussion Paper No 11 was based is that, due to the application of that rule and notwithstanding the recognition of a number of exceptions, existing law is inadequate to provide a method of enforcement where a company improperly refuses or fails to pursue a cause of action. There was no dissent amongst respondents to the Discussion Paper as to the accuracy of that proposition.

[7] The need for a change to the law has been evident for a considerable time. That need does not result from adverse economic or financial circumstances; all that corporate collapse and attendant financial loss of the kind now being experienced in Australia achieve is to bring that need into greater prominence. The Committee noted in para [2] of Discussion Paper No 11 that legislative amendment to facilitate action by, at least, a member of a company could also be useful in the general scheme of corporate regulation as an aid to protecting the interests of investors and creditors.

[8] There are, of course, statutory provisions designed to provide remedies against maladministration of companies; the more important ones, and the uncertainties as to their proper ambit, were outlined in Discussion Paper No 11.

In *Carpenter v Pioneer Park Pty Ltd* [2004] NSWSC 1007, Barrett J held that the court has an inherent power to permit proceedings to be brought in the company's name, despite the enactment of Part 2F.1A. See also *BL & GY International Co Ltd v Hypec Electronics Pty Ltd* (2003) 171 FLR 268.

[12.120] Part 2F.1A does not give an automatic right to bring a derivative action. Leave of the court must be sought under s 237. Under ss 236(1)(a), 237(1) and 238(1),[1] an application for leave to bring, or intervene in, proceedings on behalf of a company or to be substituted for a person to whom leave has been granted, may be brought by:

- a member of the company or a related body corporate;
- a former member of the company or a related body corporate;
- a person entitled to be registered as a member of the company or a related body corporate;
- an officer of the company; or
- a former officer of the company.

Note, ASIC is not provided with standing to bring an application for a derivative action as the legislation's purpose is to provide a means for investors to overcome the difficulties in *Foss v Harbottle*. See para 6.30 of the *Explanatory Memorandum to the CLERP Bill*.

Note also in *Brightwell v RFB Holdings* [2003] NSWSC 7, *Charlton v Baber* (2003) 21 ACLC 1671, *Roach v Winnote Pty Ltd (in liq)* [2001] NSWSC 822, *William Kamper v Applied Soli Technology Pty Ltd* [2004] NSWSC 891 and *Carpenter v Pioneer Park Pty Ltd* [2004] NSWSC 1007

---

1 Sections 236(1)(a) and 237(1) govern who may make an application for leave to bring, or intervene in, proceedings, while s 238(1) governs an application to substitute a person who has been granted such leave.

the courts asserted that Part 2F.1A could apply to a company in liquidation.

Grounds for an application

[12.130] Once an applicant has sought leave to bring, or intervene in, proceedings on behalf of the company under s 237(1), the court must grant the application if it is satisfied:
- it is probable the company will not bring the proceedings or take proper responsibility for such proceedings;
- the applicant is acting in good faith; or
- it is in the best interests of the company that the applicant be granted leave;
- there is a serious question to be tried; and
- at least 14 days before the application the applicant gave the company written notice of the intention to apply for leave and the reasons for such (unless the court believes an order granting leave is appropriate despite no such notice being given): s 237(2).

Company will not bring proceedings

[12.140] In regard to the first requirement, that the company will not bring the proceedings may be evident from a board resolution or a refusal of a request of the applicant to bring the proceedings: *Swansson v Pratt* (2002) 20 ACLC 1594. In the absence of such the court will need to consider if this conclusion may be inferred. See also *Goozee v Graphic World Group Holdings Pty Ltd* (2002) 20 ACLC 1502; *Isak Constructions v Faress* [2003] NSWSC 784; and *Brightwell v RFB Holdings* [2003] NSWSC 7.

Notice

[12.150] This first requirement is interrelated with the last notice requirement. While this is designed to give the company an opportunity to consider the matter and perhaps decide to litigate without the need of a derivative action, an applicant may also use this prerequisite as a means of demonstrating that the company would not itself instigate proceedings if despite the notice the company still refuses to litigate.

As stated in the legislation, the court may grant leave even though notice has not been given to the company. In *Isak Constructions v Faress* [2003] NSWSC 784, Barrett J asserted that leave should only be given without the required notice where the company was already aware of the relevant matters associated with the application or where there was good reason to allow the applicant to represent the company without the company's knowledge. In that case notice had incorrectly been given to the company's solicitor, rather than the company. It had also not been given within 14 days before the application. However, as the company was well aware of the applicant's intentions and reasons Barrett J granted the applicant the leave sought.

Good faith

[12.160] As to the second prerequisite, the subjective requirement of 'good faith' in s 237(2)(b) is determined in light of the objective requirement in s 237(2)(c) that it is in the best interests of the company that the applicant be granted leave: *Talisman Technologies Inc v Qld Electronic Switching P/L* [2001] QSC 324. Thus, if the plaintiff is bringing the proceedings for its own benefit, rather than the benefit of the company, the plaintiff will not be acting in good faith: *Talisman Technologies*. Palmer J in *Swansson v Pratt* (2002) 20 ACLC 1594 at 1061-1062 discussed those factors that are important to a consideration of this requirement:

[1061] Good faith – principles

32. There is no elaboration in s 237 as to what matters the Court should take into account in determining whether an applicant is "acting in good faith". That phrase is one which occurs in very many different contexts in the law: it must take its content in any particular case from the context in which it is used.

33. As I have observed, prior to the commencement of Pt 2F1A only current shareholders could take advantage of the exceptions to the rule in *Foss v Harbottle*. Pt 2F.1A now gives a right to initiate proceedings to some persons who, but for those provisions, would have had no such right at all under the general law. Such persons are all those within the categories created by s 236(1)(a) who are not shareholders of the company when the application for leave is made. Further, there is no requirement in s 236 that a person seeking leave must have been a shareholder or officer when the alleged wrong was committed against the company. Accordingly, under Pt 2F1A a former shareholder or director may seek to sue in the company's name for a wrong which was committed after he or she had disposed of all shares in the company or had ceased to hold office.

34. The Court is not given power in Pt 2F.1A to grant final relief in a suit instituted in a company's name to any person other than the company itself. Accordingly, applicants for leave who are not current shareholders of the company cannot gain by increase in the value of their shares if the derivative action succeeds and the company recovers compensation. Likewise, applicants who are former officers of the company cannot obtain orders resolving conflicts in which they themselves are engaged. Yet such persons are entitled to be given leave if they satisfy the requirements of s 237(2). The section, therefore, suggests that it must be possible for persons to satisfy the requirement of good faith even when they have no financial interest in the company and no present involvement in its management.

35. At this early stage in the development of the law on the statutory derivative action created by Pt 2F.1A it would be unwise to endeavour to state compendiously the considerations to which the Courts will have regard in determining whether applicants in all categories defined by s 236(1) are acting in good faith. The law will develop incrementally as different factual circumstances come before the Courts.

36. Nevertheless, in my opinion, there are at least two interrelated factors to which the Courts will always have regard in determining whether the good faith requirement of s 237(2)(b) is satisfied. The first is whether the applicant honestly believes that a good cause of action exists and has a reasonable prospect of success. Clearly, whether the applicant honestly holds such a

belief would not simply be a matter of bald assertion: the applicant may be disbelieved if no reasonable person in the circumstances could hold that belief. The second factor is whether the applicant is seeking to bring the derivative suit for such a collateral purpose as would amount to an abuse of process.

37. These two factors will, in most but not all, cases entirely overlap: if the Court is not satisfied that the applicant actually holds the requisite belief, that fact alone would be sufficient to lead to the conclusion that the application must be made for a collateral purpose, so as to be an abuse of process. The applicant may, however, believe that the company has a good cause of action with a reasonable prospect of success but nevertheless may be intent on bringing the derivative action, not to prosecute it to a conclusion, but to use it as a means for obtaining some advantage for which the action is not designed or for some collateral advantage beyond what the law offers. If that is shown, the application and the derivative suit itself would be an abuse of the Court's process ... **[1062]** The applicant would fail the requirement of s 237(2)(b).

38. Where the application is made by a current shareholder of a company who has more than a token shareholding and the derivative action seeks recovery of property so that the value of the applicant's shares would be increased, good faith will be relatively easy for the applicant to demonstrate to the Court's satisfaction. So also where the applicant is a current director or officer: it will generally be easy to show that such an applicant has a legitimate interest in the welfare and good management of the company itself, warranting action to recover property or to ensure that the majority of the shareholders or of the board do not act unlawfully to the detriment of the company as a whole.

39. However, where the applicant is a former shareholder or officer with nothing obvious to gain directly by the success of the derivative action, the Court will scrutinise with particular care the purpose for which the derivative action is said to be brought.

40. For example, a creditor may happen to be a former shareholder of the company and may seek, by the derivative action, to place the company in a financial position to repay the debt. There would be no abuse of process in commencing and maintaining the derivative action itself in that the action is commenced and maintained in order to achieve the purpose for which it is designed, namely, to recover property for the company. However, it may well be said that, in making an application for leave under Pt 2F.1A, the applicant is not acting in good faith because he or she is, in reality, seeking to vindicate his or her interest as a creditor and not whatever interest he or she may have as a former shareholder.

41. To take another example: a derivative action sought to be instituted by a current shareholder for the purpose of restoring value to his or her shares in the company would not be an abuse of process even if the applicant is spurred on by intense personal animosity, even malice, against the defendant: it is not the law that only a plaintiff who feels goodwill towards a defendant is entitled to sue ... On the other hand, an action sought to be instituted by a former shareholder with a history of grievances against the current majority of shareholders or the current board may be easier to characterise as brought for the purpose of satisfying nothing more than the applicant's private vendetta. An applicant with such a purpose would not be acting in good faith.

42. If a wrong appears to have been done to a company and those in control refuse to take proceedings to redress it, the Court should permit a derivative action to be instituted only by those within the categories allowed by s 236(1) who would suffer a real and substantive injury if the action were

not permitted. The injury must be necessarily dependent upon or connected with the applicant's status as a current or former shareholder or director and the remedy afforded by the derivative action must be reasonably capable of redressing the injury.

43. Further, if an applicant for leave under s 237 seeks by the derivative action to receive a benefit which, in good conscience, he or she should not receive, then the application will not be made in good faith even though the company itself stands to benefit if the derivative action is successful. Such a benefit would include, for example, a double recovery by the applicant for a wrong suffered or recompense for a wrongful act inflicted upon the company in which the applicant was a direct and knowing participant with the proposed defendant in the derivative action. In such a case the law would not permit the applicant to derive a benefit from his or her own wrongdoing.

See also *Isak Constructions v Faress* [2003] NSWSC 784.

Best interests of the company

[12.170] As to the third requirement, the court in *Swansson v Pratt* (2002) 20 ACLC 1594 at 1604-1605 asserted that the 'best interests of the company' requirement in s 237(2)(c) imposed a high threshold:

[1604] **The best interests of the company ...**
55. At the outset, it is important to note that s 237(2)(c) requires the Court to be satisfied, not that the proposed derivative action may be, appears to be, or is likely to be, in the best interests of the company but, rather, that it is in its best interests. ...

56. The requirement of s 237(2)(c) that the applicant satisfy the Court that the proposed action is in the best interests of the company is a far higher threshold for an applicant to cross. It requires the applicant to establish, on the balance of probabilities, a fact which can only be determined by taking into account all of the relevant circumstances. Accordingly, the enquiry will normally require the applicant to adduce evidence at least as to the following matters.

57. First, there should be evidence as to the character of the company: different considerations may well apply depending on whether the company is a small, private company whose few shareholders are the members of a family or whether it is a large public listed company. If the company is a closely held family company, it may be relevant to take into account the effect of the proposed litigation on the purpose for which the company was established and on the family members who are the shareholders. If the company is a public listed company, such considerations will be irrelevant. Again, the company may be a joint venture company in which the venturers are deadlocked so that the proposed derivative action is seen as being for the purpose of vindicating one side's position rather than the other's in a way which will not achieve a useful result: see eg *Talisman Technologies Inc v Queensland Electronic Switching Pty Ltd* [2001] QSC 324.

58. Second, there should be evidence of the business, if any, of the company so that the **[1605]** effects of the proposed litigation on its proper conduct may be appreciated.

59. Third, there should be evidence enabling the Court to form a conclusion whether the substance of the redress which the applicant seeks to achieve is available by a means which does not require the company to be

brought into litigation against its will. So, for example, if the applicant can achieve the desired result in proceedings in his or her own name it is not in the best interests of the company to be involved in litigation at all. This was the case in *Talisman Technologies* in which it appeared from the evidence that the most desirable outcome for the applicant was to obtain an order for specific performance of a contract, which it could do in a suit in which the company did not need to be a party.

60. Fourth, there should be evidence as to the ability of the defendant to meet at least a substantial part of any judgment in favour of the company in the proposed derivative action so that the Court may ascertain whether the action would be of any practical benefit to the company.

See also *Brightwell v RFB Holdings* [2003] NSWSC 7; *Charlton v Baber* [2003] NSWSC 745; *Carpenter v Pioneer Park Pty Ltd* [2004] NSWSC 1007.

[12.180] Section 237(3) specifies a rebuttable presumption as to when such derivative litigation is *not* in the best interests of the company. This provides a presumption where the company has decided not to bring or defend proceedings, or to settle proceedings against a third party (note, it must be proceedings against a third party, not a related party: s 237(4)) and all the directors who participated in the decision:

- acted in good faith for a proper purpose;
- did not have a material personal interest in the decision;
- informed themselves about the subject matter of the decision to the extent that they reasonably believed appropriate; and
- rationally believed that the decision was in the best interests of the company: s 237(4).

A director's belief that the decision was in the best interests of the company is a rational one unless the belief is one that no reasonable person in their position would hold. In essence, these prerequisites echo those prescribed under the business judgment rule, discussed in Chapter 10, which provides a defence to a claim of a breach of the directors' duty of care.

Serious question to be tried

[12.190] As to the fourth prerequisite, the requirement is that there be a serious question to be tried, rather than establishing a *prima facie* case. This approach is designed to ensure an application for leave is not a costly mini-trial (*Swansson v Pratt* (2002) 20 ACLC 1594; *Goozee v Graphic World Group Holdings Pty Ltd* (2002) 20 ACLC 1502; *Carpenter v Pioneer Park Pty Ltd* [2004] NSWSC 1007) and that frivolous or vexatious claims cannot be pursued by applicants for some ulterior motive through Part 2F.1A.

Substitution of litigant

[12.200] As noted above, Part 2F.1A is not confined to derivative actions. Where subsequent events indicate it would be prudent to substitute another person for a person who has previously been granted leave to bring a derivative action, an application for such may also be made under Part 2F.1A. Section 238(2) provides that an order substituting the applicant for a person to whom leave has been granted to bring a derivative action 'may' be made where the court is satisfied that the applicant is acting in good faith and it is appropriate to make the order in all the circumstances.

Ratification

[12.210] That the company has ratified or approved the conduct that the applicant seeks to challenge through a derivative action under Part 2F.1A does not prevent a successful application for a derivative action being made: s 239(1). While under s 239(2) such ratification may be taken into account in determining the application, from s 239(2)(a) and (b) the concern is to ensure that the ratification was made by a fully informed meeting, acting for a proper purpose.

Court's powers

Independent investigator

[12.220] Under s 241 the court may make any orders or directions it considers appropriate. In particular, the court is empowered to appoint an independent person to investigate, and report to the court, as to the company's financial position, the acts and circumstances giving rise to the cause of action and the costs involved in the proceedings. To ensure such an investigator may effectively carry out his or her duties, the investigator is conferred a right to inspect the books of the company for any purpose connected with their appointment: s 241(2). See also s 241(3). This will ensure that the court can make its decision whether to grant leave in light of independently provided information: *Explanatory Memorandum to the CLERP Bill* paras 6.62-6.64.

Costs

[12.230] Under s 242, when the court grants an application for leave to bring a derivative action it may also make an order as to the costs in relation to the proceedings brought or intervened in or the application for leave itself. Such an order may be made against the person who was granted leave to bring the derivative action, the company or any other party to the proceedings or application. Moreover, such an order may entail that one party indemnify another for such costs. These powers enable the court to protect a *bona fide* applicant from the costs involved in a derivative action, while also providing the court with another mechanism to discourage potentially frivolous actions or actions perhaps based on ulterior motives: *Explanatory Memorandum to the CLERP Bill* para 6.69. However, as the proceedings are derivative in nature, the legislation does not empower the court to provide any further type of relief to an applicant: *Swansson v Pratt* (2002) 20 ACLC 1594.

Leave to settle proceedings

[12.240] Where an applicant is granted leave to bring or intervene in proceedings, s 240 provides that such litigation may not be discontinued, compromised or settled without leave of the court. This limited form of case management is designed to ensure a successful applicant does not, *inter alia*, settle proceedings so as to benefit himself or herself, rather than acting in the company's best interests.

Oppression

Oppressive or unfairly prejudicial or discriminatory conduct

[12.250] In a bid to combat the limitations embodied in the rule in *Foss v Harbottle* (1843) 2 Hare 461; 67 ER 189, a statutory form of relief was introduced to allow, *inter alia*, minority shareholders to seek relief from oppressive conduct. Today the oppression remedy is embodied in ss 232-235 but extends well beyond oppressive conduct. Under s 232 relief may be sought where:

- the affairs (defined broadly in s 53) of the company are being conducted in a manner that is oppressive, unfairly prejudicial to, or unfairly discriminatory against, a member(s), or contrary to the interests of the members as a whole; or
- an act, omission or resolution or proposed act omission or resolution is oppressive, unfairly prejudicial to, or unfairly discriminatory against, a member(s), or contrary to the interests of the members as a whole.

When these prerequisites are established, s 233 confers on the court a broad discretion to make such orders as it thinks fit to remedy the situation.

Standing under s 234

[12.260] Section 234 specifies who may apply for an order under s 233:
- a member of the company;
- a person who has been removed from the register of members because of a selective reduction under s 256B(2);
- a person who has ceased to be a member if the application relates to the circumstances in which they ceased to be a member;
- a person to whom a share has been transmitted under a will or by operation of law; or
- a person whom ASIC thinks appropriate given their investigations into the company's affairs or matters connected with the company's affairs.

[12.270] Generally, to be a member that person must be registered on the company's share register: *Niord Pty Ltd v Adelaide Petroleum NL* (1990) 8 ACLC 684 at 689; *Titlow v Intercapital Group (Australia) Pty Ltd* (1996) 14 ACLC 1065. In *Re Independent Quarries Pty Ltd* (1993) 12

ACLC 159, however, the court held the applicant was a member even though he was not registered on the share register. As the applicant had share certificates properly sealed in his name and a rival faction was controlling the share register, the court did not require an application for rectification of the share register before finding the applicant to be a member.

[12.280] The applicant need not be a member at the time of the subject conduct. It suffices that the person is a member at the time of the application: *Re Spargos Mining NL* (1990) 8 ACLC 1218 at 1219-1123.

Re Spargos Mining NL
Supreme Court of Western Australia: Murray J
(1990) 8 ACLC 1218

An application was made by a shareholder of Spargos Mining NL for relief under the predecessor to s 232. The applicant asserted that the directors of the company had acted in an oppressive manner. To this end the applicant pointed to a number of transactions that the board had approved that appeared not to be for the benefit of Spargos Mining NL, but rather other companies in the same corporate group. The conduct complained of took place between January 1998–March 1990. The applicant only became a member of the company in November 1989. The issue in this hearing was whether the applicant had to be a member of the company at the time of the alleged oppressive conduct.

Murray J held that it was sufficient that the applicant was a member at the time of the application.

> **Murray J:** [1219] This is a petition by a shareholder in Spargos Mining NL ("Spargos") for relief pursuant to the Companies (Western Australia) Code sec 320. The application is made by one David Jenkins who since 6 December 1989 has with his wife been jointly registered as the holder of 90,000 fully paid 25 cent shares in Spargos. He makes the application, as his evidence to the Court asserts, by reason of perceived oppression as he understood it to be, arising out of the activities of the directors of Spargos over a period of time. Mr Jenkins conceded that all of the matters, except for a sale of a half share in Spargos' principal asset, the operating Bellevue Gold Mine, were past events at the time in late November 1989 when he acquired the shares providing the qualification to bring the petition. ...
>
> [1222] The question of standing here does not arise in the context of the administrative or public law cases. The Court is here asked to provide a remedy if it is of the opinion that the circumstances proved demonstrate what may be described as operative unfairness to a member, a group of members or the members of a company as a whole. In my view the application may within the terms of sec 320(1) be made by any person who is then a member. His interest as a member is a sufficient interest in terms of the statute to confer standing to bring proceedings which are of course at his risk, if the Court is unpersuaded to the opinion required by sec 320(2). On the other hand, the unfairness required to be established in my view quite evidently need not be to the particular member who is that applicant. It may, I think, be demonstrated with respect to any member or group of members to which the applicant need not belong. If that was established I would not think that the Court would be

entitled to deny relief, because the applicant was not a member of the particular aggrieved group of members. Similarly, if the view taken was that there was oppression to the members as a whole, it would not seem to me to be open to argue that so far as the applicant member was concerned his shareholding was so small that the nature of the oppression so far as he was concerned must be regarded as minimal. It would remain the fact that the statutory criteria for relief had been made out in proceedings which are entirely the creature of statute, although of respectable antiquity, and in my view that would be an end to the matter.

The statute has created a cause of action and conferred standing upon a person who or which is a member at the time of the application and who has a genuine belief that [1223] the provable facts will demonstrate the grounds for relief for which the statute provides. In one sense it may be that the statute should be regarded as conferring standing upon the genuinely concerned intermeddler and that is the only restriction upon the Pandora's box of meddlesome intervention of which the statute conceives. ...

It is apparent to me that Mr Jenkins was honestly of the view that the affairs of the company were being conducted oppressively and in a way which was unfairly prejudicial to and unfairly discriminatory against the shareholders and contrary to their interests as a whole, in that the company was in effect being used by the directors as a cash box to further what the directors thought were the interests of the Independent Resources Group as a whole, but in a way which Mr Jenkins genuinely considered to be inimical to the interests of the shareholders, or at least the minority shareholders, in Spargos, considered as a group in themselves. Such a belief, genuinely held, is sufficient to ground the petition and it is unnecessary in my view, except perhaps in the context of my discretion within sec 320 (if it should be necessary to consider that) to consider further Spargos' submissions with respect to the standing of the petitioner.

[12.290] Conversely, if the applicant is no longer a member, his or her right to bring an application under s 234 will have ceased, unless he or she falls with s 234(b) or (c): *Niord Pty Ltd v Adelaide Petroleum NL* (1990) 8 ACLC 684 at 697 and 698; *Mike Gaffikin Marine Pty Ltd v Princess Street Marina Pty Ltd* (1995) 13 ACLC 991 at 1004 and 1005; *Titlow v Intercapital Group (Australia) Pty Ltd* (1996) 14 ACLC 1065. In the latter case the applicant had held employee shares, but on the cessation of his employment they were transferred and his name removed from the register. He claimed that the transfer was voidable and that he was entitled to have his name restored to the register. The court found that as he was not a member at the time of the initiation of the proceedings he could not bring an action under one of the predecessors to ss 232-235, s 260. Today, the applicant in *Titlow v Intercapital Group (Australia) Pty Ltd* (1996) 14 ACLC 1065 could have fallen within s 234(c) as the conduct of which he complained related to his cessation of membership.

[12.300] Creditors and other persons who may be affected by the acts and omissions of directors or majority shareholders have no standing under the section unless they are members of the subject company: *Mike Gaffikin Marine Pty Ltd v Princess Street Marina Pty Ltd* (1995) 13

ACLC 991; *Ruralcorp Consulting Pty Ltd v Pynery Pty Ltd* (1996) 21 ACSR 161 at 169.

[12.310] There is no requirement that the member be a minority shareholder. Contra *Re Polyresins Pty Ltd* (1998) 16 ACLC 1,674 at 1683. The contrary view expressed in that case is clearly incorrect. Conceivably, a majority shareholder may be oppressed by a minority shareholder where, for example, beneficial ownership does not coincide with voting rights. Moreover, as s 232 extends to acts or omissions that are contrary to the interests of the company as a whole, there is no need for the applicant to be hurt by the oppressor's conduct: *Re Spargos Mining NL* (1990) 8 ACLC 1218.

[12.320] The legislation now applies whether the member is affected in his or her capacity as a member or 'in a capacity other than as a member': s 234(A)(i). See also *Re G Jeffrey Pty Ltd* (1984) 2 ACLC 421; *Thomas v Mackay Investments* (1996) 22 ACSR 294 at 302. While this would appear to enable a member to bring an application when affected in a non-corporate capacity, such as a creditor, where the action is brought merely to achieve a collateral purpose, for example, to pressure the company to repay a loan, the application will be dismissed as an abuse of process: *Re Bellador Silk Ltd* [1965] 1 All ER 667.

[12.330] While most applications involve the conduct of small proprietary companies, members of public companies may also seek relief: *Cumberland Holdings Ltd v Washington H Soul Pattinson & Co Ltd* (1977) 13 ALR 561. The legislation applies to all types of companies, whether limited by shares or guarantee: *ASC v Multiple Sclerosis Society of Tasmania* (1993) 11 ACLC 461. Applications may not, however, be brought after the company is in liquidation: *Webb v Stanfield* (1990) 8 ACLC 715; *Zempilas v JN Taylor Holdings Ltd (in liq) (No 6)* (1991) 9 ACLC 835.

Who may be the oppressor?

[12.340] While the legislation originally confined the availability of relief to members affected by the conduct of oppressive directors, today the legislation no longer specifies who the oppressor must be, nor the capacity in which that person must be acting. '[A]nyone who is taking part in the conduct of the affairs of the company, whether *de facto* or *de jure*' may be the subject of application: *Re HR Harmer Ltd* [1958] 3 All ER 689 at 698. See also *Re East West Promotions Pty Ltd* (1986) 4 ACLC 84 at 88. Moreover, as the section extends to resolutions or proposed resolutions and acts 'by or behalf of the company', the oppressor may be other members or classes of members or even the company itself.

Scope of s 232

Objective test

[12.350] Whether the conduct complained of is oppressive, unfairly prejudicial or unfairly discriminatory is determined objectively, from the position of a hypothetical reasonable person/director: *Wayde v NSW Rugby League Ltd* (1985) 3 ACLC 799 at 804 and 806; *Morgan v 45 Flers Avenue Pty Ltd* (1986) 10 ACLR 692 at 704; *Dynasty Pty Ltd v Coombs* (1994) 12 ACLC 915; (1995) 13 ACLC 1290 at 1296.

Act or omission

[12.360] As noted above, the legislation is not confined to positive acts. Under s 232(b), an omission that has the prescribed impact may trigger an application. Adopting a passive policy of starving the company of the materials it needed to conduct its business was held to be oppressive in *Scottish Co-op Wholesale Society Ltd v Meyer* [1959] AC 324. See further the case extracts below. Similarly, in *Re Bright Pine Mills Pty Ltd* [1969] VR 1002, the foregoing of a corporate opportunity so that it could be adopted by another company in which the director was interested was held to be an unfairly prejudicial omission.

Isolated past conduct or continuous course of conduct

[12.370] While originally the legislation required the conduct to be continuous up to the date of the application, today the conduct may be isolated and may have occurred in the past, even prior to the shareholder becoming a member: *Re Spargos Mining NL* (1990) 8 ACLC 1218; *Re Norvabron Pty Ltd (No 2)* (1986) 5 ACLC 184 at 212. Whether the act or omission complained of continues will, however, be relevant to the relief sought: *Re Spargos Mining NL*. The legislation now also expressly extends to proposed acts: s 232(b) and (c).

Ultra vires, illegal or want of probity

[12.380] It is not necessary that the conduct be *ultra vires*, illegal or involve a want of probity before it may be the subject of an application. Hence, the directors may be acting consistently with the company's constitution but nevertheless be held to be acting oppressively in light of members' expectations stemming from agreements or understandings: *Ebrahimi v Westbourne Galleries Ltd* [1973] AC 360; *Re M Dalley & Co Pty Ltd* (1968) 1 ACLR 489. In this regard see further the discussion of *Ebrahimi v Westbourne Galleries Ltd* in Chapter 13.

Discriminatory

[12.390] While s 232 extends to acts or omissions that are unfairly discriminatory, it is not a prerequisite for the operation of the Part that the member be singled out for ill treatment: *Re HR Harmer Ltd* [1958] 3 All ER 689. Conduct which affects all members equally, including the 'oppressor', may be oppressive: *Scottish Co-op Wholesale Society Ltd v Meyer* [1959] AC 324. This is supported by the extension of s 232(d) to acts and omissions that are contrary to the interests of the members as a whole.

Oppressive conduct

[12.400] As noted above, the predecessors to s 232 were originally confined to oppressive conduct. While s 232 now extends beyond such, as noted above, oppressive conduct continues to be a basis for an application for relief under s 232. While generally, definitions of 'oppressive' conduct have required some element of *mala fides* on the oppressor's part (*Scottish Co-operative Society v Meyer* [1959] AC 324), as noted above *bona fide* actions of the directors can be oppressive: *Re M Dalley & Co Pty Ltd* (1968) 1 ACLR 489. In essence, oppression includes conduct which 'lacks the degree of probity which [the members] are entitled to expect in the conduct of the company's affairs': *Re Jermyn Street Turkish Baths Ltd* [1971] WLR 1042 at 1059. Greater clarification of this term may be obtained from an examination of a leading case, *Scottish Co-operative Society v Meyer* [1959] AC 324.

Scottish Co-operative Society v Meyer
House of Lords: Viscount Simonds, Lords Morton of Henryton, Keith of Avonholm and Denning
[1959] AC 324

The board of directors was constituted by the two respondents and three nominee directors of the appellant society. As a result of the rejection of a share offer made by the appellant, seeking to buy further shares in the company, relations on the board became hostile. The appellant established within itself a new department that competed with the company and diverted the produce from its mills to this body, rather than the company. The appellant declined to supply the company the cloth it needed, except at non-competitive prices. The effect of creating the new department and passive policy of non-supply was to take business from the company and starve it of the materials it needed to conduct its business. With the downturn in business, the value of the company's shares plummeted. While the nominee directors were aware of the appellant's policy, they did nothing to remedy the situation.

The respondents sought relief under the s 210 of the *Companies Act* 1948 (UK) on the ground that the affairs of the company were being conducted in an oppressive manner. The court at first instance agreed and ordered the appellants to purchase the respondents' shares. On appeal the House of Lords agreed that by adopting this passive policy the directors had subordinated the interests of the company to those of the Society and in turn acted in an oppressive manner. The House of Lords also asserted that the order granted constituted the most appropriate form of relief, rather than winding the company up.

> **Lord Denning**: **[366]** Again, when the co-operative society determined to set up its own rayon department, competing with the business of the company, the duty of the three directors to the company was to do their best to promote its business and to act with complete good faith towards it; and, in consequence, not to disclose their knowledge of its affairs to a competitor, and not even to work for a competitor, when to do so might operate to the disadvantage of the

company ... whereas they were under the self-same duties to the society. It is plain that, in the circumstances, these three gentlemen could not do their duty by both companies, and they did not do so. They put their duty to the society above their duty to the company in this sense, at least, that they did nothing to defend the interests of the company against the conduct of the society. They probably thought that 'as nominees' of the co-operative society their first duty was to the co-operative society. In this they were wrong. By subordinating the interest of the company to those of the society, they conducted the affairs of the company in a manner oppressive to other shareholders.

It is said that these three directors were, at most, only guilty of inaction – of doing nothing to protect the company. But the affairs of a company can, in my opinion, be conducted oppressively by the directors doing nothing to defend its interests when they ought to do something – just as they can conduct its affairs oppressively by doing something injurious to its interests when they ought not to do it. ...

[368] So I would hold that the affairs of the company were being conducted in a manner oppressive to the respondents. The crucial date is, I think, the date on which the petition was lodged – 14 July 1953. If the respondents had at that time a petition to wind up the company compulsorily, the petition would undoubtedly have been granted. The facts would plainly justify such an order on the ground that it was 'just and equitable' that the company should be wound up ... But such an order would unfairly prejudice the respondents because they would only recover the break-up value of their shares. So, instead of petitioning for winding-up order, they seek to invoke the new remedy given by s 210 of the Companies Act 1948. But what is the appropriate remedy? ...

The object of the remedy is to bring 'to an end the matters complained of', that is, the oppression, and this can be done even though the business of the company has been brought to a standstill. If a remedy is available when the [369] oppression is so moderate that it only inflicts wounds on the company, while leaving it active, so also, it should be available when the oppression is so great as to put the company out of action altogether. Even though the oppressor by his oppression brings down the whole edifice – destroying the value of his own shares with those of everyone else – the injured shareholders have, I think, a remedy under s 210.

One of the most useful orders mentioned in the section – which will enable the court to do justice to the injured shareholders – is to order the oppressor buy their shares at a fair price; and a price would be, I think, the value of which the shares would have had at the date of the petition, if there had been no oppression.

Unfairly prejudicial or discriminatory conduct

[12.410] The scope of the legislation was significantly extended by including conduct that is, *inter alia*, unfairly prejudicial or unfairly discriminatory: s 232(e). Mere prejudice or discrimination does not, however, suffice to place conduct within this category. There must also be proof of unfairness: *Wayde v New South Wales Rugby League Ltd* (1985) 3 ACLC 799.

Wayde v New South Wales Rugby League Ltd
High Court of Australia: Mason ACJ, Wilson, Deane,
Dawson and Brennan JJ
(1985) 3 ACLC 799

The directors of the New South Wales Rugby League ('League') decided that the number of teams in the Winfield Cup premiership competition in 1985 should be limited to 12. The decision was to make the competition more efficient and to make it more attractive to the public. The board also determined that the application by the Western Suburbs District Rugby League Football Club ('Wests') for entry into that competition should be rejected. Members of the League representing Wests sought an order restraining the League from acting upon the decision on the basis that it was oppressive, unfairly prejudicial to, or discriminatory against, Wests under a predecessor to s 232, s 320.

The court at first instance agreed that the conduct was oppressive, unfairly prejudicial to, or discriminatory against, Wests and granted an order restraining the League from acting on the board's decision. This finding was set aside on appeal to the Court of Appeal. On further appeal the High Court agreed, finding that the conduct was not oppressive, unfairly prejudicial or unfairly discriminatory. While Wests may have been prejudiced by the decision, it had not been unfairly prejudiced. The board had in good faith used its power to determine which clubs should participate in the competition to further the League's object of promoting the sport's best interests. As Wests fully appreciated that it had no secure right to participate in the premiership competition, the decision was not unfair.

Mason ACJ, Wilson, Deane, Dawson JJ: [803] It is conceded that the Board made the decisions which are under attack in good faith. There is no suggestion that, in exercising the power conferred by Art 76, it failed to have regard to relevant considerations or that it took irrelevant considerations into account. It is a point of great importance that the decisions were made in the exercise of a power that is expressly conferred on the Board, a power to determine the nature and extent of the competition that was to take place in 1985 and the clubs that were to be permitted to participate in it. It is not a case where the directors of a company, in the exercise of the general powers of management of the company, might bona fide adopt a policy or decide upon a course of action which is alleged to be unfairly prejudicial to a minority of the members of the company. In that kind of case it may well be appropriate for the Court, on an application for relief under sec 320, to examine the policy which has been pursued or the proposed course of action in order to determine the fairness or unfairness of the course which has been taken by those in control of the company. The Court may be required in such circumstances to undertake a balancing exercise between the competing considerations disclosed by the evidence: cf *Thomas v HW Thomas Ltd* (1984) 2 ACLC 610 at pp 618, 620.

But here the decision to limit the premiership competition to twelve participants — and this was the critical decision — was taken honestly in pursuit of the object of fostering the game of rugby league and serving its best interests (cl 3(b), memorandum of association). The Board was not only empowered but obliged to face up to the difficulties presented by a competition which occupied too long a period of the year and to exercise the power expressly bestowed upon it in a manner which it considered to be in the best interests of the game. It is not seriously suggested that the Board overlooked the extreme consequences which the decision would visit upon Wests, amounting perhaps to its virtual extinction. The appellants' contention is that, while the Board could reasonably conclude that a competition confined to twelve clubs was preferable to one involving thirteen clubs, the facts that the latter was not wholly unworkable and that Wests was a viable competitor lead to the conclusion that the prejudice to Wests so outweighs the perceived benefits to the League as to be unfair. They submit that the exclusion of a viable club, such exclusion not being required to render the competition workable, would promote "purposes foreign to the company's operations, affairs and organizations" adopting the meaning ascribed to the phrase "benefit of the company as a whole" by Dixon J in *Peters American Delicacy Co Ltd v Heath* (1939) 61 CLR 457 at p 512.

The answer to this contention is that no amount of sympathy for Wests can obscure the fact that the League was expressly constituted to promote the best interests of the sport and empowered to determine which clubs should be entitled to participate in competitions conducted by it. It was upon this basis that the clubs, including Wests, chose to incorporate. Indeed, the 1984 correspondence between Wests and the League which is in evidence plainly shows that Wests itself fully appreciated that it had no secure right to participate in the premiership competition. In truth, the Board was confronted with a conflict of immediate interest between Wests on the one hand and the League as a whole on the other and the exercise of the power conferred by Art 76 must **[804]** necessarily be prejudicial to one or the other. Given the special expertise and experience of the Board, the bona fide and proper exercise of the power in pursuit of the purpose for which it was conferred and the caution which a Court must exercise in determining an application under sec 320 of the Code in order to avoid an unwarranted assumption of the responsibility for management of the company, the appellants faced a difficult task in seeking to prove that the decisions in question were unfairly prejudicial to Wests and therefore not in the overall interests of the members as a whole. It has not been shown that those decisions of the Board were such that no Board acting reasonably could have made them. The effect of those decisions on Wests was harsh indeed. It has not, however, been shown that they were oppressive or unfairly prejudicial or discriminatory or that their effect was such as to warrant the conclusion that the affairs of the League were or are being conducted in a manner that was or is oppressive or unfairly prejudicial. That being so, the appellants have failed to make good their second submission.

The appeal must be dismissed.

Brennan J: **[804]** As the power conferred by Art 76 is of such a nature that its exercise may discriminate among the clubs wishing to compete and may prejudice a club which is excluded from a competition, an exercise of the power is not necessarily invalid because a club is discriminated against and prejudiced by being excluded from a competition. The countervailing considerations of efficient organization of the competition and the interests of the respective clubs which wish to compete must be weighed by the directors (cf *Mills v Mills* (1938) 60 CLR 150 at p 164) and a decision made as to which interest shall prevail or as to how the interests should be adjusted. The resolution of the countervailing considerations was a function entrusted to the directors by the constitution of the League and the members of the League were entitled to have their directors perform that function according to their own judgment. If we leave aside for the moment sec 320 of the *Companies (New South Wales) Code*, there is no foundation for the order sought by Wests to restrain the Board of Directors from acting on their resolution to exclude Wests. As Lord Wilberforce said in delivering the judgment of the Judicial Committee in *Howard Smith Ltd v Ampol Ltd* [1974] AC 821 at p 832:

> [805] "There is no appeal on merits from management decisions to courts of law; nor will courts of law assume to act as a kind of supervisory board over decisions within the powers of management honestly arrived at."

That proposition does not apply, of course, where the statute requires a decision to be confirmed by the court and the court gives or withholds confirmation according to its opinion of the fairness of the decision – for example, a decision to reduce capital (cf *Poole v National Bank of China, Limited* [1907] AC 229 at p 239; *Carruth v Imperial Chemical Industries, Ltd* [1937] AC 707 at pp 744, 763, 770). But in the absence of statutory authority, the court may not intervene and hold the decision invalid on the ground that the court thinks the decision unreasonable. If the decision is such that no reasonable board of directors could think the decision to be substantially for a purpose for which the power was conferred, the court may infer that the directors did not make the decision in good faith for a purpose within the power and intervene on that ground (see *Shuttleworth v Cox Brothers & (Maidenhead)* [1927] 2 KB 9 at pp 23, 24). The dictum of Latham CJ in *Peters' American Delicacy Co Ltd v Heath* (1939) 61 CLR 457 at p 481, with respect to a decision which "no reasonable man could have reached" relied on *Shuttleworth*, and should not be understood as asserting a wider ground for intervention. In the present case the good faith of the directors was conceded and Wests' complaint was not that the directors failed to consider the object of fostering the game or failed to take into account the impact of their decision on Wests. In essence, the attack on the decision is founded on the submission that the directors unreasonably failed to give the disability which their decision placed on Wests sufficient weight. The validity of an exercise of power cannot be challenged merely because too little weight is given to some matters which properly fall for consideration and too much to others, for the court will not substitute its discretion for the discretion exercised in good faith by the directors. As Barwick CJ, McTiernan and Kitto JJ said in *Harlowe's Nominees Pty Ltd v Woodside (Lakes Entrance) Oil Co N* (1968) 121 CLR 483 at p 493:

> "Directors in whom are vested the right and the duty of deciding where the company's interests lie and how they are to be served may be concerned with a wide range of practical considerations, and their judgment, if exercised in good faith and not for irrelevant purposes, is not open to review in the courts."

Section 320, however, extends the grounds for curial intervention. It provides a wide range of remedies when the Court is of the opinion, *inter alia*, that a resolution or a proposed resolution "was or would be oppressive or unfairly prejudicial to, or unfairly discriminatory against, a member or members ... or was or would be contrary to the interests of the members as a whole" (subsec (2)(b)). The remedies for which sec 320 provides are available whether or not the resolution complained of is a valid resolution. To say that the resolution was adopted in good faith and for a purpose within the power conferred is relevant to but not conclusive of the question whether relief should be granted under sec 320.

In earlier times, the statutory precursors of sec 320 empowered the court to grant a remedy when the affairs of the company were being conducted "in a manner oppressive to one or more of the members" (see, for example, sec 186 of the *Companies Act* 1961 (NSW)). In that context, Viscount Simonds defined oppressive to be "burdensome, harsh and wrongful" (*Scottish Co-operative Wholesale Society Ltd v Meyer* [1959] AC 324 at p 342). The strength of those epithets confined the grounds on which the court might intervene, but sec 320 (both in its original 1981 form and in its amended 1983 form) broadens the grounds of intervention. Clearly the legislature intends to provide a greater measure of curial protection to members of a company, especially if they be in a minority, than the protection afforded under earlier *Companies Acts*. In *Thomas v HW Thomas Ltd* (1984) 2 ACLC 610, the Court of Appeal of New Zealand held that under a similar but not identical provision (sec 209 of the Companies Act 1955 (NZ)) it was not necessary for a complainant to point "to any actual irregularity or to an invasion of his legal rights or to a lack of probity or want of good faith towards him on the part of those in control of the company": per Richardson J at p 617. I **[806]** would respectfully adopt that observation and apply it to sec 320. Section 209 of the New Zealand Act provides a remedy in cases where the Court "is of the opinion that it is just and equitable" to grant a remedy. Although notions of what is just and equitable are relevantly to be considered in applying sec 320, the just and equitable requirement does not appear in the analogous provisions of the Australian Companies Codes. That textual difference may be material, but I do not pause to consider it now, for it does not affect the view which I take of the present case.

Here, the appellants seek to restrain the exercise of a power of such a nature that its exercise is apt to discriminate among the clubs whose representatives are members of the League and to prejudice any club which is excluded from the Premiership Competition. The expression "the interests of the members as a whole" is not likely to provide a criterion for intervention in respect of a decision made in exercise of a power that is conferred to resolve a conflict of interests between one or more members on the one hand and the League's object of fostering the game on the other. In that context the interests of the members as a whole "tends to become a cant expression", to adopt the words of Rich J in *Richard Brady Franks Ltd v Price* (1937) 58 CLR 112 at p 138. In the present case, the relevant expressions are "oppressive or unfairly prejudicial to, or unfairly discriminatory against, a member". Where the directors of a company are empowered to discriminate among its members and to prejudice the interests of one of them, the adoption of a resolution which has that effect and which is made in good faith and for a purpose within the power is not, without more, "oppressive or unfairly prejudicial to, or unfairly discriminatory against, a member". Section 320 requires proof of oppression or proof of unfairness: proof of mere prejudice to or discrimination against a member is insufficient to attract the Court's jurisdiction to intervene. In the case of some discretionary powers, any prejudice to a member or any discrimination against him may be a badge of unfairness in the exercise of the power, but not when the discretionary power contemplates the effecting of prejudice or discrimination. It is not necessary now to decide whether "oppressive" carries in the context of sec 320 the meaning which it carried in the context of the statutory precursors of sec 320. At a minimum, oppression imports unfairness and that is the critical question in the present case.

It is not necessarily unfair for directors in good faith to advance one of the objects of the company to the prejudice of a member where the advancement of the object necessarily entails prejudice to that member or discrimination against him. Prima facie, it is for the directors and not for the Court to decide whether the furthering of a corporate object which is inimical to a member's interests should prevail over those interests or whether some balance should be struck between them. The directors' view is not conclusive, but an element in assessing unfairness to a member is the agreement of all members to repose the power to affect their interests in the directors: see sec 78 of the Code. Nevertheless, if the directors exercise a power – albeit in good faith and for a purpose within the power – so as to impose a disadvantage, disability or burden on a member that, according to ordinary standards of reasonableness and fair dealing is unfair, the Court may intervene under sec 320. The question of unfairness is one of fact and degree which sec 320 requires the Court to determine, but not without regard to the view which the directors themselves have formed and not without allowing for any special skill, knowledge and acumen possessed by the directors. The operation of sec 320 may be attracted to a decision made by directors which is made in good faith for a purpose within the directors' power but which reasonable directors would think to be unfair. The test of unfairness is objective and it is necessary, though difficult, to postulate a standard of reasonable directors possessed of any special skill, knowledge or acumen possessed by the directors. The test assumes (whether it be the fact or not) that reasonable directors weigh the furthering of the corporate object against the disadvantage, disability or burden which their decision will impose, and address their minds to the question whether a proposed decision is unfair. The Court must determine whether reasonable directors, possessing any special skill, knowledge or acumen possessed by the directors and having in mind the importance of furthering the corporate object on the one hand and the disadvantage, disability or burden which their decision will impose on a member [807] on the other, would have decided that it was unfair to make that decision.

The question here is whether the resolutions which were manifestly prejudicial to and discriminatory against Wests, were also unfair – that is, so unfair that reasonable directors who considered the disability the decision placed on Wests would not have thought it fair to impose it. The decision by the League's directors to reduce the number of competitors to 12 and to exclude Wests was in fact taken with full knowledge of the disability that that decision would place on Wests. But the directors also knew that the larger competition was burdensome to, and perhaps dangerous for, players and that a shorter season was conducive to better organization of the Premiership Competition. The directors had to make a difficult decision in which it was necessary to draw upon the skills, knowledge and understanding of experienced administrators of the game of rugby league. The Court, in determining whether the decision was unfair, is bound to have regard to the fact that the decision was admittedly made by experienced administrators to further the interests of the game. There is nothing to suggest unfairness save the inevitable prejudice to and discrimination against Wests, but that is insufficient by itself to show that reasonable directors with the special qualities possessed by experienced administrators would have decided that it was unfair to exercise their power in the way the League's directors did. The appeal should be dismissed.

[12.420] Whether conduct is unfair will depend on the history of the association and the parties' expectations: *Thomas v HW Thomas Ltd* (1984) 2 ACLC 610 at 618:

> Fairness cannot be assessed in a vacuum or simply from one member's point of view. It will often depend on weighing conflicting interests of different groups within the company. It is a matter of balancing all the interests involved in terms of the policies underlying the companies legislation in general and [ss 232-235] in particular: thus to have regard to the principles governing the duties of a director in the conduct of the affairs of a company and the rights and duties of a majority shareholder in relation to the minority; but to recognise that [ss 232-235 are] ... remedial provision[s] designed to allow the court to intervene where there is a visible departure from the standards of fair dealing; and in light of the history and structure of the particular company and the reasonable expectations of the members whether the detriment occasioned to the complaining member's interests arising from the acts or conduct of the company in that way is justifiable.

[12.430] While the courts have stressed that they should not take a narrow view of the facts when determining whether there has been unfairness within s 232, as evidenced in *Wayde v New South Wales Rugby League Ltd* (1985) 3 ACLC 799, in determining whether conduct is unfair the courts are reluctant to second guess a *bona fide* decision by the board as to what is in the company's best interests. See also *Dosike Pty Ltd v Johnson* (1996) 22 ACSR 752 at 757. Thus, the making of a bad business decision will not, of itself, be oppressive or unfair: *Shirim v Fesena* [2002] NSWSC 10.

[12.440] Conduct that has been held to be oppressive, unfairly prejudicial or discriminatory includes:

- altering the company's constitution to extinguish a member's voting rights (*Shears v Phosphate Co-operative Co of Aust Ltd* (1988) 14 ACLR 747);
- issuing shares to dilute a member's interest (*Re Dalkeith Investments Pty Ltd* (1984) 9 ACLR 247; *Kokotovich Constructions Pty Ltd v Wallington* (1995) 13 ACLC 1113);
- removing a director from a 'quasi-partnership' (*Ebrahimi v Westbourne Galleries Ltd* [1973] AC 360 – see further the extracts in Chapter 13); *Aloridge Pty Ltd (prov liq apptd) v West Australian Gem Explorers Pty Ltd (in liq)* (1996) 22 ACSR 484 at 490);
- preventing the minority shareholder/director participating in meetings (*John J Starr (Real Estate) Pty Ltd v Robert A Andrew (A'Asia) Pty Ltd* (1991) 9 ACLC 1372; *Shirim v Fesena* [2002] NSWSC 10); and
- the payment of unreasonable emoluments to directors at the expense of dividends (*Sanford v Sanford Courier Service Pty Ltd* (1987) 5 ACLC 394). See also *Re Bagot Well Pastoral Co Pty Ltd* (1993) 11 ACLC 1; *Roberts v Walter Developments Pty Ltd* (1997) 15 ACLC 882; *Cooke v Fairbairn* [2003] NSWSC 232.

Note in regard to the latter point that the non-payment of dividends will not always of itself be unfairly prejudicial. In *Thomas v HW Thomas Pty Ltd* (1984) 2 ACLC 610 and *Re G Jeffrey (Mens Store) Pty Ltd* (1984) 2

ACLC 421, the directors' decision to manage the subject companies in a financially conservative manner was held not to fall within the parameters of the legislation. The courts held there to be nothing unfair about making the applicants abide by the directors' decisions as to appropriate distributions.

Contrary to interests of members as a whole

[12.450] The inclusion of the phrase 'contrary to the interests of the members as a whole' significantly widens the scope of s 232 as it allows the court to order relief where all members are equally prejudiced by the conduct through, for example, the dissipation of corporate assets. The courts' reluctance to reassess the board's view as to the benefits of a transaction will, however, limit the occasions when this aspect of s 232 will be utilised.

Nature of relief under s 233

[12.460] Section 233(1) confers on the court a broad discretion to make such order(s) 'that it considers appropriate'. Section 233(1)(a)-(j) provides a non-exhaustive list of orders that the court may make individually or in combination:

- the company be wound up;
- the company's constitution be modified or repealed;
- the affairs of the company be regulated;
- the shares of a member or a person to whom the shares are transmitted by will or under operation of law be purchased by another member;
- shares be purchased by the company and its share capital be correspondingly reduced;
- proceedings be instituted, prosecuted, defended or discontinued by the company;
- proceedings be instituted, defended or discontinued in the name of the company and on its behalf by a member or a person to whom the shares are transmitted by will or under operation of law;
- a receiver or a receiver and manager of property be appointed;
- restraining a person engaging in specified conduct or doing a specified thing; or
- requiring a person to do a specified act.

Note, in *In the Matter of Sutherland v NRMA* [2003] NSWSC 829, the court used the oppression remedy to amend the company's constitution to delete clauses that were held to be oppressive, unfairly prejudicial or unfairly discriminatory to the applicant and other shareholders in his age bracket.

Where an order is made under s 233, the applicant must lodge a copy of the order with ASIC within 14 days after it is made: s 235.

Injunctions

Introduction

[12.470] While s 1324 provides aggrieved shareholders with a speedier form of relief than ss 232-235, there being no need to engage in the lengthy process of proving oppressive conduct, strangely this section, and its predecessor s 574, have rarely been used. Section 1324(1) allows ASIC or a person 'whose interests have been, are or would be affected by the conduct' to apply for an injunction or interim injunction (s 1324(4)) restraining a person who engages in conduct which, in essence, directly or indirectly involves a contravention of the *Corporations Act*. Under s 1324(2), the court may require a person who fails or refuses to do an act required by the *Corporations Act* to do that act or thing. The section extends to past, present and proposed breaches of the *Corporations Act*: s 1324(1) and (2). Relief may be ordered under s 1324(1) or (2) whether or not it appears:

- the person will continue to engage, or refuse/fail to engage, in that conduct;
- the person has previously engaged, or refused/failed to engage, in that conduct; and
- there is an imminent danger of substantial damage to any person if that person engages, or refuses/fails to engage, in that conduct: s 1324(6) and (7).

Standing to apply for injunction

[12.480] Section 1324 extends standing to seek an injunction to ASIC and any 'person whose interests have been, are or would be affected by the conduct'. The latter phrase allows a wider group of applicants to seek this form of relief than s 234. In particular, the section allows third parties, such as creditors, to seek injunctive relief: *Allen v Atalay* (1994) 12 ACLC 7; *Airpeak Pty Ltd v Jetstream Aircraft Ltd* (1997) 23 ACSR 715.

[12.490] The section does not appear to require the applicant to be affected directly, nor does it prescribe the nature of the person's interest. Thus, there is nothing in the section that suggests such a limitation and given the section is remedial in nature, an expansive interpretation is preferable. This view finds support in Black CJ's comments as to the scope of s 1324 in *Cullen v Wills, Adler and Jooste* (1991) 9 ACLC 1450 at 1458 and the broad interpretation adopted in *Broken Hill Proprietary Co Pty Ltd v Bell Resources Ltd* (1984) 2 ACLC 157.

Broken Hill Proprietary Co Pty Ltd v Bell Resources Ltd
Supreme Court of Victoria: Hampel J
(1984) 2 ACLC 157

Broken Hill Proprietary Co Pty Ltd ('BHP') was the target company of a proposed takeover offer by Bell Resources Ltd ('Bell'). BHP's shareholders had been approached with a view to them exchanging their shares for shares in another company that was also a member of BHP. BHP sought an injunction preventing Bell distributing documents amongst BHP's members that allegedly did not comply with the prospectus requirements. Bell challenged BHP's standing to bring the application on the basis that the members, not the company, were affected by the proposed share swap.

The court held that BHP had standing to seek the injunction. It was asserted that s 1324 should be broadly interpreted and, as 7% of its issued share capital was affected by the share swap, the applicant had a sufficient nexus with the transaction to render it a person affected within s 1324.

Hampel J: [160] Mr Hulme of Queen's Counsel who, with Mr Callaway, appeared for the respondent, submitted that the applicant had no *locus standi*, essentially because a company is a separate entity from its shareholders. It was argued that on the material in this case it has not shown how the applicants' interests are or could be affected by the conduct of the respondent. Mr Hulme relied on the decision of Gillard J in *Colotone Holdings Ltd v Calsil Ltd* [1965] VR 129. That case concerned a takeover scheme which contained a number of conditions. The notice to the offeree corporation which outlined the scheme differed materially from the scheme itself. There was therefore a contravention by the offeror corporation of sec 184(2)(a) of the *Companies Act*. His Honour held that although there had been such a contravention, the scheme was not thereby invalidated and any acceptance constituted a valid contract between the shareholder and the offeree corporation. Colotone had brought proceedings seeking a declaration that the scheme was void and the proceedings before his Honour were by way of an interlocutory injunction to restrain Colotone from proceeding with registration of any transfers received in response to the takeover offer.

In dismissing the application for an interlocutory injunction sought by the company and one shareholder, his Honour held that "neither plaintiff has shown any invasion of any personal right of a proprietary nature or of a right analogous thereto and neither plaintiff has shown any special injury arising from a breach by Calsil in failing to notify Calsil of the terms of the actual offer it proposed to make to the shareholders of Colotone. In the absence of the Attorney-General (or a representative on behalf of all shareholders at least) neither Colotone nor the plaintiff, Hansen, is competent to sue for an injunction".

It was Mr Hulme's submission that sec 574(1)(b) when referring to the interest which may be affected by the conduct is to be interpreted as referring to the interest of the kind contemplated by Gillard J in the *Colotone case*.

Mr Chernov submitted that sec 574 ought to be interpreted more liberally on the question of locus standi. He argued that the Companies Code was new legislation intended to give the widest possible protection to the public and that sec 574 should be reviewed as giving the Court wide powers to deal with any conduct which may contravene the Code. It followed that the class of persons who, apart from the Commission, could move the Court to act under the section should be as wide as possible and therefore subsec (1)(b) should not be read down to refer only to interests of the kind contemplated in the *Colotone case*.

The question of *locus standi* has received considerable attention in recent times, particularly in relation to legislation which can be said to be concerned primarily with the [161] protection of the public. ...

The *Companies Code*, in my view, is legislation which is clearly concerned in the [162] broadest sense with the protection of the public in respect of commercial activities of corporations. The whole legislative scheme is designed to ensure that the greatest possible protection is afforded in many instances by the provision to the public of information relevant to those commercial activities. Severe penalties are imposed by many sections of the Code for non-compliance with it and sec 574, in my view, is intended to enable interested persons to obtain relief in the form of injunctive relief to prevent actual or proposed conduct in contravention of the Code. It follows that in interpreting sec 574(1)(b) a broad interpretation consistent with the objectives of the Act should be adopted and not the more restricted interpretation of the kind adopted by Gillard J before the enactment of this much more far-reaching and comprehensive *Companies Code*.

In my view the interests referred to in this subsection are interests of any person (which includes a corporation) which go beyond the mere interest of a member of the public. It is not necessary that personal rights of a proprietary nature or rights analogous thereto are or may be affected nor need it be shown that any special injury arising from a breach of the Act has occurred.

The applicant in this case is a company whose shareholders have been approached with a view to their exchanging their shares in that company for shares in another company which is also the applicant's shareholder. The offer refers to fully paid ordinary shares in BHP together with all rights including the rights issue announced on 3 February 1984 and other entitlements. It is made in respect of a large quantity of shares, namely some 7% of the issued share capital of BHP. In those circumstances I accept Mr Chernov's submission that there is a sufficient nexus between the applicant company and the transaction with which these proceedings are concerned to bring the applicant within the scope of sec 574(1)(b) as a person whose interests have been or would be affected by the conduct. To hold otherwise would, in my view, be quite contrary to the scheme of this legislation and to the interest which the public has in ensuring that persons who have more than a mere general interest are able to invoke the powers of the Court given by sec 574. I hold therefore that the applicant has *locus standi* to make the present application.

Thus, under this view, any person who has an interest which goes beyond the mere interests of a member of the public may make an application. See also *QIW Retailers Ltd v David Holdings Pty Ltd (No 2)* (1992) 8 ACSR 333; *Airpeak Pty Ltd v Jetstream Aircraft Ltd* (1997) 23 ACSR 715 at 720.

[12.500] The scope of s 1324 was again scrutinised in *Mesenberg v Cord Industrial Recruiters Pty Ltd* (1996) 19 ACSR 483 at 488-489. Here, Young J suggested the section should not be interpreted as an exception to the rule in *Foss v Harbottle* (1843) 67 ER 189:

> I have extreme disquiet as to whether the legislature really intended that whenever there is a breach of even a minor part of the *Corporations Law*, any shareholder or creditor of the company, because he or she can say that he or she has a stronger interest than the ordinary member of the company, should be able to displace the role of the directors or the liquidators and make the

decision to prosecute a breach. ... I doubt very much, however, whether the legislature intended to abrogate the rule in *Foss v Harbottle* for internal disputes where sections of the Law repeat in a statutory form (sometimes making them criminal offences as well) what were the general law obligations of officers of a company.

Ultimately, Young J had to accept that the trend was to allow shareholders and creditors wide standing and to bring proceedings under s 1324, even for purely internal matters.

[12.510] Young J, however, went on to deny the applicant the ability to invoke s 1324 when the alleged breach of the *Corporations Act* supporting the application under s 1324 was a civil penalty provision. In that case, the plaintiff relied on an alleged breach of s 232(2), now s 181(1)(a). As this is a civil penalty provision, Young J held that only ASIC had authority to enforce this provision. He consequently held that the applicant lacked standing to seek an injunction under s 1324 upon the basis of this section. This view was subsequently rejected in *Airpeak Pty Ltd v Jetstream Aircraft Ltd* (1997) 15 ACLC 715.

Airpeak Pty Ltd v Jetstream Aircraft Ltd
Federal Court of Australia: Einfeld J
(1997) 15 ACLC 715

Airpeak Pty Ltd ('Airpeak') was a member of the Air Transportation Group. Airpeak had commenced an action against Jetstream Aircraft Ltd ('Jetstream') for breach of contracts. Jetstream cross-claimed for breaches of contract by Airpeak and for moneys lent to the Group. Jetstream also claimed directors of the Air Transportation Group had acted in contravention of certain duties of directors. Jetstream applied for orders under s 1324 for the return of various moneys received by these directors as a result of their alleged breaches of duty.

In turn these directors applied to the court to have that part of Jetstream's claim alleging a breach of director's duties by them struck out. They argued that Jetstream did not have standing pursuant to s 1324 to bring a claim alleging a breach of directors' duties under s 232(4) and (6) relying upon Young J's decision in *Mesenberg v Cord Industrial Recruiters Pty Ltd* (1996) 14 ACLC 519. In reply Jetstream claimed that it had standing because s 1324 gave the court power to grant injunctions on the application of 'any person whose interests have been, or would be affected' by certain types of conduct. As a creditor of the Air Transportation Group, Jetstream was a person 'whose interests had been affected' by the actions of the directors.

The court held that 'interests' in s 1324 had to be broadly interpreted as the interests of any person with an interest over and above a member of the public and that a creditor of a company had been recognised as such a person. To say that s 1324 could only be used by ASIC for a breach of a civil penalty provision was contrary to the plain terms of s 1324 which expressly gave anyone with an interest above the interests of a member of the public the right to apply for an injunction. Thus, the court refused to follow *Mesenberg v Cord Industrial Recruiters* and held Jetstream had standing under s 1324.

Einfeld J: [719] Standing for an action under sections 232(4) & (6)
Throughout the challenged paragraphs, Jetstream asserts that the McGowans' actions have caused detriment to Air Transportation thus affecting Jetstream's ability as a creditor to recover against it. Jetstream says that it is consequently a person whose interests have been affected within the meaning of section 1324 of the Corporations Law. Jetstream emphasises that it is not seeking damages, but various orders requiring money received by the McGowans in breach of the Act to be returned to the company and an order setting aside the Callmoon Agreement so that the assets transferred under its terms could be returned to the companies.

Standing to seek injunctions for contravention of the Corporations Law in general is set out in section 1324. This section gives the Court power to grant injunctions upon the application of the Australian Securities Commission (the Commission) or of any person whose interests have been, are or would be affected by certain conduct of specified types of individuals. The "interests" referred to in section 1324(1) and 1324(2)(b), on which Jetstream relies for its standing, has been interpreted broadly by the courts. In *Broken* **[720]** *Hill Proprietary Company Limited v Bell Resources Limited* (1984) 2 ACLC 157; 8 ACLR 609, Hampel J in the Victorian Supreme Court reasoned that the Companies Code, now replaced by the Corporations Law, was intended to enable interested persons to obtain injunctions to prevent actual or proposed contraventions of the Code. Consequently, "interests" in section 574 of the Code, now section 1324 of the Law, was interpreted (at 162) as referring to "interests of any person (which includes a corporation) which go beyond the mere interest of a member of the public". See also *QIW Retailers Ltd v Davids Holdings Pty Ltd (No 2)* (1992) 10 ACLC 1,162; 37 FLR 57; 109 ALR 377. In *Allen v Atalay* (1994) 12 ACLC 7, a case also involving an alleged contravention of section 232 of the *Corporations Law*, Hayne J stated at 10:

"... it is in my view arguable that a creditor having a right to prove in the liquidation of a company may be a person whose interests are affected by a contravention which is alleged to have led to the diminution in the value of his claim against the company."

Through its cross-claim, Jetstream asserts that it is a creditor of the applicants and that, in breaching their duty as directors of Air Transportation, the McGowans have caused detriment to Air Transportation, consequently making the company less able to meet Jetstream's claims. Thus, if Jetstream establishes itself as a creditor of Air Transportation by successfully defending the action brought by the applicants, that meets, so the argument goes, the requirements for standing under section 1324.

The applicants' argument that Jetstream does not have standing for the injunctions sought was based on a recent judgment by Justice Young of the NSW Supreme Court in *Mesenberg v Cord Industrial Recruiters Pty Ltd* (1996) 14 ACLC 519; 39 NSWLR 128; 19 ACSR 483. In consequence, the applicants assert, standing for an action for breach of these sections is exclusively defined by Part 9.4B of the Corporations Law entitled "Civil and Criminal Consequences of Contravening Civil Penalty Provisions'".

The argument proceeded thus. Section 232(6B) identifies subsections (4) and (6) of section 232 as civil penalty provisions as defined by section 1317DA of Part 9.4B which provides for civil and criminal consequences of contravening these provisions, or of being involved in a contravention of them. Pursuant to section 1317EB(1), only the Commission, its delegate or a person authorised by the Minister, may apply for a civil penalty order for the breach of a civil penalty provision. In *Mesenberg* Justice Young held that breaches of section 232 are dealt with exclusively by the civil penalty provisions in Part 9.4B. His Honour's reasoning was that it is more appropriate for regulators such as the Commission rather than for shareholders or creditors to commence proceedings for breach of section 232 because to allow otherwise would invite the mischief that the rule in *Foss v Harbottle* had been introduced to eradicate. Commenting on the decision in *Allen v Atalay*, Justice Young said at ACLC 525; NSWLR 134:

"I have extreme disquiet as to whether the legislature really intended that whenever there is a breach of even a very minor part of the Corporations Law any shareholder or creditor of the company, because he or she can say that he or she has a stronger interest than the ordinary member of the company, should be able to displace the role of the directors or the liquidators and make the decision to prosecute a breach."

While allowing the Court to order compensation to be paid to the disadvantaged company on the application for a civil penalty order (section 1317HA), Part 9.4B makes no provision for an injunction to be granted. The Commission or its delegate can only seek an injunction under section 1324. His Honour thus concluded at ACLC 526; NSWLR 137 that:

"... except in so far as s 1324 can be used by the Commission in aid of its rights under Part 9.4B, or a delegate of the minister is a person affected, there is no longer any right for a person affected (not being the Commission or person referred to in s 1317EB) to seek an injunction in respect of an alleged contravention of s 232."

I respectfully agree with Justice Young that only the Commission, its delegate or a person authorised by the Minister, is entitled to apply for and enforce civil penalty orders. However, it seems to me with due respect, as it appears to do to Hampel and Hayne JJ, to go against the plain terms of section 1324 (expressly giving anyone with an interest above the interests of a member of the public the right to apply for an [721] injunction) to say that it can only be used by persons having standing under Part 9.4B when section 232 is being activated. The concern that shareholders or creditors should not be allowed through litigation to interrupt the proper running of a company is certainly valid. However, the Court has the ultimate discretion in these matters as to whether to grant an injunction, in that it can choose to award damages instead of an injunction, or even refuse relief altogether if it considers the circumstances to be unworthy of intervention.

I therefore hold that Jetstream has standing pursuant to section 1324 of the Corporations Law to bring its claims for contravention of subsections (4) and (6) of section 232 of the Corporation Law, and thus refuse the application to strike out paragraphs 19-22, 59-61 & 69-75 of Jetstream's cross claim.

Applying this approach, the court held that a creditor had standing to bring an application under s 1324 even though it was based on an alleged breach of s 232. See also *Emlen Pty Ltd v St Barbara Mines Ltd* (1997) 24 ACSR 303 at 306.

Nature of relief under s 1324

[12.520] As with s 233, s 1324 provides the court with a broad discretion to make an order restraining or requiring a person to act on such terms as it thinks appropriate: s 1324(1) and (2). Such an order may be discharged or varied at any time: s 1324(5). Moreover, the court has power to grant both final and interim injunctions: *Liquorland (Aust) Pty Ltd v Anghie* (2002) 20 ACLC 58. The court may also order the person to pay damages to any other person in lieu of or in addition to an order under s 1324(1) and (2): s 1324(10).

Right to Inspect Books

Members' right to inspect books

[12.530] Members do not have an inherent right to inspect the company's books to enable them to determine whether, for example, the above shareholder remedies may be utilised. Thus, the source of such rights must be found in the company's constitution or the *Corporations Act*.

[12.540] Under replaceable rule, s 247D, the directors of the company or the general meeting through the passage of an ordinary resolution, may authorise a member to inspect the company's books.

[12.550] If a company is not governed by the replaceable rules and has no provision in its constitution echoing s 247D, the member will need to turn to s 247A. Under this provision, a member may apply to the court for an order enabling the member or another person, such as an accountant, on the member's behalf, to inspect the company's books. See also s 247A(4). The court's discretion extends not only to whether leave should be granted but also the width of such an order for inspection and therefore which books of the company should be made available: *Majestic Resources NL v Caveat Pty Ltd* [2004] WASCA 201. See also *Ito v Shinko (Australia) Pty Ltd* [2004] QSC 268.

[12.560] Such an order, however, may only be made if the applicant is acting in good faith and the inspection is for a proper purpose: s 247A(1) and (5). See *Re Augold NL* [1987] 2 Qd R 297 at 309; *Re Claremont Petroleum NL* [1990] 2 Qd 31; *Knightswood Nominees Pty Ltd v Sherwin Pastoral Co Ltd* (1989) 7 ACLC 536; *Ito v Shinko (Australia) Pty Ltd* [2004] QSC 268. Moreover, the inspection must be in connection with the bringing of a derivative action under s 237, discussed above: s 247A(5)(b). Thus, while s 247A(1) states that an application can be made by a member of a company or registered managed investment scheme, s 247A(2) states that standing to make such an application is confined to a person who has been granted leave, has applied for leave, or is eligible to apply for leave to bring a statutory derivative action. These sections make it clear that s 247A was intended to complement the granting of leave to bring a derivative action under s 237.

[12.570] In determining if the applicant is acting in good faith and for a proper purpose, the courts will consider whether the applicant has a *bona fide* interest in accessing the documents or access is sought for personal benefit and whether the member has had a previous opportunity to access the material. See, for example, *Knightswood Nominees Pty Ltd v Sherwin Pastoral Co Ltd* (1989) 7 ACLC 536; *Tinios v French Caledonia Travel Services Pty Ltd* (1994) 12 ACLC 622; *Czerwinski v Syrena Royal Pty Ltd* (2000) 18 ACLC 337. See further ss 247B and 247C.

Directors' right to inspect books

[12.580] Under s 290(1), directors have a right to access the company's financial records at all reasonable times. In a manner akin to s 247A, under s 290(2) a court may authorise a person to inspect the company's financial records on the director's behalf.

[12.590] Under s 198F(1) and (2), directors have access to the company's books for the purposes of legal proceedings where:
- the director is a party;
- the director proposes in good faith to bring the proceedings; or
- the director has reason to believe the proceedings will be brought against him or her.

This provision allows directors to access company information in regard to litigation that may affect them personally and thus the use of the information may not strictly be for carrying out directors' duties. See further *Stewart v Normandy NFM Ltd* (2000) 18 ACLC 814.

[12.600] In *Stewart v Normandy NFM Ltd*, Burley J held that s 198F could not be used where the applicant proposes to bring a derivative action. In such cases, s 247A, discussed above, must be utilised.

[12.610] The ability to bring such an application extends for seven years after the applicant ceased to be a director: s 198F(2). As access to financial records is authorised under s 290, s 198F does not extend to such records.

Review questions

1. Gertie and Fred ran a successful wine-making business together before deciding to incorporate Wine Pty Ltd in 1997. The decision to incorporate was based on personal liability and tax considerations. Gertie and Fred are the company's only two directors and shareholders. However, in recent times they have found it difficult to work together. Gertie wants to sell the business. Fred's response is: 'No way, we have come too far to sell this business!' In turn Gertie has begun using company funds to establish a new business in competition to Wine Pty Ltd. Advise Fred and Gertie as to any cause of action open to the parties under the *Corporations Act* to resolve these difficulties?

2. Things have become worse in the relationship. Gertie resigned her directorship, but still continued her management of part of Wine Pty Ltd's business, whilst developing her new business. Soon after Gertie's resignation, Fred appointed his son as a director and they in turn agreed to an increase in director's fees. At the same time, they recommended against Wine Pty Ltd paying a dividend that year, although the company had always paid dividends in the past. Gertie was angry that no dividends would be paid. Advise Gertie as to any causes of action Gertie has under the *Corporations Act* to resolve these difficulties?

Further reading

Baxt, 'The New Remedy in Oppression – A Reworded Provision or a New Remedy?' (1985) 3 *C&SLJ* 21

Baxt, 'Will Section 574 of the Companies Code Please Stand Up (and will Section 1324 of the Corporations Law Follow Suit)' (1987) 7 *C&SLJ* 388

Boros, Minority Shareholders' Remedies (1995)

Cameron 'Rugby League Footballers and Oppression or Injustice' (1985) 8 *UNSWLJ* 236

Cassidy, *Concise Corporations Law* (4th ed, Federation Press, Sydney, 2003) ch 12

Corkery, 'Oppression or Unfairness by Controllers – What Can a Shareholder Do About it? Analysis of s 320 of the Companies Code' (1985) 9 *Adel L Rev* 437

Companies and Securities Law Review Committee Report No 12, *Enforcement of the Duties of Directors and Officers of a Company By Means of a Statutory Derivative Action (*November 1990)

Ford, Austin and Ramsay, *Ford's Principles of Corporations Law* (11th ed, Butterworths, Sydney, 2003) ch 11

Ford, Austin and Ramsay, *An Introduction to the CLERP Act 1999* (Butterworths, Sydney, 2000)

Hill, 'Protecting Minority Shareholders and Reasonable Expectations' (1992) 10 *C&SLJ* 86

Norman, 'Access to Corporate Information' (1986) 4 *C&SLJ* 149

Prince, 'Australia's Statutory Derivative Action – Using the New Zealand Experience' (2000) 18 *C&SLJ* 493

Ramsay, 'Enforcement of Corporate Rights and Duties by Shareholders and the ASC: Evidence and Analysis' (1995) 23 *ABLR* 174

Ramsay, 'Can a Majority Shareholder Bring an Oppression Action' (1999) 17 *C&SLJ* 187

Ramsay, 'An Empirical Study of the Use of the Oppression Remedy' (1999) 27 ABLR 174

Rees, 'Directors' Unfair Conduct as a Ground for Remedy under the Companies Act' (1985) 3 *C&SLJ* 63

Sinnot and Duns, 'Shareholders' Right of Access to Corporate Books' (1990) 8 *C&SLJ* 73

Wishart, 'A Fresh Approach to Section 320' (1987) 17 *UWALR* 94

13

External Administration

Overview

This chapter is concerned with the means by which companies may be externally administered. These schemes are governed by Chap 5 of the *Corporations Act* 2001 (Cth) ('*Corporations Act*'). The types of external administration discussed are:

- receiverships;
- schemes of arrangements;
- administration; and
- winding up.

A common thread in the examination of these forms of external administration is the consequent appointment of a person(s) to administer the company and/or its property or business. To this end the chapter briefly considers the appointment, powers and duties of receivers, administrators and liquidators. Another interrelated thread in the discussion is the effect of appointing such persons has on the management of the company. For example, it will be seen that the board of directors' management powers are curtailed to the extent that such powers are exercisable by a receiver: *Hawkesbury Development Co Ltd v Landmark Finance Co Pty Ltd* [1969] 2 NSWR 782 at 790. Similarly, when a company is under administration, the administrator controls the company's business, property and affairs generally and the appointment has the effect of suspending the board's powers: ss 437A(1)(a) and (b) and 437C. As with other forms of external administration, in a winding up, while the directors continue to hold office, control of the company's affairs shifts from the board to the liquidator.

The chapter also considers different types of winding up. Companies may be wound up by order of the court for reasons of insolvency (under Part 5.4 of the *Corporations Act*) or other grounds specified in s 461 (under Part 5.4). Alternatively a company may be wound up voluntarily on the application of the members (when the company is solvent) or the creditors (when the company is not solvent).

The chapter concludes with a discussion of deregistering companies under Chap 5A. Under Part 5A a company may be deregistered, rather than wound up. Deregistration may be voluntary (s 601AA) or at the instigation of ASIC: s 601AB. This process provides an easy and inexpensive way to dissolve, *inter alia*, defunct companies.

While generally these mechanisms will be utilised when a company is in financial difficulties, this is not always the case. It will be seen that schemes of arrangement may be used, *inter alia*, to reconstruct a company or amalgamate with another company, while a winding up may be spurred by non-financial reasons such as a breakdown of relations between the parties conducting the company's affairs. Similarly, the deregistration provisions are aimed at solvent, but defunct, companies.

Receivership

Appointment of receiver

Appointment by creditor

[13.10] As discussed in Chapter 8, a receiver may be appointed under a lending instrument, such as a debenture, when its terms have been breached. The receiver is appointed to protect the secured creditor's interests by taking control of the property over which they are appointed and assuming responsibility for incoming profits and the payment of outgoings.

The manner in which the receiver is to be appointed is determined by the terms of the lending instrument. It may, for example, specify that the appointment is to be in writing. The lending instrument will also determine whether a receiver or a receiver and manager may be appointed. As discussed below, the distinction between these two offices has been rendered largely insignificant by the broad powers conferred under s 420(2).

[13.20] In contrast to a court-appointed receiver, discussed below, a person appointed pursuant to a lending instrument will owe his or her primary duties to the appointor. In addition the receiver has a duty to the company: *Expo International Pty Ltd v Chant* [1979] 2 NSWLR 820.

Appointment by a court

[13.30] Alternatively, a receiver may be appointed by a court. The appointment of a receiver is an equitable remedy that courts can make exercising their inherent jurisdiction, now echoed in the *Supreme Court Acts*. The power is normally exercised on the application of a debenture holder or mortgagee when the security or other assets are in jeopardy. Such an application may be made even where the creditor has a right to appoint a receiver under a lending instrument where, for example, the lending instrument does not provide the receiver with sufficient powers or there is some doubt as to the ability to so appoint a receiver. Note in regard to the latter point that, where there is some doubt as to the validity of a receiver's appointment, s 418A(1) allows the receiver, company or creditor of the company to seek a court order under s 418A(2) clarifying, *inter alia*, the validity of the appointment. Thus, despite the board of directors' managerial powers being displaced by the appointment of a receiver and manager, the directors retain the power to commence proceedings in the name of the company to challenge the validity of an appointment of a receiver and manager: *Ernst & Young (Reg) v Tynski Pty Ltd (CAN 008 162 123) (Receivers and Managers Appointed)* [2003] FCAFC 233.

In light of the consequences of appointing a receiver, the courts exercise this power with extreme caution. The court in *Bond Brewing Holdings Ltd v National Australia Bank* (1990) 8 ACLC 330 noted this need to exercise caution is particularly so when considering *ex parte* applications to appoint a receiver.

Bond Brewing Holdings Ltd v National Australia Bank
Supreme Court of Victoria: Kaye, Murphy and Brooking JJ
(1990) 8 ACLC 330

The case concerned the receivership of the Bond Brewing group that had borrowed $880 million from the plaintiffs, a syndicate of banks. The banks alleged that covenants in the loan agreements had been breached. On 29 December 1989 the banks faxed the defendants' solicitors (in Perth) a letter indicating that an application would be made to the Supreme Court of Victoria as soon as convenient for the appointment of receivers and managers to the defendants. The application was heard *ex parte* by Beach J. By the time the lawyers representing the defendants arrived at the court the order appointing a receiver had already been granted. The Bond Brewing group in turn applied to Beach J to set aside the order of appointment. Beach J refused to set aside the appointment but made certain variations to the earlier order that effectively provided for the continuation of the receivership pending the trial of the action that the banks had commenced against the corporate group.

The Bond Brewing group appealed to the Full Court. They argued that the ability to appoint a receiver was confined to applicants that had a proprietary interest in the subject matter of the application. The defendants also argued that a receiver should not be appointed, particularly *ex parte,* when the companies were insolvent or of doubtful solvency. While the first argument was rejected, the Full Court agreed with the second proposition that receivers should not have been appointed and set aside Beach J's order.

> **Kaye, Murphy and Brooking JJ**: **[340]** The appointment of a receiver is one of the oldest remedies of the Court of Chancery, and a very useful remedy it is. But its very efficacy means that a corresponding caution must attend its employment. Where a receiver is sought to protect property of which no one is in actual **[341]** possession, no one will be ousted by the appointment and probably no great harm will be done. But where the subject matter is in the defendant's hands he may suffer an irreparable wrong by being dispossessed and of course this danger will weigh with a judge from whom the remedy is sought. The appointment of a receiver which is to be, so to speak, at the expense of the defendant's possession and without his consent is a step never to be taken without proper consideration of the defendant's position. (*Owen v Homan* (1853) 4 HL Cas 997 at pp 1032-1033; 10 ER 752; compare the views expressed a little earlier by a'Beckett J. in Marquis of *Ailsa v Watson* (1846) 1 Shad 77 at p 78 and *Atkins v Smith* (1851) 5 Shad 103 at pp 104-105.) Where

a receiver is sought, not merely of a particular asset of the defendant, but of all his assets, particular caution is required and where, as in the present case, the receiver is to possess himself of and to manage the assets and undertaking of a collection of companies which, whether they are solvent or not, are in a very large way of business, very great circumspection is required. Of course in a strong enough case the court might, without warning to a trading company, divest it of control of its undertaking and assets. But it must always be borne in mind that the appointment of a receiver in such a case authorises an irresistible invasion and that even if the army of occupation is withdrawn after only a short time things may never be the same again. Rights of property and the company's privacy are violated. Only the most pressing need can warrant such an invasion without notice. Quite apart from the taking out of the companies' hands of control of their assets and the management of their businesses, there was in the present case the added consideration (which will not infrequently be present where a receiver is appointed to a company) that the making of the order might well have most serious legal consequences for the companies or for related companies having regard to the terms of securities given by them. And in addition to the legal consequences there was the commercial consideration that, as Picarda, *Receivers and Managers* p 4 has observed, the receiver is often seen not as the company doctor but as the undertaker, so that a blow is struck to the standing and credit of the defendants.

In the present case the order sought, although interim or interlocutory, was one with extremely grave consequences for the defendants. Putting to one side a winding up order, which will in the normal course ultimately result in a company's being given its quietus, we cannot for the moment think of an order of greater consequence to a company than one which, until further order, robs it of its control over its own assets and business.

No court will make such an order unless convinced of its necessity. A case for some kind and degree of interlocutory relief may be made out which falls short of this extremely drastic remedy; for example, the court may not be satisfied – and it is of course for the applicant to persuade the court that nothing less than what he seeks will do – that in all the circumstances it should do more than grant an injunction. At times the court will be induced to refuse the remedy of a receiver by undertakings offered by the defendant. ...

[345] We know of no principle which allows the appointment of a receiver only on the application of a person who asserts some proprietary interest in the property concerned. Of course from the very nature of the remedy the basis of the application for a receiver will often be that the court should make an order designed to protect property at the request of one who has an interest in it. The right for the protection of which the remedy is sought will, in other words, often be an interest in the property: compare Spry, *Equitable Remedies* (3rd ed) p 326 as to injunctions in aid of proprietary rights. But on principle all that need be shown to give rise to the discretion to appoint a receiver – how that discretion should [346] be exercised is another matter – is that the applicant has a right which will be protected or enforced by the grant of that remedy and that no adequate remedy at law is available. (If there is an adequate remedy available in equity, for example the grant of an injunction, then that may induce the court not to exercise its discretion in favour of appointing a receiver.) You can if you like speak of the need for an interest, in the widest sense, in the property in question as a prerequisite to the appointment of a receiver, but this is we think correct only in the sense that the applicant must

show that he has some legal or equitable right which will be protected or enforced by the making of the order sought and that no other available remedy is adequate for that purpose. (We are not for the moment speaking of the special case where consent, or something close to consent, may induce the court to exercise a jurisdiction that it would not otherwise exercise.) ...

[349] These authorities support the view that, at all events in the absence of consent or at least the absence of opposition from the company for whom a receiver is sought, orders are not to be made by way of the appointment of a receiver for the administration of the affairs of companies in financial difficulties.

[350] Nothing that we say, either here or elsewhere in these reasons, is concerned with receivers appointed in the exercise of statutory powers. In our opinion, courts of equity would not, and, whatever view may be taken of the effect of the Judicature Acts and sec 37(1) of the *Supreme Court Act* 1986, the Supreme Court will not appoint a receiver and manager of the undertaking of a company by way of establishing a regime to administer the affairs of a company in financial difficulties somewhat akin (the analogy must not be taken too far) to official management, where the company opposes that course. Equity would not, we think, have done so before the Judicature Acts and, even on the widest view of the effect of the Judicature Acts and of sec 37(1), a court now administering law and equity should act on the same principle. We do not think that before the fusion of law and equity the Court of Chancery made available its remedy of receive, or that after the fusion it should be made available, as a means of establishing a scheme for the administration of the estate of an insolvent or financially embarrassed corporate debtor where that debtor resists the appointment.

The Full Court's decision was upheld on appeal to the High Court: *National Australia Bank v Bond Brewing Holdings Ltd* (1990) 8 ACLC 365.

[13.40] The *Corporations Act* also specifically authorises the appointment of a receiver in certain cases. As discussed in Chapter 12, one form of relief available under ss 232-235 for oppressive or unfairly prejudicial or discriminatory conduct is the appointment of a receiver or receiver and manager: s 233(1)(h).

In addition, under s 1323(1) the court may on an interim (s 1323(3)) or final basis appoint a receiver or receiver and manager to the company's property or part of its property to protect the interests of an 'aggrieved person' where the company, the 'relevant person', is being investigated, prosecuted or sued civilly for a breach of the Act and is liable to pay money or account for securities, futures contracts or other property. Section 1323 allows the court to appoint a receiver over the assets of natural persons, such as directors, not just a company. Thus, in *CAC v Lombard Nash International Pty Ltd (No 3)* (1987) 5 ACLC 1020, the Commission appointed a receiver over the assets of two directors of a company where the company assets were stripped and money had been shifted to overseas bank accounts in the names of the directors and a company controlled by the directors. As the court explained, the idea behind what is now s 1323(1) is to preserve the assets of a person, whether that be the company or natural persons, until creditors' claims can be dealt with: at 1022-1023.

[13.50] A receiver appointed by a court is an officer of the court: *Duffy v Super Centre Development Corp Ltd* [1967] 1 NSWR 382 at 383. In addition, under s 9 the receiver is an officer of the company and thus is subject to the duties discussed in Chapter 10.

A court-appointed receiver enjoys such powers as the court specifies in the appointing order: s 1323(1)(h). In addition, the receiver enjoys those powers conferred by ss 420-421, discussed below.

The court's supervisory role in the case of a receiver appointed by a court and the difference between a court-appointed receiver and a privately appointed receiver were highlighted by Street J in *Duffy v Super Centre Development Corp Ltd* [1967] 1 NSWR 382 at 383-384:

> The receiver and manager is appointed as an officer of the court to undertake in that capacity the management of the business of the company as well, of course, as undertaking the care of the company's assets. To the extent to which he makes decisions from time to time, they are in effect made under the authority of the Court itself, and they are subject to review and control by the Court should a proper case be made out requiring such intervention. Whilst this Court does, therefore, have an ultimate control over the day-to-day actions of a receiver and manager, it is a control which is not in my view to be too freely exercised. If, of course, there can be shown to be some defect in the manner in which the receiver and manager is conducting his duties – a defect arising either out of some want of good faith or out of some erroneous approach in law or in principle – then that is clearly a ground on which the Court would entertain an application by one of the interested parties for appropriate directions or some other form of remedial order. Where, however, the challenge made is that there has been an absence of prudence and wisdom in the receiver's decisions, a far heavier onus rests upon the party who seeks to challenge the decision in question. The Court will not concern itself with minor and ordinary decisions that he may have made: it must be shown that there is a decision of real significance in the affairs of the company and as to which there are real and substantial grounds for questioning its correctness before the Court will embark upon an investigation of what, if any, directions ought to be given. ... There is some contrast to be borne in mind between the function of a privately appointed receiver and the function of a court appointed receiver, and I use the word 'receiver' as a compendious word encompassing a receiver and manager. To some extent a privately appointed receiver, particularly in current commercial practice, makes an effort to restore the financial prosperity of the company whose affairs he has been appointed to administer by a debenture **[384]** holder. A court appointed receiver does not fill the same position. He is not so much what might be described as a company doctor, but rather his functions is that of company caretaker. His function is not so much to restore profitability. It is rather to preserve those assets of the company upon which its fortunes may be dependent, and to preserve its potentiality for earning profits in the future.

[13.60] Note, a receiver must be a registered liquidator (s 418(1)(d)) unless the receiver is a body corporate authorised by law to act as receiver of the subject property: s 418(3). See further s 418(1) for those persons excluded from being appointed as a receiver.

ASIC must be notified of the appointment or termination of a receiver: s 427. As soon as practicable after appointment, the receiver must also serve notice of the appointment on the company: s 429(2)(a).

The company must also set out in every public document or negotiable instrument of the company a statement after the company's name where it first appears, that a receiver or receiver and manager has been appointed: s 428(1).

Impact of appointment on directors' powers

[13.70] While the appointment of a receiver does not terminate the company's life (*George Barker (Transport) Ltd v Eyon* [1973] 3 All ER 374 at 380), nor displace the board of directors, as Street J noted in *Hawkesbury Development Co Ltd v Landmark Finance Co Pty Ltd* [1969] 2 NSWR 782 at 790, the appointment significantly impacts upon the board's ability to manage the company and to conduct its ordinary business:

> Receivership and management may well dominate exclusively a company's affairs in its dealings and relations with the outside world. But it does not permeate the company's internal domestic structure. That structure continues to exist notwithstanding that the directors no longer have authority to exercise their ordinary business management functions. A valid receivership and management will ordinarily supersede, but not destroy, the company's own organs through which it conduct its affairs. The capacity of those organs to function bears a direct inverse relationship to the validity and scope of the receivership and management.

Traditionally, a distinction has been drawn between a 'receiver' and a 'receiver and manager'. The latter appointee enjoys, in addition to the responsibilities of a receiver, the power to manage the company and may conduct its business as a going concern: *Re Manchester & Milford Railway Co* (1880) 14 Ch D 645. As discussed below, s 420(2), however, renders the distinction essentially meaningless by conferring broad powers of management on receivers unless expressly excluded under the terms of the appointment. The legislation also deems the receiver of corporate property to be a manager if the receiver manages, or has under the terms of his or her appointment power to manage, the affairs of the company.

Termination of appointment

[13.80] The power to terminate a receiver's appointment under a lending instrument will usually be contained in the appointing document. The termination will not be effective, however, unless the receiver is given written notice.

In addition, under s 423(1) the court has a broad discretion to make such orders as it thinks fit, including an order removing a receiver, where it appears to the court or ASIC that a receiver is not faithfully performing his or her functions or is breaching a requirement of a court order, the instrument under which it was appointed or the Act.

If the receiver wishes to cease to act, notice must be lodged with ASIC within seven days and published in the Gazette within 21 days of the termination: s 427(4). Final accounts must be lodged with ASIC within one month of ceasing to act: s 432(1)(b).

Receiver's powers

[13.90] If the person has been appointed under a lending instrument, that document will usually provide a source of wide powers. These will commonly include a general authority to act as the company's agent, to conduct the company's business and to realise corporate assets. A receiver appointed under a lending instrument may seek directions from the court in relation to any matter arising in connection with the performance or exercise of the receiver's functions and powers: s 424(1).

[13.100] The *Corporations Act* supplements any express authority by extending to all receivers broad powers that are applicable unless expressly prohibited under the appointment. Section 420(1) provides receivers with a general power to do 'all things necessary or convenient to be done for or in connection with, or as incidental to, the attainment of the objectives' underlying the receiver's appointment. Subject to the terms of the court order or lending instrument under which the receiver is appointed, receivers may utilise in addition to those powers conferred under the order or instrument the specific powers detailed in s 420(2) in furthering the objectives of the appointment. The conferral of these powers does not, however, affect any rights persons other than the company have in the subject property: s 420(3). See also ss 420B and 420C.

Receiver's duties

[13.110] In addition to the general duty to act in the interests of the appointing creditors and the company, discussed above, the *Corporations Act* also imposes certain specific duties on receivers. Under s 421(1), a receiver is obliged to establish a bank account bearing, *inter alia*, the title of 'receiver', into which any money that comes under the receiver's control is to be paid.

[13.120] Under s 429(2)(b), the receiver is to be forwarded a report of the company's affairs, compiled by the directors and secretary, within 14 days of the company's receiving notice of the appointment. The receiver must respond by lodging with ASIC the report, with a notice containing any comments on the report, within one month of its receipt: s 429(2)(c)(i). A copy of the notice must be sent to the company and, in certain cases, to the trustee of debenture holders: s 429(2)(c)(ii) and (iii). To assist in preparing this report, the receiver may require officers, former officers, employees, former employees and persons involved in the formation of the company to verify and report on specified matters: s 430(1).

[13.130] A managing receiver/controller must also prepare and lodge with ASIC a report as to the company's affairs within two months of appointment: s 421A(1). Notice of the preparation and lodging of the report must be published in a national newspaper or a newspaper in each jurisdiction: s 421A(3)(a). In addition, the receiver must report to ASIC any information indicating:

- an offence may have occurred in relation to the company by a past or present officer or member;
- that a person who has taken part in the formation, promotion, administration, management or winding up of the company may have misapplied, retained or become liable for corporate money/ property; or
- that a person who has taken part in the formation, promotion, administration, management or winding up of the company may have been guilty of negligence, default, breach of duty or trust in relation to the company: s 422(1).

If the receiver does not lodge such a report and it appears to the court that these matters have occurred, on the application of an interested person or on its own motion, the court may order the receiver to lodge such a report: s 422(3).

The receiver must also report any other matters believed to be desirable to be brought to ASIC's notice: s 422(2).

[13.140] The receiver is required to lodge six monthly accounts with ASIC: s 432(1). These must detail, *inter alia*, the aggregate receipts and payments and the amount owing under any instrument pursuant to which the receiver was appointed: s 432(1A). The Commission may, of its own motion or on the application of the company or creditor, cause these accounts to be audited: s 432(2).

[13.150] When a receiver is authorised to sell corporate property, s 420A(1) imposes a duty on the receiver to take all reasonable care to sell the property at not less than its market value or, at least, at the best price reasonably obtainable having regard to the circumstances when the property is sold. This duty is in addition to the receiver's general duties: s 420A(2).

As noted by Young CJ in *Ultimate Property Group Pty Ltd v Lord* [2004] NSWSC 114, the consequences of breaching s 420A are not specified in the section. In turn he suggested that a breach of s 420A may nevertheless support a private action for equitable damages. See further *Ultimate Property Group Pty Ltd v Lord*.

Receiver's liability

[13.160] Under s 423, the court has an overriding supervisory role over receivers' conduct. If it appears to the court or ASIC that a receiver is not faithfully performing his or her functions, not observing a requirement of the order or instrument under which he or she was appointed, or not observing a requirement of the court or the Act, or the receiver is the subject of a complaint to ASIC or court, ASIC or court may inquire into the matter and the court take such action as it thinks fit: s 423(1). Under s 423(2), ASIC may report to the court any matter that in its opinion constitutes a misfeasance, neglect or omission by the receiver. In response, the court may order the receiver to make good any consequent loss to the company and such other order(s) as it thinks fit: s 423(2). The court's supervisory role is supported by broad powers of investigation, detailed in s 423(3).

[13.170] Notwithstanding any agreement to the contrary, the receiver is also liable for the debts incurred in the course of the receivership, services rendered and goods purchased, hired etc: s 419(1). This does not, however, prejudice the receiver's rights as against the company: s 419(1). Nor is the receiver personally liable for debts incurred before the appointment unless personal liability is specifically accepted. See *Re Diesels & Components Pty Ltd* (1985) 3 ACLC 555.

Schemes of Arrangement

Defining compromise or arrangement

[13.180] The directors/members of a company may wish to enter into a 'compromise' or 'scheme of arrangement' under Part 5.1 of the *Corporations Act* because, *inter alia*, (i) the company is in financial difficulty or (ii) they wish to restructure the company or amalgamate it with another company. See further s 413(1). Neither the term 'compromise' nor 'scheme of arrangement' is defined in the Act. The ordinary meaning of a 'compromise' would suggest it is suited to the first scenario as it would involve accommodating conflicting claims by adjusting, for example, members' or creditors' rights. The term 'arrangement', however, would appear to entail a broader array of underlying purposes and means of effecting such and thus may be directed to the second scenario. See further s 413, in particular to the courts' powers when facilitating reconstructions and amalgamations.

Agreement to scheme

Convening meeting to consider proposal

[13.190] Under s 411(1), where a compromise or arrangement is proposed, on the application of the company or any creditor or member, the court may order that a meeting(s) of the company's creditors or members, or class(es) of creditors or members, be held to determine whether they agree to the compromise or arrangement. Where the proposed compromise or arrangement involves a group of companies, subject to certain preconditions, s 411(1A) and (1B) allow the court to order consolidated meetings of the companies' creditors/members. See further s 411(1A). The court's power to order this meeting(s) extends to directing the manner in which the meeting(s) is to be conducted: *Re Hills Motorway* [2002] NSWSC 897.

[13.200] An order for a meeting(s) may not be made unless ASIC has had a reasonable opportunity to examine and make submissions to the court on the proposed compromise or arrangement: s 411(2). The court may go further and prescribe as a precondition to convening the meeting that ASIC or any other person provide a report on the terms of the compromise or arrangement, the conduct of the officers of the company(s) concerned and any other matters that ASIC or other person believes ought to be brought to the court's attention: s 415(2)(a). See also *Re NRMA Ltd (No 1)* (2000) 156 FLR 349 at 354-356 and *Re International Goldfields Ltd* [2003] WASC 86.

Explanatory statement

[13.210] Where a meeting is convened under s 411, s 412(1) requires that a statement explaining the compromise or arrangement accompany the notice of the meeting and be sent to each creditor (unless their debts do not exceed $200) or member: s 412(2). The statement must detail, *inter alia*, any material interests the directors have in the compromise or arrangement and any information within the directors' knowledge that is material to the creditors'/members' decision: s 412(1)(a).

Court's discretion to approve compromise or arrangement

[13.220] If participants of the meeting agree to the compromise or arrangement, the court may order that the compromise or arrangement is binding on all parties, including any dissenting minority: s 411(4)(b). The approval will not have effect, however, until lodged with ASIC: s 411(10). The order shall then be effective from that date or such earlier date prescribed by the court: s 411(10).

[13.230] While this power of approval is discretionary, the courts are reluctant to second guess the decision of an informed meeting of creditors/ members. As the court stated in *In re English, Scottish and Australian Chartered Bank* [1893] 3 Ch 385 at 409:

> If the creditors are acting on sufficient information and with time to consider what they are about, and are acting honestly, they are, I apprehend, much better judges of what is to their commercial advantage than the court be ... While, therefore, I protest that we are not to register their decisions, but, to see that they are properly convened and have been properly consulted, and have considered the matter from a proper point of view ... the court ought to be slow to differ from them.

[13.240] The court will not, however, allow an unreasonable scheme to be forced on the creditors/members. As Bowen LJ stated in *Re Alabama New Orleans Texas and Pacific Junction Railway Co* [1891] 1 Ch 213 at 243:

> A reasonable compromise must be a compromise which can, by reasonable people conversant with the subject, be regarded as beneficial to those on both sides who are making it ... I have no doubt at all that it would be improper for the court to allow an arrangement to be forced on any class of creditors, if the arrangements cannot reasonably be supposed by sensible business people to be for the benefit of that class as such.

If the participants have, for example, been misled as to the consequences of the scheme, it will not be approved by the court: *Re Dorman Long & Co* [1934] Ch 635.

Re Dorman Long & Co
Chancery Division: Maugham J
[1934] Ch 635

The company sought approval of a scheme of arrangement involving an amalgamation with another company, South Durham Steel and Iron Co ('South Durham'). It was provisionally agreed that Dorman's would acquire South Durham's undertaking (business) and assets. Two schemes of arrangement were prepared: one between Dorman and its debenture stockholders and shareholders and one between South Durham and its debenture stockholders and shareholders. The schemes had been approved in class meetings of the shareholders and debenture stockholders. A circular distributed to Dorman's debenture stockholders and shareholders indicated that the scheme had the approval of the trustee of the debenture stockholders. The statement did not disclose how the companies' assets had been revalued, nor that being Dorman's bankers, the trustees served to profit from the scheme.

Confirmation of the schemes was sought from the court. The court refused to do so because, *inter alia*, the circular was insufficient as it should have stated the amount of the revaluation. It was also misleading in its reference to the scheme being approved by the trustees. A fresh meeting was ordered.

> **Maugham J**: [655] I will first state my view as to the function of the Court in determining whether the compromise or arrangement should be sanctioned by the Court. It is plain that the duties of the Court are two-fold. The first is to see that the resolutions are passed by the statutory majority in value and number, in accordance with s 153, sub-s 2, at a meeting or meetings duly convened and held. Upon that depends the jurisdiction of the Court to confirm the scheme. The other duty is in the nature of a discretionary power ...
>
> [657] In my opinion, then, so far as this second duty is concerned, what I have to see is whether the proposal is such that intelligent and honest man, a member of the class concerned and acting in respect of his interest, might reasonably approve. The schemes before me are attacked on both grounds. It is said that the resolutions have not been duly passed and that the Court in considering the nature of the schemes ought to come to a conclusion that a reasonable businessman would not approve of them. ...
>
> [665] I now pass to an important question – namely, the question in relation to the explanatory circular sent out by the directors. ...
>
> [670] I have anxiously considered the terms of the circular and have weighed the arguments which have been presented to me. In my opinion the circular was not sufficient in the particular circumstances of this case, and it was in one important respect misleading. The most serious matter, in my opinion, is the reference on page 4 to the trustees for the stockholders. It is in these terms. "The terms of the scheme have been referred to the trustees for the stockholders who, after making a careful investigation of the whole position recommend the proposals for the approval of the stockholders." ...

Barclays Bank Ld, were the trustees. They were owed a week ago a sum of about 1,411,000, and as a result of a provisional agreement entered into by the company, partly referred to and explained in the circular under the heading of "Bankers", they are beyond all doubt getting great advantages if the scheme goes through. In my opinion it was quite wrong to say that the scheme had been referred to the trustees for the stockholders who, after a careful investigation, "recommend the proposals for the approval of the stockholders," without telling them, or reminding them if they already knew, that Barclays Bank Ld were the trustees and that they had the strongest interest in recommending the scheme from their own point of view as bankers. ... **[671]** [T]he ordinary reader of the clause which I have read would necessarily draw the inference that the independent trustees had, after a careful investigation of the whole position, come to the conclusion that the reader should vote for it, and that it might properly be approved or ought to be approved by the stockholders. ... I think it most unfortunate that in the present case it has been impossible for the debenture stockholders to have the opinion of a really independent trustee to guide them in the matter which is before them. ...

[675] I have deliberately refrained from expressing any opinion of my own on the question whether the scheme is one which the stockholders should or should not support, because, in my opinion, that is a matter which is not within the function of the Court. It is for the stockholders, I repeat, to deal with the matter, and if I have taken so long in considering the general features of the case it is because I should be unwilling to let the matter go back for further consideration if the scheme were such that ultimately the Court would decline to approve it. ...

[679] My opinion therefore is that if I am asked to do so I ought to direct fresh meetings to be summoned on the present **[680]** petition ...

Administration of Company

Appointment of administrator

[13.250] Part 5.3A, incorporated by the *Corporate Law Reform Act* 1992 (Cth), introduced a mechanism through which an administrator may be appointed to take responsibility for the affairs of a company of doubtful solvency. An administrator may be appointed by a:

- resolution of directors where they believe the company is insolvent or likely to be insolvent: s 436A;
- liquidator or provisional liquidator where it is believed that the company is insolvent or likely to be insolvent: s 436B; or
- chargee entitled to enforce a charge over the whole or substantial portion of the company's property: s 436C.

In *Downey v Crawford* [2004] FCA 1264 the court held that in regard to an appointment of an administrator under s 436A the question is not whether the company is actually insolvent. Rather, the question is whether the directors 'genuinely believed, on reasonable grounds, that the company was insolvent or likely to become so in the future': at [189]. The test required the application of an 'objective standard' – that of a 'director of ordinary competence': at [190].

[13.260] The appointment of an administrator is designed to stabilise the company's position and maximise its chances of continuing (s 435A(a)) with a view to persuading creditors to enter into a deed of arrangement. If, however, the administrator concludes that the company's position indicates that it is not possible for the company, or its business, to continue, the administrator's task is to ensure a better return for the company's creditors and members than that consequent to an immediate winding up of the company: s 432A(b).

[13.270] As with a receiver, an administrator must be a registered liquidator: s 448B. In addition, the administrator must consent to the appointment: s 448A. See further s 448C as to persons who are ineligible for appointment.

Upon the appointment, the administrator must lodge notice of the appointment with ASIC before the end of the next business day. In addition, within three days of the appointment the administrator must publish notice of the appointment in a national newspaper or a newspaper in each jurisdiction in which the company has a registered office or carries on business: s 450A(1).

As soon as practicable after the appointment, and not later than the end of the next business day, written notice of the appointment must be given to the company and person(s) who holds a charge(s) over the whole or substantial portion of the company's property: s 450A(2) and (3). The company must in turn set out in every public document or negotiable instrument of the company a statement after the company's name where it first appears, that an administrator has been appointed: s 450E(1). Under s 447A(1) a court may dispense with the requirement in s 450E(1): *In Re Brashs Pty Ltd* (1994) 15 ACSR 477; *In the Matter of Multelink Aust Ltd (Admin Appt)* (2003) 21 ACLC 1661. However, as s 450E(1) is designed to protect the interests of persons who become creditors while the company trades under the deed of arrangement, such an order will not be made to promote the interests of existing creditors and other persons interested in the company's affairs: *In the Matter of Multelink Aust Ltd (Admin Appt)*.

As with the appointment of a receiver, where there is doubt as to the validity of an appointment, on the application of the administrator, the company or any of the company's creditors, the court may direct whether or not the purported appointment was valid: s 447C(1) and (2).

Impact of appointment on directors' powers

[13.280] While the company is under administration, the administrator controls the company's business, property and affairs generally: s 437A(1)(a) and (b). As with the appointment of a receiver and manager, this has the effect of suspending the board's powers: s 437C. Under s 437C(1), the company's officers may only exercise their powers or perform their functions with the administrator's written approval. Any unapproved dealing with the company's property is void and the officer may be liable for any loss arising from the transaction: ss 437D and 437E. The suspension of the board's powers does not, however, effect a removal of the directors from their offices: s 437C(2). Moreover, the appointment of the administrator does not affect the continued conduct of the company's business.

[13.290] Note also in regard to the company's members that while the company is under administration, they are unable to deal in their shares in the company: s 437F. Any transaction contrary to this prohibition is void: s 437F. In regard to the impact on creditors' rights, as discussed below, the appointment also effects a moratorium on creditors' claims.

Termination of appointment

[13.300] It will be seen that the court enjoys a broad discretion to make such orders it thinks fit where it is satisfied that an administrator is acting in a manner prejudicial to the creditors' or members' interests: s 447E(1). Such powers could be used to remove an administrator from office. A more specific power of removal exists in s 449B which allows the court to remove an administrator on the application of ASIC or a creditor.

A vacancy in the office of an administrator may be filled by the entity that initially appointed the administrator, whether that be a court, the company, liquidator, provisional liquidator or chargee: s 449C(1) and (2).

Committee of creditors

[13.310] Within five business days of the appointment, the administrator must convene a meeting of the company's creditors to determine whether they are to appoint a committee of creditors and, if so, its membership: s 436E(1) and (2). At the meeting the creditors may, in addition, resolve to remove the administrator from office and appoint someone else where, for example, they do not believe the administrator to be impartial: s 436E(4).

If appointed, the committee of creditors receives and considers reports from the administrator and generally adopts a consultative role: s 436F(1). The committee may not, however, give directions to the administrator, except to require that person to report to them on matters pertaining to the company's administration: s 436F(2) and (3).

As discussed below, an additional meeting of the company's creditors must be convened to determine the company's future: s 439A.

Administrator's powers

[13.320] As noted above, the administrator controls the company's business, property and affairs generally: s 437A(1)(a). This control includes the ability to conduct the business and to dispose of all or part of the company's business or property: ss 437A(1)(b) and (c) and 437D(2)(a). The administrator also may perform any function, or exercise any power, that the company or its officers could have utilised were the company not under administration: s 437A(1)(d). These powers must only be exercised for the purpose of carrying Part 5.3A into effect and only for proper purposes within s 181 and the general law duties discussed in Chapter 10. See *Blundell v Macrocam Pty Ltd* [2004] NSWSC 895. In carrying out these functions, the administrator is acting as the company's agent: s 437B. See also the extracts from *Patrick Stevedores Operations No 2 Pty Ltd v Maritime Union of Australia* (1998) 16 ACLC 1041 below.

Administrator's duties

[13.330] One of the administrator's primary tasks is to investigate the company's business, property, affairs and financial circumstances as soon as practicable after the appointment and form an opinion as to which course of action would best serve the creditors' interests. The administrator must consider whether:
- the company should enter into a deed of company arrangement;
- the administration should end; or
- the company should be wound up: s 438A.

To assist in this task, within seven days of commencing the administration, or such longer period as the administrator allows, the directors must give the administrator a report of the corporation's business, property, affairs and financial circumstances: s 438B(2). The administrator may also seek further support from the directors by requiring them to meet with the administrator and to provide additional information on these matters: s 438B(3). The administrator is also entitled to inspect the corporation's books: ss 438B(1) and 438C(1). See also the extracts from *Patrick Stevedores Operations No 2 Pty Ltd v Maritime Union of Australia* (1998) 16 ACLC 1041 below.

[13.340] In addition, the administrator must lodge a report with ASIC, coupled with any supporting information, where the administrator believes:
- a past or present officer or member of the company may have been guilty of an offence in relation to the company;
- a person who has taken part in the formation, promotion, administration, management or winding up of the company may have misapplied, retained or become liable for corporate money/property; or
- a person who has taken part in the formation, promotion, administration, management or winding up of the company may have been guilty of any negligence, default, breach of duty or trust in relation to the company: s 438D(1).

If the administrator does not lodge a report and it appears to the court that these matters have occurred, on the application of an interested person or on its own motion, the court may order the administrator to lodge the necessary report: s 438D(3).

The administrator must also report any other matters believed to be desirable to bring to ASIC's notice: s 438D(2).

Administrator's liability

[13.350] As with receivers, the court has a general supervisory role over the administrator's conduct. If the court is satisfied that an administrator has:
- managed or is managing the company's business, property or affairs in a manner that is prejudicial to the interests of some or all of its creditors or members;
- did an act, or made an omission, or proposed such, that is or would be prejudicial to these interests;

on the application of ASIC, a creditor or member of the company, the court may make such orders as it thinks fit: s 447E(1).

[13.360] While considered to be acting as the company's agent, the administrator is nevertheless personally liable for debts incurred and services, goods or property obtained or used in the course of the administration: ss 443A-443BA. This is notwithstanding any agreement with the company to the contrary; though any rights the administrator may have against the company are preserved (s 443A(2)) and the administrator may have a right to be indemnified out of corporate assets: s 443D(a).

The powers, duties and liability of an administrator were discussed by the High Court in *Patrick Stevedores Operations No 2 Pty Ltd v Maritime Union of Australia* (1998) 16 ACLC 1041.

Patrick Stevedores Operations No 2 Pty Ltd v Maritime Union of Australia
High Court of Australia: Brennan CJ, McHugh, Gummow, Kirby, Hayne and Callinan JJ
(1998) 16 ACLC 1041

Central to the issue before the court was the interplay between the *Workplace Relations Act* 1996 (Cth) and Part 5.3A of the *Corporations Act*. The Maritime Union of Australia claimed the employer companies in the Patrick Group had committed conspiracy to dismiss the union workforce in breach of s 298K of the *Workplace Relations Act*. Administrators had been appointed to the employers and the Union advised the Federal Court that the administrators intended to dismiss the employees. The Federal Court found there was a serious question to be tried in regard to the allegations and orders were made against the employers and operators, *inter alia*, preventing the termination of the employee's employment and disposing of the companies' assets other than in the ordinary course of business.

An appeal to the Full Court of the Federal Court was dismissed. A further appeal was made to the High Court on the basis that the Federal Court lacked power to make the orders and had failed to consider the impact of the orders on the administration of the company.

The High Court held that any orders of the Federal Court should not interfere with the lawful exercise of the administrator's powers under Part 5.3A. While it was appropriate for the Federal Court to give leave under s 440D to prosecute proceedings against the employer companies under administration, the orders contained an appealable error as they fettered the discretion conferred on the administrators by s 437A; that is, to determine whether or not the employer companies should resume trading.

Brennan CJ, McHugh, Gummow, Kirby and Hayne JJ: [1055] 40. When the employer companies were placed under administration, the Administrators were invested with the powers prescribed by ss 437A and 442A of the Corporations Law. Section 437A ... reposes in the Administrators the duty of determining whether, during the period of administration, the employer companies should attempt to continue to trade. ...

[1056] 43. ... Part 5.3A and other provisions of the *Corporations Law* are concerned to regulate the control and distribution of the assets of a company in the interests not only of the statutory entity itself, the company, and its members but also in the interests of the company's creditors. The company is an entity brought into existence to provide the vehicle for organising, deploying and distributing its assets. The *Corporations Law* prescribes the regime which defines and protects the interest of third parties – the creditors – in the deployment and distribution of a company's assets. Another law which governs conduct in which companies and natural persons may engage and relationships which companies and natural persons may enter should not be construed as intending to affect or modify a regime that affects the interests of third parties. Prima facie, a law which deals indifferently with companies and natural persons does not affect the regimes prescribed by laws dealing with bankruptcy and insolvency; a law of the former kind would have to manifest clearly an intention to affect those regimes before it would be held to do so.

44. It follows that the orders which might properly be made by the Federal Court under s 298U(e) of the Act or s 23 of the Federal Court Act ought not to interfere with the exercise by the Administrators of their powers in respect of the employer companies provided the Administrators act lawfully. Relevantly, that means that the Administrators cannot dismiss the employees for the reason, or for reasons which include the reason, that they are members of the MUA.

45. Section 440D(1) of the *Corporations Law* forbids the commencement or prosecution of proceedings against a company during administration except, inter alia, with the leave of a court. North J gave leave and that was an appropriate order in so far as it allowed the prosecution of a proceeding designed to remedy the effects of an alleged contravention of s 298K(1) of the Act. However, the other orders made with respect to the business of the employer companies during administration require some qualification as will subsequently appear.

46. The orders appear to assume that the Administrators will remain in office for a significant period of time (if not for the whole of the time until the action is tried). They are also designed to assist the bringing back of the employer companies to profitable operation. Further, the orders (as varied by the Full Court) are intended to relieve the Administrators of personal liability for the wages that the employees of those companies will earn pending the trial of the action.

47. There are some features of the operation of Pt 5.3A of the Corporations Law which should be noted. First, voluntary administration [1057] under Pt 5.3A is intended to be a temporary measure. There are times within which steps in the administration must be taken. Thus, there are times set within

which meetings of creditors must be convened. That period can be extended by court order or a meeting of creditors can agree that the meeting will be adjourned. But the meeting cannot agree to adjourn to a day more than 60 days after the first day on which the meeting was held.

48. Next, the fate of a company in voluntary administration is in the hands of its creditors – at least in the sense that it is that group which decides whether the company will execute a deed of company arrangement or the administration will end or that the company will be wound up. No doubt that is subject to the supervision of the Court in various ways. But in the end it must always be remembered that the company that is subject to voluntary administration is one that the board has resolved is insolvent or is likely to become insolvent at some future time. Any step that the Federal Court takes to prevent the frustration of its jurisdiction must be taken having regard, *inter alia*, to the interests of creditors of the company. It must also be taken in light of the fact that the board of the company has concluded that its debts cannot be paid as and when they fall due now or at some future time.

49. Ordinarily, administrators of companies are not in office very long. They must decide quickly whether the company and its business is beyond rescue. If the company or some or all of its business might be rescued, a deed of company arrangement will be proposed. It is the creditors of the company who decide whether the company should make that deed of company arrangement. The administrator will ordinarily become the administrator of the deed but the affairs of the company are then regulated by the deed. Although the creditors may resolve otherwise, the deed will ordinarily provide for the application of money received under the deed in the order of priorities that would apply in a winding up.

50. If the company and its business cannot be rescued, the company will go into liquidation and its assets will be realised and the proceeds distributed among creditors in the manner prescribed by the *Corporations Law*. The entitlements of employees are then to be paid in priority to the debts of third parties.

51. Although an administrator has power to conduct the business of the company during administration the administrator is personally liable under s 443A for debts he or she incurs in doing so. The administrator then has a right of indemnity against the company's assets, ranking in priority to unsecured debts and, generally speaking, debts secured by a floating charge. The administrator has a lien over the company's property to secure that right. But if an administrator forms the view that the company is and is likely to remain insolvent, it is unlikely that a decision would – or ought – be taken to continue trading. Personal liability of the administrator for the debts incurred would be the price of unsuccessful trading by an insolvent company. If the employer companies are indeed insolvent and if there be no prospect of supplying their employees' labour to a stevedore under a profitable contract, the Administrators are not likely to incur debts in carrying on trading, without a third party indemnity.

52. An administrator has the power to carry on trading though the company is insolvent, the personal liability of the administrator being the protection given by the *Corporations Law* to the company's creditors. But the statutory protection of the creditors generally cannot be set aside by a court's order in litigation between a plaintiff party and the company purporting to suspend s 443A of the *Corporations Law*; nor can a court order an administrator to incur, or to run the risk of incurring, a personal liability under s 443A

in order to preserve the rights of a plaintiff against the company. The administrator must act impartially as among all parties having or claiming to have an interest in the present or future assets of the company and must make those decisions which, in the light of contemporary circumstances, best serve those interests. It is for the administrator, in exercise of the discretionary powers conferred by s 437A, to decide whether or not to carry on the company's business and the form in which it should be carried on during the administration.

53. The central difficulty about the orders made by the primary judge is that they are orders which took away from the Administrators of the employer companies the discretions conferred upon them by s 437A of the *Corporations Law*. At least on one view of the effect of the orders, they would oblige the Administrators to continue to trade while the **[1058]** employer companies were insolvent. Freeing the Administrators from personal liabilities for wages incurred by employees – pursuant to the undertaking given by the employees – was not to the point. The companies themselves would remain liable for those wages.

54. It is one thing to restrain Patrick Operations from giving effect to the termination of labour supply contracts and restraining those companies in ways that would, if the employees were to succeed at trial, permit the making of orders that would undo the transactions alleged to have been undertaken as a party to a conspiracy to engage in conduct in contravention of s 298K of the Act. But it is a very different thing to fetter the discretion of the Administrators (and of the creditors) in the exercise of the powers they possess under the Corporations Law. It is for the Administrators and the creditors (including the majority creditors, the employees) to take the decisions about continued trading. ...

[1059] 60. The parlous condition of the employer companies means that a continuation of trading runs the risk of causing detriment to third party creditors or the risk of the Administrators becoming personally liable for any losses incurred. But s 437A confers on the Administrators a power to be exercised in their discretion to continue or to desist from trading. That power is to be exercised in the interests of those affected (general creditors as well as employee creditors and shareholders) and having regard to the object of Pt 5.3A ...

61. The orders made by North J fettered the discretion. In particular, order 5 precluded the Administrators from deciding whether, if trading were resumed, it would be feasible to retain the whole workforce of the employer companies. Decisions of that kind are for the Administrators to make, not the Court. They are to be made having regard to all of the circumstances known at the time.

62. It was submitted on behalf of the employees that if the Administrators wanted to exercise their powers they could always approach the Federal Court pursuant to the liberty to apply that was reserved. If they could justify their proposed course of conduct, the orders could then be varied to permit it. This contention identifies an error in the orders made by the courts below. The Administrators cannot be deprived of the discretion which the *Corporations Law* reposes in them. True, they must obey the general law in exercising their discretions, including the law governing the dismissal of redundant employees, but that is not to say that their discretionary power is subject to court approval. No doubt, a decision made by an administrator may be challenged by appeal under s 1321 of the *Corporations Law* but there is a radical

difference between a challenge to an exercise of discretion under s 1321 and a denial of the administrator's discretionary power without the court's prior approval.

63. Section 447A of the *Corporations Law* empowers the Court to "make such order as it thinks appropriate about how [Pt 5.3A] is to operate in relation to a particular company". Assuming that the Federal Court could exercise that power, it would not support an order taking away the discretionary powers of the Administrators. The Full Court invoked s 447A to support an order to exonerate the Administrators from personal liability under s 443A for wages and other benefits for which the employees (including the MUA) undertook not to hold the Administrators liable. It is unnecessary to consider the validity of the Full Court's order as the order was unnecessary. The undertaking related to the enforcement of claims for wages and other benefits, not the existence of claims susceptible of enforcement. The employees' claims for the wages and the other benefits for which the employer companies would be liable in the event of resumed trading were understood to remain enforceable against the relevant employer companies.

See also *Re Ansett Airlines Ltd and Mentha* (2001) 19 ACLC 1678 and *Re Ansett Airlines Ltd and Korda* (2002) 20 ACLC 1187.

Moratorium

[13.370] As noted above, one of the effects of appointing an administrator is the imposition of a moratorium. As explained in the *Explanatory Memorandum to the Corporate Law Reform Bill* 1992 (Cth), this is designed to shield the company from claims by individual creditors and owners or lessors of property, until its future is determined in the creditors' meeting, discussed below. It gives the company 'breathing space' to enable a decision to be made as to whether creditors would be better served under a deed or through winding up: *Cinema Plus v ANZ Bank* [2000] NSWSC 658.

[13.380] Except where a transition occurs from administrator to liquidator under s 446A, during this period the company cannot be wound up: s 440A(1). The legislation also prohibits without the administrator's written approval or leave of the court:

- the enforcement of charges: s 440B;
- steps taken by the owner or lessor of property used by the company to recover that property: s 440C;
- court proceedings, other than criminal and prescribed proceedings: s 440D;
- the initiation or proceeding of an enforcement process against corporate property: ss 440F and 440G(2); and
- the enforcement of a guarantee against a director or spouse or relative of such a director: s 440J.

Termination of administration

[13.390] Under s 435C(1)(b), the administration of a company ends on the happening of certain specified events, whichever occurs first:

- a deed of company arrangement is executed by both the company and the deed's administrator;
- the company's creditors resolve under s 439C(b) that the administration is to end;
- the company's creditors resolve under s 439C(c) that the company is to be wound up;
- a court orders that the administration is to end;
- a meeting of creditors fails to be convened in accordance with s 439A within the period prescribed by s 439A(6) or any extension granted by a court;
- the meeting of creditors fails to make a resolution under s 439C as to the company's future;
- the company contravenes s 444B(2) by failing to execute a proposed deed of company arrangement;
- a court appoints a provisional liquidator of the company; or
- a court orders that the company be wound up: s 435C(2) and (3).

Where the creditors resolve to wind up the company or to terminate a deed of company arrangement and wind up the company, under s 446A(2) the company is deemed to have resolved that it be wound up voluntarily. The administrator is deemed to have been nominated as liquidator of the company: s 446A(4).

Where the creditors resolve that the company should execute a company deed of arrangement, the administrator will be the administrator of the deed unless the creditors appoint someone else: s 444A(2).

Creditors' meeting

[13.400] As noted above, the administrator must convene a meeting of the creditors within five business days of the period prescribed in s 439A(5) to determine the company's future: s 439A(1) and (2). The notice of the meeting must be accompanied by a copy of the administrator's report on the company's business, property and affairs and a statement of the administrator's opinion, and reasons for such, as to whether it would be in the creditors' interests for:

- the company to execute a deed of company arrangement;
- the administration to end; or
- the company to be wound up: s 439A(4).

At the meeting, the creditors may resolve to adopt any of these courses of action: s 439C.

As noted above, if the meeting is not convened or fails to pass the requisite resolution, pursuant to s 435C(3)(b)-(e) the administration is terminated.

Winding Up

Types of winding up

[13.410] Winding up is the process by which a company is dissolved by law. The process involves the appointment of a liquidator, the

realisation of the company's assets, the payment of corporate debts and the distribution of any surplus amongst the members. The formal winding up of a company is a statutory process, governed by Parts 5.4–5.9. These Parts detail two ways in which a company may be wound up:
- by order of the court, 'compulsory winding up'; or
- through a 'voluntary winding up' at the instance of either the members or creditors.

Part 5.4 is concerned with the winding up of a company by the court on the grounds of insolvency, while Part 5.4A governs compulsory winding up on other grounds. Part 5.4B contains further general provisions equally applicable to both modes of compulsory winding up. Part 5.5 governs voluntary modes of winding up. Further principles governing all modes of winding up are contained in Parts 5.6 and 5.7A-5.9.

Certain aspects of the winding up of companies are not considered in this text. In particular, creditors' rights, the proving and ranking of their claims (Div 6 of Part 5.6), void and voidable transactions (Div 7 of Part 5.6 and Divs 1 and 2 of Part 5.7B) and insolvent trading, discussed in Chap 10 (Divs 3-7 of Part 5.7B), are not considered.

Appointment of liquidator

[13.420] In the case of voluntary liquidations, the liquidator is appointed by the members/creditors: ss 495 and 499.

Section 472(1) provides in the case of a court-appointed liquidator that the court may appoint an official liquidator once an order is made for the company to be wound up. Section 473(7) also allows the court to fill a vacancy in the office of a court-appointed liquidator. Section 502 provides the court with a general power to appoint a liquidator where, for any reason, no liquidator is acting. This is supplemented by s 503 which allows a court to replace a liquidator when cause is shown.

The relevant principles relating to the appointment of a liquidator were outlined by Debelle J in *Re JN Taylor Holdings Ltd* (1991) 9 ACLC 1 at 12-13:

> **Relevant principles**
> The exercise of the power to appoint a provisional liquidator pursuant to s 372 is a serious intrusion upon the company. From a commercial point of view, the practical effect of the appointment is to paralyse the company: *Re London, Hamburg & Continental Exchange Bank, Emmerson's Case* (1866) LR 2 Eq 231 at 237, *Re Capital Services Ltd* (1983) 1 ACLC 1,270. In the present case, the appointment of a provisional liquidator might not be as dramatic as in other cases because of the present state of assets and liabilities of the company.
>
> Generally speaking, a provisional liquidator will be appointed only if the court is satisfied that there is a valid and duly authorised winding up application and there is a reasonable prospect that a winding up order will be made. *Re McLennan Holdings Pty Ltd* (1983) 1 ACLC 786; (1983) 7 ACLR 732, *Montgomery Windsor (NSW) Pty Ltd v Ilopa Pty Ltd* (1984) 2 ACLC 224. However, as Young J observed in *Alessi v Original Australian Art Co Pty Ltd* (1989) 7 ACLC 595, this is not a rule of law and in the appropriate extraordinary circumstances the court will appoint a provisional liquidator,

notwithstanding that it is unlikely that the company will finally be wound up. In *Re Brylyn No 2 Pty Ltd* (1988) 6 ACLC 505; (1987) 12 ACLR 697, Senior Master Lee QC came to a like conclusion. In that case, the application was made to wind up the company on the just and equitable ground. Master Lee decided that the fact that the court might grant a remedy other than a winding up order was no reason for not deciding to appoint a provisional liquidator if, in all the circumstances, the application was justified. In such a case, if the applicant has made a prima facie case for relief, be that relief a winding up order or some other order, the court may appoint a provisional liquidator. Other examples of where a provisional liquidator has been appointed notwithstanding that there was a real possibility that the winding up proceedings might not ultimately proceed are *Tickle v Crest Insurance Co of Australia Ltd* (1984) 2 ACLC 493, admittedly, a case on its own special circumstances; *Re Nerang Investments Pty Ltd* (1985) 3 ACLC 497; (1985) 9 ACLR 646, where a provisional liquidator was appointed because there was a strong possibility that, unless the appointment was made, the affairs of the company would be conducted for the benefit of one of the directors and not for the benefit of the company as a whole; and *South Downs Packers Pty Ltd v Beaver* (1984) 2 ACLC 541, where it was not possible for the directors to meet civilly and discuss and manage the affairs of the company. In short, the circumstances in which a provisional liquidator might be appointed are various: see, for example, the observations of Bright J in *Re Club Mediterranean Pty Ltd* (1975-1976) CLC ¶40-204 at 28,238; (1975) 11 SASR 481 at 484, where the fact of the conflict of interest between the directors and the proper interests of **[13]** the company was recognised as a ground to justify the appointment of a provisional liquidator. Such is the variety of commercial affairs that it would be imprudent to limit the circumstances in which a provisional liquidator might be appointed.

It is usually necessary to establish that the assets of the company are in some jeopardy. *Re Roadmakers Pty Ltd* (1985) 3 ACLC 591. *Re Adnot Pty Ltd* (1982) 1 ACLC 307; (1982) 7 ACLR 212. *Pitt v Bachmann; Re Lockyer Valley Fresh Foods Co-operative Association Ltd* (1980) CLC ¶40-671. In one sense, the need to demonstrate that the assets are in some jeopardy reflects the fact that the primary duty of a provisional liquidator is to preserve the status quo pending the hearing and determination of the application to wind up the company so that the assets of the company are preserved for the benefit of those who may ultimately be found entitled to them. *Re Carapark Industries Pty Ltd (in liq)* [1967] 1 NSWR 337, *Garden Mews-St Leonards Pty Ltd v Butler Pollnow Pty Ltd (No 4)* (1984) 2 ACLC 682, *Re Obie Pty Ltd (No 2)* (1984) 2 ACLC 67; [1984] 1 Qd R 371, *Re Rothwells Ltd* (1989) 7 ACLC 545 at 549-550; (1989) 15 ACLR 142 at 147; and generally as to the powers and duties of the provisional liquidator, see the note by Dr O'Donovan in (1987) 5 C & SLJ 253 at 259-261. Thus, an appointment will be refused if the court is satisfied that the assets of the company can be preserved by appropriate undertakings. The assets of the company might be in jeopardy if there is a conflict of interest between directors and the company: *Re Nerang Investments Pty Ltd* (1985) 3 ACLC 497; (1985) 9 ACLR 646.

In deciding whether to appoint a provisional liquidator, the court has a very wide discretion: *Re McLennan Holdings Pty Ltd* (1983) 1 ACLC 786; (1983) 7 ACLR 732; *Pitt v Bachmann; Re Lockyer Valley Fresh Foods Co-operative Association Ltd* (1980) CLC ¶40-671, and *Re Highfield Commodities Ltd* [1984] 3 All ER 884 at 893.

[13.430] In essence, the primary role of a liquidator is to provide an orderly liquidation of the company. The liquidator is to take possession of, and protect, the company's assets, determine creditors' claims, apply any proceeds to satisfy these debts and distribute surpluses, if any, to the company's members.

[13.440] Only a natural person may hold the office of liquidator. Moreover, to be eligible for appointment, the individual must be registered with ASIC or be a registered liquidator of the company under s 1282(3): s 532(1). Note, this does not apply in the case of a member's voluntary winding up of a proprietary company: s 532(4). See further s 532 as to who is ineligible to be a liquidator.

Before a person may be appointed as a liquidator, the person must consent in writing: s 532(9).

The liquidator must lodge notice of his or her appointment with ASIC within 14 days of the appointment: s 537. In addition, within 14 days of his or her appointment, the liquidator must notify the Commissioner of Taxation of the appointment: s 215 of the *Income Tax Assessment Act* 1936 (Cth).

During the course of liquidation, the company must set out in every public document or negotiable instrument after the company's name where it first appears, the expression 'in liquidation': s 541.

Impact of appointment on directors' powers

[13.450] As with other forms of external administration, the completion of the liquidator's role necessitates that the liquidator assume total control of the company's assets and affairs. While the directors continue to hold office, control of the company's affairs shifts from the board to, in this case, the liquidator. To this end s 471A(1) states that while a company is being wound up in insolvency, in the absence of court approval, a person cannot perform or exercise a function or power as an officer of the company. See *HVAC Construction (Qld) Pty Ltd v Energy Equipment Engineering Pty Ltd* [2002] FCA 1638.

While the directors' primary role may cease, the process of winding up does not affect the company's legal identity. This does not end until the process of dissolution is complete.

Termination of liquidator's appointment

[13.460] Under ss 473(1) and 503, the court is authorised to remove a liquidator where cause is shown. In addition, under s 536(1) the court has a broad discretion to make such orders as it thinks fit, including an order removing a liquidator, where it appears to the court or ASIC that a liquidator has not faithfully performed his or her functions, has breached a requirement of a court order or the Act or is the subject of a complaint to the court or ASIC.

Once all the company's property has been realised, the creditors and contributories (members) have been paid and the winding up has been finalised, the liquidator may apply to the court to be released from his or her office and for the company to be deregistered: s 480.

Section 473(1) also provides for the resignation of a court-appointed liquidator. If a liquidator resigns or is removed from office, notification of such must be lodged with ASIC within 14 days: s 537(2).

Liquidator's powers

[13.470] Under s 477(1), liquidators are conferred certain general powers. These include the ability to:
- carry on the company's business as far as necessary for the beneficial disposal or winding up of the business;
- pay creditors;
- make any compromise or arrangement with creditors; and
- subject to s 477(2A), compromise any existing, future or potential debts, liabilities or claims.

Note, however, the approval of the court, the committee of inspection or a resolution of creditors is required before the liquidator may compromise debts of more than $20,000 or enter into agreements having effect for more than three months: s 477(2A) and (2B). Section 477(2) confers specific powers on liquidators, including the ability to bring legal proceedings in the name, and on behalf, of the company and to sell or dispose all or any part of the company's property. See further s 477(2). See also the specific powers conferred under ss 474, 475, 484, 488, 506, 507, 535, 567 and 568.

Note, under s 511 the liquidator may apply to the court for instructions.

Liquidator's duties

[13.480] The liquidator, as an agent and officer of the company, is subject to the general fiduciary duties imposed on persons in such positions, discussed in Chapter 10. A liquidator in a compulsory winding up is also an officer of the court who, therefore, owes duties to that body depending on the function being exercised: *Tanning Research Laboratories Inc v O'Brien* (1987) 5 ACLC 820 at 827.

[13.490] The *Corporations Act* also imposes specific duties on a liquidator. These include a duty to:
- within two months of receiving the statement of affairs from the director and secretary pursuant to s 475, prepare a preliminary report as to, *inter alia*, the company's position and, if it has failed, the causes of the failure: s 476;
- lodge six monthly statements detailing receipts and payments and a statement as to the position of the winding up: s 539;
- report on any apparent breaches of the Act or duties owed to the company by directors, members or promoters: s 533;
- call a meeting of creditors, if so requested, for the appointment of the committee of inspection: s 548;
- collect the company's property and apply it to the discharge of liabilities: s 478(1);

- if necessary, prepare a list of contributories (present and certain past members): ss 478(1) and (1A) and 506(1)(c); and
- call a final meeting when the affairs of the company are fully wound up: s 509.

Liquidator's liability

[13.500] As with other external administrators, the court has a supervisory role and may take such action as it thinks fit where, as noted above, the court or ASIC is satisfied that the liquidator is not faithfully performing his or her functions or has not observed a requirement of the court or the Act or a complaint has been made as to the liquidator's performance: s 536(1). When exercising this supervisory role the court may order a liquidator to be personally liable for costs wrongly incurred: *Hypec Electronics Pty Ltd (in liq) v Mead* [2004] NSWSC 731. In addition, ASIC may report to the court any matter that in its opinion constitutes a misfeasance, neglect or omission by the liquidator: s 536(2).

[13.510] Where a liquidator has failed to meet his or her responsibilities under the Act, on the application of any contributory (member), creditor or ASIC, the court may direct the liquidator to make good the default: s 540(1).

[13.520] The liquidator may be personally liable for the claims of a creditor whom the liquidator has failed to notify. As long as the creditor has been invited to prove the debt, the liquidator will not be liable if the creditor fails to so act.

[13.530] Liquidators enjoy a limited form of privilege in relation to statements made in the course of their duties which may protect the liquidator from defamation actions: ss 89 and 535.

Winding up by the court

Court's power to wind up a company

[13.540] As noted in Chapter 12, one of the forms of relief available for oppressive or unfairly prejudicial or discriminatory conduct is an order that the company be wound up: s 233(1)(a) (formerly s 246AA(2)(c)). In addition, Parts 5.4 and 5.4A provide two more specific sources of power for a company to be wound up. Part 5.4 governs winding up on the ground of insolvency, while Part 5.4A, in particular ss 461 and 464, governs a compulsory winding up on other grounds.

Winding up in insolvency

[13.550] An application to have a company wound up in insolvency may be made under s 459P. Section 459P(1) provides that the following persons may apply to have the company wound up:
- the company;
- a creditor;

- a contributory (member);
- a director;
- a liquidator or provisional liquidator of the company;
- ASIC; and
- a prescribed agency.

Leave of the court is required, however, for an application by a creditor whose debt is contingent or prospective, a contributory, a director or ASIC: s 459P(2). Leave may only be granted where the court is satisfied that there is a *prima facie* case that the company is insolvent.

[13.560] While s 459A provides that an order that a company be wound up under Part 5.4 may only be made where the company is insolvent, the company's insolvency need not be the sole reason for the application. Where an application is made under ss 233, 462 or 464, discussed below, the court may nevertheless wind up the company under Part 5.4 as long as the company is insolvent.

[13.570] Under s 95A, a company is insolvent when it is unable to meet its debts as and when they fall due. See the discussion of insolvency in Chapter 10.

[13.580] Establishing the requisite insolvency is assisted by s 459C(2) and (3) which provide that the court may presume that a company is insolvent, unless the contrary be proved, if during or after the three months ending on the day the application for winding up was made:
- the company failed to comply with a statutory demand;
- execution or other process issued on a judgment etc in favour of a creditor was returned wholly or partly unsatisfied;
- a receiver or a receiver and manager of corporate property was appointed pursuant to the terms of an instrument relating to a floating charge;
- an order was made appointing such receiver or a receiver and manager for the purpose of enforcing the charge;
- a person entered into possession, or assumed control, of the property for this purpose; or
- a person was appointed to enter into possession, or assume control of that property (whether or not as agent of the chargee).

In determining the company's solvency, the court may have regard to any contingent or prospective liability of the company: s 459D.

[13.590] On hearing the application, the court may:
- dismiss the application, with or without costs;
- adjourn the hearing conditionally or unconditionally; or
- make an interim order or other order it thinks fit: s 467(1).

See also s 467A.

[13.600] Even after a winding-up order is made, the court may exercise the powers detailed in Div 3 of Part 5.4B. These include the power to:
- stay, indefinitely or for a limited period, or terminate the winding up: s 482(1);

- require a contributory, trustee, receiver, banker, agent or officer of the company to pay, deliver, convey, surrender or transfer to the liquidator any property, money or books *prima facie* belonging to the company: s 483(1);
- make calls on all or any contributories: s 483(3); and/or
- appoint a special manager with respect to the company's business or property: s 484(1).

Winding up on other grounds

[13.610] Under s 462(2), an application for the company to be wound up pursuant to s 461 may be made by:
- the company;
- a creditor, whether contingent or prospective;
- a contributory;
- the liquidator of the company;
- ASIC pursuant to s 464 (that is, in response to its investigation into the company's affairs);
- ASIC pursuant to s 462(2A) (that is, if the company has no members and the Commission has given the company one month's written notice of its intention to apply for the order); or
- the Australian Prudential Regulation Authority pursuant to s 462(3).

An application by a contingent or prospective creditor may only be heard by the court where reasonable security for costs has been given and a prima facie case for winding up the company has been established: s 462(4). Similarly, the Australian Prudential Regulation Authority's ability to bring an application is limited to cases where an inspector has been appointed to investigate the company and its liabilities exceed its assets:

[13.620] The grounds for an order winding up a company under Part 5.4A are detailed in s 461:
- the company has resolved by special resolution to be wound up by the court;
- the company has not commenced business within a year of incorporation or has suspended its business for a whole year;
- the company has no members;
- directors have acted in the affairs of the company in their own interests, rather than the interests of the members as a whole, or in any other manner which appears unfair or unjust to other members;
- the conduct of the affairs of the company is oppressive, unfairly prejudicial to, or unfairly discriminatory against, a member(s) or is contrary to the interests of members as a whole;
- an act or omission by, or on behalf of, the company, or a resolution of a class of members, is oppressive or unfairly prejudicial to, or unfairly discriminatory against, a member(s) or contrary to the interests of members as a whole;

- ASIC has reported that the company is insolvent or should be wound up and it is in the interests of the public, members or creditors that the company be wound up;
- on the application of the Australian Prudential Regulation Authority, the court believes that it is in the interests of the public, members or creditors that the company be wound up; or
- in the opinion of the court it is just and equitable that the company be wound up.

It will be evident that the grounds for a winding up specified in s 461(1)(e)-(g) echo the grounds for relief under s 233(1). In this way s 461 provides shareholders with a further means of controlling directors' and majority shareholders' abuses of powers.

[13.630] The general 'just and equitable' basis is the most commonly used for winding up a company. An examination of the cases considering the just and equitable ground for winding up a company reveals four distinct grounds for invoking an exercise of this power:
- expulsion from office: *Ebrahimi v Westbourne Galleries Ltd* [1973] AC 360; *Re Lundie Bros Ltd* [1965] 1 WLR 1051; *Re Wonderflex Textiles Pty Ltd* [1951] VLR 458;
- justifiable loss of confidence based on lack of probity in the controller's conduct of affairs: *Loch v John Blackwood Ltd* [1924] AC 783; *Stapp v Surge Holdings Pty Ltd* (1999) 17 ACLC 896;
- a deadlock in the company's management preventing the conduct of the company's business: *Loch v John Blackwood Ltd* [1924] AC 783; *Stapp v Surge Holdings Pty Ltd* (1999) 17 ACLC 896; *Johnny Oceans Restaurant Pty Ltd v Page* [2003] NSWSC 952; and
- failure of substratum: *Re Bleriot Aircraft Co* (1916) 32 TLR 253; *Re Haven Gold Mining Co* (1882) 20 Ch D 151; *Re German Date Coffee Co* (1882) 20 Ch D 169; *Re Tivoli Freeholds Ltd* [1972] VR 445; *Strong v J Brough & Son (Strathfield) Pty Ltd* (1991) 9 ACLC 1018.

The above four categories are not exhaustive. In *Thomas v Mackay Investments* (1996) 22 ACSR 294 at 300, Owen J stressed that '[t]he classes of conduct which will justify a winding up order on the just and equitable ground are not closed. Much will depend on the circumstances of each case'. '[T]here is no necessary limit to the generality of the words "just and equitable". They are to be applied in their ordinary meaning as calling for their exercise of judgment in the conventional way': *Thomas* at 302.

The scope and application of this ground was explained by Menhennitt J in *Re Tivoli Freeholds Ltd* [1972] VR 445.

Re Tivoli Freeholds Ltd
Supreme Court of Victoria: Menhennitt J
[1972] VR 445

The subject company had been incorporated with the main object of public entertainment. New controllers, however, involved the company in lending surplus funds and in profitable corporate raiding. A minority shareholder petitioned the court for an order winding up the company on the grounds that the company's affairs were being conducted in an oppressive manner and that it was just and equitable that the company be wound up. In reply to the just and equitable basis for the winding up the respondents asserted that for such a claim to be made out the company must be acting *ultra vires* and that the predecessors to ss 124 and 125 had the effect of preventing an application being based on claims that the company was acting outside the common intention of the members or on the ground of a failure of substratum.

The Court rejected both of the latter propositions and indicated that it was just and equitable that the company be wound up. The matter was adjourned and during the period of adjournment a settlement was reached whereby the majority shareholders acquired the minority shareholders' shares.

Menhennitt J: [468] In relation to the ground that it is just and equitable that the company be wound up, the following propositions appear to me to be applicable to this case and to be established by authority:

(1) The ground is that it is just and equitable to wind up the company. These are well known words and there is no adequate equivalent for them. They give the court a wide discretion which must of course, be exercised judicially ... The question involved is basically a question of fact and all the circumstances must be looked at ...

(2) The facts rendering it just and equitable that a company be wound up and the decisions on that ground cannot be resolved into an exhaustive set of categories ...

(3) At the same time, in so far as decisions binding on me have defined basic elements necessary to constitute a particular concept, those decisions are of course to be observed by me and in so far as a case involves one concept alone such decisions might well indicate the only conclusion that was open to me. However, before reaching such a conclusion it would be necessary to have regard to changing circumstances and developments in relation to company practices including any relevant changes in law.

(4) It has been recognized that it may be just and equitable to wind a company up if the company engages in acts which are entirely outside what can fairly be regarded as having been within the general intention and common understanding of the members when they became members ... The [469] cases on loss or failures of substratum are an illustration of this more basic concept ... This more basic concept is not, it appears to me, confined to cases of 'partnership' companies or 'main object' companies. Whilst it may be easier to find the general intention and common understanding in those cases I can see no reason in principle why it should be confined to such cases and I am not aware of any decision that it is so confined. ...

[470] (6) The question in issue and the tests to be applied in ascertaining the general intention and common understanding of the members or what is the substratum of the company are different from those determining whether or not an act is *ultra vires*. The submission for the respondents that the question in issue and the tests involved are the same is contrary to the highest authority ... At 521 his Lordship said [in *Cotman v Broughman* [1918] AC 514]: 'For the purpose of determining whether a company's substratum be gone, it may be necessary to distinguish between power and object and to

determine what is the main or paramount object of the company, but I do not think this is necessary where a transaction is impeached as *ultra vires*.' ...

[471] (7) It was contended for the respondents that since the enactment of ss 19 and 20 of the *Companies Act* 1961 the provisions of those sections produce the result that it is never just and equitable to wind a company up on the ground that what is being done is entirely outside what can fairly be regarded as having been within the general intention and common understanding of the members or on the grounds that the substratum of the company has failed or gone, or alternatively, that since 1962 those grounds are confined to cases of 'partnership' companies or companies with a main object or companies which exclude the application of the powers in the Third Schedule to the Companies Act 1961. In my view, such contentions are not well founded. In part they were based on the contention, which I have rejected, that the tests for determining whether an act is *ultra vires* are identical with the tests for ascertaining general intention and common understanding among members and for determining what is the company's substratum. ... [T]he issue as to whether it is just and equitable that the company be wound up is, it appears to me, a quite different one from the question of power and the consideration that trading acts of a company cannot be outside power or cannot be relied upon by a member in winding up proceedings as being outside power does not affect the basic considerations which may still make it just and equitable that a company be wound up because of a complete departure from what was within the original general intention and common understanding of the members or because the company's substratum failed or gone. ...

(8) All the authorities appear to me to recognize that the prime source for ascertaining the general intention and common understanding of the members is the company's memorandum of association which among other things states its objects. The authorities also recognize the distinction between the objects of the company strictly so called and what are really powers although they may be termed objects. Next, as was stated by Lord Parker in *Cotman v Brougham* at 521: 'It may be necessary to distinguish between power and object and to determine what is the main or paramount object of the company'. ...

[472] (9) Whether it is permissible to go beyond the company's memorandum at ascertain the prime or main object or the general intention and common understanding of members is a matter on which there is a conflict of authority. ... However, a basic consideration is that the material being looked at must establish something general or common to all members and this consideration of itself precludes something passing between only the company and a particular shareholder unless it can be concluded that it was a matter common to all shareholders. The company's course of conduct may be relevant but it could not prevail against the conclusion to be drawn from the memorandum. On the other hand, it may be useful to remove ambiguity in relation to the issue of main objects or statutory purposes. ...

[474] [T]he main objects of the company were to carry on the entertainment business in its various forms with associated or ancillary activities and to acquire, either in the vicinity of Bourke and Little Collins Streets, Melbourne, or possibly within the area of the city of Melbourne, land on which theatres were erected together with adjoining premises. Indeed, I think there is much to be said for the view that those, with probably the addition of the acquisition of land in any form anywhere, are the only objects of the company in the proper sense, as distinct from powers. ...

[475] What I have described reveals, in my view, that more than 70 per cent of the company's funds have been committed to a use completely different in every was from anything within the company's objects (within the real sense of that term) and what was the general intention and common understanding of the members. ... When there is coupled with this departure the desire of about 93 per cent of the minority shareholders to dissociate themselves with these new activities and have their moneys returned to them, the conclusion that follows, in my view, that it would be just and equitable to wind up the company unless to do so would result in disproportionate injustice and inequity to the majority shareholders ... [I]n my view, by winding up the company no real injustice or injury would be done to the majority shareholders and certainly none sufficient to outweigh the matters to which I have referred making it just and equitable, from the point of view of the minority shareholders, to wind up the company.

See also *Scottish Co-operative Society v Meyer* [1958] AC 324 extracted in Chapter 12.

[13.640] From Menhennitt J's fourth point it will be evident that, typically, this ground will be invoked by disgruntled members of 'quasi-partnerships' who find their expectations as to a secure, continued involvement in the business have been undermined by their former partners. This term is used to refer to small proprietary companies that have grown out of a partnership where the relations between the incorporators are based on mutual confidence which gives rise to certain expectations: *Ebrahimi v Westbourne Galleries Ltd* [1973] AC 360. See also *Re Wonderflex Textiles Ltd* [1951] VLR 458 at 465. For a company to be wound up on this basis there must have been a relationship of mutual trust and confidence when the applicant entered into the corporate structure: *Guerinoni v Argyle Concrete & Quarry Supplies Pty Ltd* (unreported, WASC, 1999, Master Sanderson). In the absence of such a relationship it will not be just and equitable to wind a company up under this ground.

Ebrahimi v Westbourne Galleries Ltd
House of Lords: Lords Wilberforce, Pearson, Cross and Salmon and Viscount Dilhorne
[1973] AC 360

The subject business had been originally conducted as a partnership between the applicant and Nazar. Soon after the incorporation of the business, Nazar's son was appointed as a third director. The company was profitable and all proceeds were distributed as directors' remuneration. After a dispute with the applicant, Nazar and his son combined their voting power to remove Ebrahimi from his office as director. Ebrahimi petitioned for relief under provisions equivalent to ss 232-235 and 461.

The court held that while the removal was pursuant to the constitution, Ebrahimi had a legitimate expectation that these powers would not be so exercised in this manner and that the shared management of the business would continue. It was legitimate for the court when considering the just and equitable ground for winding up a company to take into account the personal relationship between the parties which may suggest it to be inequitable for one party to insist on his or her legal rights and exercise them in a certain manner. In this case, in light of Ebrahimi's legitimate expectations, it was just and equitable to wind up the company.

Lord Wilberforce: **[374]** This petition was based in the first place upon section 210 of the *Companies Act* 1948, the relief sought under this section being an order that Mr Nazar and his son be ordered to purchase the appellant's shares in the company. In the alternative it sought an order for the winding up of the company. The petition contained allegations of oppression and misconduct against Mr Nazar which were fully explored at the hearing before Plowman J. The learned judge found that some were unfounded and others unproved and that such complaint as was made out did not amount to such a course of oppressive conduct as to justify an order under section 210. However, he made an order for the winding up of the company under the "just and equitable" provision. I shall later specify the grounds on which he did so. The appellant did not appeal against the rejection of his case under section 210 and this House is not concerned with it. The company and the individual respondents appealed against the order for winding up and this was set aside by the Court of Appeal. The appellant now seeks to have it restored.

My Lords, the petition was brought under section 222 (f) of the *Companies Act* 1948, which enables a winding up order to be made if "the court is of the opinion that it is just and equitable that the company should be wound up." This power has existed in our company law in unaltered form since the first major Act, the *Companies Act* 1862. Indeed, it antedates that statute since it existed in the *Joint Stock Companies Winding up Act* 1848. For some 50 years, following a pronouncement by Lord Cottenham LC in 1849, the words "just and equitable" were interpreted so as only to include matters *ejusdem generis* as the preceding clauses of the section, but there is now ample authority for discarding this limitation. There are two other restrictive interpretations which I mention to reject. First, there has been a tendency to create categories or headings under which cases must be brought if the clause is to apply. This is wrong. Illustrations may be used, but general words should remain general and not be reduced to the sum of particular **[375]** instances. Secondly, it has been suggested, and urged upon us, that (assuming the petitioner is a shareholder and not a creditor) the words must be confined to such circumstances as affect him in his capacity as shareholder. I see no warrant for this either. No doubt, in order to present a petition, he must qualify as a shareholder, but I see no reason for preventing him from relying upon any circumstances of justice or equity which affect him in his relations with the company, or, in a case such as the present, with the other shareholders.

One other signpost is significant. The same words "just and equitable" appear in the *Partnership Act* 1892, section 25, as a ground for dissolution of a partnership and no doubt the considerations which they reflect formed part of the common law of partnership before its codification. The importance of this is to provide a bridge between cases under section 222(f) of the Act of 1948 and the principles of equity developed in relation to partnerships.

The winding up order was made following a doctrine which has developed in the courts since the beginning of this century. As presented by the appellant, and in substance accepted by the learned judge, this was that in a case such as this the members of the company are in substance partners, or quasi-partners, and that a winding up may be ordered if such facts are shown as could justify a dissolution of partnership between them. The common use of the words "just and equitable" in the company and partnership law supports this approach. ...

[379] My Lords, in my opinion these authorities represent a sound and rational development of the law which should be endorsed. The foundation of it all lies in the words "just and equitable" and, if there is any respect in which some of the cases may be open to criticism, it is that the courts may sometimes have been too timorous in giving them full force. The words are a recognition of the fact that a limited company is more than a mere judicial entity, with a personality in law of its own: that there is room in company law for recognition of the fact that behind it, or amongst it, there are individuals, with rights, expectations and obligations inter se which are not necessarily submerged in the company structure. That structure is defined by the *Companies Act* and by the articles of association by which shareholders agree to be bound. In most companies and in most contexts, this definition is sufficient and exhaustive, equally so whether the company is large or small. The "just and equitable" provision does not, as the respondents suggest, entitle one party to disregard the obligation he assumes by entering a company, nor the court to dispense him from it. It does, as equity always does, enable the court to subject the exercise of legal rights to equitable considerations; considerations, that is, of a personal character arising between one individual and another, which may make it unjust, or inequitable, to insist on legal rights, or to exercise them in a particular way.

It would be impossible, and wholly undesirable, to define the circumstances in which these considerations may arise. Certainly the fact that a company is a small one, or a private company, is not enough. There are very many of these where the association is a purely commercial one, of which it can safely be said that the basis of association is adequately and exhaustively laid down in the articles. The superimposition of equitable considerations requires something more, which typically may include one, or probably more, of the following elements: (i) an association formed or continued on the basis of a personal relationship, involving mutual confidence – this element will often be found where a pre-existing partnership has been converted into a limited company; (ii) an agreement, or understanding, that all, or some (for there may be "sleeping" members), of the shareholders shall participate in the conduct of the business; (iii) restriction upon the transfer of the members' interest in the company – so that if confidence is lost, or one member is removed from management, he cannot take out his stake and go elsewhere. ...

[380] My Lords, this is an expulsion case, and I must briefly justify the application in such cases of the just and equitable clause. The question is, as always, whether it is equitable to allow one (or two) to make use of his legal rights to the prejudice of his associate(s). The law of companies recognises the right, in many ways, to remove a director from the board. Section 184 of the *Companies Act* 1948 confers this right upon the company in general meeting whatever the articles may say. Some articles may prescribe other methods: for example, a governing director may have the power to remove (cf *In re Wonderflex Textiles Pty Ltd* [1951] VLR 458). And quite apart from removal powers, there are normally provisions for retirement of directors by rotation so that their re-election can be opposed and defeated by a majority, or even by a casting vote. In all these ways a particular director-member may find himself

no longer a director, through removal, or non-re-election: this situation he must normally accept, unless he undertakes the burden of proving fraud or mala fides. The just and equitable provision nevertheless comes to his assistance if he can point to, and prove, some special underlying obligation of his fellow member(s) in good faith, or confidence, that so long as the business continues he shall be entitled to management participation, an obligation so basic that, if broken, the conclusion must be that the association must be dissolved. And the principles on which he may do so are those worked out by the courts in partnership cases where there has been exclusion from management (see *Const v Harris* (1824) Tur & Rus 496, 525) even where under the partnership agreement there is a power of expulsion (see *Blisset v Daniel* (1853) 10 Hare 493, *Lindley on Partnership*, 13th ed (1971), pp 331, 595).

I come to the facts of this case. It is apparent enough that a potential basis for a winding up order under the just and equitable clause existed. The appellant after a long association in partnership, during which he had an equal share in the management, joined in the formation of the company. The inference must be indisputable that he, and Mr Nazar, did so on the basis that the character of the association would, as a matter of personal relation and good faith, remain the same. He was removed from his directorship under a power valid in law. Did he establish a case which if he had remained in a partnership with a term providing for expulsion, would have justified an order for dissolution? ...

[381] Reading this in the context of the judgment [of Ploughman J] as a whole, which had dealt with the specific complaints of one side against the other, I take it as a finding that the respondents were not entitled, in justice and equity, to make use of their legal powers of expulsion and that, in accordance with the principles of such cases as *Blisset v Daniel*, 10 Hare 493, the only just and equitable course was to dissolve the association. To my mind, two factors strongly support this. First, Mr Nazar made it perfectly clear that he did not regard Mr Ebrahimi as a partner, but did regard him as an employee. But there was no possible doubt as to Mr Ebrahimi's status throughout, so that Mr Nazar's refusal to recognise it amounted, in effect, to a repudiation of the relationship. Secondly, Mr Ebrahimi, through ceasing to be a director, lost his right to share in the profits through directors' remuneration, retaining only the chance of receiving dividends as a minority shareholder. It is true that an assurance was given in evidence that the previous practice (of not paying dividends) would not be continued, but the fact remains that Mr Ebrahimi was henceforth at the mercy of the Messrs Nazar as to what he should receive out of the profits and when. He was, moreover, unable to dispose of his interest without the consent of the Nazars. All these matters lead only to the conclusion that the right course was to dissolve the association by winding up.

I must deal with one final point which was much relied on by the Court of Appeal. It was said that the removal was, according to the evidence of Mr Nazar, bona fide in the interests of the company; that Mr Ebrahimi had not shown the contrary; that he ought to do so or to demonstrate that no reasonable man could think that his removal was in the company's interest. This formula "bona fide in the interests of the company" is one that is relevant in certain contexts of company law and I do not doubt that in many cases decisions have to be left to majorities or directors to take which the courts must assume had this basis. It may, on the other hand, become little more than an alibi for a refusal to consider the merits of the case, and in a situation such as this it seems to have little meaning other than "in the interests of the majority." Mr Nazar may well have persuaded himself, quite genuinely, that the company would be better off without Mr Ebrahimi, but if Mr Ebrahimi disputed this, or thought the same with reference to Mr Nazar, what prevails is simply the majority view. To confine the application of the just and equitable clause to proved cases of mala fides would be to negative the generality of the words. It is because I do not accept this that I feel myself obliged to differ from the Court of Appeal.

I would allow the appeal and restore the judgment of Plowman J. I propose that the individual respondents pay the appellant's costs here and in the Court of Appeal.

[13.650] Where an application is successfully made under s 461, the court's powers are the same as those detailed above with respect to a winding up in insolvency. In this context, however, the courts have stressed that winding up is a 'remedy of last resort and ought not to be granted if some other less drastic form of relief is available and appropriate': *Re Dalkeith Investments Pty Ltd* (1985) 3 ACLC 74 at 79. To this end s 467(4) prescribes that where an application is made by members as contributories on the ground that it is just and equitable (s 461(1)(k)) or that the directors have acted in a manner that appears to be unfair or unjust to other members (s 461(1)(e)), the court must consider whether some other remedy is available to the applicants and whether they are acting unreasonably in seeking the company be wound up instead of pursuing that other remedy: *Re a Company* [1983] 1 WLR 927 at 932. In particular, a rejection of an offer to have the member's shares purchased at a fair value as an alternative to winding up will be considered unreasonable: *Re a Company* at 936. See also *Cooke v Fairbairn* [2003] NSWSC 232; *Host-Plus Pty Ltd v Australian Hotels Association* [2003] VSC 145.

Voluntary winding up

Application by members

[13.660] A company may be voluntarily wound up on the application of either the members or the creditors. If the company is solvent, the members may resolve, by the passage of a special resolution, to wind the company up: s 491(1). A prerequisite to this procedure is a declaration of solvency by the directors, asserting that the company will be able to pay its debts as and when they fall due within 12 months of the commencement of the winding up: s 494(1). The declaration of solvency must have attached to it a statement of the company's affairs showing:

- the company's property and expected realisation value;
- the company's liabilities; and
- the estimated expenses of winding up: s 494(2).

[13.670] A liquidator is also appointed by the company in general meeting: s 495(1). If the liquidator forms the opinion that the company will not be able to pay its debts, then he or she must:

- apply for the company to be wound up in insolvency;
- appoint an administrator pursuant to s 436B; or
- convene a meeting of the company's creditors: s 496(1).

Application by creditors

[13.680] If the company is insolvent, the directors may call a general meeting at which the members may resolve by special resolution that, in light of the company's liabilities, it should be wound up. Upon this resolution a liquidator may be appointed. A meeting of creditors must then be summoned within 24 hours of the resolution: s 497(1). A full statement of the company's affairs must be put before this meeting (s 497(5)) and this statement lodged with ASIC within seven days of the meeting: s 497(7). A director, appointed for this purpose, and the secretary must be in attendance at the meeting to disclose to the meeting the company's affairs and the circumstances leading to the proposed winding up: s 497(6). At the meeting the creditors may nominate a liquidator. If they do not nominate a liquidator, the person appointed by the members will continue to be the liquidator: s 499.

Court's powers

[13.690] On the application of the liquidator, contributory or creditor, the court has a broad discretion to determine any question arising out of the winding up and to exercise any of the powers that would be exercisable were the company wound up by the court: s 511(1).

Deregistration

Types of deregistration

[13.700] Under Part 5A a company may be deregistered, rather than wound up. Deregistration may be voluntary (s 601AA) or at the instigation of ASIC: s 601AB. Upon deregistration the company ceases to exist: s 601AD(1). The company's property vests with ASIC (s 601AD(2)) and must be applied in accordance with s 601AE. This process provides an easy and inexpensive way of dissolving defunct companies.

Voluntary deregistration

[13.710] An application to deregister a company may be lodged with ASIC by:
- the company;
- a director or member; or
- a liquidator: s 601AA(1).

An application may be made where all of the following conditions are satisfied:
- all members agree;
- the company is not carrying on business;

- the company's assets are worth less than $1000;
- all fees and penalties payable under the Act have been paid;
- the company has no outstanding liabilities; and
- the company is not a party to any legal proceedings.

[13.720] If ASIC is not aware of any failure to comply with the above prerequisites, notice of the deregistration must be given on ASIC database and the in Gazette: s 601AA(4). After two months of the latter notice ASIC may deregister the company and notify the applicant or person nominated on the application: s 601AA(4) and (5).

Deregistration initiated by ASIC

[13.730] ASIC may deregister a company if the following conditions are satisfied:

- the company's annual return is at least six months late;
- the company has not lodged any other documents under the Act in the last 18 months; and
- the Commission has no reason to believe the company is carrying on business: s 601AB(1).

Alternatively, ASIC may deregister a company where it is being wound up and the Commission believes:

- the liquidator is no longer acting;
- the company's affairs have been fully wound up and the liquidator's return is at least six months late; or
- the company's affairs have been fully wound up under Part 5.4 and the company has no property or not enough to cover the costs of obtaining a court order for the company's deregistration: s 601AB(2).

[13.740] If ASIC decides to deregister a company, notice must be given to the company, the liquidator (if any) and the directors and this must be detailed on ASIC database and in the Gazette: s 601AB(3). After two months have passed since the notice in the Gazette, ASIC may deregister the company: s 601AB(3). Notice of the deregistration must be given to the liquidator (if any) and the directors: s 601AB(5).

[13.750] ASIC may also deregister a company if ordered by a court pursuant to ss 413(1)(d), 481(5)(b) or 509(6): s 601AC(1). ASIC is also required to deregister a company if three months have passed since the liquidator lodged a return under s 509 and no order has been made under s 509(6): s 601AC(2).

Reinstatement

[13.760] Reinstatement may occur if ASIC believes the company should not have been deregistered: s 601AH(1). A court may also order that ASIC reinstate a company where, on the application of a person aggrieved by the deregistration or a former liquidator of the company, the court is satisfied that it is just that the company be reinstated: s 601AH(2).

[13.770] In relation to standing under s 601AH, the court in *Krstevska v ACN 010505012 Pty Ltd* (2002) 20 ACLC 292 said that the test is satisfied if the 'applicant's legal rights have been affected by the deregistration and if it has a genuine grievance that the dissolution has affected its interests'. In this case this test was satisfied as the applicant wished to sue the deregistered company for personal injuries incurred as an employee. In determining if it is just to reinstate the company, regard must be had to 'what will happen if the company stays deregistered and what ... will happen if it comes out of deregistration'. In this case there was no risk that reinstatement would lead to the company engaging in insolvent trading and without reinstatement the applicant could not claim against the company (the liability was covered by an insurance policy).

[13.780] If the court makes an order for reinstatement, it may also validate anything done between the deregistration of the company and its reinstatement or make such other orders it considers appropriate: s 601AH(3). The effect of the reinstatement is to put the company in the position it would have been in had it not been deregistered: s 601AH(5). Thus, if before deregistration the company had been in liquidation, when reinstated the company will again be in liquidation (*Krstevska v ACN 010505012 Pty Ltd* (2002) 20 ACLC 292) and the previous liquidator would return to his/her office: *ACCC v ASIC* [2000] NSWSC 316. A person who was a director immediately before deregistration becomes a director again on reinstatement: s 601AH(5).

Review questions

1. Discuss from the points of view of both an insolvent company and a creditor the relative merits of receivership, a scheme of arrangement, voluntary administration and winding up as forms of administration.
2. Gertie and Fred ran a successful wine-making business together before deciding to incorporate Wine Pty Ltd in 1997. The decision to incorporate was based on personal liability and tax reasons. Gertie and Fred are the company's only two directors and shareholders. However, in recent times they have found it difficult to work together. Gertie wants to sell the business. Fred's response is: 'No way, we have come too far to wind this business up!' In turn Gertie has began using company funds to establish a new business in competition to Wine Pty Ltd. Advise as to any causes of action open to the parties under the *Corporations Act* to resolve these difficulties?
3. Things have become worse in the relationship and Gertie resigned her directorship, but still continued his management of part of Wine Pty Ltd business whilst developing her new business. Soon after Gertie's resignation, Fred appointed his son as a director and they in turn agreed to an increase in director's fees. At the same time, they recommended against Wine Pty Ltd paying a dividend that year, although the company had always paid dividends in the past.

Gertie was angry that no dividend would be paid. Is there any cause of action open to the parties under the *Corporations Act* to resolve these difficulties?

Further reading

Anderson, 'Commencement of the Part 5.3A Procedure: Some Considerations from an Economics and Law Perspective' (2001) 9 *ILJ* 4

Anderson, *Crutchfield's Corporate Voluntary Administration Law* (3rd ed, Thomson Legal & Regulatory, Sydney, 2002)

Austin and Vann (eds), *The Law of Public Finance* (Law Book Co, Sydney, 1986)

Australian Law Reform Commission, *General Insolvency Inquiry* (1988, ALRC 45)

Bennetts, 'Dealing with Winding Up Applications Following the Appointment of an Administrator' (2000) 18 *C&SLJ* 41

Blanchard and Geyde, *The Law of Company Receiverships in Australia and New Zealand* (2nd ed, Butterworths, Wellington, 1994)

Callaway, *Winding Up on the Just and Equitable Ground* (Law Book Co, Sydney, 1978)

Cassidy, *Concise Corporations Law* (4th ed, Federation Press, Sydney, 2003) ch 13

Companies and Security Advisory Committee, *Voluntary Administration Insolvency Administration* Discussion Paper (1997)

Ford, Austin and Ramsay, *Ford's Principles of Corporations Law* (11th ed, Butterworths, Sydney, 2003) chs 25, 26 and 27

Keay, *McPherson: Law of Company Liquidation* (4th ed, LBC Information Services, Sydney, 1999)

Lipton, 'Voluntary Administration: Is There Life After Insolvency for the Unsecured Creditor?' (1993) 1 *ILJ* 87

O'Donovan, *Company Receivers and Managers* (2nd ed, Lawbook Co, Sydney, 2000)

Routledge 'Part 5.3A of the Corporations Law (Voluntary Administration): Creditors' Bargain or Creditors' Dilemma?' (1998) 6 *ILJ* 127

Stevenson, 'Receivers' (1973) 47 *ALJ* 438

Tomasic and Whitford, *Australian Insolvency and Bankruptcy Law* (2nd ed, Butterworths, Sydney, 1997)

Index

ABN: 5.40-5.50

ACN: 5.40-5.50

Administrator: 13.250-13.400
    appointment: 13.250-13.290
    duties: 13.330-13.340, 13.360
    liability: 13.350-13.360
    powers: 13.320, 13.360
    termination of administration: 13.390
    termination of appointment: 13.300

Alternate director: 9.270

Amending the constitution: 6.30, 6.60-6.210

Annual general meeting: 2.290, 2.300, 5.220

Appointment of directors: 5.60, 5.140, 9.310-9.360, 9.640-9.690

Articles of association: 6.10

Associate director: 9.250

Auditor: 2.290-2.330, 5.160

Australian Business Number: 5.40-5.50

Australian Company Number: 5.40-5.50

Australian jurisdictional and administrative arrangements: 1.130

Authorised share capital: 7.240-7.250

Benefits and shortcomings of incorporation: 2.210-2.280

Benefits and shortcomings of public and proprietary companies: 2.290-2.300

Board meetings: 11.80-11.220

Board of directors, *see also* Directors: 9.10-9.30
    board meetings: 11.80-11.220
    division of power between board and general meeting: 9.20-9.30, 12.30, 12.110
    role of board of directors: 9.10

Breach of warranty of authority: 4.70

Business organisations: 2.10-2.300

Certificate of registration: 5.110, 7.40

Chairperson: 9.260, 11.730

Charges: 8.50-8.110

Chief executive officer: 9.230

Classes of shares: 7.50-7.230

Class meetings: 7.180-7.190

Common seal: 5.130

Company: 2.110-2.300

Company limited by guarantee: 2.140

Company limited by shares: 2.130

Company limited by shares and guarantee: 2.140

Company name: 5.40-5.50

Company lending money on security of its own shares: 7.380-7.400

Company liability: 3.50-3.130, 4.190-4.230

Company purchasing its own shares: 7.280-7.370

Company secretary: 5.60, 5.140, 9.280-9.300, 9.360

Conflict of interests: 10.390-10.690

Constitutional law position: 1.60-1.120

Constructive notice: 6.220

Corporate constitution: 5.70, 5.90, 6.10-6.240
    articles of association: 6.10
    altering: 6.30, 6.60-6.210
    legal effect: 6.50, 6.130-6.240
    memorandum of association: 6.10
    model articles: 6.10
    replaceable rules: 6.20-6.60, 6.130-6.140, 6.170-6.210
    statutory contract: 6.130-6.210, 6.240
    ultra vires: 6.220-6.240

Corporate personality: 2.210, 3.10-3.130

Corporate trustee: 2.50, 3.190

Creditors
    directors' duty to: 10.110
    directors' liability for insolvent trading: 10.960-10.970

Criminal liability of company: 3.50-3.130

Cross-vesting: 1.110

Debentures: 8.30-8.40

Debt capital: 8.10-8.110
    debentures: 8.30-8.40
    charges: 8.50-8.110
    negative pledges: 8.80, 8.110

De facto directors: 9.40-9.80

Deferred shares: 7.70

Deregistration of company: 2.230, 13.700-13.780

Derivative action: 12.20, 12.50, 12.110-12.240

Directors, *see also* Board of directors and Directors' duties and officers
    alternate: 9.270
    appointment: 5.60, 5.140, 9.310-9.360, 9.640-9.690
    associate: 9.250
    chairperson: 9.260
    chief executive officer: 9.230
    contract of service: 6.130-6.170, 9.700-9.800, 9.970-9.1010, 10.390-10.690
    contracts with the company: 10.390-10.690
    definition of director: 9.40-9.80
    delegation: 10.750-10.780
    disqualification: 9.370-9.620, 10.220
    duties: Chapter 10
    executive: 9.190
    financial benefits: 10.390-10.690
    governing: 9.240
    managing: 9.200-9.220
    non-executive: 9.190
    payments for loss of office: 9.970-9.1010
    qualifications: 9.310-9.360
    removal: 9.880-9.1010
    remuneration: 9.700-9.800, 9.970-9.1010
    resignation: 9.810-9.840
    statutory contract: 6.130-6.170
    vacation of office: 9.120-9.140
    validation of director's actions: 9.150-9.180

Directors' duties: Chapter 10
    business judgment rule: 10.730-10.740
    consequences of breach: 9.370-9.620, 10.160, 10.210-10.270, 10.340-10.370, 10.430, 10.500, 10.540, 10.590-10.600, 10.620, 10.730, 10.790, 10.960-10.990
    contracting with the company: 10.390-10.690
    delegation: 10.750-10.780
    disclosure requirements: 10.420-10.590
    duty of care, skill and diligence: 10.700-10.790
    duty not to fetter discretion: 10.270
    duty to act honestly and in the best interests of the company: 10.10-10.260
    duty to avoid a conflict of interests: 10.390-10.690
    employee entitlements: 10.860
    fiduciary duties: 10.10-160, 10.270-10.370, 10.390-10.430, 10.600-10.650
    insolvent trading: 3.170-3.180, 10.800-10.990
    proper purpose doctrine: 10.280-10.380
    ratification: 10.350, 10.420-10.430, 10.620, 12.210
    reliance on others: 10.750-10.780
    use of position for profit: 10.660-10.690

Disclosure document: 2.300, 8.130-8.560
    advertising: 8.470-8.540
    definition: 8.170

Disclosure document (*cont*)
    excluded offers: 8.140-8.160
    false or misleading conduct: 8.400-8.460
    hawking securities: 8.550-8.560
    image advertising: 8.490
    offer information statement: 8.170, 8.250-8.260
    offers that need disclosure: 8.130
    professional investors: 8.160
    profile statement: 8.230-8.240, 8.170
    prospectus: 8.170-8.220
    replacement document: 8.280-8.300, 8.330-8.360
    restrictions on advertisements: 8.470-8.540
    securities: 8.120
    short form prospectus: 8.170, 8.210-8.220
    small scale offerings: 8.150
    sophisticated investors: 8.160
    stop orders: 8.350-8.360
    supplementary document: 8.280-8.320, 8.350-8.360

Discount share issues: 7.240

Disqualification of directors: 9.370-9.620

Dividends: 7.490-7.660
    definition of profits: 7.530-7.640
    interim dividend: 7.650
    legal effect: 7.510, 7.630
    procedure for declaring/announcing: 7.490-7.500

Employee share schemes: 7.150, 7.470

Equal reduction of share capital: 7.300

External administration: Chapter 13
    administration of corporation: 13.250-13.400
    deregistration: 13.700-13.780
    schemes of arrangement: 13.180-13.240
    receivership: 13.10-13.170
    winding up: 13.410-13.690

Extraordinary meetings: 11.280

Financial assistance for the purchase of shares: 7.410-7.480

Financial product: 8.570-8.600

Financial services: 8.570-8.600

Foreign corporations: 5.270

Forfeiture of shares: 2.160

Fraud on minority: 12.40

General meetings: 11.280-11.810

Governing director: 9.240

Governor's shares: 7.140

Group companies: 3.180, 3.260, 7.640, 10.80-10.100
    directors' duties: 10.80-10.100

Hawking securities: 8.550-8.560
Historical development of Australian company law: 1.40-1.80
Historical development of company law: 1.10-1.30
Image advertising: 8.490
Indoor management rule: 6.50, 9.130-9.140
Injunctions: 12.470-12.520
Insolvent trading: 3.170-3.180, 10.800-10.990
Insolvent under administration: 9.440-9.460
Inspection of books: 12.530-12.610
Interim dividends: 7.650
Joint stock companies: 1.20
Joint ventures: 2.90-2.100
Large proprietary company: 2.200
Liquidator: 13.410-13.530
    appointment: 13.410-13.450
    duties: 13.480-13.490
    liability: 13.500-13.530
    powers: 13.470
    qualifications: 13.440
    termination of appointment: 13.460
Limited liability: 1.30, 2.130, 2.220, 3.20
Listed company: 2.170, 9.770-9.800
Maintenance of share capital: 7.280-7.660
Managing a corporation: 2.280, 9.370-9.390
Managing director: 9.200-9.220
Mandatory rules: 6.50
Meetings: Chapter 11
    annual general meeting: 2.290-2.300, 5.220
    board meetings: 11.80-11.220
    class meetings: 7.180-7.230, 11.20
    convening: 11.280-11.380
    definition: 11.10-11.50
    extraordinary meetings: 11.280
    general meetings: 11.280-11.810
    minutes: 11.210-11.220, 11.740-11.750
    notice: 11.110-11.140, 11.370-11.510
    proxies: 11.590-11.650
    quorum: 11.160-11.190, 11.520-11.560
    representatives: 11.660-11.690
    requisitioning: 11.290-11.300
    resolutions: 11.60-11.70, 11.500-11.510, 11.570-11.580
    validating procedural irregularities: 11.770-11.810
    voting: 11.200, 11.700-11.730

Members' remedies: 7.220, 9.950, Chapter 12, 13.610-13.690
    derivative action: 12.20, 12.50, 12.110-12.240
    discriminatory conduct: 7.220, 9.950, 12.250-12.390, 12.410-12.440, 12.460, 13.610-13.690
    injunctions: 12.470-12.520
    inspection of books: 12.530-12.610
    oppressive, unfairly prejudicial or unfairly discriminatory conduct: 7.220, 9.950, 12.250-12.460, 13.610-13.690
    proper plaintiff rule: 12.10-12.30, 12.110
    personal rights: 12.60-12.100
    rule in Foss v Harbottle: 12.10-12.30, 12.110
    types of proceedings: 12.60
    winding up: 13.610-13.650

Memorandum of association: 6.10

Minimum membership: 5.30

Mining purposes: 2.160

Minority shareholders, *see* Shareholders' remedies

Negative pledges: 8.80, 8.110

No liability company: 2.160

Nominee directors: 10.60-10.70

Non-cash consideration for shares: 5.90

Notice of meetings: 11.110-11.140, 11.370-11.510

Objects clause
    generally: 6.220-6.240
    no liability company: 2.160

Offer information statement: 8.170, 8.250-8.260

Officers, *see also* Directors: 9.90-9.110
    definition: 9.90-9.110
    types of company officers: 9.190-9.300
    validation of acts: 9.150-9.180
    validation of appointment: 9.120-9.140

Oppressive, unfairly prejudicial or unfairly discriminatory conduct: 7.220, 9.950, 12.250-12.460, 13.610-13.690

Option to purchase securities: 8.120

Ordinary shares: 7.80

Organic theory: 3.80-3.110

Par value: 7.240-7.250

Partnership: 2.60-2.80

Perpetual succession: 2.230

Personal rights: 12.60-12.100

Piercing the corporate veil: 3.140-3.280

Poll: 11.710

INDEX **379**

Preference shares: 7.90-7.130
Pre-registration contracts: 4.50-4.230
    common law: 4.50-4.70
    Corporations Act: 4.90-4.230
Premium share issues: 7.240
Privilege against self-incrimination: 3.130
Professional investors: 8.160
Profile statement: 8.170, 8.230-8.240
Profits: 7.530-7.640
Promoters: 4.10-4.40
    definition: 4.10
    duties: 4.20-4.30
    liability: 4.10-4.40, 4.60, 4.190-4.230, 8.400-8.460
    reimbursement of costs: 4.80
Proper plaintiff rule: 12.10-12.30, 12.110
Proprietary company: 2.170, 2.190, 2.290-2.300
Prospectus: 8.170-8.220
Proxies: 11.590-11.650
Public company: 2.170-2.180, 2.300
Public officer: 10.150
Qualification of directors: 9.310-9.360
Quorum: 11.160-11.190, 11.520-11.560
Receiver: 13.10-13.170
    appointment: 13.10-13.70
    duties: 13.110-13.150
    liability: 13.160-13.170
    powers: 13.90-13.100
    receiver and receiver and manager: 13.70
    termination of appointment: 13.80
Receivership: 13.10-13.170
Redeemable preference shares: 7.130
Reduction of share capital: 7.280-7.660
Registrable Australian bodies: 5.260
Registration of corporations: 5.10-5.270
    legal effect: 5.120
    post-registration requirements: 5.130-5.220
    prerequisites to registration: 5.20-5.70, 9.360
    registration process: 5.40-5.120
    registration of existing companies: 5.230-5.240
    registration of foreign corporations: 5.270
    registration of non-companies: 5.250
    registration of registrable Australian bodies: 5.260
Registers: 5.170-5.180

Registration of shares: 7.30
    proper purposes doctrine: 10.330-10.370
Regulated companies: 1.20
Removal of directors: 9.880-9.1010
Remuneration of directors: 9.700-9.800, 9.970-9.1010
Replaceable rules: 6.20-6.60, 6.130-6.140, 6.170-6.210
    altering: 6.30, 6.60
    legal effect: 6.50, 6.130
Representatives: 11.660-11.690
Resignation of directors: 9.810-9.840
Resolutions: 11.60-11.70, 11.500-11.510, 11.570-11.580
Rule in Foss v Harbottle: 12.10-12.30, 12.110
    exceptions to Foss v Harbottle: 12.40-12.100
Schemes of arrangement: 13.180-13.240
Securities: 8.120
Selective reduction of share capital: 7.300
Shadow directors: 9.40, 9.60
Sham: 3.150
Share
    certificate: 7.30-7.40
    classes: 7.50-7.230
    cumulative preference: 7.100
    deferred: 7.70
    employee: 7.150
    governor: 7.140
    issue: 5.90, 5.200, 7.50, 10.280-10.380
    nature: 7.10-7.20
    non-cash consideration: 5.90
    ordinary: 7.80
    participating preference: 7.100
    preference: 7.90-7.130
    redeemable preference: 7.130
Share buy-backs: 7.340-7.370
Share capital maintenance: 7.280-7.660
Share qualification: 9.350
Shareholders' remedies
    see Members' remedies
Shelf companies: 4.130, 5.10
Short form prospectus: 8.170, 8.210-8.220
Small proprietary company: 2.200
Small scale offerings: 8.150
Sole proprietorship: 2.10-2.20

Sophisticated investors: 8.160
Statutory contract: 6.130-6.210, 6.240
Stop orders: 8.350-8.360
Termination payments for directors: 9.970-9.1010
Tortious liability of corporation: 3.50-3.110
Trusts: 2.30-2.50, 3.190, 3.270
Types of companies: 2.120-2.300
Ultra vires doctrine: 4.180, 6.220-6.240
Unlimited company: 2.150
Vacation of director's office: 9.850-9.870
Variation of class rights: 7.160-7.230
Voting: 11.200, 11.700-11.730
Winding up: 13.410-13.690
    winding up by the court: 13.410-13.650
    winding up in insolvency: 13.540-13.600
    winding up on other grounds: 13.610-13.650
    voluntary winding up: 13.660-13.690

Also available from The Federation Press

Business Law
12th edition

Peter Gillies

Gillies *Business Law* is established as an excellent and accessible guide to business law in Australia. New editions are published every two years so that it is always largely up to date. The current edition, the 12th, was published in July 2004.

Reviews of earlier editions

> As a work for people in business, the work is an invaluable source of basic principle, easily found by reason of the clear layout of the work and easily understood by reason of the clear and lucid expression of the author.
>
> NSW Bar News

> It would be difficult to find another text that provides so much for such a reasonable price.
>
> Law Institute Journal Victoria

> Gillies has dealt with his topic of business law accurately ... its treatment is complete
>
> South Australian Law Society Journal

> An excellent and concise source of legal principles in over 40 areas of law ... a text which can be resorted to time and again ...
>
> Victorian Bar News

> *very clear and useful*
>
> Queensland Bar News

2004 • ISBN 1 86287 514 6 • PB • 1056 pp • $85

Uniform Evidence Law: Text and Essential Cases
Peter Bayne

This new work is a clear account of the law of evidence as it applies in the uniform evidence law jurisdictions of NSW, the Commonwealth, the ACT and Tasmania. A significant feature of the book is that author Peter Bayne has integrated discussion of the provisions of the Uniform Acts with discussion of evidentiary principles. The result is a seamless analysis of the Uniform Evidence Law.

Practitioners who work in uniform evidence law jurisdictions will find the seamless exposition of the Code and principle valuable.

Teachers and students will value the fact that the exposition is augmented by extracts of essential cases. Bayne's practical teaching experience informs every aspect of the structure, content and approach of the discussion.

Reviews

... This is the second book that I have reviewed dealing with the uniform evidence law but this one deals with the nuts and bolts of it, rather than trying to compare differences between the old and the new or between States. The name does not say it all. It is much more than text accompanied by essential cases. The author has on a number of occasions, considered and dissected decisions, including relatively recent High Court decisions and, by analysis, suggested that in some cases their rationale is perhaps flawed or that subsequent decisions might see the interpretation of the Act, applied differently in the future.

This is not an annotation of the Act, but more an in depth analysis of issues such as credibility, hearsay, prior inconsistent statements, prior consistent statements, admissions and denials, identification evidence, witnesses and privileges and the course of trial.

On occasions the author considers sections of the Act in a group, particularly when looking at issues such as hearsay statements which may be admissible under one of several sections of the Act. Similarly, he has discussed a number of decisions, which have included, where appropriate, the summing up of the trial judge, so that practitioners may more readily understand in simple terms, how judges have explained the application of the various provisions of the Act, to the particular factual circumstances.

This is a first rate book. I can only echo the sentiments of Justice Carolyn Simpson who said in the foreword, "I commend Peter Bayne for this worthwhile attempt to refine the principles under which we now must act, and look forward personally to benefiting, in a practical way, from his efforts in this regard."
Tasmanian Law Society Newsletter, February 2004

This is a good book. ... It is always a pleasure to read texts such as Peter Bayne's where one can understand the point in a paragraph without multiple re-readings.

Quite clearly, if you reside in uniform evidence law jurisdictions, this text is an excellent one ... this text is also of vital importance for those who serve in the Australian Defence Force, who have to deal with the matters that arise out of the Defence Force Discipline Act. ... I would highly recommend this text ...
Ethos (Law Society of the ACT), March 2004

2003 • ISBN 1 86287 458 1 • PB • 656pp • $77

Intellectual Property: Text and Essential Cases
2nd edition
Rocque Reynolds and Natalie Stoianoff

Intellectual Property: Text and Essential Cases takes the reader to the forefront of this dynamic area of law. As in the first edition it provides a comprehensive, in-depth and engaging exposition of the principles of Intellectual Property Law and selected case extracts that illustrate the law's evolution and challenges. It covers Copyright, Moral Rights, Performers' Protection, Patents, Trade Marks, Passing Off and related actions, Designs, Plant Breeder's Rights, Circuit Layouts and Confidential Information.

This second edition of *Intellectual Property: Text and Essential Cases* includes detailed consideration of the changes introduced by the *US Free Trade Agreement Implementation Act* 2004 including

- copyright and moral rights for live performers in sound recordings;
- copyright and moral rights for performers of expressions of folklore;
- a new definition of reproduction and material form;
- an extension of the duration of copyright protection;
- new laws relating to electronic rights management, encoded broadcasts and carriage service providers; and
- the protection of patents for therapeutic goods.

The application of the new *Designs Act* 2003, the abolition of the food exemption and the attack on farmer's rights under the *Plant Breeder's Rights Act* 1994, as well as the exciting developments in the law of confidential information are also explored.

In the field of trade marks the important question of whether the law can adequately protect cultural icons is discussed within the context of current debates. The proposed introduction of moral rights for indigenous communities is considered as a matter of legal principle.

Reviews of the first edition

> ... *This is a comprehensive and thoroughly researched text which provides the reader with a well-structured and detailed analysis of the current state of intellectual property law in Australia. It promises to be of invaluable assistance to every lawyer or student with an interest in the area.*
>
> The Queensland Lawyer, Vol 24, 2003

> ... *the good sprinkling of cases, which appears here, provides a useful starting point for analysis. ... ... This is a student text and in that category it is an excellent overview of this fascinating area of law.*
>
> Tasmanian Law Society Newsletter, November 2003

> Intellectual Property: Text and Essential Cases *is a comprehensive work that provides ready access to the law of intellectual property in an Australian context. ... [T]he work provides a useful overview of the law of intellectual property for practitioners and others ... This work does not suffer from the pitfalls of many text and materials case books ... Readers will find the text clear and concise. ... [It] is commended ...*
>
> Victorian Bar News, No 128, Autumn 2004

2005 • ISBN 1 86287 546 4 • PB • 592pp • $77

Income Tax: Text, Materials and Essential Cases
5th edition
Michael Kobetsky, Ann O'Connell and Miranda Stewart

Kobetsky, O'Connell and Stewart's *Income Tax* is an established tax book, which has received very positive reviews in leading law journals. The book is designed to explain the principles of Australian taxation law in plain English. The book provides students with concise extracts and other materials to illustrate the application of the income tax principles.

All chapters in the fifth edition of this established text have been fully revised to include the latest developments in taxation law. Three chapters have been completely rewritten: see the chapters on anti-avoidance, international taxation and tax administration.

Reviews of the 4th edition:

The important aspect of this book is the clear and concise presentation of the law, facts and extracts from leading authorities. ... the capital gains tax and GST chapters have particular interest. ... as the authors demonstrate, the existence of a GST discourages certain forms of tax avoidance. ... An excellent addition to any law library.
Tasmanian Law Society Newsletter, December 2003

This is the fourth edition of this book. The preface states that "the aim of this book is to introduce and explain the principles of tax law." The book achieves its aim.
Australia's tax laws are contained in more than 10,000 pages of legislation and so a book that is only 670 pages is doing very well if it can provide an overview of our complex tax laws. This book not only provides an overview of the principles of Australia's tax laws but also manages to examine some issues in greater detail.
The best features of the book are:

- *Its framework. Each chapter is devoted to a fundamental principle of tax law. This is a much easier way to read and understand the relevant concept ...*

- *The use of extracts from cases and Australian Tax Office rulings. One of the best features of the book is that each discussion of a principle of tax law is supported by appropriate extracts of relevant cases and tax office rulings. ...*

- *Its use of plain English. The language in this book is clear, concise and easy to read. Principles are explained clearly and without using verbose language.*

- *Its reference to additional reading material. ...*

The book covers the major areas of taxation including income and deductions, fringe benefits tax, capital gains tax, goods and services tax and taxation of the various entities ... Another good feature of the book is that three main types of income, namely personal services, business and property income, are discussed separately in different chapters. To round off, the book also has chapters on anti-avoidance and tax administration.
In summary a complex topic is introduced and then its fundamental principles are overviewed in a clear and concise manner.
Law Institute Journal (Victoria), Vol 77(11), November 2003

2005 • ISBN 1 86287 545 6 • PB • 768pp • $77

Labour Law
4th edition
Breen Creighton and Andrew Stewart

The new edition of this leading text provides a valuable guide to the complex network of laws that regulate our workplaces. As with previous editions, it offers an authoritative analysis of key principles and policy issues, backed by extensive reference to other writings in the field.

In charting the continuing development of Australian labour law, the new edition takes account of the many changes to Federal and State legislation over the past five years, as well as the more significant court decisions during this period. It also looks ahead to some of the further reforms that can be expected from the Howard Government as it moves into its fourth term in office.

Features include new or expanded sections on the regulation of bargaining tactics, dispute resolution under certified agreements, monitoring and privacy at the workplace, securing employee entitlements, and protection for whistleblowers. New chapters have also been created to break up the treatment of agreement-making, and of termination of employment, so as to make those parts of the book more accessible.

Contents
- The Role of Law in Labour Relations
- The Evolution of Australian Labour Law
- International Standards and Australian Labour Law
- The Constitutional Framework
- Institutional Structures and Arrangements
- Dispute Resolution and Award Regulation
- Agreement-Making
- Certified Agreements
- Australian Workplace Agreements
- Enforcement of Federal Awards and Agreements
- The Creation and Categorisation of Employment Relationships
- Sources of Employment Obligations
- Individual Rights and Obligations
- Unfair Employment Practices
- Termination of Employment Contracts
- Remedies for Wrongful or Unfair Termination
- Regulation of Trade Unions
- Sanctions Against Industrial Action
- Occupational Health and Safety

2005 • ISBN 186287 543 X • PB • 784pp • $85